Data Retention in Europe and Beyond

Data Retention in Europe and Beyond

Law and Policy in the Aftermath of an Invalidated Directive

Edited by

ELENI KOSTA

Professor of Technology Law and Human Rights, Tilburg Institute for Law, Technology and Society (TILT, Tilburg University), The Netherlands

IRENE KAMARA

Assistant Professor of Cybercrime Law and Human Rights, Tilburg Institute for Law, Technology and Society (TILT, Tilburg University), The Netherlands

Great Clarendon Street, Oxford, OX2 6DP,
United Kingdom

Oxford University Press is a department of the University of Oxford.
It furthers the University's objective of excellence in research, scholarship,
and education by publishing worldwide. Oxford is a registered trade mark of
Oxford University Press in the UK and in certain other countries

© The multiple contributors 2025

The moral rights of the authors have been asserted

All rights reserved. No part of this publication may be reproduced, stored in a retrieval system, transmitted, used for text and data mining, or used for training artificial intelligence, in any form or by any means, without the prior permission in writing of Oxford University Press, or as expressly permitted by law, by licence or under terms agreed with the appropriate reprographics rights organization. Enquiries concerning reproduction outside the scope of the above should be sent to the Rights Department, Oxford University Press, at the address above.

You must not circulate this work in any other form
and you must impose this same condition on any acquirer

Public sector information reproduced under Open Government Licence v3.0
(https://www.nationalarchives.gov.uk/doc/open-government-licence)

Published in the United States of America by Oxford University Press
198 Madison Avenue, New York, NY 10016, United States of America

British Library Cataloguing in Publication Data

Data available

Library of Congress Control Number: 2024947087

ISBN 9780198897736

DOI: 10.1093/9780191998980.001.0001

Printed and bound by
CPI Group (UK) Ltd, Croydon, CR0 4YY

The manufacturer's authorised representative in the EU for product safety is Oxford University Press España S.A. of El Parque Empresarial San Fernando de Henares, Avenida de Castilla, 2 – 28830 Madrid
(www.oup.es/en or product.safety@oup.com). OUP España S.A. also
acts as importer into Spain of products made by the manufacturer.

Foreword I

Data Retention in Europe and Beyond: Law and Policy in the Aftermath of an Invalidated Directive

The pathway which led to the adoption of Directive 2006/24/EC (Data Retention Directive) shows the typical elements of emergency legislation processes.

Adopted by the European legislator in 2006 as a response to the terrorist attacks to London and Madrid, the Directive triggered a debate which presents the most classic features of the conflict between the needs of security and the protection of fundamental rights.

By requiring the retention of specific categories of data for a time period between six months and two years, the Directive considerably impacted not only on telecommunications operators and Internet Service Providers, but on individuals as well, having profound repercussions on the exercise of rights, *in primis* privacy and data protection, and liberties, such as freedom of expression.

In 2014 it is the Court of Justice, with the well-known ruling of the *Digital Rights Ireland* case, which marks a turning point in the EU data retention regime with the invalidation of the Data Retention Directive for the violation of the principle of proportionality. It is a crucial moment, when it clearly emerges that traffic data, even though not related to the content of the communications, can nevertheless reveal very relevant information about the person, deducible from the types, the place, the frequency and the addressees of her communications. With this judgment, which constituted the basis for many national procedures, which in turn challenged the Data Retention Directive and resulted in a number of further significant CJEU judgments, the centrality of the right to the protection of personal data is therefore enhanced in a sector—such as that of fighting crime—in which greater limitations on freedoms and rights are permitted for reasons of general interest.

The tension between fundamental rights on one side, and law enforcement and national security interests on the other, as well as the necessity to reconcile such a contrast, are of course tangible in the EU legal framework. Starting from Article 4(2) of the Treaty on European Union (TEU) which explicitly provides that national security remains in the sole hands of each Member State, there are clear legislative examples which, in the field of data protection, show the need to ensure that the restrictions to individuals' rights justified by objectives of general interest are framed within a solid and foreseeable legislation and endowed with specific safeguards.

Evoking and developing the pattern outlined by Article 8(2) of the European Convention on Human Rights and by Article 52 of the Charter of Fundamental Rights of the EU, the data protection legal framework has increasingly required that data subjects rights—although not absolute—can only be limited for qualified and relevant interests, by measures which ensure the foreseeability of their effects, respect the essence of the right to data protection and are necessary and proportionate in a democratic society.

Having all this as background, this unique book, moving from the disruptive ruling that invalidated the Data Retention Directive, answers to the need to reconstruct the whole data retention legal framework, including the following case law in the field, characterised by highly complex topics, starting from the definition of 'national security' which, although frequently mentioned in EU law, still reveals uncertain features.

The book has the great merit of providing a 360-degree analysis of data retention issues, not only by delving into the extensive jurisprudence on mass surveillance that followed the *Digital Rights Ireland* case, both at the level of the CJEU and the ECtHR, but also by making a careful assessment of different regulatory approaches of Member States, which, also in the light of their respective legal tradition on the matter, have variously reacted to the invalidation of the Directive. The rulings of the Court of Justice have indeed profoundly influenced data retention legal frameworks, giving rise to forms of reluctance and diversified regulatory processes, at times particularly tortuous and long, which clearly reflect the sensitivity of the balancing exercise between fundamental rights and relevant public interests that is behind data retention legislative choices.

Moreover, the delicacy of this exercise was also fully revealed by the debate which marked the proposed ePrivacy Regulation, where considerable effort has been devoted by Member States to the attempt of influencing its provisions, also as a reaction towards the position of the CJEU, as very well explained in the volume.

Not only that, but to integrate the analysis provided, the book opens up to the examination of the international framework and assesses the legislation of third countries, each of which is of great interest due to the respective peculiarities they bear. From the United States, where the topic is intertwined with the access to data by third countries for law enforcement reasons, to Japan, where currently applicable or upcoming legislation regarding detention of data is here assessed with a specific focus on telecommunication and healthcare service providers, to India, whose quite fragmented regulatory instruments are evaluated in the book according to the Supreme Court's position on the right to privacy.

Finally, to complete the examination of the international framework, the perspective of the Council of Europe could not fail to play a fundamental role, just considering the importance of Article 8 of the European Convention on Human Rights and its evolutive interpretation as a landmark in the pathway to reconcile private life and data protection with relevant public interests such as national security.

The very high level contributors coming from a wide range of authorities, academia, and legal practices, skilfully coordinated by Eleni Kosta and Irene Kamara, the remarkable geographical scope of the book, the extremely accurate and rich analysis of the implications of data retention and mass surveillance both for society as a whole and individuals, make this book uniquely comprehensive and a particularly valuable resource for anyone interested in understanding the present and future of data retention. This, being aware that it is precisely on this ground that a very important game is being played for the protection of fundamental rights and the correct balance between the interests at stake.

Alessandra Pierucci
Member and former Chair of the Council of
Europe Consultative Committee of Convention 108

Foreword II

For any lawyer with even a passing interest in European Union law, the legal questions surrounding data retention are familiar. They encapsulate virtually all the challenges posed by the use of new technologies. First and foremost, there is a need to ensure the protection of personal data and the right to privacy of internet users, that is to say, without exceptions, all of us. Furthermore, a clear and reliable scope of mechanisms for combating crime must be established—in order to be able to pursue both crimes of a very serious nature, such as terrorism or child sex abuse, and crimes of a lesser magnitude, such as IP infringements. While it is certainly relatively straightforward to find a consensus on restrictions to online privacy concerning the first category, the same cannot be said about the second one. Yet, it should be remembered that it is the internet which makes crimes from both categories much easier to commit. This must be kept in mind when the extent of curbing privacy online and the justification of related restrictions is determined. In addition, we are also dealing here with the need to balance the various fundamental rights whose protection is guaranteed by the EU Charter of Fundamental Rights, by the European Convention on Human Rights, by the Member States' conventions, and by national constitutions. Finally, we have to cope here with one of the fundamental challenges for the internet, namely its 'de-territorialisation'. Where the internet is concerned, the distinction between what is territorial and what is extraterritorial has become blurred.

All of us lawyers certainly have a lot to say about this. For me too, the temptation is big to share some of my thoughts on this extremely important topic with the readers, by way of the present introduction. However, due to cases currently pending before the CJEU and in which I am acting as Advocate General, I am compelled to resist this temptation. Instead, I can—with full conviction—recommend to the readers the collection of excellent studies on the most varied topics related to data retention. These studies will certainly be of interest to all those who are looking for answers to various legal challenges arising from new technologies. The editing of this book was undertaken by Professor Eleni Kosta and Dr Irene Kamara, for which they deserve credit.

Maciej Szpunar
First Advocate General to the Court of Justice of the European Union

Editors' Preface

The regulation of retention of traffic and location data by electronic service providers for law enforcement purposes has been in the centre of the European policy agenda for more than 25 years. The Data Retention Directive reflects the intention of the European legislator to regulate the issue at EU level, an aspiration that was soon proven to be futile, after the invalidation of the Directive by the Court of Justice of the European Union (CJEU). This book aims at providing an overview of issues surrounding the regulation of the obligations on the retention of traffic and location data by electronic service providers to safeguards that should surround the access to retained data by competent authorities, in accordance with national laws and the CJEU case law.

This idea for this book was brewing for several years, as data retention was a topic very close to the research heart of the editors for almost two decades; it was based on early publications around the Data Retention Directive[1] but it matured at a conference in May 2022 in Rome, at the Campus di Viale Pola of LUISS, co-organised by the editors, together with Professor Dr Sofia Ranchordas and Professor Dr Antonino Gullo. In the months that followed, prominent scholars and practitioners enthusiastically embraced the idea of an edited volume dedicated to data retention, law enforcement, and national security. We are grateful to all the contributors to this book for their excellent work, their tireless efforts in making this book a unique volume on the topic of data retention, and for their eternal patience in reworking their contributions to include the latest developments in the field. We decided to end the research at the end of April 2024, when two seminal judgments were published by the CJEU, *La Quadrature du Net 'II'* and *Bolzano*.

Particular thank you goes to Alessandra Pierucci, Member and former Chair of the Council of Europe Consultative Committee of Convention 108, and Maciej Szpunar, First Advocate General to the Court of Justice of the European Union, who wrote the forewords for this volume. We would like to thank the excellent colleagues that functioned as reviewers for all chapters in this volume, for their comments and constructive feedback, which contributed significantly to the overall quality of the book. We would thus like to thank Marco Bassini, Elif Biber Sumeyye, Magda Brewczyńska, Colette Cuijpers, Lorenzo Dalla Corte, Silvia De Conca, Katerina Demetzou, Simona Demkova, Diana Dimitrova, Laura Drechsler, Ana-Maria Hriscu, Bert-Jaap Koops, Magdalena Kogut-Czarkowska, Taner Kuru, Mark Leiser, Christiana Markou, Maria-Helen Murphy, Anja Møller-Pedersen, Bryce Newell, Suzanne Nusselder, Anuj Puri, Juraj Sajfert, Dimitra Stefanatou, Aimen Taimur, Xavier Tracol, Maria Tzanou, Sascha van Schendel, Monica Vilasau Solana, Plixavra Vogiatzoglou, and Teresa Quintel.

---

[1] See eg Elini Kosta and Peggy Valcke, 'Retaining the Data Retention Directive' (2006) 22(5) Computer Law & Security Review 370–80; Elini Kosta, Fanny Coudert, and Jos Dumortier, 'Data Protection in the Third Pillar: In the Aftermath of the ECJ Decision on PNR Data and the Data Retention Directive' (2007) 21(3) International Review of Law Computers and Technology 347–62; Lexi Pimenidis and Eleni Kosta, 'The Impact of The Retention of Traffic and Location Data on The Internet User: A Critical Discussion' (2008) 32(2) Datenschutz und Datensicherheit-DuD 92–97.

We are also thankful for the support of Oxford University Press, in particular Peter Daniell and Charlotte Kershaw, and the anonymous referees for their feedback. This work would not have been possible without the support of our academic home, the Tilburg Institute for Law, Technology, and Society (TILT) at Tilburg Law School.

Eleni Kosta and Irene Kamara
Tilburg, July 2024

Contents

Table of Cases	xxiii
Table of European and International Legal Instruments	xxvii
List of Contributors	xxix

1. Introduction: Data Retention in the EU and Beyond: An Evolving Landscape 1
   Eleni Kosta and Irene Kamara
   1. The EU Data Retention Directive and the *Digital Rights Ireland* Case 1
   2. Rationale and Structure of this Book 3
   3. Data Retention in the Aftermath of *La Quadrature du Net 'II'* 8
      3.1 Ireland 8
      3.2 Belgium 9
      3.3 In anticipation of future developments 10

PART I. THE EVOLUTION OF CASE LAW IN CJEU AND EUROPEAN COURT OF HUMAN RIGHTS

2. The Evolution of the CJEU Case Law on Data Retention: Towards the Regulation of Access 13
   Eleni Kosta
   1. Introduction 13
   2. The Prohibition on Blanket Data Retention 14
   3. Retention and Access to Retained Data 15
   4. Evolving Rules on Data Retention 16
      4.1 Prohibiting blanket retention on a preventative basis 16
      4.2 Applicability of EU law on measures relating to the safeguarding of national security 17
      4.3 Civil identity data 18
      4.4 Expedited retention 19
   5. Retention of IP Addresses 20
   6. Key Safeguard for Access to Retained Data: Prior Review 21
   7. Targeted Retention 23
   8. Conclusion 24

3. Data Retention and the Judicial Parameters of Mass Surveillance in EU Law 27
   Valsamis Mitsilegas
   1. Introduction 27
   2. Annulling the Data Retention Directive: *Digital Rights Ireland* 27
   3. Rejecting National Legislation on Generalised Data Retention: *Tele2 Sverige* 30
   4. Rejecting the National Security Argument: *La Quadrature du Net 'I'* 35
   5. Rejecting Generalised Retention to Fight Serious Crime: *Garda Síochána* 39

xii   CONTENTS

    6. Rejecting National Claims on the Compatibility of 'Limited' Data Retention with EU Law: *SpaceNet* 41
    7. Conclusion 43

4. A Critical Comment on Proportionality in the Mass Surveillance Jurisprudence of the CJEU and the ECtHR 45
Lorenzo Dalla Corte
    1. Introduction 45
    2. Proportionality and Limitations Analysis 47
    3. The Suitability Assumption 49
    4. Focusing on Necessity rather than on Proportionality *Stricto Sensu* 53
    5. Merging Lawfulness and Necessity 56
    6. The Marginal Role of the Essence 58
    7. Conclusion 61

5. Proportionality and Strict Proportionality in the Case-law of the Court of Justice of the European Union on Data Retention 63
Daniele Nardi
    1. Introduction 63
    2. The Principle of Proportionality throughout the Case-law on Generalised Retention of Communication Data 65
        2.1 Proportionality of measures limiting the fundamental rights to privacy and data protection before data retention: *Schecke* 65
        2.2 *Digital Rights Ireland*: The retention of communication metadata cannot be considered 'strictly necessary' 66
        2.3 *Tele2 Sverige* and the attempt to systematise and revive the 'classical' proportionality test: The Opinion of Advocate General Saugmansgaard Øe 68
        2.4 The judgment in *Tele2 Sverige*: 'Strict necessity' decoupled and beyond the assessment of the existence of less restrictive measures 70
        2.5 Serious interferences require serious objectives: *Ministerio Fiscal* 72
        2.6 The Court lays down the hierarchy of objectives in the field of retention and access of Metadata: *La Quadrature du Net 'I'* 73
        2.7 *Prokuratuur*: The Court explains why retention and access need to be considered as a one and only interference 77
        2.8 *Garda Síochána* and *SpaceNet*: The assessment of proportionality in the field of retention of metadata for criminal law purposes is final 79
        2.9 *La Quadrature du Net 'II'* 81
            2.9.1 Advocate General Szpunar's two Opinions 81
            2.9.2 The full Court judgment 84
    3. Conclusions 91

6. Data Retention in the Proposed ePrivacy Regulation Caught between the Well-established Case Law of the Court of Justice and the Deep Disagreements of the EU Legislature: For a Legally Compliant Way Forward 95
Xavier Tracol
    1. Introduction 95
    2. Proposal of the Commission for an ePrivacy Regulation 97
        2.1 Broad definition of electronic communications metadata in the Proposal of the Commission for an ePrivacy Regulation 97
        2.2 Misleading explanatory memorandum on data retention 98
    3. Opinion of the EDPS on the Proposal for an ePrivacy Regulation 99

4.	Report of Parliament on the Proposed ePrivacy Regulation		100
5.	Council: Member States Divided in Cacophony		100
	5.1	Initial discussion	101
	5.2	Bulgarian Presidency of the Council: no common position of the Council	102
	5.3	Romanian Presidency of the Council: An Attempt to Reach a Compromise	102
	5.4	Finnish Presidency of the Council: Non-adoption of the General Approach submitted to the COREPER	103
	5.5	*La Quadrature du Net* and *Privacy International* judgments of the Court of Justice and German Presidency of the Council	104
		5.5.1 *La Quadrature du Net* and *Privacy International* judgments of the Court of Justice	104
		5.5.2 Compromise proposal made by the German Presidency of the Council	105
	5.6	Portuguese Presidency of the Council: four controversial proposals	106
		5.6.1 Proposed amendments to Article 2(2) of the draft regulation	106
		5.6.2 Proposed deletion of Article 7(4) of the draft regulation	107
		5.6.3 Proposed reintroduction of Article 7(4) of the draft Regulation	107
		5.6.4 Proposed amendments on national security	108
6.	Strongly Worded Statement of the EDPB		109
7.	Trilogues Going Nowhere		110
8.	Initiatives of Both the Commission and the Council		110
	8.1	Non-paper of the Commission	111
	8.2	High-Level Expert Group	111
9.	Conclusion: For a Legally Compliant Way Forward		112

PART II. DATA RETENTION IN THE EU MEMBER STATES AND INTERNATIONAL PERSPECTIVES

7. Data Retention in Germany: Not a Never-ending Story After All?   117
Matthias Bäcker
1. Introduction   117
2. The First Data Retention and the Judgment of the *BVerfG*   117
3. The Second Data Retention   120
4. The Legal Proceedings Against the Second Data Retention   121
   4.1 Types of action and scopes of review   121
   4.2 Development of the proceedings   122
      4.2.1 Proceedings before the *BVerfG*   122
      4.2.2 Proceedings before the administrative courts and the CJEU   123
      4.2.3 The final judgments of the *BVerwG*   125
5. Status of the Political Debate in Germany   125
6. Conclusion and Outlook   127

8. The Long Way to the Compliance of Data Retention with European Union Law: The Italian Case   129
Luigi Montuori and Veronica Tondi
1. Introduction   129
2. Data Retention in the Court of Justice Decisions   130
3. Brief Remarks on the Constitutional Jurisprudence Concerning Article 15 of the Constitution   131

xiv CONTENTS

    4. Italian Case Law and the Resistance to the Full Implementation of European Union Law   133
        4.1 The legality requirement and the controversial balancing approach in the concrete case   134
        4.2 The notion of judicial authority and the role of the public prosecutor   136
        4.3 The usability of data collected in violation of European Union law   138
    5. The Role of the Italian Supervisor and its Decisions   141
    6. Compatibility of the Italian Legislation with the Canon of Proportionality and with the Principles Sanctioned by the Court of Justice   143
    7. Conclusions   147

9. Consequences of the Collapse of a Directive: The Aftermath of CJEU Data Retention Case Law on Cypriot Jurisprudence   151
Christiana Markou
    1. Introduction   151
    2. The Landmark Supreme Court Judgment of 2021 and its Aftermath   153
        2.1 The 2021 judgment   153
        2.2 The aftermath of the 2021 judgment   154
    3. Data Retention in Cyprus in 2023   155
        3.1 Post-*Tele2 Sverige* CJEU case law   155
        3.2 A change in the Cypriot judicial approach   157
        3.3 Assessing the 2023 court judgment   158
        3.4 Repercussions on the future of data retention law in Cyprus   161
    4. Concluding Remarks   163

10. Data Retention in Ireland: When European Law Meets National Recalcitrance   165
TJ McIntyre
    1. Introduction   165
    2. Legislative Context: The Communications (Retention of Data) Act 2011   166
    3. Challenges to the Communications (Retention of Data) Act 2011   167
        3.1 *Digital Rights Ireland*   167
        3.2 *Dwyer*   167
    4. Data Retention and the Criminal Justice System after *Tele2 Sverige*   172
        4.1 Police continued to have access to data without independent authorisation   172
        4.2 Retained data continued to be admitted in criminal trials   173
        4.3 Designated judge did not exercise effective oversight   175
        4.4 Data Protection Commissioner did not intervene to prevent operation of data retention system   175
    5. Political Responses after *Tele2 Sverige*   176
        5.1 Communications (Retention of Data) (Amendment) Act 2022   178
    6. Conclusion   179

11. A Clash Between the French System and the CJEU Case Law on Data Retention?   181
Maxime Lassalle
    1. Introduction: *La Quadrature du Net 'I'* and the (il)Legitimacy of EU Law   181
    2. *La Quadrature du Net 'I'*'s Aftermath   183
        2.1 The Council of State and French constitutional identity   184
            2.1.1 The necessity to protect national security   184
            2.1.2 The French way to data protection   184

		2.2	The Parliament: A New Law in 2021	185
		2.3	The Constitutional Council: Ensuring the constitutionality of the new law?	188
		2.4	The Court of Cassation: Ensuring that criminal investigations will not be impacted	190
			2.4.1 General data retention grounded on a continuous terrorist threat since 1995	190
			2.4.2 Quick freeze as a way to use data outside the context of national security	191
	3.	The Absence of Alternatives to Data Retention?		191
		3.1	The (alleged) low operational use of targeted retention	192
		3.2	The technical feasibility of targeted retention	192
		3.3	The specificity of IP addresses	193
	4.	Conclusion: The Clash Did Not Take Place, Yet		195

12. Data Retention Amid the Erosion of the Constitutional Order: The Case of Poland — 197
    Magdalena Brewczyńska
    1. Introduction — 197
    2. The Origins and Current Shape of the General Regulatory Regime for Measures Created to Fight Terrorism — 199
       2.1 Background — 199
       2.2 Telecommunications confidentiality — 201
    3. Two Decades of Expansion of Telecommunications Surveillance — 203
       3.1 From fighting terrorism through combatting crime to performing any statutory tasks — 203
       3.2 Judgment of the 'old' Constitutional Tribunal: a missed opportunity for breaking the mass surveillance pattern — 205
       3.3 A 'deform' instead of a 'reform' of the Polish data retention law — 206
       3.4 One last PiS attempt to further expand surveillance powers — 209
    4. Data Retention in the Light of the Erosion of the Rule of Law — 210
    5. Conclusion — 212

13. The Impact—or No Impact—of the CJEU Case Law on Data Retention in Spain — 213
    Lorena Bachmaier Winter and Antonio Martínez Santos
    1. Introduction — 213
    2. Legal Framework for Data Retention in Spain — 214
    3. Data to be Retained — 215
    4. Data Retention Time Limits — 215
    5. Transfer of Data to 'Authorized Agents' — 217
    6. Protection and Security of Retained Data — 220
    7. Registration of Prepaid Card Users — 220
    8. Impact of the Case Law of the Court of Justice — 221
    9. Conclusion — 223

14. Data Retention and Law Enforcement in the Netherlands — 225
    Marc van der Ham and Esther Baars
    1. Introduction — 225
    2. Telecommunications Data Retention Act in Retrospect — 226
    3. Access to Data by Law Enforcement Authorities — 227
    4. Ruling of the Preliminary Relief Judge of the District Court of The Hague — 228

	4.1	Policy developments and legislative initiatives after the TDRA was suspended	230
		4.1.1 General observations	230
		4.1.2 Adjustments to the retention obligations in the old TDRA	231
		4.1.3 Adjustments to the access to the retained data	231
	4.2	Developments in case law requiring further adjustments	232
5.	Impact on the Availability of Telecommunications Data in Criminal Investigations		234
6.	Future Perspectives		235
7.	Conclusion		236

15. **To Retain or (not) to Retain Data? The Danish Case** 237
    Ayo Næsborg-Andersen
    1. Introduction 237
    2. The Content of the Danish Retention Rules 238
       2.1 Retention Order and Guidance of 2006 238
       2.2 Interlude: *Digital Rights Ireland* and *Tele2 Sverige* 239
       2.3 2022 revision 240
    3. Is there Something Rotten in the State of Denmark? 241
       3.1 The (lack of) revision 241
          3.1.1 The postponed revision 241
          3.1.2 The urgent revision 243
       3.2 Proportionality 245
          3.2.1 Amount of data 245
          3.2.2 Length of retention 247
          3.2.3 Justifications of retention 247
       3.3 What is not in the rules? 249
    4. Conclusion 249

16. **Belgium's New Data Retention Legislation: Third Time Lucky, or Three Strikes and You're Out?** 251
    Vanessa Franssen and Catherine Van de Heyning
    1. Introduction 251
    2. The Belgian Legislator in Search of EU-Proof Data Retention Legislation 253
       2.1 Main features of the old data retention regime 253
       2.2 The Belgian legislator sent back to square one by the CJEU 255
          2.2.1 Introduction 255
          2.2.2 New red card for general and indiscriminate retention of traffic and location data 255
          2.2.3 Targeted retention of traffic and location data for the purposes of fighting serious crime: A difficult 'tactic' to implement 256
          2.2.4 Green card for general and indiscriminate retention of identification data 259
          2.2.5 Conditions for access to retained data: Indispensable but not enough 260
          2.2.6 New 'game' opportunities created by the CJEU: National security and IP addresses of the source of the connection 262
    3. The National Impact of *La Quadrature du Net 'I'*: A Hard Ball to Catch 263
       3.1 The inevitable strike home of the Constitutional Court 263
       3.2 Belgian authorities playing extra time? 264
    4. Third Attempt: Playing Ball in the CJEU's Courtyard 265
       4.1 Main features of Belgium's new data retention regime 265

	4.2 A new pitch to the Constitutional Court and the CJEU: Meatball or curveball?	268
	5. Conclusion	273
17.	The Swedish Data Retention Saga: From EU Initiator to Penalty Payments, Reviewed and Revised National Rules	275
	Maria Bergström	
	1. Introduction	275
	2. The Swedish Support for EU Data Retention Rules, Swedish Parliamentary Control, and the Extended Implementation Process	276
	3. A Swedish Commissioner, Penalty Payments for Non-implementation, and the Adoption of Swedish Implementing Legislation	282
	4. Invalidation of National Legislation after the Annulment of the 2006 EU Data Retention Directive?	287
	5. The Request for a Preliminary Ruling from the Stockholm Administrative Court of Appeal and the Continuous Clarification by the CJEU of the Required Safeguards for Data Retention to be Lawful, and Revised National Legislation in the Absence of a General EU Legislative Framework	289
	6. Conclusions—Trial and Error or Business as Usual? Multilevel Governance, Judicial Dialogue, and Dynamic EU Lawmaking towards Legally Acceptable Requirements for Data Retention?	293
18.	Data Retention and Law Enforcement Access to Personal Data in India	295
	Shweta Reddy Degalahal	
	1. Introduction	295
	2. Right to Privacy in India	297
	3. Data Protection Legislation in India	299
	3.1 General obligations	299
	3.2 Exemptions under the Act	300
	4. Data Retention in India	300
	4.1 Information Technology Act 2000	301
	4.2 The Indian Computer Emergency Response Team (Cert-In) Rules	302
	5. Law Enforcement Access to Retained Personal Data	303
	5.1 Criminal Procedure Code 1973	303
	5.2 Indian Telegraph Act 1885	304
	5.3 Centralized Monitoring Systems	305
	5.4 Information Technology (Reasonable Security Practices and Procedures and Sensitive Personal Data or Information) Rules 2011	306
	5.5 Information Technology (Intermediary Guidelines and Digital Media Ethics Code) Rules 2021	307
	6. Analysis with the *Puttaswamy* Test	309
	7. Conclusion	312
19.	Regulating Data Retention in Japan	315
	Xenofon V Kontargyris	
	1. Introduction	315
	2. The Meiji Restoration and Origins of the Right to Privacy in Japan's Constitution	316
	3. The Civil Code of Japan	318
	3.1 Obligation to keep records	319
	3.2 Legal personality of entities	319

	3.3 Preservation of evidence	319
	3.4 Limitation period	319
4.	The Japanese Act on Protection of Personal Information and its Cornerstone Role for Regulating Retention in Japan	320
	4.1 A summary of the evolution of the Japanese law on data privacy	320
	4.2 How has APPI shaped thinking and regulatory treatment of data and records retention in Japan?	321
	4.3 The Commission on Protection of Personal Information and its role in enforcement of privacy legislation, including obligations relevant to data retention	323
5.	Japan's Commercial Code and its Provisions Related to Data Retention	324
6.	Rules with Relevance to Data Retention in Japan's Medical Practitioners Act	325
7.	Data Retention Requirements Applicable for Telecommunications Service Providers in Japan	326
8.	Data Retention Obligations in Japan's Healthcare Industry—Rules for Medical Device Manufacturers and Healthcare Providers	328
	8.1 Medical Device Manufacturers	328
	8.2 Healthcare providers	329
	8.3 A deep-dive into obligations related to data retention in Good Manufacturing Practice Guidelines in Japan—an attempt to safeguard quality and ensure accountability in the provision of healthcare	330
9.	Conclusion	331

20. Regulating Access: A Brief Overview of US Regulations on Access to Communications Data — 333
    Bryce Clayton Newell
    1. Introduction — 333
    2. Regulating Access to Communications Data in US Law — 333
        2.1 The Stored Communications Act — 334
        2.2 Content data — 335
        2.3 Non-content data — 336
        2.4 The Fourth Amendment and non-content data — 337
        2.5 Beyond the SCA — 338
    3. Connections and Conclusions — 338

PART III. PUBLIC POLICY, TECHNOLOGY, AND SOCIETAL IMPACT

21. The Judicialization of EU Data Retention Law: Epistemic Injustice and the Construction of an Unequal Surveillance Regime — 343
    Maria Tzanou
    1. Introduction — 343
    2. The Judicialization of Data Retention — 345
        2.1 The judicialization of the EU: theories, impact, and resistance — 345
        2.2 The judicialization of data retention: from *constitutionalization* to *resistance* — 348
    3. A Hierarchy of Surveillance: The 'Targeted Retention' Problem and its Consequences — 352
        3.1 Mass versus targeted surveillance and the underlying assumptions — 352
        3.2 The problem with the targeted surveillance of geographical spaces — 353
        3.3 The judicialization of data retention and epistemic injustice — 356

	4. Re-imagining Data Retention	358
	5. Conclusion	359
22.	Data Retention as a Matter of Constitutional Law	361
	Marco Bassini	
	1. Introduction	361
	2. Constitutional Pride	364
	3. Lack of Constitutional Pride?	368
	4. From Constitutional Indifference to Constitutional Obedience	372
	5. Concluding Remarks	375
23.	Passenger Name Records: Necessary Data Retention to Fight Crime and Terrorism, or Threatening Privacy and Data Protection?	377
	Lucas M Haitsma, Oskar J Gstrein, and Heinrich Winter	
	1. Introduction and Methodology	377
	2. The Regulation of PNR Data	379
	2.1 Historical context	379
	2.2 The PNR Directive	380
	2.3 The right to privacy and data protection	382
	3. *Ligue des droits humains*	382
	3.1 Interference with the right to private life and data protection	383
	3.2 The pursuit of an objective interest	384
	3.3 Appropriateness of the processing of PNR data for meeting the objective interest	384
	3.4 Sufficiently clear and precise terminology	384
	3.5 The scope of application of the PNR Directive	385
	3.6 The retention period of PNR data	386
	3.7 Processing PNR data with algorithmic systems and artificial intelligence	386
	4. Discussion: Is the PNR System Compatible with European Data Retention Case Law?	387
	4.1 Aligning the PNR Directive with European data retention case law	387
	4.1.1 PNR Canada	388
	4.1.2 Analogies to data retention case law from the electronic communications sector	388
	4.2 Does the PNR Directive contribute to the fight against serious crime and terrorism?	390
	4.2.1 Obstacles to the PNR Directive's effectiveness	390
	4.2.2 Demonstrating the effectiveness of the PNR Directive	391
	4.2.3 Is the PNR Directive necessary?	393
	5. Conclusion	394
24.	Data Retention and Automated Processing of Personal Data: Unpacking the CJEU's Approach	397
	Niovi Vavoula	
	1. Introduction	397
	2. Automated Analysis: The Evolution of the CJEU Case Law	398
	2.1 The first steps: *PNR Canada*	398
	2.2 The second step: *La Quadrature du Net 'I'*	400
	2.3 The third step: *Ligue des droits humains*	403
	2.4 The fourth step: *La Quadrature du Net 'II'*	408
	3. The Potential and Limitations of the CJEU's Approach	410
	3.1 The transplantation of the CJEU's standards to multiple contexts	410

		3.2	Room for further elaboration	413
			3.2.1 Auditing algorithms	413
			3.2.2 Assessing the reliability of databases	414
			3.2.3 Intersectional discrimination	414
			3.2.4 The 'human in the loop'	416
			3.2.5 The 'human over the loop'	417
		3.3	The relationship with the right not to be subject to automated decision-making	418
		3.4	The relationship with the AI Act	420
	4.	Conclusion		420

25. **Automated Analysis in the AFSJ and Digital Single Market Monitoring: An Effaced Nexus** — 423
    Maria Grazia Porcedda
    1. Introduction — 423
    2. Automated Analysis in CJEU Data Retention and ECtHR Mass Surveillance Case Law — 425
        2.1 Automated analysis in the CJEU data retention saga after *La Quadrature du Net 'I'* — 425
        2.2 Automated analysis in the ECtHR judgments of *Big Brother Watch* and *Centrum för Rättvisa* — 430
        2.3 Automated analysis, electronic communication and intermediation services — 433
    3. Automated Analysis in the Digital Single Market: E-communication, Online Intermediation Services, and Monitoring — 435
        3.1 The evolution of rules on digital service provision and monitoring: from neat distinction to blurred lines between ECSs, ISSs and monitoring clauses — 436
        3.2 2008–2017: The uneasy divide between ECSs and ISSs begins to show — 440
        3.3 After 2018: ECSs and ISSs overlapping *de facto*, but not *de iure* — 443
        3.4 Summary of the regulatory overlap of telecommunication and intermediation services — 448
    4. Automated analysis, the Single market-AFSJ nexus, and the effacement of technology from EU law: ways forward — 449
    5. Conclusion — 452

26. **On Administrative and Surveillance Vulnerability and the Digital Government in the EU** — 455
    Maria-Lucia Rebrean and Gianclaudio Malgieri
    1. Introduction — 455
    2. Digitalizing Public Services in the European Union — 457
    3. From Administrative to Surveillance Vulnerability — 460
    4. Transparency and Explainability as Possible Safeguards for Administrative and Surveillance Vulnerability — 463
        4.1 Transparency over surveillance measures — 464
        4.2 Transparency over the consequences of surveillance — 465
    5. Challenges to Implementing Transparency as a Safeguard for Administrative and Surveillance Vulnerability — 466
    6. From Transparency and Explainability to Accountability — 467
    7. Conclusion — 469

27. Data Retention and the 'Chilling Effect' in the Context of Mass Surveillance and a Tacit Sift Towards a Hobbesian state in Western Democracies   471
Ivan Manokha
   1. Introduction   471
   2. Digital Technology and a Shift Towards a 'Hobbesian' State   473
   3. The Chilling Effect   480
   4. Conclusion   485

Index   487

Table of Cases

COURT OF JUSTICE OF THE EUROPEAN UNION

Opinion of Advocate General Léger of 22 November 2005, Parliament v Council and
Commission (C-317/04 and C-318/04) ECLI:EU:C:2005:710 ('*AG Opinion
Parliament v Council*') 56n.67
CJEU, Judgment of 30 May 2006, Parliament v Council and Commission
(C-317/04 and C-318/04) ECLI:EU:C:2006:346 ('*Parliament v Council*') 35n.65, 399n.14
CJEU, Judgment of 16 December 2008, Satakunnan Markkinapörssi and Satamedia
(C-73/07, ECR 2008 p. I-9831) ECLI:EU:C:2008:727 ('*Satakunnan*') 65n.11, 69, 72
CJEU, Judgment of 16 December 2008 (C-524/06) Heinz Huber v Bundesrepublik
Deutschland, ECLI: EU:C:2008:724 ('*Huber*') 417
CJEU, Judgment of 10 February 2009, Ireland / Parliament and Council
(C-301/06, ECR 2009 p. I-593) ECLI:EU:C:2009:68 ('*Ireland vs Parliament
and Council*') 29–30, 277n.12, 361–62
CJEU, Judgment of 04 February 2010, European Commission v Kingdom of Sweden
(C-185/09) ECLI:EU:C:2010:59 ('*European Commission v Kingdom of Sweden*') 280n.34
CJEU, Judgment of 29 July 2010, European Commission v. Republic of Austria (C-189/09)
ECLI:EU:C:2010:455 ('*European Commission v Republic of Austria*')..................... 285
CJEU, Judgment of 9 November 2010, Volker und Markus Schecke and Eifert
(C-92/09 and C-93/09, ECR 2010 p. I-11063) ECLI:EU:C:2010:662
('*Schecke*')... 65n.9, 65–66, 67, 69, 72
CJEU, Judgment of 19 April 2012, Bonnier Audio AB and Others v Perfect Communication
Sweden AB (C-461/10) ECLI:EU:C:2012:219 ('*Bonnier Audio*') 286
CJEU, Judgment of 30 May 2013, European Commission v Kingdom of Sweden
(C-270/11) ECLI:EU:C:2013:339 ('*European Commission v Kingdom of Sweden II*') ... 284n.66
Opinion of Advocate General Cruz Villalón of 12 December 2013, Digital Rights Ireland,
(C-293/12) ECLI:EU:C:2013:845 ('*AG Opinion Digital Rights Ireland*').................... 56
CJEU, Judgment of 8 April 2014, Digital Rights Ireland and Seitlinger and others
(C-293/12 and C-594/12) ECLI:EU:C:2014:238 ('*Digital Rights Ireland*') 2–3, 4, 8–9, 13,
14, 15, 21–22, 24, 27–30, 32–33, 34, 43–44, 60–61, 64, 66–68, 69, 70, 72, 78,
96–97, 98, 100, 107, 112, 121, 134, 135, 152, 154, 165, 167, 179, 205, 213, 221,
225, 228–30, 236, 238, 239–40, 242–43, 245–46, 248–49, 251–52, 253, 254–55,
287–88, 289–90, 349, 350, 361–62, 363, 364–66, 367–68,
370–71, 372–73, 387–88, 389, 403, 441, 442
Opinion of Advocate General Wathelet of 16 September 2015, WebMindLicenses
Kft.(C-419/14) ECLI:EU:C:2015:606 ('*AG Opinion WebMindLicenses*)................ 56n.66
CJEU, Judgment of 6 October 2015, Maximillian Schrems v Data Protection
Commissioner (C-362/14) ECLI:EU:C:2015:650 ('*Schrems I*') 59, 60
Opinion of Advocate General Saugmansgaard Øe of 19 July 2016 in
Tele2 Sverige (C-203/15 and C-698/15), ECLI:EU:C:2016:572
('*AG Opinion Tele2 Sverige*')... 49n.22, 68n.29, 70n.38
CJEU, Judgment of 21 December 2016, Tele2 Sverige (C-203/15 and C-698/15)
ECLI:EU:C:2016:970 ('*Tele2 Sverige*') 5, 8, 15, 16–17, 19, 20, 21–22, 23, 24–30,
32–34, 36, 38, 41–42, 49, 51, 52, 53, 56, 60–61, 68, 70–72,
74, 76, 79, 85, 92, 100, 112, 123–24, 135, 152, 153–54,
155–56, 163, 165, 167–68, 169, 170, 172–79,
222–23, 232–34, 236, 239–40, 243, 253, 255, 256–57,
289, 290–91, 292, 349, 352, 370–71, 387–88, 389.

xxiv   TABLE OF CASES

CJEU, Judgment of 24 November 2016, (C-443/15) Parris v Trinity College and
others ECLI:EU:C:2016:897 ('*Parris*') 415–16
Opinion of Advocate General Mengozzi of 8 September 2016 (Opinion procedure 1/15)
ECLI:EU:C:2016:656 ('*AG Opinion PNR Canada*') 56n.67, 388–89
CJEU, Opinion 1/15 (EU-Canada PNR Agreement), of 26 July 2017 (Digital Reports)
ECLI:EU:C:2017:592 ('*PNR Canada*') 36n.71, 56, 74, 378, 384–85, 387–88, 392–93, 400,
404, 410, 414–15, 418–19
CJEU, Judgment of 2 October 2018, Ministerio Fiscal (C-207/16)
ECLI:EU:C:2018:788 ('*Ministerio Fiscal*')......... 18, 33n.44, 37n.81, 50–51, 72, 73, 74, 75, 135,
223, 257–58, 259, 291, 349
CJEU, Judgment of 5 June 2019, Skype Communications (C-142/18)
ECLI:EU:C:2019:460 ('*Skype Communications*') 435n.70, 445n.136
CJEU, Judgment of 13 June 2019, Google (C-193/18)
ECLI:EU:C:2019:498 ('*Google*') 435n.70, 445n.137
CJEU, Judgment of 3 October 2019, Glawischnig-Piesczek (C-18/18)
ECLI:EU:C:2019:821 ('*Glawischnig-Piesczek*') 446n.142
CJEU, Judgment of 24 June 2019, *Commission/Poland*
(Independence of the Supreme Court) (C-619/18) ECLI:EU:C:2019:531 .... 198n.8
CJEU, Judgment of 5 November 2019, *Commission/Poland*
(Independence of ordinary courts) (C-192/18) ECLI:EU:C:2019:924.................. 198n.8
Opinion of Advocate General Saugmandsgaard Øe of 19 December 2019,
Facebook Ireland and Schrems (C-311/18) ECLI:EU:C:2019:1145
('*AG Opinion Schrems II*') 56n.67, 59n.93, 60n.98, 60n.98
CJEU, Judgment of 16 July 2020, Facebook Ireland and Schrems (C-311/18)
ECLI:EU:C:2020:559 ('*Schrems II*') 409n.93
CJEU, Judgment of 6 October 2020, La Quadrature du Net and others
(C-511/18, C-512/18 and C-520/18) ECLI:EU:C:2020:791
('*La Quadrature du Net I*') 64–65, 85–86, 104–5, 124, 135, 153, 170–71, 181, 183,
222–23, 240–41, 252–53, 291, 370, 389n.118
Opinion of Advocate General Campos Sànchez-Bordona of 5 January 2020, Ordre des
barreaux francophones et Germanophone (C-520/18) ECLI:EU:C:2020:7
('*AG Opinion Ordre des barreaux francophones et Germanophone*') 51n.43
CJEU, Judgment of 6 October 2020, Privacy International (C-623/17)
ECLI:EU:C:2020:790 ('*Privacy International*') 104–5, 170–71, 291, 349–50, 425
CJEU, Judgment of 24 November 2020, R.N.N.S. v. Minister van Buitenlandse
Zaken (C-225/19 and C-226/19) ECLI:EU:C:2020:951 ('*Minister van
Buitenlandse Zaken*') 407n.87
Opinion of Advocate General Pitruzzella of 21 January 2020, H.K. v Prokuratuur,
(C-746/18) ECLI:EU:C:2020:18 ('*AG Opinion Prokuratuur*') 51n.43
CJEU, Judgment of 2 March 2021, Prokuratuur (C-746/18) ECLI:EU:C:2021:152
('*Prokuratuur*')........... 22–23, 42–43, 77, 79, 83–84, 135–36, 140, 155n.20, 170n.47, 228, 261,
267–68, 291, 351
CJEU, Judgment of 15 July 2021, *Commission / Poland* (Régime disciplinaire des juges)
(C-791/19) ECLI:EU:C:2021:596.. 198n.8
Opinion of Advocate General Carlos Campos-Sanchez Bordona of 18 November 2021
in case Commissioner of An Garda Síochána (C-140/20), ECLI:EU:C:2021:942
('*AG Opinion Garda Síochána*') 51n.43, 80n.75
CJEU, Judgment of 5 April 2022, Commissioner of An Garda Síochána (C-140/20)
ECLI:EU:C:2022:258 ('*Garda Síochána*') 18–19, 64, 134, 156, 222–23, 244–45, 257, 351
Opinion of Advocate General Pitruzzella of 27 January 2022, Ligue des droits humains
(C-817/19) ECLI:EU:C:2022:65 ('*AG Opinion Ligue des droits humains*') 386n.90
CJEU, Judgment of 21 June 2022, Ligue des droits humains ASBL v Conseil des ministers
(C-817/19), ECLI:EU:C:2022:491 ('*Ligue des droits humains*') 60n.103, 198n.6, 378n.9
CJEU, Judgment of 20 September 2022, VD SR (C-339/20 and C-397/20)
ECLI:EU:C:2022:703 ('*VD and SR*').....................................170, 213, 425n.10
CJEU, Judgment of 27 October 2022, SpaceNet (C-793/19 and C-794/19)
ECLI:EU:C:2022:702 ('*SpaceNet*') 16–17, 18–19, 41–42, 79, 122, 123–24, 125, 156, 270,
292–93, 366–67

Opinion of Advocate General Szpunar of 27 October 2022, C-470/21, *La Quadrature du Net 'II'*, ECLI:EU:C:2022:838 (*'First AG Opinion La Quadrature du Net 'II''*) 82n.86, 195n.67
CJEU, Judgment of 22 November 2022, WM and Sovim SA v Luxembourg Business Registers (C-37/20 and C-601/20) ECLI:EU:C:2022:912 (*'WM and Sovim'*) 398n.13
CJEU, Judgment 4 June 2023, ZZ (C-300/11) ECLI:EU:C:2013:363 (*'ZZ'*)................. 407n.87
CJEU, Judgment of 5 June 2023, *Commission / Poland* (Indépendance et vie privée des juges) (C-204/21) ECLI:EU:C:2023:442.. 198n.8
Opinion of Advocate General Pikamäe of 15 June 2023, Direktor na Glavna direktsia 'Natsionalna politsia' pri MVR – Sofia (C-118/22) ECLI:EU:C:2023:483 (*'AG Opinion Direktor na Glavna direktsia 'Natsionalna politsia' pri MVR'*) 60n.104
CJEU, Judgment of 7 September 2023, Lietuvos Respublikos generalinė prokuratūra (C-162/22) ECLI:EU:C:2023:631 (*Lietuvos Respublikos generalinė prokuratūra*) 43n.133
Opinion of Advocate General Szpunar of 28 September 2023, C-470/21, *La Quadrature du Net 'II'* ECLI:EU:C:2023:711 (*'Second AG Opinion La Quadrature du Net 'II''*)............................. 52n.45, 82n.88, 195n.68, 222–23, 351n.89
CJEU, Judgment of 30 April 2024, *La Quadrature du Net a.o. c. Premier Ministre and Ministre de la Culture* (C-470/21) ECLI:EU:C:2024:370 (*'La Quadrature du Net 'II'*).. 126–27, 159n.42, 397, 425
CJEU, Judgment of 30 April 2024, *Procura della Repubblica presso il Tribunale di Bolzano* (C-178/22) ECLI:EU:C:2024:371(*'Bolzano'*)........ 8, 16, 88, 89–90, 222–23, 257, 258–59, 262, 274, 389, 393–94

EUROPEAN COURT OF HUMAN RIGHTS

ECtHR, Klass and Others v. Germany, 6 September 1978, Series A no. 28 .... 16n.28, 51–52n.44, 134n.24
ECtHR, The Sunday Times v. the United Kingdom (no. 1), 26 April 1979, Series A no. 30..... 56n.66
ECtHR, Malone v. the United Kingdom, 2 August 1984, Series A no. 82.................... 134n.27
ECtHR, Leander v. Sweden, 26 March 1987, Series A no. 116.................... 464n.77, 465n.80
ECtHR, Kruslin v. France, 24 April 1990, A no. 176-A...................................... 56n.67
ECtHR, Valenzuela Contreras v. Spain, no.58/1997/842/1048, 30 July 1998................ 134n.27
ECtHR, P.G. and J.H. v. the United Kingdom, no. 44787/98, ECHR 2001-IX 56n.67
ECtHR, Weber and Saravia v. Germany, no. 54934/00, ECHR 2006-XI 16n.28, 58n.85
ECtHR, Wisse v. France, no. 71611/01, 20 March 2006 .... 134n.26
ECtHR, Association for European Integration and Human Rights and Ekimdzhiev v. Bulgaria, no. 62540/00, 28 June 2007..51–52n.44
ECtHR, Liberty and Others v. the United Kingdom, no. 58243/00, 1 July 2008 .... 56n.67
ECtHR, S. and Marper v. the United Kingdom, nos. 30562/04 and 30566/04 4 December 2008 ....398, 432
ECtHR, Kvasnica v. Slovakia, no. 72094/01, 9 June 2009 57
ECtHR, Kennedy v. the United Kingdom, no. 26839/05, 18 May 2010. .... 57, 337n.27
ECtHR, Uzun v. Germany, no. 35623/05, 2 September 2010............................. 134n.25
ECtHR, M. K. v. France, no. 19522/09, 18 April 2013 .... 398n.13
ECtHR, Roman Zakharov v. Russia [GC], no. 47143/06, 04 December 2015 .... 16n.28, 49n.26, 51–52n.44, 57
ECtHR, Szabó and Vissy v. Hungary, no. 37138/14, 12 January 2016 .... 49n.26, 249n.65
ECtHR, Ben Faiza v. France, no. 31446/12, 8 February 2018 .... 134n.25
ECtHR, Breyer v. Germany, no. 50001/12, 30 January 2020 .... 398n.13
ECtHR, Big Brother Watch and Others v. the United Kingdom [GC], nos. 58170/13 and 2 others, 25 May 2021 .... 49n.20, 388n.107
ECtHR, Centrum för rättvisa v. Sweden [GC], no. 35252/08, 25 May 2021 .....49n.26, 398n.13, 425n.8
ECtHR, Ekimdzhiev and Others v. Bulgaria, no. 70078/12, 11 January 2022 .... 51–52n.44
ECtHR, Glukhin v. Russia, no. 11519/20, 4 July 2023 .... 398n.13
ECtHR, Podchasov v. Russia, no. 33696/19, 13 February 2024......................... 398n.13
ECtHR, Škoberne v. Slovenia, no. 19920/20, 13 February 2024 .... 50n.32, 398n.13

Table of European and International Legal Instruments

Charter of Fundamental Rights of the European Union. 26.10.2012, OJ C 326/391 ('CFR' or 'CFREU' or 'Charter')..... 47n.14, 382n.48, 428n.18, 455n.6

Convention for the Protection of Human Rights and Fundamental Freedoms (European Convention on Human Rights, as amended) ('*ECHR*')...... 41–42, 47–48, 55, 135, 176, 228–29, 279, 382, 430–32

Council Decision 2006/230/EC of 18 July 2005 on the conclusion of an Agreement between the European Community and the Government of Canada on the processing of API/PNR data [2006] OJ L82/14......... 399n.15

Directive 95/46/CE of the European Parliament and of the Council of 24 October 1995 on the protection of individuals with regard to the processing of personal data and on the free movement of such data [1995] OJ L 281/31 ('*Data Protection Directive*')............... 30, 362, 436, 443

Directive 2002/58/EC of the European Parliament and of the Council of 12 July 2002 concerning the processing of personal data and the protection of privacy in the electronic communications sector (Directive on privacy and electronic communications) [2002] OJ L 201/37 ('*ePrivacy Directive*')........ 2, 3, 4, 13–14, 15, 17, 24, 25, 30–34, 35–37, 64, 68–69, 72, 74, 75, 76–77, 78, 80, 82, 84, 95–99, 100, 104–5, 107, 110, 123, 124, 130, 141, 144, 155–56, 157, 170–71, 173, 175–76, 182, 224, 228, 233, 251, 258–59, 262, 264–65, 278, 279, 362–63, 367–68, 372–74, 375, 376, 418–19, 429–30, 434–35, 436, 439, 440, 441, 442, 443, 444, 445, 447, 448, 449–50.

Directive 2006/24/EC of the European Parliament and of the Council of 15 March 2006 on the retention of data generated or processed in connection with the provision of publicly available electronic communications services or of public communications networks and amending Directive 2002/58/EC [2006] OJ L 105/54 ('*Data Retention Directive*')......v–vi, ix, 1–3, 4, 5–6, 13–14, 15, 24, 27–31, 34, 43–44, 60–61, 66, 67, 68, 69, 96–98, 99, 117–18, 119–21, 151–52, 153–54, 156, 158–59, 163, 166, 167, 199–200, 205, 206, 213, 222, 226–27, 228–29, 236, 242, 245–46, 251–52, 257–58, 259, 260, 275–82, 283, 284–89, 293, 294, 333–34, 343, 348–49, 361–62, 363, 364–69, 372–74, 435, 436, 441, 442, 477–79, 485–86

Directive 2016/681 of 27 April 2016 on the use of passenger name record (PNR) data for the prevention, detection, investigation and prosecution of terrorist offences and serious crime [2016]OJ L 119/32 ('*PNR Directive*')............ 377n.6, 379, 380–81n.29, 381, 383–94, 403–4, 405, 407–8, 418–19

Directive 2016/680 of 27 April 2016 on the protection of natural persons with regard to the processing of personal data by competent authorities for the purposes of the prevention, investigation, detection or prosecution of criminal offences or the execution of criminal penalties, and on the free movement of such data, and repealing Council Framework Decision 2008/977/JHA [2016] OJ L 119/89 ('*LED*').................154n.18, 398n.10

Directive 2024/1640 of the European Parliament and of the Council of 31 May 2024 on the mechanisms to be put in place by Member States for the prevention of the use of the financial system for the purposes of money laundering or terrorist financing, amending Directive (EU) 2019/1937,

and amending and repealing
Directive (EU) 2015/849 [2024]
OJ L 2024/1640 ('*6th Anti-Money
Laundering Directive*') 410–11
European Commission, Proposal for
a Regulation of the European
Parliament and of the Council
concerning the respect for private
life and the protection of personal
data in electronic communications
and repealing Directive 2002/58/
EC (Regulation on Privacy and
Electronic Communications) [2017]
COM/2017/010 final – 2017/03
(COD), 10 January 2017 ('*ePrivacy
Proposal or proposed ePrivacy
Regulation*') .... vi, 97, 99
European Commission, 'Proposal
for a Regulation of the European
Parliament and of the Council laying
down rules to prevent and combat
child sexual abuse' (COM)2022 209
final ('*CSAM Proposal*') 412–13
Regulation 2016/679 of the European
Parliament and of the Council of 27
April 2016 on the protection of natural
persons with regard to the processing
of personal data and on the free
movement of such data, and repealing
Directive 95/46/EC (General Data
Protection Regulation) [2016] OJ L
119/1 ('*GDPR*') 98–99, 100, 101–2, 107,
129, 141, 146, 299, 320,
322, 418–19, 433
Regulation 2018/1240 of the European
Parliament and of the Council of
12 September 2018 establishing a
European Travel Information and
Authorisation System (ETIAS) and
amending Regulations (EU) No
1077/2011, (EU) No 515/2014, (EU)
2016/399, (EU) 2016/1624 and (EU)
2017/2226 [2018] OJ L 236/1 ('*ETIAS
Regulation*') 411
Regulation 2021/784 of the European
Parliament and of the Council of
29 April 2021 on addressing the
dissemination of terrorist content
online [2021] OJ L 172/79 ('*TERREG
Regulation*') 412
Regulation 2021/1134 of the European
Parliament and of the Council of 7 July
2021 amending Regulations (EC) No
767/2008, (EC) No 810/2009, (EU)
2016/399, (EU) 2017/2226, (EU)
2018/1240, (EU) 2018/1860, (EU)
2018/1861, (EU) 2019/817 and (EU)
2019/1896 of the European Parliament
and of the Council and repealing
Council Decisions 2004/512/EC
and 2008/633/JHA, for the purpose
of reforming the Visa Information
System [2021] OJ L 248/11 ('*revised
VIS Regulation*') 412
Regulation 2024/1689 of the European
Parliament and of the Council of 13
June 2024 laying down harmonised
rules on artificial intelligence and
amending Regulations (EC) No
300/2008, (EU) No 167/2013, (EU)
No 168/2013, (EU) 2018/858, (EU)
2018/1139 and (EU) 2019/2144
and Directives 2014/90/EU, (EU)
2016/797 and (EU) 2020/1828
(Artificial Intelligence Act) [2024] OJ
L 2024/1689 ('*AI Act*') 410, 420
Treaty on European Union, (consolidated
version), OJ C 326, 26.10.2012
('*TEU*') 17, 32, 35–37, 75,
349–50, 374, 434
Treaty on the Functioning of the European
Union (consolidated version),
OJ C 326, 26.10.2012, p. *47–390*,
('*TFEU*') ... 8–9, 258n.58, 279–81, 284, 466

Contributors

Esther Baars is National Public Prosecutor on Hightech Crime, The Netherlands.

Matthias Bäcker is Professor of Public Law and Information Law, Johannes Gutenberg-Universität, Mainz, Germany.

Lorena Bachmaier Winter is Professor in Justice Systems and Procedure at the Law Faculty, Complutense University Madrid, Spain.

Marco Bassini is Assistant Professor of Fundamental Rights and Artificial Intelligence, Tilburg Institute for Law, Technology, and Society (TILT), Tilburg University, Tilburg, The Netherlands. https://orcid.org/0000-0002-9901-604X

Maria Bergström is Associate Professor in European Law, Faculty of Law, Uppsala University, Sweden.

Magdalena Brewczyńska, PhD is Postdoctoral researcher at Tilburg Institute for Law, Technology, and Society (TILT), Tilburg University, The Netherlands. https://orcid.org/0000-0001-5734-3862

Lorenzo Dalla Corte is Assistant Professor in Data Protection and Cybersecurity Law, Tilburg Institute for Law, Technology and Society (TILT), Tilburg, The Netherlands. https://orcid.org/0000-0003-2221-2971

Shweta Reddy Degalahal, BA, LLB(Hons), LLM is PhD researcher, Tilburg Institute for Law, Technology and Society (TILT), Tilburg, The Netherlands.

Vanessa Franssen, PhD is Professor of Criminal Law and Criminal Procedure, University of Liège, Liège, Belgium, Affiliated Senior Researcher, Institute of Criminal Law, KU Leuven, Leuven, Belgium.

Oskar J Gstrein is Associate Professor 'Human Dignity in the Digital Age', Department of Governance and Innovation, University of Groningen, Campus Fryslân, The Netherlands. https://orcid.org/0000-0003-0546-8684

Lucas M Haitsma, LLM is PhD Candidate, Department of Constitutional Law, Administrative Law and Public Administration, Faculty of Law, University of Groningen, Groningen, The Netherlands. https://orcid.org/0000-0002-3313-545X

Irene Kamara, PhD is Assistant Professor Cybercrime Law and Human Rights, Tilburg Institute for Law, Technology and Society (TILT, Tilburg University), The Netherlands. https://orcid.org/0000-0003-2452-5162

Xenofon Kontargyris, PhD is Global GRC Senior Director, Olympus Corporation, Tokyo, Japan.

Eleni Kosta is Professor of Technology Law and Human Rights, Tilburg Institute for Law, Technology and Society (TILT Tilburg University), The Netherlands. https://orcid.org/0000-0001-6439-4617

Maxime Lassalle is Associate Professor, University of Burgundy, Dijon, France.

Gianclaudio Malgieri, PhD is Associate Professor of Law at Leiden University. Co-Director of the Brussels Privacy Hub. Associate Editor CLSR, Leiden University, Leiden, The Netherlands.

Ivan Manokha is Professor of International Relations and Diplomacy, Schiller International University, Paris, France. https://orcid.org/0000-0001-7675-3613

Christiana Markou, PhD is Associate Professor, European University Cyprus, Cyprus.

Antonio Martinez Santos is Professor of Procedural Law, Department of Procedural Law, Universidad Nacional de Educacion a Distancia, Madrid, Spain. https://orcid.org/0000-0003-4301-9441

TJ McIntyre is Associate Professor, Sutherland School of Law, University College Dublin, Ireland. https://orcid.org/0000-0001-5041-6053

Valsamis Mitsilegas is Professor of European and Global Law and Dean, School of Law and Social Justice, University of Liverpool, United Kingdom. https://orcid.org/0000-0001-6424-7289

Luigi Montuori, PhD is Director of the Department Health and Research, Garante per la protezione dei dati personali (Italian DPA), Rome, Italy.

Ayo Næsborg-Andersen is Associate Professor of Law at the Department of Law, University of Southern Denmark, Denmark.

Daniele Nardi, University La Sapienza of Rome, LLM College of Europe (Natolin), is Legal service officer at the secretariat of the European Data Protection Supervisor, Brussels, Belgium.

Bryce Clayton Newell, PhD, JD is Associate Professor, School of Journalism and Communication, University of Oregon, Eugene, United States, Researcher, Tilburg Institute for Law, Technology and Society (TILT, Tilburg University), The Netherlands. https://orcid.org/0000-0002-6096-1175

Maria Grazia Porcedda is Assistant Professor in IT Law, Trinity College Dublin, Ireland.

Maria-Lucia Rebrean, MSc, LLM is Doctoral Researcher at eLaw Centre for Law and Digital Technologies., Leiden University, Leiden, The Netherlands.

Veronica Tondi, PhD is a Post-Doc Researcher at Law Department, Luiss Guido Carli, Rome, Italy.

Xavier Tracol, PhD is Senior Legal Officer, EUROJUST, The Hague, The Netherlands. https://orcid.org/0000-0002-2828-2586

Maria Tzanou, LLM, PhD is Associate Professor (Senior Lecturer), School of Law, University of Sheffield, United Kingdom. https://orcid.org/0000-0001-5360-2038

Marc van der Ham, LLM is External PhD candidate, eLaw - Center for Law and Digital Technologies, Leiden University, Leiden, The Netherlands, Dutch Public Prosecution Service, Rotterdam, The Netherlands.

Catherine Van de Heyning is Substitute Public Prosecutor in Antwerp, Belgium, Assistant Professor of European Fundamental Rights law, University of Antwerp.

Niovi Vavoula is Associate Professor, Chair in Cyber Policy, University of Luxembourg, Luxembourg.

Heinrich Winter is Professor of Public Administration, Department of Constitutional Law, Administrative Law and Public Administration, Faculty of Law, University of Groningen, Groningen, The Netherlands.

1
Introduction: Data Retention in the EU and Beyond

An Evolving Landscape

Eleni Kosta and Irene Kamara

1. The EU Data Retention Directive and the *Digital Rights Ireland* Case

The issue of regulation of data retention in the European Union has been part of the European policy agenda for more than 25 years, long before the adoption of the Data Retention Directive[1] in 2006. In 2004, France, Ireland, Sweden, and the United Kingdom (still a member of the EU at that time) prepared a proposal for the adoption by the Council of a 'Framework Decision on the retention of data processed and stored in connection with the provision of publicly available electronic communications services or data on public communications networks for the purpose of prevention, investigation, detection and prosecution of crime and criminal offences including terrorism'.[2] However, the European Commission considered a legal instrument regulating data retention as one primarily aiming at the harmonisation of obligations of providers for the retention of traffic and location data. Following a rigorous debate on the first- or third-pillar legal basis of the initiative dealing with the retention of traffic and location data,[3] the Commission presented on 21 September 2005 a proposal for a directive on the retention of data processed in connection with the provision of public electronic communication services and amending Directive 2002/58/EC.[4]

On 15 March 2006, the European Council adopted the Directive on the retention of traffic and location data by providers of publicly available electronic communications services or of public communications networks (hereafter 'providers'), with a view to making

---

[1] Directive 2006/24/EC of the European Parliament and of the Council of 15 March 2006 on the retention of data generated or processed in connection with the provision of publicly available electronic communications services or of public communications networks and amending Directive 2002/58/EC [2006] OJ L 105/54 ('Data Retention Directive').

[2] Council of the European Union, Framework Decision on the retention of data processed and stored in connection with the provision of publicly available electronic communications services or data on public communications networks for the purpose of prevention, investigation, detection and prosecution of crime and criminal offences including terrorism, Brussels, 28 April 2004, available at <https://db.eurocrim.org/db/en/doc/417.pdf> accessed 17 July 2024.

[3] Commission Staff Working Document '*Annex to the:* Proposal for a Directive of the European Parliament and of the Council on the retention of data processed in connection with the provision of public electronic communication services and amending Directive 2002/58/EC *EXTENDED IMPACT ASSESSMENT*', 21 September 2005, available at <https://www.europarl.europa.eu/registre/docs_autres_institutions/commission_europeenne/sec/2005/1131/COM_SEC(2005)1131_EN.pdf> accessed 21 September 2024.

[4] Proposal for a Directive on the retention of data processed in connection with the provision of public electronic communication services and amending Directive 2002/58/EC, available at <https://eur-lex.europa.eu/legal-content/en/ALL/?uri=CELEX%3A52005PC0438> accessed 21 September 2024.

them available for law enforcement purposes. The Directive was part of a broader strategy on fighting organised crime and terrorism, its importance bolstered by the terrorist attacks in Madrid and London in 2004 and 2005 respectively.[5] Data held in the hands of providers are viewed as a valuable source of intelligence in crime investigation[6] and requests for non-content data from law enforcement authorities, are in, practice often granted.[7] The Directive regulated the retention of traffic and location data, as well as data necessary to identify the subscriber or registered user by the aforementioned providers. Content data, thus data that concern the content of communications, were explicitly excluded from retention obligations.[8] The Data Retention Directive, imposing data retention obligations for periods of between six months and up to two years on providers, did not only have significant consequences for providers, but also for citizens, whose data would be retained and potentially made available to law enforcement agencies.

Even before the adoption of the Data Retention Directive, Article 15 of the ePrivacy Directive[9] allowed EU Member States to derogate from the principle of confidentiality of communications, by adopting legislative measures for the retention of traffic and location data when such measures 'constitute... a necessary, appropriate and proportionate measure within a democratic society to safeguard national security... defence, public security, and the prevention, investigation, detection and prosecution of criminal offences or of unauthorised use of the electronic communication system'.[10] These conditions, under which data retention measures may be adopted, resemble significantly the exceptions to the right to privacy laid out in Article 8(2) of the European Convention on Human Rights (ECHR).[11]

The adoption of the Data Retention Directive was met with scepticism,[12] and its national implementations were challenged in national courts in various Member States.[13] In April

---

[5] European Council, Declaration on Combatting Terrorism, 25 March 2004 <https://www.consilium.europa.eu/uedocs/cms_data/docs/pressdata/en/ec/79637.pdf> accessed 20 May 2024.

[6] Recital 11 of the Proposal for a Directive of the European Parliament and of the Council on the retention of data processed in connection with the provision of public electronic communications services and amending Directive 2002/58/EC, COM (2005) 438 final.

[7] European Commission, Directorate-General for Migration and Home Affairs, C Dupont, V Cilli, E Omersa, et al, 'Study on the Retention of Electronic Communications Non-content Data for Law Enforcement Purposes— Final Report', Publications Office 2020 <https://data.europa.eu/doi/10.2837/384802> accessed 17 July 2024, 119.

[8] Art 5(2) Data Retention Directive (n 1).

[9] European Parliament and the Council of the European Union, Directive 2002/58/EC of 12 July 2002 concerning the processing of personal data and the protection of privacy in the electronic communications sector (Directive on privacy and electronic communications) [2002] OJ L201/37 (31 July 2002) ('ePrivacy Directive').

[10] ePrivacy Directive (n 9) Art 15. The ePrivacy Directive was amended by Art 11 Data Retention Directive (n 1), by adding a new paragraph on the non-applicability of Art 15 ePrivacy Directive to retained data under the Data Retention Directive. However, as the Commission has acknowledged, the distinction of the data retention obligations in the two regimes in practice had been a challenging endeavour. European Commission, Report from the Commission to the Council and the European Parliament, Evaluation report on the Data Retention Directive (Directive 2006/24/EC), COM(2011) 225 final.

[11] Convention for the Protection of Human Rights and Fundamental Freedoms (European Convention on Human Rights, as amended) (ECHR), Article 8: '1. Everyone has the right to respect for his private and family life, his home and his correspondence. 2. There shall be no interference by a public authority with the exercise of this right except such as is in accordance with the law and is necessary in a democratic society in the interests of national security, public safety or the economic well-being of the country, for the prevention of disorder or crime, for the protection of health or morals, or for the protection of the rights and freedoms of others.'

[12] L Mitrou, 'Communications Data Retention: A Pandora's Box for Rights and Liberties?' in Digital Privacy, 431–456 (Auerbach Publications 2007); E Kosta and P Valcke, 'Retaining the Data Retention Directive', Computer Law & Security Report, vol 22, issue 5, 2006, 370–80 (Elsevier).

[13] See O Lynskey, 'The Data Retention Directive is Incompatible with the Rights to Privacy and Data Protection and is Invalid in its Entirety: Digital Rights Ireland', Common Market Law Review 51, no 6 (2014); E Kosta, 'The Way to Luxemburg: National Court Decisions on the Compatibility of the Data Retention Directive with the

2014, in its landmark *Digital Rights Ireland* judgment, the Court of Justice of the European Union (CJEU) marked a turning point in the data retention policy in the EU.[14] The CJEU invalidated the Data Retention Directive in its entirety, and ruled that the Data Retention Directive entailed a serious interference with the fundamental rights to privacy and data protection as safeguarded in the Charter of Fundamental Rights of the European Union ('the Charter').[15]

The judgment of the CJEU did not automatically result in the invalidation of national implementations of the Data Retention Directive. It served nevertheless as the basis for a number of national procedures that challenged the empowering authority of the Data Retention Directive as rationale for national rules, after *Digital Rights Ireland*. Several of those actions at national level resulted in a number of national and, most importantly, CJEU judgments,[16] which are addressed in this book. The rich jurisprudence on data retention has raised this topic into an issue of great importance for the protection of fundamental rights and freedoms of individuals.[17] Retention of data for law enforcement and national security purposes remains relevant in the EU, not only because of a regulatory gap at the EU level after the invalidation of the Data Retention Directive, but also the remaining Article 15(1) ePrivacy Directive, and the different practices and approaches at the Member States. At the same time, several countries outside the EU have developed their own systems with a view to allow competent authorities to access traffic and location data that are available in the hands of providers. The contributions to this volume (Chapter 18 by Shweta Degalahal on India, Chapter 19 by Xenofon Kontargyris on Japan, and Chapter 20 by Bryce Newel on the United States) illustrate that the legislator is mainly concerned on the facilitation of the access to the data that are already in the hands of providers, instead of introducing new data retention obligations on providers.

2. Rationale and Structure of this Book

This book aims at answering the overarching question of how the invalidated Data Retention Directive has impacted the law and policy of data retention and accessibility for law enforcement purposes, including national security, combating organised crime, and preventing serious threats to public security. This book provides a thorough analysis of the jurisprudence of the CJEU but also the European Court of Human Rights (ECtHR), and the impact of data retention practices and regulatory approaches on law and policy. The book addresses the challenges that European and international communications providers

---

Rights to Privacy and Data Protection', *SCRIPTed* 10 (2013) 339; H Hijmans and A Scirocco, 'Shortcomings in EU Data Protection in the Third and the Second Pillars: Can the Lisbon Treaty be Expected to Help?' Common Market Law Review 46, no 5 (2009).

[14] CJEU, Judgment of 8 April 2014, *Digital Rights Ireland and Seitlinger and others* (C-293/12 and C-594/12) ECLI:EU:C:2014:238.
[15] Charter of Fundamental Rights of the European Union OJ C83, vol 53, European Union 2010, p 380; *Digital Rights Ireland* (n 14) paras 65 and 69.
[16] See among many: Judgment of 6 October 2020, *La Quadrature du Net and others* (C-511/18, C-512/18 and C-520/18) ECLI:EU:C:2020:791 ('*La Quadrature du Net 'I'*'); CJEU, Judgment of 5 April 2022, *Commissioner of An Garda Síochána* (C-140/20) ECLI:EU:C:2022:258.
[17] See eg CJEU, Judgment of 21 December 2016, *Tele2 Sverige* (C-203/15 and C-698/15) ECLI:EU:C:2016:970.

face when requested to retain data for law enforcement and provides approaches to the regulation of data retention in Europe and beyond. The volume is structured in three parts.

Part I (Chapters 2–6) traces the evolution of the case law in the CJEU and the ECtHR, following the annulment of the Data Retention Directive in 2014. chapters in this section analyse the case law on data retention, its impact on the interpretation of EU data retention-related provisions, and provide critical assessments on the Courts' approach on the proportionality principle, the limitations to fundamental rights, the concepts of serious crime and national security, and positive obligations of countries to protect fundamental rights. The part commences with Chapter 2 by Eleni Kosta, which provides an overview of the evolution of the CJEU case law on data retention. This chapter starts with the reasoning of the CJEU in *Digital Rights Ireland* and continues with a thorough analysis of the evolution of the CJEU case law that links inextricably the retention of traffic and location data with its subsequent access by law enforcement authorities and introduces key safeguards for such access depending on the purpose and in some cases the types of retained data. In Chapter 3, Valsamis Mitsilegas provides a step-by-step analysis of the case law of the CJEU on data retention, identifying the Court's decisiveness in applying EU law in the face of states' national security objections. In the context of the European Union, Article 4(2) of the Treaty on European Union (TEU) explicitly provides that national security remains the sole responsibility of each Member State. Mitsilegas explains how the Court has prioritised—through its case law—the rejection of mass surveillance based on generalised and indiscriminate data retention.

The following two chapters focus on proportionality in the CJEU jurisprudence. Lorenzo Dalla Corte in Chapter 4 argues that the nature of mass surveillance challenges the application of the proportionality test by the CJEU and the ECtHR to its related case law. Dalla Corte suggests that this challenge leads to a proceduralisation of the safeguards and a controlled legitimisation of mass surveillance. On the same thematic, Daniele Nardi argues in Chapter 5 that proportionality is central to the assessment of the CJEU and traces the evolution of the proportionality test applied in the data retention case law. The author ultimately pleads for a more explicit recourse to the strict proportionality test in cases involving fundamental rights.

Given the importance of the ePrivacy Directive in the context of data retention, Xavier Tracol, in Chapter 6, focuses on the ePrivacy legislation and in specific the stalled legislative process on the Proposal for an ePrivacy Regulation, replacing the ePrivacy Directive. The author discusses, inter alia, how the Proposal for ePrivacy Regulation falls short in maintaining the substance of the current Article 15(1) ePrivacy Directive. In view of the non-successful negotiations, including due to the lack of agreement with regard to the data retention matters, and taking into account the evolving rich case law on data retention, Tracol proposes that the CJEU case law is codified in the future ePrivacy Regulation.

The invalidation of the Data Retention Directive, as mentioned earlier, did not result in the corresponding invalidation of national data retention regimes. Member States maintained their national data retention legislation even after *Digital Rights Ireland*, while several of those introduced new rules not only on data retention obligations on providers, but also on the access to the retained data by competent authorities, two topics closed intertwined in the CJEU case law.

Part II of this book (Chapters 7–20) focuses on the one hand on data retention in selected EU Member States—covering different legal traditions and geographic areas—and on the other hand, on three countries outside the European Union, namely India, Japan, and the United States. This second part delves into the adaptations of policy and amendments to legislation in the selected jurisdictions, with diverse traditions in their legal systems as regards data retention, offering an understanding of the existing regulations of data retention, weaknesses, benefits, and potential future solutions.

Matthias Bäcker in Chapter 7 reports the debate on data retention and related legal proceedings in Germany. The author argues that in general data retention is a benchmark case at the Federal Constitutional Court that offers lessons for the Europeanisation of fundamental rights in Germany. In Chapter 8, Montuori and Tondi look into the Italian approach to data retention, one of the first countries in the EU to adopt data retention legislation, and discuss the Italian legislation and case law with a particular focus on the principles of legality and proportionality, the control by an impartial authority, and the usability of data acquired in violation of European law. Christiana Markou, in Chapter 9, presents the developments in Cyprus, where the national legislation was modified only after *Tele2 Sverige*, resulting in data access orders being annulled or the granting of leave, allowing in this manner their challenge through certiorari applications. In her chapter, Markou highlights that the Cyprus Supreme Court, under the influence of *La Quadrature du Net 'I'*, found that to the extent that the Cypriot law provided for the general and indiscriminate retention of IP addresses, it was not incompatible with EU law.

TJ McIntyre in Chapter 10 examines the development of data retention in Ireland, a country associated with many of the crucial CJEU preliminary rulings. The author is critical of the role of the Irish Data Protection Commissioner, and argues that the Irish State essentially did not comply for years with the safeguards introduced by the CJEU in *Tele2 Sverige*, presenting the tale of a state that complies with the EU law requirements when forced. Maxime Lassalle in Chapter 11 provides a thorough study of the French legal regime and the (lack of) impact of the CJEU case law on it. France has been the initiator of seminal judgments by the CJEU on data retention, and Lassalle analyses how the French Council of State interpreted the *La Quadrature du Net 'I'* judgment in a narrow way in order to justify the choices of the national French legislator. An attitude that can be considered as provoking the CJEU into taking a more conciliatory position in *La Quadrature du Net 'II'*.[18]

Magdalena Brewczyńska's contribution (Chapter 12) navigates the reader through the maze of Polish legislation related to retention of data. In the shadow of a legal and political crisis in the country, law enforcement authorities and security services were enjoying excessive access to retained data. Brewczyńska uses the example of Poland to warn of the dangers when effective safeguards do not accompany rules on data retention and the access to the retained data. Lorena Bachmaier and Antonio Martinez Santos in Chapter 13 report that the Spanish data retention approach has not changed despite the invalidation of the Data Retention Directive, which has sparked a national debate on the necessity for amending the national law. Through a thorough analysis of both data retention and criminal law rules, they reach the conclusion that the Spanish legal framework on data retention does not meet the requirement of the CJEU case law and criticise the hesitation of Spanish courts to file a request for a preliminary ruling to the CJEU. Marc Van der Ham and Esther Baars in Chapter 14 provide an overview of the Dutch Telecommunications Data Retention Act

---

[18] CJEU, Judgment of 30 April 2024, *La Quadrature du Net aoc Premier Ministre and Ministre de la Culture* (C-470/21) ECLI:EU:C:2024:370 ('*La Quadrature du Net 'II'*').

(TDRA), which implemented the Data Retention Directive in the Netherlands. They analyse the suspension of the TDRA by the District Court of The Hague and the implications from the lack of a comprehensive data retention framework in the Netherlands, especially as regards criminal investigations.

Chapters 15 and 16 are dedicated to EU Member States that have introduced data retention laws after *La Quadrature du Net 'I'*, making use of the finding of the CJEU on the permissibility of legislative measures for the targeted retention of traffic and location data 'which is limited, on the basis of objective and non-discriminatory factors, according to the categories of persons concerned or using a geographical criterion, for a period that is limited in time to what is strictly necessary'.[19] In Chapter 15, Ayo Næsborg-Andersen provides a critical assessment of the evolution of the Danish legislative framework on data retention. She closely studies the 2022 revision of the Danish law that implemented the Data Retention Directive and questions whether the targeted retention scheme it introduces that covers over 67% of the Danish population is compatible with fundamental rights. In Chapter 16, Vanessa Franssen and Catherine van de Heyning delve into a thorough analysis of the Belgian 2022 Data Retention Act, which was adopted in response to *La Quadrature du Net 'I'*. They critically assess the introduction of the targeted retention scheme in Belgium that effectively covers almost the entire territory—and consequently the entire population—of Belgium, and reflect on the impact of *La Quadrature du Net 'II'* on the Belgian rules regarding the retention of IP addresses.

In Chapter 17 Maria Bergström presents the legislative history and jurisprudential evolution of data retention in Sweden, one of the first countries to enact national rules on data retention already in the 1990s. Bergström provides a critical analysis of the interplay between the Swedish and European law and politics through the lens of data retention, up to the recent proposal for national rules on geographical targeted retention.

Acknowledging that data retention for law enforcement purposes, including national security, combating serious crime, and preventing serious threats to public security, is far from being an EU matter only. This book also offers international perspectives on the matter, with country-specific chapters on India, Japan, and the United States, countries with no dedicated data retention framework similar to the European one. Although India does not have a comprehensive law on data retention, Shweta Reddy Degalahal in Chapter 18 discusses the requirements on the retention and subsequent law enforcement access to retained personal data that can be found in fragmented regulations. Degalahal assesses those requirements under the threefold test that was developed by the Indian Supreme Court in the *Puttaswamy* judgment to conclude that the existing requirements, if challenged, would not pass the aforementioned test. In Chapter 19, Xenofon Kontargyris discusses the retention of data in the telecommunications and healthcare sector and reflects on the trend that Japan increasingly follows the example of the EU in regulating issues relating to data and the enforcement of relevant rules. Bryce Clayton Newell provides, in Chapter 20, a brief overview of the choice of the US legislator to focus on regulating access to communications data. As the United States does not have a data retention law at the federal level, Newell mainly analyses relevant provisions in the Stored Communications Act and discusses the safeguards that are in place for accessing data in the hands of service

---

[19] *La Quadrature du Net 'I'* (n 16) para 144.

providers, providing a brief comparison with safeguards introduced in the CJEU case law on data retention.

Last but not least, Part III (Chapters 21–27) shifts the focus to overarching issues relating to data retention, including on the role of the courts in shaping data retention regimes, societal impact and surveillance, matters of automated analysis, and public policy linked to data retention.

Maria Tzanou and Marco Bassini focus on the role of the courts in the context of data retention. In Chapter 21, Maria Tzanou studies the European regulation on data retention through the theoretical framework of judicialisation, that is, the reliance on courts and judicial means for addressing public policy questions and political controversies. Tzanou concludes that the adoption of a different starting point for the judicial assessment of targeted geographical surveillance compared to the one used for mass surveillance should be rejected and suggests challenging the institutional and social assumptions that create unequal structural conditions and institutional (judicial) epistemic injustice. Chapter 22, authored by Marco Bassini, analyses the relationship between constitutional courts in several Member States and the CJEU and discusses how national courts had to look at the positions of the CJEU on data retention, after the latter started publishing judgments on data retention, with the first one being *Digital Rights Ireland*. Bassini criticises the EU legislator for leaving a legislative vacuum open for too long that essentially allowed (or forced?) the CJEU to judicial activism.

In Chapter 23, Lucas Haitsma, Oskar Gstrein, and Heinrich Winter consider the Passenger Name Record (PNR) Directive, which establishes a regime for the reuse of data held by airlines for law enforcement purposes. The authors consider the safeguards introduced by the CJEU in *Ligue des droits humains* in the light of the CJEU's established case law on PNR, highlighting the parallels and differences with the case law on data retention.[20] They argue that while recent jurisprudence ensures formal compatibility with fundamental rights by building on the safeguards developed in the context of data retention, the PNR system as such appears to be unsuited to the fight against serious crime and terrorism.

Remaining in the realm of PNR data, Niovi Vavoula in Chapter 24 discusses the automated analysis of personal data, as examined in *La Quadrature du Net 'I'*. Vavoula embarks on an analysis of both *La Quadrature du Net 'I'*, as well as the case law on the automated processing of PRN data, and systematises the safeguards established by the CJEU on automated processing of personal data. Vavoula concludes that the CJEU would be required to develop more in-depth safeguards in order to meet the challenges of fast-paced technological developments and Artificial Intelligence.

Maria Grazia Porcedda remains in the same thematic of automated analysis of the retained data and in Chapter 25 provides a thorough study of the case law of the CJEU and the ECtHR on the automated analysis of retained data as a measure of mass surveillance. Porcedda provides a detailed explanation on the distinction between electronic communications service providers and online intermediaries, arguing that the regulatory silos that exist in the European legal landscape hamper effective protections against surveillance.

In Chapter 26, Maria-Lucia Rebrean and Gianclaudio Malgieri approach the retention of individual's data as intrinsic facet of administrative vulnerability, given that vulnerable

---

[20] CJEU, Judgment of 21 June 2022, *Ligue des droits humains ASBL v Conseil des ministres* (C-817/19), ECLI:EU:C:2022:491.

individuals cannot refuse, postpone or control, as rule, such retention. Next to the CJEU requirement for notification, they propose transparency and explainability as safeguards for administrative and surveillance vulnerability.

Chapter 27, the final chapter of this edited volume, is authored by Ivan Manokha, who builds on the legal analyses conducted in the book, and examines the structural context within which different surveillance and data retention measures are implemented by public and private actors which cause a chilling effect.

3. Data Retention in the Aftermath of *La Quadrature du Net 'II'*

The research for this book was completed on the 30 April 2024, when the Court delivered two seminal judgments in the field of data retention, *La Quadrature du Net 'II'* and *Bolzano*.[21] However, developments at national level are not brought to a standstill. There are two interesting judgments delivered in June 2024, one by the Irish Supreme Court and one by the Belgian Court of Cassation, that are worth briefly discussing here as illustrative of current and future trends in the EU legal and jurisprudential developments.

3.1 Ireland

After the text for this book was finalised at the end of April 2024, the Irish Supreme Court gave another judgment on data retention in *DPP v Smyth*.[22] In a remarkable decision, the majority of the Supreme Court held that traffic data was admissible in a criminal prosecution despite being accessed under provisions of the 2011 Act, which were subsequently declared invalid. According to Collins J, the Irish state had not been 'reckless'[23] or 'grossly negligent'[24] in deciding to maintain general and indiscriminate retention and access without independent authorisation following the CJEU judgment in *Tele2 Sverige*. The claim was that the meaning of *Tele2 Sverige* was not entirely clear, as evidenced by the fact that the Supreme Court itself asserted that general and indiscriminate retention was permissible in its preliminary reference in *Dwyer v Commissioner of An Garda Síochána & Others*,[25] which is discussed in detail in Chapter 10, authored by TJ McIntyre.

While *DPP v Smyth* is most important for the domestic law of evidence, it also highlights a continued failure by much of the Irish judiciary to give full effect to EU law in this area. The majority judgment was replete with criticisms of the data retention case law and the rejection of the points made by the Supreme Court in the *Dwyer* reference, culminating in the complaint that '[t]he Article 267 [TFEU] reference procedure constitutes an important "judicial dialogue" between the CJEU and the national courts but it is difficult to avoid the conclusion that the dialogue here has been rather one-sided'.[26] It is notable

---

[21] See respectively: *La Quadrature du Net 'II'* (n 18) and CJEU, Judgment of 30 April 2024, *Procura della Repubblica presso il Tribunale di Bolzano* (C-178/22) ECLI:EU:C:2024:371.
[22] Credit is due to TJ McIntyre for this section, the input and analysis of the Irish judgment on *DPP v Smyth*, as part of this introductory chapter: *DPP v Smyth* [2024] IESC 22.
[23] ibid para 77.
[24] ibid para 77.
[25] *Dwyer v Commissioner of An Garda Síochána & Others* [2020] IESC 4.
[26] *DPP v Smyth* (n 22) para 97.

that the dissenting judge, Hogan J, described the approach of the majority as undermining 'the rule of law and respect for the application of EU law in general and the Charter in particular',[27] and as being 'tantamount to saying that these breaches of Article 8 of the Charter were immaterial and [failing] to give due weight to the import of a series of decisions of the Court of Justice commencing with *Digital Rights Ireland*'.[28]

3.2 Belgium

In Belgium, one burning question related to the way how the CJEU jurisprudence would impact ongoing investigations, in particular communication data driven investigations.[29] Relying on the Luxemburg jurisprudence, lawyers requested the Belgian courts in the *Sky ECC* cases to exclude telecommunication data, in particular IP addresses, if retained on the basis of the annulled Belgian 2016 data retention legislation, which is discussed in detail in Chapter 16 by Vanessa Franssen and Catherine van de Heyning. These cases resulted from a JIT (Joint Investigation Teams) investigation into the use of the encrypted software by criminal organisations whereby the confiscation of the server in France was relied upon in hundreds of serious drugs and organised crime cases.[30] The CJEU had indicated in *La Quadrature du Net 'I'* that national judges maintain a wide margin of discretion on the appreciation and, thus, exclusion of evidence. Yet, the Court set out three minimum criteria that national judges are to take into account: namely whether the suspects are able to comment effectively on that evidence, the evidence pertains to a field of which the judges have knowledge, and whether the evidence has a preponderant influence on the findings of fact.[31]

As the appreciation of criminal evidence falls within the discretion of the national courts, it was to be awaited how supreme courts would react. The Belgian Court of Cassation opted for balancing a loyal approach towards Luxembourg, while preserving the national rules on the appreciation of evidence.[32] In the *Sky ECC* cases, the Court of Cassation highlighted in that respect the discretionary margin of Member States to decide on the exclusionary rules of evidence in criminal cases.[33] As such, the Court indicated that retained data needed to be assessed in the light of the national criteria set out in Code of Criminal procedure, in particular whether the seriousness of the crime outweighs the importance of the infringement and whether the infringement was intentionally committed or not. At the same time,

---

[27] Judgment of Mr Justice Gerard Hogan delivered on 17 June 2024 on case *DPP v Smyth* [2024] IESC 22, para 48, available at <https://www.courts.ie/viewer/pdf/9d3c6ba6-f2c0-47f3-aeee-18e027e7a72b/2024_IESC_22_Hogan%20J..pdf/pdf#view=fitH> accessed 17 July 2024.
[28] ibid.
[29] Credit is due to Catherine van de Heyning for this section, the input and analysis of the *Belgian Sky ECC* cases, as part of this introductory chapter.
[30] Eurojust, 'New major interventions to block encrypted communications of criminal networks', Press release, 10 March 2021 <https://www.eurojust.europa.eu/news/new-major-interventions-block-encrypted-communications-criminal-networks> accessed 17 July 2024.
[31] *La Quadrature du Net 'I'* (n 16) paras 221–28.
[32] First references to the exclusionary criteria of *La Quadrature du Net 'I'* were mentioned in Court of Cassation 25 January 2022, P.21.1353.N, ECLI:BE:CASS:2022:CONC.20220125.2N.3; Court of Cassation 29 March 2022, P.21.1422.N, ECLI:BE:CASS:2022:ARR.20220329.2N.1; Court of Cassation 29 March 2022, P.22.0078.N, ECLI:BE:CASS:2022:ARR.20220329.2N.15.
[33] Court of Cassation 11 June 2024, P.24.0200.N, ECLI:BE:CASS:2024:ARR.20240611.2N.1 and Court of Cassation 18 June 2024, P.24.0240.N., ECLI:BE:CASS:2024:ARR.20240618.2N.

the Court highlights the importance of the CJEU case law and requires national courts to take these criteria into account. The Court of Cassation finds that neither the CJEU nor the national criteria are decisive on their own, but need to be evaluated together in a holistic way from the perspective of the fairness of the procedure as a whole. Whereas judges are not required to justify their decision to allow or exclude retained data by applying the several criteria separately on the case, the Court of Cassation demands that judges show that they took the CJEU criteria into account. Again, the Belgian legal order shows a tendency to marry loyalty to the CJEU with seeking a margin of discretion to uphold the established checks and balances on the use of retained telecommunication data.

3.3 In anticipation of future developments

While national courts seem in turmoil when called upon to implement in practice the requirements established by the CJEU, the High-Level Group (HLG) on access to data for effective law enforcement published its recommendations in May 2024.[34] These recommendations focus mainly on how to ensure that national law enforcement authorities have access to retained data, not paying sufficient attention to the safeguards developed by the CJEU on the actual retention of the data. At the time of writing this book, and as very vividly explained by Xavier Tracol in Chapter 6, the European Commission does not have any concrete plans to launch new legislation on data retention. However, the lack of an EU instrument regulating the retention of traffic and location data and their subsequent access by law enforcement authorities has led the CJEU to what Bassini calls in Chapter 22 'CJEU judicial activism'. Several authors in this book suggest that the current trend to leave the assessment of various and diverging interpretations of Article 15 ePrivacy Directive to the CJEU has placed the Court more in the political arena that its constitutional role should allow. In this book, several contributors have reflected on how concrete aspects of data retention and access to the retained data could be interpreted in a way that is compatible with EU law and have cast ideas that can help the European legislator in taking the next steps in a new attempt to regulate the issue. It remains to be seen, whether the European Commission will make a new attempt to codify the safeguards and requirements that are already present in the existing case law of the European Union and strike a balance between the needs of law enforcement authorities and the protection of fundamental rights and freedoms of individuals.

---

[34] High-Level Group (HLG) on access to data for effective law enforcement, Recommendations of the High-Level Group on Access to Data for Effective Law Enforcement, May 2024, available at <https://home-affairs.ec.europa.eu/document/download/1105a0ef-535c-44a7-a6d4-a8478fce1d29_en?filename=Recommendations%20of%20the%20HLG%20on%20Access%20to%20Data%20for%20Effective%20Law%20Enforcement_en.pdf> accessed 17 July 2024.

PART I
THE EVOLUTION OF CASE LAW IN CJEU AND EUROPEAN COURT OF HUMAN RIGHTS

2
The Evolution of the CJEU Case Law on Data Retention

Towards the Regulation of Access

Eleni Kosta

1. Introduction

Regulating data retention has become one of the most controversial issues in the policy arena in the European Union. In 2006, the European Parliament and European Council attempted to regulate the issue of data retention with the Data Retention Directive.[1] The Directive aimed to harmonize national rules on the retention of traffic and location data by telecom operators and internet service providers for law enforcement purposes, and more specifically, for the purpose of the investigation, detection, and prosecution of serious crime, as defined by each Member State in its national law. After a turbulent period of national higher court cases that invalidated (parts of the) laws that transposed the Data Retention Directive in various Member States, the Court of Justice of the European Union (CJEU) annulled the Data Retention Directive in its seminal *Digital Rights Ireland* judgment.[2]

After the invalidation of the Data Retention Directive, Member States could still adopt data retention rules on the basis of Article 15(1) of the ePrivacy Directive,[3] which allows Member States to adopt legislative measures to restrict certain rights and obligations established in the ePrivacy Directive[4] for 'a limited period'[5] to 'safeguard national security (ie State security), defence, public security, and the prevention, investigation, detection, and prosecution of criminal offences or of unauthorised use of the electronic communication system'.[6] These restrictions must be necessary, appropriate, and proportionate measures within a democratic society.[7] Based on this provision, the CJEU was asked by national

---

[1] Directive 2006/24/EC of the European Parliament and of the Council of 15 March 2006 on the retention of data generated or processed in connection with the provision of publicly available electronic communications services or of public communications networks and amending Directive 2002/58/EC [2006] OJ L 105/54 ('Data Retention Directive').
[2] CJEU, Judgment of 8 April 2014, *Digital Rights Ireland and Seitlinger and others* (C-293/12 and C-594/12) ECLI:EU:C:2014:238.
[3] Directive 2002/58/EC of the European Parliament and of the Council of 12 July 2002 concerning the processing of personal data and the protection of privacy in the electronic communications sector (Directive on privacy and electronic communications) [2002] OJ L 201/37 ('ePrivacy Directive').
[4] Article 5, Article 6, Article 8(1) (2) (3) and (4) and Article 9 ePrivacy Directive (n 3).
[5] Article 15(1) ePrivacy Directive (n 3).
[6] Article 15(1) ePrivacy Directive (n 3).
[7] On the proportionality and necessity principles in the data retention case law of the CJEU, please see Lorenzo Dalla Corte (Chapter 4) and of Danielle Nardi (Chapter 5).

courts to interpret several provisions on data retention in national legislation of Member States in a number of cases discussed in this chapter.

The CJEU has been dealing with data retention cases since 2012, with its first judgment being published in 2014 in the famous *Digital Rights Ireland* case, which invalidated the Data Retention Directive. The CJEU's most recent decisions, at the time of writing, were published in April 2024.[8] In these ten years, the CJEU has dealt with numerous aspects of data retention, stemming from the interpretation of Article 15(1) of the ePrivacy Directive, which serves as the legal basis for data retention legislation after the annulment of the Data Retention Directive. It is noteworthy that the CJEU considers data retention an issue of utmost importance, thus deciding these cases in Grand Chamber[9] or, in one case, even in Full Court.[10] This chapter, through a critical examination of the rich case law of the CJEU, distils the requirements and safeguards introduced by the CJEU in relation to various types of data and for specific purposes. It concludes that the European legislator can rely on these as the basis for a new legislative framework, which covers both the data retention obligations on providers and the safeguards on the access to the retained data.

2. The Prohibition on Blanket Data Retention

In the *Digital Rights Ireland* judgment, the CJEU analysed the provisions of the Data Retention Directive. The CJEU criticized the fact that the Data Retention Directive did not provide for any exceptions to its application. Rather, it was applicable even to persons whose communications were subject to obligations of professional secrecy in line with relevant national laws.[11] Furthermore, the Data Retention Directive did not 'require any relationship between the data whose retention is provided for and a threat to public security'.[12] The CJEU also found it illustrative that the Directive did not include provisions that could limit the retention of data based around a 'particular time period and/or a particular geographical zone and/or to a circle of particular persons likely to be involved, in one way or another, in a serious crime',[13] when the retention of such data could contribute to the prevention, detection, or prosecution of serious offences.

The CJEU took issue with the retention period in the Directive because it provided retention periods that were not 'based on objective criteria in order to ensure that it is limited to what is strictly necessary'.[14] The Court also criticized the lack of any 'objective criterion by which to determine the limits of the access of the competent national authorities to the data and their subsequent use'[15] along with the lack of specific provisions that would ensure

---

[8] CJEU, Judgment of 30 April 2024, *La Quadrature du Net a.o.c. Premier Ministre and Ministre de la Culture* (C-470/21) ECLI:EU:C:2024:370 ('*La Quadrature du Net 'II'*'); CJEU, Judgment of 30 April 2024, *Procura della Repubblica presso il Tribunale di Bolzano* (C-178/22) ECLI:EU:C:2024:371.
[9] Xavier Tracol, 'The Joined Cases of Dwyer, SpaceNet and VD and SR before the European Court of Justice: The Judgments of the Grand Chamber about Data Retention Continue Falling on Deaf Ears in Member States' (2023) 48 *Computer Law & Security Review* 105773, 14.
[10] *La Quadrature du Net 'II'* (n 8).
[11] *Digital Rights Ireland* (n 2) para 58.
[12] ibid para 59.
[13] ibid para 59.
[14] ibid para 64.
[15] ibid para 60.

a high level of protection and security of the retained data[16] and any obligation for irreversible destruction of the data.[17] Finally, the CJEU introduced an implicit requirement that retained data should be stored within the European Union in order for European independent supervisory authorities to exercise their compliance control powers.[18] The CJEU concluded that the European legislator in the Data Retention Directive 'exceeded the limits imposed by compliance with the principle of proportionality in the light of Articles 7, 8 and 52(1) of the Charter'[19] of Fundamental Rights of the European Union ('EU Charter'),[20] and found the Directive invalid.

3. Retention and Access to Retained Data

Following *Digital Rights Ireland*, several Member State national courts found that provisions of national data retention laws and, in some cases, even full national data retention laws that transposed the Data Retention Directive were invalid.[21] At the same time, some Member States proceeded with the adoption of new national data retention laws, relying on Article 15(1) of the ePrivacy Directive. One prominent example was the United Kingdom, which was still a member of the European Union at the time, and which only three months after the invalidation of the Data Retention Directive adopted the UK Data Retention and Investigatory Powers Act 2014 (DRIPA). This legislation was at the core of a second CJEU judgment, joined with a Swedish case, *Tele2 Sverige*, in which the CJEU made firm statements that national data retention legislation should meet key minimum requirements in line with the EU Charter.

In *Tele2 Sverige*, the CJEU built on its decision in *Digital Rights Ireland* and linked the establishment of rules imposing data retention obligations on providers with rules on subsequent access to that data by law enforcement authorities. Although the Data Retention Directive left the introduction of rules on access to the retained data by competent national authorities up to the national legislators,[22] the CJEU considered these two issues—data retention rules for providers and safeguards relating to access to the retained data—as inseparable. In *Tele2 Sverige*, the CJEU reiterated its position that general and indiscriminate retention of traffic and location data is not allowed under the EU Charter.[23]

However, Member States may adopt data retention rules to cover situations where individuals are 'suspected of planning, committing or having committed a serious crime or of being implicated in one way or another in such a crime'[24] and when key safeguards are put in place to govern subsequent access to the retained data. First, access to the retained data may be allowed only following prior review carried out either by a court or by an

---

[16] ibid para 67.
[17] ibid para 67.
[18] ibid para 67.
[19] ibid para 69.
[20] Charter of Fundamental Rights of the European Union, OJ C83, vol 53, European Union, 2010, 380.
[21] For an overview of national cases before *Digital Rights Ireland*, see Eleni Kosta, 'The Way to Luxemburg: National Court Decisions on the Compatibility of the Data Retention Directive with the Rights to Privacy and Data Protection', SCRIPTed 10(3) October 2013, 339.
[22] Article 4, Data Retention Directive (n 1).
[23] Charter of Fundamental Rights of the European Union (n 20) 380.
[24] CJEU, Judgment of 21 December 2016, *Tele2 Sverige* (C-203/15 and C-698/15) ECLI:EU:C:2016:970 para 125.

independent administrative body.[25] This requirement was further elaborated in the CJEU case law on data retention and is discussed in more detail below.[26] The CJEU introduced a second safeguard, requiring national authorities that were granted access to retained data to notify the affected persons as soon as such notification would not jeopardize the investigation.[27] This requirement is in line with the case law of the European Court of Human Rights (ECtHR),[28] which has established a similar requirement in cases of targeted and covert surveillance.[29] The difficulties of how this can be realized in practice is left to the national legislators, legal practitioners, and courts. The CJEU also made the requirements on the security of data more concrete in *Tele2 Sverige*, introducing a third safeguard, requiring providers to take appropriate technical and organizational measures to ensure that retained data is effectively protected against risks of misuse and unlawful access; in this context, such data must be retained within the European Union and destroyed at the end of the retention period.[30]

It should be noted that the notion of serious crime, which is quintessential to the application of data retention rules, is left to the Member States to specify, with some limited guidance coming from the Court only in much later cases.[31] In *Bolzano* the Court explained that, 'in view of the division of competences between the European Union and the Member States under the FEU Treaty and the considerable differences among the legal systems of the Member States in the area of criminal law, it must be found that it is for the Member States to define "serious offences" for the purposes of applying Article 15(1) of Directive 2002/58'.[32]

4. Evolving Rules on Data Retention

4.1 Prohibiting blanket retention on a preventative basis

The CJEU has developed established case law that general and unconditional data retention cannot pass the necessity and proportionality test applied to fundamental rights, and in particular the rights to privacy and to data protection. In *Tele2 Sverige* the CJEU declared

---

[25] ibid para 120.
[26] See section 6 in this chapter.
[27] *Tele2 Sverige* (n 24) para 121.
[28] See a.o. *Roman Zakharov v Russia* (2015) Application no 47143/06, para 287; *Szabó and Vissy v Hungary* (2016) Application no 37138/14, para 86; *Klass and Others v Germany* (1978) Series A no 28 Application no 5029/71, para 58; *Weber and Saravia v Germany* 2006-XI Application no 54934/00, para 135.
[29] F Boehm and P de Hert, 'Notification, An Important Safeguard Against the Improper Use of Surveillance - Finally recognised in Case Law and EU Law' (2012) 3(3) European Journal of Law and Technology.
[30] *Tele2 Sverige* (n 24) para 122.
[31] For instance, in *La Quadrature du Net 'I'*, the CJEU presented as examples of serious crime 'cases involving particularly serious child pornography offences, such as the acquisition, dissemination, transmission or making available online of child pornography', CJEU, Judgment of 6 October 2020, *La Quadrature du Net and others* (C-511/18, C-512/18 and C-520/18) ECLI:EU:C:2020:791 ('*La Quadrature du Net 'I'*'). In *La Quadrature du Net 'I'*, the CJEU was confronted with the automated analysis of traffic and location data for national security purposes (para 172) and the obligation in France on providers to collect real-time traffic and location data (para 170). Although both these actions give access to French law enforcement authorities to data, they do not require service providers to actually retain data and are therefore not discussed further in this chapter.
[32] *Bolzano* (n 8) para 46. In *Bolzano*, the CJEU argued that the definition of serious crime in national law 'must not be so broad that access to those data becomes the rule rather than the exception. Thus, that definition cannot cover the vast majority of criminal offences, which would be the case if the minimum period above which the maximum term of imprisonment for an offence justifies its classification as a serious offence were set at an excessively low level' (para 55).

that the fight against serious crime 'cannot in itself justify that national legislation providing for the general and indiscriminate retention of all traffic and location data should be considered to be necessary for the purposes of that fight'.[33] In *SpaceNet*,[34] the CJEU clearly reaffirmed the prohibition on 'general and indiscriminate'[35] retention of traffic and location data for the purposes of 'combating serious crime and preventing serious threats to public security'[36] on a *preventative* basis.

4.2 Applicability of EU law on measures relating to the safeguarding of national security

In its case law following *Tele2 Sverige*, the CJEU was confronted with more complex questions relating to data retention, with processing activities 'ranging from data retention to data transmission and automated data analysis',[37] measures both targeted and indiscriminate, measures of different types of data, including IP addresses, and more. Thus, the CJEU further elaborated its positions regarding data retention, building on the safeguards established in *Tele2 Sverige*, analysing data retention rules for the purposes of safeguarding national security, combating serious crime and preventing serious threats to public security.

In the context of the European Union, Article 4(2) of the Treaty on European Union (TEU) explicitly provides that national security remains the sole responsibility of each Member State. In *Privacy International*, the CJEU examined national legislation enabling a Member State authority to require providers of electronic communications services to forward traffic data and location data to the security and intelligence agencies for the purpose of safeguarding national security.[38] A number of European governments argued in *Privacy International* that 'the activities of the [national] security and intelligence agencies are essential State functions relating to the maintenance of law and order and the safeguarding of national security and territorial integrity, and, accordingly, are the sole responsibility of the Member States'.[39] Therefore, national measures concerning the safeguarding of national security cannot be considered falling within the scope of the ePrivacy Directive. However, the CJEU concluded that 'although it is for the Member States to define their essential security interests and to adopt appropriate measures to ensure their internal and external security, the mere fact that a national measure has been taken for the purpose of protecting national security cannot render EU law inapplicable and exempt the Member States from their obligation to comply with that law'.[40] A similar conclusion was reached in *La Quadrature du Net 'I'*.[41]

---

[33] *Tele2 Sverige* (n 24) para 103.
[34] CJEU, Judgment of 27 October 2022, *SpaceNet* (C-793/19 and C-794/19) ECLI:EU:C:2022:702.
[35] ibid para 131.
[36] ibid para 131.
[37] Sarah Eskens, 'The Ever-Growing Complexity of the Data Retention Discussion in the EU: An In-Depth Review of La Quadrature du Net and others and Privacy International' (2022) 8(1) EDPL 145.
[38] CJEU, Judgment of 6 October 2020, *Privacy International* (C-623/17) ECLI:EU:C:2020:790.
[39] ibid para 32.
[40] ibid para 44.
[41] *La Quadrature du Net 'I'* (n 31) para 99.

4.3 Civil identity data

In its case law, the CJEU has not treated all types of retained data in the same way. In *Ministerio Fiscal*,[42] the CJEU was confronted with questions in the context of a police investigation relating to the theft of a wallet and a mobile phone and reflected on whether retained data can be accessed in order to assist such an investigation. The CJEU found that with regard to data relating to the identity of the owners of SIM cards of mobile phones 'traffic data may include, *inter alia*, the name and address of the person sending a communication or using a connection to carry out a communication. Data relating to the identity of owners of SIM cards can also prove necessary in order to bill for the electronic communications services provided and therefore form part of traffic data'.[43] In this case, the Spanish police aimed at accessing 'only the telephone numbers corresponding to those SIM cards and to the data relating to the identity of the owners of those cards, such as their surnames, forenames and, if need be, addresses. . . . [T]hose data do not concern, . . . the communications carried out with the stolen mobile telephone or its location'.[44]

The CJEU therefore reflected on the seriousness of the interference with the fundamental rights to privacy and data protection through a detailed examination of the information that can be derived from the data to which the Spanish police wished to get access, namely the data that only allows the linking of the SIM card(s) with the identity of the owners of these SIM cards. The CJEU concluded that the interference with the rights to privacy and data protection is not 'serious', as '[w]ithout [the requested] data being cross-referenced with the data pertaining to the communications with those SIM cards and the location data, those data do not make it possible to ascertain the date, time, duration and recipients of the communications made with the SIM card or cards in question, nor the locations where those communications took place or the frequency of those communications with specific people during a given period. Those data do not therefore allow precise conclusions to be drawn concerning the private lives of the persons whose data is concerned'.[45] This way the CJEU created a two-tiered categorization of data, distinguishing between data relating to the identity (of SIM card owners, in the given case), such as names and addresses, and data that can reveal information about the private lives of individuals, suggesting that access to the former category of data could be permissible under EU law.[46]

The CJEU got the opportunity to reflect on similar types of data, namely data relating to the *civil identity* of the users of electronic communications systems, in *La Quadrature du Net 'I'*. In line with the Court's reasoning in *Ministerio Fiscal*, the CJEU found that such data 'does not, in itself, make it possible to ascertain the date, time, duration and recipients of the communications made, or the locations where those communications took place or their frequency with specific people during a given period, with the result that it does not provide, apart from the contact details of those users, such as their addresses, any information on the communications sent and, consequently, on the users' private lives'.[47] Based on this reasoning, the CJEU concluded that any interference by the retention of such data

---

[42] CJEU, Judgment of 2 October 2018, *Ministerio Fiscal* (C-207/16) ECLI:EU:C:2018:788.
[43] ibid para 42.
[44] ibid para 59.
[45] ibid para 60.
[46] ibid para 64.
[47] *La Quadrature du Net 'I'* (n 31) para 157.

is not serious. As such, the CJEU opened a clear door for national legislators to adopt laws requiring the general and indiscriminate retention of data relating to the *identity* of users of electronic communications systems for the purposes of safeguarding national security, combating crime, and safeguarding public security.[48] This position has been confirmed by the CJEU in *SpaceNet* and *Garda Síochána*.[49]

One of the most prominent positions of the CJEU relates to general and indiscriminate data retention rules for the purposes of safeguarding national security. In both *La Quadrature du Net 'I'* and in *SpaceNet*, the CJEU found that national legislators can enact general and indiscriminate data retention measures for the purposes of safeguarding of national security under specific safeguards. More concretely Member States can take legislative measures that 'allow recourse to an instruction requiring providers of electronic communications services to retain, generally and indiscriminately, traffic and location data'[50] for a limited period, when the said Member State faces a genuine and present of foreseeable serious threat to *national security*. In line with the safeguards established in *Tele2 Sverige*, a court or an independent administrative body is entrusted with effective review of this decision, during which the reviewing body will examine the correct application of these exceptional measures and will ensure the conditions and established safeguards are respected.[51] The CJEU did not make explicit reference to any notification of the affected persons in this context. Furthermore, it is noteworthy that these measures can be extended when the threat to national security persists.[52] Such exceptions would allow for rolling warrants, for instance, or for laws that can be extended for long periods of time.

4.4 Expedited retention

The CJEU gave power to Member States to introduce laws that allow, for a specified period of time in compliance with the principle of strict necessity,[53] the *expedited retention* of traffic and location data in the possession of electronic communications service providers, also known as 'quick freeze' for the purposes of combating serious crime, preventing serious threats to public security,[54] and safeguarding national security.[55] These measures must be limited and national legislators shall adopt clear and precise national rules requiring compliance with substantive and procedural conditions and entrust the persons concerned with effective safeguards against the risks of abuse.[56] In *SpaceNet* and *Garda Síochána* the CJEU refers to expedited retention that the Court considers synonymous to 'quick freeze'. However, the CJEU did not define this notion and did not clarify how this differs from the expedited preservation that the CJEU refers to in *La Quadrature du Net 'I'*, an omission that Tracol finds 'regrettable'.[57]

---

[48] ibid para 229; *SpaceNet* (n 34) para 132.
[49] CJEU, Judgment of 5 April 2022, *Commissioner of An Garda Síochána* (C-140/20) ECLI:EU:C:2022:258.
[50] *La Quadrature du Net 'I'* (n 31) para 229; *SpaceNet* (n 34) para 132.
[51] ibid.
[52] ibid.
[53] *La Quadrature du Net 'I'* (n 31) para 164.
[54] *SpaceNet* (n 34) para 118; *Garda Síochána* (n 49) para 89.
[55] *SpaceNet* (n 34) para 132; *Garda Síochána* (n 49) para 129.
[56] *SpaceNet* (n 34) para 132.
[57] Tracol (n 9) 6.

In *La Quadrature du Net 'I'*, the CJEU referred to expedited retention that it relates to expedited preservation, as understood under the Cybercrime convention,[58] and recognized Member States had the power to introduce laws that allow 'only for a period that is limited in time to what is strictly necessary ... for the purposes of combating serious crime and, a fortiori, safeguarding national security, recourse to an instruction requiring providers of electronic communications services, by means of a decision of the competent authority that is subject to effective judicial review, to undertake, for a specified period of time, the expedited retention of traffic and location data in the possession of those service providers'.[59] Although the CJEU had not initially included the purpose of preventing serious threats to public security for the expedited retention in *La Quadrature du Net 'I'*,[60] the CJEU extended the scope of expedited retention to the purpose of preventing serious threats to public security in *SpaceNet* and *Garda Síochána*.[61]

5. Retention of IP Addresses

Building on its position in *Tele2 Sverige* that general and indiscriminate retention can be allowed for specific purposes and when certain key safeguards are in place, the CJEU developed concrete case law on the retention of IP addresses. Thus, one of the most prominent and crucial exceptions to the general prohibition relates to the 'general and indiscriminate retention' of IP addresses assigned to the source of an internet connection'.[62] In *La Quadrature du Net 'I'*, the CJEU carried out an analysis of the role of IP addresses as traffic data, as defined in the ePrivacy Directive, and came to the conclusion that in the case in question 'only the IP addresses of the source of the communication are retained and not the IP addresses of the recipient of the communication, those addresses do not, as such, disclose any information about third parties who were in contact with the person who made the communication. That category of data is therefore less sensitive than other traffic data'.[63] Such general and indiscriminate retention of IP addresses of the source of a communication can be allowed through the adoption of legislative measures for specific purposes, namely for the safeguarding of national security, the combating of serious crime, and the prevention of serious threats to public security, and shall take place only for a limited period of time that is strictly necessary.[64] The CJEU found that '[i]n the light of the seriousness of the interference entailed by th[e] retention [of IP addresses] with the fundamental rights enshrined in Articles 7 and 8 of the Charter, only action to combat serious crime, the prevention of serious threats to public security and the safeguarding of national security are capable of justifying that interference'.[65] So, even if the CJEU allowed for the retention of IP addresses of the source of a communication, this was still considered a serious interference with fundamental rights and was only allowed for the aforementioned purposes.

---

[58] Convention on Cybercrime (ETS No 185).
[59] *La Quadrature du Net 'I'* (n 31) para 229.
[60] ibid.
[61] *SpaceNet* (n 34) para 132; *Garda Síochána* (n 49) para 129.
[62] *La Quadrature du Net 'I'* (n 31) para 229; *SpaceNet* (n 34) para 132; *Garda Síochána* (n 49) para 129.
[63] *La Quadrature du Net 'I'* (n 31) para 152.
[64] ibid para 229; *SpaceNet* (n 34) para 132; *Garda Síochána* (n 49) para 129.
[65] *La Quadrature du Net 'I'* (n 31) para 156.

However, in *La Quadrature du Net 'II'*, the CJEU relaxed even more the protections surrounding IP addresses, departing from the distinction between IP address of the source or the destination of a communication. The CJEU noted that 'the general and indiscriminate retention of a set – even a vast set – of static and dynamic IP addresses used by a person in a given period does not necessarily constitute, in every case, a serious interference with the fundamental rights guaranteed by Articles 7, 8 and 11 of the Charter'[66] and that 'the general and indiscriminate retention of IP addresses may ... be justified by the objective of combating criminal offences in general where it is genuinely ruled out that that retention could give rise to serious interferences with the private life of the person concerned due to the possibility of drawing precise conclusions about that person by, inter alia, linking those IP addresses with a set of traffic or location data which have also been retained by those providers'.[67] The CJEU in *La Quadrature du Net 'II'* made a clear statement that not every retention of IP addresses would constitute *per se* a serious interference with fundamental rights. In the view of the Court, the danger lies mainly in the potential combination of IP addresses with other types of data.[68] To avoid such combination, the CJEU recommends that the various categories of retained data are stored in a way that ensures 'a genuinely watertight separation'.[69] If this is ensured, then the accessing of IP addresses can be allowed not for the strict list of purposes identified in *La Quadrature du Net 'I'*, but potentially also for 'public-interest imperatives, such as the maintenance of public order and the prevention of crime or the protection of the rights and freedoms of others'.[70] The CJEU's reasoning in this last case broadens the types of data for which general and indiscriminate retention can be allowed and the purposes for which such retained data can be further accessed.

6. Key Safeguard for Access to Retained Data: Prior Review

The CJEU has been confronted several times with questions regarding access to the retained data. In *Digital Rights Ireland*, the CJEU criticized the lack of a requirement for prior review by a court or an independent administrative body[71] before competent national authorities were allowed to access data. In particular, on the issue of access, the CJEU elaborated its position in *Tele2 Sverige* that 'general access to all retained data, regardless of whether there is any link, at least indirect, with the intended purpose, cannot be regarded as limited to what is strictly necessary'[72] and required prior review carried out either by a court or by an independent administrative body before access was allowed to retained data, as one of the key safeguards regarding the law enforcement access to the retained data.[73] In *Tele2 Sverige*, the CJEU concluded that Member States cannot adopt national laws which allow for the general and indiscriminate retention of all traffic and location data of all subscribers and registered users relating to all means of electronic communication.[74] Member

---

[66] *La Quadrature du Net 'II'* (n 8) para 79.
[67] ibid para 82.
[68] ibid para 83.
[69] ibid paras 84, 164.
[70] ibid para 116.
[71] *Digital Rights Ireland* (n 2) para 62.
[72] *Tele2 Sverige* (n 24) para 119.
[73] ibid para 119.
[74] ibid para 134.

States are also not allowed to adopt national legislation governing, inter alia, access to the retained data by law enforcement authorities in absence of specific access requirements. Such exceptional access is restricted solely to fighting serious crime, and subject to prior review by a court or an independent administrative authority, and when the law includes a requirement that the data concerned should be retained within the European Union, requirement already introduced by the CJEU in *Digital Rights Ireland*.[75]

In *Privacy International*, the CJEU clarified that 'general access to *all* retained data, regardless of whether there is any link, at least indirect, with the aim pursued, cannot be regarded as being limited to what is strictly necessary'[76] and that that access to retained data shall be granted to national authorities based on objective criteria that define the circumstances and conditions to allow such access.[77] The CJEU also addressed the issue of access to retained data by security and intelligence agencies and found that Member States cannot establish an obligation requiring electronic service providers to disclose traffic data and location data to such agencies 'by means of general and indiscriminate transmission',[78] as this would not pass the strict necessity test and would not be considered justified within a democratic society.

The CJEU further elaborated its position on prior review by a court or an independent administrative body in later data retention judgments.

In *La Quadrature du Net 'I'*, the CJEU relied on its position in *Tele2 Sverige* regarding real-time collection of traffic and location data and stressed that 'it is essential that the implementation of the measure authorizing real-time collection be subject to a prior review carried out either by a court or by an independent administrative body whose decision is binding, with that court or body having to satisfy itself, inter alia, that such real-time collection is authorized only within the limits of what is strictly necessary'.[79] In the same judgment, the CJEU recognized that effective prior review in real-time cases cannot always be obtained, hence requiring in cases of 'duly defined urgency'[80] that such review by a court or an independent administrative body shall take place within a short time after access,[81] without however providing any guidance about the timeframe within which such review must take place.

In *Prokuratuur*,[82] the CJEU had the opportunity to reflect on the issue of independence aspect of prior review by an independent administrative body. The CJEU found that such a body should be objective and impartial and should not have any external influences by the authority that requests data.[83] The CJEU presented the Public Prosecutor's Office as an example, stating that 'the authority entrusted with the prior review, first, must not be involved in the conduct of the criminal investigation in question and, second, has a neutral stance vis-à-vis the parties to the criminal proceedings'.[84] Consequently, the Public Prosecutor's Office cannot be regarded as an independent authority to review and authorize the access to

---

[75] ibid para 134.
[76] *Privacy International* (n 38) para 78.
[77] ibid para 79.
[78] ibid para 81.
[79] *La Quadrature du Net 'I'* (n 31) para 189.
[80] ibid.
[81] ibid.
[82] CJEU, Judgment of 2 March 2021, *Prokuratuur* (C-746/18) ECLI:EU:C:2021:152.
[83] ibid para 54.
[84] ibid para 54.

traffic and location data for criminal investigations. The requirement for independence and impartiality were repeated by the CJEU when assessing the role of a police officer in *Garda Síochána*, which was also not found to fulfil the independence criterion when he/she 'is assisted by a unit established within the police service which has a degree of autonomy in the exercise of its duties, and whose decisions may subsequently be subject to judicial review'.[85]

7. Targeted Retention

The CJEU, in *Tele2 Sverige*, recognized the powers of Member States to adopt laws introducing targeted retention measures related to traffic and location data for the purpose of investigating serious crime; these measures must, however, be limited with respect to 'the categories of data to be retained, the means of communication affected, the persons concerned and the retention period adopted, to what is strictly necessary'.[86] In its subsequent case law, the CJEU further elaborated its position on targeted retention. The CJEU felt keen to allow ('does not preclude') national laws that introduce rules for targeted retention of traffic and location data for the purposes of safeguarding national security, combating serious crime and preventing serious threats to public security.[87] Such retention shall however be limited and be decided on the basis of 'objective and non-discriminatory factors, according to the categories of persons concerned or using a geographical criterion, for a period that is limited in time to what is strictly necessary, but which may be extended'.[88] The CJEU did not introduce any limits on what such extension may entail.

The CJEU offered some guidance on these criteria. With regard to geographic areas, the CJEU clarified that '[t]hose areas may include places with a high incidence of serious crime, places that are particularly vulnerable to the commission of serious criminal offences, such as places or infrastructure which regularly receive a very high volume of visitors, or strategic locations, such as airports, stations or tollbooth areas'.[89] The CJEU elaborated in *Garda Síochána* on the average crime rate in a given area, in relation to the geographical criterion, arguing that it is not necessary for the authorities to have 'specific indications as to the preparation or commission, in the areas concerned, of acts of serious crime'[90] and that 'the criterion drawn from the average rate of serious crime is entirely unconnected with any potentially discriminatory factors'.[91] In any event, the CJEU pointed out that the definition of geographic areas is not a static exercise and that these 'must be amended in accordance with changes in the circumstances that justified their selection, thus making it possible to react to developments in the fight against serious crime'.[92]

This acknowledgment by the CJEU that for the purposes of safeguarding national security, combating serious crime and preventing serious threats to public security, measures can be allowed for the targeted retention of traffic and location data using a geographical

---

[85] *Garda Síochána* (n 49) para 114.
[86] *Tele2 Sverige* (n 24) para 108.
[87] *La Quadrature du Net 'I'* (n 31) para 229; *SpaceNet* (n 34) para 132; *Garda Síochána* (n 49) para 129.
[88] *La Quadrature du Net 'I'* (n 31) para 229; *SpaceNet* (n 34) para 132; *Garda Síochána* (n 49) para 129.
[89] *La Quadrature du Net 'I'* (n 31) para 150.
[90] *Garda Síochána* (n 49) para 80.
[91] ibid para 80.
[92] ibid para 82.

criterion or categories of concerned persons, have opened a window of opportunity for national legislators to introduce new or adapt existing data retention laws. Some Member States soon after *La Quadrature du Net 'I'* introduced targeted retention rules for the processing of traffic and location data using the criteria presented by the CJEU (a geographical criterion or categories of concerned persons). Belgium and Denmark have already introduced retention schemes based on these criteria, with Franssen and van de Heyning reporting that the Belgian law effectively covers almost the entire population.[93] Similarly, Denmark has established new data retention rules that effectively lead to the retention of data of more than 67 per cent of the Danish population.[94] More countries are considering the introduction of similar rules, with Sweden having already proposed new data retention obligations for geographical targeted retention that could potentially cover over 70 per cent of the population.[95]

It is doubtful whether the CJEU actually had such broad applications of the criteria in mind, which would lead to such broad targeted retention schemes. In fact, such schemes are rather unlikely to pass the scrutiny of the CJEU, shall (any of) these come in front of the Court.

8. Conclusion

The invalidation of the Data Retention Directive by the CJEU in *Digital Rights Ireland* was only the beginning of a series of CJEU judgments on data retention, as the Court was asked to answer questions regarding national provisions on data retention based on Article 15(1) of the ePrivacy Directive. In its case law, the CJEU already since *Tele2 Sverige* linked the actual retention obligations on providers with the subsequent access by law enforcement authorities to the retained data.

While acknowledging that general and indiscriminate retention of traffic and location data is unacceptable on fundamental rights grounds, the CJEU introduced in its data retention judgments key safeguards that would justify the retention of specific categories of data and their subsequent access by law enforcement authorities. This chapter conducted a critical examination of the rich case law of the CJEU, and distilled the requirements and safeguards introduced by the Court in relation to various types of data and their subsequent access by law enforcement authorities for specific purposes. The CJEU remains solid in its position that general and indiscriminate retention of traffic and location data, and especially as preventative measure, is as a rule prohibited. It has however come to acknowledge justified pleas from national governments and their law enforcement authorities that accessing specific types of retained data does not constitute a serious interference with fundamental rights and shall therefore be allowed for well-specified purposes and under strict safeguards.

In this context the CJEU ruled on the general and indiscriminate retention of data relating to the civil identity of the affected individuals and on the IP address of the source of a communication for national security purposes, for fighting serious crime, and for the

---

[93] See Vanessa Franssen and Catherine van de Heyning in Chapter 16 on the Belgian legal framework.
[94] See Ayo Næsborg-Andersen, Chapter 15, on the Danish legal framework in this volume.
[95] See Maria Bergström on Sweden in Chapter 17.

protection of public order against serious threats under specific conditions. However, the case law of the Court evolves and on the later point of retention of IP addresses of the source of a communication, the CJEU in the 2024 *La Quadrature du Net 'II'* went even further and opened the door for the general and indiscriminate retention of IP addresses, as long as they are stored in a way that ensures 'a genuinely watertight separation' and for a broad range of purposes, such as public order or the prevention of crime, not necessarily serious one. This evolution in the case law creates the anticipation that the CJEU may be ready to recognize legislative measures for general and indiscriminate retention of other categories of data, and potentially for new purposes as well, especially in view of technological advancements and the use of (self-learning) algorithms.[96]

The CJEU has developed its case law on targeted retention based on categories of persons concerned or a geographical criterion, as discussed above in section 7. Current implementations of such targeted retention schemes in Belgium and in Denmark are illustrative of how these criteria can lead to a manipulation of the intentions of the CJEU and lead to the setting of extensive retention areas, covering almost the whole population of a country. The examples of Belgium and Denmark show that (at least some) national legislators are keen to take advantage of any opportunity the see in the CJEU judgments that would allow them to adopt rules on targeted retention that would in essence be general and indiscriminate retention rules in disguise.

The CJEU clearly performs its judicial role in engaging with the request for preliminary rulings by national courts. However, in absence of a concrete European legal framework on data retention and on the subsequent access to the retained data by law enforcement authorities, the CJEU is in essence setting new rules on data retention and access. Through its case law, as elucidated in this chapter, the CJEU has developed a set of safeguards and requirements that can serve as the basis for the European legislator to rely on and propose a new legal instrument for data retention and access. It is undoubted that a political compromise on a new data retention and access legal instrument at the EU level will be a difficult task. However, leaving the issue for much longer in the hands of the Member States that introduce inconsistent interpretations of Article 15(1) ePrivacy Directive or make narrow interpretations of the safeguards introduced by the CJEU,[97] may turn the task of the CJEU into a Herculean one.

---

[96] In *La Quadrature du Net I* (n 31) the CJEU was confronted with the automated analysis of traffic and location data for national security purposes (para 172) and the obligation in France on providers to collect real-time traffic and location data (para 170). Although both these actions give access to French law enforcement authorities to data, they do not require service providers to actually retain data and are therefore not discussed further in this chapter. On this issue see Niovi Vavoula (Chapter 24) and Maria Grazia Porcedda (Chapter 25).

[97] Illustrative on this point is the position of the French Council of State in the aftermath of *La Quadrature du Net 'I'* (n 31) see Maxime Lassalle (Chapter 11).

3

Data Retention and the Judicial Parameters of Mass Surveillance in EU Law

Valsamis Mitsilegas

1. Introduction

Setting parameters to surveillance based on data retention has been a key focus of the Court of Justice of the European Union (CJEU or 'the Court') in the past decade. In a number of landmark cases, the Court has been asked to interpret EU and national data retention law and its compatibility with fundamental rights. Litigation has been ongoing in view of the reluctance of Member States to accept the limits placed by the Court to mass surveillance based on indiscriminate, generalised data retention. The Court's annulment of the Data Retention Directive[1] has been followed by repeated references by national courts on the compatibility of national data retention schemes, in the absence of an EU instrument on data retention, with EU law. The CJEU insistence on prohibiting indiscriminate, generalised surveillance has been met with reluctance by national executives to accept. This persistence on maintaining generalised data retention legislation at national level has resulted in an escalation of litigation before the CJEU, with the Court being asked to address national justifications on generalised retention on the basis of the objective to fight crime, serious crime, and to protect national security. The present contribution will focus on the evolution of the CJEU case law on data retention, by providing a step-by-step analysis on how the Court of Justice has developed parameters to mass surveillance in the face of pressure by Member States. The key features of this judicial evolution will be analysed in the Court's attempt to protect fundamental rights in the face of considerable pressure by the executive to limit protection on security grounds.

2. Annulling the Data Retention Directive: *Digital Rights Ireland*

The first key CJEU ruling determining the parameters of mass surveillance under data retention has been *Digital Rights Ireland*.[2] *Digital Rights Ireland* is a landmark judgment not

---

[1] Directive 2006/24/EC of the European Parliament and of the Council of 15 March 2006 on the retention of data generated or processed in connection with the provision of publicly available electronic communications services or of public communications networks and amending Directive 2002/58/EC [13.4.2006] OJ L 105, p 54 ('Data Retention Directive').

[2] CJEU, Judgment of 8 April 2014, *Digital Rights Ireland and Seitlinger and others* (C-293/12 and C-594/12) ECLI:EU:C:2014:238.

only because the CJEU annulled the Data Retention Directive as such, but also because the Court set some key markers on the perils that the model of privatised mass surveillance put forward by the Directive entails for a number of fundamental rights including privacy, data protection, and freedom of expression.[3] In *Digital Rights Ireland*, the CJEU set clear constitutional limits to mass surveillance that have formed key benchmarks in the further evolution of EU and national law in the field. The Court expanded on the invasive impact of the pre-emptive mass surveillance paradigm introduced by the Data Retention Directive by noting from the outset that 'data, taken as a whole, may allow very precise conclusions to be drawn concerning the private lives of the persons whose data has been retained, such as the habits of everyday life, permanent or temporary places of residence, daily or other movements, the activities carried out, the social relationships of those persons and the social environments frequented by them'.[4]

Echoing the findings of national constitutional courts,[5] the CJEU acknowledged that the interference of this model of pre-emptive mass surveillance with the rights to privacy and data protection set out in Articles 7 and 8 of the EU Charter of Fundamental Rights (Charter) must be considered to be particularly serious as 'the fact that data are retained and subsequently used without the subscriber or registered user being informed is likely to generate in the minds of the persons concerned the feeling that their private lives are the subject of constant surveillance'.[6] Interference with the rights to privacy and data protection is thus viewed in conjunction with the assault on citizenship that mass surveillance entails in a democratic society.

The Court went on to undertake a detailed assessment of the compatibility of the Data Retention Directive with the principle of proportionality. Assessing the necessity of the interference on privacy caused by the Directive, the Court focused on the latter's wide reach, noting that it required the retention of all traffic data concerning fixed telephony, mobile telephony, internet access, internet email, and internet telephony; that it therefore applied to all means of electronic communication, the use of which is very widespread and of growing importance in people's everyday lives; and that it covers all subscribers and registered users.[7] According to the Court, the Directive entailed an interference with the fundamental rights of practically the entire European population.[8] The Directive covered, in a generalised manner, all persons and all means of electronic communication as well as all traffic data without any differentiation, limitation, or exception being made in the light of the objective of fighting against serious crime.[9] The Directive affected all persons, even persons for whom there is no evidence capable of suggesting that their conduct might have a link, even an indirect or remote one, with serious crime.[10] Neither did the Directive require any relation between the data retained and a threat to public security. In particular, the data retained was not required to be in relation to data pertaining to a particular time

---

[3] ibid paras 28–29.
[4] ibid para 27.
[5] See Valsamis Mitsilegas, 'The Privatisation of Surveillance in the Digital Age' in V Mitsilegas and N Vavoula (eds), *Surveillance and Privacy in the Digital Age: European, Transatlantic and Global Perspectives* (Hart 2021) 101–58.
[6] *Digital Rights Ireland* (n 2) para 37.
[7] ibid para 56.
[8] ibid para 57.
[9] ibid para 57.
[10] ibid para 58.

period and/or a particular geographical zone and/or to a circle of particular persons likely to be involved, in one way or another, in a serious crime, or to persons who could, for other reasons, contribute, by the retention of their data, to the prevention, detection or prosecution of serious offences.[11]

The Court combined its findings on the wide reach of and lack of limits to retention with similar findings regarding the *access* and *use* of retained data by competent authorities—noting that the Directive failed to lay down any objective criterion, or any substantive or procedural conditions, by which to determine the limits of the access of the competent national authorities to the data and their subsequent use.[12] In particular, access by the competent national authorities to the data retained was not made dependent on a prior judicial or independent administrative review.[13] The Court further criticised the provision on the retention period, noting that it did not make any distinction between categories of data on the basis of their possible usefulness for the purposes of the objective pursued or according to the persons concerned[14] and that it was not stated that the determination of the period of retention must be based on objective criteria in order to ensure that it is limited to what is strictly necessary.[15] On the basis of this analysis, the Court found that the Data Retention Directive failed the necessity test in that it entailed a wide-ranging and particularly serious interference with those fundamental rights in the legal order of the EU, without such an interference being precisely circumscribed by provisions to ensure that it is actually limited to what is strictly necessary.[16] The Court found that the EU legislator exceeded the limits imposed by compliance with the principle of proportionality in the light of Articles 7, 8, and 52(1) of the Charter[17] and annulled the Directive with immediate effect.

Digital Rights Ireland is a landmark judgment setting clear limits to the privatised, pre-emptive, generalised surveillance of everyday behaviour and activity.[18] The judgment is significant in expressly rejecting pre-emptive surveillance on the basis of the generalised, undifferentiated retention of personal data by private providers without the establishment of concrete and specific links to serious crime. The Court's reasoning has been criticised in assessing the proportionality of the Directive in light of its 'material objective', crime prevention, rather than its stated objective, market harmonisation, thus sitting uncomfortably with its finding in *Ireland v Parliament and Council*[19] and in allegedly incorrectly applying Article 8 of the Charter by disregarding law-enforcement exceptions to the Data Protection Directive.[20] Both these objections are unfounded. The Court rightly and inevitably focused on the impact of the Data Retention Directive on fundamental rights and to do so a substantive assessment of the fundamental rights consequences of its provisions in view of its ultimate law-enforcement function was essential. To limit proportionality assessment to

---

[11] ibid para 59.
[12] ibid paras 60–61.
[13] ibid para 62.
[14] ibid para 63.
[15] ibid para 64.
[16] ibid para 65.
[17] ibid para 69.
[18] Mitsilegas, 'The Privatisation of Surveillance in the Digital Age' (n 5).
[19] CJEU, Judgment of 10 February 2009, Ireland/Parliament and Council (C-301/06, ECR 2009 p. I-593) ECLI:EU:C:2009:68.
[20] Orla Lynskey, 'Joined Cases C-293/12 and 594/12 *Digital Rights Ireland* and *Seitlinger and Others*: The Good, the Bad and the Ugly' (*European Law Blog*, 8 April 2014) <https://www.europeanlawblog.eu/pub/joined-cases-c-29312-and-59412-digital-rights-ireland-and-seitlinger-and-others-the-good-the-bad-and-the-ugly/release/1> accessed 25 September 2024.

market harmonisation would artificially divide the two issues, and would turn a blind eye to the actual impact of the Data Retention Directive.

The argument that the Court has inadequately taken into account the law-enforcement provisions of the Data Protection Directive fails to do justice to the constitutional significance of the Court's approach to privacy and data protection: rather than focusing on the provisions of the (at times fragmented and multiplied) EU secondary law *acquis* on data protection, the Court constitutionalised its fundamental rights scrutiny by adopting the Charter as a key benchmark for the proportionality assessment of the Directive. In this process of constitutionalisation, the Court elevated the right to privacy as the key benchmark, encompassing within it privacy specific data-protection benchmarks including those enshrined in Article 8 of the Charter—with the latter used in cases where details of privacy protection (such as independent control) are evoked. The emphasis of the Court on a broader right to privacy in dealing with mass surveillance and large-scale data retention and access is welcome in allowing a 'big picture' and holistic assessment of the impact of surveillance on the individual, which could be lost if fundamental rights scrutiny was based exclusively on individual instances of data processing on the basis of data-protection rules.[21] The focus on privacy serves to address more fully the broader effects of mass pre-emptive privatised surveillance, not only in terms of profiling but also in terms of the transformation of citizenship, trust, and the relationship between the individual and the state that generalised surveillance entails.

3. Rejecting National Legislation on Generalised Data Retention: *Tele2 Sverige*

The immediate annulment of the Data Retention Directive sent shockwaves in executive and law-enforcement authorities in Member States, where data retention had been viewed as a key counterterrorism and security tool. With the Commission refraining from tabling replacement legislation and in the absence of secondary EU law in the field, a number of EU Member States continued to apply national legislation on data retention.[22] In view of the potential conflict of national data-retention measures with EU law as developed in *Digital Rights Ireland*, it was a matter of time before questions of compatibility of *national* data-retention law and practice with EU law would reach the CJEU. A key issue was whether EU law was applicable in the first place, in cases where national legislation applied in the absence of specific secondary EU law on data retention. The CJEU had the opportunity to address these issues in responding to two requests from preliminary rulings from Swedish and UK courts in its judgment in the joint cases of *Tele2 Sverige*.[23]

The first step in the Court's judgment in *Tele2 Sverige* was to establish the applicability of EU law. After all, the questions for a preliminary ruling involved national data-retention legislation operating in an era where no secondary EU law on data retention existed any

---

[21] Valsamis Mitsilegas, 'The Transformation of Privacy in an Era of Pre-emptive Surveillance' (2015) 20(1) Tilburg Law Review 35; Valsamis Mitsilegas 'The Value of Privacy in an Era of Security. Embedding Constitutional Limits on Pre-emptive Surveillance' (2014) 8 International Political Sociology 104.
[22] Arianna Vedaschi, 'Privacy versus Security: Regulating Data Collection and Retention in Europe' in BJ Goold and L Lazarus (eds), *Security and Human Rights* (2nd edn, Hart 2019).
[23] CJEU, Judgment of 21 December 2016, *Tele2 Sverige* (C-203/15 and C-698/15) ECLI:EU:C:2016:970.

longer. States had either continued the applicability of existing data-retention legislation or introduced new legislation arguably in the face of, and disobeying, the CJEU. The Court first established the applicability of EU law by placing its assessment of national law within the framework of compliance with the ePrivacy Directive,[24] to which the Data Retention Directive introduced a series of derogations.[25] But even if EU law would in principle be applicable in this context, the CJEU was called to engage with the argument that national legislation fell ultimately outside of the scope of the ePrivacy Directive on the grounds that it concerned criminal law and public and national security. In particular, it was argued that Article 1(3) of the ePrivacy Directive excluded from its scope 'activities of the State' in specified fields, including the activities of the state in areas of criminal law and in the areas of public security, defence, and state security[26] and that Article 15 of the ePrivacy Directive allowed Member States to restrict its provisions, including via the adoption of data-retention measures, to achieve crime control and security objectives which substantially overlapped with those stated in Article 1(3) of the same Directive.[27]

These arguments were not accepted by the CJEU. The latter noted from the outset that the measures referred to in Article 15 ePrivacy Directive did fall within its scope, otherwise it would be deprived of any purpose.[28] In establishing the applicability of the ePrivacy Directive in the cases before it, the Court focused on the *activities* of private providers, which are governed by Article 15 of the ePrivacy Directive[29] and on the fact that *processing* of personal data is involved in this context. The Court noted that the scope of the ePrivacy Directive extended, in particular, to a legislative measure, such as that at issue in the main proceedings, that required such providers to retain traffic and location data, since to do so necessarily involves the processing, by those providers, of personal data.[30] Importantly, in establishing the applicability of EU law, the Court expressly linked retention of data by the private sector with *access* to this data by state authorities, by treating retention and access as a continuum of activity. According to the Court, the scope of the ePrivacy Directive extended to a legislative measure relating, as in the main proceedings, to the *access* of the national authorities to the data retained by the providers of electronic communications services.[31] Access to the data retained by those providers concerns the processing of personal data by those providers, and that processing falls within the scope of the ePrivacy Directive.[32] Since data is retained only for the purpose, when necessary, of making that data accessible to the competent national authorities, national legislation that imposes the retention of data necessarily entails, in principle, the existence of provisions relating to access by the competent national authorities to the data retained by the providers of electronic communications services.[33] By adopting a holistic approach to the establishment of data-retention schemes and highlighting the link between retention and access by focusing on

---

[24] Directive 2002/58/EC concerning the processing of personal data and the protection of privacy in the electronic communications sector and Regulation (EC) No 2006/2004 on cooperation between nationals authorities responsible for the enforcement of consumer protection laws [2009] OJ L337/11 ('ePrivacy Directive').
[25] Data Retention Directive (n 1) Art 3(1).
[26] *Tele2 Sverige* (n 23) para 69.
[27] ibid paras 71–72.
[28] ibid para 73.
[29] ibid para 74.
[30] ibid para 75.
[31] ibid para 76.
[32] ibid para 78.
[33] ibid para 79.

national measures on mass, pre-emptive surveillance, the CJEU sent another clear signal that EU law is applicable in these circumstances and that national legislation is subject to the scrutiny of the Court and to the fundamental rights benchmarks of EU law.

In terms of the substantive analysis on the compatibility of national data-retention requirements with EU law, *Tele2 Sverige* built upon the findings in *Digital Rights Ireland*. Greater emphasis was placed on the impact of data retention on freedom of expression, which acquires equal footing with the rights to private life and data protection, even though it did not form part of the questions referred for a preliminary ruling.[34] The Court made specific reference to the importance of freedom of expression in any democratic society, asserting that the fundamental right to freedom of expression guaranteed in Article 11 of the Charter 'constitutes one of the essential foundations of a pluralist, democratic society, and is one of the values on which, under Article 2 Treaty on European Union (TEU), the Union is founded'.[35] In its subsequent assessment, the Court examined the degree of interference of national data-retention measures not only with the rights to privacy and data protection, but also with the right to freedom of expression.[36]

In terms of the methodology of its assessment, the Court followed its approach in *Digital Rights Ireland* by undertaking a proportionality assessment.[37] The Court went a step further to *Digital Rights Ireland* by expressly accepting that the generalised preventive retention of data leads to profiling.[38] However, the Court stopped short of accepting that the retention of metadata leading to profiling is actually a breach of the essence of the rights to private life, data protection, and freedom of expression, and proceeded with a proportionality assessment, as the Court noted that the national legislation in question did not permit the retention of content data.[39] Shying away from engaging fully with the impact of generalised data retention on the essence of fundamental rights was a missed opportunity and disregarded the particularly serious impact of the retention of metadata on the rights in question. This impact was in fact acknowledged by the Court, which stated that metadata is no less sensitive, having regard to the right to privacy, than the actual content of communications[40] and, more directly, by Advocate General Saugmandsgaard Øe, who noted with specific examples that the risks associated with the retention of and access to metadata may be as great or even greater than those arising from access to content data as metadata 'facilitate the *almost instantaneous cataloguing of entire populations*, something which the content of communications does not'.[41]

Continuing with its proportionality assessment, the Court largely followed the same route it did in *Digital Rights Ireland*. The Court accepted that the interference entailed by national data-retention legislation in question in the fundamental rights enshrined in Articles 7 and 8 of the Charter was very far-reaching and must be considered to be particularly serious, with the fact that the data was retained without the subscriber or registered user being informed is likely to cause the persons concerned to feel that their private

---

[34] ibid para 92.
[35] ibid para 93.
[36] ibid paras 101, 107, and 125.
[37] ibid paras 94–96.
[38] ibid para 99.
[39] ibid para 101.
[40] ibid para 99.
[41] Opinion of Advocate General Saugmansgaard Øe of 19 July 2016 in *Tele2 Sverige* (n 23) para 259 (emphasis added) and paras 254–258.

lives are the subject of constant surveillance.[42] The Court added that these measures could have an effect on the right to freedom of expression under Article 11 of the Charter.[43] The Court went on to note the absence of any link of data retention with the fight against serious crime. The Court further noted that in view of the seriousness of the interference with fundamental rights by national legislation, only the objective of fighting serious crime was capable of justifying such measures,[44] and even so, the fight against serious crime could not in itself justify that national legislation providing for the general and indiscriminate retention of all traffic and location data should be considered to be necessary for the purposes of that fight.[45] The Court opined that the effect of national legislation was that the retention of traffic and location data was the rule, whereas the system put in place by the ePrivacy Directive required the retention of data to be an exception.[46]

The Court followed further its approach taken in *Digital Rights Ireland* by finding that national legislation in this case which covered, in a generalised manner, all subscribers and registered users and all means of electronic communication as well as all traffic data, provided for no differentiation, limitation, or exception according to the objective pursued. Such legislation affects all persons using electronic communication services, even though those persons who are not, even indirectly, in a situation that is liable to give rise to criminal proceedings and applies even to persons for whom there is no evidence capable of suggesting that their conduct might have a link, even an indirect or remote one, with serious criminal offences.[47] Such legislation did not require there to be any relationship between the data that must be retained and a threat to public security.[48] On the basis of the above considerations, the Court found that national legislation such as that at issue in the main proceedings exceeded the limits of what was strictly necessary and could not be considered to be justified, within a democratic society, as required by Article 15 of the ePrivacy Directive read in the light of Articles 7, 8, *and* 11 (and Article 52(1)) of the Charter.[49]

The Court, however, did not stop here. Perhaps conscious of the negative reactions that a second ruling in a row against generalised preventive data retention would cause among law-enforcement and government circles, the Court attempted in *Tele2 Sverige* to develop guidance and conditions under which preventive data retention would be proportionate. The Court noted that Article 15(1) of the ePrivacy Directive, read in the light of Articles 7, 8, 11, and 52(1) of the Charter, did not prevent a Member State from adopting legislation permitting, as a preventive measure, the *targeted* retention of traffic and location data, for the purpose of fighting serious crime, provided that the retention of data is limited, with respect to the categories of data to be retained, the means of communication affected, the persons concerned, and the retention period adopted, to what is strictly necessary.[50] The Court put forward three main criteria aiming to set parameters and limits on preventive data retention. Firstly, national legislation must lay down clear and precise rules governing

---

[42] *Tele2 Sverige* (n 23) para 100, by reference by analogy to *Digital Rights Ireland* (n 2) para 37.
[43] *Tele2 Sverige* (n 23) para 101.
[44] ibid para 102, by reference to *Digital Rights Ireland* (n 2) para 60. See also CJEU, Judgment of 2 October 2018, *Ministerio Fiscal* (C-207/16) ECLI:EU:C:2018:788.
[45] *Tele2 Sverige* (n 23) ,para 103, by reference to *Digital Rights Ireland* (n 2) para 51.
[46] ibid para 104.
[47] ibid para 105, by reference to *Digital Rights Ireland* (n 2) paras 57–58.
[48] ibid para 106 by reference to *Digital Rights Ireland* (n 2) para 59.
[49] ibid para 107.
[50] ibid para 108.

the scope and application of such a data retention measure and imposing minimum safeguards, and indicate in particular in what circumstances and under which conditions a data-retention measure may, as a preventive measure, be adopted, thereby ensuring that such a measure is limited to what is strictly necessary.[51] Second, data retention must continue to meet objective criteria that establish a connection between the data to be retained and the objective pursued—such conditions must be shown to be such as actually to circumscribe, in practice, the extent of that measure and, thus, the public affected.[52]

Third, with regard to the setting of limits on such a measure with respect to the public and the situations that may potentially be affected, the national legislation must be based on *objective evidence* which makes it possible to identify a public whose data is likely to reveal a link, at least an indirect one, with serious criminal offences, and to contribute in one way or another to fighting serious crime or to preventing a serious risk to public security. Such limits may be set by using a geographical criterion where the competent national authorities consider, on the basis of objective evidence, that there exists, in one or more geographical areas, a high risk of preparation for or commission of such offences.[53] The Court added to these requirements of specificity in data retention procedural requirements regarding access to such data. These include independent review by a court or an independent judicial authority,[54] notification linked to the right to an effective remedy,[55] data security requirements,[56] and general review by an independent authority of compliance with EU data-protection law.[57] In this manner, the Court attempted to put forward clear constitutional limits to both preventive data retention and access to this data.

The ruling of the CJEU in *Tele2 Sverige* is of considerable constitutional significance. The Court affirmed its stance against mass surveillance in the face of a backlash by law-enforcement authorities and governments to its ruling in *Digital Rights Ireland* and in the face of the insistence of Member States to maintain in national legislation data retention obligations similar or identical to those introduced by the Data Retention Directive, which was annulled by the CJEU. In *Tele2 Sverige,* the Court upheld its main findings in *Digital Rights Ireland*, now applicable to *national* data-retention legislation whose compatibility with secondary EU data-protection law and with the Charter was assessed. The Court thus tackled head on Member States' disobedience and effective refusal to comply with the main thrust of *Digital Rights Ireland*. A key step in *Tele2 Sverige* was to establish the applicability of EU law; the 'private' framing of the data-retention obligations was central in this context. Another significant step has been the link that the Court made between retention of and access to personal data. Framing both retention and access within a 'privatised' framework—with the key criterion for applicability of EU law being the activity of private providers and the processing of data by them—is significant in bringing a wide range of state activity—including access of data in the context of criminal investigations—within the scope of EU law.[58]

---

[51] ibid para 109, by reference to *Digital Rights Ireland* (n 2) para 54.
[52] ibid para 109.
[53] ibid para 111.
[54] ibid para 120.
[55] ibid para 121.
[56] ibid para 122.
[57] ibid para 123.
[58] See *Ministerio Fiscal* (n 44).

4. Rejecting the National Security Argument: *La Quadrature du Net 'I'*

Resistance by Member States to the limits placed on large-scale surveillance via data retention by the Court of Justice persisted after *Tele2 Sverige*. The next step was for Member States to argue that EU law as developed by the CJEU was not applicable at national level as national data retention schemes were justified on the grounds of protecting national security. These arguments were tested in litigation leading to the CJEU ruling in *La Quadrature du Net 'I'*, where Member States argued that national security is a matter for Member States under Article 4(2) TEU and not for the European Union to regulate.[59] The Court refuted this claim. The Court reiterated that Article 15(1) of the ePrivacy Directive covers national measures which regulate the activity of providers of electronic communications services[60] and thus the scope of that Directive extends not only to a legislative measure that requires providers of electronic communications services to retain traffic and location data, but also to a legislative measure requiring them to grant the competent national authorities access to that data.[61] Such legislative measures necessarily involve the processing of the data by those providers and cannot, to the extent that they regulate the activities of those providers, be regarded as activities characteristic of States, as referred to in Article 1(3) of that directive.[62] Hence, the Court focused on the centrality of the activities of the private sector to trigger the applicability of EU law, and extended the scope of the concept not only to retention, but also to enabling access to data by state authorities.[63]

The Court went on to find that national security arguments based on Article 4(2) of the TEU cannot invalidate that conclusion—the mere fact that a national measure has been taken for the purpose of protecting national security cannot render EU law inapplicable and exempt the Member States from their obligation to comply with that law.[64] The Court declined to apply here its case law on the Passenger Name Record (PNR) legal basis litigation[65] and noted that all operations processing personal data carried out by providers of electronic communications services fall within the scope of the ePrivacy Directive, including processing operations resulting from obligations imposed on those providers by the public authorities.[66] The *source* of the obligation imposed on the private sector is thus immaterial; what matters in order for EU law to apply is the actual activity performed by the private sector. The Court attempted to distinguish private sector activity, where EU law is applicable, from cases where Member States *directly* implement measures *without imposing processing obligations* on providers of electronic communications services.[67] In these cases, national law applies, which must comply with national constitutional law and the ECHR.[68]

---

[59] CJEU, Judgment of 6 October 2020, La Quadrature du Net and others (C-511/18, C-512/18 and C-520/18) ECLI:EU:C:2020:791 ('*La Quadrature du Net 'I'*').).
[60] ibid para 95, by reference to *Ministerio Fiscal* (n 44) para 34.
[61] ibid para 96, by reference to *Ministerio Fiscal* (n 44) paras 35 and 37.
[62] ibid.
[63] Valsamis Mitsilegas, Elspeth Guild, Elif Kuskonmaz, and Niovi Vavoula, 'Data Retention and the Future of Large-Scale Surveillance: The Evolution and Contestation of Judicial Benchmarks' (2023) 29 European Law Journal 176–211.
[64] *La Quadrature du Net 'I'* (n 59) para 99.
[65] Judgment of 30 May 2006, Parliament/Council (C-317/04 and C-318/04, ECR 2006 p. I-4721) ECLI:EU:C:2006:346, paras 56–59.
[66] *La Quadrature du Net 'I'* (n 59), para 101.
[67] ibid para 103.
[68] ibid para 103.

The Court thus opined that national legislation which requires providers of electronic communications services to retain traffic and location data for the purposes of protecting national security and combating crime, such as the legislation at issue in the main proceedings, falls within the scope of the ePrivacy Directive.[69] By focusing on the central role of the private sector in domestic data retention schemes, and defining such role substantively to include both retention and access by the state in its scope, the Court recognised the privatisation of surveillance as a key factor to ensure the applicability of EU law. In this manner, the Court sent a strong signal against Member States' insistence in enacting large-scale data retention measures in domestic law and in thus breaching their fundamental rights obligations under EU law.

In terms of the impact on fundamental rights, the Court began by reiterating and developing some key principles regarding the interpretation of Article 15(1) of the ePrivacy Directive. The Court reiterated its finding in *Tele2 Sverige* that the interpretation of Article 15(1) of the ePrivacy Directive must take account of the importance both of the right to privacy, guaranteed in Article 7 of the Charter, and of the right to protection of personal data, guaranteed in Article 8 thereof, as derived from the case law of the Court, as well as the importance of the right to freedom of expression, given that that fundamental right, guaranteed in Article 11 of the Charter, constitutes one of the essential foundations of a pluralist, democratic society, and is one of the foundational values of the EU.[70] The retention of traffic and location data constitutes, in itself, on the one hand, a derogation from the prohibition laid down in Article 5(1) of the ePrivacy Directive and, on the other, an interference with the fundamental rights to respect for private life and the protection of personal data, enshrined in Articles 7 and 8 of the Charter, irrespective of whether the information in question relating to private life is sensitive or whether the persons concerned have been inconvenienced in any way on account of that interference.[71] Whether or not the retained data has been used subsequently is also irrelevant.[72] Reiterating its earlier case law, the Court highlighted the strong profiling potential of data retention.[73] The Court added that data retention for policing purposes is liable, in itself, to infringe the right to respect for communications, enshrined in Article 7 of the Charter, and to deter users of electronic communications systems from exercising their freedom of expression, guaranteed in Article 11 of the Charter.[74] The Court added in view of the significant quantity of traffic and location data that may be continuously retained under a general and indiscriminate retention measure, as well as the sensitive nature of the information that may be gleaned from that data, the mere retention of such data by providers of electronic communications services entails a risk of abuse and unlawful access.[75]

Addressing the compatibility of measures providing for preventive data retention for the purpose of safeguarding national security with EU law, the Court proceeded in *La Quadrature du Net 'I'* to make a distinction between national security on the one hand and public/internal security on the other. The Court noted that national security remains

---

[69] ibid para 104.
[70] ibid para 114. *Tele2 Sverige* (n 23) para 55.
[71] ibid. CJEU, Opinion 1/15 EU-Canada PNR Agreement of 26 July 2017 (Digital Reports) ECLI:EU:C:2017:592 paras 124 and 126.
[72] ibid para 116.
[73] ibid para 117 by reference to *Digital Rights Ireland* (n 2) para 21; *Tele2 Sverige* (n 23) para 99.
[74] ibid para 118.
[75] ibid para 119.

under Article 4(2) TEU the sole responsibility of Member States. This responsibility corresponds to the primary interest in protecting the essential functions of the State and the fundamental interests of society and encompasses the prevention and punishment of activities capable of seriously destabilising the fundamental constitutional, political, economic, or social structures of a country and, in particular, of directly threatening society, the population or the State itself, such as terrorist activities.[76] The importance of the objective of safeguarding national security, read in the light of Article 4(2) TEU, goes beyond that of the other objectives referred to in Article 15(1) of the ePrivacy Directive, inter alia the objectives of combating crime in general, even serious crime, and of safeguarding public security. Threats such as those referred to in the preceding paragraph can be distinguished, by their nature and particular seriousness, from the general risk that tensions or disturbances, even of a serious nature, affecting public security will arise. Subject to meeting the other requirements laid down in Article 52(1) of the Charter, the objective of safeguarding national security is therefore capable of justifying measures entailing more serious interferences with fundamental rights than those which might be justified by those other objectives.[77]

Data retention for national security purposes is not precluded by EU law if a series of conditions are applicable: data retention takes place for a limited period of time, as long as there are sufficiently solid grounds for considering that the Member State concerned is confronted with a serious threat, to national security which is shown to be genuine and present or foreseeable. Even if such a measure is applied indiscriminately to all users of electronic communications systems, without there being at first sight any connection with a threat to the national security of that Member State, it must nevertheless be considered that *the existence* of that threat is, in itself, capable of establishing that connection.[78] Preventive mass data retention must be limited in time to what is strictly necessary. Although it is conceivable that an instruction requiring providers of electronic communications services to retain data may, owing to the ongoing nature of such a threat, be renewed, the duration of each instruction cannot exceed a foreseeable period of time. Moreover, such data retention must be subject to limitations and must be circumscribed by strict safeguards making it possible to protect effectively the personal data of the persons concerned against the risk of abuse. Thus, that retention cannot be systematic in nature.[79] Decisions giving an instruction to providers of electronic communications services to carry out such data retention must be subject to effective review, either by a court or by an independent administrative body.[80]

The Court distinguished preventive data retention for national security purposes from preventive data retention for the purposes of combating crime and safeguarding public security, which merits a higher level of protection. Citing consistent case law, the Court stated that only action to combat serious crime and measures to prevent serious threats to public security are capable of justifying serious interference with the fundamental rights enshrined in Articles 7 and 8 of the Charter; thus only non-serious interference with those fundamental rights may be justified by the objective of preventing, investigating, detecting, and prosecuting criminal offences in general.[81] National legislation providing for the general

---

[76] ibid para 135.
[77] ibid para 136.
[78] ibid para 137 (emphasis added).
[79] ibid para 138.
[80] ibid para 139.
[81] ibid para 140 by reference to *Tele2 Sverige* (n 23) para 102. *Ministerio Fiscal* (n 44) paras 56 and 57; *PNR Canada* (n 71) para 149.

and indiscriminate retention of traffic and location data for the purpose of combating serious crime exceeds the limits of what is strictly necessary and cannot be considered to be justified, within a democratic society.[82] The deterrent effect of preventive data retention in terms of the exercise of fundamental rights and the seriousness of the interference of such retention with these rights mean that mass preventive data retention is the exception, and not the rule in a democratic society.[83] That conclusion applies even having regard to the objectives of combating serious crime and preventing serious threats to public security and to the importance to be attached to them.[84] The Court reiterated in this context its consistent stress of the fact that legislation providing for the general and indiscriminate retention of traffic and location data covers the electronic communications of practically the entire population without any differentiation, limitation, or exception being made in the light of the objective pursued. It therefore applies even to persons with respect to whom there is no evidence capable of suggesting that their conduct might have a link, even an indirect or remote one, with that objective of combating serious crime and, in particular, without there being any relationship between the data whose retention is provided for and a threat to public security.[85]

The Court developed its case law further to state unequivocally that even the positive obligations of the Member States which may arise, depending on the circumstances, from Articles 3, 4, and 7 of the Charter and relating to the establishment of rules to facilitate effective action to combat criminal offences cannot have the effect of justifying interference that is as serious as that entailed by legislation providing for the retention of traffic and location data with the fundamental rights, enshrined in Articles 7 and 8 of the Charter, of practically the entire population, without there being a link, at least an indirect one, between the data of the persons concerned and the objective pursued.[86] The Court went on to permit that *targeted* data retention for the purposes of combating serious crime, preventing serious threats to public security, and equally of safeguarding national security.[87] The Court used the retention criteria developed in *Tele2 Sverige*[88] and clarified that the persons thus targeted may, in particular, be persons who have been identified beforehand, in the course of the applicable national procedures and on the basis of objective evidence, as posing a threat to public or national security in the Member State concerned.[89] In order to comply with the principle of proportionality, the duration of targeted data retention must not exceed what is strictly necessary in the light of the objective pursued and the circumstances justifying them without prejudice to the possibility of extending those measures should such retention continue to be necessary.[90] The Court further reiterated the *Tele2 Sverige* strict limits to the real-time collection of personal data.[91]

In *La Quadrature du Net 'I'*, the Court attempted to address Member States security concerns by distinguishing between national security on the one hand and public/internal

---

[82] ibid para 141 by reference to *Tele2 Sverige* (n 23) para 107.
[83] ibid para 142.
[84] ibid para 142.
[85] ibid para 143 by reference to *Digital Rights Ireland* (n 2) paras 57 and 58 and *Tele2 Sverige* (n 23) para 105.
[86] ibid para 144.
[87] ibid para 147.
[88] *Tele2 Sverige* (n 23) paras 108, 111.
[89] *La Quadrature du Net 'I'* (n 59) para 149.
[90] ibid para 151.
[91] ibid para 188 by reference to *Tele2 Sverige* (n 23) para 119.

security on the other, and allowing mass surveillance on the basis of preventive data retention for national security purposes under a number of strict conditions. The evocation of national security considerations by states did not render EU law inapplicable, but allowed, under strict conditions, mass surveillance based on data retention. In a further attempt to accommodate Member states' concerns, the Court allowed the retention—for the purposes of both national and public security and combating crime—the general and indiscriminate retention of IP addresses;[92] the general and indiscriminate retention of data relating to the civil identity of users of electronic communications systems;[93] and expedited data retention.[94] At the same time, the Court reiterated the key fundamental rights principles developed in its earlier case law, in particular in *Digital Rights Ireland* and in *Tele2 Sverige*, and held on to the principle that mass surveillance in principle does not have a place in a democratic society, as it does not only undermine fundamental rights protection, but it also has a deterrent effect in the exercise of these rights. In order to address ongoing Member States' concerns, the Court proceeded into a very detailed ruling on the various options available to national authorities to achieve their objectives and attempted to find a compromise without undermining the core of its earlier case law. As will be seen further below, this delicate balancing act is an ongoing challenge for the Court.

5. Rejecting Generalised Retention to Fight Serious Crime: *Garda Síochána*

The Court's ruling in *La Quadrature du Net 'I'* has not stopped efforts to limit the reach of the fundamental rights protected by the Court therein. In a subsequent, case, *Garda Síochána*,[95] it was submitted by the European Commission that particularly serious crime could be treated in the same way as a threat to national security.[96] The CJEU rejected this argument. The Court stated that it is clear from the Court's case law, and in particular *La Quadrature du Net 'I'*, that there is a hierarchy amongst the public interest objectives that may justify restrictions to rights protection according to their respective importance and that the importance of the objective pursued by such a measure must be proportionate to the seriousness of the interference that it entails.[97] The Court reiterated the factors distinguishing national security from public order and the fight against serious crime in *La Quadrature du Net 'I'*.[98] The CJEU went on to state that criminal behaviour, even of a particularly serious nature, cannot be treated in the same way as a threat to national security— to treat those situations in the same way would be likely to create an intermediate category between national security and public security for the purpose of applying to the latter the requirements inherent in the former.[99] The Court reiterated its findings in *La Quadrature*

---

[92] ibid paras 153–156. The Court has recently clarified further the conditions under which public authorities responsible for the protection of copyright and related rights against infringements of those rights committed on the internet can access data, retained by providers of publicly available electronic communications services, relating to the civil identity associated with IP addresses.
[93] ibid paras 157–159.
[94] ibid paras 163–167.
[95] CJEU, Judgment of 5 April 2022, *Commissioner of An Garda Síochána* (C-140/20) ECLI:EU:C:2022:258.
[96] ibid para 60.
[97] ibid para 56.
[98] ibid paras 61–62 by reference to *La Quadrature du Net 'I'* (n 59) paras 135–137.
[99] ibid para 63.

du Net 'I' that the general and indiscriminate retention of traffic and location data for the purposes of combating serious crime exceeds the limits of what is strictly necessary and cannot be considered to be justified within a democratic society and that those data should not be retained systematically and continuously.[100] The Court stressed again that the general and indiscriminate retention of traffic and location data covers the electronic communications of practically the entire population without any differentiation, limitation or exception being made in the light of the objective pursued. Such legislation affects all persons using electronic communication services, and therefore applies even to persons with respect to whom there is no evidence capable of suggesting that their conduct might have a link, even an indirect or remote one, with that objective of combating serious crime.[101]

In insisting on the limits it posed on mass surveillance for the purposes of combating serious crime, the Court had to consider the argument put forward by the referring court that only the general and indiscriminate retention of traffic and location data allows serious crime to be combated effectively.[102] The Irish and French governments argued that this point was valid even after the Court's concessions in *La Quadrature du Net 'I'* allowing targeted data retention, as well as the general and indiscriminate retention of IP addresses and of data relating to civil identity.[103] In order to address these arguments, the Court embarked on engaging with what would constitute effective law enforcement per se. The Court observed that the effectiveness of criminal proceedings generally depends not on a single means of investigation but on all the means of investigation available to the competent national authorities for those purposes.[104] At the same time, the Court appeared to grant Member States a greater leeway in terms of the interpretation of geographical indications and targeted surveillance.[105] However, the Court stuck to its guns regarding the extent of the exceptions to the prohibition of mass surveillance for the purposes of combating serious crime set in *La Quadrature du Net 'I'*. The Court noted in particular that the fact that it may be difficult to provide a detailed definition of the circumstances and conditions under which targeted retention may be carried out is no reason for the Member States, by turning the exception into a rule, to provide for the general retention of traffic and location data.[106] In particular the Court noted that a targeted retention measure covering places or infrastructures which regularly receive a very high volume of visitors, or strategic places, such as airports, stations, maritime ports, or tollbooth areas, allows the competent authorities to collect traffic data and, in particular, location data of all persons using, at a specific time, a means of electronic communication in one of those places.[107] Moreover, the Court stated that the geographic areas covered by such a targeted retention measure may, and where appropriate must, be amended in accordance with changes in the circumstances that justified their selection, thus making it possible to react to developments in the fight against serious crime.[108] Finally, the Court allowed Member States to provide further distinctive criteria for targeted retention other than a personal or geographic criterion—these criteria must be

---

[100] ibid para 65 by reference to *La Quadrature du Net 'I'* (n 59) paras 141–142.
[101] *Garda Síochána* (n 95) para 66 by refence to *La Quadrature du Net 'I'* (n 59) paras 143–144.
[102] ibid para 68.
[103] ibid para 68.
[104] ibid para 69.
[105] Julie Teyssedre, 'Strictly Registered Retention and Access Regime for Metadata: Commissioner of the Garda Siochána' (2022) 66 CMLRev 569 at 583, 587.
[106] *Garda Síochána* (n 95) para 84.
[107] ibid para 81.
[108] ibid para 82.

objective and non-discriminatory in order to ensure that the scope of targeted retention is as limited as strictly necessary and to establish a connection, at least indirectly, between serious criminal acts and the persons whose data are retained.[109]

By expanding the parameters of targeted retention, the Court attempted to recognise law enforcement operational imperatives in data retention while maintaining its 'red line' in prohibiting generalised, indiscriminate data retention. The Court however rejected governmental arguments to allow mass data retention for the purposes of fighting serious crime. The Court noted that the fight against serious crime is of lesser importance in the hierarchy of objectives set out in *La Quadrature du Net 'I'*.[110] The Court noted again that the establishment of rules to facilitate effective action to combat criminal offences cannot have the effect of justifying interference that is as serious as that entailed by legislation providing for data retention with the fundamental rights enshrined in Articles 7 and 8 of the Charter, of practically the entire population, in circumstances where the data of the persons concerned are not liable to disclose a link, at least an indirect one, between those data and the objective pursued.[111] The Court reiterated that, subject to the exceptions set out in *La Quadrature du Net 'I'*, EU law precludes legislative measures which provide, as a preventive measure, general and indiscriminate data retention for the purposes of combating serious crime and for the prevention of serious threats to public security.[112]

6. Rejecting National Claims on the Compatibility of 'Limited' Data Retention with EU Law: *SpaceNet*

Another way of States seeking further concessions in favour of mass surveillance after *La Quadrature du Net 'I'* has been to argue in favour of the compatibility of national surveillance schemes which they deemed to provide with certain limits and safeguards to surveillance. In the case of *SpaceNet*,[113] the referring court distinguished national data retention legislation at stake from the one which gave rise to the *Tele2 Sverige* litigation in that the national legislation at issue in the main proceedings: did not require the retention of all telecommunications traffic data of all subscribers and users in relation to all means of electronic communications; excluded the retention of the content of communications; and provided that data relating to websites visited, the data from electronic mail services and the data underlying social or religious communications to or from certain lines could not be retained.[114] The referring Court further noted the limited retention period in national law[115] and the inclusion of contains strict limitations as regards the protection of retained data and access thereto.[116] The referring court further sought to justify national data retention law on the basis of a series of constitutional arguments: on the basis of the right to security enshrined in Article 6 of the Charter;[117] claiming that precluding general data

---

[109] ibid para 83.
[110] ibid paras 99–100.
[111] ibid para 95.
[112] ibid para 101.
[113] CJEU, Judgment of 27 October 2022, *SpaceNet* (C-793/19 and C-794/19) ECLI:EU:C:2022:702.
[114] ibid para 32.
[115] ibid paras 33–34.
[116] ibid para 35.
[117] ibid para 36.

retention would restrict the discretion of the national legislature in an area concerning the prosecution of crimes and public security, which, in accordance with Article 4(2) TEU, remains the sole responsibility of each Member State;[118] and arguing that the ECHR did not preclude national provisions providing for the bulk interception of cross-border flows of data, in view of the threats currently facing many States and the technological tools which terrorists and criminals may now use in order to commit wrongdoings.[119]

The CJEU put forward a constitutionally significant finding on the relationship between EU law and ECHR law in this context. The Court held that ECHR rights corresponding to Charter rights must be taken into account when interpreting the Charter only as the minimum threshold of fundamental rights protection—as Article 52(3) of the Charter is intended to ensure the necessary consistency between the rights contained in the Charter and the corresponding rights guaranteed in the ECHR, without adversely affecting the autonomy of EU law.[120] Moreover, the CJEU reiterated its findings in *La Quadrature du Net 'I'* that EU law is applicable in the present proceedings concerning national legislation which requires providers of electronic communications services to retain traffic and location data for the purposes, inter alia, of protecting national security and combating crime.[121] The CJEU reiterated the hierarchy of objectives put forward in *La Quadrature du Net 'I'*,[122] the distinction between the national security and public order objectives,[123] as well as the proportionality requirement[124] and the strict parameters permitting generalised data retention.[125]

The Court further rejected the arguments put forward by the referring court that safeguards included in national legislation aiming to limit the reach of data retention rendered the former compatible with the Charter. The Court held that generalised data retention which is limited to certain categories of data does not amount to targeted retention.[126] The Court noted that the retention of traffic and location data provided for by that national legislation concerns practically the entire population.[127] Moreover, the shorter length of generalised and indiscriminate data retention is not sufficient to justify the measure under EU law. The Court held again that the seriousness of the interference stems from the risk, particularly in view of their number and variety, that the data retained, taken as a whole, may enable very precise conclusions to be drawn concerning the private life of the person or persons whose data have been retained and, in particular, provide the means of establishing a profile of the person or persons concerned, information that is no less sensitive, having regard to the right to privacy, than the actual content of communications.[128] The Court relied here in its earlier ruling in *Prokuratuur*,[129] where it held that data retention is in any

---

[118] ibid para 37.
[119] ibid para 38.
[120] ibid para 125.
[121] ibid para 48. *La Quadrature du Net 'I'* (n 59) para 104.
[122] ibid para 71 by reference to *Garda Síochána* (n 95) para 56.
[123] ibid para 92 by reference to *Garda Síochána* (n 95) para 61.
[124] ibid para 92.
[125] ibid para 130.
[126] ibid para 84.
[127] ibid para 83.
[128] ibid para 87.
[129] ibid para 88 by reference to CJEU, Judgment of 2 March 2021, *Prokuratuur* (Conditions d'accès aux données relatives aux communications électroniques) (C-746/18) ECLI:EU:C:2021:152. The Court has recently held that Article 15(1) of Directive 2002/58/EC must be interpreted as not precluding a national provision which requires a national court, acting in the context of a prior review carried out following a reasoned request for access to a set of traffic or location data—which are liable to allow precise conclusions to be drawn concerning the private life of a

event serious regardless of the length of the period in respect of which access to those data is sought and the quantity or nature of the data available in respect of such a period, when, as in the main proceedings, that set of data is liable to allow precise conclusions to be drawn concerning the private life of the person or persons concerned.[130] The Court referred further to the finding in *Prokuratuur* that even access to a limited quantity of traffic or location data or access to data in respect of a short period may be liable to provide precise information on the private life of a user of a means of electronic communication.[131]

The CJEU was further asked on a request by the Danish government that data initially retained in a general and indiscriminate way for national security purposes is subsequently accessed by national authorities for the purpose of fighting serious crime. The Court rejected this request by noting that the objective of fighting serious crime is of lesser importance in the hierarchy of objectives of public interest than that which justified the retention (namely the safeguarding of national security); the Court held that to authorise in that situation access to retained data would be contrary to the hierarchy of the public interest objectives outlined by the Court.[132] In its subsequent ruling in *Lietuvos Respublikos generalinė prokuratūra*,[133] the Court reiterated this hierarchy of objectives, this time distinguishing between access to retained data for the purposes of fighting serious crime and access for the purposes of fighting crime. The Court based this distinction heavily on the proportionality principle,[134] and applied its earlier case law *mutatis mutandis* to the case in question to preclude access to data retained for the purposes of fighting serious crime for the purpose of fighting crime generally and of preventing non-serious threats to public security.[135] The Court held that the objective in question in the present case, namely combating corruption-related misconduct in office, was of lesser importance to the hierarchy of public interest objectives than the objective of combating serious crime and preventing serious threats to public security; and that to authorise access for this purpose would be contrary to this hierarchy of public objectives.[136]

7. Conclusion

Rejecting mass surveillance has been a key priority for the Court of Justice in the protection of fundamental rights under EU law. In *Digital Rights Ireland*, the Court set out a key

---

user of a means of electronic communication and retained by providers of electronic communications services—submitted by a competent national authority in the context of a criminal investigation, to authorise such access if it is requested for the purposes of investigating criminal offences punishable under national law by a maximum term of imprisonment of at least three years, provided that there is sufficient evidence of the commission of such offences and that those data are relevant to establishing the facts, on condition, however, that that court is entitled to refuse such access if it is requested in the context of an investigation into an offence which is manifestly not a serious offence, in the light of the societal conditions prevailing in the Member State concerned: CJEU, Judgment of 30 April 2024, *Procura della Repubblica presso il Tribunale di Bolzano* (C-178/22) ECLI:EU:C:2024:371.

[130] *Prokuratuur* (n 129) para 39.
[131] *SpaceNet* (n 113) para 89 by reference to *Prokuratuur* (n 129) para 40.
[132] *SpaceNet* (n 113) para 129 and reference to *Garda Siochana* (n 95) para 99.
[133] CJEU, Judgment of 7 September 2023, *Lietuvos Respublikos generalinė prokuratūra* (C-162/22) ECLI:EU:C:2023:631.
[134] ibid, in particular paras 35 and 37.
[135] ibid paras 38 and 41.
[136] ibid para 41.

red line against mass surveillance based on generalised, indiscriminate data retention. The Court's bold move to annul the Data Retention Directive has been followed by numerous attempts by Member States to reintroduce generalised and indiscriminate data retention in national law, justifying this introduction on internal and national security grounds. The CJEU has consistently rejected these developments, by maintaining in principle its red line against mass surveillance while offering states a degree of leeway in terms of generalised retention on national security grounds, and in terms of allowing generalised retention in specific circumstances and regarding limited categories of personal data. A constant feature in this case law has been the Court's decisiveness in applying EU law—and the Charter—in the face of states' national security objections. In the evolution of its case law, the Court has increasingly been drawn to discussing not only the constitutional and fundamental rights framework, but practical guidance to states as to what constitutes effective law enforcement. While this move is understandable in view of the Court's perceived need to respond to criticisms by the executive as regards its limited understanding of law enforcement needs and practice on the ground, these arguments should not detract from the importance of the Court's safeguarding of a number of fundamental rights from mass surveillance, not should they detract from the importance of continuing to draw a red line against privatised mass surveillance in a democratic society.

4
A Critical Comment on Proportionality in the Mass Surveillance Jurisprudence of the CJEU and the ECtHR

Lorenzo Dalla Corte

1. Introduction

Over the past decade, particularly after the 2013 'Snowden Revelations'[1] which exposed the extent to which states engaged in large-scale surveillance practices, European apex courts[2] have increasingly been grappling with the task of balancing individual rights and collective interests in controversies pertaining to bulk collection, retention, access, and analysis of personal data for law enforcement and national security purposes. The debate surrounding mass surveillance practices and their legitimacy reflects one of the primary dilemmas of contemporary liberal democracies: the tension between individual rights, such as the right to the respect of private life and to the protection of personal data, and competing public interests, such as national or public security and crime prevention.

Courts face daunting questions: when should privacy take precedence over security, 'in this data age in which digital technologies enabled huge amounts of personal data to be collected and analysed for predictive purposes?'[3] To what extent should public authorities be allowed to interfere with individual freedoms for the collective good? How should courts go about comparing seemingly incomparable values, like the respect for people's private lives with the protection of national security, or, as it were, 'the length of a line with the weight of a stone'?[4]

To be sure, courts are not guideless, and their discretion is far from being unfettered. After the Second World War, constitutional law, and particularly the process through which constitutional and quasi-constitutional courts determine the legitimacy of a measure interfering with a fundamental right (limitations analysis),[5] went through a process of gradual

---

[1] See eg David Wright and Reinhard Kreissl, 'European Responses to the Snowden Revelations' in David Wright and Reinhard Kreissl (eds), *Surveillance in Europe* (Routledge 2014). See also Zygmunt Bauman and others, 'After Snowden: Rethinking the Impact of Surveillance' (2014) 8 International Political Sociology 121.

[2] ie EU Member States' constitutional courts, the Court of Justice of the European Union (CJEU), and the European Court of Human Rights (ECtHR).

[3] Opinion of Advocate General Pitruzzella of 27 January 2022, *Ligue des droits humains* (C-817/19) ECLI:EU:C:2022:65, para 2.

[4] See Niels Petersen, 'How to Compare the Length of Lines to the Weight of Stones: Balancing and the Resolution of Value Conflicts in Constitutional Law' (2013) 14 German Law Journal 1387.

[5] I borrow the term from T Jeremy Gunn, 'Deconstructing Proportionality in Limitations Analysis' (2005) 19 Emory International Law Review 465.

globalisation.[6] Limitations analysis increasingly converged into a model (the 'post-War paradigm')[7] where judicial review and the balancing of competing rights became centred on proportionality reasoning.[8]

Proportionality, despite criticism to the contrary,[9] is meant to be a rigorous standard-based doctrine: it is historically rooted in legal formalism,[10] and aspires at reducing the subjectiveness inherent in the exercise of power and at increasing the reproducibility of legal reasoning.[11] In other words, the function of proportionality is to provide a logical framework to ground the reasoning of the judiciary, thus shielding individuals from random, arbitrary, or capricious judicial decision-making.

However, secret surveillance, particularly when carried out through automated or semi-automated means and on a large scale, challenges the extent to which judicial limitations analysis and proportionality reasoning allow to pursue an appropriate equilibrium between privacy and security. The secret nature, massive scale, and (semi-)autonomous nature of the surveillance carried out by public authorities are bound to influence courts' reasoning by influencing both the input of the process (the information available to the judiciary) and the process itself. This chapter thus investigates how, in the data retention jurisprudence of the Court of Justice of the European Union (CJEU) and the European Court of Human Rights (ECtHR), courts have been carrying out their proportionality reasoning and limitations analysis. How does the peculiar nature of the subject matter at hand impact the way in which courts reason about limiting fundamental rights and freedoms?

Through a systematic hermeneutical analysis of the case law of the CJEU and the ECtHR,[12] this chapter provides a critical overview of (some of) the peculiar characteristics of the proportionality reasoning and limitations analysis carried out by both apex courts when adjudicating cases relating to mass surveillance matters.[13] The chapter is structured

---

[6] See eg Anne-Marie Slaughter, 'Judicial Globalization' (1999) 40 Virginia Journal of International Law 1103.

[7] See Moshe Cohen-Eliya and Iddo Porat, 'American Balancing and German Proportionality: The Historical Origins' (2010) 8 International Journal of Constitutional Law 263.

[8] See eg Alec Stone Sweet and Jud Mathews, 'Proportionality Balancing and Global Constitutionalism' (2008) 47 Columbia Journal of Transnational Law 72; Anne Peters, 'Proportionality as a Global Constitutional Principle' in Anthony F Lang Jr and Antje Wiener (eds), *Handbook on Global Constitutionalism* (Edward Elgar 2017).

[9] Most notably Jürgen Habermas, *Between Facts and Norms: Contributions to a Discourse Theory of Law and Democracy* (John Wiley & Sons 2015), originally published in 1992. See also eg Stavros Tsakyrakis, 'Proportionality: An Assault on Human Rights?' (2009) 7 International Journal of Constitutional Law 468. With respect to privacy and personal data protection, see eg Filippo Fontanelli, 'The Mythology of Proportionality in Judgments of the Court of Justice of the European Union on Internet and Fundamental Rights' (2016) 36 Oxford Journal of Legal Studies 630; Audrey Guinchard, 'Taking Proportionality Seriously: The Use of Contextual Integrity for a More Informed and Transparent Analysis in EU Data Protection Law' (2018) 24 European Law Journal 434.

[10] Cohen-Eliya and Porat, 'American Balancing and German Proportionality' (n 7) 275; Moshe Cohen-Eliya and Iddo Porat, *Proportionality and Constitutional Culture*, vol 7 (CUP 2013) 31.

[11] See the numerous attempts at tying proportionality reasoning and formal logic, eg Matthias Klatt and Moritz Meister, *The Constitutional Structure of Proportionality* (OUP 2012). See also eg Giovanni Sartor, 'The Logic of Proportionality: Reasoning with Non-Numerical Magnitudes' (2013) 14 German Law Journal 1419.

[12] While there are differences between how the ECtHR and the CJEU deal with mass surveillance, the judicial dialogue between the two apex courts (and national constitutional courts) has been quite intense: see generally Jan Podkowik, Robert Rybski, and Marek Zubik, 'Judicial Dialogue on Data Retention Laws: A Breakthrough for European Constitutional Courts?' (2021) 19 International Journal of Constitutional Law 1597. This dialogue has led to a substantial convergence of the two courts' case law: see eg Monika Zalnieriute, 'A Dangerous Convergence: The Inevitability of Mass Surveillance in European Jurisprudence' (2021) *EJIL:Talk!* <https://www.ejiltalk.org/a-dangerous-convergence-the-inevitability-of-mass-surveillance-in-european-jurisprudence/> accessed 5 June 2023.

[13] This chapter does not aim, for reasons of space and scope, to summarise the surveillance case law of the Courts, nor to provide alternatives to the approach they elect to follow. It is also not meant as criticism, but as critique. On the one hand, providing an alternative to the Courts' approach to proportionality testing is beyond the

as follows: after this introduction, section 2 briefly recapitulates the elements of the limitations analysis carried out by the Strasbourg and Luxembourg courts; the chapter then moves on to the substantive discussion of the suitability test (section 3), the focus on necessity rather than on *stricto sensu* proportionality (section 4), and the merger of the legality and necessity tests (section 5). Section 6 deals with the concept of essence of the rights to private life and data protection, and section 7 concludes the chapter.

2. Proportionality and Limitations Analysis

In European constitutionalism, the restriction of fundamental rights, which have constitutional (or quasi-constitutional) status, is based on limitation clauses of equivalent hierarchical standing: only a (quasi-)constitutional limitation clause can serve as a basis for the limitation of a (quasi-)constitutional right. European supranational apex courts (ie the CJEU and the ECtHR), in their limitations analysis, thus rely on the textual hooks that are present in both the Charter of Fundamental Rights of the EU[14] ('Charter' or 'CFR' hereinafter) and in the European Convention on Human Rights (ECHR).[15]

The Charter has a single general limitation clause in its Article 52(2), which mandates that 'any limitation on the exercise of the rights and freedoms recognised by this Charter must be provided for by law and respect the essence of those rights and freedoms', and that '(s)ubject to the principle of proportionality, limitations may be made only if they are necessary and genuinely meet objectives of general interest recognised by the Union or the need to protect the rights and freedoms of others'. The ECHR, conversely, pairs each qualified right (eg Article 8(1) ECHR) with a specific limitation clause, such as Article 8(2) ECHR, which sanctions that '(t)here shall be no interference by a public authority with the exercise of this right except such as is in accordance with the law and is necessary in a democratic society in the interests of national security, public safety or the economic well-being of the country, for the prevention of disorder or crime, for the protection of health or morals, or for the protection of the rights and freedoms of others'.

The limitation clause in the Charter and the ones in the ECHR embody the traditional structure of the proportionality test of Germanic origin.[16] Regardless of their different wording, both courts assess the *lato sensu* proportionality of an interference following three sequential sub-tests: suitability, necessity, and proportionality in the strict sense, or *sensu stricto*.[17] The first sub-test is suitability, which evaluates whether a measure is effective,

---

author's abilities; on the other hand, it might not be sensible to ask a court to do what is essentially a lawmaker's job. It should be the EU legislature's task to adopt secondary data retention legislation, both to provide legal clarity and uniformity across the Union: see also Xavier Tracol, 'The Joined Cases of Dwyer, SpaceNet and VD and SR before the European Court of Justice: The Judgments of the Grand Chamber about Data Retention Continue Falling on Deaf Ears in Member States' (2023) 48(105773) Computer Law & Security Review 14.

[14] Charter of Fundamental Rights of the European Union [2012] OJ C 326/391.
[15] Council of Europe, European Convention for the Protection of Human Rights and Fundamental Freedoms, 4 November 1950, ETS 5.
[16] See generally Robert Alexy, *A Theory of Constitutional Rights* (OUP 2009); Aharon Barak, *Proportionality: Constitutional Rights and Their Limitations* (CUP 2012); Cohen-Eliya and Porat, *Proportionality and Constitutional Culture* (n 10).
[17] This chapter refers to the whole proportionality test as *lato sensu* proportionality, and to the balancing part of the whole proportionality test (ie proportionality in the strict sense) as proportionality *stricto sensu*.

that is, whether it pursues a proper purpose and whether it is rationally appropriate for its achievement. A limitation upon a right is legitimate only if it aims at achieving a goal deemed worthy of pursuit by the polity of reference (for instance the protection of national or public security) and if it is genuinely fit for that purpose.

The second component of the *lato sensu* proportionality test is the necessity sub-test, which assesses whether that measure is, amongst all the suitable alternatives, the one that interferes the least with the right it restricts. The necessary measure is the least restrictive one: is it possible to envision an alternative option that, while still suitable, does not encroach upon people's rights and freedoms as much as the measure assessed does? If so, the necessity sub-test should fail. If, conversely, there is no suitable alternative, within the legally and factually possible, that would still achieve its goal while resulting in a smaller restriction of the rights it interferes with, then the necessity sub-test should pan out.

Finally, the *stricto sensu* proportionality test—the courts' balancing exercise, proportionality in the strict sense—is meant to assess whether the societal benefits deriving from a measure that is both suitable and necessary outweigh the damage to the protection and realisation of the rights it restricts. Does the collective good that comes from a particular data retention regime justify the negative externalities, at both the individual and the societal level, that such regime brings forth?[18]

Notably, while the first two sub-tests are ideally meant to be threshold requirements, which are either met or not, proportionality in the strict sense implies a value judgment: it is based on axiological reasoning, and forces courts to make a value-laden choice about the society they shape. This last point is central to the chapter's argument. Suitability checks the rationality of the measure, and necessity whether there is an alternative less restrictive of the rights it interferes with. It is only at the *stricto sensu* proportionality stage that courts should determine whether the benefits deriving from the measure assessed, however appropriate and necessary for the purposes it pursues, also outweigh its social costs.

It must also be underlined that limitations analysis as a whole has become broader than proportionality testing alone. Both courts also assess elements other than a measure's suitability, necessity, and proportionality in a strict sense. Courts also check a measure's lawfulness, that is, whether it is sufficiently clear, accessible, and foreseeable, and whether it respects the essence of the rights it restricts, too.[19] While formally distinct and separate from proportionality reasoning, considerations about data retention's lawfulness and about the respect for the essence of the rights it interferes with interact with the *lato sensu* proportionality test.

The following sections discuss some of the peculiarities of the limitations analysis carried out by the CJEU and the ECtHR in mass surveillance judgments: their suitability test, the merger of the lawfulness test and the necessity one, the lack of proportionality in the strict sense, and the role of the concept of 'essence of a right'.

---

[18] This chapter espouses an admittedly expansive view about what *stricto sensu* proportionality test ought to be: a discussion about the values that should underlie the society we want, rather than a mere judicial cost–benefit analysis.

[19] Article 52(1) of the Charter makes explicit that limitations upon fundamental rights and freedoms must respect the essence of the rights they restrict. While that requirement is not explicitly mentioned in the ECHR, it may be argued that the respect for the essence of Convention rights in implicit: see generally Sébastien Van Drooghenbroeck and Cecilia Rizcallah, 'The ECHR and the Essence of Fundamental Rights: Searching for Sugar in Hot Milk?' (2019) 20 German Law Journal 904.

3. The Suitability Assumption

When it comes to the suitability sub-test, both the CJEU and the ECtHR do not contest the efficacy and rationality of mass surveillance measures, and rather concentrate their scrutiny on whether the purposes of the measure assessed are framed precisely and genuinely. Both courts recognise that (meta)data retention regimes allow public authorities to exercise considerable power over the individuals and groups whose data is retained, and ultimately over society at large.

For instance, in the *Big Brother Watch* case, the ECtHR remarked that bulk interception regimes are 'a valuable technological capacity to identify new threats in the digital domain',[20] in light of 'the proliferation of threats that States currently face from networks of international actors, using the Internet both for communication and as a tool, and the existence of sophisticated technology which would enable these actors to avoid detection'.[21] Likewise, in his Opinion in the *Tele2 Sverige* case,[22] where, following the *Digital Rights Ireland* judgment,[23] the CJEU addressed the incompatibility with the Charter of national legislation mandating indiscriminate metadata retention, Advocate General (AG) Saugmandsgaard Øe pointed out how 'the retention of communications data gives the authorities a certain ability to "examine the past" by accessing data relating to communications which a person has effected even before being suspected'.[24]

Both the CJEU and the ECtHR also acknowledge that this ability to 'examine the past' is inherently dangerous.[25] The Strasbourg court has oftentimes warned that 'a system of secret surveillance set up to protect national security ... may undermine or even destroy the proper functioning of democratic processes under the cloak of defending them'.[26] Likewise, the Luxembourg court is aware that large-scale personal data collection and automated processing risk 'favouring a gradual slide towards a "surveillance society"'.[27] That is, however, besides the point of the suitability sub-test, which ascertains only whether a measure interfering with a fundamental right does so in pursuit of a deserving purpose, and whether it is appropriate to achieve that purpose.[28] In that respect, courts seem to hold that the ability to 'examine the past' is indispensable in the modern information and communication society.[29]

---

[20] ECtHR, *Big Brother Watch and others v the United Kingdom* [GC] nos 58170/13, 62322/14, and 24960/15, § 323, 25 May 2021.
[21] ECtHR, *Big Brother Watch* (n 20) para 340.
[22] Opinion of Advocate General Saugmansgaard Øe of 19 July 2016 in *Tele2 Sverige* (C-203/15 and C-698/15) ECLI:EU:C:2016:572.
[23] CJEU, Judgment of 8 April 2014, *Digital Rights Ireland and Seitlinger and others* (C-293/12 and C-594/12) ECLI:EU:C:2014:238).
[24] *AG Opinion Tele2 Sverige* (n 22) para 3. Also in paras 178, 180, 181, 208, 261, and footnotes 3 and 53.
[25] See eg Neil M Richards, 'The Dangers of Surveillance' (2013) 126 Harvard Law Review 1934; Christopher Parsons, 'Beyond Privacy: Articulating the Broader Harms of Pervasive Mass Surveillance' (2015) 3 Media and Communication 1.
[26] ECtHR, *Centrum för rättvisa v Sweden* [GC] no 35252/08, § 253, 25 May 2021. See also ECtHR, *Roman Zakharov v Russia* [GC] no 47143/06, § 232, 04 December 2015; ECtHR, *Szabó and Vissy v Hungary*, no 37138/14, § 57, 12 January 2016; *Big Brother Watch* (n 20) para 339.
[27] *AG Opinion Ligue des droits humains* (n 3) para 80.
[28] Barak splits the suitability test into two distinct elements, 'proper purpose' and 'rational connection': see Barak (n 16).
[29] eg in the context of the rise of 'stochastic terrorism' see Molly Amman and J Reid Meloy, 'Stochastic Terrorism' (2021) 15 Perspectives on Terrorism 2. For a discussion about the decentralised (and decentred) nature of modern 'digital' subversion, see Thomas Rid, *Cyber War Will Not Take Place* (OUP 2013).

When it comes to assessing the appropriateness of a measure allowing bulk collection and government access to retained data, European apex courts seem to move from the assumption of the efficacy and rationality of the measures considered, particularly when it comes to national security matters.[30] It may very well be nearly impossible to determine precisely the effectiveness of surveillance technology,[31] especially when it comes to bulk data retention, collection, and analysis for preventive purposes. Yet, both the CJEU and the ECtHR accept its suitability without particular scepticism.[32] The capacity to 'see the past' grants law enforcement and intelligence agencies the ability of identifying unknown dangers, rather than merely investigating known threats. As the Venice Commission puts it, '(h)erein lies both the value it can have for security operations, and the risks it can pose for individual rights'.[33]

The effectiveness of mass surveillance thus appears to be somewhat taken for granted by Strasbourg and Luxembourg alike, and crime prevention and investigation and the safeguard of national and public security are undeniably proper purposes in a democratic society. Yet, the suitability test is still a core element of both courts' decision-making process—'the alpha and omega of the principle of proportionality'.[34] The reason is that the extent to which an interference upon a right can be deemed as justified depends, inter alia, from the goals it pursues. There is a hierarchal order in the importance that the objectives that bulk data collection, retention, and access regimes can serve, which conditions the uppermost magnitude of the interference that can be deemed acceptable for their protection. Judicial control over the definition of those objectives takes place within the suitability sub-test.

The European (quasi-)constitutional tradition requires, for a limitation upon a qualified fundamental right to be justified, more than its mere legality, that is, the fact that it must be provided for by law.[35] It also requires its legitimacy: the goals advanced by the measure considered must be deemed worth pursuing in a constitutional democracy, and the means such measure employs must be rationally adequate to achieve them.[36] Bulk retention and access regimes are, by default, agnostic to the purposes for which they take place: it is for a state's legislature and public authorities in general to set limits upon their purposes, means, and methods, and for the judiciary to determine whether those purposes and means are rational, appropriate, and genuinely framed.

From the *Ministerio Fiscal* judgment onwards, the CJEU remarked that in the areas of prevention, investigation, and prosecution of criminal offences, only the objective of fighting serious crime is capable of justifying public authorities' access to personal data retained by providers of electronic communications services: the objective pursued by

---

[30] With respect to the ECtHR, see Chao Jing, 'The ECtHR's Suitability Test in National Security Cases: Two Models for Balancing Human Rights and National Security' [2023] Leiden Journal of International Law 1.

[31] See Michelle Cayford and Wolter Pieters, 'The Effectiveness of Surveillance Technology: What Intelligence Officials Are Saying' (2018) 34 The Information Society 88.

[32] See eg ECtHR, *Škoberne v Slovenia*, App no 19920/20, §135, 15 February 2024: '[a]*lthough this point has not been demonstrated by any empirical data*, the Court has no doubt that the tracing of telecommunications traffic ... could be of considerable importance for effective law enforcement and effective public security measures' (italics added).

[33] European Commission for Democracy Through Law (Venice Commission), 'Report on the Democratic Oversight of Signals Intelligence Agencies' (Council of Europe 2015) 719/2013 3.

[34] Jonas Christoffersen, *Fair Balance: Proportionality, Subsidiarity and Primarity in the European Convention on Human Rights* (Brill 2009) 163.

[35] In the wording of Article 52(1) of the Charter, or 'in accordance with the law' in the wording of Article 8(2) of the ECHR.

[36] See Barak (n 16) 245ff.

legislation governing that access must be proportionate to the seriousness of the interference with the fundamental rights that it entails.[37] 'Serious' interferences can be justified only by the objective of fighting 'serious' crime. Conversely, interferences that are not 'serious' may be justified by the objective of fighting 'criminal offences' more generally.[38]

In both the *La Quadrature du Net 'I'* and the *Privacy International* judgments,[39] similarly, the CJEU held that the importance of the objective of safeguarding national security weighs more than other objectives, such as combating crime, even serious crime, and safeguarding public security. Threats to national security and to the public constitutional order are of a higher magnitude, and the objective of preventing or responding to them is therefore capable of justifying more serious interferences than those which might be justified by other objectives.[40]

In turn, European apex courts (most notably the CJEU, but also the ECtHR)[41] evaluate the objectives pursued by the measure they assess 'genuinely and strictly'. They do not merely accept the reasons put forth by the Member States or by the contracting parties, but rather require a precise and granular identification of the objectives pursued by the measures scrutinised. The Luxembourg court, in particular, has used the specific qualifier 'genuinely and strictly' for the first time in its *Tele2 Sverige* judgment,[42] and since then has referred to it in several other data protection judgments and opinions.[43] All those cases, notably, revolve around bulk retention and access to private communications (meta)data by public authorities specifically, as opposed to privacy and data protection matters in general.

The power to 'examine the past' is inherently prone to abuse,[44] and mass surveillance regimes may easily lead governments and public authorities to engage in slippery slopes.

---

[37] CJEU, Judgment of 2 October 2018, *Ministerio Fiscal* (C-207/16) ECLI:EU:C:2018:788, paras 54–55. See also Xavier Tracol, 'Ministerio Fiscal: Access of Public Authorities to Personal Data Retained by Providers of Electronic Communications Services' (2019) 5 Eur. Data Prot L Rev 127. Most recently, see CJEU, Judgment of 30 April 2024, *La Quadrature du Net aoc Premier Ministre and Ministre de la Culture* (C-470/21) ECLI:EU:C:2024:370 ('*La Quadrature du Net 'II'*').

[38] *Ministerio Fiscal* (n 37) paras 56–57. See also *La Quadrature du Net 'II'*, ibid.

[39] CJEU, Judgment of 6 October 2020, *La Quadrature du Net and others* (C-511/18, C-512/18 and C-520/18) ECLI:EU:C:2020:791 ('*La Quadrature du Net 'I'*'); CJEU, Judgment of 6 October 2020, *Privacy International* (C-623/17) ECLI:EU:C:2020:790. See also Xavier Tracol, 'The Two Judgments of the European Court of Justice in the Four Cases of Privacy International, La Quadrature Du Net and Others, French Data Network and Others and Ordre Des Barreaux Francophones et Germanophone and Others: The Grand Chamber Is Trying Hard' (2021) 41(105540) Computer Law & Security Review.

[40] *Privacy International* ibid para 75; *La Quadrature du Net 'I'* ibid para 136.

[41] The Strasbourg Court is conditioned by the margin of appreciation doctrine, particularly after the introduction of the subsidiarity principle in Protocol No 15.

[42] CJEU, Judgment of 21 December 2016, *Tele2 Sverige* (C-203/15 and C-698/15) ECLI:EU:C:2016:970 para 115.

[43] After *Tele2 Sverige* ibid the Court used the wording 'genuinely and strictly' eg in *Ministerio Fiscal* (n 37) para 52; *La Quadrature du Net 'I'* (n 39) para 112; CJEU, Judgment of 5 April 2022, *Commissioner of An Garda Síochána* (C-140/20) ECLI:EU:C:2022:258 para 41; and CJEU, Judgment of 27 October 2022, *SpaceNet* (C-793/19 and C-794/19) ECLI:EU:C:2022:70 para 58. The Attorneys General used the wording 'genuinely and strictly' in Opinion of Advocate General Campos Sànchez-Bordona of 5 January 2020, *Ordre des barreaux francophones et Germanophone* (C-520/18) ECLI:EU:C:2020:7 para 54; Opinion of Advocate General Pitruzzella of 21 January 2020, *HK v Prokuratuur* (C-746/18) ECLI:EU:C:2020:18 para 58; Opinion of Advocate General Carlos Campos-Sanchez Bordona of 18 November 2021 in case *Commissioner of An Garda Síochána* (C-140/20) ECLI:EU:C:2021:942 para 50; and recently in Opinion of Advocate General Szpunar of 27 October 2022, C-470/21, *La Quadrature du Net 'II'* (n 37) para 57.

[44] The ECtHR, in particular, has remarked about 'the risk of abuse which is inherent in any system of secret surveillance' in *Zakharov* (n 26) para 302; ECtHR, *Ekimdzhiev and others v Bulgaria*, no. 70078/12, § 294, 11 January 2022; ECtHR, *Association for European Integration and Human Rights and Ekimdzhiev v Bulgaria*, no. 62540/00, § 93, 28 June 2007; ECtHR, *Malone v the United Kingdom*, 2 August 1984, § 81, Series A no. 82 ('*Malone*'). See also ECtHR, *Klass and others v Germany*, 6 September 1978, § 56, Series A no. 28 ('*Klass*'): 'a field where abuse

An infrastructure initially implemented to thwart threats to national security can easily be repurposed towards other objectives, like the prevention of serious crime, to the investigation of crimes in general, and even potentially to matters like intellectual property enforcement.[45] In that sense, the Court's statement can be read as a context-specific warning against the function and purpose creep[46] that may be accelerated by the intrinsically agnostic nature of bulk data collection, retention, and access.

It could also be argued that the fact that the CJEU makes explicit that it evaluates the objectives of a measure interfering with fundamental rights 'genuinely and strictly' only in its surveillance case law is simply due to its recurring reference to the *Tele2 Sverige* judgment.[47] The court, in that reading, would be simply repeating the wording used in a prior decision without ascribing particular contextual meaning to it. However, the CJEU is quite precise with its wording, and generally ascribes precise meaning to the phrases and sentences it chooses to repeat in its subsequent case law. Accordingly, this chapter favours the first reading: it is the nature of mass surveillance itself that warrants the court's specific warning about the 'genuine and strict' nature of the suitability test it carries out.

To summarise: when carrying out the suitability sub-test, neither the CJEU nor the ECtHR seem to be overly concerned with contesting mass surveillance's ability to achieve the goals it pursues, from the prevention of national security threats to the investigation and prosecution of serious crimes. That is not surprising, as the suitability sub-test only aims at assessing *efficacy*, not effectiveness: courts only evaluate whether the measure assessed can work, not whether it is the most efficient or whether its benefit overshadow its drawbacks. Those are the subsequent sub-tests of the *lato sensu* proportionality test (ie necessity and proportionality *stricto sensu*). Irrespective of what can be said about mass surveillance from an ethical perspective,[48] arguing about its efficacy vis-à-vis the objectives of, for instance, safeguarding national security or preventing serious crime, does not seem to be the ideal avenue for contestation.

That is not to say that the suitability sub-test in matters of bulk data retention and access is insubstantial: on the contrary, the Courts exert their judicial control by requiring a precise delineation ('genuine and strict') of each of the specific objectives the measure assessed aims at achieving.[49] The extent to which individuals can be required to tolerate an

---

is potentially so easy in individual cases and could have such harmful consequences for democratic society as a whole'. As for the CJEU, see *Privacy International*, para 73: 'the mere retention of that data by the providers of electronic communications services entails a risk of abuse and unlawful access'.

[45] With respect to data retention for IP enforcement purposes, see *La Quadrature du Net 'II'* (n 37) and both the Opinions of Advocate General Szpunar: *First AG Opinion La Quadrature du Net 'II'* and Opinion of Advocate General Szpunar of 28 September 2023, C-470/21, *La Quadrature du Net 'II'* ECLI:EU:C:2023:711 ('*Second AG Opinion La Quadrature du Net 'II'*').

[46] See Bert-Jaap Koops, 'The Concept of Function Creep' (2021) 13 Law, Innovation and Technology 29. See also Maria Tzanou, 'The EU as an Emerging "Surveillance Society": The Function Creep Case Study and Challenges to Privacy and Data Protection' (2010) 4 ICL Journal 407.

[47] *Tele2 Sverige* (n 42) para 115.

[48] See eg Marie-Helen Maras, 'The Social Consequences of a Mass Surveillance Measure: What Happens When We Become the "Others"?' (2012) 40 International Journal of Law, Crime and Justice 65; John Guelke, 'The Ethics of Mass Surveillance', *The Routledge Handbook to Rethinking Ethics in International Relations* (Routledge 2020); Peter Königs, 'Government Surveillance, Privacy, and Legitimacy' (2022) 35 Philosophy & Technology 8.

[49] While the preceding paragraphs focused on the CJEU, the same holds true for the ECtHR: it has been noted (with reference to *Malone* (n 44) para 75) how '(a)ccording to the ECtHR, surveillance requires laws that need a considerable amount of detail'—Gianclaudio Malgieri and Paul de Hert, 'One European Legal Framework for Surveillance: The ECtHR's Expanded Legality Testing Copied by the CJEU' in Valsamis Mitsilegas and Niovi

interference upon their fundamental rights depends on what, precisely, that interference is meant to accomplish. As mass surveillance's purpose and function are inherently expansive, Luxembourg and Strasbourg, in their suitability sub-test, focus more on checking its goals and whether they have been framed precisely enough (the 'proper purpose' element)[50] than on arguing about whether it works or not (the 'rational connection' one).[51]

4. Focusing on Necessity rather than on Proportionality *Stricto Sensu*

Once a lawful measure interfering with a fundamental right is deemed suitable for the achievement of its objectives, courts assess whether it is also necessary, that is whether, amongst all suitable measures, it is the least restrictive one.[52] If the measure assessed passes the necessity sub-test as well, courts then evaluate whether it is proportionate in a strict sense, ie whether the benefits deriving from the measures outweigh the impairment to the protection and realisation of the rights it restricts.

The data retention case law of the CJEU and the ECtHR shows a marked focus on the necessity sub-test, and little attention to the *stricto sensu* proportionality one. That may be problematic, as the necessity and the *stricto sensu* proportionality tests have different purposes, follow different logical structures, and ultimately seek to answer complementary questions. In his Opinion in *Tele2 Sverige*, AG Saugmandsgaard Øe underlines the difference between proportionality *stricto sensu* and the necessity requirement through a dystopian hypothetical: let us imagine an EU Member State mandating 'every person residing within its territory to have a geopositioning electronic chip injected into their body, one that enabled the authorities to retrace the comings and goings of the wearer'.[53] Such a measure, even if it were considered 'necessary' due to the lack of other measures capable of achieving the same results, would still be disproportionate within a democratic society.

The necessity test should be a binary threshold assessment: a 'yes or no question', the purpose of which is just to check that the objectives pursued by the specific data retention measure considered could not be achieved by other means less restrictive of the rights interfered with.[54] Conversely, the *stricto sensu* proportionality test is meant to be a nuanced value judgment, based on axiological reasoning. Its purpose is to determine that a (mass) surveillance measure that is both suitable and necessary is also overall 'worth it'—whether the benefits deriving from public authorities' ability to 'examine the past' by accessing data retained at scale surpass its negative externalities for the individuals involved and for society at large.[55]

Vavoula (eds), *Surveillance and Privacy in the Digital Age: European, Transatlantic and Global Perspectives* (Hart Publishing 2021) 261.

[50] Barak (n 16) 245ff.
[51] ibid 303ff.
[52] 'It is settled case-law that a measure may be regarded as necessary only if no other measures exist that would be equally appropriate and less restrictive': *AG Opinion Tele2 Sverige* (n 22) para 185.
[53] ibid fn 81.
[54] See generally Janneke Gerards, 'How to Improve the Necessity Test of the European Court of Human Rights' (2013) 11 International Journal of Constitutional Law 466.
[55] *AG Opinion Tele2 Sverige* (n 22) para 223: 'the requirement of necessity implies the rejection of any measure that is inefficient. In that context there can be no question of any "overall assessment", or of "compensation" or of "weighing up", which come into play only when proportionality stricto sensu is assessed'. See also Julian Rivers, 'Proportionality and Variable Intensity of Review' (2006) 65 The Cambridge Law Journal 174.

Both Courts concentrate on the necessity sub-test, and seem conversely hesitant in qualifying the *stricto sensu* proportionality of the data retention measures they assess.[56] The data retention case law of the CJEU and the ECtHR follows a very similar blueprint: both Strasbourg and Luxembourg deal with the *lato sensu* proportionality of data retention mostly by requiring a set of safeguards and protection mechanisms of an eminently procedural nature, tuned to the importance of the objective pursued by the specific measure assessed.[57]

The CJEU, in its data retention case law, begins by 'laying out different clusters of public interest objectives and pairing them with different data retention measures based on its reading of different threat levels and seriousness that denote each objective'.[58] It then underlines the need for a set of safeguards and guarantees against abuse that are less concerned with balancing the benefits, damages, and values that mass surveillance brings forth, and more with determining its least restrictive configuration.[59] The ECtHR, in its judicial dialogue with both the CJEU and the supreme courts of the Convention's contracting parties,[60] follows the same approach, focusing on the development of end-to-end procedural safeguards.[61]

In a way, both the CJEU and the ECtHR appear to see mass surveillance as a necessary element of the *status quo*, and as a standalone kind of interference, ontologically distinct[62] from other forms of non-preventative monitoring, as opposed to being the most intrusive configuration surveillance activities can take. Both courts seem to operate under the assumption that mass surveillance is a necessity in contemporary constitutional democracies, inherently suitable for the objectives its legal bases aim at achieving, and largely focused their scrutiny and the development of their case law on finding its 'least restrictive' form.

---

[56] See eg *AG Opinion Tele2 Sverige* (n 22) para 223: 'the ... argument arises from confusion between the requirement of necessity and the requirement of proportionality stricto sensu, which the Court did not consider in Digital Rights Ireland'. With regard to how the CJEU dealt with *stricto* sensu proportionality in Opinion 1/15, see also Hielke Hijmans, 'Data Protection and Surveillance: The Perspective of EU Law' in Valsamis Mitsilegas and Niovi Vavoula (eds), *Surveillance and Privacy in the Digital Age: European, Transatlantic and Global Perspectives* (Hart Publishing 2021) 242 and fn 43: 'this assessment is similar to a test of the necessity of a measure.' and 'in Opinion 1/15 the Court assessed the necessity, not the proportionality, of a measure, although the substance of the test is the same'.

[57] The objectives are divided into the following general categories: 1. safeguarding national security; 2. fighting serious crime and preventing serious threats to public security; 3. fighting crime and safeguarding public security in general. To each objective, the CJEU ties a range of permissible mass surveillance measures, from the bulk retention of traffic and location data of all types (for national security purposes, see *La Quadrature du Net 'I'* (n 39) paras 137ff), to the targeted retention of traffic location data (for fighting serious crime and preventing serious threats to public security, see eg *SpaceNet* (n 43) para 75), to the mass retention of data on civil identities (to combat crime and safeguard public security in general, see eg *Ministerio Fiscal* (n 37) para 62, and *La Quadrature du Net 'II'* (n 37)).

[58] Valsamis Mitsilegas and others, 'Data Retention and the Future of Large-scale Surveillance: The Evolution and Contestation of Judicial Benchmarks' (2022) European Law Journal 6.

[59] See eg *Digital Rights Ireland* (n 23) paras 60–68; *Tele2 Sverige* (n 42) paras 109ff. In general, the CJEU allows various kinds of data retention measures, tuning their intrusiveness to the importance of the public interest objective pursued, on condition that they 'ensure, by means of clear and precise rules, that the retention of data at issue is subject to compliance with the applicable substantive and procedural conditions and that the persons concerned have effective safeguards against the risks of abuse': see eg *La Quadrature du Net 'I'* (n 39) para 168; judgment in *Garda Síochána* (n 43) para 67; CJEU, Judgment of 7 September 2023, *Lietuvos Respublikos generalinė prokuratūra* (C-162/22) ECLI:EU:C:2023:631 para 31.

[60] See generally Podkowik, Rybski, and Zubik (n 12). See also Marcin Rojszczak, 'The Uncertain Future of Data Retention Laws in the EU: Is a Legislative Reset Possible?' (2021) 41 Computer Law & Security Review.

[61] See eg *Centrum för rättvisa* (n 26) paras 264ff; *Big Brother Watch* (n 20) paras 350ff. See also Monika Zalnieriute, 'Big Brother Watch and Others v. the United Kingdom' (2022) 116 American Journal of International Law 585.

[62] *Big Brother Watch* (n 20) paras 343ff.

Neither the CJEU nor the ECtHR ever really question whether even the least restrictive configuration of a data retention and access regime, suitable and necessary to achieve the objectives it pursues, would still be disproportionate in the strict sense in light of its effects on the rights of the people concerned and of society as a whole.

That may be due to several reasons, some of which are inherent to proportionality in general: both the CJEU and the ECtHR base their analysis on the wording of the CFR and the ECHR, respectively, which does not exactly mirror the tripartite structure of the traditional *lato sensu* proportionality test, despite embodying its logic.[63] Moreover, as constitutional doctrine often remarked, the necessity sub-test on the ground does not often result in the binary, value-neutral assessment that is portrayed in the books.[64]

The limited role of the *stricto sensu* proportionality sub-test as compared to the necessity one may also be explained by reference to the nature of data retention in particular. The objectives mass surveillance is meant to pursue—from investigating and prosecuting crimes of varying seriousness to preventing threats to public or national security—are manifold and multifaceted, and its benefits relative to targeted surveillance difficult to quantify. The societal consequences of large-scale data retention regimes, on the other hand, are both potentially far-reaching and hard to predict. Judicial proceedings might thus not be the optimal venue for a political issue such as balancing the advantages of mass surveillance and its negative externalities.

Be as it may, safeguards and limitations do not necessarily bring mass surveillance in the realm of the *stricto sensu* proportionate. Necessity is a threshold test, meant to ascertain whether there is an alternative that, despite being as suitable as the measure assessed, is less restrictive of the rights it impacts; proportionality in the strict sense, conversely, is meant to be an axiological judgment, where competing values and interests are pitted against each other to ascertain whether the societal gains deriving from the measure surpass the damage it inflicts on the people whose rights are interfered with.

When compared to targeted surveillance, all (suitable) mass, preventive surveillance measures are bound to go beyond what is strictly necessary for their purpose: they are, in other words, over-inclusive[65] by definition. In those cases, legitimacy issues should also be assessed in light of the measure's proportionality in the strict sense. Yet what both courts do, in essence, is focus on the necessity sub-test, setting out procedural criteria for the pursuit of the 'least restrictive' mass surveillance measures. To a large extent, they limit their *stricto sensu* proportionality test to grouping permissible data retention measures according to the seriousness of the objective they pursue, rather than evaluating their effect on society.

---

[63] Article 52(1) of the CFR reads that '[a]ny limitation on the exercise of the rights and freedoms recognised by this Charter must be provided for by law and respect the essence of those rights and freedoms. Subject to the principle of proportionality, limitations may be made only if they are necessary and genuinely meet objectives of general interest recognised by the Union or the need to protect the rights and freedoms of others'. Article 8(2) reads that 'There shall be no interference by a public authority with the exercise of this right except such as is in accordance with the law and is necessary in a democratic society in the interests of national security, public safety or the economic well-being of the country, for the prevention of disorder or crime, for the protection of health or morals, or for the protection of the rights and freedoms of others'.

[64] See eg Barak (n 16) 317ff.

[65] ie it is not possible to distinctly identify the one least restrictive measure, as all suitable measure go beyond what is strictly necessary for the achievement of their objectives, and, conversely, all measures that do not are unsuitable: see Barak (n 16) 335. See also Lorenzo Dalla Corte, 'On Proportionality in the Data Protection Jurisprudence of the CJEU' (2022) 12 International Data Privacy Law 259.

The limited role of the *stricto sensu* proportionality sub-test is arguably compounded by the fact that, in cases which revolve around secret surveillance, both courts assess the necessity of the interference jointly with its lawfulness.

5. Merging Lawfulness and Necessity

Besides being proportionate, an interference upon a fundamental right must also be lawful.[66] When testing the legitimacy of surveillance measures, both the CJEU and the ECtHR read the lawfulness requirement in a peculiar fashion,[67] interpreting it in light of surveillance's necessarily opaque and secret nature. What is most notable, with regard to their case law on bulk data retention and access, is how both courts merge the lawfulness test and the necessity one, thus arguably twisting the traditional structure of the proportionality test.

In the Opinion in the *Schrems II* case, for instance, AG Saugmandsgaard Øe examines the foreseeability of section 702 of the US Foreign Intelligence Surveillance Act (FISA),[68] and argues that 'that problem also concerns the strict necessity of the interferences'.[69] In that same Opinion, the AG points out[70] that the CJEU, in both *Tele2 Sverige*[71] and *PNR Canada*,[72] framed the foreseeability requirement 'as being intrinsically linked with the condition that the interference must be necessary and proportionate',[73] in accordance with the approach historically followed by the ECtHR on the same sort of controversies. Successive CJEU case law on mass surveillance matters did not deviate from this approach, which appears now an established *modus decidendi* in Luxembourg and Strasbourg alike.[74]

The CJEU's merger between the legality and the necessity tests has indeed been borrowed from the ECtHR.[75] The Strasbourg court, in its case law on bulk interception of

---

[66] 'Provided for by law' in the wording of the CFR, and 'in accordance with the law' in the ECHR. Their meaning is to be interpreted identically: see Opinion of Advocate General Wathelet of 16 September 2015, *WebMindLicenses Kft.* (C-419/14) ECLI:EU:C:2015:606 ('*AG Opinion WebMindLicenses*') paras 134ff. See also ECtHR, *The Sunday Times v the United Kingdom* (no. 1) 26 April 1979, § 48, Series A no. 30.

[67] The ECtHR's burgeoning case law on lawfulness in surveillance judgments includes *Malone* (n 44) paras 66ff; ECtHR, *Leander v Sweden*, 26 March 1987, § 50ff, Series A no. 116; ECtHR, *Kruslin v France*, 24 April 1990, § 27ff, Series A no. 176-A; ECtHR, *P.G. and J.H. v the United Kingdom*, no. 44787/98, § 35ff, ECHR 2001-IX; ECtHR, *Liberty and others v the United Kingdom*, no. 58243/00, § 59ff, 1 July 2008; *Big Brother Watch* (n 20); *Szabò and Vissy*. As for the CJEU, see the following AG Opinions and the cases they refer to: Opinion of Advocate General Léger of 22 November 2005, *Parliament v Council and Commission* (C-317/04 and C-318/04) ECLI:EU:C:2005:710 ('*AG Opinion Parliament v Council*') paras 215ff; Opinion of Advocate General Cruz Villalón of 12 December 2013, *Digital Rights Ireland* (C-293/12) ECLI:EU:C:2013:845 ('*AG Opinion Digital Rights Ireland*') paras 108ff; Opinion of Advocate General Mengozzi of 8 September 2016 (Opinion procedure 1/15) ECLI:EU:C:2016:656 ('*AG Opinion PNR Canada*') paras 190ff; Opinion of Advocate General Saugmandsgaard Øe of 19 December 2019, *Facebook Ireland and Schrems* (C-311/18) ECLI:EU:C:2019:1145 ('*AG Opinion Schrems II*') paras 263ff; *AG Opinion Ligue des droits humains* (n 3) paras 85ff.

[68] 50 U.S.C. § 1801 et seq.

[69] *AG Opinion Schrems II* (n 67) para 268.

[70] ibid fn 145.

[71] *Tele2 Sverige* (n 42) paras 116–117.

[72] CJEU, Opinion 1/15 (EU–Canada PNR Agreement) of 26 July 2017 (Digital Reports) ECLI:EU:C:2017:592 ('*PNR Canada*') paras 140–141. See also Xavier Tracol, 'Opinion 1/15 of the Grand Chamber Dated 26 July 2017 about the Agreement on Passenger Name Record Data between the EU and Canada' (2018) 34 Computer Law & Security Review 830.

[73] *AG Opinion Schrems II* (n 67) fn 145.

[74] See most notably *La Quadrature du Net 'I'* (n 39) with respect to the CJEU, and *Big Brother Watch* (n 20) with respect to the ECtHR.

[75] See Malgieri and de Hert (n 49).

communications (meta)data, has often carried out the lawfulness and the necessity tests together. According to the case law of the ECtHR, both the 'foreseeability' requirement of the lawfulness test, and necessity of the interference deriving from the existence of surveillance powers, are benchmarked against the existence of effective legal safeguards against abuse. When assessing those safeguards, the ECtHR thus examines lawfulness and necessity jointly.[76]

In *Kvasnica*, a case revolving around telephone wiretapping, the ECtHR remarked that 'the applicant's arguments concerning the lawfulness of the interference are closely related to the question as to whether the "necessity" test was complied with in his case'.[77] *Kvasnica* was then referenced in *Kennedy*, a case revolving around the UK Regulation of Investigatory Powers Act 2000 (RIPA), where the Court was asked to examine 'the proportionality of the RIPA legislation itself and the safeguards built into the system allowing for secret surveillance, rather than the proportionality of any specific measures taken in respect of the applicant'.[78] Strasbourg held that, in those circumstances, the lawfulness of the interference is closely related to the 'necessity' test as performed upon the RIPA regime itself, rather than upon the facts of the case, and thus addressed jointly the 'in accordance with the law' and 'necessity' requirements.

The merger of lawfulness and necessity in the Court's limitations analysis then became standard practice in controversies revolving around bulk interception regimes. Central to this development is *Zakharov*, where the ECtHR again held that, where legislation permitting secret surveillance is contested, the measure's necessity is closely related to its lawfulness, and it is thus fitting to address jointly the 'in accordance with the law' and 'necessary in a democratic society' requirements. The 'quality of law' requirement implies not only the law's accessibility and foreseeability, but also 'that secret surveillance measures are applied only when "necessary in a democratic society", in particular by providing for adequate and effective safeguards and guarantees against abuse'.[79]

The same approach was then followed in the *Szabó and Vissy*,[80] *Centrum för rättvisa*,[81] and *Big Brother Watch* judgments.[82] In *Big Brother Watch*, for instance, the ECtHR again remarked that, in the assessment of the legitimacy of legislation permitting secret surveillance, the lawfulness of the interference also depends on whether the 'necessity' test has been complied with. Those two requirements must thus be assessed jointly, as '"quality of law" in this sense implies that the domestic law ... must also ensure that secret surveillance

---

[76] See *AG Opinion Schrems II* (n 67) fn 145, and the case law cited therein.
[77] ECtHR, *Kvasnica v Slovakia*, no. 72094/01, § 84, 9 June 2009.
[78] ECtHR, *Kennedy v the United Kingdom*, no. 26839/05, § 155, 18 May 2010.
[79] *Zakharov* (n 26) para 236.
[80] 'The Court ... is required to examine this legislation itself and the safeguards built into the system allowing for secret surveillance, rather than the proportionality of any specific measures taken in respect of the applicants. In the circumstances, the lawfulness of the interference is closely related to the question whether the "necessity" test has been complied with': *Szabó and Vissy* (n 26) para 58.
[81] 'In cases where the legislation permitting secret surveillance is contested before the Court, the lawfulness of the interference is closely related to the question whether the "necessity" test has been complied with and it is therefore appropriate for the Court to address jointly the "in accordance with the law" and "necessity" requirements. The "quality of law" in this sense implies that the domestic law must not only be accessible and foreseeable in its application, it must also ensure that secret surveillance measures are applied only when "necessary in a democratic society", in particular by providing for adequate and effective safeguards and guarantees against abuse': *Centrum för rättvisa* (n 26) para 248.
[82] *Big Brother Watch* (n 20) para 501: 'the Court will now – in line with its usual methodology ... assess, jointly, the foreseeability and necessity of the intelligence sharing regime'.

measures are applied only when "necessary in a democratic society", in particular by providing for adequate and effective safeguards and guarantees against abuse'.[83]

In that same case, the ECtHR also clarified what those adequate and effective safeguards must be: 'in addressing jointly "in accordance with the law" and "necessity" as is the established approach in this area',[84] the Strasbourg court examines whether the domestic legal framework clearly defined the grounds on which bulk interception may be authorised; the circumstances in which an individual's communications may be intercepted; the procedure to be followed for granting authorisation; the procedures to be followed for selecting, examining, and using intercept material; the precautions to be taken when communicating the material to other parties; the limits on the duration of interception, the storage of intercept material, and the circumstances in which such material must be erased; the procedures and modalities for supervision by an independent authority, and its powers; and the procedures for independent *ex post facto* review and the powers vested in the competent body.[85]

Granted, courts have valid reasons for addressing lawfulness and necessity jointly in mass surveillance cases. The interference assessed might derive from general complaints about the rules and not from any actual interception activity taking place, and in those cases courts are required to examine the legislation itself and the safeguards it contains, rather than the proportionality of any specific measures taken in respect of the applicants.[86]

Yet, the logical structure of the judiciary's limitations analysis is bound to influence the outcome of the assessment: it is common wisdom in general semantics that 'a map is not the territory',[87] but '(i)f our methods and models are now part of the system, they become part of the real thing'.[88] Apex courts do not only adjudicate controversies, but also perform a 'nomopoietic' function: their methods and models make and shape the law. The decision of assessing jointly whether a measure is lawful and whether it is necessary (ie the least restrictive construction amongst all the suitable alternatives) is bound to shape the outcome of the assessment. Particularly with respect to a value-laden and sensitive subject matter like mass surveillance, evaluating the necessity of a system rather than its effect on the *polis* of reference is not a neutral approach.

6. The Marginal Role of the Essence

This chapter, so far, has pointed out the thinness of the axiological layer of the limitations analysis carried out by the CJEU and the ECtHR in their mass surveillance judgments. In

---

[83] ibid para 334.
[84] ibid para 361.
[85] ibid para 361. Those eight criteria go beyond the six safeguards listed by the Court in ECtHR, *Weber and Saravia v Germany*, no. 54934/00, § 95, ECHR 2006-XI ('the nature of the offences which may give rise to an interception order; a definition of the categories of people liable to have their telephones tapped; a limit on the duration of telephone tapping; the procedure to be followed for examining, using and storing the data obtained; the precautions to be taken when communicating the data to other parties; and the circumstances in which recordings may or must be erased or the tapes destroyed').
[86] See *Szabó and Vissy* (n 26) para 58. It is also beyond this chapter's purpose to provide alternative approaches to assessing limitations to fundamental rights: it merely points out some peculiar characteristics of how courts assess interferences deriving from bulk collection and access regimes.
[87] A Korzybski, *Science and Sanity: An Introduction to Non-Aristotelian Systems and General Semantics* (International Non-Aristotelian Library Publishing Company 1933) 58.
[88] Michael Batty, 'A Map Is Not the Territory, or Is It?' (2019) 46 Environment and Planning B: Urban Analytics and City Science 599, 601.

other words, it contended that the way in which both apex courts evaluate the legitimacy of bulk retention and access regimes is focused eminently on the necessity sub-test, and does not elaborate sufficiently on elements of the analysis that would rather belong to proportionality *stricto sensu*. Yet, aside from being (*lato sensu*) proportionate, a measure providing for the legal basis for mass surveillance powers must also respect the essence of the rights it restricts.[89] One might thus wonder whether the essence test is liable to introduce a proper value judgment in the Courts' limitations analysis—whether, in other words, the axiological depth that is arguably missing in their *lato sensu* proportionality assessment may be found in their essence test.

While the concept of essence of a right was discussed by the CJEU well before the drafting of the Charter,[90] the first time the CJEU actually operationalised the essence requirement was with the *Schrems I* judgment.[91] In *Schrems I*, the CJEU confirmed that even non-absolute Charter rights contain an inviolable essence that cannot be interfered with. Interferences upon the essence of a right cannot be justified by proportionality reasoning: the essence is an absolute boundary that must be tested before[92] the *lato sensu* proportionality assessment. The essence test is thus, in theory, conceptually separate from proportionality: the essence of a right should be defined in absolute terms, and any measure interfering with it should be deemed unjustifiable before (and regardless of) the outcome of the proportionality test.[93]

The CJEU, however, seems to use the same criteria usually employed in proportionality reasoning, basing its essence test on the factual limb of the case examined, as opposed to defining in absolute terms what the core of a right entails.[94] When evaluating whether a mass surveillance measure interferes with the essence of a fundamental right, the Court assesses both the intensity and the extent of the interference, just as it does when it judges its proportionality. In other words, the CJEU differentiates between interferences upon the essence of a right and interferences upon its periphery quantitatively, rather than qualitatively,[95] and

---

[89] While Article 52(1) of the Charter mentions the essence of fundamental rights explicitly, the ECHR does not; yet, the respect for a right's essence is arguably an implicit requirement for any measure interfering with a Convention right: see *AG Opinion Ligue des droits humains* (n 3) para 90 and Van Drooghenbroeck and Rizcallah (n 19).

[90] See the case law cited in *AG Opinion Ligue des droits humains* (n 3) para 90; see also Maja Brkan, 'The Essence of the Fundamental Rights to Privacy and Data Protection: Finding the Way Through the Maze of the CJEU's Constitutional Reasoning' (2019) 20 German Law Journal 864, 867; Koen Lenaerts, 'Limits on Limitations: The Essence of Fundamental Rights in the EU' (2019) 20 German Law Journal 779, 780.

[91] CJEU, Judgment of 6 October 2015, *Maximillian Schrems v Data Protection Commissioner* (C-362/14) ECLI:EU:C:2015:650 ('*Schrems I*'). See also Tuomas Ojanen, 'Making the Essence of Fundamental Rights Real: The Court of Justice of the European Union Clarifies the Structure of Fundamental Rights under the Charter: ECJ 6 October 2015, Case C-362/14, *Maximillian Schrems v Data Protection Commissioner*' (2016) 12 European Constitutional Law Review 318. However, 'there are cases pre-dating the entry into force of the Charter where one may argue that the CJEU found, albeit implicitly, that the EU or national measure in question did not respect the essence of the fundamental right at issue'—Lenaerts (n 90) 781.

[92] *AG Opinion Ligue des droits humains* (n 3) para 92.

[93] That is what the CJEU did in *Schrems I*, explicitly following the absolute approach to the concept of essence: see also *AG Opinion Schrems II* (n 67) para 272; *AG Opinion Ligue des droits humains* (n 3) para 91; Takis Tridimas and Giulia Gentile, 'The Essence of Rights: An Unreliable Boundary?' (2019) 20 German Law Journal 794; Lenaerts (n 90); Maja Brkan, 'The Concept of Essence of Fundamental Rights in the EU Legal Order: Peeling the Onion to Its Core' (2018) 14 European Constitutional Law Review.

[94] To be clear, this is not an issue: recognising that violations of the essence of a right cannot be justified through proportionality reasoning (ie through clauses like Article 8(2) ECHR or Article 52(1) CFR) does not mean that they cannot be assessed against the same criteria through which courts determine violations of that right in general.

[95] *AG Opinion Ligue des droits humains* (n 3) paras 92–93.

relatively to the case at hand, not in absolute terms. The essence test could thus, in theory, integrate the value judgment that is lacking from the Courts' *stricto sensu* proportionality assessment. In practice, however, the essences of the rights to private life and to data protection are framed too narrowly for that to happen.

In general, the CJEU interprets the concept of essence restrictively, 'so that it continues to perform its role as a bastion against attacks on the very substance of those rights'.[96] At the time of writing, the *Schrems I* judgment is the only case where the Luxembourg court, in its surveillance case law, found a violation of the essence of a fundamental right.[97] Even there, the court did not find an interference with the essence of the right to data protection *ex* Article 8 CFR, but only of the rights to private life and to a fair trial *ex* Articles 7 and 47 CFR.[98] The essence test thus had a limited role on its own, made even narrower by the tight framing of the essences of the rights to the respect for private life and to the protection of personal data.

In *Digital Rights Ireland*, for instance, the CJEU adopted a very limited framing of what the essence of private life is: despite annulling the Data Retention Directive,[99] the CJEU did not find that it interfered with the essence of the right to private life, as it did not involve the retention of the communications' content, but only their metadata.[100] Successively, in the judgments following *Tele2 Sverige*, the Luxembourg Court began to abandon the content/metadata dichotomy,[101] which does not reflect the extent to which metadata retention and access is liable to interfere with people's fundamental rights.[102] The Court now holds that the retention of data involving only certain aspects of a person's private life is not an interference liable to encroach upon the essence of Article 7 CFR,[103] as it does not portray a 'complete picture' of an individual's personal life.[104] The CJEU thus broadened its framing of the essence of the right to private life by moving away from the content/metadata

---

[96] ibid para 98.

[97] What can be gathered by the CJEU's references to the essences to the rights to the respect for private life and to the protection of personal data thus derives from interpreting *a contrario* judgments and opinions where the court did not find that the essence was interfered with.

[98] *Schrems I* paras 94–95. Interestingly, AG Saugmandsgaard Øe remarked that 'a national measure that granted the public authorities general access to the content of communications would also to my mind infringe the essential content of the right enshrined in Article 8 of the Charter': *AG Opinion Schrems II* (n 67) fn 147.

[99] Directive 2006/24/EC of the European Parliament and of the Council of 15 March 2006 on the retention of data generated or processed in connection with the provision of publicly available electronic communications services or of public communications networks and amending Directive 2002/58/EC [2006] OJ L 105/54 ('Data Retention Directive').

[100] *Digital Rights Ireland* (n 23) para 39. See also *Tele2 Sverige* (n 42) para 101.

[101] The CJEU began to state that data that provides the means of establishing a profile of the individuals concerned is no less sensitive, than the actual content of communications in *Tele2 Sverige* (n 42) para 99, it developed that approach in *La Quadrature du Net 'I'* (n 39) para 117; *Garda Síochána* (n 43) para 45; *SpaceNet* (n 43) para 61; VD SR, Joined Cases C-339/20 and C-397/20, 20 September 2022, ECLI:EU:C:2022:703, para 90. The ECtHR also rejects the content/metadata dichotomy: see eg *Big Brother Watch* (n 20) para 363.

[102] As Michael Hayden famously remarked, 'we kill people based on metadata': *The Johns Hopkins Foreign Affairs Symposium Presents: The Price of Privacy: Re-Evaluating the NSA* (Directed by Johns Hopkins University 2014) <https://www.youtube.com/watch?v = kV2HDM86XgI> accessed 25 January 2024.

[103] *PNR Canada* (n 72) para 150. See also *AG Opinion Schrems II* (n 67) para 278, and the judgment CJEU, Judgment of 21 June 2022, *Ligue des droits humains ASBL v Conseil des ministers* (C-817/19) ECLI:EU:C:2022:491 para 120.

[104] See Opinion of Advocate General Pikamäe of 15 June 2023, Direktor na Glavna direktsia 'Natsionalna politsia' pri MVR—Sofia (C-118/22) ECLI:EU:C:2023:483 ('*AG Opinion Direktor na Glavna direktsia 'Natsionalna politsia' pri MVR*') para 48: 'the nature of the information contained in the police record is limited to a specific aspect of that private life relating to the criminal past of the person concerned, which does not allow conclusions to be drawn in general about the private life of that person ... and, thereby, to establish a profile of that individual'. See also *AG Opinion Ligue des droits humains* (n 3) para 93.

distinction, and towards assessing whether the data at hand is all-encompassing or, conversely, limited to specific aspects of people's lives. Regardless, the considerations underlying that test are still too narrow to substitute the value judgment around which the *stricto sensu* proportionality (sub-)test should revolve.

The same can be said about the right to data protection under Article 8 CFR, whose essence is not interfered with, according to the CJEU, when the measure assessed limits the purposes of the processing, on the one hand, and establishes rules ensuring personal data security, on the other.[105] As long as a data retention and access regime provides for a minimum set of rules channelling the reasons for and the extent to which personal data are processed by (or on behalf of)[106] public authorities—ie security and purpose limitation—the Luxembourg Court seems to believe that the core of the right to personal data protection is left intact.[107] Regardless of whether the essence of the right to data protection can be boiled down to a couple of data quality principles,[108] that framing is, yet again, too narrow to allow the essence test to be a meaningful substitute of *stricto sensu* proportionality reasoning.

To summarise: in its essence test, the CJEU follows an absolute approach, where interferences upon the essence of a right cannot be justified through proportionality. Yet, the criteria it uses to assess whether a measure interferes with the essence of a right are the same criterial it uses in its *lato sensu* proportionality test. The essence test could thus, in principle, allow to integrate the deficiencies of its *stricto sensu* proportionality sub-test[109] by providing an additional layer of axiological reasoning—a deeper value judgment about the social consequences of mass surveillance. However, the Court's framing of the concept of essence of a right in general, and of the essences of the rights to privacy and data protection in particular, seems to be too narrow for that to actually be the case.[110]

7. Conclusion

The inherently secret and indiscriminate nature of mass surveillance challenges the extent to which the CJEU and the ECtHR are able to follow the traditionally formal structure of limitations analysis and proportionality testing. Courts are developing their jurisprudence coherently, and adapting the traditional structure of proportionality to the characteristics of mass surveillance in a way that, this chapter argues, stretches it close to its conceptual

---

[105] *Digital Rights Ireland* (n 23) para 39; *Ligue des droits humains* (n 103) para 120. *AG Opinion Schrems II* (n 67) paras 279–280.

[106] On the privatisation of surveillance see eg Valsamis Mitsilegas, 'The Privatisation of Surveillance in the Digital Age' in Valsamis Mitsilegas and Niovi Vavoula (eds), *Surveillance and Privacy in the Digital Age: European, Transatlantic and Global Perspectives* (Hart Publishing 2021); Valsamis Mitsilegas, 'The Transformation of Privacy in an Era of Pre-Emptive Surveillance' (2015) 20 Tilburg Law Review 35.

[107] See *AG Opinion Direktor na Glavna direktsia 'Natsionalna politsia' pri MV* (n 104) para 48: 'the national legislation at issue limits the purposes of the data processing and lays down an exhaustive list of the data retained and of the rules designed to ensure that they can be accessed, amended or erased. In those circumstances, the interference entailed in the data retention provided for in that legislation does not undermine the essence of the fundamental rights'. See also *AG Opinion Ligue des droits humains* (n 3) para 94.

[108] On the topic, see Lorenzo Dalla Corte, 'A Right to a Rule - On the Substance and Essence of the Fundamental Right to Personal Data Protection' in Dara Hallinan and others (eds), *Data Protection and Privacy: Data Protection and Democracy* (Hart Publishing 2020).

[109] ie its overreliance on its necessity/legality 'hybrid' test.

[110] That would not need to be a factor if the Luxembourg court focused on the *stricto sensu* proportionality of the surveillance measures assessed as it does with its necessity, and interferences that fail the essence test would fail the *lato sensu* proportionality test anyway.

breaking point. Lawfulness and necessity are assessed together: the indiscriminate nature of mass surveillance lead the ECtHR to consider the existence of effective safeguards against abuse as part of both the requirements of 'foreseeability' and 'necessity in a democratic society', and the CJEU to linking the foreseeability requirement with the necessity and proportionality ones.

Both courts thus evaluate compliance with those conditions jointly, rather than as separate elements, each of which with its own distinct benchmarks. Similarly, although not as explicitly, both courts arguably conflate the necessity and *stricto sensu* proportionality sub-tests. There is hardly a clear distinction between necessity, ie the threshold assessment of whether a less restrictive measure exists, and proportionality in the strict sense, ie an evaluation of whether the benefits deriving from a mass surveillance regime overshadow the interference to the rights it restricts.

The courts' approach has led to a controlled legitimisation of mass surveillance and to the 'proceduralisation'[111] of its safeguards. That is due, to a large extent, to pressure by EU Member States and ECHR contracting parties: the CJEU has to tread lightly in areas traditionally reserved to the competence of the EU's Member States, and the ECtHR must respect the margin of appreciation reserved to national authorities. Both courts are likely concerned with the possibility of being perceived as political, too. Yet, despite frequent pronouncements about the dangers of mass surveillance, there is arguably a value vacuum in the courts' judgments. That might be due to the peculiarities of (mass) surveillance which, compared to other kinds of interferences, challenge the formal structure of proportionality testing. It might also be due, however, to the approach that both courts elected to follow in their limitations analysis: the peculiar decision model they follow is bound to influence the outcome of their judgments.

---

[111] What has been elsewhere dubbed as 'procedural fetishism': Monika Zalnieriute, 'Procedural Fetishism and Mass Surveillance under the ECHR: Big Brother Watch v. UK' [2021] Verfassungsblog <https://verfassungsblog.de/big-b-v-uk/> accessed 28 June 2023.

5
Proportionality and Strict Proportionality in the Case-law of the Court of Justice of the European Union on Data Retention

*Daniele Nardi**

1. Introduction

Limitations to the exercise of fundamental rights are governed, in the EU legal order, by Article 52(1) of the Charter of Fundamental Rights of the European Union ('Charter'). This provision requires such limitations to be provided for by law and they must respect the essence of fundamental rights. Subject to the principle of proportionality, limitations may only be made if they are necessary and genuinely meet objectives of general interest recognised by the Union or the need to protect the rights and freedoms of others. The principle of proportionality is therefore central to any assessment performed by the Court of Justice of the European Union (the Court or CJEU) of the justifications for any limitations to fundamental rights within the scope of EU law.

The case-law of the Court traditionally considers that the principle of proportionality is respected if two tests are passed: the test of suitability and the test of necessity.[1]

Once an objective of general interest is validly identified as worthy of protection—which is not in itself a self-evident operation—the test of suitability aims at verifying whether the limitation, or interference, with a fundamental right is capable of attaining that objective of general interest.[2] This first prong of the test is also called the 'appropriateness' test.

Subsequently, it must be assessed whether the limitation is necessary. This means that the objective cannot be achieved with less restrictive means than those deployed by the measure under scrutiny. This is where it could be said—in extreme synthesis—that the prevailing case-law of the Court, essentially, stops. Appropriateness and necessity may seem the criteria used to verify compliance with the principle of proportionality.

In reality, under the notion of 'necessity', the Court has often conflated the necessity of a measure with the third prong of the test: the strict proportionality test (or proportionality

---

* The views expressed in this chapter are personal and cannot be attributed to the European Data Protection Supervisor.
[1] See CJEU, Judgment of 8 April 2014, *Digital Rights Ireland and Seitlinger and others* (C-293/12 and C-594/12) ECLI:EU:C:2014:238 para 46.
[2] For the purpose of this contribution, we will not analyse separately the 'need to protect the rights and freedom of others', which often overlaps with the notion of 'objectives of general interest'. See Sacha Prechal and Steve Peers, 'Commentary to Article 52', in Steve Peers, Tamara Hervey, Jeff Kenner, and Angela Ward (eds), *The EU Charter of Fundamental Rights: A Commentary* (2nd edn, Hart Publishing 2021) 1628.

stricto sensu).[3] Under this specific test, to be found *lato sensu* proportionate, a measure which has already been found appropriate and necessary, still needs to cause more benefits to the objective pursued than costs in terms of interferences with fundamental rights. This is the part of the test where competing rights, or rights competing with objectives of general interest worthy of protection, are balanced against each other.

The now rich body of case-law concerning measures providing for the retention of 'metadata' of electronic communications by private entities for important public objectives of general interest, in particular law enforcement purposes, appears to be an example of this conflation of the necessity and the strict proportionality test. Metadata is a term normally understood as referring to the information of who was communicating, when, for how long, and where. The Court, refers to this form of personal data as 'traffic and location data' according to the definitions provided in the ePrivacy Directive.[4] This chapter will analyse the evolution of the proportionality test applied throughout the 'data retention' case-law to this kind of data.

Striking the right balance between the possibility to detect, investigate, and prosecute crimes through processing of vast amounts of metadata, and keeping the high level of protection for privacy and for personal data as required by Articles 7 and 8 of the Charter is not an easy task. However, the proliferation of preliminary references on the issue of proportionality of data retention obligations with which the Court has been confronted has exposed a profound cleavage between the Court of Justice and law enforcement authorities at Member State level. The overall outcome of the balancing between privacy and law enforcement as resulting from the assessment of the Court (spanning from the seminal *Digital Rights Ireland*[5] case to the recent judgments in *Commissioner An Garda Síochána*[6]) is very different from the outcome desired not only by many governments of EU Member States, but also by many of their highest national Courts. From the requests for preliminary rulings submitted to the Court transpires a clear attempt to demonstrate that measures providing for generalised retention of communication metadata are strictly necessary to fight crime effectively.

Despite the openings progressively made by the Court, notably with the ruling in *La Quadrature du Net 'I'*,[7] there are still difficulties in objectively giving effect to the requirement of 'targeted retention' and the issue of data retention remains one of the reasons why the proposal for an ePrivacy Regulation was still blocked at the time of writing.[8] This

---

[3] For Takis Tridimas, '[t]he tripartite test has received judicial support, but in practice the Court does not necessarily distinguish between the second and the third conditions. Also, in some cases the Court finds that a measure is compatible with proportionality without searching for less restrictive alternatives or even where such alternatives seem to exist': Takis Tridimas, 'The Principle of Proportionality', in Professor Robert Schütze, and Professor Takis Tridimas (eds), *Oxford Principles of European Union Law: The European Union Legal Order: Volume I* (OUP 2018) 247.

[4] Directive 2002/58/EC of the European Parliament and of the Council of 12 July 2002 concerning the processing of personal data and the protection of privacy in the electronic communications sector (Directive on privacy and electronic communications) [2002] OJ L 201/37 ('ePrivacy Directive').

[5] *Digital Rights Ireland* (n 1).

[6] CJEU, Judgment of 5 April 2022, *Commissioner of An Garda Síochána* (C-140/20) ECLI:EU:C:2022:258.

[7] CJEU, Judgment of 6 October 2020, *La Quadrature du Net and others* (C-511/18, C-512/18 and C-520/18) ECLI:EU:C:2020:791 ('*La Quadrature du Net 'I'*'). The case is called *La Quadrature du Net 'I'* to distinguish it from the other case: CJEU, Judgment of 30 April 2024, *La Quadrature du Net aoc Premier Ministre and Ministre de la Culture* (C-470/21) ECLI:EU:C:2024:370 ('*La Quadrature du Net 'II'*').

[8] See H Kranenborg, Commentary to Article 8, in Steve Peers, Tamara Hervey, Jeff Kenner, and Angela Ward (eds), *The EU Charter of Fundamental Rights: A Commentary* (2nd edn Hart Publishing 2021) 288.

contribution aims at tracking the birth of the notion of 'strict necessity' and of the heightened standard of review to which interferences with the fundamental right to protection of personal data have been subjected.

This chapter will question whether, under the cloak of 'strict necessity', the Court had not in essence already engaged de facto in a strict proportionality assessment, weighing costs and benefits, thus inevitably foraying into the political or ethical field. Anticipating growing difficulties for the legislator to be able to timely regulate disruptive data-intensive technologies, first and foremost the development of Artificial Intelligence, is important for the Court and the legislator to be equipped with a flexible but predictable 'toolkit' in the form of the principle of proportionality. It will be argued that part of this effective toolkit should be an explicit recognition, and use of, the strict proportionality part of the test.

2. The Principle of Proportionality throughout the Case-law on Generalised Retention of Communication Data

2.1 Proportionality of measures limiting the fundamental rights to privacy and data protection before data retention: *Schecke*

Before looking at the case-law on data retention, and looking at the broader field of data protection, the *Schecke*[9] ruling appears to be an important milestone. In that ruling the Court referred to the principle of proportionality as follows: 'It is settled case-law that the principle of proportionality, which is one of the general principles of EU law, requires that measures implemented by acts of the European Union are appropriate for attaining the objective pursued and do not go beyond what is necessary to achieve it'.[10]

The Court had to deal with the publication of personal data of beneficiaries of EU agricultural funds together with the amounts received, up to a significant level of detail. By reference to its earlier *Satakunnan*[11] ruling, the Court found that 'derogations and limitations in relation to the protection of personal data must apply only in as far as is *strictly* necessary' (emphasis added). The Court had to assess the 'balance' struck by the legislator between, on the one hand, the interest in guaranteeing the transparency of its acts and ensuring the best use of public funds, and, on the other, the interference with their fundamental rights under Articles 7 and 8 of the Charter. To do so it examined whether the condition of necessity had been fulfilled according to the traditional test of the 'least restrictive measure'. In that case it found that the legislator had not conducted ostensibly any such test and that in the Court's view some less restrictive measures did exist.[12] Therefore, the Court found that the measures providing for publication failed the strict necessity test and invalidated them as being not proportionate. The *Schecke* case represents a case of relatively straightforward application of the traditional notion of the necessity test. In that case, whether the

---

[9] CJEU, Judgment of 9 November 2010, *Volker und Markus Schecke and Eifert* (C-92/09 and C-93/09, ECR 2010 p. I-11063) ECLI:EU:C:2010:662 ('*Schecke*').
[10] ibid para 74.
[11] CJEU, Judgment of 16 December 2008, *Satakunnan Markkinapörssi and Satamedia* (C-73/07, ECR 2008 p. I-9831) ECLI:EU:C:2008:727.
[12] *Schecke* (n 9) para 81.

measures were necessary to achieve that aim was a matter of binary choice. In principle, whether least restrictive measures exist or not can be conceived as a threshold requirement; in other words a matter of 'yes' or 'no'.[13] In that case, however, the legislator failed *ex-ante* by not analysing sufficiently whether such least restrictive measures existed. That is to say, the Court did not need to correct any assessment of necessity as wrong in substance. It could simply invalidate the measures at stake because of the absence of that assessment, in light of the strict standard of review applicable to limitations of the fundamental right to protection of personal data.

2.2 *Digital Rights Ireland*: The retention of communication metadata cannot be considered 'strictly necessary'

The seminal case, which inaugurated a line of CJEU judgments on the legality of retention of personal data for law enforcement purposes, is *Digital Rights Ireland*.[14] With that judgment the Court decided on two preliminary references brought by the Irish High Court and the Austrian Constitutional Court. Both national courts questioned the validity of Directive 2006/24/EC,[15] the Data Retention Directive, because of its alleged incompatibility with Articles 7, 8, and 11 of the Charter. That Data Retention Directive, in essence, amended the ePrivacy Directive to introduce an obligation of retention of several sets of 'metadata' related to electronic communications, incumbent upon providers of electronic communications services. The Court assessed the seriousness of the interferences with the fundamental rights by closely looking at the data in question and their potential for affecting privacy, which was undeniable:

> [T]he data which providers of publicly available electronic communications services or of public communications networks must retain ... make it possible, in particular, to know the identity of the person with whom a subscriber or registered user has communicated and by what means, and to identify the time of the communication as well as the place from which that communication took place. They also make it possible to know the frequency of the communications of the subscriber or registered user with certain persons during a given period.[16]

The Court distinguished the interference resulting from the mere retention from the further interference resulting in the access to the retained data.[17] Both interferences however were not such as to affect the essence of the fundamental rights in question, because the content of the communication was not retained, and certain principles of data protection

---

[13] See in that sense Lorenzo Dalla Corte, 'On Proportionality in the Data Protection Jurisprudence of the CJEU' 12(4) International Data Privacy Law (2022) 261: 'Necessity, too, is a threshold requirement that results in a binary outcome: the measure considered is either the least restrictive one amongst all the suitable options, in which case it is necessary, or it is not, in which case the sub-test fails.'
[14] *Digital Rights Ireland* (n 1).
[15] Directive 2006/24/EC of the European Parliament and of the Council of 15 March 2006 on the retention of data generated or processed in connection with the provision of publicly available electronic communications services or of public communications networks and amending Directive 2002/58/EC [2006] OJ L 105/54 ('Data Retention Directive').
[16] *Digital Rights Ireland* (n 1) para 26.
[17] ibid para 35.

and data security had to be respected by providers of publicly available electronic communications services or of public communications networks according to the provisions of the Directive.[8]

Then the Court moved on to analysing the proportionality *lato sensu* and considered the appropriateness (suitability) of the measures. It found that the retention of data for the purpose of allowing the competent national authorities to have access to those data, as required by the Data Retention Directive, genuinely satisfied an objective of general interest.[19]

The Court assessed, first, the appropriateness of retention in relation to the further interference consisting in the access, and not the appropriateness/suitability of retention per se to achieve an objective in the general interest as per Article 52(1) of the Charter. This approach can be seen as consistent with the nature of retention of data in relation to access to the same data: if indeed retention and access are separate interferences, one needs to ascertain whether the logically and chronologically first interference (retention) is proportionate before assessing the second interference (access). Nevertheless, overstressing the distinct nature of these two types of interference is ultimately artificial. Indeed, it can be argued that retention without access simply does not make sense.

Every processing of personal data is an interference with the fundamental right to data protection and must have a purpose, as the text of Article 8 of the Charter itself mandates. Any purpose of data processing can only be genuinely realised when the data is accessed, that is, seen and used. Retention per se does not and cannot have any purpose: it is a form of processing that, while constituting a separate interference, cannot be really appraised independently from the interference which alone is able to achieve a purpose, and can thereby be justified under Article 52(1) of the Charter.

The considerations by the Court in the *Digital Rights Ireland* ruling do not appear to help to shed further light on how the proportionality test should be performed in relation to the separate but inextricable interferences provoked by retention and access. The Court moved on to assess retention and quotes the standard formulation of the proportionality test (as already seen in *Schecke*).[20] Then it repeated the assessment of appropriateness/suitability of retention but this time not in relation to a further interference, but rather in relation to the true objective of general interest pursued by the data retention directive, in short: the prosecution of crime. As seen above, however, retention per se cannot achieve that objective as only access by the competent authorities allows the data retained to be used. This constitutes a first choice made by the Court, which—it is submitted—has created a first conceptual problem that will continue to be found in the subsequent cases.

A second choice made—that would also mark the following cases— regards the form taken by the necessity assessment performed by the Court. In fact, the Court—differently from *Schecke*—drew direct inspiration from the case-law of the European Court of Human Rights (ECtHR). Instead of looking for least restrictive measures, the Court defined 'strict necessity' as the requirement to lay down clear and precise rules governing the scope and application of the measure in question and imposing minimum safeguards so that the persons whose data have been retained have sufficient guarantees to effectively protect their personal data against the risk of abuse and against any unlawful access and use of that data.[21]

---

[18] ibid paras 39 and 40.
[19] ibid para 44.
[20] ibid para 46.
[21] ibid para 54.

Applying this test to the Data Retention Directive, the Court found that it applied to all means of electronic communications, as well as all traffic data, and it was not restricted to data pertaining to a particular time period, a particular geographic area, or a particular circle of persons.[22] Furthermore, there was no objective criterion by which to determine when data access should be allowed, as the directive simply referred in a general manner to serious crime as defined by each Member State.[23] The Court also highlighted that the Directive did not contain substantive and procedural conditions relating to the access of the competent national authorities to the data.[24] The Directive also failed to lay down any objective criterion to limit the number of persons authorised to access and subsequently use the data retained[25] and to set a data retention period.[26] The Directive thus failed the strict necessity test.

2.3 *Tele2 Sverige* and the attempt to systematise and revive the 'classical' proportionality test: The Opinion of Advocate General Saugmansgaard Øe

Once the Data Retention Directive was invalidated, two cases were raised in Sweden and the United Kingdom, which led to the issuance of two requests for preliminary ruling to the CJEU in case C-203/15, *Tele2Sverige*, and in case C-698/15, *Watson*, which the Court decided to treat jointly.[27] The preliminary questions for the Court concerned in essence whether the Swedish and British legislations providing for the generalised retention of metadata related to electronic communications (essentially, traffic and location data) were in line with Article 15 of the ePrivacy Directive, especially after the issuance of the *Digital Rights Ireland* ruling.

The Court found at the outset that the national legislations at stake fell within the scope of the ePrivacy directive.[28] It interpreted Article 15(1) ePrivacy Directive in the light of Articles 7, 8, 11, and 52 of the Charter. The Court reminded that the ePrivacy Directive established the principle of confidentiality of communications in its Article 5(1). This principle entails that any person other than the user of an electronic communication service is prohibited from storing the traffic data related to the electronic communications, unless consent to such storage is given by the data subject. Contrary to the position expressed by the Advocate General Saugmansgaard Øe in his Opinion,[29] the Court found that Article 15(1) ePrivacy Directive was an exception to the rule of confidentiality found in Article 5(1) of the same Directive, which must be subject to a strict interpretation. The Court underlined very clearly that the exception cannot become the rule, if the principle of confidentiality of communications 'is not to be rendered largely meaningless'.[30] The Court moved on to consider not just the importance of the fundamental rights to

---

[22] ibid paras 56–59.
[23] ibid para 60.
[24] ibid para 61.
[25] ibid para 62.
[26] ibid paras 63–64.
[27] CJEU, Judgment of 21 December 2016, *Tele2 Sverige* (C-203/15 and C-698/15) ECLI:EU:C:2016:970.
[28] ibid paras 65–81.
[29] Opinion of Advocate General Saugmansgaard Øe of 19 July 2016 in *Tele2 Sverige* (C-203/15 and C-698/15) ECLI:EU:C:2016:572 ('*AG Opinion Tele2 Sverige*') para 110.
[30] *Tele2 Sverige* (n 27) para 89.

privacy and protection of personal data, but also of the fundamental right to freedom of expression.

Having laid down these premises, the Court started its assessment under Article 52(1) of the Charter and in particular of the proportionality of the limitations imposed by the measures in question to fundamental rights: limitations may be imposed on the exercise of those rights and freedoms only if they are *necessary* and if they *genuinely meet objectives of general interest* recognised by the European Union or the need to protect the rights and freedoms of others' (emphasis added).[31]

The reiteration of the *Satakunnan* and *Schecke* formulation of the 'bipartite' proportionality test contrasts starkly with the structure of the proportionality test suggested by the Advocate General in his Opinion. Indeed, Advocate General Saugmansgaard Øe tried to appraise the facts of the case under a more analytical notion of proportionality. He clearly distinguished the necessity test from the test of balancing competing costs and benefits, that is, the 'strict proportionality' test. More generally, his Opinion represents one of the clearest jurisprudential attempts at systematising—and making more predictable—the assessment of proportionality of measures limiting fundamental rights, specifically in the field of privacy and protection of personal data. The Court however did not follow the Advocate General, not only on the articulation of the proportionality assessment.

When tackling the question of the necessity of the data retention measures, the Advocate General had to deal with the notion of 'strict' necessity, recurrent in the case-law but not yet sufficiently defined.[32] The Court, for the Advocate General, had invalidated the Data Retention Directive in *Digital Rights Ireland* because of the combined effect of the generalised retention of data and the lack of safeguards,[33] and not because of issues intrinsic to the nature of generalised retention of metadata. Once he dealt with the reading of 'strict necessity in *Digital Rights Ireland* in this way, he could finally analyse the existence of less restrictive measures under the 'classical' understanding of the necessity test. In a very deferential move to the Member States and their main competence to fight against crime, he considered that the assessment of the existence of less restrictive measures should have been carried out 'in the specific context of each national regime providing for a general data retention obligation'.[34] The role played by the notion of 'strict' necessity was ultimately reduced to a 'reminder' to the national Courts to apply a strict standard of review.

Then the Opinion openly deals, in a standalone fashion—a relatively rare occurrence in the jurisprudence[35]—with the balancing exercise necessary to decide whether the advantages of reaching the objective of general interest through the measures in question outweigh the costs in terms of the unavoidable interferences with the fundamental rights concerned. This is an operation famously labelled by the Judge of the US Supreme Court Antonin Scalia as 'determining whether a particular line is longer than a particular rock is

---

[31] ibid para 94.
[32] ie to be strictly necessary, the legislation 'must lay down clear and precise rules governing the scope and application of the measure in question and imposing minimum safeguards so that the persons whose data have been retained have sufficient guarantees to effectively protect their personal data against the risk of abuse and against any unlawful access and use of that data'. See *AG Opinion Tele2 Sverige* (n 29) paras 188–205.
[33] ibid para 202.
[34] ibid para 208.
[35] See, however, the judgments quoted in footnote 78 of ibid.

heavy'.[36] The Advocate General, in the same vein, and in very frank and pedagogical terms, attempts to provide legal guidance, and sketches a rational analysis of the respective costs and benefits of generalised data retention measures, stopping just short of recognising the political and moral nature of such an exercise.[37] He concludes, as for the necessity test, that the outcome of the strict proportionality test should have been determined by the referring courts, taking account of all the relevant characteristics of the national regimes at issue; at the national, and not at the EU, level.[38]

This heavy reliance on the assessment by national judges, based on their 'local' conditions to determine applicability of EU law, might have been a factor contributing to the Opinion not being followed by the Court.[39] Be as it may, the ensuing ruling of the Court further consecrated the refusal of the Court to engage in an open discussion of 'strict proportionality', while still not refraining from conducting balancing operations between different values protected by the legal order—comparing the length of lines and the weight of stones.

2.4 The judgment in *Tele2 Sverige*: 'Strict necessity' decoupled and beyond the assessment of the existence of less restrictive measures

The Court dealt with the question of proportionality of a system of generalised retention of metadata of electronic communications separately from the question of the proportionality of the access by the law enforcement authorities to the data so retained.

After recalling the simple and 'bipartite' formulation of the proportionality test *lato sensu* and the need for the measures to be strictly necessary, the Court dealt with the seriousness of the interference. Repeating its findings in *Digital Rights Ireland*, the CJEU reminded that the data retained allowed to draw very precise conclusions concerning the private lives of the persons.[40] The interference entailed by such legislation in the fundamental rights enshrined in Articles 7 and 8 of the Charter was very far-reaching and had to be considered particularly serious. The Court further stipulated that the fact that the data was retained without the subscriber or registered user being informed is likely to cause the persons concerned to feel that their private lives are the subject of constant surveillance, and this has an impact on the freedom of expression of the users.[41]

At paras 102 and 103 of the judgment the Court engages clearly in a balancing exercise that does not easily fit under the 'plain' notion of the necessity test—even under its 'strict'

---

[36] *Bendix Autolite Corp v Midwesco Enter Inc*, 486 US 888, 897 (1988) quoted in Niels Petersen, 'How to Compare the Length of Lines to the Weight of Stones: Balancing and the Resolution of Value Conflicts in Constitutional Law' (2013) 14 German Law Journal 1387.
[37] See in particular the following extract from para 248 of the *AG Opinion Tele2 Sverige* (n 29): 'By contrast with the requirements relating to the appropriateness and necessity of the measure in question, which call for an evaluation of the measure's effectiveness in terms of the objective pursued, the requirement of proportionality *stricto sensu* implies weighing the advantages resulting from the measure in terms of the legitimate objective pursued against the disadvantages it causes in terms of the fundamental rights enshrined in a democratic society. This particular requirement therefore opens a debate about the values that must prevail in a democratic society and, ultimately, about what kind of society we wish to live in.'
[38] *AG Opinion Tele2 Sverige*' (n 29) paras 261–62.
[39] Another perhaps even more important factor—not at the core of the subject of the present chapter—might have been the finding that generalised data retention regimes are not precluded per se by Article 15(1) ePrivacy Directive, a choice that the Court manifestly did not share.
[40] *Tele2 Sverige* (n 27) para 99.
[41] ibid para 100.

form. The Court stated that, in the light of the seriousness of the interference entailed by the retention of traffic and location data, only the objective of fighting serious crime was capable of justifying such a measure. Conversely, the importance of that objective could not in itself justify national legislation providing for the *general* and *indiscriminate* retention of all traffic and location data. This, the Court said, cannot be considered necessary.

The Court then took issue with the preventive nature of the data retention obligations. In an important statement the Court underlined how the legislation imposing the retention obligations applies indiscriminately, that is 'to persons for whom there is no evidence capable of suggesting that their conduct might have a link, even an indirect or remote one, with serious criminal offences'.[42] The Court also found that this type of legislation does not require 'any relationship between the data that must be retained and a threat to public security'.[43] These considerations led the Court to conclude that that legislation 'exceeds the limits of what is strictly necessary'.[44] After having closed that door, the Court indicates the conditions under which a data retention regime could be considered strictly necessary. National legislation must lay down clear and precise rules indicating the circumstances and the conditions under which data retention measures may be adopted as a preventive measure. The retention of data furthermore must continue to meet objective criteria that establish a connection between the data to be retained and the objective pursued, and such objective connection should be justified in the legislation, for instance by indicating the geographical areas to which the measures could be limited in light of the higher risk of perpetration of serious criminal offences. These detailed 'instructions' from the Court on how to enact data retention measures for law enforcement purposes showcase in the author's opinion a 'regulatory' approach by the Court and proved extremely contentious to be complied with.

The Court finally dealt with the conditions for *access* to the retained data, clarifying from the outset that such conditions should apply irrespectively of whether retention is generalised or targeted, and essentially applied the same approach to strict necessity as for retention: it weighed that only serious crimes can justify access by the competent authority. The fact that access requests have the purpose of fighting serious crime for the Court is not sufficient: the legislation must lay down the substantive and procedural conditions governing access:

- access can be granted solely to fight serious crime;[45]
- access should be subject to prior review by a Court or by an independent administrative body, charged of verifying that access is only granted upon a reasoned request of the competent authority, showing the existence of a link with the intended purpose, in particular because the request concern data of individuals suspected of planning, committing or having committed a serious crime or being implicated in one way or another in such a crime;[46]
- the data must be retained in the EU.[47]

---

[42] ibid para 105.
[43] ibid para 106.
[44] ibid para 107.
[45] ibid para 115.
[46] ibid para 121.
[47] ibid para 122.

After *Tele2 Sverige*, the notion of strict necessity—which had been before an unspecified 'warning' in the case law of the Court, such as *Satakunnan* and *Schecke*—clearly did not consist anymore of a verification of the existence of least restrictive measures. Rather, the Court established limits and required safeguards specific to the legislation governing retention and access to metadata of electronic communications, in the light of the intrusiveness of both retention and access to the data—considered separately—for the fundamental rights to privacy and data protection. These safeguards stem from a balancing of cost and benefit rather than from a binary assessment of whether least restrictive measures exist. In this regard, *Tele2 Sverige* represents a judgment in which the Court structures its reasoning without sticking to the traditional tripartite form of the *lato sensu* proportionality test. Rather, by employing the notion of strict necessity in relation to a balancing exercise it would appear to blur both the methodological usefulness, and most importantly the predictability that stems from keeping the three prongs of the test distinct. As had already been observed in the doctrine in relation to the *Digital Rights Ireland* judgment, such an approach followed by the Court amounts to introducing a spurious element at the outset of the necessity test.[48] Furthermore, this would amount to substituting a proportionality assessment with the different concept of the 'guarantee of minimum' safeguards.[49] This is remarkable considering that the Opinion of the Advocate General as discussed in the previous section was structured along the lines of the 'classical' understanding of the proportionality test *lato sensu*.

2.5 Serious interferences require serious objectives: *Ministerio Fiscal*

In a judgment delivered in 2018 the Court tackled briefly how a balancing exercise requires verification of the strict necessity of measures interfering with Articles 7 and 8 of the Charter.

The case referred to the Court in the *Ministerio Fiscal* case[50] concerned a specific instance of 'ordinary' criminality. The referring judge enquired as to whether the public authorities' access to data for the purpose of identifying the owners of SIM cards activated with a stolen mobile telephone (such as the surnames, forenames, and, if need be, addresses of the owners of the SIM cards) constituted an interference with their fundamental rights. In particular, the judge wondered if such an interference would have to be qualified as sufficiently serious; this would have entailed access being limited to the objective of fighting serious crime. The referring judge also enquired against which criteria the seriousness of the offence at issue should be assessed. Again, it was a matter of interpreting Article 15(1) of the ePrivacy Directive.

The case indeed appeared more straightforward: it was not a matter of generalised retention of metadata of communication, although, significantly, it got attributed again to the Grand Chamber of the Court.

---

[48] Filippo Fontanelli, 'The Mythology of Proportionality in Judgments of the Court of Justice of the European Union on Internet and Fundamental Rights' (2016) 36 Oxford J Legal Studies 655: 'The Court then introduced a spurious element at the outset of the necessity test: the obligation for the EU legislator to provide in its acts minimum safeguards against the risk of abuse of fundamental rights'.

[49] Fontanelli ibid 656, by reference to R Alexy, 'Constitutional Rights and Proportionality' (2014) 22 *Revus. Journal for Constitutional Theory and Philosophy of Law/Revija za ustavno teorijo in filozofijo prava* 51–65.

[50] CJEU, Judgment of 2 October 2018 *Ministerio Fiscal* (C-207/16) ECLI:EU:C:2018:788.

The Court found that the data at stake concerned an individual criminal case and did not allow very precise conclusions concerning the private life of the persons concerned to be drawn. Therefore, the interference with their fundamental rights could not be considered as serious. Access by the competent authority to this kind of data needed not to be limited to the prosecution of serious crimes.[51]

The case is striking because while certainly constituting a 'common sense' solution of the concrete case at stake it is based on the dichotomy of serious versus non-serious interference which, while intuitively pertinent for the solution of the case, does not necessarily provide an accurate and predictable criterion for the resolution of future cases. The notions of serious or non-serious interference entail a threshold assessment as to when a quantitative assessment (a given 'degree' of seriousness) becomes relevant for a more qualitative assessment. Seen under that light, *Ministerio Fiscal* is a judgment that at its core applies the strict proportionality assessment to achieve a rather understandable outcome, but without providing guidance as to the tenets and criteria used to perform the balancing.

2.6 The Court lays down the hierarchy of objectives in the field of retention and access of Metadata: *La Quadrature du Net 'I'*

The tension between the need for law enforcement authorities to analyse vast troves of communication metadata to fight crime on the one hand, and the need to ensure effective protection to the fundamental rights of the persons using electronic communication systems—ie virtually everyone in developed societies—on the other, generated further requests for preliminary rulings.

The next 'batch' of requests addressed to Luxembourg with a clear request to lift the prohibition of mass retention of metadata established in *Tele2 Sverige* came from France with the joined cases C-511/18 and C-512/18 *La quadrature du Net aoc Premier Ministre ao* (*La Quadrature du Net 'I'*) and Belgium, with case C-520/18 *Ordre des barreaux francophones et germanophones aov Conseil des Ministres*. The two French cases had been joined originally by the Court and were also joined for the purposes of the hearing and the ruling with the Belgian cases.[52] In great synthesis, the questions referred in the three cases concerned whether not only the objective of fighting crime, but also the objective of protecting national security, was able to justify generalised retention of metadata of electronic communications.

With the ruling issued in these cases in 2020 the Court created a complex 'taxonomy' of objectives allowing different types of retention of metadata of communication. This may be seen as an indicator of how the Court needed to interpret—and in reality, stretch—the notion of strict necessity well beyond its literal meaning, as will be explained below.

---

[51] ibid paras 60–61.
[52] The hearing was also joint with that of another important preliminary request received from the United Kingdom that led to a separate CJEU judgment: CJEU, Judgment of 6 October 2020, *Privacy International* (C-623/17) ECLI:EU:C:2020:790. This latter important case was solved by the Court with a much shorter ruling than the one in *La Quadrature du Net 'I'* (n 7). While its importance in determining the scope of application of the ePrivacy Directive and more generally of EU law vis-à-vis activities of Member States in the area of national security should be acknowledged, it is less relevant for purposes of the present chapter.

The Court started by providing an interpretation of Article 15(1) of the ePrivacy Directive largely reiterating the findings of *Digital Rights Ireland* and *Tele2 Sverige*. It rebutted the vigorous requests by many intervening Member States not to consider separately the retention of data from their access. With references to the jurisprudence of the ECtHR as well as its own *PNR Canada* Opinion,[53] the Court indeed declares: 'Whether or not the retained data has been used subsequently is also irrelevant... since access to such data is a separate interference with the fundamental rights referred to in the preceding paragraph, irrespective of the subsequent use made of it.'[54] The identification and delimitation of the interference with the fundamental rights plays obviously a crucial role in the conduct of any *lato sensu* proportionality assessment.

Building inter alia on the wording of recital 11 of the ePrivacy Directive (the importance of which Advocate General Saugmansgaard Øe had tried to downplay in his Opinion in *Tele2 Sverige*[55]), the Court reiterated that derogations and limitations to the protection of personal data may apply only in so far as strictly necessary. It immediately added however that a proper *balancing* the objective of general interest against the rights at issue had to be performed, again showing a conceptual osmosis between the notions of necessity and proportionality *stricto sensu*. According to the *dictum* first found in *Ministerio Fiscal*, the Court defines the balancing in rather simple terms: the seriousness of the interference should be 'measured' and the importance of the public interest objective pursued by that interference should be verified as being 'proportionate' to that seriousness.[56] The Court stressed that the data should be retained according to objective criteria capable of establishing a connection between it and the objective pursued.

It is against this notion of strict necessity, blurring the 'necessity' and 'strict proportionality' prongs of the proportionality test *lato sensu*, now sufficiently codified in the case-law, that the Court assesses the data retention measures. This notion would essentially appear to constitute the specific proportionality test applicable in the field of data protection and more specifically in the field of retention of metadata of communications. This 'legal toolkit' mixes apparent threshold tests (resulting in pass/no pass 'scores') with the more delicate issue of the balancing competing rights and interests inevitably implying ethical or political assumptions.

On the one hand, the call for the rules being clear and precise, so that the persons will be protected against the risks of abuse, can be subsumed under the 'classic' understanding of the necessity test as a 'threshold test. Faced with governments (and jurisdictions) more than ready to blindly accept serious interferences with fundamental rights simply in the name of the fight against crime, and the possibilities offered by the ever-increasing availability of data, the Court sanctioned the lack of precision of the legislation.[57] The more the objective

---

[53] CJEU, Opinion 1/15 (*EU-Canada PNR Agreement*), of 26 July 2017 (Digital Reports) ECLI:EU:C:2017:592 ('*PNR Canada*').
[54] *La Quadrature du Net 'I'* (n 7) para 116.
[55] *AG Opinion Tele2 Sverige* (n 29) paras 107, 108, and 110.
[56] *La Quadrature du Net 'I'* (n 7) para 131.
[57] See in that connection para 117 of *Tele2 Sverige* (n 27) quoted in para 132 of *La Quadrature du Net 'I'* (n 7). The clearest statement in that sense remains the rather blunt one found in para 103 of *Tele2 Sverige*: 'while the effectiveness of the fight against serious crime, in particular organised crime and terrorism, may depend to a great extent on the use of modern investigation techniques, such an objective of general interest, however fundamental it may be, cannot in itself justify that national legislation providing for the general and indiscriminate retention of all traffic and location data should be considered to be necessary for the purposes of that fight'.

of the legislation is vague, the more difficult it is to pass the necessity test—including when it consists in the search of less restrictive measures achieving the same objective. Indeed, the first requirement to set up a threshold is that the threshold shall be clearly recognisable. This was certainly not the case with the legislation in any of the cases dealt with by the Court and analysed up until now in the present chapter.

On the other hand, by relying on the rather 'basic' definition of the balancing test elaborated in *Ministerio Fiscal*, already noted in this chapter, the Court appears to give very little guidance on how to perform it, and it never acknowledges that this balancing is to be considered *separately* from the assessment of the strict necessity.

However, the preliminary references before the Court in the joined *La Quadrature du Net 'I'* cases contained a vast arsenal of arguments in favour of public authorities being able to avail themselves of metadata of communications. They evoked concrete examples of crimes detected and punished only thanks to the metadata of persons who were not suspected of any crimes, but which were retained and thus available for ex-post analysis. The point that such form of retention is the sole tool to detect or effectively prosecute threats to national security or to detect and prosecute certain crimes had been made forcefully. The Court therefore had a challenging testing ground to apply its notion of 'strict necessity'.

The Court tackled first the preventive retention of traffic and location data for the purpose of safeguarding national security. This was a novelty: the Court had clarified (on the same day) in *Privacy International* that the ePrivacy Directive applies, including where the purpose of the measure (in this case, retention of metadata) was to protect national security.[58] Even if according to Article 4(2) TEU national security remains the sole responsibility of Member States, as long as the Member States impose *processing obligations* on the providers of electronic communication services subject to the ePrivacy directive and the principle of confidentiality, that Directive needs to apply.

In what has been called 'a win' for the public authorities' camp[59] as opposed to the 'camp' of the privacy advocates, the Court essentially accepted legislation allowing for the preventive and generalised retention of traffic and location data for the purpose of safeguarding national security, albeit under apparently strict conditions.

For the Court the importance of safeguarding national security trumps all the others and is capable of justifying more serious interferences than the fight against serious crimes. The responsibility to ensure national security 'corresponds to the primary interests in protecting the essential functions of the State and the fundamental interests of society'.[60] This 'importance' is as such sufficient to overrule even the important requirement of an objective connection between the data retained and the objective pursued, which had been central in prohibiting generalised retention of metadata for law enforcement purposes.

The requirement of strict necessity in the form of safeguards has been somehow 'saved' because the Court required that generalised retention must be limited in time, as long as the Member State is confronted with a serious threat to national security which must be genuine and present, or at least foreseeable. The decision to carry out this limited form

---

[58] *Privacy International* (n 52) para 49.
[59] Juraj Sajfert, *Bulk data interception/retention judgments of the CJEU—A victory and a defeat for privacy* in European Law Blog (26 October 2020) <https://europeanlawblog.eu/2020/10/26/bulk-data-interception-retention-judgments-of-the-cjeu-a-victory-and-a-defeat-for-privacy/> accessed 5 August 2023.
[60] *La Quadrature du Net 'I'* (n 7) para 135.

of generalised retention must also be subject to effective review by a court or by an independent administrative authority.

Moving on to the preventive retention of metadata for the purpose of combating crime and safeguarding public security the Court essentially confirmed its findings in *Tele2Sverige*. It nuanced them, however, in relation to a particular subset of traffic data: IP addresses and data relating to the civil identity used in the fight against crime or to safeguard public security.

In particular with regard to IP addresses, the Court noted that IP addresses are part of traffic data, but essentially serve to identify the natural persons who own the terminal equipment from which a communication is made. If only the IP address of the source of the communication is retained, but not the IP address of the recipient, the interference with the fundamental rights to privacy and data protection is lesser, as the categories of data are less sensitive per se.[61] Rather surprisingly the Court stated immediately afterwards that 'IP addresses [without specifying whether of the source or of the recipient or both] may be used ... to track an Internet user complete clickstream and therefore enable a detailed profile of the user to be produced'.[62]

Nevertheless, to 'strike a balance' in the case at stake, the Court considered necessary to take into account that where an offence is committed online, the IP address may be the only means to identify the potential offender.[63] However the Court considered the interference resulting from retention of IP addresses as being very serious, but again without specifying very precisely what IP addresses determine such a serious interference: the addresses of the source, of the recipient, or both? To profile users it would seem that it is necessary to have available both the source address (for instance, who accesses the internet) and the destination address (for instance, the address of the website visited). This point would have received clarification only in 2024 with the full Court judgment delivered in *La Quadrature du Net 'II'*.[64]

In the *La Quadrature du Net 'I'* judgment of 2020, the balancing has been performed by the Court through carving out from the family of traffic data a specific subset (IP addresses). The justification for the finding of the seriousness of the interference provoked by this specific subset is not entirely clear, but the Court allowed this subset to be used only for the prosecution of serious crimes; in addition, the criterion of being 'the only means' to detect certain crimes has been added to the analysis.

Thus, here too the Court mixed a pure balancing operation with a new test—'the only means'—which is more in line with the classical notion of necessity: clearly no less restrictive measures may exist where an objective can be achieved through an 'only means'.

Another form of retention which was allowed by the Court is the 'expedited' retention. This form of retention refers to data which, during their normal period of storage by the providers as per the national laws transposing the ePrivacy Directive, may objectively contribute to shed light on committed serious criminal offences or acts adversely affecting national security, or where such acts have not yet been committed but may only be reasonably suspected. In such cases the 'objective connection' requirement is fulfilled, and the Court

---

[61] ibid para 152.
[62] ibid para 153.
[63] ibid para 154.
[64] See section 2.10 in this chapter.

allows such forms of retention for a limited duration of time, even if the interference with the fundamental rights provoked remains serious, and accordingly only serious crimes, terrorism, or threats against national security may be countered with measures of expedited data retention. The Court clarified a further important safeguard that can be seen as part of its own balancing: access to such data cannot be granted for the purpose of prosecuting and punishing ordinary criminal offences, and vice versa. 'Moving up' in the hierarchy of objectives—that is, accessing data originally collected for the prosecution of serious crimes for the purpose of the safeguard of national security—remains possible.[65] Similar considerations have been developed by the Court for the other forms of retention at stake in the case and rather granularly discussed in the ruling: the automated analysis of metadata, enabled by the French legislation and treated by the Court according to the same criteria as for the generalised retention of metadata. As for the possibility of real-time collection of metadata, the Court required the collection to be possible only in presence of an objective connection and only for terrorist crimes.[66]

The aforementioned summarised paragraphs of the ruling lend themselves to varying forms of compliance. For the purposes of the present chapter it should be highlighted how the fact that the Court clearly felt the need to lay down a hierarchy of objectives, with the corresponding degrees of interference that each may allow, can be seen as a direct result of the application of the mixed balancing/strict necessity test that this chapter tries to decode. Sometimes, like for the threats to national security, the upfront 'balancing' of the competing interests is so clear that the objective connection criteria is simply overruled; some other times, for example for IP addresses, the fact it of being the only means to prosecute certain crimes allows certain forms of retention. The end result is a very prescriptive and complex ruling—a good example *of ius praetorium*: the proportionality test in the field of data retention risks assumed in the *La Quadrature du Net 'I'* ruling a sectorial meaning and its predictability may have ultimately suffered. This is because of the lack of explicit structuring of the overall proportionality test on the basis of the three 'classic' prongs. This is noteworthy considering that the 'only means' criterion presents no difficulties in being framed under the classic form of the necessity test, as the Court would have recognised in later case-law.

2.7 *Prokuratuur*: The Court explains why retention and access need to be considered as a one and only interference

In the *Prokuratuur*[67] ruling the Court had the opportunity to clarify an important aspect—whether the length of the retention measures, and other aspects such as the quantity and data available in respect of a determined period of time, had any impact on the seriousness of the interference and thus on the outcome of the balancing exercise.

---

[65] *La Quadrature du Net 'I'* (n 7) para 166.
[66] For a more complete 'mapping' of the landscape of data retention as emerging from the *La Quadrature du Net 'I'* ibid ruling, see in particular the summary tables made in Valsamis Mitsilegas, Elspeth Guild, Niovi Vavoula, and Elif Kuskonmaz, 'Data Retention and the Future of Large-scale Surveillance: The Evolution and Contestation of Judicial Benchmarks' (2022) 1(36) European Law Journal 7. See also Maria Tzanou and Spyridoula Karyda, *Privacy International and Quadrature du Net: One Step Forward Two Steps Back in the Data Retention Saga?* (2022) 28(1) European Public Law 28 no. 1 123–54 at 132–36.
[67] CJEU, Judgment of 2 March 2021, *Prokuratuur (Conditions d'accès aux données relatives aux communications électroniques)* (C-746/18) ECLI:EU:C:2021:152.

The referring Court inquired whether 'Article 15(1) of Directive 2002/58, read in the light of the Charter, must be interpreted as meaning that the access of State authorities to data making it possible to identify the source and destination of a telephone communication from a suspect's landline or mobile telephone, to determine the date, time, duration and type of that communication, to identify the communications equipment used and to establish the location of the mobile communication equipment used amounts to interference with the fundamental rights at issue which is so serious that such access should be restricted to combating serious crime, *regardless of the period in respect of which the State authorities have sought access to the retained data*'[68] (emphasis added).

The Court replied in a rather peremptory way, and rejected that the length of the retention period would be a variable able to influence the outcome of the balancing it had already performed several times.[69] Then the Court made explicit an assumption which is arguably at the core of the balancing test that it performed across the entire body of case-law analysed in this chapter. At para 40 of the ruling, it stated that '*the assessment of the seriousness of the interference that the access constitutes is necessarily carried out on the basis of the risk generally pertaining to the category of data sought for the private lives of the persons concerned*, without it indeed mattering whether or not the resulting information relating to the person's private life is in actual fact sensitive'[70] (emphasis added).

This statement probably helps to understand the root of the decision taken by the Court already in the *Digital Rights Ireland* ruling, and in particular the stubborn resistance in defending a rather artificial separation, almost a conceptual 'Chinese wall' between retention and access—despite the objection, expressed in this chapter and put forward to the Court in various instances, that retention cannot be conceived as an end per se. No public interest objective is achieved by retaining but not accessing any type of data, and thus under Article 52(1) of the Charter an interference so shaped can hardly be justified.

Paragraph 40 of the *Prokuratuur* ruling helps therefore to further understand the value judgment which is at the core of the assessment of the strict proportionality (implicitly) performed by the Court: the risk for the fundamental rights to privacy and protection of personal data involved is simply *too big as such*. This is because of the Court's own assessment of the gravity of the 'conclusions' that the data about the who, where, and when of communications allow the State authorities to draw. This must of course be understood against the backdrop of the ePrivacy Directive and the basic hermeneutical criterion according to which the exception cannot swallow the rule, a legal hurdle often overlooked by the defenders of generalised retention of metadata for law enforcement purposes.[71]

No weight on the opposite plate of the balance can match this risk. This holds true for the Court, despite the fact that safeguards could well allow access to be tailored and, under the control of a judge, only granted to the datasets for which the objective connection with the objective pursued can be thoroughly demonstrated. After all, the targeted forms of

---

[68] ibid para 21.
[69] ibid para 39.
[70] ibid para 40.
[71] This raises the question (that would go beyond the scope of the present chapter) as to whether the Union legislator would enjoy a certain discretion in easing up the basic rule of confidentiality in Article 5 ePrivacy Directive, or whether, as it seems more probable, the finding of the Court is made on the basis of constitutional principles stemming from primary law.

retention that the Court allowed still entail the same risks of abuse. Even in the case of targeted retention measures, such risks are only partially mitigated by their non-general scope. In other words, given that forms of targeted retention may still qualify as bulk processing, the risks of abuse are not very different in quality, and only marginally different in quantity than those deemed unacceptable by the Court. This value judgment is striking as it exposes a certain mistrust for the effectiveness of legal safeguards that can frame access to data and thus could limit the concrete extent of the interference.

To a certain extent, the Court appears not to trust enough that any safeguards may be able to outweigh the risks for privacy intrinsic in the generalised retention of metadata of communications. The Court might have in mind inevitable risks of abuse, or in any event it considers that any failure of the safeguards—regardless of whether such a failure is due to original design flaws or compliance issues—represents an unacceptable risk in a democratic society, having regard to the intrusiveness of the data at stake. Against this backdrop it is not an exaggeration to state that the Court based its balancing on a presumption that unlawful or insufficiently regulated access is inevitable. This reading ultimately presupposes that, at least to a certain extent, the rule of law in the Union is an objective to be reached, rather than a stable *acquis*.

2.8 *Garda Síochána* and *SpaceNet*: The assessment of proportionality in the field of retention of metadata for criminal law purposes is final

The combined effect of the *La Quadrature du Net 'I'* and *Prokuratuur* rulings could have been to put an end to the debate of whether preventive and generalised retention of metadata is allowed in EU law. However, before the issuance of both rulings three further preliminary references had reached the Court on very similar matters.

In the case *GD v Commissioner An Garda Síochána*[72] the Irish Supreme Court put forward to the Court that strict compliance with the standard laid down in *Tele2Sverige* would have made impossible to achieve the objective to prevent, investigate, detect, and prosecute at least certain types of crimes. The case was a high-profile one, in which only recourse to metadata of communications allowed the authorities to find the killer of a 13-year-old girl.

At the same time, two joined preliminary requests from Germany in cases *SpaceNet AG* and *Telekom Deutschland*[73] enquired as to whether the national telecommunications law, laboriously adapted to attempt compliance with both the Court's case-law as well as a ruling of the Federal Constitutional Court, was effectively compliant with the Court's case-law. The German provisions were expected to have a better chance of being found compliant in reasons of their level of increased precision, at least if compared to the other national measures previously submitted to the Court. They excluded from the categories of data to be retained certain specific (and in reality, essentially marginal) datasets, provided for restrictive security measures and highly regulated conditions for access, and perhaps—most importantly—provided for very limited retention periods (four weeks for location data and ten weeks for other metadata).

---

[72] *Garda Síochána* (n 6).
[73] CJEU, Judgment of 27 October 2022, *SpaceNet* (C-793/19 and C-794/19) ECLI:EU:C:2022:702.

These further precisions however did not prove sufficient to allow for a modification of the Court's established position. The Court found that the scope of the German provisions corresponded in substance to the scope of the provisions already adjudicated by the Court and the minor differences in the data retained could not alter the fact that the conclusion as to the seriousness of the interference had to be the same.[74] Concerning the relevance of the shorter retention period, the Court had to simply quote the finding in *Prokuratuur* (see previous section).

The ruling in *Garda Síochána* is striking for the rather 'defensive' tone adopted by the Court.[75] Whatever the reasons, the *Garda Síochána* ruling consists essentially of the reiteration of the now settled case-law on data retention. The Court felt, however, that it was necessary to provide further explanations of its now established position. It stated rather apodictically that 'the effectiveness of criminal proceedings generally depends not on a single means of investigation but on all the means of investigation available to the competent national authorities'.[76] It also provided even further detailed guidance on how it is possible to implement targeted retention. In rather strong words it sought to remind that 'there can be no question of reinstating... the general and indiscriminate retention of traffic and location data'[77] and 'the fact that it may be difficult to provide a detailed definition of the circumstances and conditions under which targeted retention may be carried out is no reason for the Member States, by turning the exception into the rule, to provide for general retention of traffic and location data'.[78]

In what is a very interesting twist, the Court refers in para 93 of the ruling to the fact that 'according to the Court's *settled case-law*', the proportionality of the measures adopted pursuant to Article 15(1) ePrivacy Directive 'requires... compliance not only with the requirements of aptitude and of necessity *but also with that of the proportionate nature of those measure in relation to the objective pursued*' (emphasis added).[79] It is remarkable how the Court refers to 'settled case-law'—in particular, it refers to *La Quadrature du Net 'I'*, but without pointing to any specific paragraph thereof—that would have established the 'tripartite' version of the proportionality test in the field of data retention. As the reader will have noticed, in no case under review in this chapter the autonomous status of the proportionality test *stricto sensu* had been explicitly and unambiguously recognised. The references to 'balancing', 'striking a balance', and similar expression were inextricably linked to the notion of strict necessity.

Be as it may, the two paragraphs that follow such a 'recognition' explain where specifically in the case-law the Court had conducted the strict proportionality test. In para 94 of

---

[74] ibid para 83.
[75] See in that sense Julie Teyssedre, 'Strictly Regulated Retention and Access Regimes for Metadata: Commissioner of An Garda Síochána' (2023) in Common Market Law Review 60: 569–88, Kluwer Law International. This may be explained also by the fact that, as one learns from the Opinion of the Advocate General Campos Sanchez Bordona, the Court had formally asked both Courts whether, following the *La Quadrature du Net 'I'* (n 7) ruling, it intended to maintain the preliminary reference or, rather, the preliminary questions had to be considered without object. While the German Federal Administrative Court motivated their maintaining of the preliminary references with circumstantiated arguments, the Irish Supreme Court apparently provided a very laconic reply. See the Opinion of Advocate General Carlos Campos-Sanchez Bordona of 18 November 2021 in case *Commissioner of An Garda Síochána* (C-140/20) ECLI:EU:C:2021:942 ('*AG Opinion Garda Síochána*').
[76] *Garda Síochána* (n 6) para 69.
[77] ibid para 83.
[78] ibid para 84.
[79] ibid para 93.

the *Garda Síochána* ruling, the Court recalled that, ever since the *Digital Rights Ireland*,[80] it considered that the objective of general interest that is the fight against serious crime 'however fundamental it may be, does not, in itself, justify that a measure providing for the general and indiscriminate retention of all traffic and location data, such as that established by Directive 2006/24, should be considered to be *necessary*' (emphasis added). This appears as the outcome of a weighing of competing interests (the length of lines and the weight of stones), but one cannot but notice that the words 'necessary' appears again, perhaps to the detriment of clarity.

Paragraph 95 of the *Garda Síochána* ruling underlines, by reference to para 145 of *La Quadrature du Net 'I'* that even where positive obligations exist under the Charter to establish rules to facilitate effective action to combat criminal offences, such obligations 'cannot have the effect of justifying interference that is as serious as that entailed by legislation providing for the retention of traffic and location data with the fundamental rights, enshrined in Articles 7 and 8 of the Charter, of practically the entire population.'[81] This finding is certainly the outcome of a 'strict proportionality' assessment and it should be welcome that the Court eventually labels it as such.

2.9 La Quadrature du Net 'II'

2.9.1 Advocate General Szpunar's two Opinions

The case *La Quadrature du Net 'II'*[82] concerns whether a complex system devised by the French legislator to detect and sanction (ultimately, criminally) uploaders of copyrighted materials on 'peer to peer networks' was laying down a proportionate interference with the right to protection of personal data. The data of the persons concerned consisted in the IP address of the device through which they accessed the internet and the peer-to-peer network. Under the provision of the French law at stake,[83] sworn officers working within rightsholders' organisations (ie the organisations for the defence of the copyright holders) roam the peer-to-peer networks and collect the IP addresses of the devices from which copyright protected works are uploaded in such networks. The IP address from which the protected work was uploaded, together with the date and time of the infringement and the title of the work in question, are sent to what was at the time of the facts the 'Haute Autorité pour la diffusion des oeuvres et la protection des droits sur internet' ('Hadopi').

After an automated check, Hadopi may obtain from the electronic communication service provider the identity and contact details of the holder of the internet subscription that was used to commit the infringement. Such a holder may subsequently receive a recommendation reminding them of the duty foreseen under French law[84] to make sure that the subscription is not used illegally. A second recommendation may be sent, if the same address is found in breach again and, in case of further infringements, Hadopi may refer the matter

---

[80] ibid, specifically its para 51.
[81] ibid para 95.
[82] *La Quadrature du Net 'II'* (n 7).
[83] The national provisions at stake were essentially the French Intellectual Property Code (Code de la Propriété Intellectuelle) and the implementing regulations that the Government issued to give effect to it.
[84] Article L-336-3 of the Code de la Propriété Intellectuelle (Article L-336-3 of the Intellectual Property Code).

to the Public Prosecutor's Office in order for the latter to bring criminal proceedings. This mechanism has been called the 'graduated response' mechanism in light of its paedagogical approach and increasing level of gravity of the reaction by the public authority to the copyright infringement, potentially culminating in criminal proceedings.

Against this background, the referring Court asked essentially whether IP addresses, given their not particularly sensitive character, should still be subject to review by a Court or by an independent administrative body as required by the case-law examined in this chapter. The referring Court highlighted that a systematic review would have inevitably jeopardised the fulfilment of the mission of Hadopi to effectively protect copyrights on the internet.

In what is a rather exceptional instance, Advocate General Szpunar issued two different opinions on the same case, on request of the Court. His first opinion indeed seems to have played a role in motivating the Court to reopen the oral procedure and thus convene a second hearing, and also to reattribute the case to the Full Court in a rather exceptional move which occurs rarely in the Court's practice.[85]

In the first Opinion[86] the Advocate General links—with a tight logic—retention of the data and access. The preliminary questions did not concern the retention of IP addresses by the providers of electronic communication services, but were limited to the condition of access by Hadopi to such data. The Commission and France insisted that it was not necessary to deal with any retention issue to answer the preliminary questions. Nevertheless, Advocate General Szpunar deems that the issue of access cannot be separated from the preliminary issue of the retention of the data by the providers, since access is dependent on retention.[87] It is therefore necessary in his view to assess first whether the retention is compatible with EU law and only after this test is passed, the compatibility of conditions for access to the retained data can be assessed. This is quite a clarification: although it could certainly have been inferred from the prior case-law quoted by the Advocate General, its reaffirmation in the context of preliminary questions that were avoiding—perhaps deliberately—any reference to the lawfulness of the retention cannot be underestimated.

In the second Opinion[88] issued in this case, the Advocate General develops the line presented in the first one and thus does not dwell anymore on the differences between retention and access and deal with them together. He declares that at the heart of the data retention case-law lies the requirement of proportionality, and he clearly attempts at building a bridge towards the classical three prongs of suitability, necessity, and strict proportionality. In his view, the Court in the context of Article 15(1) ePrivacy Directive has underlined the specific 'aspects' of the seriousness of the interference and the necessity of the measure at issue.[89]

---

[85] Other elements have certainly played a role for determining attribution to the full Court and this will remain a matter for speculation. Early analyses of the ruling mention in that connection also the dialogue opened with the French Council of State (Conseil d'État) which applied *La Quadrature du Net 'I'* (n 7) in a rather creative way, if not actually rebelling against the CJEU. See 'The Devil is in the (Procedural) Details – the Court's Judgment in La Quadrature du Net' by Xavier Groussot and Annegret Engel (13 May 2024) in EU Law Live, available at <https://eulawlive.com/op-ed-the-devil-is-in-the-procedural-details-the-courts-judgment-in-la-quadrature-du-net-by-xavier-groussot-and-annegret-engel/> accessed 5 June 2024.

[86] Opinion of Advocate General Szpunar of 27 October 2022, C-470/21, *La Quadrature du Net 'II'*, ECLI:EU:C:2022:838 ('*First AG Opinion La Quadrature du Net 'II'*').

[87] ibid para 45.

[88] Opinion of Advocate General Szpunar of 28 September 2023, C-470/21, *La Quadrature du Net 'II'* ECLI:EU:C:2023:711 ('*Second AG Opinion La Quadrature du Net 'II'*').

[89] ibid paras 41 and 43.

The Advocate General deals in the first place with the strict proportionality requirement and assesses the seriousness of the interference with the importance of the objective pursued. There, he clarifies a point left open by the somehow prescriptive findings of the Court in *La Quadrature du Net 'I'* on the interferences with the fundamental rights of Articles 7 and 8 of the Charter in relation to the retention and access of IP addresses. The Court had indeed stated in that ruling that 'IP addresses [without specifying whether of the source or of the recipient or both] may be used ... to track an Internet user complete clickstream and therefore enable a detailed profile of the user to be produced'.[90] The Advocate General usefully notes that this should not be read as meaning that retention of, and access to, IP addresses always generates a serious interference, but a serious interference exists 'only where the IP addresses may result in the exhaustive tracking of the user's clickstream and in very precise conclusions being drawn about his or her private life'.[91] This was not the case for the IP addresses linked to the uploading of copyrighted material on peer-to-peer networks: the graduated response mechanism of the French law did not involve the general surveillance of member of peer to peer networks, but only that of users uploading infringing files in those networks. Furthermore, the information revealed to those eventually able to link the IP address to the civil identity of the owner of the internet subscription is not that intrusive for the Advocate General.

Nevertheless, the case can be made of a member of a household in which the owner of the subscription, following the access to such data by the Hadopi, receives a recommendation that informs him or her of the title of the work illegally uploaded. That title itself may, once associated with the identified user of the peer-to-peer network in that household, reveal for instance sexual or political inclinations previously unknown to the other members of their household. However, in many other cases, possibly the majority of them, revealing the title of the work illegally downloaded will not provide any particularly sensitive detail about the private life of the persons concerned, other than the fact of having been in breach of copyright laws.

In this case it might be difficult to apply the lesson of the *Prokuratuur* ruling[92] according to which the assessment of the seriousness of the interference should be carried out on the basis of the risk for the private lives of the persons concerned generally pertaining to the category of data sought. The category of data in question (work illegally uploaded: videogames, software, music, videos, etc) is so varied that the assessment of the seriousness of the interference might need to be done on other bases, yet to be found. The relevance of such an aspect shows the role and weight of the room for discretion left to the Court in assessing whether the interference is 'serious'. For Advocate General Szpunar, the linking of IP address, civil identity data, and the extracts from the work illegally uploaded, realises a serious interference,[93] but the passage where this is put forward is probably one of the few of his two remarkable Opinions not buttressed by a convincing argumentation, in this author's opinion. Indeed, even if the Advocate General qualifies the interference as 'serious' in the first Opinion, perhaps in an attempt not to distance himself too much from the *La Quadrature du Net 'I'* ruling on IP addresses, in the second Opinion[94] he considers that the information related to the work illegally uploaded does not allow precise conclusions to be drawn about the private

---

[90] See section 2.6 in this chapter.
[91] *Second AG Opinion La Quadrature du Net 'II'* (n 88) para 55.
[92] See section 2.7 in this chapter.
[93] *First AG Opinion La Quadrature du Net 'II'* (n 86) para 94.
[94] *Second AG Opinion La Quadrature du Net 'II'* (n 88) para 57.

life of the person and he admits that the interference at stake is of 'limited seriousness'.[95] However, the possibility or not to draw such precise conclusion is the criterion previously retained in the case-law to separate serious from non-serious interferences.

In any event, for the Advocate General, where a serious interference amounts to be the sole means to prosecute a crime committed online, it means that such interference is limited to what is strictly necessary, in accordance with the Court's case law on data retention. The two Opinions insist on the fact that access to IP addresses are indispensable for identifying persons suspected of having committed an infringement online. In this regard, the Advocate General adopts a traditional notion of strict necessity test, which is interpreted as the assessment of the existence of less intrusive means.

This 'traditional' reading seemed to have required him to deal with the previous case-law that does not distinguish the strict necessity assessment from the material and procedural guarantees on which the Court insisted. For the Advocate General the 'strict proportionality' of the measure is not in itself sufficient to render it compatible with Article 15(1) ePrivacy Directive, because the case-law requires, for traffic and location data, that access is subject to prior review by a Court or by an independent administrative body. He sees this as a requirement apparently separate from the proportionality assessment. The material and procedural guarantees constitute rather an inherent and specific requirement applicable to Article 15(1) ePrivacy Directive. In particular, the requirement of prior review would not need to be applied systematically, but only where the seriousness of the interference at issue so requires. In that regard, it appears quite fundamental that the previous case-law on data retention providing for that requirement concerned access to personal data of persons suspected of having committed an infringement for the purpose of finding them. By way of contrast, the case in *La Quadrature du Net 'II'* is concerned with allowing the identity of an already found perpetrator of an infringement already established to be revealed.[96] Ultimately the Advocate General calls for a 'necessary and limited development of the case-law', without 'reconsidering' it but accepting that a more nuanced solution might be identified in very limited circumstances.

The most relevant circumstance requires that access to certain personal data would be the only means, or the least intrusive means to prosecute infringements committed exclusively online. This distinguishes the interference at stake with the one resulting from the other criminal prosecutions for which the Court stated that their effectiveness depends not on a single means of investigation.[97] Furthermore, this interpretation of Article 15(1) ePrivacy Directive would not call into question the case-law that applies to a wider range of data and pursuing other objectives. This should be elevated as a more generally valid dictum, also with a view to remedying to what the Advocate General called 'a somewhat case-by-case approach' followed by the Court in the data retention case-law on the interpretation of Article 15(1) ePrivacy Directive.

2.9.2 The full Court judgment

The conclusion of this chapter, written immediately afterwards the delivery of the full Court ruling, will continue to focus on how the Court structured its analysis of the proportionality test *lato sensu*.

---

[95] ibid para 63.
[96] ibid para 73.
[97] ibid para 60.

Firstly, the CJEU builds on the abundant body of case law-on the matter of conservation and access of IP addresses. It begins by performing a balancing test, or rather, it 'refines' the balancing test performed notably in relation to the seriousness of the interference with the fundamental rights of privacy, data protection, and freedom of expression provoked by such conservation and access.

There are separate sections of the ruling dedicated respectively to conservation and access following the argumentative structure inherited from the *Tele2 Sverige* ruling. The reader finds, immediately after a summary of the relevant point of the *La Quadrature du Net 'I'*, a recognition that the circumstances of the access by the Hadopi of the data retained are relevant to assess the interference consisting in the conservation.

The provisions governing the said conservation are strikingly out of the proceedings, since the preliminary reference only contained questions about access by the Hadopi. In other words, the question about what the legal base in French law was which allowed the IP addresses and the corresponding civil identity data of the potential offenders to be available to the providers of the electronic communication services, for them to be transmitted to the Hadopi, remains open in the ruling. The Court seems aware that such an 'elephant in the room' needed to be addressed, but it keeps—at least formally—a tight separation between the assessment of the proportionality *lato sensu* of conservation and that of access. It thus states that access by Hadopi 'necessarily *presupposes* that the providers have the IP addresses as well as the data relating to the identity of the holders of those addresses'.[98] Thus, the Court continues its analysis on the basis of the logical presumption that the data to which Hadopi had access is available because is conserved 'somehow'.[99]

As noted in section 2.7, the Court had considered the interference resulting from retention of IP addresses as being very serious, but without specifying very precisely *what* IP addresses determine such a serious interference: the addresses of the source, the recipient, or both. The Court had previously said (in this author's view, without fully providing convincing reasons) that 'IP addresses may be used, among other things, to track an Internet's user complete clickstream'.[100] This justified the conclusion according to which '[i]n the light of the seriousness of the interference entailed by that retention [of IP addresses of the source of a connection] with the fundamental rights enshrined in Articles 7 and 8 of the Charter, only action to combat serious crime, the prevention of serious threats to public security and the safeguarding of national security are capable of justifying that interference'.[101] In *La Quadrature du Net II* the Court reassesses these paragraphs as follows:

> It is true that, in paragraph 156 of the judgment of 6 October 2020, *La Quadrature du Net and Others* (C-511/18, C-512/18 and C-520/18, EU:C:2020:791), the Court held that ... Article 15(1) of Directive 2002/58 precludes the general and indiscriminate retention of only IP addresses assigned to the source of a connection for purposes other than action to combat serious crime, the prevention of serious threats to public security

---

[98] ibid para 71.
[99] It cannot be excluded that the Hadopi is able to request the IP addresses and corresponding civil identities within the tight timeframe (few weeks) in which electronic communications service providers are entitled to keep such data in accordance with Article 6 of the ePrivacy Directive, in particular for the purposes of subscriber billing and interconnection payments.
[100] *La Quadrature du Net 'I'* (n 7) para 153.
[101] ibid para 156.

or the safeguarding of national security. However, in reaching that conclusion, the Court expressly relied on the serious nature of the interference with the fundamental rights enshrined in Articles 7, 8 and 11 of the Charter which such retention of IP addresses is likely to entail.[102]

However, it could be argued that in the *La Quadrature du Net 'I'* ruling, the serious nature of the interference was derived merely from the intrinsic feature of IP addresses of the source of a connection (namely, the capacity to reveal the 'full clickstream' of a person). The full Court ruling thus 'broadens the field of view'. It explains that the first ruling concerned national legislation that allowed to retain other data, and the possibility of combining those various data allowed to draw precise conclusions about the private life of the persons whose data were concerned, thereby determining the high level of seriousness of the interference.[103] In any event, the (welcome) introduction of this contextual nuancing sits uncomfortably with the previous affirmative findings of points 153 and 156 of *La Quadrature du Net 'I'*. It constitutes a clear change in the case-law, consecrated in para 82 of *La Quadrature du Net 'II'*. The Court now admits that 'the general and indiscriminate retention of IP addresses may, as the case may be, be justified by the objective of combating *criminal offences in general* where it is genuinely ruled out that that retention could give rise to serious interferences with the private life of the person concerned due to the possibility of drawing precise conclusions about that person' (emphasis added).[104]

Indeed, the applicant La Quadrature du Net has expressed discontent with this jurisprudential change,[105] which however appears to reflect more faithfully the reality, since it is difficult to justify the simple 'equation' inherited from *La Quadrature du Net 'I'* between conservation of IP address of the source and the seriousness of the interference without further qualifying it.

This relative softening of the requirements for conservation of IP addresses and related civil identity data comes anyway assorted with a new string of mandatory procedural safeguards that Member States must ensure to keep the interference with the fundamental rights to privacy and data protection at a not serious level. The existence of such new procedural safeguards[106]—unassumingly labelled by the Court as 'clarifications' concerning

---

[102] *La Quadrature du Net 'II'* (n 7) para 77.
[103] ibid paras 80 and 81.
[104] ibid para 82.
[105] The non-governmental organisation states on its website:
'Whereas in 2020, the CJEU considered that the retention of IP addresses constituted a serious interference with fundamental rights and that they could only be accessed, together with the civil identity of the Internet user, for the purpose of fighting serious crime or safeguarding national security, this is no longer true. The CJEU has reversed its reasoning: it now considers that the retention of IP addresses is, by default, no longer a serious interference with fundamental rights, and that it is only in certain cases that such access constitutes a serious interference that must be safeguarded with appropriate protection measures'. See <https://www.laquadrature.net/en/2024/04/30/surveillance-and-hadopi-eu-court-buries-online-anonymity-a-little-further> accessed 1 June 2024.
[106] The safeguards are enumerated at paras 86–89 of *La Quadrature du Net 'II'* (n 7) and consist in:
  1. keeping separate from each other each category of data retained (para 86);
  2. such a separation must be 'genuinely watertight' (para 87);
  3. the linking the retained IP addresses with the civil identity of the person concerned must be permitted 'only through the use of an effective technical process which does not undermine the effectiveness of the watertight separation' (para 88);
  4. the reliability of that watertight separation must be subject to regular review by a public authority other than that which seeks to obtain access to the personal data retained (para 89).

'retention arrangements'[107]—is therefore determinative of the seriousness of the interference stemming from the conservation of such data. This is a central element for assessing how the proportionality test is applied by the Court and will be further discussed below.

When assessing the interference consisting in the access to the IP addresses and civil identity data, the Court reminds that such access may not be granted if the data was retained for objectives higher importance: data retained for purposes of fight against serious crime cannot be accessed for purposes of the fight against crime in general.[108] It requires, importantly, that 'national legislation must also lay down clear and precise rules capable of ensuring that the IP addresses retained in accordance with Directive 2002/58 can be used only to identify the person to whom a particular IP address was assigned, while precluding any use that allows the surveillance, by means of one or more of those addresses, of that person's online activity'.[109] With this safeguard concerning access, added to the ones that must also be respected for conservation, the Court concedes that the general and indiscriminate retention of IP addresses does not constitute a serious interference with the privacy of the holders of those addresses, since those data do not allow precise conclusions to be drawn about their private life.[110]

However, in the system of the graduated response the Hadopi was not only receiving the identity of a potential offender; it was also receiving information about the title of the work illegally made available on the peer to peer network. Invoking the assessment performed by the ECtHR in the *Benedik*[111] ruling, the Court deems necessary to look at that data as part of the context necessary to assess the extent of the interference provoked by the access. Sometimes indeed the knowledge of the title of the work illegally uploaded, especially in case of repeated offences, may be revealing intimate aspects of the private life in a rather precise manner. The Court however underlines that this would happen only in 'atypical situations,[112] which seems to be the key consideration that distinguishes this case from the other cases discussed in this chapter, where the seriousness of the interference was arguably the rule, and not the exception.

In addition, however, the Court evokes a bundle of indicators[113] that also help to conclude that the interference at stake 'is not necessarily of a high degree of seriousness'.[114] The said conclusion is then supported also by arguments that once again perhaps show, in this author's opinion, the liberty of the Court in performing the proportionality assessment *latu sensu*. The Court provides 'indicators' of the non-serious character of the interference. It starts by quoting the general principle according to which no fundamental right

---

[107] *La Quadrature du Net 'II'* (n 7) para 85.
[108] ibid para 97.
[109] ibid para 101.
[110] ibid para 103.
[111] ECtHR, Judgment of 24 April 2018, *Benedik v Slovenia* (62357/14) CE:ECHR:2018:0424JUD006235714.
[112] *La Quadrature du Net 'II'* (n 7) para 111.
[113] The indicators evoked by the Court are:
  1. access is restricted to a limited number of authorised and sworn officials of Hadopi, a public authority with independent status (*La Quadrature du Net 'II'* (n 7) para 113);
  2. the sole purpose of that access is to identify a person suspected of having engaged in an activity infringing copyright or related rights (para 113);
  3. access to the personal data at issue is strictly limited to the data necessary for that purpose (para 113);
  4. Hadopi officials who have access to the data and information concerned are bound by an obligation of confidentiality (para 114).
[114] *La Quadrature du Net 'II'* (n 7) para 113.

is absolute,[115] then it highlights the fact that no other means exist to prosecute this type of infringements and follows the Advocate General in his assessment of the strict necessity of the measure;[116] finally, the risk of systemic impunity is considered a relevant factor for the purposes of assessing the strict proportionality of the measure. In the space of three paragraphs, general considerations (no fundamental right is absolute), strict necessity in the 'orthodox' or classical sense (lack of less intrusive measure to achieve the objective), and risk factors pertaining to a strict proportionality test become criteria to determine the seriousness of the interference.

The above liberty taken in the structuring of the test may be in part explained that the Court when conducting the proportionality assessment takes now more explicitly into account elements of context. This is an important and perhaps welcome departure from the abstract approach followed in *La Quadrature du Net 'I'* end even more visibly in *Prokuratuur*. In the latter judgment, the Court required the assessment of the seriousness of the interference on the basis of the risk generally pertaining to the category of data and refused to give relevance to a contextual element such as the duration of the retention period.[117]

While the metaphor of the scale may be reductive, it remains that every balancing cannot be correct without placing all the required weights on the two plates of the scale, and more contextual assessments diminish the risks of 'forgetting' to place some weight on one of the plates. The reference to the *Benedik* ruling[118] of the ECtHR assumers perhaps particular importance[119] in a full Court ruling and adds particular dignity to the assessment of the context.[120]

In the *Bolzano* judgment,[121] delivered on the same day as *La Quadrature du Net 'II'*, the Court goes perhaps even further in recognising that the assessment of the strict proportionality is a circumstantial one. In order for the balancing to be brought to a satisfactory outcome a 'court or independent administrative body, acting in the context of a prior review carried out following a reasoned request for access [in that case, access to retained traffic data of mobile telephony], must be entitled to refuse or restrict that access where it finds that the interference with fundamental rights which such access would constitute is serious even though it is clear that the offence at issue does not actually constitute serious crime'.[122]

For the Court in *Bolzano* it is the entity called to perform such prior review which takes the role of the guarantor of the balancing between fight and criminality and protection of

---

[115] ibid para 116.
[116] ibid para 117.
[117] See section 2.7 in this chapter.
[118] ECtHR, Judgment of 24 April 2018, *Benedik v Slovenia* (62357/14) CE:ECHR:2018:0424JUD006235714, quoted at paras 73 and 107 of *La Quadrature du Net 'II'* (n 7).
[119] See in the same sense Groussot and Engel, 'The Devil is in the (Procedural) Details' (n 85) available at <https://eulawlive.com/op-ed-the-devil-is-in-the-procedural-details-the-courts-judgment-in-la-quadrature-du-net-by-xavier-groussot-and-annegret-engel/> accessed 5 June 2024.
[120] This may fit into a specific trend observed in other important rulings in the field of data protection in which the Court values more and more elements of context, even on issues related to the assessment of the applicability of data protection law *ratione materiae*, such as the assessment as to whether information constitutes or not 'personal data'. Examples of this trend may be: CJEU, judgments of 7 March 2024 *OC v Commission* (C-479/22 P) ECLI:EU:C:2024:215, see in particular paras 60 and 61 thereof; and of 9 November 2023 *Gesamtverband Autoteile v Scania* (C-319/22) ECLI:EU:C:2023:837, see in particular paras 48 and 49 thereof.
[121] CJEU, Judgment of 30 April 2024, *Procura della Repubblica presso il Tribunale di Bolzano* (C-178/22) ECLI:EU:C:2024:371.
[122] ibid para 60.

fundamental rights[123] (ie the strict proportionality test). The proper conduct of such a test in the context of a specific case allows the reviewing entity to de facto 'set aside' provisions of national law where such provisions would not allow it to exclude access to the data provoking a serious interference when the offence being prosecuted is manifestly not a serious offence 'in the light of the societal conditions prevailing in the Member State concerned'.[124] This rather disruptive finding may be rooted in the indirect recognition that sometimes the best balancing can only be performed by a judge mastering the specific factual circumstances of the case, that is, the relevant context.

The two rulings issued on the same day still may expose a certain tension between them: the Court in *La Quadrature du Net 'II'* defines rather minutiously the characteristics (the safeguards) that national legislation in the Member State must provide to ensure (strict) proportionality. By way of contrast, in *Bolzano* the role of the judge or the entity carrying out the prior review is highlighted somehow to overrule national legislation, which moreover in that case was simply reproducing the (Court-approved[125]) criterion that the seriousness of a criminal offence may be determined in relation to a minimum threshold of the maximum period of imprisonment.

It is true that the Court makes a convincing case in *Bolzano* that, when the law allows a certain latitude so that it could capture both 'serious' and 'not serious' interferences, which was the case for the Italian provisions in question,[126] the discretion left to the judge needs to be guaranteed, without this meaning that the rules are *per se* not proportionate. However, the same could have been said of the much more detailed rules establishing the system of the 'graduated response' at stake in *La Quadrature du Net 'II'*. The system was devised with very articulated rules, triggering reactions of increased intensity by the French public authority: first, the Hadopi itself would have sent a recommendation and then the file could have been 'moved up' to the public prosecutor for proper criminal action.

The discriminating factor between the two cases however appears clearly from a comparison of the two judgments, and lies in the independent nature of the reviewer. In other words: *who* is tasked with placing the weight on the balance? In the main proceedings leading to the *Bolzano* judgment, such a task was clearly conferred on an independent judge;[127] vice-versa, it seems it is not acceptable for the Court that, as soon as the interference becomes serious, an occurrence that cannot be ruled out[128] in the context of the system of the 'graduated response' at stake in *La Quadrature du Net 'II'*—there was no truly independent assessment of that balancing. The Court therefore places upon the national legislator the requirement to provide for a prior review by a court or an independent administrative body 'at a certain stage of that procedure, in order to rule out the risks of disproportionate interferences with the fundamental rights to the protection of privacy and

---

[123] ibid para 61.
[124] ibid para 63.
[125] '[A] definition according to which "serious offences", for the prosecution of which access to data may be granted, are those for which the maximum term of imprisonment is at least equal to a period determined by law, is based on an objective criterion. That is consistent with the requirement that the national legislation concerned must be based on objective criteria in order to define the circumstances and conditions under which the competent national authorities are to be granted access to the data in question' *Bolzano*, ibid, para 54.
[126] ibid para 59.
[127] The judge in charge of preliminary investigations at the District Court, Bolzano, Italy ('Giudice delle indagini preliminari presso il Tribunale di Bolzano').
[128] *La Quadrature du Net 'II'* (n 7) para 135.

personal data of the person concerned'.[129] The specific stage is identified by the Court at the moment in which the public authority decides to transfer the file to a public prosecutor, following two recommendations sent to the subscriber of the internet account used to illegally upload protected materials on peer-to-peer networks. At that stage the Court deems that the Hadopi needs to associate the civil identity to the titles of the work illegally uploaded[130] (these pieces of information, the Court also requires, must be kept beforehand in the hand of separate entities within Hadopi[131]). Because of the existence of risk of serious interferences with the rights to privacy and data protection provoked by the linking of identities with the type of work uploaded, that linking must be authorised by an independent review before the file is sent to the public prosecutor.

To conclude, three remarks can be made in relation to the approach followed applying the proportionality test *lato sensu* in *La Quadrature du Net 'II'*. Firstly, this judgment at least indirectly confirms the relatively more conscious and 'appeased' recognition that the existence (or not) of procedural safeguards is not germane to the classic notion of 'necessity' or of 'strict necessity'. Rather, the existence of safeguards impacts directly on the assessment of strict proportionality. Methodologically speaking, this is a welcome development insofar as it allows the legal reasoning to follow a more cogent and predictable logic, despite the structuring of the test as performed in the judgment is not itself exempt of difficulties. Safeguards are tools to reduce the cost in terms of the interference with the fundamental rights in question and even up the balance with the other conflicting fundamental rights or objectives of general interest.

Nevertheless, and secondly, the very fact that the outcome of strict proportionality test is made dependent upon the existence of safeguards seems to contradict the rationale of a 'pure balancing' exercise. Safeguards—especially if mandatory—can be conceptually equated to rules, and where new rules are required, the matter becomes one of compliance with such rules rather than assessing costs against benefits.[132] In other words, if one follows the distinction introduced by Alexy between 'rules' and 'principles',[133] an assessment of 'costs' and 'benefits' legally relevant should intervene where compliance with existing provisions has already been decided, and the balancing should ideally come as a logically subsequent step. What remains to be done is the application of the strict proportionality test as a method to optimise the coexistence of conflicting principles. The approach followed in *La Quadrature du Net 'II'*, not different to the earlier case law analysed in this chapter, consists in mandating certain safeguards deducted from the context in a very sophisticated manner. Only the existence of certain specific safeguards allows to ensure a correct outcome of the balancing exercise. The Court clearly states that 'the degree of interference with the fundamental rights concerned entailed by access to the personal data in question and the degree of sensitivity of those data must also influence the substantive and procedural safeguards to which that access has to be subject, including the requirement of a prior review by a court or an independent administrative body'.[134]

---

[129] ibid para 141.
[130] ibid para. 143.
[131] ibid para 142.
[132] Giovanni Ratti, 'An Antinomy in Alexy's Theory of Balancing' (2023) 36 Ratio Juris 48–56.
[133] Robert Alexy, 'Constitutional Rights and Proportionality' (2014) 22 Revus: Journal for Constitutional Theory and Philosophy of Law [iv]. See contra, for a criticism of the distinction between 'rules' and 'principles' Ratti, ibid.
[134] *La Quadrature du Net 'II'* (n 7) para 130.

However, in a 'pure balancing' logic, the costs in terms of effectiveness of achieving the objective of general interest in conflict should be simultaneously considered, but there is no clear trace of this in the ruling.[135] This absence can only be explained if one considers that the 'starting situation' is one of imbalance, in which the Court *assumes* that without the safeguards there is a disproportionate interference with the fundamental right that needs to be made even. In that regard, in *La Quadrature du Net 'II'* holds the rudder firmly to maintain the course of guaranteeing effectivity to the right of data protection amidst a political trend which would like the outcome of the balancing to favour other legitimate interests of general interests over true protection of privacy and data protection.

Thirdly, the full Court ruling is once again a very prescriptive ruling. The ruling could be seen as performing a complex 'surgery' on an already complicated 'body', the 'graduated response system', which was carefully elaborated by the French legislator.

To be clear, this author agrees that the French law at stake, no matter how refined and thought through, did not fully consider the risks for privacy and for the protection of personal data of the persons concerned that it entailed. Nevertheless, the level of refinement of the prescribed safeguards (watertight separation of roles, prior review, etc) is worthy of note. One could hardly blame the French legislator for gross negligence in relation to the protection of privacy and of the personal data of the person concerned: the bar for the national legislator is set very high.

Furthermore, contextual assessments can be framed and conceptualised up to a certain point, and naturally lend themselves to accentuate the elements politically prevalent in a given timeframe. It can be difficult for the legislator to incorporate the safeguards that the Court will consider necessary for the balancing to be correct.

A more structured and coherent abstract approach to the performance of the proportionality test *lato sensu* could help in partially reducing the role of the 'circumstances' and of the 'context', which ultimately remain vague notions, and could possibly contribute to provide normative benchmarks more predictable. Given that its complexity might be one of the biggest enemy for its effective enforcement, data protection law would benefit from more consistent and structured application of the proportionality principle.

3. Conclusions

Whether the information about the where, when, and who of communications can be retained for legitimate purposes in the public interest has certainly become one of the most recurrent subject matters of the jurisprudence of the CJEU. Communication metadata may be very intrusive for the private life of the individuals concerned. So can be information on

---

[135] In the same sense, although perhaps oversimplifying the complexity of the judgment, see Marco Mauer, 'The Unbearable Lightness of Interfering with the Right to Privacy. ECJ on Data Detention in La Quadrature du Net II', in <https://verfassungsblog.de/the-unbearable-lightness-of-interfering-with-the-right-to-privacy/> accessed 15 July 2024.
According to Mauer, 'what the Court presents as nuance is a complete abstention from proportionality assessment for certain categories of data. It does not balance the non-severe interference caused by the retention of IP addresses against the competing interest of combating ordinary crime. Instead, it stops its assessment once it has established the seriousness of the interference. In doing so, the Court is even more permissive than in *LQdN I*, where it used a positive obligation to prosecute certain crimes as a counterweight to justify the retention of IP addresses'.

the political or sexual preference that can be inferred from the titles of movies and music shared on peer-to-peer networks. Against this rather non-contentious background, the Court has applied the proportionality test under Article 52(1) of the Charter and Article 15(1) ePrivacy Directive in a rather unstructured manner.

This contribution has shown that the Court has:

- defined an interference with the fundamental rights rather broadly, by determining *ex ante* the threshold of the acceptable risk as very high. For the Court, no matter the legal safeguards for access to the data, the potential for harm to the fundamental rights—not only to privacy and data protection, but also to freedom of expression—intrinsic in the mere retention of communications metadata, is not acceptable in a democratic society when it is of a generalised nature. The unacceptability of a risk of this magnitude seems to have been the real starting point of the Court in all the cases analysed. This has not been fundamentally altered with the *La Quadrature du Net 'II'* ruling where the Court has maintained a close watch on risks of serious interferences even where they are not immediately apparent.
- adapted the application of the principle of proportionality to the fundamental assumption of what constitutes an acceptable risk, which constitutes in essence a value judgment, the outcome of a balancing of competing interests 'front-loaded' at the early stage. This might explain the conflation of the notion of strict proportionality—the natural home of any balancing exercise—into the relatively novel one of 'strict necessity' and a certain flexibility, or osmosis, between the two notions, maintained notably despite the call of Advocate-General Saugmansgaard Øe in the *Tele2 Sverige* case, and to a certain extent also of Advocate General Szpunar in *La Quadrature du Net 'II'* to more clearly distinguish each step.

The assumption that the risks involved with generalised retention of metadata are too high could be considered an application of what has been called by critics of proportionality as the principle of 'definitional generosity'.[136] According to this view, it is sufficient to consider what is conceivable as risk, and possibly the worst case-scenario (in our case, total presumed failure of all safeguards for access to the data) and then the proportionality test starts to be applied on that basis. However, this entails that judges incorporate a moral judgement in the first step of the proportionality test—identifying whether an objective of public interest exists and attributing a value to it. This in the end undermines the hermeneutical value of the proportionality test and its possibility of constituting a form of rational guidance for the legislator. This approach has already been criticised before the data retention case-law, including by promoters of the usefulness of the principle of proportionality.[137] However, the proliferation of preliminary references—all trying to show the necessity of

---

[136] See Stavros Tsakyrakis, 'Proportionality: An Assault on Human Rights?' 7(3) International Journal of Constitutional Law (2009) 468–93.

[137] Audrey Guinchard in particular underlines how in rulings such as *Schecke* (n 9) or *Google Spain* the Court did not carefully analyse the objective of general interest pursued by the processing operations causing the interferences with the fundamental rights. Rather, it adopted a rather cavalier approach and did not pay sufficient attention to the context and the analysis of the concrete data flows relevant in each case. See Audrey Guinchard, 'Taking Proportionality Seriously: The Use of Contextual Integrity for a More Informed and Transparent Analysis in EU Data Protection Law' (2018) European Law Journal 1–24 (Wiley Online).

generalised data retention measures—has put under strain the theoretical tenets at the basis of the reliance of the Court on the notion of 'strict necessity'. As this chapter has tried to show, this notion lacks very solid foundations and has become some sort of a 'security valve' to which the Court has recourse when flexibility is required. The opinions issued by Advocate-General Szpunar in the *La Quadrature du Net 'II'* cases attempt at reconciling a more foreseeable formula of the proportionality test, and in particular of the notion of strict necessity, with the now abundant and prescriptive body of case-law on data retention, while advocating, if not a *revirement*, a distinctive evolution or nuancing. The judgment of the Court in the same case does not succeed, however, in providing stable abstract benchmarks for the application of the proportionality principle. It rather gives a clear policy direction and a reminder to always integrate 'data protection by design' in every legislation. More and more detailed guidance had to be issued to referring Courts and governments eager to equip law enforcement authorities with effective tools to fight crime or other infringements.

A more explicit recourse to the strict proportionality limb of the proportionality test *lato sensu* could however help make more predictable the application of that crucial principle to the benefit of legal certainty. This could ultimately contribute to legitimise further the choices—including of a moral and political nature—that Courts having a constitutional role, such as the CJEU, must inevitably make.

6
Data Retention in the Proposed ePrivacy Regulation Caught between the Well-established Case Law of the Court of Justice and the Deep Disagreements of the EU Legislature

For a Legally Compliant Way Forward

Xavier Tracol*

1. Introduction

On 10 January 2017, the European Commission ('Commission') proposed an ePrivacy Regulation[1] which would replace ePrivacy Directive.[2] The latter remains in force until the ePrivacy Regulation enters into force.[3] The draft regulation aims to update the provisions of the ePrivacy Directive to all relevant technological developments since 2002, align the applicable regime to that of the General Data Protection Regulation (GDPR) and supplement the GDPR with specific provisions on both electronic communications and electronic communication services. Like the GDPR and unlike the ePrivacy Directive, the ePrivacy Regulation would directly apply in all Member States. If and when the ePrivacy Regulation enters into force, it would become the exclusive basis for the processing of personal data on electronic communication services. The ePrivacy Regulation was supposed to start applying at the same time as the GDPR, that is, on 25 May 2018.

For the time being, Article 15(1) of the ePrivacy Directive gives Member States an option to retain data in the electronic communications sector. This provision sets out that traffic and location data may both be exceptionally retained for a limited period on the basis of a

---

* The views expressed herein are those of the author in his personal capacity and do not necessarily reflect those of EUROJUST or the European Union in general.

[1] Proposal for a regulation of the European Parliament and of the Council concerning the respect for private life and the protection of personal data in electronic communications and repealing Directive 2002/58/EC (Regulation on Privacy and Electronic Communications), COM(2017) 10 final, 10.1.2017 ('EC Proposal ePrivacy Regulation').

[2] Directive 2002/58/EC of the European Parliament and of the Council of 12 July 2002 concerning the processing of personal data and the protection of privacy in the electronic communications sector (Directive on privacy and electronic communications) [2002] OJ L 201, 37 ('ePrivacy Directive'). The ePrivacy Directive was amended by Directive 2009/136/EC of the European Parliament and of the Council of 25 November 2009 [18.12.2009] OJ L 337 11–36. The amendments are however not relevant to data retention.

[3] Availability of data and issues related to data retention—elements relevant in the context of e-Privacy, WK 11127/2017 INIT, 10.10.2017 (12.01.2018) 1. Document partially accessible to the public.

specific legislative measure taken by Member States. The retention is only allowed when it 'constitutes a necessary, appropriate and proportionate measure within a democratic society to safeguard national security (i.e. State security), defence, public security, and the prevention, investigation, detection and prosecution of criminal offences or of unauthorised use of the electronic communications system'. All these measures shall be in accordance with the general principles of EU law, pursuant to Article 15(1) in fine of the ePrivacy Directive.

The Data Retention Directive[4] was intrinsically linked to the ePrivacy Directive. Such a link was already reflected in the title of the Data Retention Directive 'amending' the ePrivacy Directive. In addition, recital 15 of the Data Retention Directive mentioned that the ePrivacy Directive continued 'to apply to data, including data relating to unsuccessful call attempts, the retention of which is not specifically required under this Directive and which therefore fall outside the scope thereof, and to retention for purposes, including judicial purposes, other than those covered by this Directive'. The Data Retention Directive was more specifically linked to Article 15(1) of the ePrivacy Directive. Recital 12 of the Data Retention Directive made clear that this provision was 'fully applicable to the data retained in accordance with' the Data Retention Directive. More specifically, Article 11 of the Data Retention Directive added paragraph 1a to Article 15 of the ePrivacy Directive. This paragraph provided that Article 15(1) of the ePrivacy Directive 'shall not apply to data specifically required by' the ePrivacy Directive 'to be retained for the purposes referred to in Article 1(1) of that Directive'.[5]

After the Court of Justice invalidated the Data Retention Directive in its *Digital Rights Ireland* judgment of 8 April 2014,[6] Article 15(1) of the ePrivacy Directive became fully applicable again. The Commission had to determine whether it intended to propose the adoption of a new data retention directive which would have needed to take account and address the findings contained in *Digital Rights Ireland*.[7] More than ten years after the date of this judgment, the Commission has elected not to propose a new data retention directive, if not a data retention regulation which meets all the requirements set out by the Court of Justice in *Digital Rights Ireland*. The reason is that the vast majority of Member States are opposed to new EU secondary law on the subject. Only seven Member States—Estonia, Spain, The Netherlands, Luxembourg, Slovakia, Portugal,[8] and the Bulgarian Data Protection

---

[4] Directive 2006/24/EC of the European Parliament and of the Council of 15 March 2006 on the retention of data generated or processed in connection with the provision of publicly available electronic communications services or of public communications networks and amending Directive 2002/58/EC [13.4.2006] OJ L 105, p 54 ('Data Retention Directive').

[5] Article 15(1a) ePrivacy Directive (n 2), as amended.

[6] CJEU, Judgment of 8 April 2014, *Digital Rights Ireland and Seitlinger and others* (C-293/12 and C-594/12) ECLI:EU:C:2014:238.

[7] See Xavier Tracol, 'Legislative Genesis and Judicial Death of a Directive: The European Court of Justice Invalidated the Data Retention Directive (2006/24/EC), thereby Creating a Sustained Period of Legal Uncertainty about the Validity of National Laws which Enacted It', 30(6) Computer Law & Security Review (2014) 746.

[8] 'Portugal is of the opinion, following the invalidation of Directive 2006/24/EC, that the Commission should propose a new instrument on the retention of data by telecommunications operators, not agreeing with the addition, in the e-privacy proposal for a regulation, of rules on data retention, especially as such regulation will apply to telecommunications companies while the subject of retention concerns the authorities with criminal jurisdiction.' See 'Comments of the Bulgarian DPA on processing and storage of data in the context of the draft ePrivacy Regulation (FoP DAPIX – Data Retention)' Contributions by delegations, WK 9374/2017 REV 1, 15.09.2017, available at <https://www.statewatch.org/news/2017/december/eu-data-retention-and-the-eprivacy-regulation-member-state-positions-revealed/> 26.

Authority on behalf of Bulgaria[9] —favour it.[10] Portugal is the only Member State which has made public the reasons for its position on new secondary law on data retention.

Analysing data retention in the ePrivacy Regulation requires examining the role played by all the players involved in the legislative procedure, ie the Proposal of the Commission (2), the opinion of the European Data Protection Supervisor (EDPS) (3), the report of Parliament (4), the numerous different amendments on data retention proposed by Council which go in all possible directions (5), and the strongly worded statement of the European Data Protection Board (EDPB) (6), which explain why the ePrivacy Regulation has been stuck in trilogues for more than two years (7). The two initiatives taken by both the Commission and the Council are based on questionable approaches of some Member States (8). This situation therefore calls for a legally compliant way forward on data retention (9).

2. Proposal of the Commission for an ePrivacy Regulation

The Commission broadly defined electronic communications metadata in its Proposal (see section 2.1). In addition, its explanatory memorandum is misleading on data retention (see section 2.2), which fell short of providing a positive starting point for the legislative procedure.

2.1 Broad definition of electronic communications metadata in the Proposal of the Commission for an ePrivacy Regulation

The definition of electronic communications metadata in the Proposal of the Commission is broader than in the Data Retention Directive.[11] Article 4(3)(c) of the Proposal defines electronic communications metadata as 'data processed in an electronic communications network for the purposes of transmitting, distributing or exchanging electronic communications content; including data used to trace and identify the source and destination of a communication, data on the location of the device generated in the context of providing electronic communications services, and the date, time, duration and the type of communication'. Article 5(1) of the judicially invalidated Data Retention Directive provided for an exhaustive list of both traffic and location data which had to be retained. This provision defined them as including inter alia data on the source, date, time, duration, and recipient of a communication, as well as location of the communication device. It also included data on unsuccessful call attempts.[12]

---

[9] 'The Commission for Personal Data Protection as Bulgarian DPA supports the adoption of an EU legislative act on data retention for national security and law enforcement purposes'. See 'Comments of the Bulgarian DPA on processing and storage of data in the context of the draft ePrivacy Regulation (FoP DAPIX – Data Retention)', Contributions by delegations, WK 9374/2017 REV 1, 15.09.2017, available at <https://www.statewatch.org/news/2017/december/eu-data-retention-and-the-eprivacy-regulation-member-state-positions-revealed> accessed 26 September 2024, 3.

[10] Informal Outcome of Proceedings of the Informal VTC of the members of CATS on 8 February 2021, WK 2732/2021 INIT, 26.02.2021, available at <https://cdn.netzpolitik.org/wp-upload/2021/03/eu-rat-vds.pdf> accessed 26 September 2024, 3, section 6.

[11] Availability of data and issues related to data retention—elements relevant in the context of e-Privacy, WK 11127/2017 INIT, 10.10.2017, document partially accessible to the public (12.01.2018), p 1.

[12] Tracol, 'Legislative Genesis' (n 7) 738, section 3.2.2.

The broader definition of electronic communications metadata in the Proposal of the Commission implies that additional categories of such data would be retained in comparison to the Data Retention Directive. This situation is problematic since the Court of Justice considered that this directive 'applies to all means of electronic communication, the use of which is very widespread and of growing importance in people's every lives' in *Digital Rights Ireland*.[13] We are then left to wonder about the considerations of the Court of Justice on the broader definition of electronic communications metadata in the Proposal if it is seized of the matter. In this context, it is rather challenging to understand the reasons why the Commission elected to broaden the definition of electronic communications metadata in Article 4(3)(c) of the Proposal.

2.2 Misleading explanatory memorandum on data retention

The Proposal of the Commission for an ePrivacy Regulation does not include any specific provision on data retention. Its explanatory memorandum claims that the Proposal 'maintains the substance of Article 15 of the ePrivacy Directive'.[14] It mentions that Member States may keep or create domestic frameworks on the retention of personal data which provide, inter alia, for targeted measures of retention. The latter however need to comply with EU law, taking into account the case law of the Court of Justice on the interpretation of the ePrivacy directive and the Charter of Fundamental Rights.[15] The Commission specifically referred to both the *Digital Rights Ireland* and *Tele2 Sverige* judgments of the Court of Justice.[16] The latter decision permits targeted retention of traffic and location data for both preventing and fighting serious crime.[17]

The approach of the Commission set out in the explanatory memorandum is however not reflected in Article 11 of the Proposal which deals with restrictions.[18] Contrary to the mere assertion of the Commission in the explanatory memorandum, this provision certainly falls short of maintaining the substance of Article 15 of the ePrivacy Directive.[19]

---

[13] *Digital Rights Ireland* (n 6) para 56.

[14] EC Proposal ePrivacy Regulation (n 1) p 3, para 1.3.
Article 15(1) of the ePrivacy Directive (n 2) provides that 'Member States may adopt legislative measures to restrict the scope of the rights and obligations provided for in Article 5, Article 6, Article 8(1), (2), (3) and (4), and Article 9 of this Directive when such restriction constitutes a necessary, appropriate and proportionate measure within a democratic society to safeguard national security (i.e. State security), defence, public security, and the prevention, investigation, detection and prosecution of criminal offences or of unauthorised use of the electronic communication system, as referred to in Article 13(1) of Directive 95/46/EC. To this end, Member States may, inter alia, adopt legislative measures providing for the retention of data for a limited period justified on the grounds laid down in this paragraph. All the measures referred to in this paragraph shall be in accordance with the general principles of Community law, including those referred to in Article 6(1) and (2) of the Treaty on European Union'.

[15] EC Proposal ePrivacy Regulation (n 1) p 3, para 1.3.

[16] ibid, footnote 7.

[17] CJEU, Judgment of 21 December 2016, *Tele2 Sverige* (C-203/15 and C-698/15) ECLI:EU:C:2016:970, para 108.

[18] This provision sets out that 'Union or Member State law may restrict by way of a legislative measure the scope of the obligations and rights provided for in Articles 5 to 8 where such a restriction respects the essence of the fundamental rights and freedoms and is a necessary, appropriate and proportionate measure in a democratic society to safeguard one or more of the general public interests referred to in Article 23(1)(a) to (e) of Regulation (EU) 2016/679 or a monitoring, inspection or regulatory function connected to the exercise of official authority for such interests'.

[19] This situation is reminiscent of the second alternative in the following quote by the Romanian playwright Ion Luca Caragiale in *A Lost Letter*: 'One out of two, give me permission: either to revise, I accept! But let nothing change; or not to revise, I receive! But then let it change here and there, namely in the essential... points'.

The latter gives Member States an option to exceptionally retain data in the electronic communications sector for a limited period on the basis of a specific legislative measure taken by Member States in a limited number of cases in accordance with the general principles of EU law. Article 11 of the Proposal for the ePrivacy Regulation however aligns its scope with the wording of Article 23(1) of the GDPR, which provides grounds for Member States to restrict the scope of the rights and obligations in specific provisions of the ePrivacy Regulation. Article 11 of the Proposal refers to Article 23(1) of the GDPR in terms of defining general security objectives justifying the introduction of limitations to rights and obligations of electronic communication services which respect the essence of fundamental rights as required by Article 52(1) of the Charter. These restrictions could in principle be imposed in the area of fighting crime (Article 23(1)(d) of the GDPR), pursuing national security objectives (Article 23(1)(a) of the GDPR) and defence (Article 23(1)(b) of the GDPR).[20] The rights provided for in the Proposal may however also be restricted for 'other important objectives of general public interest of the Union or of a Member State' (Article 23(1)(e) of the GDPR). The latter objectives would considerably widen the scope of restrictions.[21] As the ePrivacy Directive, Articles 6(2)(b) and 7(3) of the Proposal also allow providers of electronic communications to process and retain metadata if necessary for billing and calculating interconnection payments. The approach of the Commission in the explanatory memorandum is not set out either in recital 26 of the Proposal, which provides additional information about restrictions in Article 11 of the Proposal.

3. Opinion of the EDPS on the Proposal for an ePrivacy Regulation

On 24 April 2017, the EDPS rendered opinion 6/2017 on the Proposal for an ePrivacy Regulation. The EDPS stated that 'Article 11 of the Proposal broadly corresponds to the current Article 15 of the ePrivacy Directive'.[22] As mentioned above, Article 11 of the Proposal however substantially differs from Article 15 of the ePrivacy Directive. In this context, stating that these two provisions broadly match is simply misleading.

The EDPS analysed that:

> Article 15(1) of the ePrivacy Directive allows Member States, among other things, to introduce a national data retention regime providing for the mandatory storage of electronic communication data by providers for the purposes of detecting, investigating, and prosecuting serious crime, including terrorism. Following the invalidation in the 2014 *Digital Rights* judgment of the 2006 Data Retention Directive (2006/24/EC), Member States are no longer under a legal obligation deriving from a specific Union legal instrument to introduce or maintain a data retention regime.

---

[20] See Marcin Rojszczak, 'The Uncertain Future of Data Retention Laws in the EU: Is a Legislative Reset Possible?', 41 Computer Law & Security Review (2021) 7, section 5.
[21] See Adam Juszczak and Elia Sason, 'Recalibrating Data Retention in the EU', *eurcrim* (2021) no 4, 258.
[22] EDPS Opinion on the Proposal for a Regulation on Privacy and Electronic Communications ('ePrivacy Regulation' 24.04.2017, available at <https://edps.europa.eu/data-protection/our-work/publications/opinions/eprivacy-regulation_en> p 21, section 3.7.

The EDPS would like to take this opportunity to reiterate that any national data retention regime has to comply with the requirements of the Charter, in particular Articles 7, 8, 11, 47, and 52, as set out in the relevant case law of the Court of Justice. In particular, Member States would have to comply with the *Digital Rights Ireland* jurisprudence, including the latest judgment in *Tele2 Sverige* and *Watson and others*.[23]

In any event, the EDPS considered that 'the mere fact that the intended scope of the Proposal is extended compared to the ePrivacy Directive today, should not be understood as a general mandate for the Member States to automatically extend the scope of application of any -existing or future - data retention regimes beyond the traditional electronic communications services which fall within the scope of Article 15(1) ePrivacy today. At the very least, the necessity and proportionality of any such data retention obligations would have to be demonstrated, in line with the Charter and the case law of the Court referred to above'.[24]

The EDPS thus submitted that any provision on data retention must comply with all the requirements set out in the applicable case law of the Court of Justice. The extended scope of the Proposal can accordingly not be a valid reason to also extend the scope of the specific provision on data retention without complying with such case law.

4. Report of Parliament on the Proposed ePrivacy Regulation

The Committee of Civil Liberties, Justice and Home Affairs (LIBE) is responsible for the proposed ePrivacy Regulation. The Parliament's rapporteur is MEP Birgit Sippel. On 20 October 2017, the LIBE Committee adopted its report on the proposed Regulation[25] that the plenary confirmed with a vote on 26 October 2017.

The Parliament supports a narrower and more precise list of objectives provided in Article 11 of the Proposal which may justify a restriction of rights. It therefore favours the deletion of the general clause of 'other important objectives of general public interest of the Union or of a Member State' (Article 23(1)(e) of the GDPR) from the list of grounds for restrictions.

5. Council: Member States Divided in Cacophony

The Friends of Presidency on data retention (FoP DAPIX: Working Party on Information Exchange and Data Protection) are primarily responsible for the ePrivacy Regulation including the issue of data retention. The Working Party on Telecommunications and Information Society (WP TELE) is however also involved in the matter.[26] The ePrivacy

---

[23] ibid p 21, section 3.7.
[24] ibid p 21, section 3.7.
[25] Report on the proposal for a regulation of the European Parliament and of the Council concerning the respect for private life and the protection of personal data in electronic communications and repealing Directive 2002/58/EC (Regulation on Privacy and Electronic Communications), A8-0324/2017, 20.10.2017.
[26] Joint report on common challenges in combating cybercrime as identified by Eurojust and Europol, June 2019, available at <https://www.eurojust.europa.eu/publication/common-challenges-combating-cybercrime-identified-eurojust-and-europol> accessed 26 September 2024, annex, p 21, section 2.1.a).

Regulation is accordingly not handled in the Justice and Home Affairs structure of Council despite its significant impact on law enforcement and criminal proceedings.[27]

5.1 Initial discussion

During initial discussion in the Council, Germany stated that necessary supportive action taken by operators of electronic communication networks and services in relation to activities referred to in Article 2(2) of the Proposal should be excluded from the scope of the ePrivacy Regulation rather than being subject to an exemption in Article 11 thereof.[28] Article 2(2)(a) of the Proposal provides that '[t]his Regulation does not apply to . . . activities which fall outside the scope of Union law'.[29] The UK, which was still a Member State at the time, similarly proposed an amendment to Article 2(2)(a) of the draft ePrivacy Regulation to specify that national security is an activity which falls outside the scope of EU law.[30] Poland argued that Article 7(3) of the Proposal which deals with both the storage and erasure of electronic communications metadata for the purpose of billing 'should be obligatory, i.e. it should include an obligation to store the data for this length of time'.[31] Regarding the period of retention, Poland deemed that 'data should be stored for at least 12 months',[32] whilst Slovakia considered it 'necessary to set a common minimum length of data storage (e.g. at least 6 months)'.[33] Poland proposed that 'the Regulation (e.g. in the preamble) expressly provides for the admissibility of national regulations governing the storage and use of data in criminal proceedings or for other purposes related to public or national security'.[34] The UK also proposed an amendment to Article 11(1) of the draft by removing the reference to the interests listed in Article 23(1)(a) to (e) of the GDPR,

---

[27] 'Going Dark: Justice perspectives on access to communications data for law enforcement purposes' (10.02.2023 document 6013/23, available at <https://data.consilium.europa.eu/doc/document/ST-6013-2023-INIT/en/pdf> accessed 26 September 2024, p 4.

[28] 'Data retention in the context of E-Privacy Regulation-statement by Germany', Contributions by delegations, WK 9374/2017 REV 1, 15.09.2017, available at <https://www.statewatch.org/news/2017/december/eu-data-retention-and-the-eprivacy-regulation-member-state-positions-revealed> accessed 26 September 2024, p 5.

[29] EC Proposal ePrivacy Regulation (n 1).

[30] 'UK proposals for possible solutions to ensuring the availability of communications data in context of the e-Privacy regulatory framework', Contributions by delegations, WK 9374/2017 REV 1, 15.09.2017, LIMITE, available at <https://www.statewatch.org/news/2017/december/eu-data-retention-and-the-eprivacy-regulation-member-state-positions-revealed> accessed 26 September 2024, p 12.

[31] 'PL contribution following the request of the Presidency at the DAPIX-FoP meeting on data retention of 17 July 2017', Contributions by delegations, WK 9374/2017 REV 1, 15.09.2017, available at <https://www.statewatch.org/news/2017/december/eu-data-retention-and-the-eprivacy-regulation-member-state-positions-revealed> accessed 26 September 2024, p 8, para 2.

[32] 'PL contribution following the request of the Presidency at the DAPIX-FoP meeting on data retention of 17 July 2017', Contributions by delegations, WK 9374/2017 REV 1, 15.09.2017, available at <https://www.statewatch.org/news/2017/december/eu-data-retention-and-the-eprivacy-regulation-member-state-positions-revealed> accessed 26 September 2024, p 8, para 2.

[33] 'Contribution of Slovakia to the discussions on data retention', Contributions by delegations, WK 9374/2017 REV 1, 15.09.2017, available at <https://www.statewatch.org/news/2017/december/eu-data-retention-and-the-eprivacy-regulation-member-state-positions-revealed> accessed 26 September 2024, p 12.

[34] 'PL contribution following the request of the Presidency at the DAPIX-FoP meeting on data retention of 17 July 2017', Contributions by delegations, WK 9374/2017 REV 1, 15.09.2017, available at <https://www.statewatch.org/news/2017/december/eu-data-retention-and-the-eprivacy-regulation-member-state-positions-revealed/> accessed 26 September 2024, p 8, para 2.

directly inserting the specified grounds for derogation by excluding the reference to national security.[35]

On 10 October 2017, '[d]elegations agreed that alongside developing specific legislation on data retention for the purposes of fighting crime a complementary approach could be considered in the context of the ePrivacy Regulation. The aim of such an approach would be to ensure the availability of communications metadata processed for business purposes, while not imposing a specific storage obligation on providers for the purposes of prevention and prosecution of crime as such in the draft Regulation'.[36]

5.2 Bulgarian Presidency of the Council: no common position of the Council

On 7 February 2018, the Bulgarian Presidency of the Council stated that:

'Article 11(2) requires ECS providers to establish internal procedures for responding to requests for access to end-users' data and to provide Data Protection Authority (DPA) with information about the procedures, number of requests, justification and their response. The aim of this provision is to provide the DPA with statistical information allowing for adequate monitoring of the application of Article 11(1).

Delegations raised a number of concerns with regard to this provision. Some requested clarifications on which categories of data or documents [Electronic Communications Service] ECS providers have to retain and for how long. Others asked about the purpose of the DPA collecting such data. On the other hand, there was also a proposal to provide more detailed information to the DPAs, which would allow DPAs to assess the general situation as well as individual requests for access to end-users' data.[37]

The work of the Bulgarian Presidency did not result in any common position of the Council by 23 November 2018.

5.3 Romanian Presidency of the Council: An Attempt to Reach a Compromise

On 14 February 2019, the Belgian, Estonian, Dutch, Austrian, Latvian, Danish, French, and British delegations to the Council issued a non-paper,[38] considering that the ePrivacy

---

[35] 'UK proposals for possible solutions to ensuring the availability of communications data in context of the e-Privacy regulatory framework', Contributions by delegations, WK 9374/2017 REV 1, 15.09.2017, available at <https://www.statewatch.org/news/2017/december/eu-data-retention-and-the-eprivacy-regulation-member-state-positions-revealed/> accessed 26 September 2024, p 22.

[36] Availability of data and issues related to data retention—elements relevant in the context of e-Privacy, WK 11127/2017 INIT, 10.10.2017, document partially accessible to the public (12.01.2018), p 12, section II.

[37] Council of the European Union, Document 5827/18, 07.02.2018, available at <https://data.consilium.europa.eu/doc/document/ST-5827-2018-INIT/en/pdf>, p 4.

[38] A non-paper is an informal non-legally binding document put forward in closed negotiations within EU institutions in order to seek agreement on some contentious procedural or policy issue. Often circulated by delegations of Member States to the Council or the Commission, non-papers seek to test the reaction of other parties to possible solutions, without necessarily committing the proposer or reflecting its public position.

Regulation should allow for 'the possibility for existing and future data retention regimes'.[39] They submitted that a new Article 7(2a) should be added to the draft ePrivacy Regulation which would provide that 'Union or national law may impose an obligation on the providers of the electronic communication services to retain metadata for a longer period of time, where such an obligation respects the essence of the fundamental rights and freedoms and is a necessary, appropriate and proportionate measure in a democratic society to safeguard the prevention, investigation, detection or prosecution of criminal offences'.[40]

Following a discussion in a joint meeting of the WP TELE and FoP DAPIX under the Justice and Home Affairs Council on the basis of this non-paper and taking into account the concerns raised by delegations, the Romanian Presidency of the Council has proposed on 22 February 2019 a compromise text for Article 11(1) of the draft Regulation.[41] It is accompanied by amendments to corresponding recital 26 of the draft Regulation.[42]

5.4 Finnish Presidency of the Council: Non-adoption of the General Approach submitted to the COREPER

Article 7(4) of the draft Regulation sets out that 'Union or Member state law may provide in accordance with Article 11 that the electronic communications metadata is retained for a limited period that is longer than the period set out in this Article'.[43] On 26 July 2019, the Finnish Presidency of the Council introduced in Article 7(4) of the draft Regulation the possibility for domestic law of Member States to provide that the electronic communications metadata be retained for a limited period which is longer than the period set in Article 7 of the draft Regulation.[44] It consequently deleted similar

---

[39] Council of the European Union, Document 6358/19, 14.02.2019, available at <https://www.accessnow.org/cms/assets/uploads/2019/05/ePrivacy-Access-to-Document.pdf> p 2.
[40] ibid p 5.
[41] Article 11(1) on restrictions of the draft regulation provided that 'Union or Member State law may restrict by way of a legislative measure the scope of the obligations and rights provided for in Articles 5 to 8 where such a restriction respects the essence of the fundamental rights and freedoms and is a necessary, appropriate and proportionate measure in a democratic society to safeguard one or more of the general public interests referred to in Article 23(1)(a) (c) to (e), (i), and (j) of Regulation (EU) 2016/679 or a monitoring, inspection or regulatory function connected to the exercise of official authority for such interests. **To that end and under the same conditions, Union or Member State law may, inter alia, impose an obligation on the providers of electronic communication services to retain electronic communications data to safeguard one or more of the general public interests referred to in this paragraph, for a limited period of time longer than the one provided for in Article 7**' (Council of the European Union, Document 6771/19, 22.02.2019, annex, p 62; see also Council of the European Union, Document 1001/19, 12.07.2019, annex, p 64).
[42] ibid, p 2. Recital 26 set out that 'this Regulation should not affect the ability of Member States to carry out lawful interception of electronic communications or take other measures, *such as measures providing for the retention of data for a limited period of time*, if necessary and proportionate to safeguard the public interests mentioned above, in accordance with the Charter of Fundamental Rights of the European Union and the European Convention for the Protection of Human Rights and Fundamental Freedoms, as interpreted by the Court of Justice of the European Union and of the European Court of Human Rights' (Council of the European Union, Document 6771/19, 22.02.2019, annex, p 32; see also Council of the European Union, Document 11001/19, 12.07.2019, annex, p 32).
[43] Council of the European Union, Document 11291/19, 26.07.2019, annex, p 60; see also Council of the European Union, Document 12293/19, 18.09.2019, annex, p 60; Council of the European Union, Document 12633, 04.10.2019, annex, p 62; Council of the European Union, Document 13080/19, 17.10.2019, annex, p 62; Council of the European Union, Document 13632, 30.10.2019, annex, p 69.
[44] Council of the European Union, Document 11291/19, 26.07.2019, p 4, para 5.

Article 11(1) of the draft Regulation[45] whilst recital 26 thereof remained unaltered[46] until 4 November 2020.[47]

On 8 November 2019, the Finnish Presidency of the Council removed the reference to Article 11 in Article 7(4) of the draft Regulation.[48] It, however, added a reliance on safeguarding public security. On 27 November 2019, the Finnish Presidency submitted a General Approach to the COREPER[49] which was not adopted.[50]

5.5 La Quadrature du Net and Privacy International judgments of the Court of Justice and German Presidency of the Council

On 6 October 2020, the Court of Justice rendered its two judgments in *La Quadrature du Net and others, French Data Networks and others, Ordre des Barreaux francophone and germanophone and others*, and *Privacy International* (see section 5.5.1). These two judicial decisions led to the compromise proposal made by the German Presidency of the Council (see section 5.5.2).

5.5.1 La Quadrature du Net and Privacy International judgments of the Court of Justice

In the *La Quadrature du Net 'I'*[51] and *Privacy International*[52] judgments, the Court of Justice interpreted both Article 1(3) on scope and Article 15(1) of the ePrivacy Directive in light of Article 4(2) about national security of the Treaty on the EU and Articles 7 about respect for private life, Article 8 about protection of personal data, Article 11 about freedom of expression and information, and Article 52(1) about the principle of proportionality

---

[45] Council of the European Union, Document 11291/19, 26.07.2019, annex, p 65. See also Council of the European Union, Document 12293/19, 18.09.2019, annex, p 65; Council of the European Union, Document 12633, 04.10.2019, annex, p 67; Council of the European Union, Document 13080/19, 17.10.2019, annex, p 67; Council of the European Union, Document 13632, 30.10.2019, annex, p 74; Council of the European Union, Document 13808/19, 08.11.2019, annex, p 69.

[46] Council of the European Union, Document 11291/19, 26.07.2019, annex, p 34. See also Council of the European Union, Document 12293/19, 18.09.2019, p 33; Council of the European Union, Document 12633, 04.10.2019, annex, p 33; Council of the European Union, Document 13080/19, 17.10.2019, annex, p 33; Council of the European Union, Document 13632, 30.10.2019, annex, p 40; Council of the European Union, Document 13808/19, 08.11.2019, annex, p 35; Council of the European Union, Document 14054/19, 15.11.2019, available at <https://data.consilium.europa.eu/doc/document/ST-14068-2019-INIT/en/pdf> accessed 26 September 2024, annex, p 37; Council of the European Union, Document 14068/19, 18.11.2019, available at <https://data.consilium.europa.eu/doc/document/ST-14068-2019-INIT/en/pdf> accessed 26 September 2024, annex, p 37 and 38; Council of the European Union, Document 6543/20, 06.03.2020, annex, p 40 and 41; Council of the European Union, Document 9931/20, 04.11.2020, annex, p 44 and 45.

[47] Council of the European Union, Document 9931/20, 04.11.2020, annex, p 44 and 45.

[48] Council of the European Union, Document 13808/19, 08.11.2019, p 2, para 4. Article 7(4) of the draft Regulation set out that '*Union or Member state law may provide in accordance with Article 11 that the electronic communications metadata is retained, **in order to safeguar public security**, for a limited period that is longer than the period set out in this Article*' [sic]. See Council of the European Union, Document 14068/19, 18.11.2019, available at <https://data.consilium.europa.eu/doc/document/ST-14068-2019-INIT/en/pdf>, annex, p 66; Council of the European Union, Document 5979/20, 21.02.2020, annex, p 28.

[49] Council of the European Union, Document 14068/19, 18.11.2019.

[50] Council of the European Union, Progress report, document 13106/20, 23.11.2020, available at https://data.consilium.europa.eu/doc/document/ST-13106-2020-INIT/en/pdf, p 3, para 5.

[51] CJEU, Judgment of 6 October 2020, *La Quadrature du Net and others* (C-511/18, C-512/18 and C-520/18) ECLI:EU:C:2020:791 ('*La Quadrature du Net 'I'*'), paras 90, 92, 96–98, 101, and 102.

[52] CJEU, Judgment of 6 October 2020, *Privacy International* (C-623/17) ECLI:EU:C:2020:790, paras 30, 33, 35, 39, 42, 43, 46, 47, and 49.

of the Charter. In the *Privacy International* judgment, the Court of Justice ruled that the ePrivacy Directive read in light of Article 4(2) of the Treaty on the EU 'must be interpreted as meaning that national legislation enabling a State authority to require providers of electronic communications to forward traffic data and location data to the security and intelligence agencies for the purpose of safeguarding national security falls within the scope of that directive'.[53] The Court of Justice also ruled that Article 15(1) of the ePrivacy Directive read in light of Article 4(2) of the Treaty and Articles 7, 8, 11, and 52(1) of the Charter 'must be interpreted as precluding national legislation enabling a State authority to require providers of electronic communications services to carry out the general and indiscriminate transmission of traffic data and location data to the security and intelligence agencies for the purpose of safeguarding national security'.[54] In the *La Quadrature du Net 'I'* judgment, the Court of Justice identified a diverse range of situations in which EU law permits retention of traffic and location data by providers of electronic communications services on a general and indiscriminate basis to safeguard national security provided strict requirements are met. The Court of Justice reiterated that EU law precludes general and indiscriminate retention of traffic and location data to combat crime and safeguard public security, but allows general and indiscriminate retention of IP addresses and data identifying users of electronic communications services to combat crime and safeguard public security. In addition, the Court of Justice found that EU law allows automated analysis of traffic and location data and targeted real-time collection of traffic and location data for national security purposes.[55]

5.5.2 Compromise proposal made by the German Presidency of the Council

On 4 November 2020, the German Presidency of the Council referred the Regulation to further consultations and made a compromise proposal. It proposed to delete amendments which had been previously introduced on data retention, in particular Articles 6(1)(d) and 7(4) in light of the *Privacy International* judgment.[56] The German Presidency proposed to adhere to the general content of Article 11 as initially proposed by the Commission. The German Presidency proposed to amend recital 26 of the draft Regulation.[57]

The reactions of Member States to the amendments proposed by the German Presidency were rather mixed. Many Member States would have liked to keep the provisions on data

---

[53] ibid para 83(1).
[54] ibid para 83(2).
[55] Ibid, disposition, para 2. See Sarah Eskens, 'The Ever-Growing Complexity of the Data Retention Discussion in the EU: An in-Depth Review of *La Quadrature du Net and others* and *Privacy International*' 1 European Data Protection Law Review (2022) 143, 154, and 155.
[56] Council of the European Union, Progress report, document 13106/20, 23.11.2020, available at <https://data.consilium.europa.eu/doc/document/ST-13106-2020-INIT/en/pdf> p 3, para 8, and footnote 12.
[57] '[T]*his Regulation should not affect the ability of Member States to carry out lawful interception of electronic communications, including by requiring providers to enable and assist competent authorities in carrying out lawful interceptions, or take other measures, such as legislative measures providing for the retention of data for a limited period of time,* if necessary and proportionate to safeguard the public interests mentioned above, in accordance w th the Charter of Fundamental Rights of the European Union and the European Convention for the Protection of Human Rights and Fundamental Freedoms, as interpreted by the Court of Justice of the European Union and of the European Court of Human Rights' (Council of the European Union, Document 9931/20, 04.11.2020, annex, p 44 and 45; see also Council of the European Union, Document 5008/21, 05.01.2021, available at <https://data.consilium.europa.eu/doc/document/ST-5008-2021-INIT/en/pdf> annex I, p 47; Council of the European Union, Document 5642/21, 29.01.2021, available at <https://data.consilium.europa.eu/doc/document/ST-13548-2021-INIT/en/pdf> annex I, p 4s3; Council of the European Union, Document 6087, 10.02.2021, annex I, p 30 and 31).

retention proposed by the Finnish Presidency of the Council. Other Member States requested a broader exemption of security related issues from the scope of the proposal.[58]

The Portuguese Presidency of Council subsequently specified that the subject matter of this amendment was the '[p]ossibility for union or MS law derogations. CSAM. Interception under law enforcement authorities'.[59]

5.6 Portuguese Presidency of the Council: four controversial proposals

The Portuguese Presidency of the Council made four proposals, ie it proposed amendments to Article 2(2) of the draft Regulation (see section 5.6.1), the deletion (see section 5.6.2), and then reintroduction (see section 5.6.3) of Article 7(4) of the draft Regulation as well as amendments on national security (see section 5.6.4).

5.6.1 Proposed amendments to Article 2(2) of the draft regulation

The Portuguese Presidency of the Council proposed to amend Article 2(2)(a) of the draft Regulation on material scope by providing that '[t]his Regulation does not apply to ... activities *which fall outside the scope of Union law, and in any event activities concerning national security and defence*'.[60] On 5 January 2021, the Portuguese Presidency of the Council mentioned that the amendment to Article 2(2)(a) of the draft Regulation fell under Data retention/National Security & Defense.[61] Amended Article 2(2) of the draft Regulation intends to exclude both national security and defence from the material scope of the draft Regulation.

Concerns have also been raised over the version of the draft ePrivacy Regulation of the Portuguese presidency.[62] On 25 January 2021, a cross-section of digital rights groups led by EDRi sent a letter to WP TELE, challenging the exception for national security and public order in then Article 2(2)(a) of the draft. It contended that this provision aimed at bypassing the case law of the Court of Justice on data retention. It accordingly requested WP TELE to reject this provision.[63]

The exclusion proposed by the Portuguese Presidency of the Council seems to be a direct reaction to the two *La Quadrature du Net 'I'* and *Privacy International* judgments. The scope of this exclusion would however be limited to activities of electronic communications providers which fall within the scope of EU law but are carried out on behalf of a public authority in relation to safeguarding national security and defence. Such activities would be excluded from the scope of the ePrivacy Regulation. They would, however, not be excluded from the scope of EU law.

---

[58] Council of the European Union, Progress report, Document 13106/20, 23.11.2020, available at <https://data.consilium.europa.eu/doc/document/ST-13106-2020-INIT/en/pdf> p 4, para 10.
[59] Council of the European Union, Document 5008/21, 05.01.2021, available at <https://data.consilium.europa.eu/doc/document/ST-5008-2021-INIT/en/pdf> annex II, p 113.
[60] Council of the European Union, Document 9931/20, 04.11.2020, annex, p 55.
[61] Council of the European Union, Document 5008/21, 05.11.2021, available at <https://data.consilium.europa.eu/doc/document/ST-5008-2021-INIT/en/pdf> annex II, p 113.
[62] EDRi, Strengthening privacy and confidentiality of communications, 25.01.2021, available at <https://www.euractiv.com/wp-content/uploads/sites/2/2021/01/20210125-ePrivacy-letter-EDRi.pdf> accessed 26 September 2024.
[63] ibid.

Regarding the scope of the Charter, the Court of Justice ruled in the *Pfleger* judgment of 30 April 2014 that it applies to national derogations from EU law. Importantly, the use by Member States of fundamental rights provided for by EU law to justify an obstruction of a fundamental freedom guaranteed by the Treaty must be regarded as 'implementing Union law'[64] within the meaning of Article 51(1) of the Charter.[65] In addition, the Court of Justice found in the *Digital Rights Ireland* judgment that the retention of telecommunications metadata 'falls under Article 8 of the Charter because it constitutes the processing of personal data'.[66] The Court of Justice could accordingly review the compliance of both Article 2(2)(a) of the ePrivacy Regulation as amended by Council and domestic law of Member States on activities concerning national security and defence within the meaning of this provision with Article 7 on respect for private life, Article 8 on protection of personal data and Article 52(1) on the principle of proportionality of the Charter.

5.6.2 Proposed deletion of Article 7(4) of the draft regulation

The Portuguese Presidency of Council also proposed to delete Article 7(4) of the draft Regulation[67] in light of these two judgments.[68] It stated that an 'analysis of these judgments has led the Presidency to the conclusion that the general clause on restrictions in Art. 11 enables EU and Member States to regulate data retention in conformity with EU law and there is no further need for additional provisions in the ePrivacy Regulation. Such specific provisions in the ePrivacy Regulation could even entail the risk of further restricting potential future legislation on data retention at national or EU level'.[69] If the EU legislature adopts this version of the Regulation, the Court of Justice would consider the legal validity of domestic provisions about the retention of data on the basis of Article 23 of the GDPR read in light of Article 8 of the Charter rather than Article 11 of the ePrivacy Regulation, which is the counterpart of Article 15(1) of the ePrivacy Directive. The Court would however still have jurisdiction to rule on the legal validity of domestic provisions on the retention of data in light of the Charter including the principles of proportionality and strict necessity as interpreted in its own case law.

5.6.3 Proposed reintroduction of Article 7(4) of the draft Regulation

The French delegation expressed its wishes in a working document of 12 January 2021.[70] It requested, inter alia, the reintroduction of Article 7(4) of the draft Regulation on the retention of data for criminal purposes.[71]

---

[64] CJEU, Judgment of 30 April 2014, *Pfleger* (C-390/12) ECLI:EU:C:2013:747 paras 31–36.
[65] See Tracol, 'Legislative Genesis' (n 7) 744, section 6.1.
[66] *Digital Rights Ireland* (n 6) para 29.
[67] Council of the European Union, Document 9931/20, 04.11.2020, annex, p 71. See also Council of the European Union, Document 5008/21, 05.01.2021, available at <https://data.consilium.europa.eu/doc/document/ST-5008-2021-INIT/en/pdf> accessed 26 September 2024, annex I, p 79.
[68] Council of the European Union, Document 12891/20, 20.11.2020, available at <https://data.consilium.europa.eu/doc/document/ST-12891-2020-INIT/en/pdf> accessed 26 September 2024, p 4, para 8; Council of the European Union, Document 13106/20, 23.11.2020, available at <https://data.consilium.europa.eu/doc/document/ST-13106-2020-INIT/en/pdf> accessed 26 September 2024, p 4, para 8.
[69] Council of the European Union, Document 9931/20, 04.11.2020, p 3, para 5 a).
[70] Council of the European Union, ePrivacy Regulation: FR comments (doc. 5008/21), WK 390/2021 INIT, 12.01.2021.
[71] ibid p 2.

On 29 January 2021, the Portuguese Presidency of the Council proposed the reintroduction of Article 7(4) of the draft Regulation.[72] The French delegation thus obtained the reintroduction of Article 7(4) of the draft Regulation on the retention of data for criminal purposes that it requested in the working document of 12 January 2021.[73] This provision makes clear that even where the Regulation should apply according to Council, electronic communications metadata should in principle be retained for the prosecution of criminal offences.

5.6.4 Proposed amendments on national security

On 10 February 2021, the Portuguese Presidency of the Council made amendments to the text on data retention and data processing for national security processes.[74] Recital 26 of the draft ePrivacy Regulation then provided inter alia that:

> this Regulation should not affect the ability of Member States to carry out lawful interception of electronic communications, including by requiring providers to enable and assist competent authorities in carrying out lawful interceptions, or take other measures, such as legislative measures providing for the retention of data for a limited period of time, if necessary and proportionate to safeguard the public interests mentioned above, in accordance with the Charter of Fundamental Rights of the European Union and the European Convention for the Protection of Human Rights and Fundamental Freedoms, as interpreted by the Court of Justice of the European Union and of the European Court of Human Rights.[75]

Article 6(1)(d) of the draft ePrivacy Regulation permits '[p]roviders of electronic communications networks and services ... to process electronic communications data ... if ... it is necessary for compliance with a legal obligation to which the provider is subject laid down by Union or Member State law, which respects the essence of the fundamental rights and freedoms and is a necessary and proportionate measure in a democratic society to safeguard the prevention, investigation, detection or prosecution of criminal offences or the execution of criminal penalties, and the safeguarding against and the prevention of threats to public security.[76]

---

[72] 'Union or Member state law may provide in accordance with Article 11 that the electronic communications metadata is retained, in order to safeguard the prevention, investigation, detection or prosecution of criminal offences or the execution of criminal penalties, and the safeguarding against and the prevention of threats to public security, for a limited period that is longer than the period set out in this Article. that may be extended if threats to public security of the Union or of a Member State persists' (Council of the European Union, Document 5642/21, 29.01.2021, available at <https://edri.org/wp-content/uploads/2021/02/20210129-Portuguese-Presidency-proposal-on-the-ePrivacy-5642-21-LIMITE-.pdf> accessed 26 September 2024, annex I, p 75).

[73] Council of the European Union, ePrivacy Regulation: FR comments (doc. 5008/21), WK 390/2021 INIT, 12.01.2021, p 2.

[74] Available at <https://x.com/SamuelStolton/status/1359482943224369158> accessed 25 September 2024.

[75] Council of the European Union, Proposal for a Regulation of the European Parliament and of the Council concerning the respect for private life and the protection of personal data in electronic communications and repealing Directive 2002/58/EC (Regulation on Privacy and Electronic Communications), Interinstitutional File: 2017/0003(COD), document 6087/21, 10.02.2021, available at <https://data.consilium.europa.eu/doc/document/ST-6087-2021-INIT/en/pdf> accessed 25 September 2024.

[76] Council of the European Union, Proposal for a Regulation of the European Parliament and of the Council concerning the respect for private life and the protection of personal data in electronic communications and repealing Directive 2002/58/EC (Regulation on Privacy and Electronic Communications), Interinstitutional File: 2017/0003(COD), document 6087/21, 10.02.2021, available at <https://data.consilium.europa.eu/doc/document/ST-6087-2021-INIT/en/pdf> accessed 26 September 2024.

Article 7(4) of the draft ePrivacy Regulation provides that:

Union or Member State law may provide that the electronic communications metadata is retained, including under any retention measure that respects the essence of the fundamental rights and freedoms and is a necessary and proportionate measure in a democratic society, in order to safeguard the prevention, investigation, detection or prosecution of criminal offences or the execution of criminal penalties, and the safeguarding against and the prevention of threats to public security, for a limited period. The duration of the retention may be extended if threats to public security of the Union or of a Member State persists.[77]

This provision reflects new Article 7(2a) proposed by the eight delegations to the Council in their non-paper of 14 February 2019 and the wishes of the French delegation expressed in a working document of 12 January 2021.[78] Regarding the substance, this provision does not comply with the well-established case law of the Court of Justice, since the scope of the retention of electronic communications metadata includes all criminal offences and is not limited to serious crime.[79] In addition, this provision leaves out the conditions on the retention of electronic communications metadata and falls short of drawing any distinction between categories of data. In February 2021, the German Federal Commissioner for Data Protection and Freedom of Information expressed 'concerns about the general reduction of the level of data protection'.[80]

6. Strongly Worded Statement of the EDPB

On 9 March 2021, the EDPB adopted statement 03/2021 on the ePrivacy Regulation.[81] The Board expressed concerns about processing and retention of electronic communication data for the purposes of law enforcement and safeguarding national security. With reference to both the *La Quadrature du Net 'I'* and the *Privacy International* judgments,[82] the EDPB considered that 'the ePrivacy Regulation cannot derogate from the application

---

[77] Council of the European Union, Proposal for a Regulation of the European Parliament and of the Council concerning the respect for private life and the protection of personal data in electronic communications and repealing Directive 2002/58/EC (Regulation on Privacy and Electronic Communications), Interinstitutional File: 2017/0003(COD), document 6087/21, 10.02.2021, available at <https://data.consilium.europa.eu/doc/document/ST-6087-2021-INIT/en/pdf> accessed 25 September 2024.

[78] Council of the European Union, ePrivacy Regulation: FR comments (doc. 5008/21), WK 390/2021 INIT, 12.01.2021.

[79] *Tele2 Sverige* (n 17) para 134(2); *La Quadrature du Net 'I'* (n 51), disposition, para 229(1). See Xavier Tracol, 'The Judgment of the Grand Chamber dated 21 December 2016 in the Two Joint *Tele2 Sverige* and *Watson* cases: The Need for a Harmonised Legal Framework on the Retention of Data at EU Level' (2017) 33(4) Computer Law & Security Review 541–52; 'The Two Judgments of the European Court of Justice in the Four Cases of *Privacy International*, *La Quadrature du Net and Others*, *French Data Network and Others* and *Ordre des barreaux francophones et germanophone and Others*: The Grand Chamber is Trying Hard to Square the Circle of Data Retention' (2021) 41 Computer Law & Security Review 1–13.

[80] Federal Commissioner for Data Protection and Freedom of Information (BfDI), E-Privacy Regulation, available at BfDI—Telekommunications—E-Privacy Regulation (bund.de) <https://www.bfdi.bund.de/EN/Fachthemen/Inhalte/Telefon-Internet/Positionen/ePrivacy_Verordnung.html> accessed 30 December 2024.

[81] EDPB, Statement 03/2021 on the ePrivacy Regulation, 09.03.2021, available at <https://edpb.europa.eu/our-work-tools/our-documents/statements/statement-032021-eprivacy-regulation_en> accessed 25 September 2024.

[82] ibid p 1, footnote 2.

of the latest CJEU case law, which notably provides that Articles 7, 8, 11 and 52(1) of the Charter must be interpreted as precluding legislative measures, which would provide, as a preventive measure, the general and indiscriminate retention of traffic and location data'.[83] The Board critically stated that 'providing a legal basis for anything else than targeted retention for the purposes of law enforcement and safeguarding national security is not allowed under the Charter, and would anyhow need to be subject to strict temporal and material limitations as well as review by a Court or by an independent authority'.[84]

7. Trilogues Going Nowhere

On 20 May 2021, trilogues, which are three-way inter-institutional negotiations, started between the Commission, the Parliament, and the Council. The ePrivacy Regulation has been stuck therein ever since. The point of contention between the EU two co-legislators, that is, the Parliament and the Council, deals with the capacity of law enforcement agencies to both retain and access personal data from private electronic communications. The positions of the two institutions significantly differ: the Council wants to give more leeway to law enforcement and make data retention a rule, whereas the Parliament is concerned about the surveillance implications of the measure and wants to make it a mere exception.

The Court of Justice based its relevant case law on the ePrivacy Directive read in light of both the Treaty on the EU and the Charter of Fundamental Rights. The Treaty and the Charter are part of EU primary law since the Treaty of Lisbon entered into force on 1 December 2009. New provisions of EU secondary law adopted by the EU legislature should be consistent with the well-established case law of the Court of Justice based on EU primary law and refrain from attempting to circumvent it. If the EU legislature includes in the ePrivacy Regulation—which is part of EU secondary law—provisions which do not comply with the applicable case law of the Court of Justice partly based on EU primary law and if the Court of Justice is requested to rule on the interpretation of such provisions, the Court of Justice would probably invalidate them. The EU legislature should accordingly comply with all the requirements set out by the Court of Justice in its applicable case law on data retention and simply codify it in EU secondary law.

8. Initiatives of Both the Commission and the Council

The Commission and Member States took two initiatives on data retention. On 10 June 2021, the Commission presented a non-paper about the way forward on data retention[85] (see section 8.1). On 20 March 2023, Member States proposed to establish a High-Level Expert Group on Access to Data (see section 8.2).[86]

---

[83] ibid pp 1 and 2.
[84] ibid.
[85] Council of the European Union, Document WK 7294/2021 INIT, 10.06.2021.
[86] Proposal to establish a High-Level Expert Group on Access to Data—Compilation of replies by delegations, 7184/23, 20.03.2023, LIMITE (obtenu par CONTEXTE).

8.1 Non-paper of the Commission

In its non-paper, the Commission stated that parameters such as airports, stations, or toll-booth areas,[87] transport hubs, affluent neighbourhoods, places of worship, schools, cultural and sports venues, political gatherings and international summits of heads of state or large-scale conferences, Houses of Parliament, law courts, and shopping malls may be considered for geographical targeting.[88] The Commission regarded 'expedited retention' as equivalent to 'quick freeze' or 'data preservation'.[89] It provided online child sexual abuse as an example of cybercrime.[90] It defined the phrase 'data related to civil identity' as encompassing contact details of users.[91] The Commission distinguished it from subscriber data that it defined as 'information enabling identification of the sender of a communication (e.g. name, address, username, phone number)'.[92] The Commission added that subscriber data 'can also include information such as ID number, nationality and date of birth, postal and geographic address, billing and payment data, telephone, or email, the type of service and its duration, as well as related technical data'.[93] The Commission has not specified what the mysterious latter phrase is supposed to refer to and entail.

In any case, the Commission attempted to come up with examples of areas and places that domestic legislatures of Member States may take into account for the adoption of domestic law which complies with the requirements set out by the Court of Justice in its case law on targeted retention of personal data. Whilst this attempt is laudable to assist Member States in adopting compliant domestic law, the applicable case law of the Court of Justice on data retention which already includes many examples is more relevant than the non-paper of the Commission on the matter.

8.2 High-Level Expert Group

Member States established a High-Level Expert Group on Access to Data, as confirmed by Swedish Minister of Justice Gunnar Strömmer during the 12th meeting of the Joint Parliamentary Scrutiny Group about Europol on 27 March 2023.[94] On 6 June 2023, the Commission adopted decision C(2023) 3647 final setting up a high-level group on access to data for effective law enforcement.[95]

Regarding the scope of the group, there is 'no point in talking about access to data … if there is no data retained' as aptly put by Estonia.[96] The position of France however gives

---

[87] Council of the European Union, Document WK 7294/2021 INIT, 10.06.2021, p 5.
[88] ibid p 6.
[89] ibid p 7.
[90] ibid p 7.
[91] ibid p 3.
[92] ibid p 3, footnote 16.
[93] ibid p 3, footnote 16.
[94] 'The priorities of the Swedish Presidency in the area of internal security', video available at <https://parleu2023.riksdagen.se/en/conferences/jpsg-europol--the-joint-parliamentary-scrutiny-group-on-europol/> accessed 25 September 2024.
[95] European Commission, Decision setting up a high-level group on access to data for effective law enforcement (06.06.2023) C(2023) 3647 final, available at <https://home-affairs.ec.europa.eu/system/files/2023-10/Commission%20Decision%20setting%20up%20a%20high-level%20group%20on%20access%20to%20data%20for%20effective%20law%20enforcement_en.pdf> accessed 25 September 2024.
[96] High-Level Expert Group on Access to Data (n 86) annex, p 7.

rise to concerns about the general approach proposed for this group. The French authorities stated that 'the high-level group of experts should not be a tool for transposing the now constant case law of the CJEU on data retention and access in a law enforcement context, but should be a body that will propose concrete orientations to face the challenges and difficulties that internal security forces are facing in this area.'[97] Whilst acknowledging that the case law of the Court of Justice on data retention is well established, the position of France is that the group should not focus on its implementation. The group is rather expected to make proposals on the problems faced by domestic authorities instead of contributing to the implementation of the case law.

The position of Slovakia includes a reference to 'the case-law of the Court of Justice of the European Union (derived only from secondary legislation)'.[98] This statement is however legally erroneous since relevant judgments of the Court of Justice are also based on the Treaty of the EU and the Charter of Fundamental Rights which are part of EU primary law. These two positions of France and Slovakia do therefore not represent a very positive starting point to establish a high-level expert group with a constructive approach to data retention in the ePrivacy Regulation. By 15 May 2024, the group has not yet formulated any recommendation that it was set up to formulate, pursuant to Article 5(3) of the decision.

9. Conclusion: For a Legally Compliant Way Forward

The explanatory memorandum of the Commission Proposal for an ePrivacy Regulation states that domestic frameworks on the retention of personal data which provide, inter alia, for targeted measures of retention need to comply with the case law of the Court of Justice including both the *Digital Rights Ireland* and *Tele2 Sverige* judgments. In his Opinion on the Proposal, the EDPS also states that any provision on data retention must comply with all the requirements set out in the applicable case law of the Court of Justice.[99] In its report, the Parliament supports a narrow and precise list of objectives on data retention provided in Article 11 of the Proposal which may justify a restriction of rights.

The various Presidencies of the Council have attempted to reach a compromise about the provision of the draft Regulation on data retention before the Court of Justice rendered both the *La Quadrature du Net 'I'* and *Privacy International* judgments on 6 October 2020. These two judicial decisions are legally based inter alia on both Article 4(1) of the Treaty and the Charter of Fundamental Rights which are part of EU primary law. The *La Quadrature du Net 'I'* and *Privacy International* judgments have led to strong reactions of some Member States which made proposals aimed to circumvent them in the provision on data retention of the draft ePrivacy Regulation.

In light of the situation, the EDPB adopted a strongly worded statement pointing out that the ePrivacy Regulation cannot derogate from both the *La Quadrature du Net 'I'* and the

---

[97] High-Level Expert Group on Access to Data (n 86) annex, Note of comments from the French authorities, p 16.
[98] High-Level Expert Group on Access to Data (n 86) annex, Written contributions for doc. No. 1815/23 and pertaining to doc. No. 5601/23 regarding the creation of the high-level expert group on access to data by the Slovak Republic, p 22.
[99] ePrivacy Regulation (n 22) p 21, section 3.7.

Privacy International judgments. As a matter of fact, the draft Regulation has been stuck in trilogues since 2021. The adoption of the ePrivacy Regulation therefore remains nowhere in sight. The only compliant way forward would be for the EU legislature to simply codify the well-established case law of the Court of Justice based on EU primary law in the provision on data retention of the ePrivacy Regulation.

Instead, the Commission presented a non-paper whilst Member States established a High-Level Expert Group. The positions of both France and Slovakia about the scope of the latter however give rise to concerns about their general approach to the matter.

In addition, the Commission has not proposed any new EU secondary legislation on the retention of data for more than ten years. In this context, data retention continues being governed by the well-established case law of the Court of Justice.[100] The latter must be complied with by all Member States including those which disagree with it and have been attempting to circumvent it in the provision on data retention of the ePrivacy Regulation. The EU legislature does however not manage to agree on the substance of this provision. Last, the hierarchy of norms between EU primary and secondary law implies that the EU legislature may only adopt a provision which fully complies with all the requirements set out in the applicable case law of the Court of Justice.

---

[100] See CJEU, Judgment of 30 April 2024, *La Quadrature du Net a.o. c. Premier Ministre and Ministre de la Culture* (C-470/21) ECLI:EU:C:2024:370 ('*La Quadrature du Net 'II'*').

PART II
DATA RETENTION IN THE EU MEMBER STATES AND INTERNATIONAL PERSPECTIVES

7
Data Retention in Germany
Not a Never-ending Story After All?

Matthias Bäcker

1. Introduction

As in many EU Member States, the dispute over data retention in Germany seemed like a never-ending story for a long time. The legislator twice enacted legal provisions on data retention, both of which were overturned in court proceedings after a short time. This contribution presents the history of data retention in Germany in chronological order, thus revealing a remarkable shift in the focus of the legal dispute. The court proceedings against the first data retention before the Federal Constitutional Court (*Bundesverfassungsgericht*—*BVerfG*) revolved around the constitutional limits arising from German fundamental rights (see section 2). By contrast, the proceedings against the second set of provisions on data retention (see section 3) centred on the boundaries of data retention under EU law. Consequently, it was up to the German administrative courts and the Court of Justice of the European Union (CJEU) to issue the decisive judgments, while parallel proceedings before the *BVerfG* remained ineffective (see section 4). In the current German political debate, the demand for the most far-reaching data retention possible no longer plays a role (see section 5). If a consensus can be reached on the remaining points of contention, this might pacify the discussion on data retention in Germany. By contrast, the Europeanisation of the protection of fundamental rights, which marked the more recent proceedings on data retention, appears to be relevant for many other questions of security law. This development could significantly influence the role of the *BVerfG* (see section 6).

2. The First Data Retention and the Judgment of the *BVerfG*

Until 2007, German law did not provide for the retention of telecommunication traffic and location data. Proposals to introduce data retention were unsuccessful in 1996[1] and 2002.[2] Only the Data Retention Directive[3] led to a change in the legal situation. In December

---

[1] Cf *Bundestag* document (*Bundestags-Drucksache*) 13/4438, pp 23 and 39.
[2] Cf *Bundesrat* document (*Bundesrats-Drucksache*) 513/02, p 2 et seq; *Bundestag* document (*Bundestags-Drucksache*) 14/9801, pp 8 and 13.
[3] Directive 2006/24/EC of the European Parliament and of the Council of 15 March 2006 on the retention of data generated or processed in connection with the provision of publicly available electronic communications services or of public communications networks and amending Directive 2002/58/EC. OJ L 105, 13.4.2006, p 54 ('Data Retention Directive').

2007, the legislator implemented the Directive by amending the Telecommunications Act (*Telekommunikationsgesetz—TKG*).[4] The new law ordered data storage for six months. The categories of data to be stored corresponded to the requirements of the Directive. For the use of the data, the *Telekommunikationsgesetz* contained a provision that allowed the service providers to transmit the data to certain authorities.[5] Fittingly, the statutes regulating the activities of these authorities, such as the Code of Criminal Procedure or the Police Acts of the states (*Länder*), contained authorisations to collect this data. Permissible purposes of use were the prosecution of criminal offences, provided that the offence was either of considerable significance or committed by means of telecommunications, averting dangers to public security[6] and reconnaissance by the intelligence services. The identification of a telecommunication subscriber by means of a dynamic IP address was regulated separately. The legal requirements for this use of the stored data were lower. In particular, such data use was permissible for the prosecution of any criminal offence as well as administrative offences[7] and for averting dangers to public order.[8] Service providers were obliged to store data as of 1 January 2009.

Data retention has been extremely controversial in Germany from the beginning. After the changes to the *Telekommunikationsgesetz* came into force, numerous people took legal action against them before the *BVerfG*. This was possible because German constitutional procedural law allows affected persons to file a constitutional complaint against a statute that infringes their fundamental rights.

The *BVerfG* first issued an interim decision in March 2008. In this decision, the court allowed data retention for the time being, but limited the use of the data to serious cases.[9] In March 2010, the *BVerfG* declared the provisions on data retention null and void.[10] The court stated that the general and indiscriminate retention of traffic data for a maximum period of six months could, as a matter of principle, comply with the fundamental right to the secrecy of telecommunications laid down in Article 10 of the Basic Law (*Grundgesetz*—the German constitution). Since, however, such retention constitutes a particularly serious encroachment, the principle of proportionality dictates that strict

---

[4] Act on the revision of telecommunications surveillance and other covert investigation measures and on the implementation of Directive 2006/24/EC *(Gesetz zur Neuregelung der Telekommunikationsüberwachung und anderer verdeckter Ermittlungsmaßnahmen sowie zur Umsetzung der Richtlinie 2006/24/EG)* of 21 December 2007 (Bundesgesetzblatt part I p 3198).

[5] § 113b TKG as amended on 21 December 2007.

[6] German law distinguishes the public tasks of prosecuting crimes and averting dangers. Both tasks are regulated in different laws and partly assigned to different authorities. Criminal prosecution exclusively deals with past events. Its sole aim is to solve a crime that has already been committed. If, on the other hand, a criminal offence or other damaging event is still imminent, certain authorities such as the police can intervene to avert this danger. The concept of public security includes all legally binding rules. Therefore, every imminent illegal act constitutes a danger to public security.

[7] German law distinguishes between criminal offences and administrative offences. Administrative offences are less serious violations of the law that are only punishable by a fine and not by imprisonment. There are different procedural rules for the prosecution of criminal offences and administrative offences. In particular, only a court can pass a criminal sentence, while any public authority may, within the scope of its tasks, impose a fine to sanction an administrative offence.

[8] In German law, the term 'public order' refers to fundamental social norms. Conduct may constitute a danger to public order even if it is not expressly prohibited by law. In this case, the competent authority can intervene to avert this danger.

[9] BVerfG order of 11 March 2008 – 1 BvR 256/08 – BVerfGE 121, 1.

[10] BVerfG judgment of 2 March 2010 – 1 BvR 256/08, 1 BvR 263/08, 1 BvR 586/08 – BVerfGE 125, 260, English translation available at <https://www.bundesverfassungsgericht.de/SharedDocs/Entscheidungen/EN/2010/03/rs20100302_1bvr025608en.html> accessed 15 July 2024.

requirements be placed on the use of the retained data in statutory law.[11] According to the *BVerfG*, such use is only permissible for the prosecution of serious crime, as well as for the prevention of serious harm.[12] This substantive threshold must, moreover, be accompanied by procedural safeguards. For instance, a court must order the use of retained data, and the persons concerned must have access to effective remedies where such use has taken place.[13]

By contrast, the *BVerfG* set less stringent requirements for the use of data to identify a telecommunications subscriber by means of a dynamic IP address. The court considered the encroachment on the secrecy of telecommunications to be less serious in this case, since the competent authority does not receive the stored data itself and the transmitted data are of only limited informative value. The legislator may therefore generally permit this use for criminal prosecution and for averting dangers to public security.[14]

The judgment on data retention, on the one hand, fits conclusively into the case law of the *BVerfG*. On the other hand, the court showed little sensitivity for the European legal framework of data retention.

The judgment is one of a large number of decisions of the *BVerfG* on security law that the court has handed down since 1999. These decisions have established the security constitution as a distinct sub-set of German constitutional law.[15] The judgment on data retention shares two features that characterise the case law of the *BVerfG*. Firstly, the court's reasoning consistently exhibits a 'yes, but' structure. In principle, the *BVerfG* acknowledges the need to provide the security authorities with new means to fulfil their tasks. This even applies to highly intrusive measures such as data retention. At the same time, however, the court establishes strict substantive and procedural requirements, which the legislator must implement in the statutory authorisations for these measures.[16] Secondly, the *BVerfG* describes these requirements in ever greater detail. By now, the court has issued fundamental decisions that decisively shape the legislation for certain tasks of the security authorities.[17] The judgment on data retention, in the same vein, has established detailed substantive and procedural requirements that considerably limit the legislature's regulatory leeway.

The judgment is, however, unusual and noteworthy because of the EU Law framework of the contested provisions. All other decisions of the *BVerfG* on security law dealt with powers

---

[11] ibid paras 204 et seq.
[12] ibid paras 226 et seq.
[13] ibid paras 239 et seq.
[14] ibid paras 254 et seq.
[15] Cf in detail Matthias Bäcker, 'The Security Constitution' in Matthias Herdegen, Johannes Masing, Ralf Poscher, and Klaus Gärditz (eds), *Constitutional Law in Germany* (Beck 2024, forthcoming).
[16] The case law of the *BVerfG* on security law is primarily directed at the legislature, due to the principle of legal reservation (*Gesetzesvorbehalt*). According to this central requirement of German constitutional law, every action of a public authority that encroaches on fundamental rights must have a legal basis in statutory law. Furthermore, there are stringent requirements on the clarity and specificity of statutory provisions in security law. Such statutes must lay down which measures a security authority may take, under which conditions, and which procedural requirements apply.
[17] Cf on the law of averting danger by the police BVerfG judgment of 20 April 2016—1 BvR 966/09, 1 BvR 1140/09—BVerfGE 141, 220, English translation available at <https://www.bundesverfassungsgericht.de/SharedDocs/Entscheidungen/EN/2016/04/rs20160420_1bvr096609en.html>; on the law of reconnaissance by the domestic intelligence services BVerfG judgment of 26 April 2022—1 BvR 1619/17—BVerfGE 162, 1, English translation available at <https://www.bundesverfassungsgericht.de/SharedDocs/Entscheidungen/EN/2022/04/rs20220426_1bvr161917en.html> accessed 15 July 2024.

of intervention based on autonomous regulatory decisions of German legislators. In contrast, the Data Retention Directive made data retention, though not data use, mandatory.

The German government had, accordingly, argued in the proceedings before the *BVerfG* that data retention as such was not subject to review by the court.[18] The government based its reasoning on the *Solange* case law.[19] According to this case law, the *BVerfG* does not review the implementation of mandatory European law requirements by German legislators, as long as (*solange*) European law guarantees a sufficient standard of protection of fundamental rights.[20]

The *BVerfG* nevertheless reviewed the contested provisions in full, including the rules on data retention. The court, moreover, did not consider a referral to the CJEU to be necessary. In this regard, the *BVerfG* pointed out that the validity of the Data Retention Directive was not relevant to the constitutional complaint proceedings. This was because data retention could be designed in such a way that it complied with German fundamental rights. Regarding the use of the data, on the other hand, the Directive left the Member States considerable leeway. The German legislature had to exercise this leeway in accordance with the fundamental rights of the Basic Law.

These statements are plausible from a European law point of view if one assumes that the primacy of European law only precludes the setting aside of European law requirements by Member State courts, but not a mere examination as to whether such requirements comply with Member State fundamental rights.[21] In contrast, it was hardly justifiable from this point of view that the *BVerfG* declared the German provisions null and void also with regard to data retention. As the deadline for transposition of the Data Retention Directive had already expired at that point, the court directly caused a breach of the Federal Republic's obligations under European law.

3. The Second Data Retention

The 2010 judgment of the *BVerfG* showed how data retention could be designed in accordance with the Basic Law. The legislator, however, did not take up this suggestion at first. The then Federal Minister of Justice of the liberal Free Democrats blocked new legislation until the end of her term in 2013, although Germany was obliged to implement the Data Retention Directive. The Commission therefore initiated infringement proceedings in May 2012.[22]

---

[18] Cf BVerfGE 125, 260 (n 10) paras 148 et seq.

[19] Settled case law since BVerfG order of 22 October 1986 – 2 BvR 197/83 – BVerfGE 73, 339.

[20] In the meantime, the *BVerfG* has partially amended its case law. The court held that even if an act by a German public body is mandatory under EU law, that act must comply with the guarantee of human dignity laid down in Art 1 Basic Law. The *BVerfG* guarantees the protection of this core principle of German fundamental rights protection without reservations and in every individual case by means of its so-called identity review, BVerfG order of 15 December 2015 – 2 BvR 2735/14 – BVerfGE 140, 317, English translation available at <https://www.bundesverfassungsgericht.de/SharedDocs/Entscheidungen/EN/2015/12/rs20151215_2bvr273514en.html> accessed 16 July 2024.

[21] It is in my opinion not entirely clear from the case law of the CJEU whether it is permissible to draw this distinction between the examination and the setting aside of EU law requirements, cf CJEU, Judgment of 26 February 2013, *Melloni* (C-399/11) ECLI:EU:C:2013:107, para 60; CJEU, Judgment of 29 July 2019, *Pelham and others* (C-476/17) ECLI:EU:C:2019:624, para 80 et seq.

[22] CJEU, *Commission/Germany* (C-329/12) ECLI:EU:C:2014:2034. The Commission withdrew its application on 5 June 2014, after *Digital Rights Ireland* (n 23).

The external pressure to implement the Directive was removed when the CJEU annulled it in 2014 in *Digital Rights Ireland*.[23] Nonetheless, many politicians concerned with home affairs, particularly members of the conservative Christian Democrats, pushed for a reintroduction of data retention. The governing coalition, which by then consisted of Christian Democrats and Social Democrats, finally agreed on a compromise. A statute passed in December 2015 was to reintroduce data retention as of July 2017.[24] In terms of data categories, the scope of the new rules on data retention largely coincided with the first data retention and the Data Retention Directive, with only minor changes. In contrast, these rules considerably shortened the duration of data retention. Location data had to be stored for only four weeks, the other data for ten weeks.[25] Finally, the law imposed strict requirements on the use of retained data. In principle, data may only be used to prosecute a particularly serious criminal offence from an exhaustive list or to avert a danger to life, limb, or freedom of a person or to the existence of the federation or a state (*Land*).[26] Less strict requirements applied once again to the use of data with the aim of identifying a telecommunication subscriber by means of a dynamic IP address.[27]

These rules were recognisably based on the constitutional requirements laid down in the judgment of the *BVerfG*. Regarding the duration of data retention, the law even remained considerably below the maximum period of six months which the *BVerfG* considered still permissible. Nevertheless, this law still provided for general and indiscriminate data retention. Therefore, it was disputed from the beginning whether it complied with the requirements of EU law.

4. The Legal Proceedings Against the Second Data Retention

As with the first data retention, numerous persons took legal action to seek judicial review of the new provisions. This time, however, two different kinds of action before different courts were initiated (see section 4.1). These proceedings took very different courses (see section 4.2).

4.1 Types of action and scopes of review

Most persons turned once again to the *BVerfG* with constitutional complaints, in some cases in conjunction with applications for an interim decision. These complainants, however, had to overcome the problem that the *BVerfG* had approved the general and indiscriminate retention of traffic data in its 2010 judgment. Several constitutional complaints therefore pursued a two-pronged litigation strategy. On the one hand, the complainants tried to show that the new provisions on data retention did not fully meet the constitutional requirements of the 2010 judgment. On the other hand, they argued that a general

---

[23] CJEU, Judgment of 8 April 2014, *Digital Rights Ireland and Seitlinger and others* (C-293/12 and C-594/12) ECLI:EU:C:2014:238.
[24] Act on the introduction of a retention obligation and a maximum retention period for traffic data (*Gesetz zur Einführung einer Speicherpflicht und einer Höchstspeicherfrist für Verkehrsdaten*) of 10 December 2015 (Bundesgesetzblatt part I, p 2218).
[25] § 176 TKG.
[26] § 177 TKG.
[27] § 174(1) sentence 3 TKG.

and indiscriminate retention of data contradicted the requirements of EU law. The scope of review of the *BVerfG*, however, is confined to the Basic Law. The complainants therefore argued that the *BVerfG* should use EU law as an aid to interpreting the Basic Law.[28]

The telecommunications company *SpaceNet*, which as a provider of internet access services was obliged to retain data, took a different approach.[29] SpaceNet considered that while the new provisions on data retention largely met the constitutional requirements laid down in the 2010 judgment, it was questionable whether these provisions complied with EU law. The company sought to take legal action so that EU law fell immediately within the scope of review of the competent court.

SpaceNet therefore decided not to turn to the *BVerfG*. They instead filed a lawsuit against the Federal Network Agency (*Bundesnetzagentur—BNetzA*) before the Cologne Administrative Court (*Verwaltungsgericht Köln*). The *BNetzA* is the authority tasked with enforcing the telecommunications law, including the provisions on data retention. SpaceNet requested a declaratory decision to establish that they are not obliged to retain traffic data. Within the framework of these proceedings, the administrative court must comprehensively examine whether the statutory obligation to retain data complies with higher-ranking law. This includes compliance with EU law.

4.2 Development of the proceedings

4.2.1 Proceedings before the *BVerfG*

In June 2016, a chamber of the *BVerfG* ruled on two applications for an interim decision to suspend the entry into force of the provisions on data retention and rejected them.[30] The decisions correspond to the interim proceedings against the first data retention in that the court did not suspend data retention as such. Furthermore, the court this time did not restrict the use of the data. The *BVerfG* referred to the strict legal requirements for the use of the retained data. Although an interim decision cannot be equated with a decision on the merits,[31] the reasoning of the court at least indicates that it stuck to its line of approving general and indiscriminate data retention under certain conditions. After the CJEU had declared Member State regulations on data retention to be contrary to EU law in *Tele2 Sverige*,[32] some complainants again applied for an interim decision by the *BVerfG*. The court rejected these applications as well, referring to its earlier decisions.[33]

In contrast, the *BVerfG* did not issue a decision in the main proceedings for several years. Only the use of retained data with the aim of identifying a telecommunications subscriber

---

[28] The *BVerfG* had previously accorded the status as a source of constitutional interpretation to the ECHR, BVerfG order of 14 October 2004 – 2 BvR 1481/04 – BVerfGE 111, 307, English translation available at <https://www.bundesverfassungsgericht.de/SharedDocs/Entscheidungen/EN/2004/10/rs20041014_2bvr148104en.html> accessed 25 September 2024.
[29] Full disclosure: I was SpaceNet's litigation counsel and developed their litigation strategy.
[30] BVerfG orders of the 3rd Chamber of the First Senate of 8 June 2016 – 1 BvQ 42/15 and 1 BvR 229/16.
[31] In summary proceedings directed against the enforcement of statutory law, the *BVerfG* decides primarily based on a weighing of the consequences that would occur in the case of the provisional enforcement of an unconstitutional statute on the one hand and in the case of the provisional invalidation of a statute that conforms to the Basic Law on the other hand. The substantive reasons for or against the unconstitutionality of the statute are in principle disregarded.
[32] CJEU, Judgment of 21 December 2016, *Tele2 Sverige* (C-203/15 and C-698/15) ECLI:EU:C:2016:970.
[33] BVerfG orders of the 3rd Chamber of the First senate of 13 April 2017 – 1 BvR 3156/15 and 1 BvR 141/16.

by means of a dynamic IP address was the subject of a decision in May 2020. The *BVerfG* declared the statutory provisions to be insufficient.[34] The court, however, handed down this decision in response to a constitutional complaint that was directed solely against several provisions on the use of traffic data. Data retention itself was not the subject of the proceedings.

In November 2019, the *BVerfG* issued a landmark decision on the relationship between German and EU fundamental rights. Although the subject matter of the case had no connection to security law, this decision had the potential to be highly significant for the proceedings on data retention. Deviating from its previous case law, the *BVerfG* held that German and EU fundamental rights can be applicable simultaneously. This is the case if German law serves to implement, but is not fully determined by EU law. In such cases, the *BVerfG* reviews German law primarily based on the Basic Law, including German fundamental rights. German fundamental rights, however, are to be interpreted in the light of EU fundamental rights. In particular, the level of protection German fundamental rights provide must not fall below the level of EU fundamental rights.[35]

This recent approach of the *BVerfG* met the demand of some complainants to modify the 2010 judgment on data retention in view of the more recent case law of the CJEU. The implications of this approach for the data retention case, however, were not entirely clear. This was because the EU law requirements do not stem exclusively from fundamental rights, but also from Article 15 of the ePrivacy Directive.[36] With reference to this provision, the *BVerfG* has in the meantime clarified that the interpretation and application of secondary EU law does not fall within its scope of review.[37] The court thus distinguishes between fundamental rights and secondary law requirements and considers itself competent only for the fundamental rights requirements. This approach draws on the distinction between 'specific' fundamental rights standards and mere questions of statutory law in the *BVerfG*'s case law on German fundamental rights.[38] Whether this distinction can be transferred to EU law, however, seems questionable.

4.2.2 Proceedings before the administrative courts and the CJEU

SpaceNet's administrative law proceedings yielded greater returns. In June 2017, the Higher Administrative Court of North Rhine-Westphalia (*Oberverwaltungsgericht Nordrhein-Westfalen*) issued an interim decision, according to which SpaceNet was provisionally not obliged to retain data. Based on the *Tele2 Sverige* judgment of the CJEU, the court assumed that the German provisions on data retention were contrary to EU law.[39] The result of this

---

[34] BVerfG order of 27 May 2020 – 1 BvR 1873/13, 1 BvR 2618/13 – BVerfGE 155, 119, English translation available at <https://www.bundesverfassungsgericht.de/SharedDocs/Entscheidungen/EN/2020/05/rs20200527_1bvr187313en.html> accessed 25 September 2024.

[35] BVerfG order of 6 November 2019 – 1 BvR 16/13 – BVerfGE 152, 152, English translation available at <https://www.bundesverfassungsgericht.de/SharedDocs/Entscheidungen/EN/2019/11/rs20191106_1bvr00161 3en.html> accessed 25 September 2024.

[36] Directive 2002/58/EC of the European Parliament and of the Council of 12 July 2002 concerning the processing of personal data and the protection of privacy in the electronic communications sector (Directive on privacy and electronic communications). OJ L 201, 31.7.2002, p 37 ('ePrivacy Directive').

[37] BVerfG judgment of 19 May 2020 – 1 BvR 2835/17 – BVerfGE 154, 152 para 85, English translation available at <https://www.bundesverfassungsgericht.de/SharedDocs/Entscheidungen/EN/2020/05/rs20200519_1bvr28351 7en.html> accessed 25 September 2024.

[38] Settled case law since BVerfG order of 10 June 1964 – 1 BvR 37/63 – BVerfGE 18, 85.

[39] OVG Nordrhein-Westfalen order of 22 June 2017 – 13 B 238/17.

decision was that these provisions were never implemented. Certainly, the interim decision only had direct effect *inter partes*. The *BNetzA*, however, declared that it would not enforce the legal obligation to retain data as a whole, that is, also against all other obligated companies, until the legal conclusion of SpaceNet's lawsuit. As a result, virtually all telecommunications companies operating in Germany refrained from data retention.

Following this interim decision, the largest telecommunications company in Germany, Telekom Deutschland, also brought an action for a declaratory judgment against the *BNetzA*. The actions of SpaceNet and Telekom Deutschland in the main proceedings were successful at first instance before the *Verwaltungsgericht Köln*.[40] The *BNetzA* appealed the decisions to the Federal Administrative Court (*Bundesverwaltungsgericht—BVerwG*), the highest court for administrative disputes in Germany. The *BVerwG* stayed both proceedings in September 2019 by means of identical orders and made a reference for a preliminary ruling to the CJEU. In its reference, the *BVerwG* asked whether Article 15 of the ePrivacy Directive, in the light of EU fundamental rights, precludes data retention as provided for in German law.[41] To distinguish German data retention from the provisions that the CJEU had previously assessed, the *BVerwG* referred to the limited storage period and the strict requirements for data use. Moreover, the reference revealed a discernible effort on the part of the *BVerwG* to induce the CJEU to take a more permissive stance on Member State data retention rules.

In the oral hearing before the Grand Chamber of the CJEU in September 2021, the representatives of numerous Member States (again) raised fundamental objections to the court's case law on Member State data retention. By contrast, the German government referred to *La Quadrature du Net 'I'*[42] to justify the German data retention. In a similar vein to the *BVerwG*, the government referred to the comparatively short retention period and the strict requirements for data use.

In its judgment of September 2022 on the *SpaceNet* case, the CJEU stuck to its recently found differentiated approach to Member States data retention rules.[43] Accordingly, a general and indiscriminate retention of traffic and location data can only be temporarily justified where there is a serious present or foreseeable threat to national security.[44] In contrast, the legislator may provide for the general and indiscriminate retention of IP addresses assigned to the source of an internet connection to safeguard national security, combat serious crime, and prevent serious threats to public security. Moreover, the legislator may provide for the targeted or expedited retention of traffic and location data for the same purposes.[45]

Furthermore, the CJEU rejected the German government's reasoning on the compatibility of the German data retention with the criteria laid down in *La Quadrature du Net 'I'*. The Court stated that in spite of the shortened retention period, the data still revealed sensitive information about the persons concerned. Moreover, requirements on the use of

[40] VG Köln judgments of 20 April 2018 – 9 K 3859/16 and 9 K 7417/17.
[41] BVerwG orders of 25 September 2019 – 6 C 12.18 and 6 C 13.18.
[42] CJEU, Judgment of 6 October 2020, La Quadrature du Net and others (C-511/18, C-512/18 and C-520/18) ECLI:EU:C:2020:791 ('*La Quadrature du Net 'I'*').
[43] CJEU, Judgment of 27 October 2022, SpaceNet (C-793/19 and C-794/19) ECLI:EU:C:2022:702; in the same vein previously CJEU, Judgment of 5 April 2022, Commissioner of An Garda Síochána (C-140/20) ECLI:EU:C:2022:258 ('*Garda Síochána*'). Both cases were heard orally at the same hearing.
[44] *SpaceNet* ibid para 72.
[45] ibid para 75.

the retained data could neither limit nor remedy the serious interference with fundamental rights inherent in the general and indiscriminate data retention.[46]

4.2.3 The final judgments of the *BVerwG*

In August 2023, the *BVerwG* issued the final judgments in the *SpaceNet* and *Telekom Deutschland* cases.[47] In these judgments, the court declared the German provisions on data retention inapplicable. For traffic and location data, this result followed already from the fact that these provisions provided for general and indiscriminate retention. They neither presupposed a threat to national security, nor did they provide for targeted retention based on a personal or geographical criterion.

The *BVerwG*, moreover, also objected to the obligation to retain IP addresses, even though, according to the more recent case law of the CJEU since *La Quadrature du Net 'I'*, general and indiscriminate retention is permissible in principle. The German provisions, however, allow the use of these data to an excessive extent. In particular, the competent authorities are authorised to use the data to combat any crime, to safeguard any non-negligible assets or generally for intelligence purposes.

According to the *BVerwG*, the flaws of the provisions on data use cannot be remedied by applying them in a restrictive manner. In this respect, the court comes to a markedly different conclusion than the French *Conseil d'État*, which, in its follow-up decision to *La Quadrature du Net 'I'*, held that the statutory reference in the corresponding French provisions to the principle of proportionality is sufficient to limit data use to serious cases.[48] In contrast, the *BVerwG* points out that it is up to the legislator and not the courts to determine precise conditions for data retention. This position is convincing on the merits and is in line with the case law of the *BVerfG* as well as the CJEU.[49] The solution of the *Conseil d'État* entails considerable legal uncertainty and substantial risks for fundamental rights. A mere reference to the principle of proportionality would in effect allow the competent authorities to define the scope of provisions that are precisely intended to limit their activities. Since the authorities use the retained data without the knowledge of the data subjects and there is, in the case of IP addresses, no provision demanding prior authorisation by a court, there would be no effective procedural counterweight to this far-reaching power.

5. Status of the Political Debate in Germany

Although the judgments of the *BVerwG* have direct effect only *inter partes*, it seemed clear in their aftermath that that the second data retention in Germany had failed, and the provisions would generally not be applied. Consequently, several complainants withdrew their constitutional complaints before the *BVerfG* in the absence of a need for legal protection. A chamber of the *BVerfG* had already refused in February 2023 to admit three of the constitutional complaints against the provisions on data retention for decision.[50] The chamber

---

[46] ibid paras 77 et seq.
[47] BVerwG judgments of 14 August 2023 – 6 C 6.22 and 6 C 7.22.
[48] Conseil d'État decision of 21 April 2021 – 393099, 394922, 3978444, 397851, 424717, 424718, para 39.
[49] cf *SpaceNet*, paras 69, 75, and 101; in the same vein *La Quadrature du Net 'I'*, para 168; *Garda Síochána*, para 67.
[50] German constitutional procedural law allows the *BVerfG* such a refusal if a constitutional complaint has no general constitutional significance and a decision is not required to enforce the complainant's fundamental rights.

reasoned that in *SpaceNet*, the CJEU had clarified the question of whether data retention was compatible with EU law.[51]

This left the question of whether there would be a third attempt to introduce data retention in Germany. At present, this seems uncertain. The coalition of Social Democrats, Greens, and Free Democrats, which has been in power in the federal government since 2021, has stated in its coalition agreement that 'data should be stored in a legally secure manner on an ad hoc basis and by judicial order'.[52] This wording suggests that the governing coalition rejects general and indiscriminate data retention.

Accordingly, in October 2022, the Federal Ministry of Justice drafted a bill that would eliminate the provisions on data retention.[53] Instead, the draft makes use of the option opened by the CJEU to provide for the expedited retention of traffic and location data. By contrast, the draft contains no provisions for any kind of general and indiscriminate retention of such data, nor does it provide for a targeted retention.

This draft is, however, controversial within the federal government and has not been introduced into the legislative process so far. In particular, the Federal Minister of the Interior has repeatedly called for the general and indiscriminate retention of IP addresses to combat serious crime.

On the other hand, to my knowledge, no member of the current federal government has called for the further regulatory options from the case law of the CJEU to be utilised. Even the opposition Christian Democrats, who as the governing party had pushed through the second data retention, have constantly spoken out in favour of retaining IP addresses in particular.[54] With regard to the other data categories dealt with by the CJEU, however, there have been no statements recently. A general and indiscriminate retention of traffic and location data to protect national security or a targeted data retention to combat serious crime do not seem imminent in Germany in the near future.

The recent *La Quadrature du Net 'II'* judgment of the CJEU[55] might, however, change the discussion significantly. In this judgment, the Court held, contrary to its previous case law, that the retention of Internet access data with the aim of attributing IP addresses to individuals does not necessarily constitute a serious interference with fundamental rights.[56] Member States may therefore authorise such retention for the purpose of combating criminal offences in general.[57] The reasoning in *La Quadrature du Net 'II'* raises the question of whether the German provisions on the retention of IP addresses are now applicable after all, at least insofar as they allow access to the retained data to combat crime. If this were the

---

In particular, the court will usually refuse to admit a constitutional complaint for decision if it is inadmissible or manifestly unfounded.

[51] *BVerfG* orders of the 1st Chamber of the First Senate of 14 February 2023 – 1 BvR 2683/16 and 1 BvR 2845/16; of 15 February 2023 – 1 BvR 141/16.
[52] 'Daring more progress: Alliance for freedom, justice and sustainability' ('*Mehr Fortschritt wagen: Bündnis für Freiheit, Gerechtigkeit und Nachhaltigkeit*'), coalition agreement 2021-2025 between the Social Democratic Party of Germany, Alliance 90/The Greens and the Free Democratic Party, p 87.
[53] The draft has not yet been officially published but is available at <https://cdn.netzpolitik.org/wp-upload/2022/10/2022-10-25_BMJ_RefE_Sicherungsanordnung-StPO.pdf> accessed 25 September 2024.
[54] Cf the latest parliamentary motion to reintroduce the retention of IP addresses in *Bundestag* document (*Bundestags-Drucksache*) 20/3687.
[55] CJEU, Judgment of 30 April 2024, *La Quadrature du Net a.o. c. Premier Ministre and Ministre de la Culture* (C-470/21) ECLI:EU:C:2024:370 (*La Quadrature du Net 'II'*).
[56] ibid para 79.
[57] ibid para 82.

case, data retention would partially come back into force in Germany. This would put the ball in the court of the opponents of data retention, who would need to find an unlikely political majority in favour of repealing the provisions on the retention of IP addresses.

It is, however, far from clear whether these provisions are now applicable or not. In *La Quadrature du Net 'II'*, the CJEU called for substantive and procedural safeguards to ensure that data access does not allow precise conclusions to be drawn about the private lives of the IP address holders, except in atypical situations.[58] The German provisions on data access do not contain any such guarantees. In particular, law enforcement authorities can have extensive information about the internet activities of the owner of a particular IP address. In such cases, the retained data would enable these authorities to attribute this information to an individual, which would constitute a serious interference with the fundamental rights of the person concerned. New court proceedings may be necessary to clarify this issue.

6. Conclusion and Outlook

The development of data retention in Germany is remarkable from both a constitutional and a legal policy perspective.

From a constitutional point of view, the proceedings against the second data retention have led to a partial 'dethronement' of the *BVerfG*. In Germany, this court is traditionally considered the natural guarantor of the protection of fundamental rights.[59] Regarding security law in general, the *BVerfG* has in its case law developed strict standards, which have had a decisive influence on recent legislation.

With respect to data retention, however, the 2010 judgment of the *BVerfG* is not significant anymore. This judgment is now outdated both in terms of its scope of review, which was strictly limited to German fundamental rights, and in terms of its comparatively permissive attitude to data retention. Today, the decisive standards for data retention for Germany as well as for other Member States are derived from EU law and the case law of the CJEU. What is more, institutionally the *BVerfG* has not played a significant role in the review of the second set of provisions on data retention. SpaceNet deliberately bypassed the *BVerfG* in their action, which led to the preliminary ruling of the CJEU and afterwards to the—at least temporary—de facto end of data retention in Germany, by exhausting the remedies available under German administrative procedural law.

It seems likely that the data retention case, in this respect, will not remain a single isolated phenomenon, but will set a trend in motion. For individuals in Germany seeking judicial protection of their fundamental rights against data processing activities by security authorities, remedies will often be available before both the *BVerfG* and the non-constitutional courts, whose scope of review generally includes EU law. Should the CJEU continue to draw on data protection cases to distinguish itself as a fundamental rights court, bringing actions before the non-constitutional courts will often appear attractive to these individuals. This remains true even for data retention, although the CJEU has increasingly watered down its

---

[58] ibid paras 95 et seq, 135 et seq, and 164.
[59] Cf on the significance of the *BVerfG* for the German legal system Matthias Jestaedt, Oliver Lepsius, Christoph Möllers, and Christoph Schönberger, *The German Federal Constitutional Court: The Court Without Limits* (OUP 2020).

originally very strict standards since *Tele2 Sverige*, with *La Quadrature du Net 'II'* being the most permissive judgment so far. Nevertheless, the case law of the CJEU is still significantly more restrictive than that of the *BVerfG*.

This potential development constitutes a challenge for the *BVerfG* to redefine its institutional position in the framework of fundamental rights protection in Europe. The court has already taken up this challenge by partially expanding its scope of review with respect to EU fundamental rights. It is to be hoped that the *BVerfG* will build on this approach in its future jurisprudence. Marginalising the court is not in the interest of an effective protection of fundamental rights in security law. There are good reasons to assume that in the German court system, the (domestic) last word on fundamental rights issues is best left with the *BVerfG*. The reference for a preliminary ruling by the *BVerwG* in the *SpaceNet* and *Telekom Deutschland* cases, which was borne by a recognisable unwillingness to follow the strict jurisprudence of the CJEU, exemplifies this. Furthermore, if the *BVerfG* expands its scope of review even more consistently, it can incorporate its rich experience with the protection of fundamental rights into a fruitful steady dialogue with the CJEU via the preliminary ruling procedure. The court could thus become a significant player in a Union-wide fundamental rights discussion. This might prove particularly valuable if Member States continue to exert pressure on the CJEU to water down its case law, as they have done—in part successfully—in relation to data retention. Strong national constitutional courts such as the *BVerfG* could provide some support for the CJEU and thus contribute to more consistent case law. If the *BVerfG* became more involved on the European level, it might hence strengthen both its own position and that of the CJEU.

From a legal policy perspective, the discussion on data retention in Germany currently revolves around a few relatively small-scale questions. Extreme positions have little influence in this discussion. The only major point of contention at present is the question of whether the legislature should provide for the general and indiscriminate retention of IP addresses. While this is undoubtedly an important question, the scope of the debate appears comparatively limited. The other regulatory options identified by the CJEU do not currently play a significant role in the German discussion. There are no proposals to undermine the general prohibition of general and indiscriminate data retention through circumvention strategies of the kind that can be observed in other Member States. German case law may well have contributed to this comparatively moderate state of discussion. Due to the 2010 judgment of the *BVerfG* and the 2017 interim decision of the *Oberverwaltungsgericht Nordrhein-Westfalen*, data retention only existed for a short period of time in Germany. It has been de facto abolished for over 14 years at the time of writing. To all appearances, this has not had any catastrophic effects on the security of Germany and the well-being of its inhabitants. There is hence little evidence to support extreme demands for the most comprehensive data retention possible. Should a political agreement be reached on the remaining contentious issue of the retention of IP addresses, it might be possible to pacify the discussion for the foreseeable future. Unless there is a new attempt to reintroduce data retention at European level, the seemingly never-ending story of data retention in Germany might come to an end after all.

8
The Long Way to the Compliance of Data Retention with European Union Law
The Italian Case

Luigi Montuori and Veronica Tondi*

1. Introduction

In the Italian legal system, the rules on retention of and access to telephone and telematic traffic data are contained in Article 132 of Legislative Decree n. 196/2003,[1] which has been amended several times. The provision places on the provider of the electronic communication service, for the purpose of investigating offences, the obligation to store the data for a period determined in relation to the nature of the information. In fact, periods of 24 and 12 months are provided for, respectively, telephone and telematic traffic data, and 30 days for unanswered calls. A longer retention period, extended up to 72 months, was introduced for offences of particular social alarm, that is, essentially for organised crime and terrorism offences.

Prior to the amendments introduced in 2021,[2] which will be examined below, the retention and acquisition of the above-mentioned information were not subject to any requirement of seriousness of the offences alleged to have been committed, nor to the existence of indications of a criminal offence of a certain consistency. Moreover, following Legislative Decree n 109/2008,[3] a prosecutor's decree was sufficient to access the data, while the defence lawyer was granted the possibility of requesting directly from the service provider the data in his or her client's name. When adapting to the General Data Protection Regulation (GDPR), however—by means of Legislative Decree n 101/2018—the direct access of the defence to data relating to incoming communications had been limited to cases where an actual and concrete prejudice to the conduct of the defence investigation could occur.[4]

---

* This chapter is the result of a joint discussion. However, sections 2, 5, 6, and 7 must be attributed to Luigi Montuori, while sections 1, 3, and 4 must be attributed to Veronica Tondi.

[1] Legislative Decree 30 June 2003, n. 196, 'Personal Data Protection Code'.

[2] Law Decree 30 September 2021, n. 132, 'Urgent measures on justice and defence, as well as extensions on referendum, temporary allowance and IRAP', converted with amendments by Law 23 November 2021, n. 178.

[3] Article 2, Legislative Decree 30 May 2008, n. 109, 'Implementation of Directive 2006/24/EC on the retention of data generated or processed in connection with the provision of publicly available electronic communications services or of public communications networks and amending Directive 2002/58/EC'.

[4] On the problematic issues related to the access to traffic data for defensive purposes, see Alessandro Pasta, *Luci e ombre nella disciplina dei tabulati nel processo penale* (2022), 12 *Cass. pen.* 4465.

That being said, this chapter intends to retrace the tortuous path of the adaptation of the Italian legal system to the requirements sanctioned at European level. After a brief introduction on the orientations of the Constitutional Court on the subject of Article 15 of the Italian Constitution, we then chose to dwell on certain issues, addressed by the case law on data retention, in respect of which it seemed clearer to see the emergence of friction profiles with the European Union legislation, as interpreted by the Court of Justice.

This is followed by an examination of the guidelines issued by the Italian Supervisory Authority (*Garante per la protezione dei dati personali—Garante*), and of the issues concerning the protection of the right of defence, when its exercise requires access to traffic data. On this point, we shall also consider the different articulation of the remedies that may be exercised, as a result of the legislator's latest intervention.

Finally, the most recent regulatory intervention on the subject will be analysed, which aimed to adapt the domestic legal system to European case law, albeit with some persistent critical profiles, to arrive at some conclusive reflections on the actual consistency of the chosen solutions with the requirements repeatedly affirmed by the Court of Justice.

2. Data Retention in the Court of Justice Decisions

The Court of Justice of the European Union (CJEU), in the last ten years, has intervened several times on the topic of data retention and access of traffic data, giving rise to a constant case law of the Court with decisions that represent 'milestones'.[5]

The issue of storage and access to traffic data raises issues concerning not only compliance with Articles 7 and 8 of the Charter, explicitly mentioned in the request for a preliminary ruling in question, but also the protection of freedom of expression, guaranteed by Article 11 of the Charter, as a founding value of the Union and of every democratic and pluralist society.[6]

The well-known and constant case law of the CJEU relating to the retention of and generalised and undifferentiated access to traffic and location data in Articles 5 and 15 of the ePrivacy Directive,[7] points out that the accessed data must be treated in compliance with the regulations on the matter and with the guidelines of the jurisprudence of the CJEU and that (the retention of and) the generalised access to traffic and location data cannot be considered—in the opinion of the CJEU—limited to what is strictly necessary,[8] in full compliance with the principles of necessity and proportionality, in order to be compatible with the combined provisions pursuant to Articles 15(1) of the ePrivacy Directive and Articles 7, 8, 11, and 52(1) of the Charter.[9]

---

[5] The expression can be read in the conclusions made in Court of Justice, 6 October 2020, *Privacy International* C-623/17.

[6] CJEU, Judgment of 21 December 2016, *Tele2 Sverige* (C-203/15 and C-698/15) ECLI:EU:C:2016:970, paras 92–93; CJEU, Judgment of 8 April 2014, *Digital Rights Ireland and Seitlinger and others* (C-293/12 and C-594/12) ECLI:EU:C:2014:238, para 25.

[7] Directive 2002/58/EC of the European Parliament and of the Council of 12 July 2002 concerning the processing of personal data and the protection of privacy in the electronic communications sector (Directive on privacy and electronic communications) [31.7.2002] OJ L 201/37.

[8] *Tele2 Sverige* (n 6) paras 114–18.

[9] In the Court's opinion, only in particular situations (such as cases of threats by terrorist activities of vital interests of national security, defence, or public safety) may access to data of other persons (with respect to suspects of planning, committing or to have committed a serious violation or even to be implicated in one way or another in

3. Brief Remarks on the Constitutional Jurisprudence Concerning Article 15 of the Constitution

Before delving into the individual problematic profiles of the domestic application guidelines on data retention, it may be useful to make a few brief introductory remarks concerning the ways in which the Constitutional Court has, over time, intended to delineate the scope of the protection offered by Article 15 of the Constitution. According to this provision, the freedom and secrecy of correspondence and all other forms of communication are inviolable. Thus, according to what has been repeatedly affirmed by constitutional case law, this right is enshrined among the supreme constitutional values, guaranteeing the living space that surrounds the person, and 'without which the person cannot develop in harmony with the postulates of human dignity'.[10]

The character of inviolability expressly attributed to the freedom and secrecy of communications must be understood, according to the Court, in a twofold sense: firstly, its essential content cannot be subject to constitutional review; moreover, it can only be restricted to protect a primary public interest that is also constitutionally relevant, provided that the restrictions are established by law and are ordered by the judicial authority.[11] Such interests may include the need to prevent and combat crime.[12]

Another significant point consists in the irrelevance, for the protection in question to operate, of the chosen means of communication, which may consist not only of traditional paper correspondence but also of computer and telematic tools. It has also been clarified—including in a recent ruling on the need for the authorisation of the Chamber to which the Member belongs for the acquisition of WhatsApp messages and emails stored on a mobile device and addressed to a Member of Parliament, pursuant to Article 68 of the Constitution[13]—that correspondence is a broad concept, capable of encompassing any form of communication of thought between persons, other than face-to-face

---

such a violation) be granted, where there are objective elements which allow us to believe that such data may, in a concrete case, provide a contribution effective in the fight against similar activities (ibid para 119). However, in the latter case, it is necessary that the national regulations respect the provisions deriving from Art 15(1) ePrivacy Directive, as clarified by the Court in the *Tele2 Sverige* judgment, as regards both the access of the competent national authorities to the stored data and the protection and level of security of such data (see ibid para 124); which it is for the referring courts to verify. In particular, the Court indicates certain conditions to be respected in the event of access by the police (see ibid paras 120–23), such as: limitation of access by the competent national authorities to data stored only in case of fight against serious crime (but see, in this regard, also the judgment of the Court of Justice: CJEU, Judgment of 2 October 2018, *Ministerio Fiscal* (C-207/16) ECLI:EU:C:2018:788; subjecting this access (except in duly justified cases of urgency) to prior control by a judge or an independent administrative authority, initiated upon a reasoned request from the competent national authorities, submitted, in particular, in the context of procedures prevention, investigation or prosecution; control by an independent authority of compliance with the high level of protection required by Art 8(3) of the Charter; information to the persons concerned, where such information does not jeopardise the investigation; adoption of appropriate technical and organisational measures, which make it possible to guarantee a high level of data protection and security; providing for storage in the territory of the Union; providing for the irreversible destruction of data at the end of the retention period (for further elements).

[10] Constitutional Court 24 January 2017, n. 20; 11 March 1993, n. 81; 23 July 1991, n. 366; 4 April 1973, n. 34.
[11] ibid 23 July 1991, n. 366.
[12] ibid 11 March 1993, n. 81.
[13] According to Art 68 of the Constitution, authorisation is required from the Chamber to which the Member belongs in order to proceed, inter alia, with the interception of conversations or communications and the seizure of correspondence against a Member of Parliament.

conversation. Therefore, even WhatsApp messages and e-mails can be understood as a form of correspondence.[14]

Having said this, the Constitutional Court has also made a distinction between two possible means of acquiring for criminal proceedings the communications protected by the above-mentioned Article 15 of the Italian Constitution: interception of communications, characterised by the tapping of confidential communications between several persons in a covert manner, and the seizure of correspondence. The latter—the Court recently clarified— must be used for the acquisition of messages stored on the device and already read by the addressee, because otherwise the scope of protection of Article 15 of the Italian Constitution would be almost nullified, when technical instruments are used by virtue of which reception immediately follows the sending of the communication. On the other hand, the less guaranteed instrument of seizing mere documents cannot be used.[15]

With regard, more specifically, to the external data of communications, and therefore to telephone records, constitutional jurisprudence has for many years brought them within the scope of protection of Article 15 of the Constitution. In fact, it has been observed that the guarantee of confidentiality enshrined in the provision in question cannot be limited solely to the content of communications, but also includes information concerning the identity of the persons between whom they take place, and their circumstances of time and place. Indeed, it is precisely the aforementioned inviolable nature of the right under consideration that leads to an extensive interpretation of its scope of application.[16]

It follows that at least the minimum guarantees that must be observed when restricting the inviolable right to freedom and secrecy of communications must be operative in this matter. It is therefore necessary, in the first place, that the compression of the right takes place by means of an act of the judicial authority, and, furthermore, that this measure contains a specific and adequate motivation, such as to demonstrate the concrete existence of evidentiary requirements aimed at the constitutionally protected purpose of the prevention and repression of offences.[17]

Nevertheless, as will be seen, the Constitutional Court has traditionally ruled against the necessary extension, to the acquisition of traffic data, of all the provisions applicable to the interception of communications, including the authorisation of an impartial judge. In fact, since the information in question does not relate to the content of communications, it was held that it is not such as to affect the core of the right protected by Article 15 of the Constitution, and that therefore an order by the public prosecutor, as 'judicial authority', was sufficient.[18]

---

[14] Constitutional Court (n 10) 27 July 2023, n. 170; see also, on the irrelevance of the instrument used in the communication, Constitutional Court, 11 March 1993, n. 81.

[15] ibid 27 July 2023, n. 170.

[16] ibid 11 March 1993, n. 81. See, on this judgment, Alberto Camon, *L'acquisizione dei dati sul traffico delle comunicazioni* (2005), 2 *Riv. it. dir. e proc. pen.* 594; Filippo Raffaele Dinacci, *L'acquisizione dei tabulati telefonici tra anamnesi, diagnosi e terapia: luci europee e ombre legislative* (2022), 2 *Proc. pen. giust.* 302. See also, on the constitutional case law on the matter, Alberto Macchia, *I diritti fondamentali "minacciati": lo sfondo delle garanzie in Costituzione* (2017), *Dir. pen. cont.* 5; Alessandro Pace, *Nuove frontiere della libertà di "comunicare riservatamente" (o, piuttosto, del diritto alla riservatezza)?* (1993), *Giur. cost.* 742; D. Potetti, *Corte costituzionale n. 81/93: la forza espansiva della tutela accordata dall'art. 15 comma 1 della Costituzione* (1993), 12 *Cass. pen.* 2746.

[17] ibid 11 March 1993, n. 81; 23 July 1991, n. 366; 11 June 1987, n. 223; 6 April 1973, n. 34.

[18] ibid 17 July 1998, n. 281, and 11 March 1993, n. 81.

We will return to this point in our examination of the most controversial points of Italian case law, in terms of the consistency of the domestic legal system with European requirements.

Lastly, it is worth recalling the rulings[19] with which the Constitutional Court deemed unfounded the issue of constitutionality concerning the inclusion of the acquisition of telephone records among the acts for which the authorisation of the Chamber to which the Member of the Parliament belongs is required, pursuant to the aforementioned Article 68 of the Fundamental Charter. This concerns, in particular, the hypothesis in which the data concern communications between a Member of Parliament and third parties. In this case, first of all, the judgment ruled out the possibility that there is an 'ontological difference' between the information relating to the content of the conversations and the external data of the latter, as had been argued by the judge *a quo*, and this is precisely the reason for the attraction of the latter within the scope of protection of Article 15 of the Constitution. In fact, data 'of undoubted communicative significance' are taken into consideration, which, moreover, by virtue of technological evolution, can enable the location and tracking of the user's movements. The data itself, therefore, as 'communicative facts', can also fall within the scope of application of Article 68 of the Constitution, in the part in which this norm requires the authorisation of the Chamber to which the Member of the Parliament belongs in order to subject the latter to interception of conversations or communications and seizure of correspondence.

In fact, the particular intrusiveness of the investigative activity concerning traffic data is liable to condition the free exercise of the parliamentary function, opening up glimpses into the sphere of relations, including institutional ones, of the parliamentarian himself.[20]

Awareness of the considerable suitability of the acquisition of traffic data to affect the fundamental right to freedom and secrecy of communications, as well as of the communicative significance of such information, will, however, only be brought to its full consequences following the rulings of the Court of Justice.

4. Italian Case Law and the Resistance to the Full Implementation of European Union Law

As far as Italian case law is concerned, it is possible to notice that, for years, it seemed to fail to incorporate the Court of Justice's guidance, because of the need not to restrict the use of an often-crucial tool for the proof of crimes. In fact, it is precisely the supranational rules, as developed and applied by the European apex Courts, that have proved decisive in determining the boundaries of legitimacy of measures involving the storage and acquisition of data revealing multiple aspects of a person's private life.[21]

Three main issues will be examined: the problem of full respect of the principles of legality and proportionality; the unsatisfactory conclusions reached with reference to the authority having the power to access traffic data; the solution adopted regarding

---

[19] ibid n. 83; see also ibid, 28 May 2010, n. 188.
[20] ibid 11 April 2019, n. 83, and 28 May 2010, n. 188.
[21] See, for the opinion according to which supranational dispositions reconduct the protection of personal data to a fundamental right of the individual, Tommaso Rafaraci, *Verso una* law of evidence *dei dati* (2021), 7 *Dir. pen. proc.* 853.

the usability of data obtained in violation of European Union law, as interpreted by the Luxembourg Court.

4.1 The legality requirement and the controversial balancing approach in the concrete case

One of the most relevant problems, emerged by the case law of the Court of Justice, can be considered the respect of the legality principle, in its substantive dimension.

Various judgments, from *Digital Rights Ireland*, to *Prokuratuur*[22] and *Garda Síochána*[23] cases, strongly stated the need for 'clear and precise rules governing the scope and application of the measure and imposing minimum safeguards, in order to protect individuals against the risk of abuse'.

This legitimacy condition of national law derives also, and significantly, from the safeguards which Italian Constitution, at Article 15, connects to the protection of the freedom and secrecy of communications, as already discussed in the previous section. This right, according to the mentioned provisions, can only be limited according to the law and through an order issued by a judicial authority, due to its primary importance.

Moreover, the necessity of clear and precise rules, to justify an interference with the right to respect for private and family life, was clearly stated by the European Court of Human Rights (ECtHR), in many decisions regarding secret surveillance[24] or the use of intrusive technical measures, such as electronic tracking,[25] due to the primary importance of the rule of law in the Convention. More specifically, the Strasbourg Court, though including in the notion of 'law' either written statute and unwritten law and case law,[26] stressed the importance of the 'quality' of the law itself, in terms of clarity, accessibility, and foreseeability of its provisions. So, even with reference to interception of communications or measures of secret surveillance, the different way of intending the foreseeability condition does not exclude the need for precise rules, determining the circumstances and conditions on which public authorities are empowered to resort to such instruments.[27] This is fundamental to avoid arbitrary interferences with fundamental rights: consequently, sufficient legal guarantees must be established with reference to 'the nature, scope and duration of the possible measures, the grounds required for ordering them, the authorities competent to permit, carry out and supervise them, and the kind of remedy provided by the national law'.[28]

However, the legality requirement has long been underestimated in the Italian system, in the data retention field, as well as with reference to the use of other technical instruments in the criminal procedure. Before the latest intervention of Italian legislator, Article 132 of Legislative Decree n. 196/2003 did not establish at all the conditions for the retention and

---

[22] CJEU, Judgment of 2 March 2021, *Prokuratuur* (C-746/18) ECLI:EU:C:2021:152.
[23] CJEU, Judgment of 5 April 2022, *Commissioner of An Garda Síochána* (C-140/20) ECLI:EU:C:2022:258.
[24] ECtHR, *Klass and Others v Germany*, 6 September 1978, Series A no. 28.
[25] ECtHR, *Ben Faiza v France*, no. 31446/12, 8 February 2018, para 56; ECtHR, *Uzun v Germany*, no. 35623/05, 2 September 2010, paras 60–63.
[26] ECtHR, *Wisse v France*, no. 71611/01, 20 March 2006, para 33.
[27] ECtHR, *Valenzuela Contreras v Spain*, no. 58/1997/842/1048, 30 July 1998, para 46; ECtHR, *Malone v the United Kingdom*, 2 August 1984, Series A no. 82, paras 66–68.
[28] *Uzun v Germany*, para 63.

the access to traffic and location data, in terms of seriousness of the crime concerned, or existence of sufficient evidence demonstrating its commission.

However, even after *Digital Rights Ireland* and *Tele2 Sverige* judgements, Italian case law, generally refusing the incoherence of national rules with European Union law, basically evaded this fundamental legality requirement, especially through the application of a sort of balancing technique to each concrete case. Through this kind of reasoning, Italian courts considered it possible to overcome the lack of provisions in line with the statements of the Court of Justice, by assessing their existence in the single case under consideration.[29]

So, in various occasions, even the Court of Cassation, as a judge of last resort in the Italian judiciary system, denied the violation of the requirement of the seriousness of crime, by recognising the seriousness of the offence in the concrete case at issue, even if no legal rule on the matter had been adopted by the legislator.[30]

This approach was considered justified by certain statements in the *Ministerio Fiscal* judgment,[31] concerning the need for an assessment of proportionality including the seriousness of the interference with fundamental rights deriving from the measure concerned, on the one hand, and the seriousness of the crime whose prevention and detection justifies the access to data, on the other hand. This kind of reasoning has been interpreted as necessarily implying a discretionary power of the judiciary, in reaching an adequate balance. However, as already remarked, the case law of the Court of Justice is clear, also in its latest pronouncements, in imposing a predetermination of the conditions of the retention and access to traffic data. Moreover, the access to certain kinds of information is explicitly qualified as a serious interference with the rights protected by Articles 7 and 8 of the Charter.

More specifically, the Luxembourg Court refers to 'a set of traffic or location data', which is 'indeed liable to allow precise, or even very precise, conclusions to be drawn concerning the private lives of the persons whose data has been retained, such as the habits of everyday life, permanent or temporary places of residence, daily or other movements, the activities carried out, the social relationships of those persons and the social environments frequented by them'.[32] It is true that, also in the dimension of the European Convention on Human Rights (ECHR), the concept of 'law' may include case law, as already said. Nevertheless, a case-to-case assessment of a broad concept such as the one of 'serious crime', when highly sensitive information regarding an individual's private life is concerned, appears to be inconsistent with the *ratio* of effective protection which lies under the legality requirement.

This kind of issue arose, again, after the first reactions to *Prokuratuur* case, when Italian judges had to decide if national rules were incompatible with the statements of the Court of Justice. Even if some national judgments already denied the contrast,[33] other decisions recognised the violation of EU law, but came to opposite solutions regarding the possibility of a direct implementation of the principles established in the *Prokuratuur* case. One of these

---

[29] For an example of this approach, in the case law on the merits, see Trib. Padova, 15 March 2017, critically commented by Roberto Flor, *Data retention ed art. 132 cod. privacy: vexata quaestio (?)* (2017), *Dir. pen. cont*, and Francesca Ruggieri, *Data retention e giudice di merito penale. Una discutibile pronuncia* (2017), 6 *Cass. pen.* 2483 et seq.

[30] Court of Cassation, III Sec., 25 September 2019, n. 48737.

[31] *Ministerio Fiscal* (n 9) para 56–58.

[32] *Prokuratuur* (n 22) para 36; see also CJEU, Judgment of 6 October 2020, *La Quadrature du Net and others* (C-511/18, C-512/18 and C-520/18) ECLI:EU:C:2020:791 ('*La Quadrature du Net I*') para117.

[33] Trib. Milano, VII Sec., 22 April 2021, commented by Veronica Tondi, *La disciplina italiana in materia di data retention a seguito della sentenza della Corte di Giustizia UE: il Tribunale di Milano nega il contrasto con il diritto sovranazionale* (2021), *Sist. pen.*

judgments,[34] in fact, stated that it was possible, even without an intervention of the legislator, to specify the requirement of the seriousness of the crime concerned, by referring to the list of illicit acts for which it is possible to authorise the interception of communications (Article 266 of Italian Code of Criminal Procedure).

The Court of Cassation[35] did not rule in favour of this solution, which did not seem to comply with the mentioned legality requirement, being unable to fully satisfy the certainty issues already mentioned.

The intervention of Law Decree n. 132/2021, converted, with amendments, by Law n. 178/2021, partially solved the problem, by limiting the access to data—but not their retention—to certain categories of crime, and by requiring either the existence of sufficient evidence of the perpetration of the offence and the relevance of traffic data for the reconstruction of the facts.[36] As an effect, the conditions justifying the access to data must have been specified by the law and must be adequately expressed in the decision.

The need for objective criteria for defining the circumstances and conditions under which access to the data must be granted has been very recently reaffirmed by the Court of Justice[37], even if the Luxembourg Court recognised the possibility for the national judge, in making the proportionality assessment, to exclude the access to data if the single offence, though exceeding the threshold established by law, is considered as manifestly not serious. This has been said precisely with reference to the Italian provisions on the matter.

4.2 The notion of judicial authority and the role of the public prosecutor

Even with reference to the requirement of the control by a judge or by another independent authority, as gradually clarified by the Court of Justice, the approach of Italian case law has been conservative.

More specifically, the Court of Cassation[38] denied the possibility to find a contrast with supranational law because of the conferral to the public prosecutor of the power to access traffic data, as Article 132 of the Privacy Code prescribed before the latest intervention of the legislator. The justification for such a conclusion is found, first, in Italian public prosecutor's status: the authority who owns the power to direct the investigations and to decide on the indictment belongs to the judiciary order and is independent from the executive power. Most of all, Article 107 of the Constitution, as interpreted by most scholars, makes it compulsory for the legislator to guarantee this independence.

---

[34] Trib. Roma, Judge for preliminary investigation, 25 April 2021, commented by Jacopo Della Torre, *L'acquisizione dei tabulati telefonici nel processo penale dopo la sentenza della Grande Camera della Corte di Giustizia UE: la svolta garantista in un primo provvedimento del g.i.p. di Roma* (2021), *Sist. pen;* see also, about another decree of the Judge for preliminary investigation of Rome, in different composition, Alessandro Malacarne, *Ancora sulle ricadute interne della sentenza della Corte di Giustizia in materia di acquisizione di tabulati telefonici: il G.i.p. di Roma dichiara il "non luogo a provvedere" sulla richiesta del p.m.* (2021), *Sist. pen.*
[35] Court of Cassation, II Sec., 15 April 2021, n. 28523, commented by Alberto Cisterna, *Infondata la questione di legittimità sull'utilizzo dati dopo autorizzazione* (2021), 36 *Guida dir.* 68.
[36] Art. 132 of Legislative Decree n. 196 of 2003, par. 3.
[37] CJEU, Judgment of 30 April 2024, *Procura della Repubblica presso il Tribunale di Bolzano* (C-178/22).
[38] Court of Cassation, V Sec., 24 April 2018, n. 33851; Court of Cassation, V Sec., 19 April 2019, n. 36380: see, on this judgment, Luca Luparia, *Data retention e processo penale. Un'occasione mancata per prendere i diritti davvero sul serio* (2019), 4 *Dir. Internet* 753.

As a consequence, some judgments of the Court of Cassation ruled in favour of the possibility to include, in the notion of 'judicial authority' whose control is necessary to access traffic data, both the judge and the prosecutor, also due to the reference to some allegedly ambiguous notions used in the decisions of the Court of Justice. The French and English words 'jurisdiction' and 'court' are an example, because, according to this approach, they do not necessarily refer to a judge.

Even after the *Prokuratuur* judgment,[39] the inconsistency of Italian law with EU requirements was denied by some judges of first instance, because the public prosecutor's independence would ensure sufficient guarantees as to the decision to access traffic data.[40]

However, this kind of reasoning seems not to confer the proper importance to the clear statements of the Court of Justice:[41] the supranational case law does not simply require a position of independence—interpreted as absence of interferences from the executive power—of the authority who is called to put in place a prior review of the respect of the necessity and proportionality conditions. In fact, it establishes that 'it must be a third party in relation to the authority which requests access to the data, in order that the former is able to carry out the review objectively and impartially and free from any external influence'.[42]

Indeed, although the existence of a constitutional guarantee of prosecutorial independence in the Italian legal system is widely acknowledged,[43] the idea of a claimed neutrality of the prosecutor's work has been questioned for many years.[44] Consequently, the Italian public prosecutor, as the authority who possibly requests the access to data and who directs the investigation stage, should not be considered a 'third party', in the meaning accepted by the Luxembourg Court.

In any case, the matter was the subject of a reference for a preliminary ruling by a court of first instance, though the case was removed from the register of the Court of Justice, because the reference itself referred to the text of Article 132 of the Privacy Code, as it stood prior to

---

[39] See, on this judgment, in the Italian doctrine, *ex multis*, Elena Andolina, *La sentenza della Corte di giustizia UE nel caso H.K. c. Prokuratuur: un punto di non ritorno nella lunga querelle in materia di data retention*? (2021), 5 *Proc. pen. giust.* 1204; Leonardo Filippi, *La Grande Camera della Corte di giustizia U.E. boccia la disciplina italiana sui tabulati* (2021), *Penale Diritto e Procedura*; Giulia Formici, *La disciplina della data retention tra esigenze securitarie e tutela dei diritti fondamentali* (Giappichelli 2021) 120 et seq.; Francesco Torre, "*Data retention*": una ventata di ragionevolezza da Lussemburgo (a margine della sentenza della Corte di giustizia 2 marzo 2021, C-746/18) (2021), 2 *Consulta online* 615.
[40] Trib. Milano (n 33).
[41] On the topic, Gennaro Gaeta, *Consensi e dissensi sulla indipendenza del p.m. (a proposito del potere di acquisire i tabulati telefonici)* (2021), 3 *Arch. pen.* 11.
[42] *Prokuratuur* (n 22) para 52.
[43] Also, by the Constitutional Court (n. 420 of 1995).
[44] See, on the topic, *ex multis*, Claudia Cesari, *La disciplina costituzionale*, in Alberto Camon (ed), *Fondamenti di procedura penale* (CEDAM 2021) 108; Oreste Dominioni, *Per un collegamento tra ministero della giustizia e pubblico ministero*, in Giovanni Conso (ed), *Pubblico ministero e accusa penale. Problemi e prospettive di riforma* (Zanichelli 1979) 68–69; Piero Gaeta, *L'organizzazione degli uffici di procura. Note sull'evoluzione dell'indipendenza 'interna' del pubblico ministero: verso una gerarchia funzionale* (2019), *Questione giustizia*; Antonello Gustapane, *Il pubblico ministero tra obbligatorietà ed efficienza, alla luce dei più recenti interventi del legislatore e del CSM* (Bononia University Press 2018) 142; Giuseppe Monaco, sub *art. 112 Cost.*, in Angelo Giarda, Giorgio Spangher (eds.), *Codice di procedura penale commentato*, I (Wolters Kluwer 2017) 125–26; Guido Neppi Modona, sub *art. 112 Cost.*, in Giuseppe Branca (ed.), *Commentario della Costituzione*, IV (Zanichelli 1984) 39; Ciro Santoriello, *Il pubblico ministero ed i cento talleri di Kant* (2021) 2 *Arch. pen.* 1 et seq.; Nicolò Zanon, *Pubblico ministero e Costituzione* (CEDAM 1996); Vladimiro Zagrebelsky, *Indipendenza del pubblico ministero e obbligatorietà dell'azione penale*, in *Pubblico ministero e accusa penale*, cited above, 13 et seq. See also, with specific reference to the acquisition of traffic data, Giulia Lasagni, *Dalla riforma dei tabulati a nuovi modelli di integrazione fra diritti di difesa e tutela della privacy* (2022), *Leg. pen.* 3.

the 2021 amendments.[45] Finally, the need for the authorisation of a judge was established by the legislator in 2021.

4.3 The usability of data collected in violation of European Union law

Another critical issue can be considered the one of the usability, as evidence, of data retained and collected in violation of the legitimacy conditions of the measure, according to EU law.

For years, Italian case law affirmed that a ban on the usability of such information at trial[46] could only derive from its acquisition after the expiry of the maximum period of retention established by the Privacy Code, because of the recognition of an implicit ban to use such information after this term.[47] For a period of time, the Court of Cassation[48] had affirmed the possibility to apply the dispositions regarding the interception of electronic communications, including the provision[49] which reconducts the consequence of non-usability to certain violations, such as the lack of a proper judicial authorisation, or the non-respect of some procedures of execution of these operations. Nevertheless, this approach was, later, abandoned by the Court.[50]

On the contrary, the non-compliance of the access procedure with European requirements was not considered as a valid reason to exclude such usability, even after the *Prokuratuur* case.[51] Moreover, according to the Court of Cassation's approach,[52] the absence of a duly justified order of the judicial authority, as a basis for the access to data, though interfering with the usability of information, merely affected the validity of the procedure for the acquisition of the latter, but it did not imply the invalidity of the means of proof itself. Consequently, even if normally, in the Italian legal system, no remedy should be available in the case of non-usability of evidence deriving from the violation of a ban on its acquisition, these judgments recognised the possibility to simply overcome this procedural consequence, by adopting, *ex post*, the judicial authority's decree.

However, it must be recalled that, even before the latest decisions of the Court of Justice, according to some scholars, the usability of data collected in violation of the provisions of Articles 7 and 8 of the Charter should be excluded. Following this approach, these rules lay down a 'European ban' on the acquisition of evidence in such a way as to limit the fundamental rights concerned, without respecting the conditions established by EU law.[53]

It has also been observed that the primacy of European Union law imposes the need to exclude any effect of measures based on national rules inconsistent with supranational

---

[45] Trib. Rieti, 4 May 2021.
[46] According to Art 191 of Italian criminal procedural code, the usability of evidence must be excluded in case of violation of a ban on the acquisition of such evidence, established by law.
[47] Court of Cassation, V Sec., 25 January 2016, n.7265; Court of Cassation, V Sec., 5 December 2014, n.15613; see also Court of Cassation, Un. Sec., n. 155 of 2012 and n. 52117 of 2014.
[48] Court of Cassation, Un. Sec., 13 July 1998.
[49] Art 267 of the Code of Criminal Procedure.
[50] Beginning from Court of Cassation, Un. Sec., 23 February 2000, n. 6.
[51] Trib. Milano (n 33).
[52] Court of Cassation, V Sec., 20 November 2020, n. 37552; VI Sec., 4 May 2006, n. 33519.
[53] Luca Luparia, *Data retention e processo penale* (n 38) 763; Stefano Marcolini, *L'istituto della data retention dopo la sentenza della Corte di giustizia del 2014*, in Alberto Cadoppi, Stefano Canestrari, Adelmo Manna, and Michele Papa (eds), *Cybercrime* (Giappichelli 2019) 1594.

law, and that this contrast would deprive data retention of any legal basis.[54] In fact, as recognised by the Court of Justice[55] and by Italian Constitutional Court,[56] the mechanisms which guarantee the prevalence of EU law over the contrasting national dispositions[57] must be extended to the case law of the Luxembourg judge.

Most of all, as admitted, in general terms, by the Constitutional Court and by the Court of Cassation, the possibility to use, in the criminal proceeding, evidence collected in violation of fundamental rights protected by the Constitution should be radically denied.[58] Paradoxically, in the past, Italian case law[59] affirmed that, even if a contrast between national legislative provisions on traffic data and EU law had been recognised, the access to this information would have been consistent with Article 15 of the Constitution, protecting—as already said—the freedom and secrecy of communications. However, this kind of reasoning appears not to confer the proper importance to the conditions on which this disposition admits limitations to such a fundamental right: as already observed, the law must specifically provide for the cases and the instruments of the restriction, but legal rules were very generic on the point.

Such a normative regime, consequently, formed the basis of 'explorative' acquisitions by investigative authorities.[60]

Finally, in the *Prokuratuur* judgment, the Court of Justice, even leaving discretion to national legal systems on this point, stated that, in some cases, the use of the collected data must be excluded, in compliance with the principles of primacy, equivalence, and the effectiveness of EU law. More specifically, the ban on the use of traffic data should be recognised when the information concerned are subjected to a general and indiscriminate retention or accessed in the absence of the requirements imposed by EU law, especially when a violation of the adversary principle and of fair trial can be found, and data are 'likely to have a preponderant influence on the findings of fact'.[61]

Some scholars, though retaining that traffic data are destined to be put at the disposal of the parties, and that is consequently not easy to satisfy such requirements, observed that a reference to the already cited regime of interceptions, in light of the equivalence principle, could lead to the same conclusion.[62]

---

[54] Federica Iovene, Data retention *tra passato e futuro. Ma quale presente?* (2014), 12 *Cass. pen.* 4281; Marcolini ibid.
[55] CJEU, Judgment of 19 January 2010, *Kücükdeveci* (C-555/07, ECR 2010 p. I-365) ECLI:EU:C:2010:21.
[56] Constitutional Court, n. 113 of 1985 and n. 389 of 1989.
[57] See Court of Justice, Order of 3 June 1964, *Costa/ENEL* (6/64, ECR 1964 p. 1195) (FR1964/01195 NL1964/01255 DE1964/01307 IT1964/01177 EN1964/00614) ECLI:EU:C:1964:34.
[58] See, inter alia, Constitutional Court, n. 34 of 1973; n. 81 of 1993, on traffic data; n. 229 of 1998; 149 of 2008; Court of Cassation, Un. Sec., n. 6 of 2000 and n. 5021 of 1996. In the legal doctrine, in favour of the possibility to identify bans on the acquisition of evidence rooted in the Constitution, Filippo Raffaele Dinacci, *L'inutilizzabilità nel processo penale. Struttura e funzione del vizio* (Giuffrè 2008) 75 et seq; *contra*, Novella Galantini, *L'inutilizzabilità della prova nel processo penale* (CEDAM 1991). For an application of this theory to traffic data, see Andrea Chelo, *Tabula rasa sui tabulati? Riflessioni a margine della recente giurisprudenza della Corte di giustizia dell'Unione europea* (2022), 9 *Cass. pen.* 3273; Dinacci, *L'acquisizione dei tabulati telefonici* (n 16) 309.
[59] Court of Cassation, n. 33851 of 2018 (n. 34) § 1.3.2.
[60] Dinacci, *L'acquisizione dei tabulati telefonici* (n 16) 310.
[61] See, on the topic, *ex multis*, Elena Andolina, *La sentenza della Corte di giustizia UE nel caso H.K. c. Prokuratuur: un punto di non ritorno nella lunga querelle in materia di data retention?* (2021), 5 *Proc. pen. giust.* 1209; Mattia Giangreco, Data retention, *acquisizione e utilizzabilità dei tabulati telefonici e telematici: una riflessione incrociata* (2022), 4 *Cass. pen.* 1683 et seq; Alessandro Malacarne, *Ancora sull'acquisizione dei tabulati telefonici e sull'accesso ai dati delle comunicazioni elettroniche nel processo penale* (2021), 12 *Cass. pen.* 4121.
[62] Leonardo Filippi, *La Grande Camera della Corte di giustizia U.E. boccia la disciplina italiana sui tabulati* (2021), *Penale Diritto e Procedura*.

With reference to this issue, it is possible to observe that, even if the stated principle regarding the usability of evidence—coming from a quite different case[63]—seems not fully adequate for the subject of access to traffic data,[64] the *Prokuratuur* judgment allows a link between the violation of the requirements regarding the substantial and procedural conditions for the intrusion and the prejudice to fair trial.[65] So, European case law appears to strengthen the conclusions which can derive from the principle of non-usability of evidence collected in violation of fundamental rights protected by the Constitution.

The issue under consideration has been, finally, dealt with by Italian legislator, who, at Article 132, par. 3-*quater*, established the non-usability of data collected in violation of par. 3 and 3-*bis* of the same Article: therefore, this sanction was related to the absence of the conditions for the adoption of the measure and to the failure to comply with the procedural provisions, which are indispensable to ensure the consistency of the discipline with the European Union law and the Constitution. The following requirements are taken into account, indeed: the existence of sufficient evidence of the commission of certain kind of offences; the authorisations of a judge; the relevance of the information for the assessment of facts; and the possibility for the prosecutor to collect data, without the intervention of the judge, only in case of urgency, with the need for a subsequent judicial validation. However, the problem of 'bulk data retention', in light of European case law, is still open.

Another relevant problem, in the internal legal system, arises from the principle stated by the Court of Justice in the *Garda Síochána* case, according to which the possibility, for national authorities, of limiting the effects of the conflict between national rules and EU law should be excluded.[66] Moreover, as clarified by the Court, 'the interpretation that the Court gives to a rule of EU law ... clarifies and defines the meaning and scope of that rule as it must be, or ought to have been, understood and applied from the time of its coming into force': the rule, thus interpreted, must, therefore, be applied also to legal relationships established before the judgment.[67]

Moreover, Italian jurisprudence, with reference to the usability of evidence, ruled in favour of the applicability of the *tempus regit actum* rule at the time of the decision and not at the time of the acquisition of evidence. In fact, the evidentiary process ends with the assessment of evidence, and the prohibition on the use of illegitimate evidence prevents the evaluation of the latter, even if acquired under the rules previously in force.[68]

However, Italian legislator (Article 1, par. 1-*bis*, of Law n. 178/2021) introduced a specific normative regime for traffic data accessed before the adoption of the new dispositions: even if the access was not authorised by a judge, they remain usable, but they must be evaluated in conjunction with other evidence, and only to prove an offence respecting the new seriousness standard established by the law. This norm, which prevails on the already mentioned application of the *tempus regit actum* rule, appears to be only partially compliant with the Court of Justice's statements; nevertheless, it was considered legitimate by recent

---

[63] CJEU, Judgment of 10 April 2003, Steffensen (C-276/01, ECR 2003 p. I-3735) ECLI:EU:C:2003:228.
[64] Chelo, Tabula rasa *sui tabulati?* (n 54) 3276–3277.
[65] See Dinacci, *L'acquisizione dei tabulati telefonici* (n 16) 321.
[66] *Garda Síochána*, paras 115 et seq.
[67] *Garda Síochána*, para 125.
[68] Court of Cassation, Un. Sec., 25 February 1998, n. 4265; Court of Cassation, Un. Sec., 24 September 2004, n. 5052. For a similar approach in the legal doctrine, see Dinacci, *L'inutilizzabilità nel processo penale* (n 58) 168–69.

decisions of the Court of Cassation, which refers, inter alia, to the proper implementation of the adversary principle.[69]

This is another sign of the search for practical solutions trying to identify a difficult balance between the different rights and interests at stake.

5. The Role of the Italian Supervisor and its Decisions

Particular attention has been required for the complaint presented by a data subject under investigation for some crimes and settled with the prosecutor.[70] The same person, in particular, complained about the violation—by a well-known telephone operator (which does not appear to have responded and, moreover, did not decide to comply with the invitation formulated by the Garante)—of the right of access to incoming and outgoing traffic data, which his defenders needed to conduct the defence investigations precisely with regard to these crimes. The sensitivity of this case is unquestionable also considering the well-known relevant interventions of the Court of Justice regarding the retention of traffic data and that it was the first application of the legislation in force after the full operation of the GDPR, which, as is known, entailed, through Legislative Decree n. 101/2018, some changes also to Section 132 of the Privacy Code. Moreover, this should be seen from the perspective of the *lex specialis* of reference for the matter regarding electronic communications (ePrivacy Directive), which has remained unchanged pending the adoption of the new ePrivacy Regulation, as expressly provided for by Article 95 and Recital 173 of the GDPR.

By the mentioned provision, the Garante first of all recalled the persistent validity and operation of the principles and logical-legal reasoning already contained in its general provision of 3 November 2005, '*Access to telephone data: safeguards for incoming calls*',[71] specifying that: 'By way of exception . . . requests for the exercise of rights can be presented, and granted, when they demonstrate that the response to them by the provider is necessary to avoid "effective and concrete prejudice for carrying out the defensive investigations" referred to in law 7 December 2000, n. 397', although having as their object incoming telephone traffic, meaning 'any data subjected to processing for the purpose of transmitting a communication on an electronic communications network or related invoicing'. However, on this occasion, the Garante clarified that the burden of proving the need for access is on the applicant, who should submit suitable evidence to the provider that the lack of access would cause an effective and concrete prejudice to the carrying out of the investigations. In this case, the Garante deemed that there was a close connection between the requested traffic data and the indictments by the judicial authority, and that the requested data, including incoming traffic data, were needed for carrying out defensive investigations aimed at protecting the fundamental right of defence of the complainant at that time involved in judicial proceedings against him. The provision also underlined that the continuing and unjustified failure to act by the telephone company should not reflect negatively on the

---

[69] Court of Cassation, III Sec., 31 January 2022, n. 11991. See also Court of Cassation, 3 February 2023, n. 11283.
[70] 14 May 2020 (web doc. n. 9442587) <https://www.garanteprivacy.it/web/guest/home/docweb/-/docweb-display/docweb/9442587> accessed 4 January 2025.
[71] web doc. n. 1189488.

interested party, preventing him from fully exercising his right of defence. Therefore, the telephone company was ordered to grant the access request by the complainant, and to adopt—as part of the ongoing revision of its procedures following the measures set out in the aforementioned provision of 15 January 2020—organisational and technical measures suitable for promptly responding to similar requests for access to records.

A similar problem was encountered regarding a complaint that was filed against the same telephone operator by the lawyer of a freelancer who was also subject to criminal proceedings. This case called for a more general reflection on the scope of application and practical–operational nature of Article 132 of the Privacy Code, in case of persistent inaction or refusal by the telephone operators who then find themselves forced to access the telephone/internet traffic databases after the deadlines respectively established by law have elapsed.[72]

Considering the constraint of the principle of purpose limitation weighing on this database, the wording used in the decision was prudential and also in line with the principle of accountability of the controller; accordingly, having found the illegality and seriousness of the behaviour by the Company, the Garante determined the obligation for the company to deliver the data, leaving the choice of the relevant methods to the company's own responsibility as a controller. The same approach was also followed in the decision of 11 November 2021, which also included an order to pay a fine amounting to EUR 150,000. The fine was made necessary as a follow-up to the handling of a similar complaint, regarding the impending defence needs of the accused; that complaint had been granted by the emergency decision imposing corrective measures of 27 May 2021 (see footnote 69), through which the refusal by the Company to grant requests for access to the records, even if sent by the Office, was declared illicit and the Garante ordered transmitting such data to the lawyer of the complainant in accordance with the time limits established by Article 132 of the Privacy Code.

The other decisions by the Garante[73] followed very similar approaches and came to identical conclusions. Reference should be made, however, to the aforementioned decision of 8 July, which established the obligation for the telephone company to adopt suitable technical solutions for the recovery of the records which were stored only in the database reserved for requests possibly coming from the Judicial Authority since the general 24-month period set out in the law as running from generation of the traffic had elapsed by then.

Furthermore, the Court of Cassation, by a 5 July 2022 decision, established that Article 132 of the Privacy Code contains special rules regarding retention of and access to traffic data by the controller 'for other purposes', as per the relevant heading—namely, for the specific 'purposes of detection and repression of crimes'.

In this case, Article 132, paragraphs 1 and 3, provided that the 'telephone traffic data shall be retained by the provider for twenty-four months as from the date of the communication' and within that mandatory term they 'the data may be acquired subject to an authorisation granted by the judge with a reasoned order upon the request made by the public prosecutor or else by the defence counsel, the person under investigation, the injured party, or any other civil party, on condition the data are relevant to establish the facts at issue'.

---

[72] 24 months for telephone traffic; 12 months for the electronic one: see Section 132, paragraph 1, of the Italian Privacy Code.
[73] 14 May 2020, web doc. n. 9442587 (n 70).

This is in compliance with the amendments made to the third paragraph of Article 132 by Article 1, par. 1, letter. a), of Law Decree n. 132/2021, converted, with amendments, by Law n. 178/2021, in turn following the CJEU ruling in *Prokuratuur*. The latter judgment excluded compatibility with EU legislation of the Estonian legislation, which attributed the power to acquire information to the prosecuting officer, rather than to a judge or another independent entity. The approach set out in the legislation therefore envisaged a model, in which the party concerned, through his lawyer, could request a decision from the competent public prosecutor that enabled the provider to release the data. At the time of the facts, the third paragraph of Article 132 of the Privacy Code also enabled the defence counsel to address the request for the data directly to the provider and this precisely in the cases referred to in Article 391-*quater* of the Italian Code of Criminal Procedure. A condition applying to the request for direct access to incoming communications data was the risk of 'actual and concrete prejudice for carrying out the defense investigations'. 'Otherwise, the rights referred to in Articles 12 to 22 of Regulation can be exercised in the manner set out in Article 2-*undecies*, par. 3, third, fourth and fifth sentences', that is, in the absence of the said prejudice. According to Article 2-*undecies*, par. 3 (article inserted by Legislative Decree 10 August 2018, n. 101), in turn, when the exercise of the right has been 'delayed, limited or excluded', then the rights of the interested party can also be exercised through the Garante in accordance with the methods set out in Article 160.

In this case, the Garante informs the data subject that it has carried out all the necessary checks, and that the interested party has the right to file an appeal with judicial authorities. The data controller informs the interested party of the rights referred to in this paragraph. Article 160 of the Privacy Code outlines, for its part, a special internal assessment procedure by a member designated by the DPA, which is other than the one applying to complaints under Article 141 of the Privacy Code; following the investigation, the necessary modifications and additions are communicated to the controller if the processing was found not to comply with the relevant laws or regulations. As regards the procedure indicated by Article 391- *quater* of the Code of Criminal Procedure, par. 3 of the latter provides that, in case of refusal by the Telecom operator, 'the provisions of Articles 367 and 368 of the code of criminal procedure shall be applicable': that is, the power to address requests to the public prosecutor and to solicit the decision (by the judge for preliminary investigations), consisting of the order to ensure acquisition of traffic data.

6. Compatibility of the Italian Legislation with the Canon of Proportionality and with the Principles Sanctioned by the Court of Justice

Therefore, several times in Italy the Court of Cassation has deemed the domestic legislation compatible with the canon of proportionality and compliant with principles sanctioned by the Court of Justice as, in particular, it limits the retention period and commits the effective control of the strict necessity of data acquisition to the judicial authority (in this case, the public prosecutor).

The judgment of 13 February 2020 of the Court of Cassation[74] also affirmed that 'it cannot be considered that the Italian legislation on traffic data retention (so called data

---

[74] Court of Cassation, 13 February 2020, n. 5741.

retention) is in contrast with the rulings of the Court of Justice dated 8 April 2014 and 21 December 2016 since the legislation provides for the retention of telephone traffic data for a limited period of 24 months, allows acquiring the data only for the purpose of ascertaining and suppressing crimes, and provides that the use of the said data is subject to the acquisition order issued by the Public Prosecutor—that is, a judicial body that acts in the context of a preliminary investigation activity. It follows therefore that the Italian legislation does not provide for the right of public authorities to access sensitive data indiscriminately but limits it only to cases of investigations for crimes carried out within a specific period of 24 months (increased to 72 only for crimes of particular social alarm) and makes it conditional upon the authorization from a judicial body.... The legitimacy of the national reference legislation constituted by Article 132 of the Privacy Code, since the derogation from the right to confidentiality of communications is provided for a limited period, [and] has the exclusive objective of ascertaining and prosecuting crimes and is subject to the issuance of a provision by a judicial authority'.

But with the judgment of 2 March 2021, relating to *Prokuratuur*,[75] CJEU intervened once again on the matter, clarifying two essential aspects, which risk jeopardising the argument used by the Court of Cassation, among other things in the judgment referred to above. Indeed, according to the Court, the procedural acquisition of traffic data is, on the one hand, limited only to proceedings for serious crimes or for serious threats to public safety and, on the other hand, must be subject to the authorisation of a third-party authority with respect to the requesting public authority. Indeed, the Court specifies that access by the competent national authorities to the retained data must be 'subject to a prior check carried out either by a judge or by an independent administrative body and ... the decision of that judge or of such entity [must] intervene following a reasoned request from the aforementioned authorities'. More specifically, regarding the first issue, the Court states that 'Article 15(1) of the ePrivacy Directive, read in the light of Articles 7, 8 and 11 as well as Article 52(1) of the Charter, must be interpreted as precluding national legislation which allows access by public authorities to a set of data relating to traffic or location data suitable for providing information on the communications made by a user of a medium of electronic communications or on the location of the terminal equipment used by him and to allow precise conclusions to be drawn about his private life, for the purposes of prevention, investigation, detection and prosecution of crimes, without this access being limited to procedures aimed at combating against serious crime or the prevention of serious threats to public security, and this regardless of the length of the period for which access to the aforementioned data is requested, as well as the quantity or nature of the data available for that period'.[76]

From the second point of view, the Court notes that the European legislation precludes 'national legislation that confers upon the public prosecutor's office, whose task is to direct the criminal pre-trial procedure and to bring, where appropriate, the public prosecution in subsequent proceedings, the power to authorise access of a public authority to traffic and location data for the purposes of a criminal investigation'.[77]

The Italian legislation did not appear to comply with these principles (Article 132 of the Privacy Code), insofar as, on the one hand, it relied on the seriousness of crimes only for

---

[75] *Prokuratuur* (n 22).
[76] ibid para 27.
[77] ibid para 46.

regulating the chronological distance of the acquisition and not the admissibility of such acquisition and, on the other hand, it empowered the public prosecutor to acquire the relevant records in the absence of scrutiny by the judge.

Sharing the need for a legislative intervention, the Garante therefore invited the legislator to 'differentiate the conditions, limits and terms of retention of telephone and Internet traffic data by having regard to the particular seriousness of the crime for which the proceeding is within maximum duration periods compatible with the aforementioned principle of proportionality', subjecting their acquisition 'to the authorization of the judge, without prejudice, in cases of urgency, to the possibility for the public prosecutor to do so by his own decree, subject to subsequent validation after Article 267, paragraph 2, of the criminal procedure code'.[78]

This led to the Law Decree n. 132/2021, dated 30 September 2021, converted, with amendments, by Law n. 178/2021.[79] It is interesting to note that already in its original text, the decree provided for the repeal of Article 2-*quinquiesdecies* of the Privacy Code, relating to the prescriptive power of the Garante to be exercised also through provisions of a general nature—in relation to processing carried out for the execution of a task of public interest that is likely to present high risks. Conversely Article 9, par. 1, lett. e), of the Law Decree n. 139/2021, as converted by Law n. 205/2021, has attributed to the Garante a general prescriptive power with reference to data retention. Following the re-introduction of par. 5 of Article 132 of the Code, in particular, it has been envisaged that the Garante regulates, with a provision of a general nature, how telecommunications service providers are required to process data relating to telephone traffic and electronic traffic for the purposes of ascertainment and prosecution of the crimes envisaged by the article itself (see par. 13.2).

Furthermore, Article 1 of the same Law Decree n. 132/2021 introduced an important innovation in the regulation of the acquisition—of telephone and electronic records—for the purpose of use in criminal proceedings. The rationale for this innovation (which amended Article 132 of the code) was the need to adapt the legislation to the principles established by the CJEU in *Prokuratuur*, which reiterated that the procedural acquisition of traffic data is on the one hand limited only to proceedings for serious crimes or for serious threats to public safety and, on the other hand, must be subject to the authorisation of a third party authority with respect to the requesting public authority.

In line with these indications, Law Decree n. 132/2021 has established, in Article 1, the full judicialisation of the acquisition procedure and the delimitation of the scope of application of the procedure itself, which can only be carried out in the context of proceedings for crimes characterised by a certain seriousness, in the presence of sufficient evidence and of the relevance of the acquisition for the purposes of establishing the facts of the case. For the purpose of determining the seriousness of the crimes legitimising the acquisition of the records, the statutory provision of a maximum custodial penalty of three years is relevant; which must be combined with the availability, in factual terms, of sufficient evidence and with the investigative relevance of the data to be acquired, with the *ad hoc* provision of the crimes of threatening and telephone harassment.

---

[78] Letter to Parliament on the regulations applying to retention of telephone and internet traffic data for purposes of justice 22/07/2021 <https://www.gpdp.it/web/guest/home/docweb/-/docweb-display/docweb/9685978>.

[79] Law Decree 30 September 2021, n. 132, published in the Official Journal 29/11/2021 n. 284.

However, this provision lends itself to significant criticism. In the Italian legal system there are many crimes, which we can hardly define as serious, but which carry a maximum statutory custodial penalty of three years, for example insult, defamation, unintentionally causing bodily injury, misuse of power, offence to a public official.

In the scenario outlined above, the Court of Justice brings some clarity with the judgment in Case C-178/22.[80] The Court confirms that access to telephone records can be granted only to the data of individuals suspected of being implicated in a serious offence, and it specifies that it is for the Member States to define 'serious offences'. However, the court responsible for authorising that access must be entitled to refuse or restrict that access where it finds that the interference with the fundamental rights to private life and to the protection of personal data which such access would constitute is serious.

The Member States cannot alter that concept of 'serious crime', in the light of the societal conditions prevailing in the Member State concerned, even though the legislature of that Member State has provided for such offences to be punishable by a maximum term of imprisonment of at least three years. The Court states, in that connection, that a minimum period fixed by reference to such a term of imprisonment does not appear to be excessively low.

The discipline of the urgent procedure safeguards, despite the peculiarity that characterises its object, the need for the full jurisdictionalisation of the acquisition procedure and its limitation only to crimes characterised by sufficient gravity. The Law Decree also provides (which was originally set out in par. 3 of Article 132 of the Privacy Code) that Article 2-*undecies*, par. 3, periods from third to fifth of the Code is applicable, in case any of the rights pursuant to Articles from 12 to 22 of the GDPR is exercised; in these particular cases the exercise of those rights is delegated to the Garante, which acts in the name of the data subject and is subject to the presence of prevailing (also) public needs. Furthermore, following the enactment of the Law Decree, a ban on using the data acquired in violation of the above acquisition rules (ordinary and emergency) was expressly provided for and a transitional regulation was introduced which conditions the usability at the trial, against the defendant, of the records already acquired before the date of entry into force of the new piece of legislation, to the coexistence of other elements of proof and for the exclusive purpose of ascertaining the crimes for which, according to the 'ordinary' regulation, the acquisition is permitted. Furthermore, with a novelty of more general scope, relating to the content of the judge's decree authorising interceptions by computer seizure (so-called trojan), it has been established that the reasons, to be indicated in the decree itself, must be specific.

Existence of the requirement of urgency which must underpin the authorisation of the judge: 'in cases of urgency, the possibility for the public prosecutor to do so with his own decree',[81] allows us to also raise some criticisms. In fact it is evident that the provision on urgency can only be used by the public prosecutor and does not mention the defence at all, with consequent possible findings also of a constitutional nature, see Article 111 of the Italian Constitution, that establishes that the 'Jurisdiction shall be implemented through due process regulated by law. All court trials shall be conducted with adversarial proceedings and parties shall be entitled to equal conditions before a third-party and impartial judge'.[82]

---

[80] *Bolzano* (n 37).
[81] Article 132, par. 3-*bis*, Legislative Decree n. 196/2003, as amended by Law Decree n. 132/2021.
[82] Article 111, para 2, Italian Constitution.

But going further, we can flag other aspects on which to focus our attention.

Law 167 of 2017, which extended the retention period of the telecommunications traffic data generated in Italy to six years (72 months), albeit with some limitations—proceedings for crimes falling within the jurisdiction of district prosecutors and the acquisition of data collected beyond the standard term is limited to this category of particularly serious crimes—creates strong doubts about the lack of proportionality between the used data, the storage time, and the pursued purposes.

Let us note how the principle of proportionality has been repeatedly underlined by the European Data Protection Supervisor (EDPS) also regarding the legislator. In December 2019, 'Guidelines on the assessment of the proportionality of measures which limit the fundamental rights to privacy and the protection of personal data' addressed the issue of the proportionality of the measures envisaged by national legislators also in terms of access to and retention of traffic data.

However, several times the Court of Cassation[83] has found the internal discipline compatible with the proportionality standard and in compliance with the established principles by the Court of Justice as, in particular, it limits the duration of storage and entrusts the judicial authority with the effective control of the strict necessity of data acquisition.[84]

It follows, according to the Court of Cassation, that the Italian legislation does not provide for the public authorities' right to indiscriminately access sensitive data but limits it only to cases of criminal investigations carried out within a given period of 24 months (72 only for offences to fundamental legal assets and so of particular social alarm) and makes it subject to authorisation from a judicial body.[85]

7. Conclusions

There are various points of interest in Italian legislation regarding data retention for the purposes of prevention and repression of crimes which are regulated by Article 132 of the Privacy Code.

Starting from the access to this data by the defence counsel, it should be noted that in the context of adaptation to the GDPR—through Legislative Decree no. 101/2018—the defence counsel's direct access to data relating to 'incoming' communications was limited to cases in which an effective and concrete prejudice to the conduct of the defence investigation could occur. The current legislation has now eliminated the possibility for the defendant's lawyer to directly ask the telephone or telematic provider for access to the data, and consequently the power of intervention of the Italian Authority for the protection of personal data, in the event of late or unjustified refusal by Telecommunications operator. Furthermore, any failure to comply with the decrees authorising the acquisition of traffic data adopted by the judicial authority now falls within the competence of the judicial authority itself—that is, it is no longer the responsibility of the Garante. Telephone traffic data, in fact, are accessible only to the judicial authority, pursuant to Article 132 of the Privacy Code, as part of the

---

[83] Court of Cassation, Sec. V, 24 April 2018, n. 273892 and Sec. III, 23 August 2019, n. 36380.
[84] See judgment n. 5741 of 13 February 2020.
[85] Court of Cassation, Sec. V, 24 April 2018.

ongoing investigations for the repression of crimes. This interpretation was confirmed by the Court of Cassation's decision 5 July 2022, n. 21314.[86]

Another aspect of interest was to see how the public prosecutor was granted the power of direct access to traffic data. With reference to the need for control by a judge or other independent authority, as gradually clarified by the Court of Justice, the approach of Italian case law has been conservative. The Court of Cassation has denied several times in the past the possibility of finding a conflict with supranational rules due to the granting of the power of access to traffic data to the public prosecutor, as required by the Article 132 of the Privacy Code before the latest intervention by the legislator.

The need for authorisation from a judge was introduced by the legislator only since May 2021, following the CJEU ruling in *Prokuratuur*; therefore, except in cases of urgency, the processing requires prior authorisation with a reasoned decree from the judge, at the request of the public prosecutor or at the request of the defence counsel.

Also, on the issue of data retention, the role of the Court of Justice was fundamental, since the Court in its rulings called for a predetermination of the conditions of retention of and access to traffic data, recalling respect for the principle of legality, in its substantial dimension. For years, Italian jurisprudence has seemed not to incorporate the guidelines of the Court of Justice, due to the need not to limit the use of an instrument that is often crucial for proving crimes, despite the fact that this condition of legitimacy of the Italian legal system also derives from the safeguards that the Italian Constitution, in Articles 15 and 14, affords to the protection of freedom and secrecy of communications and the inviolability of one's home, also conceived in its virtual dimension, as a space for projection of the individual's personality.

Before the last intervention of the Italian legislator, Article 132 of legislative decree no. 196/2003 had not established at all the conditions for the conservation and access to traffic and location data, in terms of the seriousness of the crime in question, nor the existence of sufficient evidence demonstrating its commission. Thus, on several occasions, the Court of Cassation has also denied the violation of the requirement of the seriousness of the crime, recognising the seriousness of the crime in the concrete case in question, even if no legal rule on the matter had been adopted by the legislator.

Legislative Decree n. 132 of 2021 partially resolved the problem, limiting access to data—but not their storage—to some categories of crimes, and requiring the existence of sufficient evidence of the commission of the crime and the relevance of traffic data for the reconstruction of the facts. But upon closer inspection, the legislator had some doubts about the conformity of Italian legislation with the principles dictated by EU regulations, introducing an important innovation in the regulation of the acquisition—of telephone and informatic records—for the purposes of use in criminal proceedings. The motivation for this innovation (which modified Article 132 of the Code), which reiterated that the procedural acquisition of traffic data is on the one hand limited only to proceedings for serious crimes or serious threats to public safety and, on the other, it must be subject to the authorisation of an authority third to the requesting public authority.

For the purposes of ascertaining the seriousness of the crimes that legitimise the acquisition of the documents, the legal provision of a maximum custodial sentence of three years is

---

[86] General register number 17439/2021; sect. number 2750/2022; published 5 July 2022.

relevant; this must be combined with the availability of sufficient factual evidence and the relevance of the data to be acquired for the purposes of the investigation. On the other hand, such acquisition is subject to the authorisation issued by an authority that is other than the public authority requesting the data. However, this provision was criticised from several quarters. In the Italian legal system there are several criminal offences that can hardly be defined as serious and nevertheless carry a maximum custodial sentence of three years under the law—such as slander, defamation, causing personal injuries unintentionally, misuse of power, disrespectful conduct to public officials, etc.

The aforementioned decision of the Court of Justice in Case C-178/22[87] has an important impact on Italian legislation in various aspect. First and foremost for the Court it is 'irrelevant' that the data may not be the data of the owners of the mobile telephones at issue, but the data of the persons who communicated with each other by using those telephones after their alleged theft. In fact, the decision argues, Directive 2002/58 protects all communications carried out by network users and the 'user' is 'any natural person using a publicly available electronic communications service, for private or business purposes, without necessarily having subscribed to this service'.

Another relevant aspect is how the Court interprets the serious interferences, 'only if those provisions are intended for the prosecution of serious offences, such as serious threats to public security, understood as that of the State, and other serious crime'.[88] And even if it is up to the Member States to define 'serious crimes', they cannot however distort the notion and, by extension, that of 'serious crime', by including crimes that are manifestly not serious.

Instead, the Court specifies, the threshold set with reference to the prison sentence of no less than a maximum of three years does not appear excessively low. Nor is the setting of a threshold necessarily contrary to the principle of proportionality. However, on the one hand, it is necessary that to authorise access there is a preventive control by the judge. On the other hand, the judge must be able to refuse or limit access if he finds that the interference with fundamental rights is serious, while the crime to be prosecuted is 'manifestly' not serious and, in light of the social conditions existing in the Member State concerned, does not fall under serious crime.

In fact, the judge must always 'strike a fair balance between, on the one hand, the legitimate interests relating to the needs of the investigation in the context of combating crime and, on the other hand, the fundamental rights to privacy and protection of personal data of the persons whose data are concerned by the access'.[89] In particular, 'as part of its examination of the proportionality of the interference with the fundamental rights of the person concerned caused by the request for access, that court or body must be able to exclude such access where it is sought in the context of proceedings for an offence which is manifestly not a serious offence'.[90] In fact the Court leaves it up to the national judge, Italian in the case examined, to guarantee a fair balance between the legitimate interests connected to the needs of the investigation in the context of the fight against crime and the fundamental rights of the data subjects whose data is affected by the access.

---

[87] *Bolzano* (n 37).
[88] ibid para 19.
[89] CJEU, Judgment of 30 April 2024, *La Quadrature du Net and Others (Personal data and combating counterfeiting)* C-470/21, paras 125 and the case law cited.
[90] *Bolzano* (n 37) para 62.

Another important aspect is that the terms of data retention underwent an unprecedented expansion in 2017: Article 167 of Law 167/2017 has enormously extended these terms, in addition to the 'ordinary' term, a further period of 72 months was foreseen whether it concerns telephone traffic, whether it concerns electronic traffic, or finally, whether it concerns data relating to unanswered calls, for particularly serious crimes, such as those under the jurisdiction of the District Attorney's Office (organised crime, terrorism). The problem is that, to allow access to prosecutors to records in cases of particularly serious crimes, operators must keep everyone's records for six years. With the argument of the fight against terrorism and organised crime, all citizens risk being transformed into suspects.

In short, reformation of the domestic legislation on data retention is called for in order to introduce different conditions, periods, and limitations with regard to the retention of telephone and internet traffic data, by having regard to the specific seriousness of the underlying offence. At all events, the maximum retention period should be compatible with the aforementioned proportionality requirements as interpreted by the Court of Justice.

It would be unfortunate if the data retention period of the national rules could only be modified through further intervention by the Court of Justice and not by means of a virtuous internal process which opens a dialogue in order to strike the right balance between the rights at play, security and privacy, where neither of them prevails over the other but coexists in mutual respect. This is the task of the jurist who must look at all the tools available, such as the principles of legality and proportionality enshrined in the Constitution at the national level and in the Charter at the European Union level.

9

Consequences of the Collapse of a Directive

The Aftermath of CJEU Data Retention Case Law on Cypriot Jurisprudence

Christiana Markou

1. Introduction

Even before its annulment by the CJEU, the Data Retention Directive had many detractors arguing that it failed to strike a fair balance between the fight against terrorism and serious crime on the one hand, and the fundamental rights of data protection and privacy of EU citizens on the other.[1] Still, Member States had to transpose it into their national legal orders. For this purpose, Cyprus introduced Law 183(I)/2007, a largely *verbatim* implementation of the Data Retention Directive. By application of this law, a large number of court orders have been issued authorizing police access to traffic and location data of criminal suspects. During the years before the annulment of the Data Retention Directive, the lawfulness of such orders was often challenged by persons targeted by them through certiorari applications to the Cyprus Supreme Court, which was consistently upholding them on the ground that they were permitted by the relevant data retention legislation, namely the aforementioned Law 183(I)/2007.

When in 2014, the CJEU annulled the Data Retention Directive effectively confirming that it constituted a disproportionate interference with the rights to data protection and privacy, said legislative measure disappeared from the EU legal landscape. However, this did not automatically annul the national transposition measures and as a result, Cyprus remained (and still does) with a law identical to the annulled Data Retention Directive in its legal order. In fact, shortly after the annulment of the Data Retention Directive, the Cyprus Supreme Court expressly opined that the annulment by the CJEU had no effect on the national data protection legislation, which remained in force as *national* law.[2]

---

[1] Christiana Markou, 'The Cyprus and Other EU Court Rulings on Data Retention: The Directive as a Privacy Bomb' (2012) 28(4) Computer Law & Security 468; Stephen McGarvey, 'The 2006 EC Data Retention Directive: A Systematic Failure' (2011) 10 Hibernian Law Journal 119; Arianna Vedaschi and Valerio Lubello, 'Data Retention and its Implications for the Fundamental Right to Privacy: A European Perspective' (2015) 20(1) Tilburg Law Review 14–34; Abu Bakar Munir, Siti Hajar Mohd Yasin, and Siti Sarah Abu Bakar, 'Data Retention Rules: A Dead End' (2017) 3 European Data Protection Review 71; Marie-Helen Maras, 'While the European Union was Sleeping, the Data Retention Directive was Passed: The Political Consequences of Mandatory Data Retention' (2011) 6(2) Hamburg Review of Social Sciences 1, 3–10. Notably, the European Data Protection Supervisor has characterized the Data Retention Directive as 'the most privacy invasive instrument ever adopted by the EU in terms of scale and the number of people it affects', see European Data Protection Supervisor (EDPS), Press Release, 'The "Moment of Truth" for the Data Retention Directive: EDPS Demands Clear Evidence of Necessity' at the European Commission conference 'Taking on the Data Retention Directive' (2010), Brussels <https://edps.europa.eu/sites/edp/files/edpsweb_press_releases/edps-2010-17_data_retention_directive_en.pdf> accessed 10 November 2023.

[2] Cyprus, Supreme Court, *Isaias*, Civil Appeal no 402/2012 (majority decision) 7 July 2014.

Unsurprisingly therefore, court orders issued on the basis of Law 183(I)/2007 continued to be upheld as valid and lawful even after the Data Retention Directive annulment, despite the CJEU finding that the particular measure was not compatible with Articles 7 and 8 of the EU Charter of Fundamental Rights (Charter).[3] This stance of the Cypriot judiciary was argued to be misguided; Law 183(I)/2007 is largely a reproduction of the provisions of the Data Retention Directive and accordingly, the position that that law was in line with the Charter while the (identical) Directive was not, was obviously difficult to justify. The supremacy of EU law, which is embodied in Article 1A of the Cyprus Constitution, effectively means that Law 183(I)/2007, being in conflict with the Charter, should not have been applied by the Cypriot courts (until amended by the national parliament).[4] As others rightly pointed out, 'national measures—whether they pre-existed the Data Retention Directive or were adopted to transpose it—must comply with the rights of privacy and data protection guaranteed by the Charter, as interpreted by the Court in Digital Rights Ireland'.[5]

Remarkably, even the CJEU ruling in *Tele2 Sverige*, which embodied an explicit stance against the lawfulness of national legislation providing for the general and indiscriminate retention of all traffic and location data,[6] did not lead to an immediate change of the judicial approach in Cyprus. In fact, influenced by the important role of data retention in the fight against serious crime (in that case, child pornography), the Supreme Court in 2017 rejected an application for leave for a certiorari application seeking to challenge the lawfulness of a data access order.[7] Of course, following an appeal, that decision was reversed in 2018 and leave for a certiorari application to be filed was eventually granted. The said appeal decision paved the way towards an alignment with EU case law on data retention, yet that did not happen because a certiorari application was never filed in the end.

Meanwhile, the Cypriot legislature has also remained inactive, as there has been no amendment of Law 183(I)/2007 in response to the aforementioned CJEU case law. In fact, apart from an amendment in 2008 (shortly after said law was passed), there has been no other amendment to date. Accordingly, in Cyprus, there is currently in force data retention legislation identical to the (annulled) Data Retention Directive. Ideally of course, it is the EU, which should legislatively intervene to regulate the matter for all Member States or at least assist them in that aim, something which can be achieved through the draft ePrivacy Regulation.[8] This EU process however takes time[9] and the draft's provisions on data retention have proved to be contentious.[10]

---

[3] See eg Cyprus, Supreme Court, *Syfantou*, Civil applications no 216/14 and 36/2015, 27 October 2015.
[4] For a detailed critique of the relevant stance of the Cypriot judiciary, see Christiana Markou, 'Data Retention in Cyprus in the Light of EU Data Retention Law' in Marek Zubik, Jan Podkowik, and Robert Rybski (eds), *European Constitutional Courts towards Data Retention* (Springer 2021) 8.
[5] Marie-Pierre Granger and Kristina Irion, 'The Court of Justice and the Data Retention Directive in Digital Rights Ireland: Telling Off the EU Legislator and Teaching a Lesson in Privacy and Data Protection' (2014) 39(4) European Law Review 835, 848.
[6] CJEU, Judgment of 21 December 2016, *Tele2 Sverige* (C-203/15 and C-698/15) ECLI:EU:C:2016:970 para 103.
[7] Cyprus, Supreme Court, *Artemi Kkolou*, Civil Application no 1/2017, 31 January 2017.
[8] Commission (EC), 'Proposal for a Regulation of the European Parliament and of the Council concerning the respect for private life and the protection of personal data in electronic communications and repealing Directive 2002/58/EC (Regulation on Privacy and Electronic Communications)', COM (2017) 010 final - 2017/03 (COD).
[9] On the role of this measure in the data retention landscape, see Marcin Rojszczak, 'The Uncertain Future of Data Retention Laws in the EU: Is a Legislative Reset Possible?' (2021) 41 Computer Law & Security Review 105572. See also Markou, 'Data Retention' (n 4) 85, 97.
[10] Xavier Tracol, 'The Two Judgments of the European Court of Justice in the Four Cases of Privacy International, La Quadrature du Net and Others, French Data Network and Others and Ordre des Barreaux

Against this background, this chapter will first present and explain the Supreme Court judgment of 2021, which signalled a deviation from the aforementioned judicial approach and an alignment with the CJEU case law, as it then stood (see section 2.1). The chapter will then explain its immediate aftermath on the Cypriot jurisprudence regarding data retention and the lawfulness of court orders authorizing police access to retained data issued on the basis of Law 183(I)/2007 (see section 2.2). This section will also introduce the rather unexpected (yet correct) turn that Cypriot case law took two years after the landmark 2021 judgment, specifically in 2023. Section 3 will then analyse and assess the relevant 2023 judgment in the light of more recent developments in the CJEU case law on data retention and the 2021 Supreme Court judgment. It will conclude that despite having certain weaknesses and also being somewhat controversial with regard to how the court avoided the result of the binding 2021 judgment, the 2023 ruling is correct. Accordingly, it should be expected that it will affect the relevant Cypriot jurisprudence and may even force the Supreme Court to 'correct' its 2021 judgment, thereby limiting its effect by reference to specific types of data and more recent CJEU case law.

2. The Landmark Supreme Court Judgment of 2021 and its Aftermath

2.1 The 2021 judgment

Certiorari applications challenging the lawfulness of data access orders issued by courts on the basis of Law 183(I)/2007 were adding up as was relevant CJEU case law, which reinforced the position adopted in *Tele2 Sverige*. Accordingly, the question regarding whether Law 183(I)/2007 was incompatible with EU law and thus, invalid and/or inapplicable became increasingly pressing and had to be resolved. For this purpose, a number of pending certiorari applications filled in 2018–2020 were jointly heard by the Supreme Court sitting in full plenary (all 13 judges) due to the importance of the question at stake.[11]

Taking into account *Tele2 Sverige* and the subsequent rulings of the CJEU in *La Quadrature du Net 'I'*[12] and in *Prokuratuur*[13] the Supreme Court, by majority, held that sections 3 and 6–10 of Law 183(I)/2007 (which correspond to Articles 3 and 5 of the Data Retention Directive) are incompatible with Article 15 of the ePrivacy Directive[14] and relevant CJEU case law. Said provisions of Law 183(I)/2007 provided for a general and indiscriminate data retention obligation and accordingly, finding them as not being in accord with EU law appeared inevitable. The majority rightly acknowledged that any guarantees relating to data access could not

---

Francophones et Germanophone and Others: The Grand Chamber Is Trying Hard to Square the Circle of Data Retention' (2021) 41 Computer Law & Security Review 1–13, 12.

[11] Cyprus, Supreme Court, *Hadjioannou and others*, Civil Applications no. 97/18, 127/18, 140/19-143/19, 154/19, 169/19, 36/20 και 46/20, 27 October 2021.
[12] CJEU, Judgment of 6 October 2020, *La Quadrature du Net and others* (C-511/18, C-512/18 and C-520/18) ECLI:EU:C:2020:791 ('*La Quadrature du Net 'I'*').
[13] CJEU, Judgment of 2 March 2021, *Prokuratuur* (C-746/18) ECLI:EU:C:2021:152.
[14] Directive 2002/58/EC of the European Parliament and of the Council of 12 July 2002 concerning the processing of personal data and the protection of privacy in the electronic communications sector (Directive on privacy and electronic communications) [31.7.2002] OJ L 201/ 37.

justify the disproportionality of the separate interference with human rights inherent in data retention. Moreover, it shared the view that a law transposing a Directive found incompatible with the Charter, cannot in fact be compatible with EU law.

What was somewhat surprising was that the decision of the Supreme Court was not unanimous. There was a strong minority (consisting of six judges) which opined that Law 183(I)/2007 was not inconsistent with relevant CJEU law, albeit without offering any convincing justification. More specifically, the minority emphasized that section 14 of Law 183(I)/2007 lays down significant guarantees, yet that provision is identical to Article 7 of the Data Retention Directive on data protection and data security, which had obviously not been enough to prevent the annulment of the relevant Directive by the CJEU. Moreover, it failed to acknowledge that data retention and access to retained data are two distinct interferences with individual privacy, despite the fact that this stems clearly from the relevant CJEU case law, as has been illustrated elsewhere.[15] Obviously, the approach of the minority was closer to the 'permissive interpretation'[16] of the *Digital Rights Ireland* ruling, yet even that interpretation accepts that access and data security were vaguely regulated and could not thus 'save' the Directive.[17] Quite remarkably the minority also opined that there can be no harm (or damage) by retention alone (ie if there is no access to the retained data) in effect ignoring the fact that a privacy violation per se constitutes damage (even in the absence of tangible adverse effects on the individual).[18]

Despite the fallacies, it should be accepted that the minority judgment clearly embodies (strong) judicial resistance to depriving law enforcement authorities of valuable weapons against serious crime and a stance in favour of the security of the population. In fact, as it arises from more recent case law at EU level discussed later in this chapter, such judicial resistance may have forced the CJEU to take a step back, thereby adopting a less stringent approach to data retention and readjusting the scales of privacy and security by tilting them a bit towards the side of security.

2.2 The aftermath of the 2021 judgment

After the above-discussed 2021 Supreme Court judgment (*Hadjioannou*), which found the data retention provisions of Law 183(I)/2007 incompatible with EU law and thus, invalid, it

---

[15] See Markou, 'Data Retention' (n 4) 85, 92. This has explicitly been confirmed by the CJEU among others in CJEU, Judgment of 27 October 2022, *SpaceNet* (C-793/19 and C-794/19) ECLI:EU:C:2022:702, para 91 where by reference to previous case law, the Court stated the following: 'It follows that national legislation ensuring full respect for the conditions established by the case-law interpreting Directive 2002/58 as regards access to retained data cannot, by its very nature, be capable of either limiting or even remedying the serious interference, which results from the general retention of those data provided for under that national legislation, with the rights guaranteed by Articles 5 and 6 of that directive and by the fundamental rights to which those articles give specific effect (judgment of 5 April 2022, Commissioner of An Garda Síochána and Others, C-140/20, EU:C:2022:258, paragraph 47)'.
[16] Niklas Vainio and Samuli Miettinen, 'Telecommunications Data Retention after Digital Rights Ireland: Legislative and Judicial Reactions in the Member States' (2015) 23(3) International Journal of Law and Information Technology 290, 299.
[17] ibid 290, 299–300.
[18] As is acknowledged in Recital 51 of the Law Enforcement Directive (Directive 2016/680/EE), a processing (which includes storage and retention) is considered to lead to damage among others 'where data subjects might be deprived of their rights and freedoms or from exercising control over their personal data'. The same is stated in Recital 75 of the General Data Protection Regulation (GDPR).

was expected that subsequent certiorari applications against court orders authorizing police access to retained data (issued on the basis of said law) would succeed and the relevant court orders would be set aside. Indeed, national provisions which contravene EU law are in fact inapplicable according to relevant CJEU case law.[19] Even when such orders were not similarly challenged and thus, remained valid, it was expected that the obtained evidence (in the form of telecommunications data) could not easily be used as evidence in court. Arguably, such orders had authorized access to data retained (and thus obtained) unlawfully, which could therefore be argued to be inadmissible as evidence in criminal proceedings.[20]

Indeed, applications seeking the leave of the court to file a certiorari application against data access orders tended to be quickly approved by the judges of the Supreme Court via short judgments of very similar wording granting the applicants the necessary leave to proceed with a certiorari application. At that stage, the court only needs to be satisfied that there is an arguable case of illegality, which the judges easily found by reference to the 2021 Supreme Court judgment, which is binding on them.[21]

Moreover, shortly after the 2021 Supreme Court judgment, there have also been cases concerning certiorari applications, in which the judge annulled the court order authorizing police access to retained data.[22] Interestingly, in one case, the Attorney-General, who represented the Cyprus government, did not defend the lawfulness and/or validity of the relevant order; having probably thought that the effect of the 2021 judgment could lead to no other result, the Attorney-General agreed to the annulment of the order in question.[23]

One would perceive these developments as signalling the 'death' of Law 183(I)/2007 and highlighting the need for new Cypriot data retention legislation, which would be compatible with CJEU case law, thus providing for a targeted (as opposed to a general and indiscriminate) data retention obligation.

However, after having the time to 'digest' the 2021 Supreme Court judgment as well as more recent CJEU case law, the Attorney-General of the Republic, in a more recent case concerning a certiorari application against a data access order issued on the basis of Law 183(I)/2007, exploited the recent stance of the CJEU towards the general and indiscriminate retention of IP addresses. That case, discussed in detail in section 3 of this chapter, was decided in 2023 and the relevant judgment brought back some of the uncertainty in the data retention landscape in Cyprus.

3. Data Retention in Cyprus in 2023

3.1 Post-*Tele2 Sverige* CJEU case law

In 2020, in *La Quadrature du Net 'I'*, the CJEU made it clear that Article 15(1) of the ePrivacy Directive and the Charter do not preclude national measures that 'provide, for

---

[19] CJEU, Judgment of 18 May 2021, *Asociaţia "Forumul Judecătorilor din România"* (C-83/19, C-127/19, C-195/19, C-291/19, C-355/19, and C-397/19) ECLI:EU:C:2021:393.
[20] See *Prokuratuur* (n 13) para 44; *La Quadrature du Net 'I'* (n 12) para 227.
[21] See for example Cyprus, Supreme Court, Civil Application no 98/2022, 21 July 2022; Civil Application no 8/2022, 14 March 2022; Civil Application no 196/2022, 12 December 2022; Civil Application no 68/2023, 7 June 2023.
[22] See for example, Cyprus, Supreme Court, Civil Application no 169/19, 1 March 2022.
[23] Cyprus, Supreme Court, Civil Application no 59/2022, 14 July 2022.

the purposes of safeguarding national security, combating serious crime and preventing serious threats to public security, *for the general and indiscriminate retention of IP addresses assigned to the source of an Internet connection for a period that is limited in time to what is strictly necessary*.[24] Obviously, the CJEU has, in that context, decided to loosen its stringent approach against general and indiscriminate data retention, thereby responding to the resistance exhibited by some Member States and/or their courts and purporting to strike a fair balance between the conflicting interests of security and privacy.[25] Indeed, it is clear that the Court has been influenced by the fact that 'where an offence is committed online, the IP address might be the only means of investigation enabling the person to whom that address was assigned at the time of the commission of the offence to be identified'.[26]

Notably, the 2021 Supreme Court judgment (*Hadjioannou*) did not focus on the retention of IP addresses or any other specific type of telecommunication or internet data. In fact, that judgment did not deal with the facts of any of the joined cases *at all* and approached the matter as a purely legal question of compatibility of specific national legal provisions with EU law. The CJEU ruling in *La Quadrature du Net 'I'*, including its part referring to the retention of IP addresses, though cited by the Supreme Court (*Hadjioannou*), had no influence on the reasoning or outcome of the particular case. As already mentioned, the Supreme Court found the relevant national provisions (in their entirety) to be incompatible with EU law and thus, invalid. This was unsurprising given that, similarly to the Data Retention Directive, the data retention provisions of Law 183(I)/2007 laid down a much more extensive data retention obligation than an obligation confined to the retention of IP addresses of the source of a connection (source IP addresses).

Then came *Garda Síochána*[27] and *SpaceNet*,[28] in which the CJEU has largely reiterated its ruling in *La Quadrature du Net 'I'*. It is clear from all these rulings that the green light by the CJEU is given to 'a legislative measure providing for the general and indiscriminate *retention of only IP addresses* assigned to the source of a connection'.[29] The national retention obligations at stake in those cases all went beyond retention of source IP addresses leading the Court to reinstate its stance regarding the unlawfulness of general and indiscriminate retention obligations and hinting that said national provisions were not compatible with EU law. It is true that nowhere in those judgments the CJEU has stated or even hinted that a data retention provision can be examined *in parts* or viewed as providing for (multiple) separate data retention obligations each referring to a specific piece of telecommunication (or internet) data so that one such separate obligation can be compatible with EU law while another (part of the same provision) may be not. Yet, the Court has not excluded that possibility either.

---

[24] Emphasis added.
[25] Others described this approach as a 'major concession that the CJEU made to Member States' law enforcement authorities' also arguing that it progressively re-legitimizes bulk data retention: Maria Tzanou and Spyridoula Karyda, 'Privacy International and Quadrature du Net: One Step Forward Two Steps Back in the Data Retention Saga?' (2022) 28(1) European Public Law 123, 140, 148.
[26] *La Quadrature du Net 'I'* (n 12) para 154.
[27] CJEU, Judgment of 5 April 2022, *Commissioner of An Garda Síochána* (C-140/20) ECLI:EU:C:2022:258.
[28] *SpaceNet* (n 15).
[29] *La Quadrature du Net 'I'* (n 12) para 155; *Garda Síochána* (n 27) para 74; *SpaceNet* (n 15) para 101.

3.2 A change in the Cypriot judicial approach

Though as already stated, the CJEU did not speak of the possibility of partial incompatibility with EU law, this is exactly the approach adopted by a Supreme Court judge in 2023 in *NM*.[30] More specifically, the case concerned a certiorari application challenging the lawfulness of a data access order issued under Law 183(I)/2007 in the context of the investigation of online child pornography offences. Though that order was authorizing police access to data retained in accordance with data retention provisions of Law 183(I)/2007, which were, in *Hadjioannou*, ruled to be incompatible with the ePrivacy Directive and the Charter, the Supreme Court judge has not annulled the access order in its entirety, as one would expect. It is perhaps no coincidence that said judge was among the minority of the judges, who did not agree that Law 183(I)/2007 was incompatible with the relevant EU law in 2021 in *Hadjioannou*.[31]

The court emphasized the fact that *Hadjioannou* did not annul (or cancel) the data retention provisions of Law 183(I)/2007, but only gave precedence to the relevant EU law, which was in conflict with the corresponding national provisions according to CJEU case law. This is what the principle of the supremacy of EU law dictated and according to the judge, it is also in line with relevant CJEU case law according to which national courts should give precedence to conflicting EU law[32] and refrain from applying national provisions that are not compatible with EU law.[33] Indeed, no court in Cyprus can abolish or amend legislation. In line with the constitutional principle of separation of powers,[34] only the legislator (in Cyprus, the House of Representatives)[35] has such power. Courts can only rule legislative provisions as invalid, thereby refrain from applying them and preventing the result which could be achieved by them. This is what the Supreme Court could only do (and actually did) in the landmark 2021 judgment in *Hadjioannou*. Accordingly, on this point, the line of thinking of the court in *NM* is correct and uncontroversial.

What is controversial relates to how the Supreme Court escaped the *binding* 2021 finding of incompatibility and consequent invalidity of the data retention obligation given that it had to deal with the exact same data retention provisions. Given also that there has not, in the meantime, been any change of approach at EU level,[36] courts would be expected to disapply the relevant national legislation in all subsequent cases until said legislation was abolished or amended by the parliament. However, the Court in *NM* sought to distinguish *Hadjioannou* from the case it had before it, something which is interesting (and perhaps somewhat controversial) because *Hadjioannou* has *not* been decided by reference to any specific facts. As already stated, the Cyprus Supreme Court, in that case, chose to approach the matter as a purely legal question and its outcome has clearly not been influenced by any (specific) facts at all. Accordingly, even if the facts of *NM* could be considered materially

---

[30] Cyprus, Supreme Court, Civil Application no 124/2022, 14 February 2023. For a summary of this case and a short commentary, see Thalia Prastitou, Observations regarding the Issuance of Certiorari (SC 2023), (2023) 1 *Kypriaki Nomiki Epitheorisi*, 94.
[31] See section 2 of this chapter.
[32] CJEU, Judgment of 19 November 2009, *Filipiak* (C-314/08, ECR 2009 p. I-11049) ECLI:EU:C:2009:719.
[33] *Asociatia 'Forumul Judecatorilor din Romania' v Inspectia Judiciara*.
[34] Cyprus, Supreme Court, *President of the Republic v House of Representatives*, 3 December 2015, Reference 1/2015.
[35] Article 61 of the Constitution of the Republic of Cyprus.
[36] Indeed, a general and indiscriminate data retention obligation going beyond the retention of source IP addresses and civil identity data continues to be considered incompatible with EU law.

different from those of *Hadjioannou*, that could not really allow for distinguishing the one from the other.

In effect, the Court could not in fact avoid the effect of *Hadjioannou*, which being a plenary Supreme Court decision, binds any other court in Cyprus (despite the fact that it has not acted as an appeal court). There are of course cases in which the Supreme Court can overrule a previous ruling. However, apart from the fact that this is possible in very limited cases, such as when the previous legal rule should be considered to be wrong,[37] a Supreme Court judge (hearing a case as a first instance court) cannot overrule a full plenary Supreme Court judgment.

Nevertheless, the Court in *NM* stated that the Supreme Court in *Hadjioannou* has not directly examined the compatibility of the relevant national provisions with the EU legislation and case law concerning IP addresses, as in that case the access orders at stake concerned different types of telecommunication data (not IP addresses).[38] As a result, according to the Court, *NM* materially differed from *Hadjioannou*. In this way, the Court escaped the result of *Hadjioannou*, albeit somewhat controversially, given that as it arises from the above discussion, it effectively overruled it, something which the said Court had no power and most probably, no intention to do

Indeed, in a previous case, the same Court annulled a data access order by reference to the binding of the judicial precedent of *Hadjioannou* without inquiring into the type of telecommunication (or internet) data at stake.[39] Of course, though it did not have any effect on the Court's approach and/or decision, in that case, the Attorney-General consented to the annulment of the data access order, unlike in *NM* where the Attorney-General defended its validity by reference to the CJEU case law on the retention of IP addresses.

3.3 Assessing the 2023 court judgment

The most important arising question is whether the judgment of the Court in *NM* could be considered as correct. Importantly, that would mean that the approach followed in *Hadjioannou* was somewhat simplistic leading to a wrong outcome in so far as it meant the annulment of *all* data access orders *regardless of the telecommunication data at stake*.

In *NM* the data access order was twofold. Its first part concerned police access to data related to the IP address of the source of the connection while its second part, concerned police access to the number of a call and to several details of the user of that number. The Court annulled the second part without hesitation, as it was authorizing police access to retained data in relation to which, EU law, particularly the relevant CJEU case law, prohibits a general and indiscriminate retention obligation.

Conversely, the Court upheld the first part of the order on the ground that it was allowing police access to data, namely source IP addresses, which, according to the Court, were retained in accordance with a national provision, specifically section 6(b) of Law 183(I)/2007, which is not incompatible with EU law. Section 6(b) of Law 183(I)/2007

---

[37] Cyprus, Supreme Court, *Watts and others v Laouri and others*, (2014) 1(B) CLR 1401.
[38] Notably, neither *Hadjioannou* (n 11) nor *NM* states what telecommunication or internet data was involved in the joined cases decided by the Supreme Court sitting in plenary.
[39] Cyprus, Supreme Court, Civil Application no 169/19, 1 March 2022.

corresponds to (and is identical with) Article 5(1)(a)(2) of the (annulled) Data Retention Directive. The particular provision refers to the retention of data concerning internet access, internet email, and internet telephony, specifically (i) the user ID(s) allocated, (ii) the user ID and telephone number allocated to any communication entering the public telephone network, and (iii) the name and address of the subscriber or registered user to whom an Internet Protocol (IP) address, user ID, or telephone number was allocated at the time of the communication.

One observes that the Court has considered that only section 6(b) of Law 183(I)/2007 was relevant, whereas the retention of IP addresses *as such* is obviously not mandated by said provision but (by part of) section 8(b) of Law 183(I)/2007, which is identical to Article 5(1)(c)(2)(i) of the Data Retention Directive.[40] Furthermore, though the *NM* judgment seeks to examine the lawfulness and validity of the access order by reference to the specific types of data at stake, it does not mention at all the (specific) data to which said access order in question related. Rather, it is confined to stating that said order was authorizing access to 'data relating to IP addresses' without disclosing what exactly that data was. As is explained below, the particular detail was important in the context of the judicial approach adopted and the outcome ultimately reached. This is even more so given that IP addresses form part of traffic and location data,[41] and as a result, all such data may be regarded as 'data relating to IP addresses'.

These weaknesses aside, to determine whether the judicial approach followed in *NM* is correct, the first question that should be addressed is what data retention provision the CJEU ruled that it may be permissible. The Court in *NM* put most of the emphasis on the general and indiscriminate retention of IP addresses assigned to the source of a connection. In most cases of online crime however, the IP address of a suspect is known to the police, who thus needs access to *additional* data that may be retained *together or in connection with* the IP address, in order to establish and/or confirm the identity of said suspect. Accordingly, the part of the CJEU ruling referring to IP addresses making no reference to any other associated data, does not say much about what national data retention provisions (or obligations) are thereby given the 'green light'. Understandably, a provision providing for the retention of IP addresses *only*, if not accompanied by provisions allowing for the retention of additional data, could be of little, if any, practical significance, as IP addresses do not on their own disclose the identity of the user behind them.[42]

---

[40] The said provision of the Data Retention Directive provides for the retention of data 'concerning Internet access, Internet e-mail and Internet telephony: (i) the date and time of the log-in and log-off of the Internet access service, based on a certain time zone, *together with the IP address, whether dynamic or static, allocated by the Internet access service provider to a communication*, and the user ID of the subscriber or registered user' (emphasis added).

[41] This has also explicitly been acknowledged by the CJEU in *La Quadrature du Net 'I'* (n 12) para 152.

[42] For a related critique of the CJEU ruling on IP addresses specifically as far as dynamic IP addresses are concerned, see Adam Juszczak and Elisa Sason, 'Recalibrating Data Retention in the EU' (2021) 4 Eucrim 238, who even express doubt as to whether dynamic addresses should be considered as covered by the relevant CJEU ruling (given that the identity of the user cannot often be reached without access to additional data which cannot lawfully be subject to a general and indiscriminate data retention obligation). See also CJEU, Judgment of 30 April 2024, La Quadrature du Net a.o. c. Premier Ministre and Ministre de la Culture (C-470/21) ECLI:EU:C:2024:370 ('*La Quadrature du Net 'II'*'), paras 95–122, where the Court imposes requirements regarding the separation and linking of the two data categories; said judgment however (briefly discussed below in section 3.4) concerned the purpose of combatting crime in general, not serious crime, which was the focus of national provisions subject to the Cypriot and also previous CJEU case law. It is uncertain if those requirements will acquire any relevance to cases concerning serious crime too.

Indeed, the said part of the relevant CJEU rulings is accompanied by another part referring to the permissibility of a general and indiscriminate retention of 'data relating to the civil identity of users of electronic communications systems',[43] such as data covering 'the contact details of those users, such as their addresses'.[44] Thus, though this is not highlighted in the *NM* judgment, according to the CJEU, it may be permissible—under EU law—for national laws to provide for a general and indiscriminate retention of IP addresses *and* of the identity and contact details of the users behind them for the purposes of combating serious crime and preventing serious threats to public security.[45]

The next question that should be addressed is whether sections 6 and 8 of Law 183(I)/ 2007 or even sections 6(b) and 8(b) of that law which, as explained above, related to the access order at stake in *NM*, are only providing for one such (permissible) data retention obligation, that is, a general and indiscriminate retention of IP addresses and of the identity and contact details of the users behind them. Understandably, if that were the case, said provisions could readily be considered as in accord with EU law, however this is not case. Clearly, sections 6(b) and 8(b) of Law 183(I)/2007 provide for the general and indiscriminate retention of *(much) more* than merely the IP address and civil identity of users.

Two are the options open to a court following one such conclusion: either it will consider the whole of the relevant provisions as incompatible with EU law and disapply them, or it will isolate any compatible parts of those provisions and disapply only the incompatible ones.[46] Though it did not say that expressly, the Court in *NM* obviously favoured the second of these options, and indeed, the parts of sections 6(b) and 8(b) of Law 183(I)/2007 referring to IP addresses and the name and address of the subscriber (or user) behind the IP addresses are not incompatible with EU law, as this particular type of data is clearly the data in relation to which the CJEU ruled that a general and indiscriminate retention obligation may be permissible.

The final question arises as to whether this is a permissible approach towards finding incompatibility with EU law. Most certainly, this question has not explicitly been answered by the CJEU in its relevant case law. Yet, nothing in that case law could be taken as hinting that parts of national provisions providing for something which is permissible under EU law should still be disapplied because some other parts of those provisions provide for something which is incompatible with EU law. More generally, partial incompatibility with EU law seems very well possible[47] and unless, the compatible parts are *not* 'stand-alone' and/or independent from the incompatible parts, there should not be any such thing as an automatic 'incompatibility infection' rendering the whole of the national provision and/or measure ineffective and/or inapplicable. Indeed, that would be an overly stringent

---

[43] *SpaceNet* (n 15) para 97.
[44] *La Quadrature du Net 'I'* (n 12) para 157.
[45] *SpaceNet* (n 15) para 97, adopting previous case law.
[46] Notably, the dis-application of the rule in either case must be immediate given that as the CJEU has clarified, save in very exceptional cases, national courts do not have the power to maintain even temporarily the effects of rules found to be incompatible with EU law, see *Prokuratuur* (n 13) paras 214–18. This confirms that the different approach adopted by the UK High Court a few years ago in *R (The National Council for Civil Liberties (Liberty)) v Secretary of State for the Home Department & Anor* [2018] EWHC 975 (Admin), where the court refrained from immediately disapplying the legal provisions declared incompatible with EU law to give reasonable time to the Parliament to amend (and correct) UK data retention law may have been wrong.
[47] There have been cases in which the CJEU has found national measures to be *partly* incompatible with EU law, see eg CJEU, Judgment of 17 May 2017, *X v Ministerraad* (C-68/15) ECLI:EU:C:2017:379 ('X'); CJEU, Judgment of 30 January 2020, *Köln-Aktienfonds Deka* (C-156/17, Publié au Recueil numérique) ECLI:EU:C:2020:51.

approach, which unwisely underestimates the practical effects of national rules' disapplication and which could unnecessarily result in various problems in Member States as a result of the collapse of legislation which, in most cases, serves the public interest in one way or another.[48] The principle of supremacy of EU law is certainly not intended to produce such results, when the preservation of the EU legal order and its effective application across the EU is not threatened.

In the case under discussion, the relevant provisions of Law 183(I)/2007 provide for the general and indiscriminate retention of *both* data, which EU law allows for it to be subject to one such obligation (namely, source IP address and user civil identity) and data which cannot lawfully be retained in this way. There seems to be no valid reason why the part of said provisions which concern the first type of data should also be disapplied. Indeed, the retention of source IP addresses and user civil identity data serve a vital public interest, specifically the detection of offences, including child pornography ones, committed online, which has been highlighted by national governments and acknowledged by the CJEU.[49]

In this respect, though the Court in *NM* does not explain its decision in this way, its conclusion that there is no incompatibility with EU law affecting the validity of the first part of the data access order in question can be considered correct. Of course, it should be stressed out that this is so, provided that said order was authorizing access to no data other than the IP address and user civil identity, something which, as already mentioned, does not arise clearly from the judgment of the court. Indeed, an access order authorizing police access to data lawfully retained cannot but be upheld.[50] What is more, such an approach mirrors courts handling a delicate legal situation in a way that exploits the green light given by the CJEU to certain specific indiscriminate data retention obligations, thereby achieving a balance between the competing interests involved (to the extent possible) while at the same time, respecting the supremacy of EU law.

3.4 Repercussions on the future of data retention law in Cyprus

Most certainly, the 2023 judgment (*NM*) will influence the future of the Cypriot legal landscape with regards to data retention. Indeed, whereas right after the 2021 (plenary) Supreme Court judgment (*Hadjioannou*), it appeared that courts would lean towards the quick annulment of data access orders issued under Law 183(I)/2007 without an inquiry in the specific type of telecommunication (or internet data) involved in each case, courts are now likely to consider the approach adopted in *NM* and at least some of them, will most likely adopt it. This is even more so given a more recent CJEU judgment discussed

---

[48] Related to this is the decision of the UK High Court in *R (The National Council for Civil Liberties (Liberty)) v Secretary of State for the Home Department & Anor* [2018] EWHC 975 (Admin), para 46, where the court referred to the 'chaos and damage to the public interest' that the disapplication of a part of national legislation declared incompatible with EU would cause to the country.

[49] *La Quadrature du Net 'I'* (n 12) para 154.

[50] It should be clarified that this position does not combine retention with access in way that ignores that they are two distinct interferences with privacy and data protection rights. Nor does it suggest that when access is limited, retention beyond what is compatible with EU law and thus, permissible will be remedied or become acceptable. The position expressed here refers to both access and retention being limited to what is compatible with EU law, the novelty of the approach only being that in order for retention to be considered as such, the relevant provisions must be examined in parts and not in their entirety. If seen in their entirety, a finding of incompatibility with EU is inevitable.

below. As a result, not all data access orders should now be expected to quickly or easily be annulled. Moreover, the police, taking into account *NM*, may start limiting the scope of its access requests and seek court orders authorizing access to IP addresses and/or user civil identity data only rendering it clear that no access to data retained unlawfully is sought.

Moreover, given that, as already stated, the deviation of the court from *Hadjioannou* is somewhat controversial, the possibility cannot be excluded of the Cyprus Supreme Court exploiting a chance to 'correct' *Hadjioannou*, thereby clarifying or setting the relevant legal rule right, to the benefit of all stakeholders, namely, the judiciary, the legal and law enforcement community, and criminal suspects.

It should be noted that more recently, specifically on 30 April 2024, the CJEU issued another judgment, namely *LQDN2/Hadopi*,[51] relating to the retention of IP addresses and civil identity data. Though a thorough assessment of said decision is outside the scope of the present chapter which focuses on law as of 2023, the said decision is quite important, as it perhaps necessitates new or amending legislation in Cyprus. Prior to said recent judgment, CJEU case law referred to the combatting of serious crime and threats to national security stating that it is only for these purposes that the indiscriminate retention of source IP addresses and civil identity data was compatible with EU law.

The CJEU in *LQDN2/Hadopi* essentially confined that (previous) case law, in particular *La Quadrature du Net and others*, to national legislation providing for the retention of *additional* data, which in combination with IP addresses, could 'allow precise conclusions to be drawn about the private life of the persons whose data were concerned and, consequently, to lead to a serious interference with the fundamental rights enshrined in Articles 7 and 8 of the Charter'.[52] First of all, by doing so, the CJEU seems to confirm that consistently to what has been argued above (see section 3.1), it is very well possible for a data retention obligation that goes *beyond* IP addresses and civil identity data to be considered permissible and compatible with EU law, *when it comes to its parts referring to IP addresses and civil identity data*. In this respect, the recent decision of the CJEU backs up the assessment conducted by this chapter (see section 3.3), though it also introduces some uncertainty as is explained below.

The CJEU went on to state that a general and indiscriminate retention of IP addresses may be permissible also in cases where the purpose is to combat *crime in general* (as opposed to serious crime) provided however that 'it is genuinely ruled out that that retention could give rise to serious interferences with the private life of the person concerned due to the possibility of drawing precise conclusions about that person by, inter alia, linking those IP addresses with a set of traffic or location data which have also been retained by those providers'.[53] Though the CJEU waters down the prohibition on general and indiscriminate data retention obligations even more, the extent to which it does so is not as great as it may be appear. Indeed, the condition imposed by the CJEU requires that national legislation lay down 'clear and precise rules relating to those retention arrangements, which must meet strict requirements',[54] which the CJEU later describes by reference to specific technical and other requirements ensuring watertight separation between the different categories of

---

[51] *La Quadrature du Net 'II'* (n 42).
[52] *LQDN2/Hadopi*, para 81.
[53] ibid para 82.
[54] ibid para 85.

retained data.[55] Accordingly, Cyprus (and perhaps other Member States) will need new (or amending) legislation in order to be able to take advantage of the new 'green light' given by the CJEU. Presumably, there will also be technical matters that will also have to be clarified and/or resolved before that. Indeed, Law 183(I)/2007 contains nothing close to the provisions on retention arrangements described by the Court. Moreover, said Law is also confined to the combatting of serious crime, and therefore, as it now stands, it cannot be used as the basis of orders giving access to retained data for the combatting of crime in general.

Unfortunately, *LQDN2/Hadopi* also creates some (additional) uncertainty in this area. More specifically, the extensive focus of the Court on the separation in particular, between IP addresses and civil identity, gives rise to a question regarding whether the related technical and other requirements have any relevance to the case of data retention provisions for combatting *serious crime* or if in relation to serious crime, retention and access to both IP addresses and civil identity data continue to be subject to the previous case law which imposed no similar requirements of technical separation and conditions referring to the linking between the two data categories.

4. Concluding Remarks

Following the annulment of the Data Retention Directive by the CJEU in 2014, the legal landscape concerning data retention in Cyprus has gone through various 'eras'. Since there has not been any reaction from the legislature, Law 183(I)/2007, which transposed the Data Retention Directive *verbatim*, has remained in the Cypriot legal order intact. As a result, court orders authorizing police access to retained data were being upheld as being in accordance with the law.

It was not until seven years later, specifically in 2021 and after *Tele2 Sverige*, that the data retention provisions of Law 183(I)/2007 were considered as incompatible with EU law and therefore, were disapplied in a number of cases jointly examined by the Cyprus Supreme Court, which, sitting in full plenary, annulled all data access orders in question. While, right after said judgment (and because of it forming binding precedent) similar orders were being annulled or leave was granted allowing their challenge through certiorari applications, a court in 2023 came to adopt a different approach. More specifically, relying on the more recent CJEU case law referring to the general and indiscriminate retention of IP addresses and user civil identity data, the Court looked into the specific telecommunication (or internet) data involved in the case before it and effectively found that to the extent that the Cypriot law provided for the general and indiscriminate retention of IP addresses, it was not incompatible with the EU law. Accordingly, it upheld the court authorizing police access to the relevant data.

Despite some weaknesses and though the way said Court deviated from *Hadjioannou* is somewhat controversial, the relevant approach should be considered appropriate and correct. As a result, it is very likely that it will signal a change in how the judiciary approaches cases challenging the validity of data access orders issued on the basis of Law 183(I)/2007. It may even lead to a new full plenary Supreme Court judgment seeking to vary or clarify

---

[55] ibid paras 86–93.

the rule of *Hadjioannou* (the 2021 Supreme Court judgment), thereby aligning it with the approach and outcome of *NM* (the 2023 judgment).

Additionally, the police should be expected to adjust its approach when it comes to applying to the court for data access orders so as to limit the requested access to data lawfully retained. Ultimately, when the relevant legal landscape settles and becomes clear, there will also be less, if any, certiorari applications challenging the validity of access orders on grounds relating to the compatibility of the data retention provisions with EU law.

Of course, given the most recent CJEU case law, which touches data retention for combatting crime in general, Cyprus may have to reconsider the relevant framework thoroughly, as the one currently in place is confined to serious crime alone.

10
Data Retention in Ireland
When European Law Meets National Recalcitrance

TJ McIntyre

1. Introduction

There is much already written about data retention in Ireland, primarily on the domestic law and the CJEU cases it has prompted.[1] In this chapter I take a different perspective, based on my experience campaigning on the issue as chairperson of Digital Rights Ireland. Rather than discussing the substantive law around data retention, I examine Irish recalcitrance in complying with that law. Specifically, how the State continued to enforce national data retention law for six years after *Tele2 Sverige*[2] confirmed its illegality, attempted to re-litigate the legality of indiscriminate data retention before the national courts, and reformed domestic law only when forced to act by the CJEU decision in *Garda Síochána*.[3]

Ireland is of course not the only jurisdiction to push back against the CJEU jurisprudence limiting mass surveillance. Governments across the EU have resented the CJEU for curtailing their securitarian agendas, and for the last decade there has been what Mitsilegas et al describe as a 'tug of war between Member States' desire to maintain generalised and indiscriminate data retention schemes and the upholding of fundamental rights'.[4]

However, the Irish experience is a particularly stark example of a state responding in a way which undermined the rule of law. In the words of one High Court judge: '[t]he State, rather than giving effect to EU law by disapplying the unlawful [retention and access] sections sought instead to re-litigate arguments already dismissed by the CJEU in our national courts [and] thereby kept the unlawful provisions on life support'.[5] The criminal justice system was also complicit, as the Garda Síochána (police force) continued to access illegally retained data and courts continued to admit it in evidence. When reforming legislation was eventually passed in 2022, it was rushed through the Oireachtas (Irish

---

[1] See eg TJ McIntyre, 'Data Retention in Ireland: Privacy, Policy and Proportionality' (2008) 24 Computer Law & Security Report 326; Maria Helen Murphy, 'Data Retention in the Aftermath of *Digital Rights Ireland and Seitlinger*' [2014] Irish Criminal Law Journal 105; David Fennelly, 'Data Retention in Ireland' in Marek Zubik, Jan Podkowik, and Robert Rybski (eds), *European Constitutional Courts towards Data Retention Laws* (Springer International Publishing 2021); Xavier Tracol, 'The Joined Cases of *Dwyer*, *SpaceNet* and *VD* and *SR* before the European Court of Justice: The Judgments of the Grand Chamber about Data Retention Continue Falling on Deaf Ears in Member States' (2023) 48 Computer Law & Security Review 105773.
[2] CJEU, Judgment of 21 December 2016, *Tele2 Sverige* (C-203/15 and C-698/15) ECLI:EU:C:2016:970.
[3] CJEU, Judgment of 5 April 2022, *Commissioner of An Garda Síochána* (C-140/20) ECLI:EU:C:2022:258.
[4] Valsamis Mitsilegas and others, 'Data Retention and the Future of Large-scale Surveillance: The Evolution and Contestation of Judicial Benchmarks' (2022) European Law Journal <https://doi.org/10.1111/eulj.12417> accessed 25 September 2024.
[5] Per Murphy J in *DPP v Gerard Cervi*, Bill no CCDP 0028/2019, trial transcript, 12 December 2022, p 58.

Parliament) in just four days, and still failed to address many fundamental rights concerns.[6] In this chapter I analyse this response and argue that it highlights significant problems in how the Irish legal system guarantees fundamental rights against state surveillance.

2. Legislative Context: The Communications (Retention of Data) Act 2011

Data retention first attracted public attention in 2001 when journalist Karlin Lillington revealed that telecommunications providers were storing traffic and location data for six years, contrary to the first ePrivacy Directive.[7,8] This prompted scrutiny by the Data Protection Commissioner, who threatened to take action against providers and the State unless this system was regularised. Following this intervention, data retention was given a (questionable) basis by a secret ministerial order in 2002.[9] However, the Data Protection Commissioner ('DPC') continued to press for primary legislation. This was eventually adopted as Part 7 of the Criminal Justice (Terrorist Offences) Act 2005 ('the 2005 Act'), albeit on a rushed basis with no prior notice or consultation.[10]

After the adoption of the Data Retention Directive, Part 7 of the 2005 Act was replaced with the Communications (Retention of Data) Act 2011 ('the 2011 Act'). The 2011 Act was a largely verbatim transposition of the Data Retention Directive.[11] It set different retention periods for internet data (one year) and telephony data (two years).[12] Retained data could be accessed by the Garda Síochána, the Defence Forces, the Revenue Commissioners, the Garda Síochána Ombudsman Commission (the police disciplinary body), and the Competition and Consumer Protection Commission.[13] Access to retained data was by internal authorisation: there was no requirement of approval by a judge or independent agency.[14] Instead an official of a certain rank within each body could make a 'disclosure request' to a service provider in order to access retained data in relation to State security, serious crimes,[15] complaints against police members, and saving of human life.[16]

---

[6] Cormac McQuinn, 'Concern at "Rushed" Nature of Proposed Law to Deal with Fallout from Dwyer Appeal on Data' (*The Irish Times*, 30 June 2022) <https://www.irishtimes.com/politics/oireachtas/2022/06/30/concern-at-rushed-nature-of-proposed-law-to-deal-with-fallout-from-dwyer-appeal-on-data/> accessed 2 September 2022.

[7] Directive 2002/58/EC of the European Parliament and of the Council of 12 July 2002 concerning the processing of personal data and the protection of privacy in the electronic communications sector (Directive on privacy and electronic communications) [2002] OJ L 201/37.

[8] Karlin Lillington, 'Retention of Mobile Call Records Queried' (*The Irish Times*, 7 November 2001) <https://www.irishtimes.com/business/retention-of-mobile-call-records-queried-1.336042> accessed 16 August 2023.

[9] See generally McIntyre (n 1).

[10] See generally ibid.

[11] Directive 2006/24/EC of the European Parliament and of the Council of 15 March 2006 on the retention of data generated or processed in connection with the provision of publicly available electronic communications services or of public communications networks and amending Directive 2002/58/EC [2006] OJ L 105/54.

[12] Communications (Retention of Data) Act 2011, section 3.

[13] Section 6 of ibid, as amended by sections 1(5) and 89(b)(i) of the Competition and Consumer Protection Act 2014 and as applied by section 98 of the Garda Síochána Act 2005.

[14] The operation of this system in An Garda Síochána and the role of the internal Telecoms Liaison Unit is set out in *Dwyer v Commissioner of An Garda Síochána and others* [2018] IEHC 685 at para 3.88 onwards.

[15] Including revenue offences and competition offences.

[16] See section 6 of the <?IBT>Communications (Retention of Data) Act (n 12), as amended by sections 1(5) and 89(b)(i) of the Competition and Consumer Protection Act 2014 and as applied by section 98 of the Garda Síochána Act 2005.

The 2011 Act did not require that individuals be notified of access to their data. There was limited provision for investigation and redress in case of wrongful access to data through a Complaints Referee mechanism,[17] and light-touch annual oversight by a designated judge of the High Court.[18]

3. Challenges to the Communications (Retention of Data) Act 2011

3.1 *Digital Rights Ireland*

Litigation challenging data retention was already underway when the 2011 Act was passed. Digital Rights Ireland had started a High Court action in August 2006 challenging the 2002 ministerial order and Part 7 of the 2005 Act on the basis of national constitutional law, the ECHR, and EU law. Following some procedural skirmishing, in January 2012 the High Court made a request for a preliminary ruling from the CJEU on the validity of the Data Retention Directive. This—along with the Austrian reference in *Seitlinger and others*—led in April 2014 to the well-known CJEU judgment in *Digital Rights Ireland*,[19] invalidating the Data Retention Directive.

When the matter returned to the Irish courts, Digital Rights Ireland amended its case to challenge the 2011 Act also. In November 2015 it applied for a preliminary hearing before the High Court to determine the EU law issues. However, the hearing of that application was delayed pending the CJEU decision on the *Tele2 Sverige* references from Sweden and the United Kingdom, and the High Court ultimately did not decide on it until July 2017. At that point the High Court refused the application for a preliminary hearing, finding that a full trial was more appropriate given the complex issues of law and disputed issues of fact.[20]

After that decision Digital Rights Ireland paused its litigation pending the outcome of a parallel challenge being brought by Graham Dwyer, who had been convicted of the murder of Elaine O'Hara following a prosecution which used retained traffic and location data. That case (*Dwyer v Commissioner of An Garda Síochána & others*) was being fast-tracked as Dwyer was in custody and a decision was necessary before his appeal against conviction could progress. Consequently *Dwyer* would determine the central issues about the validity of the 2011 Act sooner and would potentially make the *Digital Rights Ireland* case no longer necessary.

3.2 *Dwyer*

In *Dwyer* the plaintiff challenged two provisions of the 2011 Act: section 3, insofar as it required general and indiscriminate retention of telephony data for two years, and section 6(1)(a), insofar as it allowed for police access to retained telephony data in relation

---

[17] ibid section 10.
[18] ibid section 11.
[19] CJEU, Judgment of 8 April 2014, *Digital Rights Ireland and Seitlinger and others* (C-293/12 and C-594/12) ECLI:EU:C:2014:238.
[20] *Digital Rights Ireland Ltd v Minister for Communications, Marine and Natural Resources* [2017] IEHC 307.

to serious crime without independent authorisation. While the invalidity of these sections was clear in light of *Tele2 Sverige*, the State response was to stall and 're-litigate before the High Court issues that had already been determined by the CJEU'.[21] The State put forward expert testimony on the effectiveness of data retention and the limits of other measures such as data preservation and targeted retention, with a view to persuading the High Court to carry out its own proportionality assessment of indiscriminate retention.[22]

In December 2018 the High Court upheld the plaintiff's challenge.[23] The court declined to revisit the findings of the CJEU in *Tele2 Sverige* regarding proportionality, instead quoting with approval the plaintiff's argument that the court should not allow 'a Member State [to] make sophisticated, clear, cogent arguments before the CJEU [and] by clear implications [sic] have those arguments rejected and then come back before the courts of the Member States and effectively try the same argument again'.[24] The High Court also rejected the State's arguments that the system of internal approval within the Garda Síochána met the CJEU's requirements for independent approval of access to data,[25] and that the retrospective effect of the judgment could be limited.[26]

In January 2019 the High Court therefore made a declaration that section 6(1)(a) of the 2011 Act was invalid insofar as it applied to access to telephony data retained under section 3.[27] Significantly, however, that declaration did not declare section 3 (requiring indiscriminate retention) to be invalid. The plaintiff had not challenged retention for purposes other than the criminal law (such as state security), and the court accepted the State's argument that a narrow declaration was necessary to 'ensure that service providers do not perceive the principal judgment as a basis to destroy or to cease retaining "mobile telephony data"'.[28]

The State appealed this decision to the Supreme Court, which heard the case in December 2019.[29] The State's arguments on appeal largely reprised the case it made in the High Court, and in effect invited the Supreme Court to put itself on a collision course with the CJEU by adopting a strained reading of *Tele2 Sverige* which would allow domestic courts to make their own assessment of the proportionality of general and indiscriminate retention.

The Supreme Court, however, declined to take this approach.[30] While the Court strongly disagreed with the CJEU's ruling in *Tele2 Sverige*, the majority judgment of Clarke CJ stressed the obligation of sincere cooperation with the CJEU[31] and instead opted for a form of judicial dialogue—making a preliminary reference designed to convince the CJEU to change course.[32]

---

[21] Per Murphy J in *DPP v Gerard Cervi* (n 5) p 50.
[22] *Dwyer v Commissioner of An Garda Síochána & others* [2018] IEHC 685 para 3.65.
[23] ibid.
[24] ibid para 3.54.
[25] ibid paras 65–75.
[26] ibid paras 79–89.
[27] *Dwyer v Commissioner of An Garda Síochána & Others* [2019] IEHC 48.
[28] ibid para 6.
[29] Leave to appeal directly to the Supreme Court rather than the Court of Appeal was granted on the basis of the significance of the case: *Dwyer v Commissioner of An Garda Síochána & others* [2019] IESCDET 108.
[30] In a remarkable dissenting judgment, Charlton J argued that no reference should be made on the basis that assessing whether a national measure is a proportionate interference with Charter rights was solely a matter for the national courts, and that the CJEU lacked competence in relation to this case as it arose out of a criminal law matter.
[31] *Dwyer v Commissioner of An Garda Síochána & others* [2020] IESC 4, para 6.5.
[32] Or at least to register its objection to the CJEU's approach.

The Supreme Court decided to refer three sets of issues:

(a) Whether a system of universal retention of certain types of metadata for a fixed period of time is never permissible irrespective of how robust any regime for allowing access to such data may be;
(b) The criteria whereby an assessment can be made as to whether any access regime to such data can be found to be sufficiently independent and robust; and
(c) Whether a national court, should it find that national data retention and access legislation is inconsistent with European Union law, can decide that the national law in question should not be regarded as having been invalid at all times but rather can determine invalidity to be prospective only.[33]

The core of the reference, however, was the first set of issues: the permissibility of what the Supreme Court termed 'universal retention'.[34] In its judgment and the text of the reference itself, the Supreme Court compiled what was essentially a detailed brief arguing for the CJEU to depart from the central finding of *Tele2 Sverige* regarding indiscriminate retention. The Supreme Court was quite scathing regarding the reasoning in *Tele2 Sverige*, stating for example that:

> The conclusion ... that a regime of universal data retention in bulk is *per se* impermissible, irrespective of the terms of such retention or the conditions of access, would appear not to be a conclusion that the legitimate and important objective of investigating serious crime could be achieved by methods less intrusive of the rights of individuals, but rather a conclusion that the objective of investigating serious crime cannot justify the universal retention of bulk communications data however regulated or controlled. This is a value judgment but one not apparent from the Charter.[35]

The Supreme Court highlighted EU case law on the factual nature of assessments of proportionality[36] and noted that 'the differences of function and capacity in relation to obtaining evidence and making findings of fact'[37] between national courts and the CJEU had to be respected—indirectly arguing that the CJEU should defer to the findings of national courts in this area.[38] It went on to make numerous findings of fact supporting the necessity of data retention, which it summarised as follows:

> [I]t is not possible to access that which has not been retained. If, ... it is not permissible to have 'universal' retention of metadata, notwithstanding the robustness of any access

---

[33] *Dwyer v Commissioner of An Garda Síochána & others* [2020] IESC 4, para 7.2.
[34] A more palatable rebranding of 'general and indiscriminate retention'.
[35] *Dwyer v Commissioner of An Garda Síochána & others* [2020] IESC 4, para 6.16, per Clark CJ.
[36] ibid para 3.30.
[37] ibid para 6.5.
[38] In a curious aside Clarke CJ advanced the idea that Member States should be allowed greater leeway to introduce data retention as 'the precise extent to which such matters may have such an effect on citizens may well vary from Member State to Member State, not least because of the different experiences within Member States of pervasive scrutiny on the part of police authorities': ibid, at para 6.17. This invokes the trope that post-communist Member States have greater awareness of the risks of mass surveillance. While this may well be true as a factual matter, the implication that the Irish state can be better trusted with these powers smacks of exceptionalism.

regime, then it follows that many . . . serious crimes against women, children and other vulnerable persons will not be capable of detection or successful prosecution. Against that background, the Supreme Court has made the following findings of fact:

(i) Alternative forms of data retention, by means of geographical targeting or otherwise, would be ineffective in achieving the objectives of the prevention, investigation, detection and prosecution of at least certain types of serious crime, and further, could give rise to the potential violation of other rights of the individual;

(ii) The objective of the retention of data by any lesser means than that of a general data retention regime, subject to the necessary safeguards, is unworkable; and

(iii) The objectives of the prevention, investigation, detection and prosecution of serious crime would be significantly compromised in the absence of a general data retention regime.[39]

The reference in *Dwyer* (anonymised by the CJEU as *GD v Commissioner of An Garda Síochána & others*) was heard by the Grand Chamber in September 2021, alongside other data retention references in *SpaceNet*[40] and *VD and SR*.[41] The reference was widely viewed as the 'spearhead of an attempt by EU member States to persuade the European Court of Justice to revisit its previous case law'.[42] The State relied heavily on the argument that '[i]n contrast to the position in the references from *Tele2 Sverige/Watson* onwards, in this Reference, the Supreme Court of Ireland has had the benefit of detailed evidence, including expert evidence, on the forms and feasibility of data retention'.[43] The State's arguments were unusually aggressive, including assertions that the *Tele2 Sverige* judgment 'could not be reconciled with the concept of a Union based on the rule of law'[44] and that the CJEU was 'legislating in this field'.[45]

The CJEU Grand Chamber, however, did not engage with these claims in any detail. Its judgment largely restated its earlier findings from *La Quadrature du Net 'I'*[46] and *Prokuratuur*[47] to find that the ePrivacy Directive precludes general and indiscriminate data retention for the purpose of combating serious crime, that internal authorisation of access by an internal police unit is insufficient to meet the requirement of authorisation by an independent administrative body, and that EU law precludes a national court from limiting the temporal effects of a declaration of invalidity. Indeed, there was palpable 'fatigue

---

[39] Supreme Court of Ireland, 'Order for Reference by the Court of Certain Questions on the Interpretation of European Union law to the Court of Justice of the European Union under Article 267 of the Treaty on the Functioning of the European Union' (25 March 2020) para 8.5 <https://curia.europa.eu/juris/showPdf.jsf?text=&docid=226341&pageIndex=0&doclang=en&mode=req&dir=&occ=first&part=1&cid=1931729> accessed 25 April 2024.

[40] CJEU, Judgment of 27 October 2022, *SpaceNet* (C-793/19 and C-794/19) ECLI:EU:C:2022:702.

[41] CJEU, Judgment of 20 September 2022, *VD* and *SR* (C-339/20 and C-397/20) ECLI:EU:C:2022:703.

[42] Naomi O'Leary, 'Irish Murder Case Entangled in EU Data Power Struggle' (*The Irish Times*, 13 September 2021) <https://www.irishtimes.com/news/crime-and-law/irish-murder-case-entangled-in-eu-data-power-struggle-1.4673042> accessed 14 September 2021.

[43] 'Written Observations of the Defendants in Case C-140/20' (*AsktheEU.org*, 7 August 2020) para 28 <https://www.asktheeu.org/en/request/10950/> accessed 5 August 2023.

[44] ibid 48.

[45] ibid para 7; <https://www.asktheeu.org/en/request/written_observations_of_ireland_4> accessed 7 October 2023.

[46] CJEU, Judgment of 6 October 2020, *La Quadrature du Net and others* (C-511/18, C-512/18 and C-520/18) ECLI:EU:C:2020:791 ('*La Quadrature du Net 'I'*').

[47] CJEU, Judgment of 2 March 2021, *Prokuratuur* (C-746/18) ECLI:EU:C:2021:152.

and irritation'[48] that the Supreme Court had persisted with the *Dwyer* reference after being invited to withdraw it as unnecessary after *La Quadrature du Net 'I'*[49] and *Privacy International*.[50] Advocate General Campos Sánchez-Bordona noted that those judgments 'answered in full' all the questions referred, that they were 'recapitulatory' and 'have resolved the debate' regarding data retention, and suggested that '[a]ny other request for preliminary ruling on the same subject would therefore warrant a reasoned order [without oral argument] pursuant to Article 99 of the Rules of Procedure of the Court of Justice'.[51]

Following the CJEU decision in *Garda Síochána*, in July 2022 the Supreme Court affirmed the earlier High Court declaration of invalidity.[52] However, this left indiscriminate retention in place: as already noted the High Court declaration merely invalidated section 6(1)(a) regarding *access* to retained telephony data without independent authorisation. Consequently, even after the Supreme Court decision the 2011 Act largely remained in force, still required indiscriminate retention of telecommunications data, and police were still able to access that data for criminal investigations using other mechanisms such as search warrants or production orders.[53]

This was a remarkable outcome. In its preliminary reference the Supreme Court specifically asked whether indiscriminate data retention is permissible, but by affirming such a narrow declaration it effectively ignored the CJEU's answer. This was arguably incompatible with the judgment in *Garda Síochána* itself, in which the Grand Chamber held that the Supreme Court was *bound* to make a declaration of invalidity[54] and that:

> Maintaining the effects of national legislation such as the 2011 Act would mean that the legislation would continue to impose on providers of electronic communications services obligations which are contrary to EU law and which seriously interfere with the fundamental rights of the persons whose data have been retained.[55]

The text of the declaration, it should be noted, had been agreed by the plaintiff with the State defendants and reflected his own selfish interest in challenging his conviction and the State's desire to continue with indiscriminate retention regardless of EU law. By merely rubber-stamping the declaration the Supreme Court allowed the State to persist in its law-breaking, arguably breaching the Court's duty of sincere cooperation and the obligation to apply EU law *ex officio* where necessary to protect the public interest.[56] This highlights an important limitation of individual challenges as a means of ensuring fundamental rights: the interests of individual litigants and the wider public are not always aligned.

---

[48] Tracol (n 1) s 4.
[49] *La Quadrature du Net 'I'* (n 46).
[50] CJEU, Judgment of 6 October 2020, *Privacy International* (C-623/17) ECLI:EU:C:2020:790.
[51] *Commissioner of An Garda Síochána* (n 3) paras 5–7.
[52] Shane Phelan, 'Graham Dwyer Case: Supreme Court Will Dismiss State Appeal against Data Ruling' (Irish Independent, 26 May 2022) <https://www.independent.ie/irish-news/courts/graham-dwyer-case-supreme-court-will-dismiss-State-appeal-against-data-ruling-41691335.html> accessed 25 April 2024.
[53] Conor Gallagher, 'Garda Develop Workaround to Obtain Mobile Data Following Dwyer Ruling' (*The Irish Times*, 15 November 2021) <https://www.irishtimes.com/news/crime-and-law/garda-develop-workaround-to-obtain-mobile-data-following-dwyer-ruling-1.4728497> accessed 17 August 2023.
[54] *Commissioner of An Garda Síochána* (n 3) paras 123, 128, 129.
[55] Ibid paras 123, 122.
[56] See eg Tobias Nowak and Monika Glavina, 'National Courts as Regulatory Agencies and the Application of EU Law' (2021) 43 Journal of European Integration 739.

4. Data Retention and the Criminal Justice System after *Tele2 Sverige*

In this section I turn to consider how the criminal justice system persisted in accessing retained data and using it as evidence in the period after the judgment in *Tele2 Sverige*.

4.1 Police continued to have access to data without independent authorisation

The Garda Síochána realised almost immediately that the *Tele2 Sverige* judgment meant that use of the 2011 Act was no longer tenable. Internal correspondence on the day of the judgment flagged the issue: in January 2017 the Garda legal section confirmed that the 2011 Act was in breach of EU standards, and in March 2017 the Garda Commissioner wrote to the Department of Justice[57] stating that '[i]t is the view of An Garda Síochána that the [2011 Act] would fall foul of European Union law based on the judgment' and that 'urgent legislative change' was needed.[58]

However when no legislative change was forthcoming, the Garda Síochána persisted in accessing data under the 2011 Act, despite knowing the risks this presented for future prosecutions. Murphy J summarised this in stark terms in the 2022 murder prosecution *DPP v Gerard Cervi*, stating that:

> The obligation to disapply national rules with conflict with EU law has been restated and affirmed many times. It is applicable to national administrative authorities, such as An Garda Síochána, as well as to national courts ... On the evidence, it is clear that the Irish authorities, the Department of Justice and Equality, and An Garda Síochána were aware in early 2017 that the 2011 Act and in particular, section 3 and 6 thereof ... contravened EU law and were precluded by EU law. The gardaí were aware immediately that it had immediate implications for the continued use of the 2011 Act. Being so aware, they were under an obligation to disapply it. Notwithstanding their knowledge that sections 3 and 6 in particular, were precluded by EU law, they continued to use those provisions until December 2018 [the date of the High Court judgment in *Dwyer*].[59]

After the High Court judgment in *Dwyer*, the Garda Síochána stopped using section 6 of the 2011 Act for criminal law purposes, and instead moved to accessing retained data using judicially issued search warrants.[60] This, however, was at best a stopgap: while it addressed the issue of independent authorisation for access to data, it could not address the fact that the underlying data was still being retained illegally.

---

[57] The full name of the department varied during this period but for the sake of consistency I refer to it as the Department of Justice throughout.
[58] See Irish Human Rights and Equality Commission, 'Submissions of Amicus Curiae in the Cases of *The People (at the Suit of the DPP) v Caolan Smyth* and *The People (at the Suit of the DPP) v Gary McAreavey*' 27 <https://www.ihrec.ie/documents/submissions-of-amicus-curiae-in-the-cases-of-the-people-at-the-suit-of-the-dpp-vs-caolan-smyth-and-the-people-at-the-suit-of-the-dpp-vs-gary-mcareavey/> accessed 3 May 2023.
[59] *DPP v Gerard Cervi* (n 5) pp 59–61.
[60] Typically under section 10 of the Criminal Justice (Miscellaneous Provisions) Act 1997. See Gallagher (n 53).

4.2 Retained data continued to be admitted in criminal trials

In *Garda Síochána* the State argued that even if Irish law did not create an independent authority for *ex ante* approval of access to retained data, it nevertheless provided adequate safeguards against abuse through a supposedly 'multi-layered *ex post facto* review', including 'intense scrutiny in the context of the criminal trial'.[61] In reality, however, this did not prevent the use of illegally accessed data in prosecutions and criminal courts generally continued to admit such evidence.

The Irish law on admissibility of wrongfully obtained evidence is complex and has changed significantly over recent years.[62] In short, however, different standards apply depending on whether the trial court finds the evidence was obtained in breach of constitutional rights or merely illegally.[63] There is a presumption that unconstitutionally obtained evidence should be excluded, but the courts will take into account whether the breach of constitutional rights was deliberate and conscious, reckless or grossly negligent, or merely inadvertent, and whether the police action was lawful at the time but became unlawful due to some subsequent legal development.[64] In relation to illegally obtained evidence the courts apply a weaker balancing test which in practice leans towards evidence being admissible.[65]

Applying these standards, the courts have generally found sufficient leeway to admit communications data notwithstanding that it had been illegally retained and accessed. For example, in *DPP v Doherty*[66] the Court of Appeal held that communications data showing that the appellant had used an internet café to send emails was not personal data triggering a right to privacy, and in any event whether that data had been retained illegally was irrelevant as 'the right to privacy cannot extent to participation in criminal activity'.[67] In *DPP v Smyth and McAreavey*[68] the Court of Appeal held that the lack of independent authorisation for access could be disregarded as it was 'inconceivable that if such an authority existed, and approval had been sought, that access would have been refused',[69] and that in any event there was a very limited privacy interest in the small set of phone records accessed. In *DPP v Dwyer*[70] the Court of Appeal held that access and use of the appellant's phone data was not a direct breach of his rights under the Charter of Fundamental Rights but merely a breach of the ePrivacy Directive as read in light of the Charter. Consequently, the weaker balancing test for illegally obtained evidence applied, so that the data was admissible.[71]

---

[61] 'Written Observations of the Defendants in Case C-140/20' (n 43) para 57.
[62] See eg Claire Hamilton, 'Interpreting Change through Legal Culture: The Case of the Irish Exclusionary Rule' (2021) 41 Legal Studies 355.
[63] See most recently the restatement of these rules in *DPP v Quirke* [2023] IESC 20.
[64] ibid para 53.
[65] *People (AG) v O'Brien* [1965] IR 142.
[66] *DPP v Doherty* [2019] IECA 209.
[67] Per Edwards Ps in *DPP v Doherty* [2019] IECA 209 at paras 124–27. The proposition that there is no right to privacy in criminal activity is a particularly problematic one. While it does have some foundation in Irish cases such as *CRH Plc, Irish Cement Ltd v Competition and Consumer Protection Commission* [2018] 1 IR 521 but is incompatible with other authority such as *Benedik v Slovenia*, App no 62357/14, 27 July 2018 in which the ECtHR notes at para 99 that 'the questions raised by the Government concerning the applicability of Article 8 [to disclosure of IP addresses] are to be answered independently from the legal or illegal character of the activity in question'.
[68] *DPP v Smyth and McAreavey* [2022] IECA 182.
[69] Per Birmingham P in *DPP v Smyth and McAreavey* ibid para 28.
[70] *DPP v Dwyer* [2023] IECA 70.
[71] ibid at paras 127–30.

In at least some of these cases there has been an element of motivated reasoning as the courts seek to avoid giving full effect to the CJEU jurisprudence. This is exemplified in a remarkable July 2022 ruling by High Court judge Tony Hunt in the murder trial of *DPP v Wayne Cooney*.[72] In that case Hunt J held that retained telephony data was admissible where it had been accessed in 2019 by a search warrant. However in the course of that ruling Hunt J went on to say that the CJEU's approach 'exhibits a strange and unusual set of priorities'. He stated that there was no evidence for the CJEU's claim that phone data would 'reveal a significant amount of the private life of the person concerned', a view which he said is 'not universally held outside the membership of the CJEU'.

Hunt J rejected the argument that the law had been clear since 2016, saying that 'many reputable institutions and bodies believed the data privacy rights in question ought to yield to the public interest in the investigation of serious crimes', and that in the *Garda Síochána* case a number of Member States urged the CJEU to allow police forces to continue to access mobile phone data. Hunt J therefore said that as of 2019 the law was still in a state of flux and it was still a 'matter of considerable contention' as to whether data retention was permitted. Hunt J said that there was no sense in which gardai or the Attorney-General, the government or the mobile phone providers could be said to be guilty of a 'deliberate and conscious violation of European Union privacy rights by maintaining and operating the 2011 Act ... pending a definitive ruling by the Court of Justice'. He concluded by saying that there had been no 'legal tomfoolery' on the part of the State.

This ruling highlights a tactic frequently used by the State in the area of fundamental rights: to argue that EU law is not binding on the State until there is a ruling against it, so that in the meantime the State can avoid compliance by affecting uncertainty as to what EU law requires. There is an interesting comparison to be made with the December 2022 ruling of High Court judge Deirdre Murphy in the murder trial of *DPP v Gerard Cervi*.[73] In that case she rejected the prosecution argument that in 2018 the Garda Síochána could still treat the 2011 Act as 'presumptively Constitutional and on the Irish statute books, and presumed to be lawful and valid'. Murphy J. held that 'the logical extension of that argument is that unless and until all Member States of the European Union independently invalidate their national provisions, the decision of the CJEU [in *Tele2 Sverige*] is of no effect. This is patently not so'.[74]

At the time of writing, two of these judgments (*DPP v Smyth and McAreavey*[75] and *DPP v Dwyer*[76]) are under appeal to the Supreme Court, which will consider the admissibility of illegally retained/accessed data in light of the principle that remedies for breach of EU law must be effective and equivalent to remedies for breach of domestic law. These cases may even prompt a further preliminary reference to the CJEU on this issue. However, whatever the outcome of these cases the point remains that, when it mattered, admissibility hearings

---

[72] The transcript is not publicly available but the ruling is extensively quoted in media reports. All the following quotations are taken from: Eoin Reynolds, 'Graham Dwyer Ruling Fails to Stop Prosecution Use of Mobile Phone Evidence in Murder Trial' (*Irish Examiner*, 8 July 2022) <https://www.irishexaminer.com/news/courtandcrime/arid-40913573.html> accessed 25 August 2023; Eoin Reynolds, 'Graham Dwyer Fallout: Judge Makes Significant Ruling on Mobile Data' (*Irish Independent*, 8 July 2022) <https://www.independent.ie/irish-news/graham-dwyer-fallout-judge-makes-significant-ruling-on-mobile-data/41824994.html> accessed 29 August 2023.
[73] *DPP v Gerard Cervi* (n 5).
[74] ibid p 61.
[75] *DPP v Smyth and McAreavey* (n 68).
[76] *DPP v Dwyer* (n 70).

did not serve as an effective *ex post* safeguard to prevent or sanction illegal access to retained data.

4.3 Designated judge did not exercise effective oversight

The State's arguments in *Garda Síochána* cited the designated judge as a further component of Ireland's 'multi-layered *ex post facto* review' of access to retained data.[77] This is a role given to a judge of the High Court who is required to keep the operation of the 2011 Act under review and to ascertain whether the authorities are complying with its provisions.[78] I have argued before[79] that this model of light-touch, part-time oversight by a busy judge with no staff, specialist knowledge, or technical advisors is not fit for purpose, and the period after the *Tele2 Sverige* judgment confirms that assessment. While the judgment in *Tele2 Sverige* was delivered in December 2016, the designated judge (Baker J) did not address it until her annual report in June 2018.[80] In that report Baker J identified that the relevant parts of the 2011 Act were invalid following *Tele2 Sverige* and mentioned the need for reform. However she did not have any power to prevent the authorities from continuing to use those powers, highlighting the weakness of an oversight mechanism which cannot intervene to stop such blatant illegality.[81]

4.4 Data Protection Commissioner did not intervene to prevent operation of data retention system

Another disappointing aspect of the Irish situation was that the DPC, Helen Dixon, did not take any steps to prevent telecommunications companies from retaining data when it became clear after *Tele2 Sverige* and the Murray Review that the 2011 Act was in breach of EU law. The only response by the DPC was to recommend reform of the law.[82] (Unlike the earlier DPC Joe Meade, who threatened to take legal action against the data retention scheme in place prior to 2005.[83]) It may have been that the DPC felt that action was unnecessary as the *Dwyer* case was pending by that time: however, as we have seen, that case took a further five years to resolve during which Irish citizens were subject to serious ongoing breaches of their Charter rights. The DPC could—and should—have respected the

---

[77] 'Written Observations of the Defendants in Case C-140/20' (n 43) para 57.
[78] Communications (Retention of Data) Act (n 12) s 12.
[79] TJ McIntyre, 'Judicial Oversight of Surveillance: The Case of Ireland in Comparative Perspective' in Martin Scheinin, Helle Krunke, and Marina Aksenova (eds), *Judges as Guardians of Constitutionalism and Human Rights* (Edward Elgar 2016).
[80] Marie Baker, 'Report of Designated Judge Made Pursuant to Section 8(2) of the Interception of Postal Packets and Telecommunications Messages (Regulation) Act 1993 and Section 12(1)(c) of the Communications (Retention of Data) Act 2011' (28 June 2018) <http://opac.oireachtas.ie/AWData/Library3/TAOdoclaid02082018d_113723.pdf> accessed 6 February 2019.
[81] It is also notable that Baker J did not refer the matter to the Data Protection Commissioner, as she could have done under section 12 of the Communications (Retention of Data) Act (n 12).
[82] Data Protection Commissioner, 'Annual Report 2017' (2018) 9 <https://www.dataprotection.ie/docimages/documents/DPC%20Annual%20Report%202017.pdf> accessed 19 August 2018.
[83] McIntyre (n 1).

principle of the primacy of EU law by enforcing the ePrivacy Directive to stop indiscriminate retention much sooner.

5. Political Responses after *Tele2 Sverige*

We have already seen that the Garda Síochána sought amending legislation in March 2017, and the pressure for reform increased further in April 2017 when the former Chief Justice, John Murray, delivered a report confirming that the 2011 Act was contrary to EU law ('the Murray Review').[84] Murray had been appointed by the Minister for Justice in January 2016 to examine the legal framework around State access to journalists' communications data. This was prompted by a scandal in which the Garda Síochána Ombudsman Commission was found to have accessed journalists' phone records without a clear legal basis.[85] Murray interpreted his remit widely, and wrote a damning report which found that the 2011 Act and other aspects of Irish data retention practice constituted 'mass surveillance' which in almost all aspects was in breach of both EU and ECHR standards.[86] Indeed, in a very unusual postscript Murray went on to say that State agencies should consider whether they would continue to access this data 'pending the final resolution of issues pertaining to the status of the Act and/or any amending legislation conforming with EU law and obligations under the ECHR'.[87] Translated from the circumspect language of the judiciary, this was a strong warning that the law was so deficient that it should not be relied on any further.

Initially it seemed that reforming legislation would follow promptly. The Department of Justice published the Murray Review in October 2017 along with a general scheme of a bill to replace the 2011 Act. That bill proposed one year retention of (unspecified) categories of data based on ministerial order, judicial authorisation of access to data, and notification after access. In December 2018 the general scheme went through pre-legislative scrutiny before the Oireachtas Joint Committee on Justice and Equality where most stakeholders welcomed the commitment to reform, but criticised the proposal for leaving open the possibility of indiscriminate retention, with no safeguards for journalists, and no effective oversight. In January 2018 the Joint Committee published a report which largely adopted these criticisms.[88]

Despite this early activity, nothing emerged for another four years other than statements from successive Ministers for Justice that drafting of a bill was 'well advanced', 'at an advanced stage', or 'currently being finalised'. By late 2020 these assurances were wearing thin, and the official position became one of waiting for the outcome of the Supreme Court referral

---

[84] John Murray, 'Review of the Law on the Retention of and Access to Communications Data' (Department of Justice and Equality 2017) <http://www.justice.ie/en/JELR/Review_of_the_Law_on_Retention_of_and_Access_to_Communications_Data.pdf/Files/Review_of_the_Law_on_Retention_of_and_Access_to_Communications_Data.pdf> accessed 26 September 2024.

[85] Conor Lally, 'GSOC Trawls Journalists' Phone Records in Inquiry' (*The Irish Times*, 14 January 2016) <http://www.irishtimes.com/news/crime-and-law/gsoc-trawls-journalists-phone-records-in-inquiry-1.2495959> accessed 1 September 2016.

[86] Murray (n 84).

[87] ibid 167.

[88] Joint Committee on Justice and Equality, 'Report on Pre-Legislative Scrutiny of the Communications (Retention of Data) Bill 2017' <http://www.oireachtas.ie/parliament/media/committees/justice/2018/Data-Retention-Report-Final.pdf> accessed 2 May 2018.

to the CJEU in *Garda Síochána*. The reason given was that 'Data retention and access measures reach deep into Member States' criminal justice systems, requiring a high level of legal certainty because of their significant implications for criminal investigations and prosecutions. The CJEU's consideration of the questions referred will assist in bringing clarity to an evolving area of jurisprudence'.[89]

This was a remarkable approach—to continue indefinitely with a system which the CJEU had found to be a serious interference with Charter rights since 2016. It appears to have been motivated by a belief that the State could continue in this deliberate lawbreaking with impunity. Perhaps the most important factor was that the criminal justice system was effectively complicit in this illegality: the Garda Síochána still had access to retained data and courts largely continued to admit it in evidence. There was little political accountability, as data retention was a niche issue of interest to a relatively small number of journalists and parliamentarians.[90] There may also have been a view in Government that the CJEU had conceded some ground in *La Quadrature du Net 'I'* and would back down further when confronted with the Supreme Court's preliminary reference in *Garda Síochána*.

The Government was finally forced to act by the CJEU judgment in *Garda Síochána* on 5 April 2022, but seems to have been entirely surprised by the decision. The Government did not give approval to prepare legislation until nearly two months later, on 31 May 2022, and after that point acted in a way which was calculated to prevent effective scrutiny. There was no prior consultation with the DPC[91] or industry,[92] much less the public or civil society. There was no notification to the European Commission of the proposed law as a draft technical regulation.[93] The Minister for Justice did not publish a draft of the legislation until 21 June 2022. Despite very short notice, the Joint Oireachtas Committee on Justice carried out pre-legislative scrutiny of that draft in a public hearing on 30 June 2022, but the Minister of Justice then effectively negated that scrutiny by publishing an entirely different draft on 1 July 2022. Ultimately the amending legislation was passed as the Communications (Retention of Data) (Amendment) Act 2022 ('the 2022 Act'), having been rushed through parliament in just four days. This episode highlights disrespect by the executive towards parliament, as well as disregard of the consultation procedures required by law to ensure good governance.

---

[89] Helen McEntee TD, Written Answers 24 November 2020, available at <https://www.kildarestreet.com/wrans/?id=2020-11-24a.1972> accessed 26 September 2024.

[90] Gerard Cunningham, 'No One Cares about Garda Retaining Phonecall Data' (*Village Magazine*, 23 February 2016) <https://villagemagazine.ie/no-one-cares-about-garda-retaining-phonecall-data/> accessed 16 August 2023.

[91] Consultation was required by Article 36(4) GDPR and section 84(12) of the Data Protection Act 2018. See the submissions of Dale Sunderland, Assistant Data Protection Commissioner, in Joint Committee on Justice, 'Report on Pre-Legislative Scrutiny of the Communications (Retention of Data) (Amendment) Bill 2022' (Houses of the Oireachtas 2022).

[92] See the submissions of Ronan Lupton SC, chair of the Association of Licensed Telecommunications Operators, in ibid.

[93] Making it very likely that it will be unenforceable if and when it is challenged. See Directive (EU) 2015/1535 of the European Parliament and of the Council of 9 September 2015 laying down a procedure for the provision of information in the field of technical regulations and of rules on Information Society services (codification) [2015] OJ L 241/1, and Case C-194/94, *CIA Security International SA v Signalson SA and Securitel SPRL* ECLI:EU:C:1996:172. The State attempted to cure this problem by a retrospective notification of the Act to the Commission some months after it was passed (notification number 2022/872/IRL). However only draft legislation may be notified, so this belated notification is of no legal effect.

5.1 Communications (Retention of Data) (Amendment) Act 2022

The 2022 Act is complex and a full assessment of it is outside the scope of this chapter, but in short it amends the 2011 Act to provide for:

- 12 month general and indiscriminate retention of telephony and internet traffic and location data ('Schedule 2 data'), for State security purposes, based on a judicial retention order. The conditions for a retention order are that the Minister for Justice is satisfied there is 'a serious and genuine, present or foreseeable threat to the security of the State', makes an application to the High Court, and a High Court judge finds that retention is necessary and proportionate for State security purposes.[94]
- 12 month general and indiscriminate retention of user data and internet source data (such as names, addresses, IMSI and IMEI numbers, allocated IP addresses, and user IDs), for both State security and criminal law purposes.[95]
- Judicial temporary preservation orders (quick freeze orders) in relation to Schedule 2 data, for both State security and serious crime purposes.[96]
- An entirely new access regime for data. Access to retained Schedule 2 data is limited to State security purposes and requires authorisation by a District Court judge.[97] User data and internet source data can be accessed for both State security and criminal law purposes: on the basis of internal authorisation for user data[98] while access to internet source data must be authorised by a District Court judge.[99] There is also provision for urgent access without judicial authorisation to cell site location data, Schedule 2 data, and internet source data.[100]
- Notification of individuals whose data has been disclosed under the Act.[101]
- A new judicial 'production order' mechanism for access to Schedule 2 data which is being held by providers for a purpose other than compliance with the retention regime (for example, for billing or quality assurance)—significantly, that data can be accessed in relation to serious crime, not merely State security.[102]

Despite these changes, the 2022 Act is a minimal response to the particular issues identified by the CJEU in *Garda Síochána* rather than a wider reform of Irish law to bring it in line with international human rights standards. The 2022 Act still does not address most of the issues identified in the Murray Review. For example: it does not define 'security of the State', leaving access on this vague basis open to abuse.[103] It does not provide any safeguards

---

[94] Section 3A.
[95] Sections 3 and 3B. 'User data' and 'internet source data' are defined in section 1, but the distinction between the two is unclear as both definitions include names, addresses, and allocated IP addresses, whether static or dynamic. It should be noted that this does not require SIM card registration.
[96] Sections 7A, 7B.
[97] Section 6A.
[98] Section 6.
[99] Section 6C.
[100] Sections 6B, 6D, 6E.
[101] Section 12G.
[102] Section 7C.
[103] Compare ECtHR, *Roman Zakharov v Russia* [GC], no 47143/06, 04 December 2015, in which the European Court of Human Rights held that Russian law which failed to define national security was in breach of Article 8 ECHR. At para 248 the court noted that 'It is significant that [Russian law] does not give any indication of the circumstances under which an individual's communications may be intercepted on account of events or activities

regarding access to data for the purpose of identifying journalists' sources.[104] It does not introduce any remedy for individuals in the case of wrongful access to retained data, nor establish any sanction for wrongful access.[105] It does not regulate the downstream use or sharing of data after it has been accessed.[106] Most crucially, it does nothing to change the existing oversight system, which has already been proven inadequate.[107] In these regards the data retention regime continues to breach fundamental rights standards in a way which will store up trouble for the future.[108]

6. Conclusion

The Irish State knowingly persisted with illegal retention of data and access to data for several years after *Tele2 Sverige*. As summarised by Murphy J in *DPP v Gerard Cervi*: 'The authorities took a calculated decision to continue using sections 3 and 6 of the 2011 Act, even though they knew they would be infringing Charter rights by so doing'.[109] There was no possible excuse after the Murray Review made the illegality of the 2011 Act excruciatingly clear, but there was a systemic failure of the governance mechanisms which should have addressed this illegality. The Data Protection Commissioner did not act; the designated judge could not act; the work of parliamentary committees was largely ignored; and for the most part the criminal justice system turned a blind eye, preferring a greater chance of convictions over compliance with the law. Ultimately it was left to individual challenges to bring about change, but these were slower and weaker mechanisms to achieve compliance. In both *Digital Rights Ireland* and *Garda Síochána* it took approximately seven years from initial filing of the case to judgment of the CJEU, delays which the State fully exploited. When the law was finally amended, this was done in a rushed way calculated to minimise parliamentary scrutiny and input from the DPC. The overall pattern is one of Ireland as a scofflaw state, one which fails to comply with EU law until forced to do so by the CJEU, and even then complies only minimally and grudgingly.

---

endangering Russia's national, military, economic or ecological security. It leaves the authorities an almost unlimited degree of discretion in determining which events or acts constitute such a threat and whether that threat is serious enough to justify secret surveillance, thereby creating possibilities for abuse.'

[104] Compare *Corcoran v Commissioner of An Garda Síochána* [2023] IESC 15.
[105] Murray (n 84) 133–34.
[106] ibid 173.
[107] ibid 48. The Policing, Security and Community Safety Bill 2023 proposes relatively minor reform in this area, by merging the role of the designated judge into a wider Independent Examiner of Security Legislation. However that would not confer any new power to intervene to prevent illegal practices.
[108] In 2022 the Minister for Justice stated that her Department was in the process of drafting a further Communications (Data, Retention and Disclosure) Bill to provide 'a set of wider reforms to clarify and consolidate the law on data retention'. However there is as yet no transparency as to what is intended by this, nor whether it will introduce new safeguards. See eg 'Bill Sets Rules for Holding Communications Data' (*Law Society Gazette*, 22 June 2022) <https://www.lawsociety.ie/gazette/top-stories/2022/june/bill-sets-rules-for-holding-communications-data> accessed 23 October 2023.
[109] *DPP v Gerard Cervi*, Bill no CCDP 0028/2019, trial transcript, 12 December 2022, p 63.

11
A Clash Between the French System and the CJEU Case Law on Data Retention?

Maxime Lassalle

1. Introduction: *La Quadrature du Net 'I'* and the (il)Legitimacy of EU Law

For years, the case law of the Court of Justice of the European Union (CJEU) related to data retention was purely ignored in France.[1] It started to change when, in 2018, the French Council of State referred a preliminary ruling in the context of legal challenges targeting the legal framework related to data retention. The ruling in that case—*La Quadrature du Net 'I'*[2]—ignited a much-awaited debate about data retention.[3] The least we can say is however that the decision of the CJEU was not well received. Before addressing the impact this case had on French law, it is necessary to develop, as a way of introduction, the main features of the CJEU's decision as they can explain, at least partly, what happened next.[4]

The first question that was referred to the CJEU by the Council of State showed the reluctance of the French highest administrative court to accept the position of the CJEU on the applicability of EU law in matters related to national security. It was questioning the competence of the European Union and therefore the ability of the CJEU to rule in these matters: 'is the general and indiscriminate retention obligation . . . to be regarded . . . as

---

[1] It was surprisingly not ignored in the area of administrative access to metadata. The constitutional Council struck down several provisions and started doing so as early as 2015. See for instance French Constitutional Council, 5 August 2015, n° 2015-715 DC.
[2] All the English versions of provisions as well as considerations or findings of Court decisions in this chapter are free translations. The material content of the law of the time is extensively described in the ruling of the CJEU and there is no necessity to repeat it here. See CJEU, Judgment of 6 October 2020, *La Quadrature du Net and others* (C-511/18, C-512/18 and C-520/18) ECLI:EU:C:2020:791 ('*La Quadrature du Net I*'), paras 31–53.
[3] Loïc Azoulai and Dominique Ritleng, '« L'État, c'est moi ». Le Conseil d'État, la sécurité et la conservation des données' (2021) *Revue trimestrielle de droit européen* 349; Brunessen Bertrand 'L'audace sans le tact: jusqu'où la Cour de justice peut-elle aller trop loin? (2021) *Dalloz IP/IT* 486; Maxime Lassalle 'Conservation et réquisition des données relatives aux communications électroniques : un débat serein est-il enfin possible ?' (2022) *Recueil Dalloz* 1540.
[4] This case is not the latest decision of the Grand Chamber on data retention further to a request for a preliminary ruling by a French Court (see in particular CJEU, Judgment of 20 September 2022, *VD and SR* (C-339/20 and C-397/20) ECLI:EU:C:2022:703 ('*VD and SR*'). These more recent cases addressed however the application of the CJEU's case law on data retention in the specific context of market abuse investigations. As expected, the CJEU rejected the creation an exception in this field and the restriction of the temporal effect of the decision in national law declaring invalid data retention schemes. See also section 3.3 of this chapter on the latest case: CJEU, Judgment of 30 April 2024, *La Quadrature du Net a.o. c. Premier Ministre and Ministre de la Culture* (C-470/21) ECLI:EU:C:2024:370 ('*La Quadrature du Net 'II'*).

Maxime Lassalle, *A Clash Between the French System and the CJEU Case Law on Data Retention?* In: *Data Retention in Europe and Beyond*. Edited by: Eleni Kosta and Irene Kamara, Oxford University Press. © Maxime Lassalle 2025.
DOI: 10.1093/9780191998980.003.0011

interference justified by the right to security guaranteed in Article 6 of the Charter and the requirements of national security, responsibility which falls to the Member States alone pursuant to Article 4 TEU?'[5] In other words, if national security is a responsibility that falls to the Member States, can EU law regulate activities that are related to it? This question had not been explicitly addressed by previous cases of the CJEU relating to data retention.[6]

The CJEU knew that the Council of State expected some concessions and was keen on addressing some of the Member States' concerns. The Court asserts, with references to cases in other fields than data retention, that 'although it is for Member States to define their essential security interests and to adopt appropriate measures to ensure their internal and external security, the mere fact that a national measure has been taken for the purpose of protecting national security cannot render EU law inapplicable and exempt the Member States from their obligation to comply with that law'.[7] Yet here the ePrivacy Directive is applicable, which triggers the applicability of the Charter.[8] The CJEU however acknowledges that the interpretation of article 15(1) of the ePrivacy Directive must take into consideration the 'importance and the objective of protecting national security and combating serious crime in contributing to the protection of the rights and freedoms of others'.[9] In the EU legal framework, these rights are enshrined not only in article 6 of the Charter which 'lays down the right of every individual not only to liberty but also to security'[10] but also in articles 7 (protection of an individual's home and communications), 3, and 4 (protection of an individual's physical and mental integrity and the prohibition of torture inhuman and degrading treatment). It creates positive obligations for public authorities. The Court was therefore willing to strike a balance between the various interests and rights at stake.[11]

Even though EU law applies, the Court acknowledges that 'national security remains the sole responsibility of each member state'[12] and that there is something specific with threats against national security. Such threats must be distinguished from 'the general risk that tensions or disturbances, even of a serious nature, affecting public security will arise'[13] and they are 'capable of justifying measures entailing more serious interferences with fundamental rights'.[14] In other words, the Court accepts to create an exception to

---

[5] *La Quadrature du Net 'I'* (n 2) para 73.

[6] Previous cases (ie CJEU, Judgment of 21 December 2016, *Tele2 Sverige* (C-203/15 and C-698/15) ECLI:EU:C:2016:970) dealt with the applicability of EU law to national data retention schemes and not the specific case of national security.

[7] *La Quadrature du Net 'I'* (n 2) para 99.

[8] The CJEU based its previous decisions on the applicability of the ePrivacy Directive (Directive 2002/58/EC of the European Parliament and of the Council of 12 July 2002 concerning the processing of personal data and the protection of privacy in the electronic communications sector (Directive on privacy and electronic communications) [2002] OJ L 201/37).

[9] *La Quadrature du Net 'I'* (n 2) para 122.

[10] ibid para 123.

[11] ibid para 127. It found however that the principles already expressed in previous cases allow to strike such balance between the necessity to protect privacy and the other interests. The CJEU had already stated for instance that the Member States should consider the seriousness of an interference and verify 'that the importance of the public interest objective pursued by that limitation is proportionate to that seriousness' (*La Quadrature du Net 'I'* para 131).

[12] ibid para 135.

[13] ibid para 136.

[14] ibid para 136.

its pre-established stringent rules according to which there was no exception to the prohibition of indiscriminate data retention. While previous cases were very demanding and would consider lawful only targeted data retention schemes, the CJEU now accepts that indiscriminate data retention can be lawful under very specific circumstances, namely in case of a serious threat against national security. Such a threat can justify indiscriminate data retention for a limited time 'as long as there is sufficiently solid ground for considering that the Member States concerned is confronted with a serious threat ... to national security which is shown to be genuine and present or foreseeable'.[15]

The CJEU has therefore created a major exception to the prohibition of indiscriminate data retention in *La Quadrature du Net 'I'*. Its purpose was to address the concerns coming from national authorities. Despite these concessions, the requirements of the CJEU were still deemed excessive in France. *La Quadrature du Net 'I'* was perceived as an illegitimate application of EU law in a field that is supposed to fall to the Member States, namely national security. Yet the authority of the CJEU could not be challenged directly. It was however still possible to do it indirectly, based on the French constitutional identity: the guarantees of the French Constitution can prevail over EU law if the latter does not contain the same guarantees.[16] The implementation of the CJEU case law in the French legal system was therefore very controversial and several courts—the Council of State (Conseil d'État),[17] the Constitutional Council,[18] and the Court of Cassation[19]—had to step in, as well as the Parliament.[20] As a consequence, the developments following *La Quadrature du Net 'I'* are certainly very revealing not only of the national public authorities' disapproval regarding the strong requirements related to data retention, but also and probably more importantly of the real practical difficulties of implementing the CJEU approach at a national level.

2. *La Quadrature du Net 'I'*'s Aftermath

This chapter will start with all the decisions that have affected the current legal framework. Even though *La Quadrature du Net 'I'* was certainly not the first case of the CJEU regarding data retention, it was only after this case that the French legal system started to figure out a way to address the CJEU's approach. The Council of State, the Parliament, the Constitutional Council, and the Court of Cassation all had to step in to address different aspects of the problem.

---

[15] ibid para 137.
[16] This point is based on article on article 4 (2) of the Treaty on European Union which protects national constitutional identities and acknowledge that national security remains the sole responsibility of the Member State. The Council of State remains however very elusive on this point, see French Council of State, *French Data Network*, 4 April 2021, n°393099, para 10. For a detailed and critical analysis of this case and the context of the reference to France's constitutional identity, see Araceli Turmo, 'National security as an exception to EU data protection standards: The judgment of the Conseil d'État in French Data Network and others' 59 (2022) Common Market Law Review 203–22.
[17] *French Data Network*, ibid.
[18] French Constitutional Council, *M Habib A and others*, 25 February 2022, n° 2021-976/977 QPC.
[19] French Court of Cassation, 12 July 2022, n° 21-83.710.
[20] Paragraphs II et III of article L. 34-1 of the *code des postes et des communications électroniques*, as in force before law n° 2021-998 du 30 juillet 2021 *relative à la prévention d'actes de terrorisme*.

2.1 The Council of State and French constitutional identity

2.1.1 The necessity to protect national security

Following *La Quadrature du Net 'I'*, the French government had invited the Council of State to conduct a control *ultra vires* and to reject the jurisdiction of the CJEU in matters related to national security.[21] This request was dismissed and the Council of State, following principles established in previous cases, ruled that it would instead make an interpretation of EU law that is the most respectful of the French constitutional requirements, to the extent allowed by the rulings of the CJEU.[22] In other words, the Council of State used the margins left by the rulings of the CJEU to adopt the interpretation of EU law that was the most compliant with the principles enshrined in the French legal order. The Council of State added that should the interpretation of EU law given by the CJEU prevent the application of these constitutional requirements, this interpretation would be disregarded to the extent necessary to ensure the respect of these requirements. The message was quite simple: either it is possible to make an interpretation of EU law that is compliant with the French requirements, or the approach of the CJEU should be disregarded. The Council did not go that far—this time. In that case, the Council of State made an interpretation of EU law that conformed to the national requirement to protect national security.[23]

2.1.2 The French way to data protection

In this context, the Council of State was not willing to ban the indiscriminate retention of location and traffic data.[24] For this reason, it proposed a reinterpretation of the criterion enshrined in the case law of the CJEU. The idea is quite simple. If data retention is exceptional and can be justified only in case of a major threat to national security, one solution is to claim that there is—potentially permanently—such a major threat. The Council of State therefore ruled that France was under a major threat.[25] The only concession that was made to the CJEU was that the existence of this threat must be reassessed regularly, which was not a legal requirement at that time. Therefore, according to the French Court, the main issue with French law at that time was the absence of judicial control over the existence of the threat.[26] At the moment of the decision, the Council of State assessed the existence of this threat—without saying how—and concluded that it existed. The data had therefore been retained lawfully so far.

Since the Council of State saved data retention of traffic and location data for the purpose of fighting threats against national security, the principle of indiscriminate data retention itself was also saved. Then, if the data is retained for this purpose, can it also be used for other purposes? In principle, it should not.[27] However, according to the Council of

---

[21] *French Data Network* (n 16) para 8.
[22] ibid paras 5–7.
[23] The Council of state found that the constitutional requirements do not have an equivalent protection in EU law and should therefore guide the interpretation of EU law (ibid paras 9–10)
[24] The specific situation of IP addresses was also addressed (ibid paras 37–39, but is developed in section 3.3 of this chapter.
[25] ibid para 44.
[26] ibid paras 45–46.
[27] For other purposes—namely combating serious crime and preventing serious attacks on public security—data retention can only be targeted (*La Quadrature du Net 'I'* (n 2) para 148–50). Retention of these data is never acceptable for the purpose of combatting criminal offences (ibid para 145).

State, the CJEU acknowledged that this data can subsequently be subject to a quick freeze to change its purpose and therefore be retained and accessed for other purposes.[28] As a consequence, all the public authorities' powers were saved and there was no need to conclude that European law should be disregarded to protect the requirements of the French constitution.

2.2 The Parliament: A New Law in 2021

The Council of State is the highest administrative court. It controls the legality of administrative acts, but not the constitutionality of the law. It had jurisdiction because the implementation of statutory obligations related to data retention was made through administrative act, which could be only challenged before administrative courts.[29] Following the rulings of the CJEU and the Council of State, the Parliament chose to intervene itself to adapt the legal framework. In this piece of legislation, the French parliament decided to follow the principles that were proposed by the Council of State.[30] Since then the legal framework distinguishing different categories of data[31] and different purposes is applicable as explained in Table 11.1 below.

---

[28] Paragraph 57 of the Council of State's ruling makes reference to its paragraph 55, itself making reference to paragraph 164 of the CJEU's ruling in *La Quadrature du Net 'I'* (ibid). In that paragraph, the CJEU states that the purpose of the expedited retention no longer corresponds to the purpose for which that data was initially collected. It is therefore quite important to understand what is the purpose for which this data was initially collected. More particularly, does this mean that this technique can be used to repurpose data already collected based on data retention obligations for purposes of national security? In *La Quadrature du Net 'I'*, the Court does not state anywhere that the initial purpose is or even can be to address a threat to national security. The initial purpose of the processing of this data is actually different and is mentioned in paragraph 160 of the CJEU's ruling in *La Quadrature du Net 'I'*. This paragraph refers to articles 5, 6, and 9 of the ePrivacy Directive, according to which this data is processed and retained for the purposes of routing communications and billing and payment operations for services rendered (the Council of state acknowledges that this is the initial purpose in paragraph 51 of its ruling). In other words, expedited retention is meant to address data that is temporarily retained for technical and commercial purposes.

[29] ibid para 3.

[30] Law n° 2021-998 of the 30 July 2021 relative à la prévention d'actes de terrorisme et au renseignement JORF n°0176 31 July 2021. French data retention obligations apply to two categories of private actors, namely electronic communications operators and specific categories of service providers. As for the first category, article L32 15° of French Post and Electronic Communications Code defines an operator as 'any natural or legal person operating an electronic communications network open to the public or providing an electronic communications service to the public'. Article L32 1° defines electronic communications as 'the emission, transmission or reception of signs, signals, writing, images or sounds by cable, radio, optical or other electromagnetic means'. The second category of actor subject to data retention obligations is mentioned in articles 6 I 1 and 6 I 2 of Law n° 2004-575 of the 21 June 2004 pour la confiance dans l'économie numérique, which covers 'persons whose business is to provide access to online public communication services' as well as 'natural or legal persons who, even free of charge, make available to the public via online public communication services, the storage of signals, writings, images, sounds or messages of any kind supplied by recipients of these services'.

[31] The detail of the data to be retained by electronic communication operators can be found in Administrative Act n° 2021-1361 of 20 October 2021 relatif aux catégories de données conservées par les opérateurs de communications électroniques, pris en application de l'article L. 34-1 du code des postes et des communications électroniques, JORF n°0246 21 October 2021. See also, for the other service providers with data retention obligations, administrative act n° 2021-1362 of 20 October 2021 relatif à la conservation des données permettant d'identifier toute personne ayant contribué à la création d'un contenu mis en ligne, pris en application du II de l'article 6 de la loi n° 2004-575 du 21 juin 2004 pour la confiance dans l'économie numérique, JORF n°0246 21 October 2021.

Table 11.1 Duration of data retention based on the nature of the information and on the purpose of data retention

	For the purposes of criminal proceedings, the prevention of threats against public security, and the safeguarding of national security	For the purposes of the fight against serious crimes, the prevention of serious threats against public security, and the safeguarding of national security	For reasons relating to the safeguarding of national security, (when a serious threat, present or foreseeable, against the latter, is observed[32])
Information relating to the civil identity of the user[33]	Five years (from the end of the validity of the contract)	Five years (from the end of the validity of the contract)	Five years (from the end of the validity of the contract)
Other information provided by the user when subscribing to a contract or creating an account[34] as well as information relating to payment[35]	One year (from the end of the validity of the contract or the closing of the account)	One year (from the end of the validity of the contract or the closing of the account)	One year (from the end of the validity of the contract or the closing of the account)

[32] Administrative act n° 2022-1327 du 17 octobre 2022 *portant injonction, au regard de la menace grave et actuelle contre la sécurité nationale, de conservation pour une durée d'un an de certaines catégories de données de connexion JORF n°0242* 18 October 2022.

[33] Article R10-13 I of the code of posts and electronic communications refers to

    1° The surname and first name, the date and place of birth for a natural person or the company name, as well as the surname, first name, date and place of birth of the person acting in his name, when the account is opened in the name a legal person;
    2° The associated postal address(es);
    3° The e-mail address(es) of the user and of the associated account(s), if applicable;
    4° The telephone number(s).

See also art 2 of the aforementioned administrative act n° 2021-1362 of 20 October 2021.

[34] Article R10-13 II of the code of posts and electronic communications refers to

    1° The identifier used;
    2° The pseudonym(s) used;
    3° The data intended to allow the user to check his password or to modify it, if necessary via a double user identification system, in their latest updated version.

See also art 3 of the aforementioned administrative act n° 2021-1362 of 20 October 2021.

[35] Article R10-13 III of the code of posts and electronic communications refers to

    1° The type of payment used;
    2° The payment reference;
    3° The amount;
    4° The date, time and place in the case of a physical transaction.

See also art 4 of the aforementioned administrative act n° 2021-1362 of 20 October 2021.

Table 11.1 Continued

	For the purposes of criminal proceedings, the prevention of threats against public security, and the safeguarding of national security	For the purposes of the fight against serious crimes, the prevention of serious threats against public security, and the safeguarding of national security	For reasons relating to the safeguarding of national security, (when a serious threat, present or foreseeable, against the latter, is observed[32])
Technical data making it possible to identify the source of the connection or those relating to the terminal equipment used[36]	No data retention is allowed.	One year (from the connection or use of the terminal equipment)	One year (from the connection or use of the terminal equipment)
Certain categories of traffic data, in addition to the technical data mentioned above, and location data specified by decree[37]	No data retention is allowed.	No data retention is allowed.	Up to one year, under the condition that the Prime Minister requests electronic communications to do it for certain categories of data

---

[36] R10-13 IV of the code of posts and electronic communications refers to

    1° The IP address assigned to the source of the connection and the associated port;
    2° The user's identification number;
    3° The identification number of the terminal;
    4° The telephone number at the origin of the communication.

See also art 5 of administrative act n° 2021-1362 of 20 October 2021, adding, for the persons mentioned in article 6 I 1 of the aforementioned Law n° 2004-575 of 21 June 2004 pour la confiance dans l'économie numérique: 'a) The connection identifier; b) The identifier allocated to the subscriber by these persons; c) The IP address allocated to the source of the connection and the associated port'. The same article adds, for the persons mentioned in article 6 I 2 of the law: 'a) The connection identifier at the origin of the communication; b) The types of protocol used to connect to the service and to transfer content'.

[37] Article R10-13 V of code of posts and electronic communications refers to

    1° The technical characteristics as well as the date, time and duration of each communication;
    2° Data relating to the additional services requested or used and their suppliers;
    3° The technical data enabling the recipient(s) of the communication to be identified (. . .);
    4° For transactions carried out using mobile phones, the data enabling the location of the communication to be identified.

See also art 6 of administrative act n° 2021-1362 of 20 October 2021, adding, for the persons mentioned in article 6 I 1 of the aforementioned Law n° 2004-575 of 21 June 2004 pour la confiance dans l'économie numérique: a) 'The start and end dates and times of the connection; b) The characteristics of the subscriber's line'. The same article adds, for the persons mentioned in article 6 I 2 of the law: 'a) The identifier assigned by the information system to the content that is the subject of the operation; b) The nature of the operation; c) The date and time of the operation; d) The identifier used by the originator of the operation where this has been provided by the originator'.

This categorization follows the distinctions requested by the CJEU's case law. However, it also shows that the French parliament was not willing to accept the consequences that should follow from such categorization. Otherwise, it would also put forward criteria to justify targeted retention of the most sensitive categories of data.

2.3 The Constitutional Council: Ensuring the constitutionality of the new law?

The French Constitutional Council deals with the conformity of national law with the Constitution, but it does not have jurisdiction to assess the conformity of a national law with EU law. Furthermore, it did not get—yet—the opportunity to deal with the new law adopted in 2021 that was mentioned in the previous section, since this law was not referred to the Constitutional Council, neither before it came into force nor since then. However, the Constitutional Council has jurisdiction to deal with priority preliminary rulings on the issue of constitutionality referred by the Court of Cassation when this Court has serious concerns that a law that is applicable in a case before it does not conform to the Constitution. Yet, the Court of Cassation had to rule on the use as evidence, in criminal proceedings, of data that had been collected under the previous legal framework. Given the ruling of the CJEU, the Court of Cassation had concerns about the constitutionality of retention, access, and use as evidence of telecommunication data. It referred a question to the Constitutional Council which was therefore asked to address the constitutionality of a law that was not in force anymore. That law was deemed unconstitutional. Since the interpretation of the grounds for this decision is far from self-evident, it seems more appropriate to quote it as such:

> However, in the first place, the data[38] retained under the contested provisions relates not only to the identification of users of electronic communications services but also to the location of their communication terminal equipment, the technical characteristics, the date, time, and duration of the communications as well as the identification data of their recipients. Given their nature, their diversity, and the processing to which they may be subject, these data provide on these users as well as, where applicable, on third parties, numerous and precise information, particularly intrusive to their privacy.
>
> Secondly, on the one hand, such retention generally applies to all users of electronic communications services. On the other hand, the retention obligation applies equally to all data relating to these persons, regardless of their sensitivity and without consideration of the nature and seriousness of the offenses likely to be under investigation.[39]

At first reading, one could think that the Constitutional Council rejected the very principle of indiscriminate data retention. However, one should not forget that this proceeding was meant to control a piece of legislation that was not in force anymore. As already explained,

---

[38] The Constitutional Council refers to '*données de connexion*' in French, which is the umbrella concept used to label all the different kinds of data at stake.
[39] M Habib A and others (n 18) paras 11–12.

that law had many shortcomings. The first one was the weakness of the distinction between categories of data. That law did not distinguish, for instance, traffic and location data from other categories of data. They were subject to general retention rules. This is what is rightfully criticized in paragraph 11 of the Constitutional Council's ruling. Yet it does not have any impact on the new law enacted in 2021 which already distinguished different categories of data.

The second shortcoming of the piece of legislation that was checked is mentioned in paragraph 12 of the Constitutional Council's ruling. This paragraph is slightly more complex. On the one hand, all users of electronic communication services are affected by data retention obligations. In other words, data retention obligations are not targeted. On the other hand, all the data is retained, irrespective of its sensitivity and the purposes of the retention. This second part of the paragraph conflates two elements. The first one is that of the absence of categorization of data, which was already addressed in paragraph 11 of the ruling. The second one is the seriousness of the offenses or public interest goal for which the retention is supposed to be useful.

What does it mean? Are these different criteria cumulative? In other words, does the Constitutional Council expect the legislation to distinguish (1) different categories of data, (2) different categories of purpose, and (3) different categories of people who are targeted by data retention? This would be an interpretation of the French Constitution that is inspired by the CJEU case law. Or are these criteria alternative, meaning that the law does not have to respect all these limitations on the scope of data retention? The ruling is quite ambiguous, but the Constitutional Council was likely only willing to acknowledge that the legislator could not go backward regarding data retention. The principles established in the law in 2021—different categories of data and different categories of purposes, but an absence of different categories of targets—were « constitutionalized » by this ruling. The Constitutional Council did not have to go as far as to follow completely the requirements of the CJEU to censor the law. Other rulings related to access to the data confirmed that the Constitutional Council was not willing (at all) to follow the CJEU.[40]

There is another sign that the Constitutional Council was not willing to give too much importance to its ruling. The reason why the Court of Cassation referred a question to the Constitutional Council was that of the admissibility as evidence of the retained data that had been accessed and used even though their retention was potentially not constitutional in the first place. In this context, the ruling of the Constitutional Council could have meant that all this information should be excluded and could not be used as evidence in criminal proceedings. The Constitutional Council decided however that 'these measures cannot be challenged based on this unconstitutionality'.[41] It explicitly rejected this hypothesis based on article 62 of the Constitution which grants the possibility to the Constitutional Council not to give full consequences to a declaration of unconstitutionality. It considered that the provisions declared unconstitutional were no longer in force.[42] Moreover, the exclusion of

---

[40] The Constitutional Council refused to follow the CJEU in it famous *Prokuratuur* case (CJEU, Judgment of 2 March 2021, *Prokuratuur* (C-746/18) ECLI:EU:C:2021:152). See French Constitutional Council, *Mr Omar Y*, 3 December 2021, n° 2021-952 QPC; *Mr Lotfi H*, 20 May 2022, n° 2022-993 QPC and *M Ibrahim K*, 17 June 2022, n° 2022-1000 QPC.
[41] *M Habib A and others* (n 18) para 17.
[42] ibid para 16.

the data 'would disregard the constitutional objectives of safeguarding public order and finding perpetrators of offenses and would thus have manifestly excessive consequences'.[43]

2.4 The Court of Cassation: Ensuring that criminal investigations will not be impacted

The Court of Cassation is the highest court dealing with criminal cases. It does not judge the facts of a case. Its mission is mainly to unify the interpretation of the law made by lower courts. It was the last actor to address the issue of data retention after the CJEU's decision in *La Quadrature du Net 'I'*. Facing cases where the data that had been retained based on the previous law were used as evidence in criminal proceedings, the Court of Cassation had to decide whether this data should be excluded or could be used as evidence. The Court of Cassation could not exclude the evidence based on the unconstitutionality of the law that was the basis of their retention. As already explained, such an option was ruled out by the Constitutional Council. However, the Court of Cassation was, contrary to the Constitutional Council, habilitated to apply EU law and even had the duty to do so. In a series of major decisions, the Court of Cassation followed an approach that was directly inspired by the ruling of the Council of State.

The Court of Cassation was willing to save the data retention measures at the ground of the access measures whose legality was challenged. It followed a reasoning in two steps. First, the Court of Cassation concluded that all the data that had been retained under the previous legal framework could legally be retained based on a continuous terrorist threat in France since 1995. Second, all this data was legally retained for a purpose but could be used for other purposes based on the so-called quick freeze procedure.

2.4.1 General data retention grounded on a continuous terrorist threat since 1995

On 12 July 2022, the Court of Cassation adopted four landmark decisions related to data retention and subsequent access to that data.[44] These data had been retained based on the former legal framework, and the Court of Cassation had to check its conformity to EU law. The reasoning that was followed was explained both in the text of the decisions and in an explicative note that was exceptionally published given the practical importance of these decisions.[45]

The Court of Cassation acknowledged and formally applied the criteria put forward by the CJEU. However, in reality, this decision seems to circumvent the guarantees and limitations contained in the case law of the CJEU. In particular, the exception to the prohibition of indiscriminate data retention in case of threat to national security was used by the Court of Cassation to justify the retention measures that were undertaken. According to the Court of Cassation, traffic and location data were retained for the purposes of detection and investigation of criminal offenses affecting the fundamental interests of the Nation and acts of terrorism. Such offenses are criminalized under articles 410-1 to 422-7 of the criminal code, which pursues the purpose of safeguarding national security. In other words, the data were

---

[43] ibid para 17.
[44] French Court of Cassation, 12 July 2022, n° 21-83.710, 21-83.820, 21-84.096 and 20-86.652.
[45] French Court of Cassation, *Note explicative relative aux arrêts de la chambre criminelle du 12 juillet 2022 (pourvois n° 21-83.710, 21-83.820, 21-84.096 et 20-86.652)*.

retained for appropriate purposes. The Court of Cassation added that the general prosecutor at the Court of Cassation had regularly produced information relating to the terrorist attacks undertaken in France since 1994. Consequently, the Court of Cassation was able to conclude that there was a continuous threat to national security that preexisted the criminal offences at stake in these cases.

2.4.2 Quick freeze as a way to use data outside the context of national security

The retention of traffic and location data was therefore, according to the Court of Cassation, legal and conform to EU law. However, these data were retained for a specific purpose, namely combatting the threat to national security. Was it legal to access and use them for other purposes as well? According to the Court of Cassation, the power to issue production orders based on the code of criminal procedure has the value of quick-freeze injunctions whose availability in national law is based on the Budapest Convention.[46] These quick-freeze injunctions were considered by the CJEU as an alternative to general data retention schemes since they are targeted. They can, according to the CJEU, be used outside the context of a serious threat to national security, in particular to retain data for the purpose of combatting serious criminality.[47]

However, in the case law of the CJEU, quick-freeze injunctions do not apply to data that have already been retained based on a serious threat to national security. In other words, quick-freeze injunctions are not supposed to be used to repurpose data that have been collected for the purpose of national security. The reasoning of the Court of Cassation therefore wrongly conflates two distinct ideas put forward by the CJEU. On the one hand, general and indiscriminate data retention is legal, under certain conditions, for the purpose of national security. On the other hand, quick-freeze injunctions are viable alternatives to general and indiscriminate data retention in particular in cases related to serious criminality. This trick allows the Court of Cassation to save the data that have been used in the criminal investigations it had to deal with.

All these decisions are consistent: the requirements of the CJEU have been politely but strongly rejected. Through a very creative interpretation of *La Quadrature du Net 'I'*, the Council of State managed to find a way to make it look like a correct implementation of the ruling of the CJEU. The legislator, the Court of Cassation and most likely the Constitutional Council followed a similar reasoning. This is all based on the alleged absence of alternatives to data retention.

3. The Absence of Alternatives to Data Retention?

Reading the ruling of the Council of State, the message is clear: there is no other way. In other words, implementing the requirements of *La Quadrature du Net 'I'* would be impossible. Several grounds are mentioned to make this point. If they are not always convincing because one cannot check the data behind these reasonings,[48] they deserve to be taken into

---

[46] Arts 60-1, 60-2, 77-1-1, 77-1-2, 99-3, and 99-4 of the French code of criminal procedure.
[47] *La Quadrature du Net 'I'* (n 2) paras 160–165.
[48] The Council of State refers to « the documents in the file, in particular the investigative measures carried out by the tenth chamber of the litigation section, as well as the exchanges that took place during the oral investigation session held on March 22, 2021 » (*French Data Network* (n 16) para 50, see also paras 51 and 53).

consideration in order, to the extent that this is possible, to be compared to solutions that have been implemented in other countries.

3.1 The (alleged) low operational use of targeted retention

The Council of State's starting point is that data retention is a deciding factor in the success of criminal investigations.[49] It is in 'numerous hypotheses' the unique way to find the offenders. The Council of State referred to the data gathered during the procedure in the *French Data Network* case and stated that alternative investigative measures (spinning, surveillance techniques, searches for fingerprints and genetic traces) cannot be used to reach the same goals as efficiently. Furthermore, complex investigative measures such as real-time data capture are more intrusive than the measures based on data retention. Similarly, electronic communication is more and more encrypted, which makes it more and more complicated to identify the offenders. For this reason, *ex post* access to retained metadata is all the more crucial. Last but not least, access to metadata could be a way to lift quickly the suspicion that could exist on innocent people.

After having stated that there was no viable alternative to data retention, the Council of State addressed the alternatives proposed by the CJEU. The first alternative would be to rely on the data that electronic communication operators are allowed (and not obliged) to retain in the context of their activities. For the Council of State, however, in the absence of mandatory data retention, the data that is retained does not match the requirements of the public authorities to conduct investigations.[50] The second alternative is that of targeted retention schemes. Yet again, the operational interest of this option is deemed 'uncertain'.[51] In case of an investigation targeting a person who was not identified beforehand as a potential offender, first-time offender, or even a person using pre-paid cards, this option would not allow access to the data necessary for the criminal investigation. Moreover, it is impossible to determine geographic areas where serious crime will occur and, even though it would be possible, it would prevent investigations in other parts of the territory. It would also be contrary to the constitutional principle of equality before the law. The third option put forward by the CJEU was that of the so-called quick-freeze injunctions of the data based on the Budapest Convention. According to the Council of State, such a mechanism is effective only under the condition that the data have already been retained. If this is not the case, a quick-freeze injunction cannot be used to access data related to the period before the injunction.[52]

3.2 The technical feasibility of targeted retention

A very interesting point was made by the Council of State, based on the technical impossibility of implementing targeted data retention:

---

[49] ibid para 50.
[50] ibid para 51.
[51] ibid para 54.
[52] ibid para 56.

However, it appears from the documents in the file, in particular from the information collected from the French Telecoms Federation, that such targeted retention faces technical obstacles that compromise its implementation. Concerning targeted retention based on geographical criteria, it appears that the location of mobile telephone relay antennas and their cells is specific to each operator, that the mode of propagation of the radio waves emitted by the mobile telephone relays is not compatible with predefined geographical limits and that the location information is not systematically present in the data collected. The companies Free Mobile and Free indicate, for their part, that the traffic data stored in their information system is not associated with a particular geographical area, that moreover, this location changes over time, and that they are only able to establish a correlation between the radio 'cell' with which telecommunication metadata is associated and the geographical location of this cell only on a case-by-case basis, in response to a judicial production order. As for conservation targeted at people, the French Telecoms Federation argues that it would face an obstacle in that the information contained in the traffic data does not allow sorting according to categories of people. The companies Free and Free Mobile specify, for their part, that people are identified by data—the telephone number, the IMSI number, and the IMEI number—which can vary over time and that this data is managed separately to meet the requirements of the GDPR.[53]

The Council of State addressed here a point that is potentially very important. Is it even feasible to implement the requirements of the CJEU regarding targeted data retention? To address this question, the Council of State claims to have heard experts, especially representatives of major mobile phone companies. However, the explanations given by these professionals seemed quite convenient for the Council of State. Despite that, this point is used to dismiss, on another ground, the proposals put forward by the CJEU. According to the Council of State, even though the requirements of the CJEU were as such conform to the French Constitutional identity, it would not be technically feasible to apply them. This point could potentially be criticized based on comparative law: at the end of the day, for what reason such targeted data retention schemes are technically feasible outside of France while they are not in France?

3.3 The specificity of IP addresses

The CJEU traditionally distinguishes different categories of data to apply different sets of rules depending on the seriousness of the interference with fundamental rights that retention of these different categories of data entails. The first category is that of 'traffic and location data', whose retention is seen as a 'serious interference' with the fundamental rights enshrined in articles 7 and 8 of the Charter. At the other end of the spectrum are data relating to the civil identity of users of electronic communication systems. It is nothing new that retention of this data cannot be classified as serious.[54]

---

[53] ibid para 53.
[54] *La Quadrature du Net 'I'* (n 2) para 157.

The retention of IP addresses appears to be the most problematic category of data. The assessment of the seriousness of the interference with fundamental rights posed by retaining this data has been contested, given the practical necessity of accessing IP addresses retained under data retention obligations to tackle certain types of crime, particularly online criminality. According to the CJEU in *La Quadrature du Net 'I'*, such data 'do not, as such, disclose any information about third parties who were in contact with the person who made the communication'.[55] However, they may be used 'among other things, to track an internet user's complete clickstream and, therefore, his or her entire online activity'.[56] Access to IP addresses has something special since 'it might be the only means of investigation enabling the person to whom that address was assigned at the time of the commission of the offense to be identified'.[57] Considering this, indiscriminate data retention of this kind of data was deemed, in *La Quadrature du Net 'I'*, acceptable only for the purposes of combatting serious crime, preventing serious threats to public security, and safeguarding national security.[58] The Council of State was however not convinced by this and concluded that, since access to this data is strictly regulated, data related to IP addresses could be retained for other purposes such as combatting criminality in a broad sense.[59] The law enacted in 2021 did not follow such an extensive approach and limited retention obligations of technical data making it possible to identify the source of the connection, including IP addresses, to the purposes of the fight against serious crimes, the prevention of serious threats against public security, and the safeguarding of national security. In other words, it followed the requirements of the CJEU. However, IP addresses are still accessed in the context administrative proceedings or criminal investigations related to criminal offences in general.[60] Such a situation was contested and the Council of State referred another preliminary ruling to the CJEU in *La Quadrature du Net 'II'*. The advocate general had proposed a 'rejustment of the case law of the Court ... as regards measures for the retention of IP addresses assigned to the source of the connection'.[61] His suggestion was to extend the purposes that can ground indiscriminate retention of IP addresses to online criminal offenses, even to those that are not deemed serious.[62] The full Court extended the possibility of general and indiscriminate retention of IP addresses to the purpose of combatting criminal offences in general, including in the context of administrative proceedings, but under one condition, thus avoiding acknowledging explicitly a jurisprudence reversal.[63] It ruled that such mandatory retention of IP addresses by service providers conform to EU law 'where it is genuinely ruled out that that retention could give rise to serious interferences with the private life of the person concerned due to the possibility of drawing precise conclusions about that person by, inter alia, linking those IP addresses with a set of traffic or location data which have also been

---

[55] ibid para 152.
[56] ibid para 153.
[57] ibid para 154.
[58] ibid para 156.
[59] *French Data Network* (n 16) para 39.
[60] The CJEU has already ruled on retention of data in general in relation to investigations related to market abuse—without saying whether this kind of investigation was related to serious crime. See *VD and SR*.
[61] Opinion of Advocate-General Szpunar of 27 October 2022, C-470/21, *La Quadrature du Net 'II'*, ECLI:EU:C:2022:838 ('*First AG Opinion La Quadrature du Net 'II'*').
[62] ibid para 83. See also Opinion of Advocate-General Szpunar of 28 September 2023, C-470/21, *La Quadrature du Net 'II'* ECLI:EU:C:2023:711 ('*Second AG Opinion La Quadrature du Net 'II'*').
[63] See *La Quadrature du Net 'II'* (n 4) paras 81–82. It is only on this condition that retention will not be deemed serious and will therefore conform to EU law (ibid para 90).

retained by those providers'.[64] Consequently, any combination of the retained 'IP addresses with other data, retained in compliance with Directive 2002/58, which would allow precise conclusions to be drawn about the private life of the persons whose data are thus retained, is ruled out'.[65] It has practical consequences for the providers since 'retention must be organised in such a way as to guarantee a genuinely watertight separation of the different categories of data retained'.[66] It is still too early to understand the final impact of the Court's ruling. One thing is certain, however: the Court has made concessions in response to a new question referred by the French Council of State.

4. Conclusion: The Clash Did Not Take Place, Yet

After *La Quadrature du Net 'I'*, the Council of State, the Parliament, the Constitutional Council, and the Court of Cassation all made significant efforts and concessions to take into consideration—for the first time—the requirements of the CJEU regarding data retention. French law has been reformed, at least formally incorporating certain principles derived from EU law. Different categories of data are now distinguished, and the most sensitive data can only be retained in a general and indiscriminate way for specific purposes, such as national security. Yet, French law does not seem to match the requirements of the CJEU on this matter. Indiscriminate data retention is still the principle, while it should be, following the CJEU's approach, the exception. At present, the whole system is based on the idea that France has been facing a terrorist threat for a long time (since 1994 for the Cour de cassation) and will probably always face one. This simple idea justifies the widespread collection and retention of data. This data can then be accessed outside the context of national security. In other words, French law follows its own approach to data retention. And it is not going to change. As clearly stated by the Council of State: either this intermediary solution is accepted by the CJEU, or the French constitutional identity will be used as a shield to disregard EU law and its requirements regarding data protection. The clash did not take place yet, but it may be coming.

One should also acknowledge an evolution in the legal framework relating to access to traffic and location data. Public authorities must apply the case law of the Court of cassation, implementing the requirements of the CJUE regarding the authorization by a court or an independent authority.[67] Yet, this requirement of the Court of Justice is also very controversial, and the law was not changed by the parliament, leaving the legal framework in a strange situation: the code of criminal procedure does not require an authorization by a court or an independent authority in case of access to traffic and location data, while the case law of the Court of Cassation does.[68] This situation shows that the approach put forward by the CJEU is not rejected in a uniform way by the different stakeholders in France, and that, by tackling the issue of both data retention and data access, the Court of Justice

---

[64] ibid para 82.
[65] ibid para 83.
[66] ibid para 84. It is therefore a technical solution to what used to be a principled approach of the Court. On the technical feasibility of the solutions proposed by the Court, see above section 3.2 of this chapter.
[67] French Court of Cassation, 12 July 2022, n° 21-83.710, 21-83.820, 21-84.096, and 20-86.652.
[68] Agnès Canayer and Philippe Bonnecarrere, *Surveiller pour punir ? Pour une réforme de l'accès aux données de connexion dans l'enquête pénale*, Paris, Sénat, 2023.

has put forward particularly demanding criteria which can only be gradually incorporated into national law.

For the time being, the CJEU's firm stance has been partly (and politely) rejected in France and has certainly created a lot of confusion. The desire for conciliation expressed by the CJEU in *La Quadrature du Net 'II'* may have the merit of moving things forward both regarding data retention and data access. The CJEU has made concessions regarding both data retention and data access for a very specific category of traffic data, namely IP addresses. Someone is now going to have to make concessions regarding other categories of traffic and location data, both with regard to retention and access.

12
Data Retention Amid the Erosion of the Constitutional Order
The Case of Poland

Magdalena Brewczyńska

1. Introduction

Article 2 of the Constitution of the Republic of Poland of 1997 stipulates that Poland 'shall be a democratic state ruled by law'.[1] On the one hand, this cardinal provision establishing the principle of the rule of law has for years served the Constitutional Tribunal as a lighthouse that points to the direction in which this highly respected independent state institution should orient its decisions and as a crucial point of departure for formulating more specific fundamental for democracy principles, such as legal certainty, proportionality, or protection of citizens' legitimate expectations.[2] On the other hand, the principle of the rule of law could have been seen as one of the objects of the Constitutional Tribunal's greatest protection.[3] The last few years have shown, however, that the symbiosis between the rule of law and the role of the Constitutional Tribunal, crucial for safeguarding democratic processes and restraining legislative and executive powers, should not have been taken for granted.

In October 2015, the populist, centre-right party Law and Justice (Polish: *Prawo i Sprawiedliwość*) (PiS) came into power and, at a breathtaking pace, embarked on a series of reforms undermining the principle of the rule of law. Given the above, it came as no surprise that on the wave of the new order, next to the attempts to weaken the separation of powers, the disempowering of the Constitutional Tribunal became one of the primary goals of the ruling party. While the attacks on the impartial judiciary at all levels (including the constitutional level) were gaining momentum, the guarantee conveyed in Article 2 of the Constitution ceased to be predominantly the interest of constitutionalists. It became an important subject in the public discourse. Although it was pretty unprecedented how many talked about the rule of law and so vocally manifested resistance against the 'reforms'

---

[1] Article 2 Constitution of the Republic of Poland of 2 April 1997 published in Dziennik Ustaw No. 78 item 483.
[2] Stanisław Biernat and Monika Kawczyńska, 'The Role of the Polish Constitution (Pre-2016): Development of a Liberal Democracy in the European and International Context' in Anneli Albi and Samo Bardutzky (eds), *National Constitutions in European and Global Governance: Democracy, Rights, the Rule of Law: National Reports* (TMC Asser Press 2019) 762.
[3] One can formulate it also from the other side and consider the Polish Constitutional Tribunal as 'the centerpiece for the protection of the rule of law and constitutional checks upon majoritarian politics' (Wojciech Sadurski, 'Polish Constitutional Tribunal Under PiS: From an Activist Court, to a Paralysed Tribunal, to a Governmental Enabler' (2019) 11 Hague J Rule Law 63, 83).

infringing the foundations of democracy, the constitutional order continued to erode in the next years.

In this atmosphere, in 2021, revelations concerning the use of the Pegasus spyware by the PiS government began to unfold. It was revealed that Pegasus was illegally used against lawyers, journalists, politicians, and other persons with one common denominator—openly criticising the PiS party.[4] This secretly installed on a smartphone tool was capable of collecting vast amounts of data (including the content of emails, chat messages, files, browser history, or GPS) stored or processed on the targeted device and transmitting it to the Pegasus user—in this case—the state secret services acting upon political instructions.[5]

Employment of such intrusive spyware, compounded with the attempts of monopolising by the ruling party all public institutions designed to provide democratic safeguards against the abuse of power and the generally aggravating rule of law crisis, left seemingly little room for considerations on the regulatory developments and uncontested practices in the area of the retention of telecommunication data. While the courts of many EU Member States were submitting consecutive requests to the Court of Justice of the European Union (CJEU) for preliminary rulings on matters concerning telecommunication surveillance,[6] with respect to Poland, the CJEU had to adjudicate on the rule of law-related violations of EU law in the course of the infringement procedures launched by the European Commission.[7] Consequently, while several Member States were urged to align some specifics of their national telecommunication data retention frameworks to the standards demanded by the EU Charter of Fundamental Rights (Charter), Poland was ordered to return to the path of the rule of law and respect for other essential EU values.[8]

The goal of this contribution is to show that the discussion on data retention, albeit in the case of Poland overshadowed by many severe instances of the abuse of power, is not trivial and that the concerns it raises show their true colours exactly when democracy and

---

[4] Hendrik Mildebrath (European Parliamentary Research Service), 'Europe's PegasusGate Countering spyware abuse' 2022 <doi:10.2861/52251> 12, accessed 26 September 2024.

[5] Polish Senate, *Raport Końcowy Komisji Nadzwyczajnej ds. wyjaśnienia przypadków nielegalnej inwigilacji, ich wpływu na proces wyborczy w Rzeczypospolitej Polskiej oraz reformy służb specjalnych* from 6 September 2023 available at <https://www.senat.gov.pl/download/gfx/senat/pl/defaultaktualnosci/1924/15764/1/raport_koncowy_z_prac_komisji_nadzwyczajnej.pdf> accessed 20 September 2023.

[6] Since 2015 the CJEU decided among others on the requests for a preliminary ruling from the Supreme Court of Estonia (CJEU, Judgment of 2 March 2021, *Prokuratuur* (C-746/18) ECLI:EU:C:2021:152); from the Constitutional Court of Belgium (CJEU, Judgment of 21 June 2022, *Ligue des droits humains ASBL v Conseil des ministres* (C-817/19), ECLI:EU:C:2022:491; or from the Supreme Court of Ireland (CJEU, Judgment of 5 April 2022, *Commissioner of An Garda Síochána* (C-140/20) ECLI:EU:C:2022:258).

[7] Two infringement procedures were launched by the European Commission before the CJEU in 2018—one concerning the independence of the ordinary courts (C-192/18) and the other concerning the independence of the Polish Supreme Court (C-619/18). In 2019, the European Commission initiated the third infringement procedure due to the implementation of a new disciplinary regime for Polish judges (C-791/19). The fourth infringement procedure commenced in 2021 as a result of the continuation of the attacks on the independence and impartiality of judges through disciplinary tools (C-204/21).

[8] The infringement procedures led to four judgments, where the CJEU agreed with the European Commission on the alleged failures to comply with the rule of law principle: CJEU, Judgment of 24 June 2019, Commission/Poland (Independence of the Supreme Court) (C-619/18, *Publié au Recueil numérique*) ECLI:EU:C:2019:531; CJEU, Judgment of 5 November 2019, Commission/Poland (Independence of ordinary courts) (C-192/18, *Publié au Recueil numérique*) ECLI:EU:C:2019:924; CJEU, Judgment of 15 July 2021, Commission/Poland (*Régime disciplinaire des juges*) (C-791/19) ECLI:EU:C:2021:596; CJEU, Judgment of 5 June 2023, Commission/Poland (*Indépendance et vie privée des juges*) (C-204/21) ECLI:EU:C:2023:442). This does not mean, of course, that Polish rules on telecommunication data retention dating back to the pre-PiS times did not deserve CJEU's critical scrutiny from the point of view of their compliance with the Charter.

rule of law are in danger. Now, when the results of the parliamentary elections held on 15 October 2023 have been announced, and the democratic opposition appears to be in a position to depose the PiS, Poland may be at a decisive turning point. Poland does not only have a chance to restore the rule of law but also to establish new rules on crime control and security which will respect the constitutional and fundamental rights standards. At this moment of transition, this chapter intends to offer a critical analysis of the former and current regulatory landscape of telecommunication surveillance but, even more importantly, to flag what the new ruling, and hopefully truly democratic, majority should keep in mind to fulfil its promise of the real renaissance of the rule of law.

The chapter is structured as follows. Firstly, it introduces the origins and discusses the current shape of the data retention regulatory regime initially created to fight terrorism (section 2). Then, it shows how the telecommunication surveillance measures devised as a reaction to the 'extraordinary' threats were expanded to become readily available tools for 12 distinct public institutions and bodies (section 3). Next, the chapter offers a reflection on the problem of data retention from the rule of law perspective (section 4). Finally, it ends with a conclusion summarising the main findings and formulating a message to those who wish to direct Poland back on the democratic track.

2. The Origins and Current Shape of the General Regulatory Regime for Measures Created to Fight Terrorism

2.1 Background

After the 9/11 attacks, a number of countries across the world sought to ensure that similar tragedies would not happen again. The governments promised to find a way to anticipate risk and prevent any future instances of terrorism. The rhetoric of the 'war on terror' for years had dominated public debate and created a fertile ground for introducing legislative measures strengthening investigative and preventative powers of states' criminal law enforcement authorities and security services, including measures relying on the retention of telecommunication data.

Poland, back then not yet part of the European Union (EU), was no exception to this pattern. In January 2003, the first law on mandatory telecommunication data retention was adopted by the government under the leadership of social–democratic party Democratic Left Alliance (Polish: *Sojusz Lewicy Demokratycznej*) (SLD). Importantly, it was not a law in the form of a statute adopted in the course of a democratic parliamentary procedure but an ordinance issued by the executive organ—the Minister of Infrastructure.[9] Although the regulation formally had its legal basis in the Telecommunications Act of 2000,[10] its scope and, in particular, the fact that it provided for the indiscriminate retention

---

[9] Ordinance of the Minister of Infrastructure on the performance by operators of tasks for defence, state security and public security and order (*Rozporządzenie Ministra Infrastruktury w sprawie wykonywania przez operatorów zadań na rzecz obronności, bezpieczeństwa państwa oraz bezpieczeństwa i porządku publicznego*) of 24 January 2003 published in Dziennik Ustaw 2003 No 19 item 166.

[10] Article 40(3) of Telecommunication Act (*Ustawa Prawo Telekomunikacyjne*) of 21 July 2000 published in Dziennik Ustaw 2000 No 73 item 852.

of telecommunication data for 12 months, in itself raised serious constitutional concerns.[11] Article 31 of the Polish Constitution explicitly demands that any limitation upon the exercise of constitutional freedoms and rights should be imposed only by a statute. Despite this, the ministerial ordinance on telecommunication data retention remained in force and continued to be the source of related telecommunication service providers' obligations for over six years. In 2009, the regulation was finally replaced with a statute. This occurred when Poland (since 1 May 2004—when it became a Member State of the EU) implemented the Data Retention Directive[12] into the national legal order[13] by revising the Telecommunications Act of 2004 (hereafter the 'Telecommunications Act' or 'Act'),[14] which in a meanwhile replaced the Telecommunications Act of 2000.[15]

The primary motivation for the reform and maintaining data retention obligations was still the fight against terrorism. In the part justifying the choice of the maximum data retention period of 24 months instead of the previously required 12 months,[16] the Proposal for the revision of the Telecommunications Act explained inter alia that 'Poland is *or may be* used as a logistics base or transit point for terrorist groups. Due to Poland's geographical location, on the east-west and north-south routes, there is a very high probability of using the territory of our country in this way. This applies to both Islamists and other terrorist groups. ... Situations of a similar nature may occur in which terrorists will try to use the territory of Poland as an escape route. Due to the mentioned geographical location ... it should be considered that there is a high risk of using the territory of Poland for the described activities'.[17] Another argument was that due to the presence of Polish soldiers in Afghanistan, Poland might have become 'a new route for heroin transport to Europe', what could create a direct threat to Poland's security. According to the drafters of the Proposal, '[h]eroin sales are one of al-Qaeda's sources of funding. If Polish soldiers participated in drug smuggling, Poland's credibility as allies could be threatened. Polish soldiers would indirectly, without knowing it, help finance the activities of al-Qaeda and the Taliban'.[18] It was progress that the data retention measures finally gained a legal basis in the statute. Still, the arguments of the legislator—at that time under the lead of the centre-right liberal Civic Platform

---

[11] See eg Wojciech Klicki, Anna Obem, Katarzyna Szymielewicz (Fundacja Panoptykon) [2014] Raport *Telefoniczna kopalnia informacji. Przewodnik* <https://telefoniczna-kopalnia.panoptykon.org/> accessed 15 September 2023.

[12] Directive 2006/24/EC of the European Parliament and of the Council of 15 March 2006 on the retention of data generated or processed in connection with the provision of publicly available electronic communications services or of public communications networks and amending Directive 2002/58/EC [13.4.2006] OJ L 105/54.

[13] Act on the amendment of Telecommunications Act and other acts (*Ustawa o zmianie ustawy—Prawo telekomunikacyjne oraz niektórych innych ustaw*) of 24 April 2009 published in Dziennik Ustaw 2009 No 85 item 716.

[14] Telecommunications Act (*Ustawa Prawo telekomunikacyjne*) of 16 July 2004 published in Dziennik Ustaw 2004 No 171 item 1800 (with subsequent changes).

[15] On the implementation of the Data Retention Directive to the Polish national legal order see eg Andrzej Adamski, 'The Telecommunication Data Retention in Poland: Does the Legal Regulation Pass the Proportionality Test?' (2013) 1 ICT Przegląd Prawa Technologii Informacyjnych, ICT Law 4.

[16] Later in January 2013 (on the basis of an Act amending the Telecommunication Act and other acts [*Ustawa o zmianie ustawy Prawo telekomunikacyjne oraz niektórych innych ustaw*] of 16 November 2012 published in Dziennik Ustaw 2012 item 1445), the period of telecommunication data retention was shortened to 12 months.

[17] Justification accompanying the Governmental Proposal for the Act on the amendment of Telecommunications Act and other acts (*Ustawa o zmianie ustawy—Prawo telekomunikacyjne oraz niektórych innych ustaw*) of 30 October 2008 Document No 1448, 12, emphasis added.

[18] Justification accompanying the Governmental Proposal for the Act on the amendment of Telecommunications Act and other acts (*Ustawa o zmianie ustawy—Prawo telekomunikacyjne oraz niektórych innych ustaw*) of 30 October 2008 Document No 1448, 13.

(Polish: *Platforma Obywatelska*) (PO)—referring to abstract and hypothetical rather than concrete and imminent dangers invited questions on whether the introduced measures meet the constitutional standard of being 'necessary in a democratic state'.[19] As observed by Panoptykon—a Polish NGO on privacy and data protection matters—the reasoning of the drafters was flawed.[20] The arguments were formulated years after the most hectic period of the 'war on terror' was already over, and the proportionality of the measures was doubtful. Furthermore, Panoptykon rightly pointed out the irrationality of subjecting a society of 38 million citizens to surveillance measures due to the risk of a narrow group of soldiers hypothetically engaging in some criminal activity.[21]

Despite that, the Telecommunications Act (with several changes incorporated thereto over time) until today remains a central legal act governing the provision of telecommunication services in Poland and laying down general rules on the retention and provision of access to telecommunication information.

2.2 Telecommunications confidentiality

Among other things, the Telecommunications Act guarantees the protection of 'telecommunications confidentiality' and thereby embodies the general guarantees set out in Article 47 of the Polish Constitution, which provides for the right to protection of private life and Article 49, per which '[t]he freedom and privacy of communication shall be ensured. Any limitations thereon may be imposed only in cases and in a manner specified by statute'.[22] The limitations clause contained in Article 49 mirrors the general derogatory regime formulated in Article 31(3) of the Constitution, which provides that '[a]ny limitation upon the exercise of constitutional freedoms and rights may be imposed only by statute, and only when necessary in a democratic state for the protection of its security or public order, or to protect the natural environment, health or public morals, or the freedoms and rights of other persons. Such limitations shall not violate the essence of freedoms and rights'.[23]

In line with the Telecommunications Act, telecommunications confidentiality applies to five categories of data, namely: (1) data concerning the user; (2) content of the individual communications; (3) transmission data, including location data; (4) data concerning location other than data necessary for the transmission of communication or invoicing purposes; and (5) data on call attempts, including unsuccessful attempts.[24]

---

[19] Article 31 Constitution of the Republic of Poland.
[20] Wojciech Klicki, Anna Obem, Katarzyna Szymielewicz (Fundacja Panoptykon) [2014] Raport *Telefoniczna kopalnia informacji. Przewodnik* <https://telefoniczna-kopalnia.panoptykon.org/> accessed 15 September 2023.
[21] Wojciech Klicki, Anna Obem, and Katarzyna Szymielewicz (Fundacja Panoptykon) [2014] Raport *Telefoniczna kopalnia informacji. Przewodnik* <https://telefoniczna-kopalnia.panoptykon.org/> accessed 15 September 2023. For more on proportionality of surveillance measures used for security purposes see eg Jonida Milaj, 'Privacy, Surveillance, and the Proportionality Principle: The Need for a Method of Assessing Privacy Implications of Technologies Used for Surveillance' (2016) 30(3) International Review of Law, Computers & Technology 115; and Paul De Hert, 'Balancing Security and Liberty within the European Human Rights Framework. A Critical Reading of the Court's Case Law in the Light of Surveillance and Criminal Law Enforcement Strategies After 9/11' (2005) 1(1) Utrecht Law Review 68.
[22] Article 49 Constitution of the Republic of Poland.
[23] Article 31(3) ibid.
[24] Article 159(1) Telecommunications Act.

The right to consult, record, store, disseminate, or make any other use of any of the data protected by telecommunications confidentiality—whether data concerning the user, metadata, or content of communication—should, in principle, be reserved for the sender or recipient of each communication. An exception to this rule may apply when necessary for reasons provided for in the Telecommunications Act or other separate legal acts.[25]

Article 176 of the Telecommunications Act opens chapter VIII thereof titled 'Defence, state security and public safety and order obligations' and requires telecommunications undertakings to perform tasks and obligations related to defence, state security, public safety, and order within the scope and under the terms specified in the Telecommunications Act or in separate regulations.[26] In connection with these obligations, Article 179(3) indent 1 letter (a) of the Act exhaustively enumerates state bodies, which besides the court and public prosecutor, are authorised to get access to telecommunication data (both content and metadata) as an exception to the telecommunications confidentiality. The list of the *authorised bodies* currently encompasses ten institutions ranging from the Police through several secret security agencies to, among others, the Internal Inspectorate of the Prison Service or National Revenue Administration.[27] Notably, the vast array of authorised bodies, whose competence may not reveal any direct link to fighting terrorism, brings into question the coherence between the current regulatory landscape and the original legislators' intentions to establish measures necessary to fight terrorism expounded in the early 2000s.

While the statutes governing the functioning of each of the authorised bodies and the Code of the Criminal Procedure[28] regulate details on the collection and use of intelligence and evidence, Article 179 of the Telecommunications Act sets out the general obligations of the telecommunication service providers to ensure technical and organisational conditions for access and retention of telecommunication messages (ie content of telephone calls and other information transmitted by means of telecommunications networks[29]) sent or received by an end-user or telecommunications terminal equipment, but also other 'data related to the telecommunications messages'.[30] The latter includes transmission data, data concerning location, and data on attempted calls. The access to all these data must be concurrent and mutually independent for all authorised bodies.[31] This means that several state institutions can access and retain data of the same user without notifying each other and without any coordination.[32] Furthermore, the legislator demands that unless otherwise permitted by the authorised body, access to the data should be provided directly—primarily through dedicated interfaces, without the engagement of employees of the telecommunication service providers.[33]

---

[25] Article 159(2) ibid.
[26] Article 176 ibid.
[27] Article 179(3)(a) of the Telecommunications Act (n 24) enumerates the following 'authorised bodies': the Police, the Internal Supervision Bureau, the Border Guard, the Internal Inspectorate of the Prison Service, the State Protection Service, the Internal Security Agency, the Military Counter-Intelligence Service, the Military Gendarmerie, the Central Anti-Corruption Bureau, and National Revenue Administration.
[28] Act Code of Criminal Procedure (*Ustawa Kodeks Postępowania Karnego*) of 6 June 1997 published in Dziennik Ustaw 1997 No 89 item 555 (with subsequent changes).
[29] Article 2 indent 27a Telecommunications Act (n 24).
[30] Article 179(3)(a) ibid.
[31] Article 179(3)(a) ibid.
[32] Stanisław Piątek, *Prawo telekomunikacyjne. Komentarz* (CH Beck 2008 online) Commentary to Article 79 Telecommunications Act, point 7.
[33] Article 179(4b) Telecommunications Act (n 24).

Articles 180a–180d of the Act lay down rules on the retention and access to telecommunication metadata that is not related to the retention and access to the content of the telecommunication messages. At the constitutional level, the telecommunication metadata is protected under Article 51. According to Article 51(2) of the Constitution, '[p]ublic authorities shall not acquire, collect nor make accessible information on citizens other than that which is necessary in a democratic state ruled by law'.[34] Further, in line with Article 51(5) of the Constitution, '[p]rinciples and procedures for collection of and access to information shall be specified by statute'.[35]

This statute—and more precisely Article 180a(1) in conjunction with Article 180(c) of the Telecommunications Act—provides for an obligation of the retention of (1) data necessary to trace the network termination point, telecommunications terminal equipment, an end user, who originates the call and who is called; and (2) data that is necessary to identify the date and time of a call and its duration, the type of call, and location of telecommunications terminal equipment for the period of 12 months. Access to these data by the courts, public prosecutors, and ten other authorised bodies—the catalogue of which is the same as for the previously discussed telecommunication data—is subject to separate provisions outside the Telecommunications Act. Due to the fact that rules on access to metadata are scattered across over a dozen legal acts, a comprehensive analysis of all relevant provisions applicable to each of the authorised bodies is a rather tedious exercise, laying outside the scope of this chapter. For this reason, the next section will focus on the most essential developments and characteristics of the Polish data retention regime as a whole and only occasionally refer to rules concerning specific authorities.

3. Two Decades of Expansion of Telecommunications Surveillance

3.1 From fighting terrorism through combatting crime to performing any statutory tasks

As explained, the Polish telecommunication data retention regime was introduced as a response to terrorist threats. Regardless of this formal justification of the applicable since 2004 Telecommunication Act, neither retention of nor access to telecommunications data has ever been restricted to situations of terrorist threats. Since the beginning, telecommunication service providers have been imposed a general and indiscriminate data retention obligation. Access to these data has gradually been granted to ever more institutions, to currently be granted to 12 different bodies.

Inasmuch as access to the content of telecommunication is restricted to certain types of crime (serious crime) and requires *ex ante* judicial approval, access to metadata is nearly unlimited and not subject to any prior authorisation.[36] There is no specification of

---

[34] Article 51(2) Constitution of the Republic of Poland.
[35] Article 51(5) ibid.
[36] Marcin Rojszczak, 'Polskie przepisy inwigilacyjne w świetle najnowszego orzecznictwa Trybunału Sprawiedliwości – wnioski krytyczne po wyroku Trybunału Sprawiedliwości z 2.03.2021 r., C-746/18, Postępowanie karne przeciwko H.K.' (2021) 11 EPS 48.

circumstances when the authorities are allowed to resort to this operational measure and no differentiation between the type of accessed data, such as differentiation between, for instance, information on the identity of the owner of a specific SIM card and location data that allows for tracking all movements of that SIM card's user.[37] To give some examples of the scope of tasks for the performance of which metadata can be accessed: the Police Act[38] permits the Police to obtain any non-content telecommunication data if needed for the prevention or detection of crime and fiscal crime, or saving human life or health, or supporting search or rescue activities.[39] The Act on the Central Anti-Corruption Bureau goes, however, much further and allows the Central Anti-Corruption Bureau to access the non-content telecommunication data for the realisation of any of their broadly defined statutory tasks.[40] These tasks range from '*recognizing*, preventing and detecting crimes' to 'conducting *analytical activities* within the area of competence of the Bureau'.[41]

It follows that any non-content telecommunication data, including data which 'taken as a whole, allow precise conclusions to be drawn concerning the private lives of the persons whose data is concerned'[42] and therefore requiring more stringent protection, can in practice be accessed at any time by 12 different bodies for activities, which not only do not need to concern fighting terrorism or even combatting crime, but at times data can be related to the realisation of other statutory tasks of the requesting bodies.

This vast and easy access to telecommunication data is reflected in the reported by the Ministry of Justice numbers of submitted requests. The latest available report concerns 2022 and shows that that year metadata was requested 1,787,885 times and that the vast majority of requests originated from the Police, namely 1,335,825.[43] These numbers show the scale in which the instrument of telecommunication data retention is used in practice but do not provide any constructive insights into the way it is done. The information published in bulk neither reveals the purpose for which data was requested (whether prevention or investigation of crime) nor the type of crime that gave rise to the request. Furthermore, when considering the practical aspects of access to telecommunication data, it is worth recalling that the Telecommunication Act provides for the possibility of accessing telecommunication data directly through a dedicated interface without the involvement of employees of the telecommunication service providers.[44] This means that telecommunication service

---

[37] See eg the reasoning of the CJEU in CJEU, Judgment of 2 October 2018, *Ministerio Fiscal* (C-207/16) ECLI:EU:C:2018:788, paras 54–63.

[38] Police Act (*Ustawa o Policji*) of 6 April 1990 published in Dziennik Ustaw 1990 No 30 item 179 (with subsequent changes).

[39] Article 20c(1)(1) ibid.

[40] Article 18 of the Act on the Central Anti-Corruption Bureau (*Ustawa o Centralnym Biurze Antykorupcyjnym*) of 9 June 2006 published in Dziennik Ustaw 2006 No 104 item 708 (emphasis added). In a similar manner, a broad scope of access to non-content telecommunication data, ie access for the purpose of performance of any statutory task, is provided to the Military Counter-Intelligence Service (Article 32(1) of the Act on the Military Counter-Intelligence Service and Military Intelligence [*Ustawa o Służbie Kontrwywiadu Wojskowego oraz Służbie Wywiadu Wojskowego*] of 9 June 2006 published in Dziennik Ustaw 2006 No 104 item 709) and to the the Internal Security Agency (Article 28(1) of the Act on the Internal Security Agency and the Intelligence Agency [*Ustawa o Agencji Bezpieczeństwa Wewnętrznego oraz Agencji Wywiadu*] of 24 May 2002 published in Dziennik Ustaw 2002 No 74 item 676 [with subsequent changes]).

[41] Article 2 Act on the Central Anti-Corruption Bureau (emphasis added).

[42] CJEU, Judgment of 21 December 2016, *Tele2 Sverige* (C-203/15 and C-698/15) ECLI:EU:C:2016:970 para 99; repeated inter alia in CJEU, Judgment of 2 March 2021, *Prokuratuur* (n 6) para 40.

[43] A letter from the Minister of Justice to the Senate President of 14 July 2023, Document nr 1073, available at <https://www.senat.gov.pl/gfx/senat/userfiles/_public/k10/dokumenty/druki/1000/1073.pdf>.

[44] Article 179(4b) Telecommunications Act (n 24). This is further confirmed in the statutes governing access to telecommunication data for each of the authorised bodies—see eg Article 20c (3) Police Act, or Article 18(3) Act on the Central Anti-Corruption Bureau.

providers do not even have to be aware of when and what kind of data of their customers is accessed. Consequently, they cannot keep their own statistics of these instances, which could be compared with the officially published information.[45] This disallows undertaking such initiatives as publishing transparency reports, which could provide—alternative to the official state's information—insights into the interest of public authorities in the data of the users of telecommunication services and thereby contribute to public accountability.[46]

3.2 Judgment of the 'old' Constitutional Tribunal: a missed opportunity for breaking the mass surveillance pattern

When the CJEU decided on the invalidity of the Data Retention Directive on 8 April 2014 in *Digital Rights Ireland*,[47] a case regarding the conformity of the Polish laws governing access to telecommunication data by law enforcement and security agencies with the national Constitution was pending in front of the Polish Constitutional Tribunal. The long-awaited, complex judgment assessing in total more than 30 provisions of relevant national laws was finally delivered on 30 July 2014.[48] Firstly, the Tribunal clarified that '[c]onstitutional protection covers not only the content of the message, but also all circumstances of the communication process, which include personal data of the participants in that process, information about dialled telephone numbers, websites viewed, data showing the time and frequency of calls or enabling the geographical location of the conversation participants, and finally data about the IP number or IMEI number'.[49]

Then, bound by the extent of the application of the Human Rights Commissioner (the Ombudsman)[50] and the Prosecutor General,[51] who initiated the proceeding, the Tribunal ruled on access to the stored telecommunication data.[52] Numerous provisions concerning access and use of telecommunication metadata by law enforcement and security agencies were found incompatible with the constitutional standards enshrined in Articles 47 (right to private life), Article 49 (confidentiality of communication) and Article 51 (right to data protection).[53] The Tribunal contended that conditions for processing telecommunication

---

[45] Panoptykon claims that 'IT systems can be built in such a way that there is no trace left on the operator's side that the data has been accessed' Wojciech Klicki, Anna Obem, and Katarzyna Szymielewicz (Fundacja Panoptykon) [2014] Raport *Telefoniczna kopalnia informacji. Przewodnik* <https://telefoniczna-kopalnia.panoptykon.org/> 32 accessed 15 September 2023.

[46] For more on transparency reports see eg Paul De Hert and Dariusz Kloza, 'Corporate Transparency is Crucial, But It Must Also Become Far More Meaningful,' The Privacy Surgeon, 2014; or Eleni Kosta and Magdalena Brewczyńska, 'Government Access to User Data: Towards More Meaningful Transparency Reports' in Rosa Ballardini, Petri Kuoppamäki and Olli Pitkänen (eds), *Regulating Industrial Internet through IPR, Data Protection and Competition Law* (Kluwer Law Int 2019) 247.

[47] CJEU, Judgment of 8 April 2014, *Digital Rights Ireland and Seitlinger and others* (C-293/12 and C-594/12) ECLI:EU:C:2014:238.

[48] Decision of the Polish Constitutional Tribunal of 30 July 2014 in Case K 23/11.

[49] Justification of the Judgment Section III, para 1.4.

[50] Applications of the Human Rights Commissioner of 19 June 2011, 1 August 2011, 15 November 2011, and 27 April 2012.

[51] Applications of the Prosecutor General of 7 March 2012, 21 June 2012, and 13 November 2012.

[52] It could not adjudicate on the issue of the indiscriminate retention of this data of all users. Article 15 of the Act on the Constitutional Tribunal provides for that the Tribunal is bound by the extent of the application, question of law or complain upon which it decides the case.

[53] For more detailed analysis of the judgment in English see eg Jan Podkowik 'Privacy in the Digital Era – Polish Electronic Surveillance Law Declared Partially Unconstitutional: Judgment of the Constitutional Tribunal of Poland of 30 July 2014, K 23/11' (2015) 11 European Constitutional Law Review 577; Agnieszka Grzelak, 'Data Retention Saga Continues: Decision of the Polish Constitutional Tribunal of 30 July 2014 in Case K 23/

data by public authorities must be regulated in a possibly most precise and transparent manner to avoid arbitrariness. In the case at issue, it identified severe constitutional shortcomings due to the lack of independent supervision over authorities' access to metadata, lack or imprecision of provisions mandating the destruction of data that is not relevant for the proceedings within which it was collected, and failure to ensure destruction of the privileged information, such as information protected by professional secrecy (eg lawyer, medical, or journalistic secrecy).[54]

As regards the mechanism of control of the use of surveillance measures, the Tribunal emphasised the importance of its independence and external to the supervisees' position. In view of the judges, the secrecy of the operations of obtaining information for law enforcement or security purposes and limited public control over these activities can create a risk of abuse and lead to the infringement of fundamental rights and freedoms and therefore require impartial scrutiny. The Tribunal refrained, however, from taking a clear position on whether the supervision is necessarily to be *ex ante* or whether an *ex post* control can also meet the constitutional standards.[55]

Despite leaving room for some uncertainties, such as those concerning the matter of prior or posterior control, the overall findings of the Constitutional Tribunal on telecommunication surveillance were of the utmost importance. Their substance was welcomed by the Human Rights Commissioner and civil society organisations, for whom the decision of 2014 offered grounds for optimism for curtailing indiscriminate and practically unlimited access to metadata by the Police and other state agencies. Yet, unlike the CJEU with regard to the Data Retention Directive, the Polish Constitutional Tribunal did not declare the disputed unconstitutional provisions invalid with a retroactive or at least immediate effect. To give the legislator sufficient time to amend the framework and implement necessary safeguards while not abruptly depriving authorised law enforcement and security bodies of their—allegedly crucial—operational tool of access to metadata, the unconstitutional provisions were not to lose their binding force for another 18 months after the day of the publication of the judgment, that is, until February 2016.

3.3 A 'deform' instead of a 'reform' of the Polish data retention law

The discussed judgment of the Constitutional Tribunal, albeit not flawless, set out the major standards which the Polish telecommunication surveillance law should meet to be compatible with the Constitution. It took over a year before any legislative initiative was taken to adapt the unconstitutional framework to what was commanded in the seminal decision. A rushed (and still not satisfactory for any of the interested parties) Proposal for the Act Amending the Police Act and other Acts[56] was tabled by the Senate. This, however,

---

11' (2016) 22(3) European Public Law 475; or Bartłomiej Opaliński, 'Gromadzenie i udostępnianie danych telekomunikacyjnych w orzecznictwie polskiego Trybunału Konstytucyjnego' in Piotr Brzeziński, Bartłomiej Opaliński, and Maciej Rogalski (eds) *Gromadzenie i udostępnianie danych telekomunikacyjnych* (CH Beck 2016).

[54] Justification of the Judgment Section III, paras 10.4–10.11.
[55] Agnieszka Grzelak, 'Data Retention Saga Continues: Decision of the Polish Constitutional Tribunal of 30 July 2014 in Case K 23/11' (2016) 22(3) European Public Law 475, 485.
[56] Senate's Proposal for the Act amending the Police Act and other acts (*Senacki projekt ustawy o zmianie ustawy o Policji oraz niektórych innych ustaw*) of 29 July 2015, document 3765.

took place only at the end of July 2015. Without much further debate, the proposal was rejected and works on it were discontinued due to the election of a new parliament in October 2015.[57]

From that moment, the new parliamentary majority had only four months left to revise the unconstitutional provisions before they would lose their binding force. Parallel to the mentioned earlier controversial reforms overhauling the judicial system, undermining essential principles of the system of separation of powers and the checks and balances built in it, which gave the origins to the rule of law crisis, the new rules on access to telecommunication data were adopted. On 15 January 2016, a new Act Amending the Police Act and other Acts[58] was passed. The Act did not, however, introduce necessary changes in line with the Constitutional Tribunal's decision.

On the contrary, the new legislation, not without reason alias 'Surveillance Act' (Polish: '*Ustawa inwigilacyjna*') failed to bring Polish data retention law any closer to the constitutional standards demanded by the national judgment or standards formulated by the CJEU,[59] and in fact only further expanded state surveillance powers. Under the new regulation, there were no changes made to the retention of telecommunication non-content data, and both law enforcement and security agencies preserved full access thereto. What has changed, however, is that the fate of telecommunication metadata was now also shared by the 'internet data', defined in the Electronic Services Act.[60]

Until the adoption of the discussed legislation, the internet service providers were required to provide sought information about users upon request 'for the purposes of the [already] ongoing proceedings'.[61] Under the Surveillance Act, it became possible to request data also for preventative purposes, that is, when no proceeding has formally been initiated.[62] Importantly, the Surveillance Act also introduced the same possibility as existed already in relation to telecommunication services, that is, that access to data could be provided directly through a dedicated interface without a need for engaging employees of internet service providers.[63] According to Panoptykon, if enforced in practice, the elimination of a human in the loop, who otherwise manually had to process every data request, could open the door for unlimited access to data of all internet service users and, therefore, mass state surveillance on the internet.[64]

---

[57] For the elaborate explanation of the content and context of the Senate's Proposal and many of its reminiscences in the later adopted data retention law see Arkadiusz Nyzio, 'Wokół "ustawy inwigilacyjnej": geneza, przepisy i konsekwencje "Ustawy z dnia 15 stycznia 2016 r. o zmianie ustawy o Policji oraz niektórych innych ustaw"' (2017) 1(2) Jagielloński Przegląd Bezpieczeństwa 49, 56ff.

[58] Act Amending the Police Act and other Acts (*Ustawa o zmianie ustawy o Policji oraz niektórych innych ustaw*) of 15 January 2016 published in Dziennik Ustaw 2016 item 147.

[59] Such as those formulated in *Digital Rights Ireland* (n 47) or *Tele2 Sverige* (n 42).

[60] Article 18 of the Electronic Services Act (*Ustawa o świadczeniu usług drogą elektroniczną*) of 18 July 2002 published in Dziennik Ustaw 2002 No 144 item 1204. This provision enumerates categories of data the processing of which by the electronic service provider is permitted for establishing, shaping the content, changing, or terminating the contractual relationship with the recipient of the service. These data include: full name, identification number, address, data used to verify the electronic signature of the service recipient; electronic addresses of the recipient of the service.

[61] Article 18(6) Electronic Services Act.

[62] Article 8 Surveillance Act modifying Article 18(6) Electronic Services Act.

[63] eg Article 1 indent 2 Surveillance Act revising Article 20c (2) Police Act.

[64] Wojciech Klicki (Fundacja Panoptykon) [2017] Raport *Rok z Ustawą Inwigilacyjną. Co się zmieniło? Czy było się czego bać?* <https://panoptykon.org/sites/default/files/publikacje/fp_rok_z_tzw._ustawa_inwigilacyjna_18-01-2017.pdf> 3, accessed 20 September 2023.

As regards the crucial point of the Tribunal's judgment concerning the indispensability of control over authorities' access to data, the Surveillance Act laid down rules, which actually barely created a façade of the mechanism demanded by the Constitution. The 'control' mechanism laid down by the Surveillance Act was limited to an obligation imposed on the authorised bodies to report twice a year to a competent district court information on the data accessed.[65] The courts were to review the reports containing information on the number of times telecommunication data was accessed and information on the categories of crimes these instances of access concerned. In the course of such 'control', from which several types of user data are excluded,[66] the court is 'permitted' (rather than required) to obtain the evidence justifying authorities' access to telecommunication data. Yet, the Surveillance Act did not specify any mechanisms or procedures the courts could rely on in performing the control and, most importantly, the consequences of concluding that access to telecommunication data was unlawful. At an individual level, this renders the 'mechanism of control' a practically meaningless tool which can neither affect cases where telecommunication data was accessed in breach of the rights of the Constitution (including the rights to privacy and data protection, as well as a fair trial), nor prevent future abuses.

When it comes to the democratic scrutiny at large, the Surveillance Act requires presidents of the competent district courts to forward the received reports to the Minister of Justice, who once a year provides aggregated information on the access to telecommunication data by law enforcement and security services to the parliament and thus general public.[67] In this way, the Surveillance Act not only failed to establish a real supervision mechanism but created even more opacity in the reporting. It deemed the reports on access requests prepared by specific state institutions and submitted to courts 'classified information'.[68] At the same time, the 'reform' removed the until then existing obligation to report all instances of accessed data to the Office of Electronic Communications (Polish: *Urząd Komunikacji Elektronicznej*), whose statistics were directly available to the public. Consequently, the only available but impossible-to-verify information on the scale of the state's access to telecommunication data became an annual report of the Minister of Justice. Yet, it must be noted that since the PiS party came to power, the Minister of Justice is not only a representative of the executive branch, but he also holds the position of the general public prosecutor—a superior to all lower-rank prosecutors, including those accessing telecommunication and internet data.[69]

---

[65] eg Article 1 of the Surveillance Act introduced the discussed 'control' mechanism to the Police Act by inserting Article 20ca thereto. For other authorised bodies see the following provisions of the Surveillance Act: Article 2 indent 3 for the Border Guard; Article 3 indent 2 for the National Revenue Administration; Article 6 indent 2 for the Military Gendarmerie; Article 7 indent 4 for the Internal Security Agency; Article 10 indent 4 for the Military Counter-Intelligence Service; Article 11 indent 4 for the Central Anti-Corruption Bureau.

[66] In particular the subscribers data referred to in Articles 179(9) and 161 of the Telecommunication Act.

[67] Article 5 indent 3 Surveillance Act.

[68] Under the former data retention regulatory regime, Panoptykon used to regularly request authorised bodies to provide statistical information on telecommunication data requested every year. Under the new regime, Panoptykon's inquiry did not succeed. Information was refused on the ground of the confidentiality obligations established by the Surveillance Act. (Press article of 18 January 2017 'Panoptykon o przekazywanu danych telekomunikacyjnych: Po zmianie przepisów o inwigilacji jeszcze mniej przejrzystości' < https://serwisy.gazetaprawna.pl/telekomunikacja/artykuly/1011690,panoptykon-po-zmianie-przepisow-o-inwigilacji-mniej-przejrzystosci.html> accessed 20 September 2023.

[69] For more on the reform and problem of merging the offices of the Minister of Justice and the Public Prosecutor see eg Monitoring Committee of the Council of Europe, 'The Functioning of Democratic Institutions in Poland' (6 January 2020) paras 45–58; Karolina Kremens, *Powers of the Prosecutor in Criminal Investigation: A Comparative Perspective. Directions and Developments in Criminal Justice and Law* (Routledge 2021) 38ff.

A few months after the adoption of the Surveillance Act, the surveillance regulatory landscape was further supplemented by an Act on Counter-Terrorism Measures.[70] Among other things, this new legislation introduced an obligation to register all pre-paid SIM cards, equipped the security services with numerous additional powers, but also introduced an important change to the Code of Criminal Proceedings—it introduced a new provision explicitly sanctioning the possibility of using the so-called fruit of a poisonous tree, that is, evidence obtained illegally.[71]

3.4 One last PiS attempt to further expand surveillance powers

After years of expanding surveillance powers and failing to provide any safeguards that could protect against the risk of abuse, in December 2022, the PiS government tabled a proposal for a new Electronic Communications Law[72] that was supposed to replace the current Telecommunication Act. Formally, the proposed law aimed at implementing the European Electronic Communications Code[73] to the national legal order. However, besides provisions indeed transposing the respective EU Directive, the proposal introduced several new ways of increasing the possibility of mass surveillance of citizens. The draft legislation did not only still fail to effectively remove the faults of the telecommunication data retention framework identified by the Constitutional Tribunal, but it further extended the catalogue of data stored by the electronic service providers and available to state competent authorities. The proposal maintained the obligation to store data identifying data the user, such as name, surname, and national ID number (*Polish:* PESEL) and discussed earlier metadata for 12 months, but it also introduced a new category of service providers subject to this obligation—that is providers of publicly available services of 'interpersonal communication not using numbers'.[74] These services encompass electronic communicators, like WhatsApp, Messenger, or Signal, but also regular emails. The providers of such services were to be required to store the data—the exact scope of which was unclear—for a period of 12 months and make it available to competent authorities on request. The unclarity as to the type of data was a result of a formulation used by drafters of the proposal, who referred to 'data uniquely identifying a network user'.[75] It was delegated with full discretion to the executive branch to determine the type of data falling under the discussed notion.[76]

---

[70] Act on anti-terrorist activities (*Ustawa o działaniach antyterrorystycznych*) of 10 June 2016 published in Dziennik Ustaw 2016 item 904.
[71] Article 168a Code of Criminal Procedure.
[72] Governmental Proposal for the Act of Electronic Communications Law (*Rządowy Projekt ustawy Prawo komunikacji elektronicznej*) of 22 November 2022, Proposal No UC45 document 2861. Beyond governing the electronic data retention measures, the proposed act encompassed also rules on the radio and television broadcasting. Due to the drafters proposition for obligatory positioning of five channels of the state broadcaster on top of the electronic programming guides in all television operators, the proposal was dubbed publicly the 'Lex Remote Control' (Polish: *Lex Pilot*).
[73] Directive (EU) 2018/1972 of the European Parliament and of the Council of 11 December 2018 establishing the European Electronic Communications Code (Recast) Text with EEA relevance PE/52/2018/REV/1 OJ L 321, 17.12.2018, 36–214.
[74] Articles 43-53 Governmental Proposal for the Act of Electronic Communications Law.
[75] In Polish: '*dane jednoznacznie identyfikujące użytkownika w sieci*'.
[76] Art 46(1) indent 2 of the proposed Act.

Like the vague arguments presented by the legislator introducing data retention in the early 2000s, the rationale behind the new surveillance provisions of the discussed proposal was to 'support of the processes of detecting, identifying and combating threats emerging in cyberspace'. In practice, this will mean that a wide and not clearly defined array of data could be obtained by several state bodies in almost any situation in which that body considers (without a need for having sufficient evidence) that some threat can occur and must be prevented. Luckily, the Proposal in the discussed shape was withdrawn by its authors in the spring of 2023 and did not return for the parliamentary discussion. Regrettably, this means also, however, that the European Electronic Communications Code has still not been transposed to the national legal framework.

4. Data Retention in the Light of the Erosion of the Rule of Law

The past 20 years have shown an increase in all (representing the entire spectrum of the political stage—SLD, PO, PiS, and any coalition members) Polish governments' interest not only in the content of citizens' communications, but also in metadata. Regardless of the political affiliations of the ruling majorities, nearly all regulatory interventions in this area aimed at expanding the surveillance powers without providing any meaningful safeguards that could counterbalance the risk of potential abuse. The chance to change this trend emerged with the discusion in Section 3.2 of of the judgment of the Constitutional Tribunal in 2014. Although the judgment did not go as far as some would have wished for and, for instance, did not specify the requirement of a prior judicial approval for access to non-content data, it was clear that in light of the Polish Constitution, there needs to be some mechanism in place that could guarantee an effective rather than illusionary control over such intrusive operational tool as unlimited access to telecommunication (even if non-content) data. In this way, the Tribunal sided with the citizens and called for restraining state powers that interfere with the basic rights and freedoms of individuals enshrined in the Constitution.

Therefore, the judgment, even if not groundbreaking, could have become a turning point in the process of shaping Polish surveillance laws. Its correct and prompt implementation could have strengthened the position of individuals and set the minimum benchmark. It could have set the minimumConstitutional standards which laws providing for surveillance measures must meet. This did not happen. Conversely, with the politicisation of the Constitutional Tribunal that coincided with the deadline for the ordered revisions of the rules on access to telecommunication data, this chance was missed. Since the end of 2015, the meaning of the Constitutional Tribunal as a guardian of the principle of the rule of law and the constitutionally protected rights and freedoms has drastically been diminished. The practical consequences of the progressive depreciation of this formerly highly esteemed institution can be seen, for instance, in the retrieval of several applications for the verification of Acts constitutionality filed by the Human Rights Commissioner. One of the most important in the context of the present discussion decisions was a decision to withdraw the request for adjudicating on the conformity of the Surveillance Act of 2016 to the Constitution. Considering that the Surveillance Act not only failed to implement the old Constitutional Tribunal's decision of 2014 but seriously violated constitutional rights and freedoms, as well as infringed the EU standards, in February 2016, the Human

Rights Commissioner submitted it to the Constitutional Tribunal.[77] In the 'democratic state ruled by law', as indicated by Article 2 of the Constitution, the Tribunal would again have to balance the rights and freedoms of the individuals against the state interest in using surveillance measures, remaining independent and impartial in its assessment. Given the previous judgment and parallel developments of the case law of the CJEU on data retention measures, one can assume that the new Surveillance Act would not meet the standards set by the Polish Constitution and the Charter. However, in light of the arbitrary change in the composition of the Tribunal and the fact that two persons designated to adjudicate on the case were not authorised to be appointed as members of the Constitutional Tribunal,[78] the Human Rights Commissioner decided to withdraw his application.[79] This decision was motivated by the fact that, in view of the Commissioner, there was no chance for an independent and substantive examination of the application since the case was to be judged by persons whose not only judicial status but also impartiality could be questioned. The Commissioner explained that he 'fears that, in such a situation, the Tribunal's judgment could freeze a legal state that is incompatible with constitutional and European standards'.[80]

The above shows the very practical consequences of the erosion of the constitutional order. The obstruction of the Constitutional Tribunal, that is, the primary mechanism of control over the constitutionality of laws, has indirectly allowed for breaching the Constitution itself. This coupled with the loss of the meaning and role of the foundations of the order of the modern constitutional state, which in turn can be considered a loss of internal state sovereignty.[81] As rightly observed by Wyrzykowski, '[a] sovereign state is a state which acts on the basis and within the limits of the law and in which the rules which the state establishes for its citizens are respected. The power of sovereignty is not unlimited, because contemporary sovereignty is bound by the standards of individual rights and freedoms'.[82]

Interestingly, when it comes to the protection against the processing of individuals' personal data by public authorities, Article 51(2) of the Constitution explicitly reiterates that those authorities must not 'acquire, collect nor make accessible information on citizens other than that which is necessary in a democratic *state ruled by law*'.[83]

Yet, one can claim that given the gravity of the dismantlement of the constitutional order experienced in Poland since 2015, the wide and virtually unlimited access to mere metadata is not as concerning as scandals such as the one related to the use of Pegasus against political

---

[77] Human Rights Commissioner, Application for a declaration of incompatibility of certain provisions with the Constitution of 18 February 2016 (II.519.109.2015.KŁS/VV/AG) <https://ipo.trybunal.gov.pl/ipo/dok?dok=F-1860511071%2FK_9_16_wns_2016_02_18_ADO.pdf> accessed 20 September 2023.

[78] In brief, the constitutional crisis began in Poland in the fall of 2015 after PiS came into power. The new parliament elected three Constitutional Tribunal judges to replace the judges who had previously been legitimately elected but not yet sworn. The President of Poland refused to take the oath of these three judges and, thereby, finalise the process of their appointment. The Prime Minister, in turn, refused to publish the Constitutional Tribunal's judgments on the constitutionality of the Constitutional Tribunal Act, confirming the legality of the three judges' election.

[79] Human Rights Commissioner, Withdrawal of the Application of 18 February 2016 of 14 March 2018 (II.519.109.2015.MM) <https://ipo.trybunal.gov.pl/ipo/dok?dok=F-1734213486%2FK_9_16_wns_2018_03_14_ADO.pdf> accessed 20 September 2023.

[80] Human Rights Commissioner (*Rzecznik Praw Obywatelskich*), '*RPO wycofuje wniosek do Trybunału Konstytucyjnego w sprawie inwigilacji*' 14 March 2018 <https://bip.brpo.gov.pl/pl/content/rpo-wycofuje-wniosek-do-trybunalu-konstytucyjnego-w-sprawie-inwigilacji> accessed 20 September 2023.

[81] Miroslaw Wyrzykowski, 'Experiencing the Unimaginable: The Collapse of the Rule of Law in Poland' (2019) 11 Hague Journal on the Rule Law 417, 418.

[82] ibid.

[83] Article 51(2) Constitution of the Republic of Poland (emphasis added).

opponents and persons criticising the ruling party. This would be, however, a gross mistake to agree with such an argument. There is an undeniable link between the gradual expansion of any surveillance powers (even if seemingly less intrusive) and the failure to bring surveillance laws in conformity with the Constitutional human rights standards and the point where the democratic constraints are relaxed to the extent that nobody can feel protected against the arbitrary and unlimited use of power.

In the elections held in October 2023, the society clearly showed that it wants the rule of law instead of the 'law and justice'. It wishes for the power of the representatives of sovereignty to be limited with no exception. Every intrusion into the sphere of fundamental rights and freedoms protected by the Constitution must meet the minimum conditions set out by the principle of the rule of law.

In the case of the Polish surveillance framework, there is a lot to be done. The framework must be aligned with the standards formulated by the Constitutional Tribunal in 2014 and the CJEU. First and foremost, the access must not remain unlimited. The limitations should be threefold: they must concern the scope of retained and accessed data, types of authorities with data access competence, and situations in which such access is permissible. Secondly, there must be an independent and effective rather than illusionary mechanism of control over public authorities' access to data. As a rule, there should be a prior approval issued by some independent body, but there should also be some mechanism of transparency and accountability towards the general public established. Thirdly, the law should envisage consequences of unjustified or unlawful access to individuals' data. Such consequences need to be considered at multiple levels: consequences for those who abused the power, consequences for concerned individuals (notification mechanism or right to a legal remedy), and procedural consequences (eg whether the unlawfully obtained data can at all be used in the court proceeding). The new parliament will have to decide on these matters and be able to justify its choices to the democratic society.

5. Conclusion

The present chapter discussed the main policy developments in the area of telecommunication and electronic communication data retention for the purposes of crime control and security that took place in Poland in the past 20 years. It showed that data retention is a tool eagerly used by the Police as well as several security services. For years, the legal framework governing the use of such surveillance measures has only been expanding, while all governments were failing to provide safeguards capable of providing an effective counterbalance for those whose fundamental rights and freedoms are put in danger by these intrusive measures.

The last eight years showed the extreme combination of the abuse of power and destruction of the Constitutional Tribunal—a crucial institution in a democratic state—devised as a guardian of the constitutional order. Now, at the dawn of the promised restoration of the rule of law and Poland's return to the values respected by the EU community, the new government will have to live up to quite a challenge. It will have to prove that it indeed puts the values such as safeguarding fundamental rights and freedoms enshrined in the Charter as interpreted by the CJEU above its own interest of controlling society, including the political opponents, through the tools of unrestrained surveillance. Only then, the promise of the renaissance of the rule of law can be fulfilled.

13
The Impact—or No Impact—of the CJEU Case Law on Data Retention in Spain

Lorena Bachmaier Winter and Antonio Martínez Santos

1. Introduction

The Spanish Law on Data Retention (LDR)[1] transposed into the Spanish domestic legal order the Data Retention Directive,[2] later declared void by the judgment of the of Justice of the European Union (CJEU) in its *Digital Rights Ireland* judgment.[3] Article 3 of the Spanish law essentially reproduces Article 5 of the (now annulled) Data Retention Directive, when listing the data that service providers are obliged to retain for a period of 12 months.

Despite the CJEU judgment in *Digital Rights Ireland*, Spanish Courts have declared the validity of the provisions of the Spanish Law on Data Retention. Moreover, the post- *Digital Rights Ireland* case law on data retention, as, for example, in *Tele2 Sverige*[4] and *VD and SR*,[5] have generally not impacted Spanish legislation and practice.

As a result, the Spanish Law on Data Retention is still in force in its original version, having been subject only to three minor amendments in 2014, which are unrelated to the CJEU ruling in the *Digital Rights Ireland* case.[6] The issue is controversial, as will be addressed below, since there have also been legal scholars who claim that a correct interpretation of the CJEU rulings leads to the conclusion that Spanish law does not meet the proportionality requirements set forth in the European Charter of Fundamental Rights ('Charter') and in the European case law.

This chapter will first analyse the legal framework on data retention which is in force in Spain, addressing in detail its scope and the rules on time limits, transfer of data, protection

---

[1] Law 25/2007, of 18 October, *de conservación de datos relativos a las comunicaciones electrónicas y a las redes públicas de comunicaciones* (BOE-A-2007-18243) (Law on retention of data relating to electronic communications and public communications networks).

[2] Directive 2006/24/EC of the European Parliament and of the Council of 15 March 2006 on the retention of data generated or processed in connection with the provision of publicly available electronic communications services or of public communications networks and amending Directive 2002/58/EC. OJ L 105, 13.4.2006, p. 54.

[3] CJEU, Judgment of 8 April 2014, *Digital Rights Ireland and Seitlinger and others* (C-293/12 and C-594/12) ECLI:EU:C:2014. On the impact of this judgment in national laws see eg Adam Juszczak and Elisa Sason, 'Recalibrating Data Retention in the EU. The Jurisprudence of the Court of Justice of the EU on Data Retention – Is this the End or is this the Beginning?', eucrim 4 (2021) 238

[4] CJEU, Judgment of 21 December 2016, *Tele2 Sverige* (C-203/15 and C-698/15) ECLI:EU:C:2016:970.

[5] CJEU, Judgment of 20 September 2022, *VD and SR* (C-339/20 and C-397/20) ECLI:EU:C:2022:703.

[6] See Final Provision 4 of Law 9/2014 of 9 May (the previous Spanish Law on Telecommunications), which amended Articles 6.2, 7.3, and 10 of the LDR.

of retained data, and the registration of pre-paid card users. After setting the legal context, it will be discussed to what extent the case law of the CJEU has impacted upon the Spanish law and court decisions, and whether the Spanish approach is in conformity with the principle of proportionality, as it is established in the CJEU data retention case law. Issues on admissibility of evidence and the need for a harmonized approach at the European level to prevent that breaches of the data retention rules do not have any major impact on the adjudication of criminal cases, and shall not be addressed here.[7]

2. Legal Framework for Data Retention in Spain

The Spanish Data Retention Law—made of only ten Articles—is specifically addressed to operators providing publicly available electronic communications services or operating public communications networks (landline and mobile telephones and internet services). It defines as obliged parties those which are listed in the Public Register of Communications Operators, which depends on the *Comisión Nacional de los Mercados y de la Competencia* (National Commission for Markets and Competition((CNMC).[8]

The LDR imposes three key obligations on these operators, which are:

(a) To retain, for a minimum period of time, the traffic and location data of natural and legal persons deriving from the provision of the service, as well as the data necessary to identify subscribers or registered users.[9]
(b) To transfer the retained data to the so-called 'authorized agents' when these data are necessary for the detecting, investigating and prosecuting *serious* crimes. The order to transfer these data is subject to prior judicial warrant,[10] a general requirement for any investigative measure that affects the right to the protection of personal data (Article 18.4 of the Spanish Constitution).[11]
(c) To ensure the secure storage and protection of the retained data.[12]

---

[7] The case law of the CJEU on the data retention regime is relevant for identifying rules on admissibility of evidence at the EU level, which are necessary to be harmonized. See Lorena Bachmaier Winter, 'Mutual Admissibility of Evidence and Electronic Evidence in the EU: A new try for European minimum rules in criminal proceedings?', eucrim 2 (2023) 223 at <https://eucrim.eu/articles/mutual-admissibility-of-evidence-and-electronic-evidence-in-the-eu/>; Giulia Lasagni, 'Admissibility of Evidence in Criminal Proceedings: Lessons (and Problems) from the 'Data Retention Saga' in Lorena Bachmaier Winter and Farsam Salimi (eds), *Admissibility of Evidence in EU Cross-Border Criminal Proceedings: Electronic Evidence, Efficiency and Fair Trial Rights* (Hart Publishing 2024).

[8] The register of operators is provided in Article 7 of the current General Telecommunications Law (see Law 11/2022 of 28 June, BOE-A-2022-10757). To become an authorized communications operator the registration in this public register is mandatory.

[9] See Articles 4 and 5 LDR.

[10] See Articles 1.1, 6.1, and 7 LDR. See also Article 588 *ter* j of the Criminal Procedure Code (BOE-A-1882-6036), which regulates the incorporation into criminal proceedings of electronic data from automated files of communications service providers.

[11] The case law of the Spanish Supreme Court links the transfer of data provided for in the LDR only to the right to the protection of personal data. It considers that the measure alone does not affect the right to secrecy of communications. Vid. in this regard the judgment of the Supreme Court 348/2014, 22 January 2014 (ECLI:ES:TS:2014:348).

[12] See Article 8 LDR.

In addition to these three obligations, there is a general prohibition on the exploitation or use of the resulting records, except with the express consent of the person concerned in accordance with the provisions of the General Telecommunications Law (LGT).[13]

3. Data to be Retained

Operators are obliged to retain the data specified in Article 3 of the LDR, which merely reproduces the content of Article 5 of the Data Retention Directive.[14] There is only one difference: when the Spanish LDR refers to the data necessary to identify telephone communications, it specifies in detail the elements that must be retained by the obliged parties: type of call (whether voice transmission, voicemail, conference, or data); supplementary services, including call forwarding or call transfer; and messaging services used, including short message services and multimedia services. In other words, it transposes here the definition of 'telephone service from Article 2(2)(c) of the Data Retention Directive.[15]

According to Article 4 LDR, the obligation to retain data also extends to unsuccessful calls, but not to 'unconnected' calls (ie calls where there was no intervention by the operators involved).[16] Both the content of communications and the information consulted using electronic communications networks are expressly excluded from said obligation.[17]

4. Data Retention Time Limits

The Spanish LDR imposes on operators the obligation to retain the data referred to in Article 3 for at least 12 months from the date of the communication.[18]

Strictly speaking, the law does not set any maximum time limit, but merely provides that the obligation to retain data 'ceases after twelve months'. At first sight, it would therefore appear that the data can be retained indefinitely, provided that the operator is prepared to do so and willing to bear the cost. However, it is clear from Article 66 of the current LGT that the person concerned has the right to have his/her traffic data deleted as soon as they are no longer needed, 'without prejudice to the obligations laid down in the LDR'. Therefore, it must be understood that the 'minimum period' of retention established by the LDR does not in any case empower operators to retain data indefinitely. The same conclusion is

---

[13] Article 4.1, second paragraph of the LDR, which has to be put in relation with the current Article 66.2 of the General Telecommunications Law of 2022; which transposes the rights recognized in the ePrivacy (Directive 2002/58/EC of the European Parliament and of the Council of 12 July 2002 concerning the processing of personal data and the protection of privacy in the electronic communications sector (Directive on privacy and electronic communications). OJ L 201, 31.7.2002, p 37).

[14] This provision includes data necessary: to trace the origin and destination of the communication; to determine its duration and the date and time it occurred; to identify the type of communication and the equipment used; and to identify the location of mobile devices. See Article 3.1 LDR.

[15] Compare Article 3(1)(d) LDR with Articles 2(2)(c) and 5(1)(d) of Directive 2006/24/EC.

[16] Articles 4.2 and 4.3 LDR.

[17] Articles 1.3 and 3.2 LDR.

[18] Article 5.1 LDR.

reached by analysing the rules on personal data protection,[19] as well as the provisions of the ePrivacy Directive.[20]

The LDR enables the government to establish different retention periods (shorter and/ or longer than 12 months) for certain data or categories of data. In order to respect the time limits set out in the Data Retention Directive,[21] the LDR provided that, in these special cases, the minimum mandatory retention period imposed by the government should not be less than six months nor exceed two years.[22]

When setting reduced or extended minimum time limits by regulation, the government should consult with operators and take into consideration the cost of storing and retaining the data, as well as their potential relevance for the detection, investigation, and prosecution of serious criminal offences. We are not aware of any use of this power by the Spanish government so far.

Failure to comply with the obligation to retain data may constitute an administrative offence, which will be regarded as a very serious violation if no data have been retained at all, a serious violation in the event that data have been retained but for less than the minimum period established by law, or a less serious violation for other infringements.[23] The applicable penalties for infringements committed by operators are provided for in the General Telecommunications Law: a fine of up to 20 million euros and possible disqualification for up to five years in the case of very serious infringements, and a fine of up to two million euros in the case of serious infringements.[24] A minor breach of the obligation to retain data is punishable by a fine of up to 100,000 euros.[25] The imposition of these administrative sanctions corresponds to the Secretary of State for Telecommunications, following a 'mandatory and determining' report by the Ministry of the Interior.[26]

Finally, Article 588 *octies* of the Code of Criminal Procedure (CCP)[27] must be considered. This provision was introduced in 2015. It enables the judicial police and the Public Prosecutor's Office to directly issue data preservation orders while the judicial warrant on the appropriateness of their transfer is pending. This is a provisional measure to avoid the expiration of the data retention period in the meantime. In these cases, the operator must retain the data for a maximum period of 90 days. Such period may be extended only once and in any event for a maximum of 180 days. The Code of Criminal Procedure establishes that the operator is obliged to collaborate and to keep the confidentiality of the adoption of the securing order.[28]

---

[19] See Organic Law 3/2018 of 5 December 2018 on the Protection of Personal Data and Guarantee of Digital Rights and Regulation (EU) 2016/679 of the European Parliament and of the Council of 27 April 2016 on the protection of individuals with regard to the processing of personal data and on the free movement of such data.

[20] See especially Article 6(1) of Directive 2002/58/EC.

[21] On the aims and content of the EU Directive 2006/24/EC in Spanish, see eg Stefano Rodotà, 'La conservación de los datos de tráfico en las comunicaciones electrónicas', IDP, Rev. de Internet, Derecho y Política, (2006) 3, 53.

[22] See Article 5.1 LDR.

[23] See Article 10 LDR.

[24] See Article 109 of the General Telecommunications Law currently in force. It is important to note that, in the case of legal persons, in addition to the penalty applicable to the operator, an individual fine of up to 5,000 euros in the case of minor infringements, up to 30,000 euros in the case of serious infringements and up to 60,000 euros in the case of very serious infringements may be imposed on their legal representatives or on the persons making up the management bodies or collegiate administrative bodies involved in the agreement or decision (See Article 109.5 LGT).

[25] See Article 10.1(c) LDR in conjunction with Article 109.1(d) of the General Telecommunications Law.

[26] See Article 10.2 LDR.

[27] *Ley de Enjuiciamiento Criminal*.

[28] The data preservation order of Article 588 *octies* of the CCP is not only applicable to data retained under the LDR, but in general to any data stored in computer systems (eg data stored in social networks, email or cloud

5. Transfer of Data to 'Authorized Agents'

The LDR provides that the data retained may only be transferred upon prior judicial warrant, and only to the subjects and for the purposes specified in the law itself, that is, the detection, investigation, and prosecution of *serious* crimes. The information transmitted must be limited to what is strictly necessary for the achievement of these purposes.[29] The transfer of data should be carried out in electronic form.[30]

From the very beginning of the entry into force of the LDR there were doubts about the meaning of the term 'serious crimes' in Article 1 LDR. In principle, from a strictly legal point of view, in Spanish Criminal Law serious crimes are those punishable by a serious penalty. According to Article 33.2 of the Spanish Criminal Code (CC),[31] serious penalties are (among others) permanent revisable imprisonment, imprisonment for more than five years and absolute disqualification. Offences carrying these types of penalties include homicide, murder, kidnapping, rape, most terrorist offences, drug trafficking (in some cases), and most offences against the Crown.

However, several Provincial Courts have opted for a broad interpretation of this concept, following the case law of the Constitutional Court in relation to telephone-tapping. According to this case law, when deciding on the tapping of a telephone, the seriousness of the offence should not be determined solely by the legally established penalty—although this must undoubtedly be taken into account—but should also take into account other factors, such as the legal right or value being protected as well as its social relevance.[32]

Currently, these doubts seem to have been cleared up as a result of the legal reform of 2015, which introduced Article 588 *ter* a in the CCP. According to this Article, the interception of telephone and telematic communications can be judicially authorized when investigating one of the crimes referred to in Article 579.1 of the CCP: intentional crimes punishable with three years' imprisonment or more, crimes committed by organized groups and terrorism; or any crimes committed through computer systems, information or communication technologies, or communication services. This legal provision would also apply to LDR data transfer orders.[33]

---

accounts). In this regard, see Instruction (*Circular*) 1/2019 of 6 March 2019 of the General Public Prosecutor's Office on common provisions and security measures for technological investigative measures in the Criminal Procedure Act. For a proposal prior to the 2015 reform, see Julio Pérez Gil and Juan José González López, 'Cesión de datos personales para la investigación penal: una propuesta para su inmediata inclusión en la Ley de Enjuiciamiento Criminal', Diario La Ley, 7401 (2010).

[29] Article 6 LDR.
[30] See Order of the Ministry of the Presidency PRE/199/2013 of 29 January, defining the form for the delivery of data retained by operators of electronic communications services or public communications networks to authorized agents. In 2014, Article 6.2 LDR was amended to specify this aspect, which was not provided for in the original wording of the regulation.
[31] Organic Law 10/1995, of 23 November, on the Criminal Code (BOE-A-1999-23750).
[32] See judgments of the Spanish Constitutional Court 166/1999 of 27 September 1999 (para 3 of the legal grounds) and 299/2000 of 11 December 2000 (para 2 of the legal grounds).
[33] This is also the understanding of the Supreme Court Judgment STS 1309/2021 of 23 March 2021 (ECLI:ES:TS:2021:1309). This is a criterion also shared by the Public Prosecutor's Office (see Instruction 2/2019 of 6 March 2019 of the General Public Prosecutor on the interception of telephone and telematic communications, § 4). Several authors have also been in favour of adopting this approach. See José Luis Rodríguez Lainz, 'Hacia un nuevo entendimiento de gravedad del delito en la Ley de conservación de datos relativos a las comunicaciones electrónicas', Diario La Ley, 7789(2012); Julio Pérez Gil, 'Exclusiones probatorias por vulneración del derecho a la protección de datos personales en el proceso penal', *Justicia: garantías "versus" eficiencia?* (Tirant 2019) 399; and

As mentioned above, only so-called 'authorized agents' can be data transferees.[34] According to Article 6(2) LDR, authorized agents are:

(a) Law enforcement officers, when performing judicial police duties.
(b) Officials of the Customs Service, when acting as judicial police.
(c) The staff of the National Intelligence Centre, in the context of the security investigations it may conduct under its regulatory legislation.[35]

When these agents require data relating to communications which are in the possession of an operator within the meaning of Article 3 LDR, they must apply to the competent judicial authority for a transfer order. This judicial authority will normally be an Investigating Judge (*Juzgado de Instrucción* or *Juzgado Central de Instrucción* in cases of serious crimes where the *Audiencia Nacional* has jurisdiction). The Public Prosecutor's Office is not considered a judicial authority in Spain to this end and therefore cannot authorize this type of measure, not even in those proceedings in which it directs the criminal investigation.[36]

The LDR does not specify the contents of the application to obtain the judicial warrant, hence the general rules on the interception of communications provided in the CCP apply here, as established by the Supreme Court.[37] This means that Articles 588 *bis* b and 588 *ter* j, second paragraph CCP[38] are to be applied, and that the law enforcement agents need to show that the requested data are 'indispensable for the investigation'.

According to these rules, the request for judicial authorization made by the 'authorized officers' must in any case contain: (1) the description of the facts under investigation; (2) the detailed explanation of the reasons that justify the need for the measure in accordance with the guiding principles set forth in Article 588 *bis* a, as well as the reasonable grounds to believe that a crime has been committed, as determined during the investigation that preceded the request for the interception of communications; (3) the identity of the persons concerned by the transfer of data; (4) the identity of the operator who must comply with the request for transfer; (5) the nature of the data whose knowledge is necessary; (6) the reasons justifying the need to obtain the information to which the request refers; (7) the

---

Susana Oromí Vall-Llovera, 'Access to personal data retained by electronic communications service providers in criminal investigations according to the Court of Justice of the EU', Revista de Internet, Derecho y Política (31) (2020) 1.

[34] In its report on the draft bill on data retention, the Spanish General Council of the Judiciary criticized this nomenclature as inappropriate and imprecise. However, the legislator kept it in the LDR.

[35] See Law 11/2002, of 6 May, regulating the National Intelligence Centre, and Organic Law 2/2002, of 6 May, regulating the prior judicial control of the National Intelligence Centre.

[36] Decision of the non-jurisdictional full court meeting of the 2nd Chamber of the Supreme Court of 23 February 2010: 'Judicial authorization is required for operators providing electronic communications services or public communications networks to transfer data generated or processed for this purpose. Therefore, the Public Prosecutor's Office will need such authorization to obtain from the operators the retained data specified in Article 3 LDR'. This Decision (*Acuerdo*) was reflected a few weeks later in Supreme Court Ruling 247/2010 of 18 March. Note that Article 6 LDR did not include the Public Prosecutor's Office among the authorized agents, but this was not an obstacle for the Supreme Court to recognize this status even before the procedural reform of 2015 (see Organic Law 13/2015 of 5 October).

[37] It is important to note that these Articles of the CCP cover the cases regulated by the LDR, but also others that are not provided for in it. In this regard, see Guideline 2/2019, of 6 March of the General Public Prosecutor.

[38] Article 588 *ter* j CCP regulates the access to electronic data held by service providers and provides also for the possibility of data mining and the use of artificial intelligence for the search of data.

form in which the measure will be executed; (8) the duration of the requested interception or access to data; and (9) the officer who will carry out the measure, if known.

Upon receipt of the request from the 'authorized officers', if the judge deems it appropriate (adequacy, necessity, and proportionality), he/she shall issue the order for the transfer of data. The judicial warrant ordering the transfer of data shall be reasoned and it must specify: (1) its addressee or addressees, mentioning their duty to cooperate and to keep the order and the subsequent acts secret,[39] under penalty of incurring in an offence of disobedience; (2) the specific offence under investigation and the facts that show probable cause for the measure to be justified; (3) the identity of the persons under investigation and of any other person affected by the transfer of data, if known; (4) the purpose of the measure, ie the retained data to be transferred to the authorized officers; (5) the reasons why he/she considers the transfer of data to be necessary and proportionate;[40] and (6) the time limit for the execution of the order, depending on the urgency for the investigation and the nature and technical complexity of the operation.[41] If the judicial warrant does not specify a time limit, the transfer must take place within seven calendar days from 8:00 am on the calendar day following the day on which requesting authorities received the order. Failure to comply with the court order to transfer the data does not constitute an administrative offence under Article 10 of the LDR but could possibly entail criminal liability (disobedience).[42]

The LDR does not establish the grounds upon which the judicial authority may refuse to grant the measure to transfer the data, but here the general rules apply: the court shall not grant the judicial authorization when the measure is unnecessary, disproportionate, inadequate, ungrounded, not related to the crime, or when it is too vague, that is, when it does not clearly limit the scope of data required or when the facts which are under investigation are not sufficiently defined. Under the Spanish criminal procedural law prospective investigations such as fishing expeditions are generally prohibited.

This prohibition is derived from Article 588 *bis* a of the CCP, which also defines the principles of exceptionality, necessity, and proportionality in order to adopt the investigative measures regulated in Articles 588 *ter* a, and ff of the CCP.

Thus, according to Article 588 *bis* a of the CCP, the judge must verify that there are no other alternative measures or a less intrusive measure that could be equally useful to investigate and proof the facts. Furthermore, the judge must assess whether, in the absence of the transfer of data by the communications operator, there would be a 'serious difficulty' in discovering or verifying the act under investigation, in determining the perpetrator, or in ascertaining his/her location or the location of the evidence of the crime. Finally, as regards the principle of proportionality, the Spanish CCP establishes the elements that the judge must consider in assessing the proportionality of any measure encroaching a fundamental right. Thus he/she must make a decision taking into consideration all the circumstances

---

[39] According to Article 9(1) LDR, operators must refrain from informing data subjects that their data have been transferred to authorized agents.

[40] See Article 7(2) LDR: 'The judicial decision shall determine, in accordance with the provisions of the Criminal Procedure Act and in accordance with the principles of necessity and proportionality, the retained data to be transferred to the authorized officials'.

[41] See Article 7.3 LDR.

[42] This seems to be the meaning of Article 8.2, first paragraph *in fine* of the LDR. In this respect, see Article 556 of the Criminal Code, on the crime of disobedience to a public authority. However, this is an offence that in Spain can only be committed by natural persons (not legal persons).

of the case, that the interference of the rights and interests affected is outbalanced by the benefit to the public interest and third parties. When weighing up the possible conflicting interests, the assessment of the public interest will be based on the seriousness of the offence, its social relevance, the technological environment in which the offence has been committed,[43] the intensity of the existing evidence and the relevance of the result pursued with the restriction of the right.

6. Protection and Security of Retained Data

The LDR obliges communications operators to protect the retained data.

To this end, operators must: (1) identify the personnel specifically authorized to access the data; and (2) take technical and organizational measures to prevent: (2a) their manipulation or use for purposes other than those authorized by the LDR, (2b) their accidental loss, (2c) their destruction, whether accidental or unlawful, and (2d) their unauthorized storage, processing, or disclosure.

Article 8 LDR refers to the law on personal data protection for all issues and obligations related to ensuring the quality of the data stored, the confidentiality and security of their processing, and the level of protection that corresponds to them.[44] The references in the LDR to Organic Law 15/1999 on Personal Data Protection, now repealed, must now be understood as referring to the current Organic Law on the Protection of Personal Data and Safeguard of Digital Rights.[45]

Failure to comply with the duties imposed on operators by Article 8 LDR constitutes an administrative infringement which, once again, may be very serious, serious, or less serious, and the sanctioning regime of the General Telecommunications Law described above applies. However, in these cases, the competent authority to investigate the case and impose the sanction is the Spanish Data Protection Authority.[46]

7. Registration of Prepaid Card Users

The LDR closes with an additional provision concerning mobile telephone services by means of prepaid cards, which provides that these companies are obliged to keep a logbook with the identity of all customers who purchase this type of cards.

In the case of natural persons, the name, surname, nationality, and personal identification document number (identity card, passport, residence card, etc) must be entered in the register. In the case of legal persons, the company name and tax identification number must

---

[43] For the Spanish CCP the fact that cybercrimes can only be effectively detected and investigated by adopting measures that allow the law enforcement to access to the computer and the electronic data, determines that the gravity of the crime does not play a role in this field. It means that the fact that the crime is committed in the cyberworld requires per se the adoption of access to such computer systems and stored data, regardless the penalty that is provided for such a crime. On this understanding of the proportionality principle detached from the gravity of the criminal offence, see Lorena Bachmaier Winter, 'Remote search of computers under the new Spanish Law of 2015: proportionality principle and the protection of privacy', ZStW 129-1 (2017) 1.

[44] See Royal Decree 1720/2007 of 21 December 2007.

[45] Organic Law 3/2018 of December 5 on Protection of Personal Data and Guarantee of Digital Rights (*Ley Orgánica de Protección de Datos Personales y garantía de los derechos digitales*).

[46] Article 10.3 LDR.

be entered. Customers must be informed of the existence and content of this register before purchasing a prepaid card, and the service provider is obliged to protect the information contained therein under the terms of Article 8 LDR.

From the moment the card is activated until the obligation to retain card communications data (which is governed by the general provisions of the LDR) ceases, operators are obliged to transfer the purchaser's identification data to authorized officials, when required for the purpose of detection, investigation, and prosecution of a criminal offence.

Two issues should be noted in this respect: first, that the request for the transfer of the identification data of the purchaser of a given prepaid card is not subject to judicial authorization.[47] This is the general rule for the identification of telephone line holders by the judicial police and the Public Prosecutor's Office in Spain (as long as it does not involve data linked to communication processes). And second, that authorized officers may require the card purchaser's identification data for the investigation of any crime (not just *serious crimes*).

8. Impact of the Case Law of the Court of Justice

The judgment of the Court of Justice in the *Digital Rights Ireland* case did not have a significant impact on Spanish law and practice. Although it generated some uncertainty among scientific scholars—some authors went so far as to state that, with the CJEU ruling, the Spanish LDR had been left in a 'legal limbo'—very soon the Supreme Court made it clear that the Spanish law on data retention could be interpreted so to meet the requirements of European law.[48] However, it took several years (until 2021) for the Supreme Court to substantiate this conclusion in detail.[49]

The most recent case law of the Supreme Court has given the following reasons to support the compatibility of the LDR with the case law of the CJEU on the ePrivacy and the Data Retention Directives:[50]

(a) The Spanish legislation establishes defined time limits for data retention.
(b) Operators should only retain metadata in the strict sense of the word, ie data relating to the communications history and the equipment or device used, never relating to the content of the communication.
(c) Operators are strictly forbidden from using or exploiting the data that they are obliged to retain under the LDR. While it is true that the mere storage of communications

---

[47] In this respect, see Article 588 *ter* m of the CCP. A judicial warrant is required to link an IP address, an IMEI number or an IMSI number that the police have obtained while investigating in public networks, with a specific equipment or device (and, therefore, to identify the holder of the contract and, eventually, the person using the equipment). According to the Constitution (Article 18 SC) this requires prior judicial warrant, since it interferes with the fundamental right to privacy. See Article 558 *ter* k of the CCP and, prior to the 2015 procedural reform, Supreme Court judgment 217/2014 of 30 January 2014 (ECLI:ES:TS:2014:217) and the case law cited therein.
[48] Supreme Court Judgment 3436/2015 of 7 July 2015 (ECLI:ES:TS:2015:3436) and Supreme Court Judgment 5140/2015 of 23 November 2015 (ECLI:ES:TS:2015:5140).
[49] Judgment of the Supreme Court STS 1309/2021 of 23 March 2021 (ECLI:ES:TS:2021:1309).
[50] See Supreme Court Judgment 2800/2017 of 1 June 2017 (ECLI:ES:TS:2017:2800); Supreme Court Judgment 110/2019 of 23 January 2019 (ECLI:ES:TS:2019:110); Supreme Court Judgment 1966/2020 of 15 June 2020 (ECLI:ES:TS:2020:1966) and, especially, Supreme Court Judgment STS 1309/2021 of 23 March 2021 (ECLI:ES:TS:2021:1309), cited above.

data constitutes an act of 'processing' within the meaning of European law, it is also true that in Spain the stored data cannot be processed, disseminated, or transferred to third parties other than those provided for by law. They are simply 'hibernated' in the custody of the operator until a judge authorizes their transfer or, failing that, until they are completely erased within 12 months.

(d) Data can only be transferred to so-called 'authorized agents' (judicial police, public prosecutor's office, National Intelligence Centre). The circle of potential transferees is extremely restricted.

(e) The transfer of data is only possible for the investigation of serious crimes (in the sense of Article 579.1 CCP) and always requires individualized judicial authorization.

(f) Obtaining judicial authorization is subject to the principles of proportionality, necessity, speciality, appropriateness, and exceptionality. Access to data for prospective purposes is not allowed.

(g) The data disclosed to authorized agents is always limited to the information strictly necessary for the investigation.

(h) The law imposes an obligation on operators to protect the data retained to ensure their integrity, security, quality, and confidentiality. Failure to comply with this obligation constitutes an offence punishable by administrative sanctions, with fines of up to several million euros depending on the seriousness of the infringement.

(i) Data storage requires operators to adopt several security measures, including keeping a detailed record of access to data: identification of the user, date and time of the access attempt, file accessed, type of access and whether access was authorized or denied.[51]

(j) The technical specifications of the format in which the transfer of data must take place are regulated in detail by means of a Ministerial Order.[52]

According to the Spanish Supreme Court, these circumstances would satisfactorily address the concerns raised by the Court of Justice against the Data Retention Directive, which ultimately led to its annulment.

The Supreme Court has persisted unchanged in this position over the years, even after the judgments of the CJEU in *Tele2 Sverige*,[53] *La Quadrature du Net 'I'*,[54] *Prokuratuur*,[55] *Garda Síochána*,[56] *SpaceNet*,[57] and the more recent ones *La Quadrature du Net 'II'*[58] and *Bolzano*.[59] In the judgment of the Spanish Supreme Court of 19 October 2022,[60] a murder case where the defence questioned the validity of the traffic and geolocation data used as

---

[51] Articles 81.4 and 103 of Royal Decree 1720/2007, of 21 December.
[52] See Order of the Ministry of the Presidency PRE/199/2013 of 29 January defining the format for the delivery of data retained by operators of electronic communications services or public communications networks to authorized agents.
[53] CJEU, Judgment of 21 December 2016, *Tele2 Sverige* (C-203/15 and C-698/15) ECLI:EU:C:2016:970.
[54] CJEU, Judgment of 6 October 2020, *La Quadrature du Net and others* (C-511/18, C-512/18 and C-520/18) ECLI:EU:C:2020:791 ('*La Quadrature du Net 'I'*').
[55] CJEU, Judgment of 2 March 2021, *Prokuratuur* (C-746/18) ECLI:EU:C:2021:152.
[56] CJEU, Judgment of 5 April 2022, *Commissioner of An Garda Síochána* (C-140/20) ECLI:EU:C:2022:258).
[57] CJEU, Judgment of 27 October 2022, *SpaceNet* (C-793/19 and C-794/19) ECLI:EU:C:2022:702.
[58] CJEU, Judgment of 30 April 2024, *La Quadrature du Net a.o. c. Premier Ministre and Ministre de la Culture* (C-470/21) ECLI:EU:C:2024:370 ('*La Quadrature du Net 'II'*').
[59] CJEU, Judgment of 30 April 2024, *Procura della Repubblica presso il Tribunale di Bolzano* (C-178/22) ECLI:EU:C:2024:371 ('*Bolzano*').
[60] See Supreme Court Judgment 3822/2022 of 19 October 2022 (ECLI:ES:TS:2022:3822).

evidence, arguing that the retention of such data was contrary to the case law of the CJEU, the Supreme Court refuses this claim by stating that the right to privacy has to be counterbalanced by the right to security of the citizens. This would require the adoption of preventive measures, as the retention of data, so that the Investigating Judge can, if need be, assess later whether the crime committed is serious or not. Once the seriousness of the crime is confirmed, it would then, if requested, adopt the measure to access the retained data after checking the adequacy, necessity, and proportionality of the measure. In this judgment the Supreme Court points at the fact that according to the Spanish law the preservation of data, as it does not entail any processing of those data, does not entail a 'relevant' encroachment of the right to privacy.[61]

For their part, both the Organic Law on Personal Data Protection of 2018 and the General Telecommunications Law of 2022 have made express references to the LDR in some of their provisions, so that at present the material validity of the Spanish LDR in practice is beyond any doubt.[62]

Finally, the CJEU itself has not questioned the validity of the Spanish LDR in the cases in which it has had the opportunity to do so, since there have been some preliminary references filed to the Court regarding several provisions of the Spanish LDR.[63] We refer specifically to the judgment of the Court of Justice (Grand Chamber) in *Ministerio Fiscal*. However, the CJEU's silence can reasonably be attributed to the fact that in that case it was not necessary to rule on the validity of the Spanish law to answer the question referred for a preliminary ruling.[64]

9. Conclusion

The practical application of the Spanish LDR currently gives access to an enormous amount of information that neither the Spanish legislator nor the Supreme Court have been willing to give up. We are faced with a generalized and indiscriminate collection of traffic, location, and identification of communications data of the entire population, which is done for the sole purpose of making it available for a hypothetical future criminal investigation.

The usefulness of this approach for the prosecution of serious crimes and for the protection of national security is out of question: far-reaching data retention is undeniably helpful for the purposes of criminal investigations. It is also undeniable that the Spanish legislator has tried to strike a difficult balance, ensuring that the storage and transfer of data is protected with enough guarantees aimed at preventing abuses: prohibition or limitation of the cases where it can be used; limitation of the persons or entities that can access to the data;

---

[61] Point 12 of the paragraph 4 of the legal reasoning states that the retention of traffic and geolocation data does not have a significant impact upon the privacy of the individuals, since the data are not processed. Furthermore, there are enough safeguards for the rights of the accused since the access to the retained data required a judicial warrant.
[62] Order of the Supreme Court 5148/2018 of 22 March 2018 (ECLI:ES:TS:2018:5148A).
[63] CJEU, Judgment of 2 October 2018, *Ministerio Fiscal* (C-207/16) ECLI:EU:C:2018:788.
[64] See José Luis Rodríguez Lainz 'El régimen legal español en materia de conservación y cesión de datos para la investigación de delitos', Diario La Ley, 9291(2018); and also 'El renacer de la Ley Española sobre conservación de datos relativos a las comunicaciones', Diario La Ley, 9740 (2020).

requirement of reasoned judicial warrant for the transfer of the data, decided on a case-by-case basis; strict compliance with the principle of proportionality (albeit understood in a broad way with regard to cybercrime and other crimes committed in a digital environment), minimization of the data accessed, etc.

However, it is clear that the amount of information with potential investigative relevance collected by communications operators in Spain is clearly minimal in relation to the colossal volume of data the service providers are obliged to retain every day. The Spanish legislation does not contemplate any objective criteria to limit the retention of traffic and location data, be it geographic, temporal, or personal: in Spain, the retention of communications data is not selective, but generalized and indiscriminate by law. On the other hand, the usefulness for criminal proceedings of the stored data only becomes apparent *a posteriori*, once the law enforcement authorities show probable cause of a crime and apply for the judicial warrant for the transfer of data.

Thus, it seems questionable whether the current Spanish rules on communications data retention comply with the requirements outlined in the case law of the CJEU when interpreting the ePrivacy Directive and Articles 7, 8, and 11 of the Charter, specifically regarding the indiscriminate retention of such data.[65] However, Spanish courts have shown a different approach in this regard. Balancing the safeguards provided in the LDR against the benefits for the criminal prosecution, they have clearly decided in favour of allowing what is in our mind a disproportionate retention of communications data, as long as its storage and access is surrounded by enough safeguards. For the Spanish Courts so far, the mere retention of communication data, albeit being massive, does neither pose any fundamental rights concerns nor a breach of the proportionality principle. It remains to be seen for how long this approach will resist the general criticism of the privacy rights community, the non-governmental organizations, and the legal scholars.

In our mind, it is more than doubtful that the current Spanish legal framework on data retention of electronic and digital communications complies with the requirements outlined by the case law of the CJEU when interpreting the provisions of Directive 2002/58/EC and Articles 7, 8, and 11 of the Charter. Specifically, the massive and indiscriminate retention of these data do not seem to meet the requirements derived from the principle of proportionality. The principle of loyal cooperation should have led the Spanish Courts to file a preliminary question to the CJEU regarding the possible incompatibility of the Spanish LDR with the EU law, however this has not happened yet, and, at the sight of the Supreme Court case law, it would seem that a dialogue between courts is not to be expected.

---

[65] In the same sense, see Ignacio Colomer Hernández (2018), 'La cesión de datos de las comunicaciones electrónicas para su uso en investigaciones criminales: una problemática en ciernes', in Fernando Jiménez Conde, Olga Fuentes Soriano, and María Isabel González Cano (eds), *Adaptación del Derecho Procesal español a la normativa europea y a su interpretación por los tribunales* (Tirant 2018) 77; Juan Carlos Ortiz Pradillo, 'Europa: auge y caída de las investigaciones penales basadas en la conservación de datos de comunicaciones electrónicas' *Revista General de Derecho Procesal*, 52 (2020) 1; and Andoni Polo Roca *La conservación de datos en el sector de las telecomunicaciones. Un estudio sobre su regulación en la Unión Europea y su cabida en el Derecho de la Unión* (Aranzadi 2022).

14
Data Retention and Law Enforcement in the Netherlands

Marc van der Ham and Esther Baars

1. Introduction

The Netherlands currently lacks a general legal national data retention obligation. Since the court in summary proceedings of the District Court of The Hague suspended the Telecommunications Data Retention Act on 11 March 2015, no new law has taken its place.[1] The Dutch government did, however, attempt to introduce a new legal retention obligation, by submitting a draft legislative proposal in 2016 containing a modified general data retention obligation.[2] Additional major changes to the proposal were announced in 2018, and to date, these changes have not been submitted to the Dutch Parliament, with political decision-making at a standstill.[3] Consecutive Dutch Ministers of Justice and Security have informed Parliament that they will await discussions and possible initiatives at the European level. Additionally, since the *Digital Rights Ireland*[4] ruling by the Court of Justice of the European Union (CJEU), subsequent rulings have influenced the remaining policy space for a general legal data retention obligation. Nevertheless, since 2015, Dutch providers of electronic communications services and public electronic communications networks have ceased the general retention of user data, impacting the investigation and prosecution of criminal offences in the Netherlands.[5]

This chapter chronicles how the Data Retention Directive[6] was implemented in the Dutch Telecommunications Data Retention Act (TDRA),[7] the effects of its termination by the Court of Justice, and the legislative efforts made to reinstate a legal general data retention obligation.[8] The chapter starts with an overview of the suspended TDRA in section 2, covering its broad description and the regulation of access by law enforcement authorities

---

[1] Rb. 's-Gravenhage (vzr.) 11 March 2015, ECLI:NL:RBDHA:2015:16424.
[2] *Kamerstukken II* 2015/16, 34537, nr. 2.
[3] ibid nr. 8.
[4] CJEU, Judgment of 8 April 2014, *Digital Rights Ireland and Seitlinger and others* (C-293/12 and C-594/12) ECLI:EU:C:2014:238.
[5] This does not affect the fact that providers continue to store data to the extent necessary for their normal business operations. The extent to which they retain what is strictly necessary may differ per company.
[6] Directive 2006/24/EC of the European Parliament and of the Council of 15 March 2006 on the retention of data generated or processed in connection with the provision of publicly available electronic communications services or of public communications networks and amending Directive 2002/58/EC [2006] OJ L 105/54.
[7] *Stb.* 2009, nr. 333.
[8] Due to the authors' expertise and background, the chapter is limited to the domain of investigating and prosecuting crime and does not cover data retention in the context of national security interests and access to that data by the Dutch intelligence services.

to retained, or for business purposes stored, data (section 3). Section 4 analyses the ruling of the court in summary proceedings in The Hague, which led to the suspension of the TDRA. In section 4.1, the 2016 proposal for a new general data retention law is discussed, along with subsequent political discussions and considerations. These are then juxtaposed with recent CJEU case law in section 4.2. Section 5 explores the practical consequences of the absence of a general legal data retention obligation for investigating and prosecuting criminal offences. This section also addresses challenges related to Carrier-Grade NAT technology for criminal investigations and its interaction with the lack of a data retention obligation (section 5.1). Future developments from a Dutch perspective are examined in section 6. Concluding observations are made in section 7.

2. Telecommunications Data Retention Act in Retrospect

On 19 September 2007, the Minister of Justice sent a draft bill aimed at the implementation of the Data Retention Directive to the Parliament.[9] The draft TDRA proposed rules for the general obligation to retain data by providers of public telecommunications networks and providers of public telecommunications services, the data to be retained, the retention periods, and the protection and security of the retained data. The TDRA aimed for a literal implementation of the Data Retention Directive.[10] This means that its definitions and categorizations have been adopted. Where the Data Retention Directive did not provide definitions, existing concepts in Dutch law were followed. For example, the definition of 'data', as already defined in the Dutch Telecommunications Act, was adopted. The Data Retention Directive left room for the Member States to determine the exact retention periods for specific data categories. The legislative proposal originally proposed a retention period of 18 months, but the TDRA ultimately stipulated a retention period of 12 months.[11] Failure to comply with the regulations (eg the retention of data, retention periods, security measures) of the TDRA was sanctioned by criminalization under the Dutch Economic Offenses Act.[12] Before the TDRA was proposed, the Dutch telecommunications law already had a limited retention obligation, for so-called location data for the purpose of file analyses that should lead to the identification of specific users (eg, users of pre-paid cards). With the TDRA, the

---

[9] *Kamerstukken II* 2006/07, 31145, nr. 2.
[10] An exception to this is that the TDRA also provided for a retention obligation for data relating to failed calls. The Data Retention Directive did not provide for this.
[11] The initial proposal introduced a retention period of 18 months to 'meet the needs of the Police and the Public Prosecution Service', see *Kamerstukken II* 2006/07, 31145, nr. 3, p. 5. An amendment to the law in July 2011 subsequently made a distinction between data relating to (mobile) telephony and Internet traffic related to internet access, email over the internet, and internet telephony. A retention period of twelve months applies to the first category of data, and a retention period of six months applies to the latter. For both categories, counting starts from the date of communication.
[12] The Dutch Economic Offices Act (*Wet op de Economische Delicten*) Stb. 1950, 62, is a law that regulates the investigation, prosecution and adjudication of acts that are harmful to economic life. The law describes offences, which are mentioned in many other laws, are an economic offence (crimes or simple violations). The list of economic offences is very varied, for instance a farmer who violated manure legislation, can be prosecuted under this act. Pursuant to Article 1, sub 2, in conjunction with Article 2, paragraph 1, the intentional violation of the TDRA was punishable as a crime and otherwise as a misdemeanour. The maximum penalty for the crime was a prison sentence of not more than two years, community service or a fine of the fourth category. Pursuant Article 6 paragraph 1 sub 2 WED and Article 23, paragraph 4, of the Dutch Criminal Code, the maximum fine—as of 1 January 2024—would have been EUR 25,750.

retention period for these specific location data has been brought into line with that for user and traffic data.[13] The TDRA also prescribed that rules could be laid down in secondary legislation regarding measures for the security and destruction of, and access to, the data.[14] The TDRA was adopted by the Lower House of the Dutch Parliament on 22 May 2008, and by the Dutch Senate on 7 July 2009. It entered into force on 1 September 2009.[15]

3. Access to Data by Law Enforcement Authorities

The TDRA did not include specific provisions regarding access to the retained data. Dutch legislation already encompassed rules for accessing telecommunications data in the investigation and prosecution of criminal offenses. Consequently, access to the data retained by providers under the TDRA for law enforcement authorities is exclusively regulated through existing investigative powers in the Dutch Code of Criminal Procedure (DCCP).

Based on the DCCP, the public prosecutor holds the exclusive authority to issue an order for traffic data under Article 126n/u DCCP. The prerequisite for issuing such an order is a criminal suspicion warranting pre-trial detention, or a reasonable suspicion of organized crimes amounting to a serious breach of the legal order. Besides the public prosecutor, a police officer, based on Article 126na/ua DCCP, is independently authorized to issue an order for retained subscriber data. The application of this power by the police officer is not limited to cases involving serious forms of crime; it requires a suspicion of a crime or a reasonable suspicion that crimes are being planned or committed in an organized context. This broader power exists because access to subscriber data constitutes less of an infringement of the user's fundamental rights than with access to traffic data.[16]

Additionally, an existing specific arrangement for criminal investigations into terrorist crimes also applied to providers in scope of the TDRA.[17] Under this arrangement the public prosecutor is granted the authority to order traffic data when there are (only) *indications* of a terrorist crime (Article 126zh DCCP). In such cases, a police officer is also independently authorized to order user data (Article 126zi DCCP). For the investigation of terrorist crimes, the public prosecutor may also initiate an 'exploratory investigation'. During the preparation phase of this exploratory investigation, the public prosecutor, if the investigation demands it, can issue production orders for databases from public (and private) entities to process the data (Article 126hh DCCP). The data can subsequently be analysed to identify specific profiles and patterns of actions of individuals relevant in the fight against

---

[13] This existing limited retention obligation, currently laid down in Article 13.4, paragraph three, Telecommunications Act, is not discussed in this chapter because it has not yet been subject to specific judicial review or legislative changes. Nevertheless, it could be argued that the principles in the *Digital Rights Ireland* judgment could equally be applied to the general retention obligation for location data.

[14] For example, the Telecommunications Data Security Decree (*Besluit beveiliging gegevens telecommunicatie*) Stb. 2009, 350. The Decree requires, for instance, a security plan that maps where data is stored and what security measures have been taken, security requirements with regard to personnel (eg clearances, detailed job descriptions), logical access security (eg personal accounts, logging, and monitoring) and physical security.

[15] Stb. 2009, 360.

[16] Accessing subscriber data (eg the user's name, address, email, phone number) may be seen as less intrusive compared to traffic (eg time and duration of a call, the sender and recipient of an email) or content data (eg text of emails, contents of phone calls, documents stored in the cloud) because it typically involves basic identifying information rather than the substance of communications.

[17] *Stb.*, 2006, 731.

terrorism. However, prior authorization from the investigative judge is required for this analysis.

These existing statutory powers have not been altered because of the suspension of the TDRA. In response to the CJEU judgment in *Prokuratuur*,[18] however, recent Dutch court judgments have altered the specific regulation of the investigative powers to issue an order for location data.[19]

4. Ruling of the Preliminary Relief Judge of the District Court of The Hague

Following *Digital Rights Ireland*,[20] several Dutch public interest organizations and electronic communications services companies initiated summary proceedings at the District Court of The Hague and filed a motion for suspension of the TDRA.[21] In addition to that motion, the organizations also claimed that the Dutch state should be prohibited from gaining access to stored data, insofar as this violated the principles formulated in the *Digital Rights Ireland* judgment, as well as fundamental rights protected in the EU Charter on Fundamental Rights ('Charter') and in particular Articles 7, 8, and 11, the European Convention on Human Rights (ECHR) and in particular Articles 8 and 10, the Dutch Constitution (Article 10), the ePrivacy Directive (Article 15), and/or the Treaty on European Union (Article 6, paragraphs 1 and 2). The scope of the claim was of a general nature and extended beyond data retained under the TDRA. Additionally, the organizations claimed that companies should not be forced to retain any data prior to a modified data retention law was enacted or the TDRA was formally revoked.[22]

The claimants asserted that the TDRA clearly violated EU regulations and could not, therefore, remain in force. Since the TDRA implemented the invalidated Data Retention Directive in a literal manner, it consequently equally infringed upon Articles 7 (Respect for private life and family life) and 8 (Protection of personal data) of the Charter.[23] Additionally, the claimants argued that the retention of and access to data, in and of itself, would independently constitute violations of Article 8 (Right to respect for private and family life) ECHR. This, they contended, would result in a 'chilling effect', leading to infringements of the rights protected in Articles 10 (Freedom of expression) and 11 (Freedom of assembly and association) ECHR.[24] The claimants also asserted that it is irrelevant whether only a

---

[18] CJEU, Judgment of 2 March 2021, *Prokuratuur* (C-746/18) ECLI:EU:C:2021:152.
[19] These changes pertain to the competent authority and now more frequently necessitate the prior approval of an investigative judge before a public prosecutor can issue production orders. They will be codified into the DCCP in the coming years as elements of a comprehensive modernization effort. For a discussion of the impact of *Prokuratuur* on special investigatory powers in the DDCP, see AG van Toor, 'Prokuratuur (HvJ EU, C-746/18) – Differentiatie en beperkingen van dataretentie door telecommunicatieaanbieders en de vorderingsvoorwaarden', EHRC, p 2.
[20] *Digital Rights Ireland* (n 4).
[21] These organizations were Privacy First, Nederlands Juristen Comité voor de Mensenrechten (Dutch Section of the International Commission of Jurists), Nederlandse Vereniging van Strafrechtadvocaten (Dutch Association of Defence Counsel), Nederlandse Vereniging van Journalisten (Dutch Union of Journalists), BIT B.V., SpeakUp B.V., and VOYS B.V.
[22] Rb. 's-Gravenhage (vzr.) 11 March 2015, ECLI:NL:RBDHA:2015:16424.
[23] ibid paragraph 2.2.
[24] ibid paragraph 2.2.

small part of the stored data is actually used; the massive storage itself already constitutes a major infringement. Furthermore, there are insufficient safeguards to prevent abuse by government authorities. Lastly, the claimants referred to advice from the Council of State and the Dutch Data Protection Authority, both of which, following the *Digital Rights Ireland* ruling, concluded that the TDRA can no longer remain in force.[25] The necessity and effectiveness of the TDRA in the fight against serious crime—citing technological advancements—was also disputed by the claimants.[26]

In its judgment, the District Court of The Hague in summary proceedings first noted that, based on Article 94 of the Dutch Constitution, a law in a formal sense can only be declared inoperative in summary proceedings if and insofar as it is 'manifestly non-binding' due to conflict with provisions of treaties and decisions of international law organizations.[27] Moreover, the court stated, great restraint is required in such a judgment because, in summary proceedings, only a provisional judgment can be given. With this preliminary limitation, the court in summary proceedings acknowledged the separation of state powers as laid down in the Dutch Constitution. The court then based its assessment entirely on the *Digital Rights Ireland* judgment by applying its principles to the TDRA, which—it finds—needs to be assessed as an autonomous (national) law and should encompass the 'entire body of relevant domestic legislation'.[28] This assessment is then carried out by the court.

Some specific domestic considerations in the judgment are worth mentioning. Firstly, the court found that there is indeed secondary legislation that lays down rules on the security and oversight of the retained data, but also concluded that the requirement to store the retained data in the European Union is missing. The latter requirement is an 'essential component', according to paragraph 69 of the *Digital Rights Ireland* judgment.[29] This requirement is not met in Dutch legislation. Secondly, the court also concluded that there are insufficient guarantees in the DCCP that access to the retained data is only given for the purpose of combating serious crime, especially because no prior judicial permission is required by the DCCP to issue an order to gain access to the retained data. Finally, and in that context, the court also concluded that 'the Public Prosecution Service cannot be regarded as an independent administrative body'.[30]

Based on the principles of the *Digital Rights Ireland* judgment and these specific considerations, the court ruled that the TDRA is 'manifestly non-binding' and therefore rendered it 'inoperative'.[31]

---

[25] *Kamerstukken II* 2014/15, 33542, nr. 16 (attachment). <https://www.raadvanstate.nl/adviezen/@63280/w03-14-0161-ii-vo/> accessed 25 September 2024.
[26] Rb. 's-Gravenhage (n 22) paragraph 2.2.
[27] The Dutch State argued in its defence that a criminal court had already ruled on the TDRA, and therefore, there could be no question of it being undeniably non-binding. The court in summary proceedings does not agree with this argument because, according to the court, the criminal court only considered the existence and possible consequences for the suspect of procedural errors due to the application of the Telecommunications Act. There has been no civil law review of the provisions of the TDRA and whether it would violate provisions enshrined in international law.
[28] The invalidation of the DCD does not automatically invalidate the TDRA, see ECLI:NL:RBDHA:2015:2498, paragraph 3.3. The 'entire body of domestic legislation' should be considered because it can adequately address specific objections in the *Digital Rights Ireland* judgment, eg, regarding the security and access of the retained data.
[29] Rb. 's-Gravenhage (n 22) paragraph 3.9.
[30] ibid paragraph 3.11.
[31] ibid paragraph 3.12.

4.1 Policy developments and legislative initiatives after the TDRA was suspended

Seven months after the Digital Rights judgment, amendments to the TDRA were announced and published as a draft legislative initiative in November 2014.[32] Eventually, they were formally submitted to the Dutch Parliament in 2016 through a legislative proposal for a new general legal data retention obligation.[33] The proposal only provides a revised regulation of a data retention obligation and access to the retained data in the context of the investigation of serious crimes. In addition to the principles outlined in the *Digital Rights Ireland* judgment, the legislative proposal also addresses conclusions drawn in the March 2015 ruling by the court in summary proceedings.[34]

Nevertheless, the 2016 legislative proposal only introduces minor adjustments to the TDRA that was rendered inoperative. These are discussed in section 4.1.2. Subsequent judgments, however, assessing the validity of several domestic legal retention obligations in different EU Member States by the Court of Justice, prompted the Dutch Minister for Justice and Security in 2018 to announce additional major changes to the 2016 legislative proposal.[35] These changes, however, have not yet been finalized, published, or formally submitted to Parliament.[36]

4.1.1 General observations

Besides the introduction of changes to the suspended TDRA, the 2016 legislative proposal also includes several arguments stressing the necessity of a legal data retention obligation as such.[37] First, technological developments are mentioned. For instance, the fact that for providers of public telecommunications there are no strong business reasons to retain telecommunications data for a long time and the fact that much of that type of data would be anonymised or encrypted.[38] Second, a joint report by the Police and Public Prosecution Service (discussed in more detail in section 5), provides dozens of case-studies in which data retained under the TDRA proved instrumental for the criminal investigation or the subsequent prosecution of the suspect.[39] Third, an official evaluation by the Research and

---

[32] *Kamerstukken I* 2014/25, 31145, nr. AA.
[33] *Kamerstukken II* 2015/16, 34537, nr. 2.
[34] *Kamerstukken I*, 2014/15, 31145, nr. AA, p. 17 and Annex. The Dutch State decided not to lodge an appeal against the ruling of the court in summary proceedings. According to the Minister, an appeal could delay the consideration of the new legislative proposal and the court in summary proceedings did not contest the validity of a general data retention obligation per se. Additionally, the 2014 draft legislative proposal already addressed some of the key objections of the Digital Rights judgment and the ruling of the court in summary proceedings. See *Kamerstukken II*, 2014/15, 33542, nr. 18.
[35] Most notably Cases C-203/15 and C-698/15 *Tele2 Sverige AB and the British Secretary of State for the Home Department* [2016] ECLI:EU:C:2016:970, *Kamerstukken II* 2017/18, 34537, nr. 7.
[36] The Dutch Parliament did consistently ask, in committees and by letters, for responses by the responsible Ministers of Justice and Security, see *Kamerstukken II 2016/17*, 34537, nr. 6 and *Kamerstukken II 2016/17*, 34537, nr. 7, p. 7.
[37] The proposal does not refer to the statement by the European Commission of September 2015, in which it announced that it will not put forward a proposal for a new Data Retention Directive: European Commission, 'European Commission statement on national data retention laws' (European Commission, 16 September 2015) < https://ec.europa.eu/commission/presscorner/detail/en/STATEMENT_15_5654> accessed 14 February 2024.
[38] This also follows from obligations in the e-Privacy Directive (2002/58/EC). While this connection is not explicitly made in the explanatory memorandum to the legislative proposal, a letter from 26 March 2018 by the Minister of Justice and Security does explain this. See *Kamerstukken II* 2017/18, 34537, nr. 7, p. 5.
[39] WN Ferdinandusse, D Laheij, and JC Hendriks, 'De bewaarplicht telecomgegevens en de opsporing: het belang van historische telecommunicatie gegevens voor de opsporing', 23 March 2015, p. 15, <eerstekamer.nl>.

Data Centre (Wetenschappelijk Onderzoek en Documentatie Centrum (WODC)) of the Dutch Ministry of Justice and Security, concluded that a legal data retention obligation was necessary for the criminal investigation and prosecution of serious crimes.[40] Additionally, the legislative proposal stresses its provisions are designed to comply with the ePrivacy Directive now that the DCD is invalidated.[41] More specifically, the proposal explicitly and extensively argues how national derogations of the obligations for service providers enshrined in the ePrivacy Directive, should be designed. Therefore, the proposal addresses the requirements of the human rights test in the case-law of the European Court of Human Rights (ECtHR), and which equally applies to the applicable Charter of Fundamental Rights of the European Union.[42] The proposed adjustments to the initial 2016 legislative proposal are made based on these analyses.

4.1.2 Adjustments to the retention obligations in the old TDRA

To ensure maximum clarity and foreseeability of the legal data retention obligation in the Netherlands, the 2016 legislative proposal reintroduces a comprehensive law, instead of introducing several adjusted provisions of the suspended TDRA. First, the proposal explicitly explains why the retention periods of 12 months (for telecommunications data, which now include VoIP internet-calls) and six months (for internet communication data) remain unchanged because they are still considered 'strictly necessary'.[43] Second, the types of data within the scope of the retention obligation remains limited to subscriber and traffic data (which partially includes subscriber data).[44] However, data regarding emails over the internet are being excluded, as well as specific location data as referenced in article 13.4, paragraph 3, Telecommunications Act (except for the first Cell-ID).[45] Moreover, the definition of IP addresses is modified to ensure it refers to a subscriber or user.[46] The scope of the data retention obligations still encompasses all users, irrespective of whether there is a reasonable suspicion or any other possible involvement with crimes. With regard to the security of the data and their retention, the proposal introduces mandatory data localization within the European Union for the processing and storing of data. The supervisory roles over the providers in scope of the TDRA of the Telecommunications Agency and Dutch Data Protection Authority are reconfirmed in the proposal.[47]

4.1.3 Adjustments to the access to the retained data

The proposal stresses that access by law enforcement authorities to data retained under the TDRA is limited to the investigation and prosecution of serious crimes. This limitation

---

[40] *Kamerstukken II* 2015/16, 34537, nr. 3, p. 4; attachment to *Kamerstukken II* 2014/15, 33870, nr. 1.
[41] Infringements by the adjusted TDRA as autonomous domestic legislation on the freedom to provide services on the EU's Single Market should also be justified, as established in the *Pfleger* judgment (C-390/12 *Pfleger and others* [2014] ECLI:EU:C:2014:281.
[42] 'No interference by any public authority in the exercise of this right shall be permitted except as provided for by law and is necessary in a democratic society in the interests of, among other things, national security, public safety, or the prevention of disorder or crime', see *Kamerstukken II* 2015/16, 34537, nr. 3, p. 19. The Charter applies to domestic legislation because it is based on an exemption explicitly provided in the ePrivacy Directive.
[43] *Kamerstukken II* 2015/16, 34537, nr. 3, p. 7, 10–11.
[44] Traffic data for internet communication is limited to an IP address, the date and time of the log-on and log-off of the communication.
[45] *Kamerstukken II* 2015/16, 34537, nr. 3, p. 11. According to the explanatory report, the Police has other means to link a pre-
[46] ibid nr. 3, p. 11.
[47] ibid nr. 3, p. 17.

is met by referring to criminal offenses for which pre-trial detention is permitted under the DCCP. However, this reference is not sufficient because pre-trial detention is also possible for offenses that cannot be classified as serious crimes.[48] Therefore, additional requirements apply. Consequently, access is explicitly limited to the investigation of crimes of such seriousness that in the specific case the criminal investigation demands it that retained data is accessed.[49] This assessment is primarily the responsibility of the public prosecutor, but by introducing the condition of prior approval by an investigative judge for access to retained traffic data, an additional safeguard is proposed.[50] In emergency cases, the prior approval and issuing of the production order can be done orally (and should be confirmed in writing within three days).[51] Regarding the supervision of access to the data, in addition to the approval of the investigative judge in specific cases, there is a role for the Attorney General at the Supreme Court, who can investigate the legality of the actions of the Public Prosecution Service at system level. Finally, to enhance transparency regarding access to data, the annual report of the Ministry for Justice and Security will include data on how often retained data is used in criminal investigations.[52]

4.2 Developments in case law requiring further adjustments

The *Tele2 Sverige*[53] judgment by the Court of Justice prompted the Minister of Justice and Security to take the 2016 legislative proposal back to the drawing board. By letter of 3 February 3 2017, the Minister informed the Parliament that the Cabinet is studying the implications of the judgment for the data retention proposal under consideration and will therefor also liaise with the Police, the Public Prosecution Service and other EU Member States.[54] On 26 March 2018, a letter containing a comprehensive assessment of the implications of *Tele2 Sverige* and subsequent legislative steps was sent to the Parliament.[55] Importantly, the letter also makes reference to the 2017 government coalition agreement, which stipulates that the 2016 data retention proposal shall be reconsidered.[56]

---

[48] For instance, bicycle theft, which in the Netherlands understandably (and culturally) could be considered a serious crime, but objectively in the context of fundamental rights and freedoms, is not.
[49] *Kamerstukken II* 2015/16, 34537, nr. 3, p. 12.
[50] ibid nr. 3, p. 12. The addition of prior judicial approval will lead to substantial administrative and financial burdens on the side of the Dutch judiciary and could slow down the course of the investigation, see p. 13. For an overview of relevant CJEU case-law in relation to the requirement of prior judicial approval for the use of special investigatory powers, see KC van Horssen, 'Aan het uitkristalliseren: de betekenis van het EU-recht voor opsporingsbevoegdheden' TBS&H 2024, nr. 1, p. 5.
[51] *Kamerstukken II* 2015/16, 34537, nr. 3, p. 14.
[52] ibid nr. 3, p. 18.
[53] CJEU, Judgment of 21 December 2016, *Tele2 Sverige* (C-203/15 and C-698/15) ECLI:EU:C:2016:970.
[54] *Kamerstukken II* 2016/17, 34537, nr. 6. Almost all EU Member States established national data retention legislation based on the Data Retention Directive.
[55] ibid nr. 7.
[56] Rijksoverheid, 'Trust in the Future' (Regeerakkoord 2017) (Rijksoverheid, 10 October 2017) <https://www.rijksoverheid.nl/documenten/publicaties/2017/10/10/regeerakkoord-2017-vertrouwen-in-de-toekomst> accessed 14 February 2024. The coalition agreement says that: 'The legislative proposal for the Adjustment of Telecommunications Data Retention is being reconsidered. In doing so, the government explores to what extent European law allows for a balanced data retention requirement for certain telecommunication data, particularly data that serve to identify the user of a communication service. Special attention is given to safeguards for the personal privacy of citizens, limited access, enhanced supervision, necessity of retention periods, adequate protection and security of the data, and a reporting and evaluation obligation'.

The key conclusion of the assessment in the letter, referencing the *Tele2 Sverige* judgment, is that the 2016 general data retention proposal will have to be thoroughly revisited. The key adjustment to be made is that the scope of the retention obligation, because of—according to the Minister for Justice and Security—a strict interpretation by the Court of Justice of the ePrivacy Directive, has to be limited to subscriber data.[57] In this context, the Minister expects that future case law on the relationship between data protection and the criminal investigation of serious crime should be further clarified in the years to come.[58] The Minister concluded, through discussions with the Police and the Public Prosecution Service, that retaining the subscriber data of all users remains necessary to trace the use of a communication service back to a specific user at a specific time, 'prior to the moment when it becomes apparent'.[59] The letter clarifies: 'it is solely the data necessary to determine retrospectively which individual used, for example, a specific IP address or phone number at a particular time'.[60]

Regardless of the *Tele2 Sverige* judgment, but considering the Carrier Grade Network Address Translation (hereafter, CG-NAT) technology utilized by telecommunications service providers to allocate mobile IP addresses, as mentioned in the letter of 26 March 2018, the 2016 legislative proposal concerning the retention of subscriber data needs further adjustment. Due to CG-NAT technology, IP addresses can no longer be directly associated with specific devices at a given point in the time.[61] This significantly impedes the investigation and prosecution of any serious crimes committed using digital communication tools, where an IP address often serves as the primary lead for the investigation: 'this means that the government fails its responsibilities to address serious norm violations and towards victims of serious crimes'.[62] Consequently, the Minister announces the legal obligation for providers to retain the (subscriber) data required to link a specific 'user' to an IP address at a specific point in time—while acknowledging the impact of such an obligation on the use of CG-NAT technologies by providers.[63]

According to the Minister, a general data retention obligation for subscriber data is still in line with the *Tele2 Sverige* judgment, which explicitly addresses traffic and location data, because from these data, no precise conclusions can be drawn about the private lives of the individuals whose data has been retained.[64] Moreover, a retention obligation for this data is 'necessary and effective while the infringement on the privacy of citizens in retaining this data is minimal'.[65] Consequently, the data in scope of the 2016 legislative proposal will be modified and limited to subscriber data (and no longer will include location data or traffic data).[66] However, an amended proposal has not yet been sent to the Parliament to

---

[57] *Kamerstukken II* 2017/18, 34537, nr. 7, pp. 7–8.
[58] ibid nr. 7, p. 8.
[59] ibid 34537, nr. 7, p. 8.
[60] ibid nr. 7, p. 8.
[61] For business reasons, a public mobile IP address can be associated with thousands of *devices*. See ibid, nr. 7, p. 9. The letter uses the word 'user', but an IP address can only be associated with a device (it does not provide any information about the *user* of the device).
[62] ibid nr. 7, p. 8.
[63] ibid nr. 7, p. 10.
[64] ibid nr. 7, p. 10.
[65] ibid nr. 7, p. 11.
[66] For a short discussion of the impact of the CJEU, Judgment of 6 October 2020, *La Quadrature du Net and others* (C-511/18, C-512/18 and C-520/18) ECLI:EU:C:2020:791 ('*La Quadrature du Net 'I*'') on the parliamentary consideration of the 2016 legislative proposal and intended major amendments, see JJ Oerlemans, c.s., 'Tijd voor een nieuwe bewaarplicht' CR 2021/59, p. 157.

this day. No government position has been published either regarding the notions of 'targeted' or 'expedited' retention of traffic and location data, as suggested by the CJEU in recent judgments.[67]

5. Impact on the Availability of Telecommunications Data in Criminal Investigations

On 23 March 2015, shortly after the court ruling in summary proceedings in The Hague, the Public Prosecution Service and Police presented a report entitled: 'Data Retention and Criminal Investigations: the Importance of Historical Telecommunications Data' (hereafter 'the report').[68] The report, based on more than one hundred and thirty published and unpublished rulings in criminal cases, describes how historical telecommunications data therein have been used for the investigation and prosecution of serious crimes. Without such data, these investigations and prosecutions would likely have been significantly complicated and could have led to unresolved cases.

Uncertainty about the presence of such data, therefore, undeniably impacts the effectiveness of criminal investigations.[69] For which there are several reasons. First, there is a practical effect. Data stored for business purposes may vary from day to day and from one provider to another. It is a labour-intensive and vulnerable process to ensure that each individual police officer or public prosecutor has current knowledge on what data is available. This may result in data that is present not being requested, or to unnecessary requests and additional paperwork for non-present information.

Second, the nature of the crime or the investigation may cause some time to elapse before a relevant telephone number or IP address becomes known with the investigating team. A case derived from the aforementioned report can serve as an example. In this case, the Court of Amsterdam convicted a suspect for the sexual abuse of young children using a webcam. This occurred over a period of several years.[70] The verdict shows that investigation into the IP address used by the sender during threatening chats to the child, led to the suspect's home and thus to his computer, which contained evidence. The authors stipulate: 'The first report against this perpetrator was made more than a month after the last chats between the perpetrator and that victim, because the victim's mother only discovered these chats after some time. Being able to requisition IP addresses older than a month was thus a necessary condition for this investigation.'[71]

Another example that law enforcement practitioners increasingly face, and which consumes time is the situation where the offence involved the use of a service from a foreign service provider. This might include the use of an email address, cloud environment or a social media account. In some cases, a mutual legal assistance request to the relevant foreign

---

[67] As suggested by the CJEU in CJEU, Judgment of 27 October 2022, *SpaceNet* (C-793/19 and C-794/19) ECLI:EU:C:2022:702.

[68] Ferdinandusse, Laheij, and Hendriks (n 39) p. 15.

[69] In a recent WODC report on the impact of encryption on law enforcement, a public prosecutor was quoted saying: 'This is a typical question that we are asked very often. How many cases have you not been able to solve because there is no data retention? No idea, because you can never say what you don't have and to what extent that would or would not have led to the solution of the case', *Kamerstukken II* 2022/23, 26643, nr. 1023, p. 57.

[70] ECLI:NL:RBAMS:2015:673.

[71] Ferdinandusse, Laheij, and Hendriks (n 39) p. 15.

country is first required to obtain information, before subscriber and traffic information on a specific phone number or IP address can be requested from the appropriate (national) provider. In this regard, it happens more than once that by the time the phone numbers or IP addresses required from abroad are received, no information is available from the party by whom those numbers were provided.

Finally, investigators increasingly see cases where CG-NAT is applied by providers when issuing IP addresses. To compensate for the lack of IPv4 addresses, many providers apply this technology. As a result, the specific public IP address that is relevant within an investigation, is used (almost) at the same time by significant numbers of random users. Reducing that group of accidental users to the smallest possible group of potentially suspicious users is possible only if a correlation can be made with certain data coming from the provider. If those data are not, or no longer available, then in practice, it is difficult and not infrequently impossible to identify the actual suspect user. In the context of the intended legal obligation for providers (outlined in the letter of 26 March 2018) to link IP addresses to specific users at specific times, implementation discussions with providers have led to an assignment from the Ministry of Justice and Security to the Research and Data Centre. This assignment involved conducting research on how to achieve this in practice using retained subscriber data, without disclosing excessive (non-relevant) personal data to law enforcement authorities.

Although the research was finalized and published in October 2019, the Minister for Justice and Security has not formally responded, despite several feasible policy options being suggested. The research found that a legal obligation for providers to link an IP address to a specific device (or user) was the most desirable, as it would likely speed up the adaptation of IPv6 in the Netherlands (which is unavoidable anyway given the expected increase of online devices) and because other alternatives would lead to unnecessary privacy violations of users.[72] The State Secretary for Economic Affairs, however, informed the Parliament of the position of the government that it should be left to companies to determine when the (costly) transition to IPv6 should be made and therefore was primarily a business decision.[73]

6. Future Perspectives

While the Dutch government has not recently taken any concrete steps towards reestablishing a domestic general legal data retention obligation (limited to subscriber data), it has voiced its support for a new EU data retention obligation—'despite the regrettable constraints imposed by CJEU case law'—in light of its necessity in the fight against serious crime.[74] The existence of tangible policy options to address the CG-NAT issue, coupled with the potential for a general legal retention obligation for subscriber data in light of

---

[72] The research found that a legal obligation for providers to link an IP address to a specific device (or user) was the most desirable, as it would likely speed up the adaptation of IPv6 in the Netherlands (which is unavoidable anyway given the expected increase of online devices) and because other alternatives would lead to unnecessary privacy violations of users. WODC, '*Possibilities for identification on the internet based on IP address* (*Mogelijkheden voor identificatie op internet op basis van IP-adres*)' (WODC, 18 October 2019) < https://repository.wodc.nl/handle/20.500.12832/2447> accessed 14 February 2024.
[73] *Kamerstukken II* 2019/20, nr. 2136.
[74] *Kamerstukken II* 2020/21, 22112, nr. 3114, p. 8 and *Kamerstukken II* 2020/21, 32317, nr. 682, p. 7.

recent EU case law, raises questions about why the proposed amendments to the 2016 legislative proposal have not been finalised.[75] This is particularly puzzling given the Dutch government's strong support for a retention obligation to aid in the investigation and prosecution of serious crimes. It seems the Netherlands may be inclined to await a European initiative before proceeding. Deliberations in the 'High Level Expert Group on Access to Data for Effective Law Enforcement', in which the Netherlands actively participates, might indeed result in a new EU legislative initiative, the Dutch Minister for Justice and Security recently suggested.[76]

A related relevant development is that the Dutch government has established several 'functional requirements' for providers of new 5G networks to continue to meet existing interception capabilities. Providers of 5G networks must organize them in such a way that they can continue to comply with existing legal obligations under the Telecommunications Act. Due to the new technical architecture of these 5G networks, this may mean that providers must (*de facto*) store data in order to meaningfully intercept and correlate communications and transfer them to the police. There could be an overlap between this data and what is in scope of a future data retention law. The Dutch government has established and announced these functional requirements as part of an early public frequency auction.

7. Conclusion

The Netherlands currently does not have a legal data retention obligation. Following the annulment by the CJEU of the Data Retention Directive in its *Digital Rights Ireland* judgment and the subsequent ruling of the court in summary proceedings, which rendered the TDRA inoperative, no new legal obligation has been enacted. A formally submitted proposal to Parliament in 2016 for an adjusted legal data retention obligation was superseded by conclusions of the CJEU in its *Tele2 Sverige* judgment, and subsequent announced major amendments have not been published.

Nevertheless, letters from the Dutch Minister for Justice and Security to the Parliament are quite clear about the direction of any future legislative initiatives. A legal data retention obligation in the Netherlands will be limited to the retention of subscriber data but will be of a general nature: it will apply to all users. To meet the conditions established by the CJEU regarding access to stored data, the DCCP will require the prior approval of an investigative judge before a public prosecutor can issue a production order for the stored data. Additionally, the law will mandate that the retained data must be processed and stored within the territory of the EU.

To address the challenges of the CG-NAT technology, providers could have the legal obligation to be able to link a (mobile) IP address to a specific user (or device) at a specific moment and time. However, the political decision to go ahead with this policy option has not been taken. Finally, the active participation of the Dutch government in the new EU High Level Expert Group on Access to Data for Effective Law Enforcement shows that the Netherlands prefers a new harmonized EU legal data retention obligation and is unlikely to move fast with enacting a new national law.

---

[75] See Oerlemans (n 66).
[76] *Kamerstukken II* 2022/23, 32 317, nr. OE, p. 9.

15
To Retain or (not) to Retain Data? The Danish Case

Ayo Næsborg-Andersen

1. Introduction

This chapter examines the Danish data retention rule, focusing on their evolution, specifically the work of the Danish Parliament (Folketinget). In doing so, the main sources are from the Danish Parliament, as well as case law from the Court of Justice of the European Union (CJEU), but also drawing from sources such as civil society organisations criticising the development, as relevant.

The Danish rules on data retention can be characterised by three different phases, each with their own legislation. The first, pre-9/11, is easily summarised, as no data was generally retained, apart from what the telephone companies and internet providers needed for their bookkeeping. Access to data required a court warrant.[1] This phase will not be discussed further, as opposed to the next two phases which are the subject of the chapter.

The second phase, spanning from 2002 when the retention rules were introduced, to 2022 when the rules were revised, was heavily influenced by the shock of the so-called 9/11 attacks on the Twin Towers in New York in 2001. Preventing such a crime from happening on Danish ground became paramount, legitimising wholescale retention of data for the purpose of providing the police with as many tools as possible. This phase was characterised by an extreme reluctance to evaluate or revise the data retention rules, postponing a revision otherwise mandated by the Danish Retention Act no fewer than 10 times.

In 2022, the current Act was passed with the long-postponed revision finally happening, only to be contradicted by the Court of Justice of the European Union shortly thereafter. This phase is still characterised by a desire to retain as much data as possible, and giving the police access, albeit now at least formally tempered by case-law from the Court of Justice.

The chapter starts by outlining the content of the rules, starting with the 2002 rules and 2006 Retention Order and Guidance. The political reaction to pivotal judgments from the CJEU is described, as well as the resulting 2022 revision.

Section 2 discusses whether and to what extent, the Danish rules can be considered to be problematic, looking at the (lack of) political and legislative reaction to the CJEU judgments, the proportionality of the rules as they stand today, and potential omissions.

---

[1] *Folketingstidende 1998-99*, Tillæg A, L 41 som fremsat. Note all references to preparatory works are to Folketingstidende (Official Report of Parliamentary Proceedings), and its various appendices—Tillæg A (Appendix A) for proposals, and Tillæg F (Appendix F) for meeting minutes. All references hereto follow the official referenceguide at <https://www.folketingstidende.dk/da/guide-til-dokumenter/om-at-henvise-til-folketingstidende> accessed 2 February 2024.

The chapter ends by concluding that the current rules have significant flaws, being designed to retain as much data as possible, without considering the impact of the resulting interference on the private lives of the citizens.

2. The Content of the Danish Retention Rules

In 2002, following an intense debate constantly referencing the urgency of preventing terrorism, legislation allowing wholescale retention was passed.[2] The details were to be set out in an executive order (Logningsbekendtgørelsen, or the Retention Order), which was issued in 2006, following extensive consultations with the internet and telephone providers.[3] This Order stood, with a minor amendment in 2014 following *Digital Rights Ireland*,[4] until new legislation was passed in 2022. The following explains the main points of the 2006 Order and the 2014 amendment, followed by the 2022 revision.

2.1 Retention Order and Guidance of 2006

In September 2006 the Retention Order was published, with an accompanying guideline. The Order took full effect in 2007.[5]

The following data was to be collected:

A) **Information about landline and mobile telephony, TXT, EMS, and MMS communication**
   - Calling number (A number) and name and address of the subscriber or registered user
   - Called number (B number) and name and address of the subscriber or registered user
   - Change of dialled number (C number) and name and address of the subscriber or registered user
   - Receipts for received messages
   - The identity of the communication equipment used (e.g., IMSI and IMEI numbers)

---

[2] *Folketingstidende 2001-02,* tillæg F, møde 23 (meeting 23), pp 1321–45.
[3] Retsudvalget, (Committee for Legal Affairs) 'L 55 - Bilag 44' (appendix 44) (*Folketinget*, April 2004) <http://webarkiv.ft.dk/?/samling/20031/udvbilag/reu/l55_bilag44.htm> accessed 29 March 2023.
[4] CJEU, Judgment of 8 April 2014, *Digital Rights Ireland and Seitlinger and others* (C-293/12 and C-594/12) ECLI:EU:C:2014:238.
[5] 'Bekendtgørelse Nr 988 Af 28/09/2006 Om Udbydere Af Elektroniske Kommunikationsnets Og Elektroniske Kommunikationstjenesters Registrering Og Opbevaring Af Oplysninger Om Teletrafik (Logningsbekendtgørelsen)' [Executive Order no. 988 of 28/09/2006 Regarding Providers of Electronic Communicationnetworks and Electronic Communicationservices Registering and Retaining Information (Retention Order)] (28 September 2006) <https://www.retsinformation.dk/eli/lta/2006/988> accessed 28 March 2023; 'Vejledning Nr 74 Af 28/09/2006 Til Bekendtgørelse Om Udbydere Af Elektroniske Kommunikationsnets Og Elektroniske Kommunikationstjenesters Registrering Og Opbevaring Af Oplysninger Om Teletrafik (Logningsbekendtgørelsen)' [Guidance on the Retention Order] (28 September 2006) <https://www.retsinformation.dk/eli/mt/2006/74> accessed 28 March 2023. The 2002 Act fulfilled the requirements of the later EU Data Retention Directive, meaning the Order served as the technical fulfilment of the implementation.

- The cell(s) a mobile phone is connected to at the start and end of the communication, as well as the precise geographical or physical location of the associated masts at the time of the communication
- Time of start and end of the communication

B) **Information about the providers' own e-mail services**
   - Sending e-mail address
   - Receiving e-mail address

C) **Information about the providers' own internet services**
   - Customers' user IDs, such as subscription numbers or other information used to identify the customer to the provider.
   - The user identity and telephone number assigned to communications on public electronic communications network (IP telephony)
   - Ports and transportation protocols used in individual settings (the so-called 'session log').
   - Name and address of any subscribers or identified users assigned an IP, user ID or phone number.
   - Exact geographical location of hot spots, as well as any equipment used.
   - Time of start and end of the communication

All data was to be retained for one year, and failure to comply could be fined.

Neither the executive order, nor the accompanying guideline, contained any mention of security measures, though the Data Retention Directive[6]—they were purportedly implementing—had specific provisions hereof. These were instead regulated through a technical set of rules aimed at providers.[7] Though regulating security measures separately made updating them easier, it also potentially obscured the connection between the fundamental rights of the persons whose data were retained, and the measures ensuring their security, that is, the very measures minimising the risk of further potential violations.

The police could access the data only through a court warrant, which in cases of urgency could be obtained afterwards.[8]

2.2 Interlude: *Digital Rights Ireland* and *Tele2 Sverige*

Digital Rights Ireland did not trigger a wholesale revision of the Danish rules, but did result in the Ministry of Justice cancelling most of the session logs, only retaining IP addresses (see also section 3.2 below on proportionality) The rest of the Order remained untouched,

---

[6] Directive 2006/24/EC of the European Parliament and of the Council of 15 March 2006 on the retention of data generated or processed in connection with the provision of publicly available electronic communications services or of public communications networks and amending Directive 2002/58/EC. OJ L 105, 13.4.2006, p. 54.

[7] 'Bekendtgørelse No 1031 Af 13/10 2006 Om Udbud Af Elektroniske Kommunikationsnet Og -Tjenester' (Executive Order on Procurement of Electronic Communicationnetworks and—Services) <https://www.retsinformation.dk/eli/lta/2006/1031> accessed 31 May 2023.

[8] 'Bekendtgørelse Af Lov Om Rettens Pleje LBK No. 1261' (Administration of Justice Act) (23 October 2007) <https://www.retsinformation.dk/eli/lta/2007/1261> accessed 12 February 2023, chapters 71 and 74.

as the Minister pointed to other governments across Europe sharing the Danish interpretation of the judgment.[9]

The 2016 *Tele2 Sverige*[10] judgment caused considerable parliamentary debate, but no revision, as the government repeatedly postponed such process with different arguments (see section 4.1).[11]

2.3 2022 revision

The 2022 regulation,[12] explicitly aimed at preserving the 2006 status quo, was two-fold, containing one set of rules for general, undifferentiated retention, and another set for targeted retention.[13] The targeted retention was meant as a fall-back option, only to be activated by the Minister of Justice if the general retention was not in place. Instead, the police was initially allowed access to the general retention data, both for fighting serious crime and threats to the security of the nation. The two types of retention differ in the locations and people targeted but collect almost the same information. Compared to the 2006 Retention Order, categories A and B are identical, with the old category C being divided into two new categories, C (IP telephony) and D (IP addresses):

C) **Information about the providers' own internet telephony services (IP telephony)**
   - The assigned user identity
   - The user identity and telephone number assigned to communications on public electronic communications network
   - Name and address of the subscriber or registered user to whom an Internet Protocol address, user-identity or telephone number was assigned at the time of communication
   - Time of start and end of the communication

D) **Source IP addresses including source ports used for CG-NAT sessions.**

IP telephony (C) and landlines (part of category A) are excluded from the targeted retention; co-incidentally two categories whose practical relevance must be considered relatively minor in 2023.

The general retention can be activated in case of a serious threat against Denmark, for a period of up to one year at a time, resulting in a nationwide retention of all the abovementioned data, without any differentiation.

The targeted retention, when utilised, can cover both specific persons and geographical areas. Every person sentenced for a crime carrying a maximum custodial penalty of at least three years can be targeted for a period of three to ten years following the moment of

---

[9] Retsudvalget, 'Åbent samråd om reaktion på dommen' (n 11).
[10] CJEU, Judgment of 21 December 2016, Tele2 Sverige (C-203/15 and C-698/15) ECLI:EU:C:2016:970 ('*Tele2 Sverige*').
[11] For examples of questions raised, see 'Search for "Tele2"' (*Folketinget*) <https://www.ft.dk/da/search?msf=&q = tele2&as = 1> accessed 12 February 2023.
[12] Lov nr. 291 af 08/03/2022 om ændring af retsplejeloven og lov om elektroniske kommunikationsnet og -tjenester (Act no. 291 of 08/03/2022 on amending the Administrative Justice Act and the Act on Electronic Communication Networks and Services).
[13] *Folketingstidende 2021-22*, Tillæg A, L 93 som fremsat.

release, and persons or communication devices previously linked to a potential crime can also be targeted if the police so choose. The *La Quadrature du Net 'I'*[14] judgment allows for applying geographical criteria, based on objective and non-discriminatory factors, in combating serious crimes. As a consequence the Danish law introduced a big novelty in logging of geographic areas. Thus, the retention can be targeted to areas of 3x3 km, based on either the number of reported crimes carrying a maximum custodial penalty of three years or more, or inhabitants convicted of a such a crime, being one and a half times higher than the national average. As the average is not weighted against population density, the targeted areas will almost invariably include all denser populated areas such as cities, as more crimes are reported there than in the rural areas which include, for example, farming land and forests. Additionally, so-called critical locations can be targeted, from royal residences, over police stations and embassies, to traffic junctions such as bus stations and major roads. All in all, if all targeted areas are logged, an estimated 15% of Denmark's area, inhabited by 67% of the population, will be targeted, not counting those living outside the targeted areas who may travel to or through the targeted areas for work or leisure.[15]

The general IP retention (category D) is available for fighting all kinds of crimes, and not just serious crime.

3. Is there Something Rotten in the State of Denmark?

Several aspects of the retention rules are worth discussing. Why did the revision get continually postponed? Is the amount and extent of retained data proportional to the stated goals? And what is not covered by the rules?

3.1 The (lack of) revision

When the first comprehensive data retention legislation was adopted in 2002, both the extent and the length of the retention of data were new measures. As such, the legislation came with a sunset clause ordering an evaluation and revision in 2005–06 (the Danish parliamentary year lasts from October to September the following year).[16]

3.1.1 The postponed revision
As described, the Retention Order was not effectuated until 2006. Therefore, the revision was postponed until 2009–10, to allow for the experiences necessary to conduct a proper evaluation.[17] When the time came, however, the revision was delayed two more years, citing both lack of experience as the order had only been active for two years, and waiting

---

[14] CJEU, Judgment of 6 October 2020, La Quadrature du Net and others (C-511/18, C-512/18 and C-520/18) ECLI:EU:C:2020:791 ('*La Quadrature du Net 'I'*').
[15] Minister of Justice, 'L 93 - 2021-22 - Endeligt Svar På Spørgsmål 51' (Final Answer to Question 51) (7 February 2022) <https://www.ft.dk/samling/20211/lovforslag/L93/spm/51/svar/1853021/2524275/index.htm> accessed 12 May 2023.
[16] *Folketingstidende 2001-02, 2. samling*, Tillæg A, L 35 som fremsat.
[17] *Folketingstidende 2005-06*, Tillæg A, L 217 som fremsat

for a promised revision of the EU Retention Directive in late 2010, so as not to perform two revisions within a short time span.[18] Some parliamentarians argued for a one-year delay only, but this gained no ground with the rest of the parliament.[19] Meanwhile, the Danish Civil Security Service was said to be utilising the retained data in a 'considerable amount' of cases.[20]

In 2011, when the time was up for the delayed revision, the government proposed yet another two-year delay, to wait for a revised Retention Directive expected in Autumn 2012. Interestingly, at this time the government had changed from being mainly Liberal to Social-Democrat, and the Liberals (Venstre) who had overseen the introduction of the data retention executive order and argued for postponing its revision just three months prior, were now in opposition, arguing for an urgent revision. The debate surrounding the proposed postponement was more critical than prior, touching upon inter alia the lack of implementation of retention orders in other EU countries such as Sweden.[21] The revision was postponed only one year, and an examination of whether the Danish Retention Order over-implemented the Data Retention Directive (aka gold-plating),[22] and the usefulness of the retained data to the police and secret service was ordered.

The requested examination was provided in the form of a 2012 report, concluding that the Danish Retention Order on 'a few occasions' went further than the Data Retention Directive, specifically in the logging of internet sessions, the geographical placement of hot spots offering wireless internet access, and logging both the first and the last mast connected to a cell phone conversation (the Data Retention Directive only mandated the logging of the first mast).[23] The report also contained a somewhat cursory exploration of the usefulness of the retained data to the police and the secret service, offering examples of specific cases where the data had been useful, along with a general statement that both found the cell phone data extremely useful. The internet session logs, however, were less useful and rarely utilised due to technical issues, due to the telecommunications companies only being required to log every 500th data package of the users' communication with the internet, instead of all communication.[24] Despite these findings, which might have been ground for an urgent revision of at least the internet session logs, 2012 saw yet another two-year postponement of the revision to 2014–2015, as the promised EU revision had been postponed until late 2013, possibly 2014.[25]

Although the *Digital Rights Ireland* judgment in 2014 caused considerable debate, it only caused a minor revision, namely the removal of the aforementioned useless session logs. A proposal was put forth in May 2015 to postpone the regulation until year 2015–2016

---

[18] *Folketingstidende 2009-10*, Tillæg A, L 180 som fremsat

[19] *Folketingstidende 2009-10*, tillæg F, møde 72, pp 8–14.

[20] Ministry of Justice, 'Redegørelse Om Diverse Spørgsmål Vedrørende Logningsreglerne' (Memorandum Regarding Various Questions Concering Retention Regulations) (21 December 2012) <https://www.ft.dk/samling/20121/almdel/REU/bilag/125/1200765/index.htm> accessed 2 May 2023, p. 23.

[21] *Folketingstidende 2011-12*, tillæg F, møde 30., pp 42–55.

[22] Eva Thomann and Asya Zhelyazkova, 'Moving beyond (Non-)Compliance: The Customization of European Union Policies in 27 Countries' (2017) 24 Journal of European Public Policy 1269.

[23] Ministry of Justice, 'Redegørelse Om Diverse Spørgsmål Vedrørende Logningsreglerne' (n 24), p. 13.

[24] Ministry of Justice, 'Notat Om Betydningen Af EU-Domstolens Dom Af 8. April 2014 i de Forenede Sager C-293/12 Og C-594/12 (Om Logningsdirektivet) for de Danske Logningsregler' (Note on the Consequence of Cases C-293/12 and C-594/12 for the Danish Retention Regulation) (2 June 2014) <https://www.ft.dk/samling/20131/almdel/EUU/bilag/482/1376484/index.htm> accessed 2 May 2023, pt. 4.4.1.

[25] *Folketingstidende 2012-13*, Tillæg A, L 142 fremsættelse.

to wait for potential guidelines from the EU, but a general election was called before the proposal could become law, and the revision did not happen.[26] The introductory debate regarding the proposal did, however, not imply any resistance, so the revision would probably have passed.[27] At the end of the parliamentary year of 2015–2016, the new government proposed yet another postponement, this time to 2016–2017, in order to continue consultations on how to re-introduce session logs without putting too extraneous an economical burden on the companies.[28] This was adopted without much discussion.[29]

In December 2016, the *Tele2 Sverige* judgment was published, causing the Danish government to acknowledge the necessity of changing the national rules from general to targeted retention. The Minister of Justice, however, refused to suspend the general retention until new regulation had been passed, due to the data being 'too valuable a tool' to the police.[30] As a consequence, the scheduled revision of the retention rules was postponed yet again to the parliamentary year of 2017–2018, giving the government time to work on new legislation, consulting with both the European Commission, other EU Member States, the police and secret services, and the tele- and internet providers.[31] Thus, while *Tele2 Sverige* did not leave any doubt that the Danish rules had to be changed, it did not have any immediate effect.

Repeating a now well-established pattern, the revision, originally to be carried out in 2009, was postponed several more times. In April 2018, the government wanted to wait for guidelines from the EU Commission.[32] April 2019, those guidelines were not yet published, and while the government had started planning how a revision could be performed, they now wanted time to examine a Swedish retention legislation proposal of a few weeks earlier.[33] The April 2019 postponement was never formally passed due to a general election being called, but in December the new government proposed postponing one more year, to the parliamentary year 2020–2021, this time to wait for the (at that time) forthcoming judgment in *La Quadrature du Net 'I'* case in (reportedly) May 2020. Denmark had, along with 15 other EU Member States and the European Commission, submitted an observation to the Court, hoping it would change its opinion regarding general retention of data.[34] Had the Court followed the submitted observations, the Danish rules would not have had to change. This was, however, not the case.

3.1.2 The urgent revision
The *La Quadrature du Net 'I'* judgment of 6 October 2020 resulted in a proposal for revised legislation introduced 11 November 2021, with an intended fast legislative process, aiming at

---

[26] *Folketingstidende 2014-15, 1. samling*, Tillæg A, L 193 fremsættelse.
[27] *Folketingstidende 2014-15, 1. Samling*, Tillæg F, møde 88, pp 29–30
[28] *Folketingstidende 2016-17*, Tillæg A, L 183 fremsættelse.
[29] *Folketingstidende 2015-16*, Tillæg F, møde 100, pp 58–61.
[30] Retsudvalget, 'Åbent samråd i Retsudvalget om logning og dommen i Tele2-Watson sagen' (Open Consultation in the Legal Affairs Committee Regarding Retention and the Tele 2 Sverige Judgment) (*Folketinget*, 2 March 2017) <https://www.ft.dk/da/udvalg/udvalgene/reu/tv?s = 20161&m = td.1380023&from = 21-12-2016&to = 03-05-2017&as = 1#pv> accessed 3 May 2023 at 11:59.
[31] *Folketingstidende 2016-17*, Tillæg A, L 191 fremsættelse.
[32] *Folketingstidende 2017-18*, Tillæg A, L 218 fremsættelse.
[33] *Folketingstidende 2018-19*, Tillæg A, L 227 fremsættelse.
[34] *Folketingstidende 2019-20*, Tillæg A, L 87 fremsættelse.

an effective date of 1 January 2022. It was, however, not passed until March 2022, following lengthy parliamentary debates, and effective from a date of the Minister of Justice's choosing.[35]

Part of the 2022 regulation carried a warning of a 'substantial litigation risk' from the Ministry of Justice.[36] Such a warning had not been issued before and was the subject of much debate in the parliament, though eventually the majority deferred to the expertise of the Ministry.[37] The substantial litigation risk became reality less than a week after its adoption, when the EU Court in April 2022 handed down the *Garda Síochána* judgment.[38] Making it very clear that data retained for national security reasons could not be utilised for the prevention of serious crime, the judgment necessitated an immediate change of this practice in Denmark.[39] As the Danish regulation had relied on the general retention data to be utilised by the police for fighting serious crime, no targeted retention was in place, leaving the Minister of Justice scrambling to put together a new order for targeted retention and leaving the police with very limited access to retained data in the meantime.[40] In June, a partly targeted retention was put in place to combat serious crime, targeting geographic areas with a higher than average number of reported crimes, and 'certain critical locations'.[41] Despite a promised revision of the regulation in the next parliamentary year, this did not happen, and as of June 2023 there is no apparent schedule for a future revision.[42] Furthermore, the Retention Order of March 2022 authorising the general retention through March 2023 has seemingly not been renewed, meaning either the general retention is currently happening unauthorised, or has been stopped without any publicity whatsoever. Considering the general unwillingness of the Danish government to seize retaining as much data as possible it seems highly unlikely that the general retention has been stopped, particularly given the secret services still rating the risk of terrorism as 'severe', providing the necessary grounds for continuing the retention.[43] Thus, the presumption must be that the general retention is currently unauthorised. Considering the two periods where a legislatively mandated revision was postponed without changing the legislation, this lack of

---

[35] 'Lov Nr. 291 Om Ændring Af Retsplejeloven Og Lov Om Elektroniske Kommunikationsnet Og -Tjenester (Revision Af Reglerne Om Registrering Og Opbevaring Af Oplysninger Om Teletrafik (Logning) m.v.)' (Act Revising the Administrative Justice Act (Revising Rules on Retention and Registration of Teledata)) (3 August 2022) <https://www.retsinformation.dk/eli/lta/2022/291> accessed 12 February 2023.
[36] *Folketingstidende 2021-22*, Tillæg A, L 93 som fremsat, p 55.
[37] *Folketingstidende 2021-22*, Tillæg F, møde 21, pp 21–34
[38] CJEU, Judgment of 5 April 2022, Commissioner of An Garda Síochána (C-140/20) ECLI:EU:C:2022:258 ('*Garda Síochána*').
[39] Minister of Justice, 'Orientering' (Memorandum) (6 April 2022) <https://www.ft.dk/samling/20211/almdel/reu/spm/776/svar/1874527/2560123/index.htm> accessed 12 May 2023.
[40] Minister of Justice, 'REU, Alm.Del - 2021-22 - Endeligt Svar På Spørgsmål 842' (Final Answer to Question 842) (1 June 2022) <https://www.ft.dk/samling/20211/almdel/reu/spm/842/svar/1889619/2585479/index.htm> accessed 12 May 2023.
[41] Ministry of Justice, 'REU, Alm.Del - 2021-22 - Bilag 295' (Appendix 295) (*Folketinget*, 28 June 2022) <https://www.ft.dk/samling/20211/almdel/REU/bilag/295/2601507/index.htm> accessed 15 May 2023.
[42] 'Oversigt over forventede fremsættelser efter vinterferien' (Index over expected proposals after the winter break) (*Statsministeriet*, 2 February 2023) <https://www.stm.dk/statsministeriet/publikationer/oversigt-over-forventede-fremsaettelser-efter-vinterferien/> accessed 15 May 2023; The only mention of data retention in 2022–23 is an unanswered question to the Minister of Justice: Lisbeth Bech Nielsen, 'Spørgsmål 20' (Question 20) (*Folketinget*, 27 February 2023) <https://www.ft.dk/samling/20222/almdel/diu/spm/20/index.htm> accessed 15 May 2023; Nina Holst-Christensen, 'Logning Og Privatlivsbeskyttelse' (Retention and Protection of Privacy) [2023] Ugeskrift for retsvæsen U.2023B.93 does, however, mention an upcoming revision, without getting specific.
[43] Politiets Efterretningstjeneste, 'Terrortruslen mod Danmark er præget af nye tendenser' (Threat of terror against Denmark characterised by new tendencies) (28 March 2023) <https://pet.dk/pet/nyhedsliste/terrortruslen-mod-danmark-er-praeget-af-nye-tendenser/2023/03/28> accessed 25 May 2023.

proper authorisation would not be entirely unprecedented, although there is a difference in order of magnitude between not performing a revision and carrying out an unauthorised retention.

3.2 Proportionality

The goal of the various Danish governments since 9/11 has explicitly been to gather as much data as possible. This shows in various ways, some more overt than others. What does not show is a serious consideration of whether the invasion of privacy resulting from the retention is proportional to the stated goals of fighting terrorism and serious crime. Ensuring proportionality means considering many different aspects, some of which are discussed in the following.[44]

3.2.1 Amount of data

Pivotal to the discussion on the proportionality of retention should be the amount of data retained. This aspect has, however, very rarely been acknowledged as being particularly problematic. The first discussions on data retention in 2002, fuelled by the anxiety caused by the 9/11 attacks, did acknowledge the enormity of the interference with the right to privacy, but overall concluded that preventing another terrorist attack was more important.[45] Since 2002, however, this aspect of the debate has been near invisible. A few politicians have continually raised the issue arguing inter alia that at the very least Denmark should not be gold-plating the Data Retention Directive (see section 3.1.1), without much success.

The lack of discussion was particularly clear when, in 2014, the Court of Justice pronounced *Digital Rights Ireland*, invalidating the Data Retention Directive. As the Danish Retention Order implemented the Directive, this caused a debate on whether and to what extent the Order should be immediately revised. The Ministry of Justice provided an analysis of the judgment in relation to the Danish rules, which—while not outright false—did not present a complete picture of the judgment.[46] The analysis was accurate in presenting the procedural requirements of, for example, regulating access to the retained data and defining the period of retention, all aspects already regulated in Danish law. The amount of data collected was not discussed in any detail, though a pivotal point of the judgment. Instead, the Ministry pointed to the case being decided on several considerations, and since Denmark was within the clear on the processual requirements, the overall conclusion was that the Danish Retention Order was in line with the EU Charter.[47] As mentioned above, the only action taken was cancelling the session log due to it being useless and thus unproportional,

---

[44] The following categories are inspired by Tanja Kammersgaard Christensen, *De Retlige Rammer for Politiets Digitale Overvågning* (Regulatory Frames for the Police's Digital Surveillance) Aalborg University 2020), chapter 9.
[45] *Folketingstidende 2001-02*, Tillæg F, møde 23, pp. 1321–45.
[46] See also Jacob Mchangama, 'Revision Af Logningsreglerne' (Revision of Retentionrules) (4 September 2014) <https://www.ft.dk/samling/20131/almdel/REU/bilag/365/1396392/index.htm> accessed 2 May 2023, pointing out that the Ministry had neglected to draw on e.g., recent case-law from the European Court of Human Rights.
[47] Ministry of Justice, 'Notat Om Betydningen Af EU-Domstolens Dom Af 8. April 2014 i de Forenede Sager C-293/12 Og C-594/12 (Om Logningsdirektivet) for de Danske Logningsregler' (n 10).

but shortly thereafter, the National Danish Police put forth a set of requests for a new retention regulation, reintroducing the session log in a more comprehensive form.[48] This, however, proved to be unacceptably costly to the tele- and internet providers.[49] The request was rejected solely on the basis of cost, not privacy, with the Minister of Justice repeatedly insisting the retention would not technically qualify as surveillance, as all the data was to be collected by the providers and not the police.[50]

The stated goal of gathering as much data as possible is also reflected in the new targeted retention covering two-thirds of the population (as described in Chapter 2, section 2.3), bringing into question whether it is not, in fact, more general than targeted. While the criteria used are objective, weighing the crime statistics against population density would have provided a more accurate picture of the areas relevant for targeting, and thus also adhered closer to *La Quadrature du Net 'I'*.

Another way of ensuring as much data as possible is gathered is through redefinitions. The police can only gain access to the targeted data for the solving of serious crimes, and therefore the 2022 revision lowered the threshold for serious crimes from a maximum custodial penalty of six years to three years, drastically expanding the number of crimes eligible for that designation, and thereby also the number of potential persons surveilled. This gives the police a wider access to the targeted data and expands the potential amount of data retained since persons accused of committing serious crimes can be targeted for targeted retention. The Court of Justice has left the definition of serious crime up to the national legislatures, but expanding the definition is perhaps a somewhat contradictory reaction to the Court of Justice demanding limitations to the use of retained data.[51] An argument can perhaps be made that by only retaining targeted data, less data is collected, and thus the widening of the pool of persons surveilled is not in and of itself problematic, as the targeted retention is still less intrusive than the general retention. The fact that the definition of serious crime is specifically tailored to collect as much data as possible, instead of relying on whether a crime is particularly abhorrent or disruptive, does however speak against this argument.

The 2022 revision also removed the possibility of using anonymous top-up sim cards through a redefinition of the telephone numbers database. This was intended to fight criminals operating incognito, but in the process removed the possibility for everyone, including non-criminals, to remain anonymous while using cell phones. This part of the legislation did not receive much attention.[52]

Finally, the 2022 revision allowed for retained IP addresses to be used for combatting all kinds of crime. This part of the legislation was based on the argument that paras 152–156

---

[48] Steen A Jørgenssen, 'Søren Pind skrotter dyrt forslag om overvågning' (Søren Pind scraps expensive proposal on surveillance) (*Jyllands-Posten*, 17 March 2016) <https://jyllands-posten.dk/politik/ECE8519748/soeren-pind-forkaster-dyrt-forslag-om-sessionslogning/> accessed 3 May 2023.

[49] *Folketingstidende 2016-17*, Tillæg A, L 183 fremsættelse.

[50] '§ 20-spørgsmål US 44 Om logning af tele- og internettrafik' (Question 44 on Retention of Tele- and Internettraffic) (*Folketinget*, 9 February 2016) <https://www.ft.dk/samling/20151/spoergsmaal/US44/index.htm> accessed 2 May 2023; Sebastian Gjerding, 'Omstridt internetovervågning lagt i graven for anden gang' (Disputed internetsurveillance buried a second time) (*Information*, 17 March 2016) <https://www.information.dk/indland/2016/03/omstridt-internetovervaagning-lagt-graven-gang> accessed 3 May 2023.

[51] Tanja Kammersgaard Christensen and Lene Wacher Lentz, 'Logning af teledata – balancen mellem hensynet til kriminalitetsbekæmpelse og borgerens privatliv' (Retention of teledata - balancing crime prevention and the private life of citizens) [2022] Juristen 174.

[52] *Folketingstidende 2021-22*, Tillæg A, L 93 som fremsat, pt. 3.4

of *La Quadrature du Net 'I'* only apply to destination IP addresses, and paras 157–159 to source IP addresses, making a distinction between the seriousness of the retention of the two kinds of IP addresses, and stating that retention of IP source addresses does not, in itself, constitute a serious interference. This reading, however, ignores para 168 concluding that retention of source IP addresses should be limited to combating serious crimes and threats to national security.[53]

Overall, proportionality only seems to be a valid argument for reducing the amount of retained data when the measure is too costly for the industry, or the data in question is useless. Considerations of privacy can apparently never justify a reduction in the amount of data as long as the data might potentially be useful to the police, up to and including the forced de-anonymisation of every person owning a cell phone. For a democratic country, such lack of consideration of the importance of privacy is very undemocratic.

3.2.2 Length of retention

The 2002 legislation was partly based on a 1999 whitepaper, focused on the prevention of child pornography. It discussed the ideal length of retention; for purposes of fighting crime the suggestion was 12 months but weighing the purposes against the interference with the right to privacy, six months was considered appropriate. When legislation was subsequently introduced, however, the chosen length was 12 months, emphasising the need for fighting crime over concerns of privacy.[54] The retention period has not been changed since its initiation and has not been debated beyond a cursory rejection of any suggestion of change.

Likewise, the authorisation of general, undifferentiated retention in the 2022 legislation happens up to one year at a time, though perhaps a shorter period would be more appropriate, considering the general retention is supposed to be an exception to the rule, therefore requiring more or less constant monitoring to ensure it is needed.

The justification for the longer period is, and has been from its introduction, that crimes such as terrorism usually require a longer period of planning, and therefore the police must have access to historical data. Considerations of privacy have not been enough to outweigh this argument.

3.2.3 Justifications of retention

One of the most common arguments against accusations of invasion of privacy is that the police does not actually gain access to all the information gathered.[55] Access always requires a court warrant, and therefore the retention of data cannot, in itself, be classified as an interference with the right to privacy. Notably, the ECtHR has repeatedly repudiated this argument, from as early as 1987, and the Court of Justice has taken the same stance, multiple times. The retention may not always be a violation in itself, but since it is an interference, its proportionality needs to be carefully considered.[56] This case law has, however, never been presented in full to the Danish Parliament, especially notable in the analysis of

---

[53] *La Quadrature du Net and Others* 'I'; Jesper Lund, 'The new Danish data retention law: attempts to make it legal failed after just six days' (15 June 2022) <https://itpol.dk/articles/new-Danish-data-retention-law-2022> accessed 12 May 2023; see also Ministry of Justice, 'Bilag 192' (Appendix 192) (10 March 2022) <https://www.ft.dk/samling/20211/almdel/REU/bilag/192/2541578.pdf> accessed 24 May 2023.

[54] *Folketingstidende 2001-02*, Tillæg A, L 35 som fremsat, pp 847–54.

[55] '§ 20-spørgsmål US 44 Om logning af tele- og internettrafik' (n 56).

[56] Christensen (n 48), pp 133–35.

the *Digital Rights Ireland* case. The argument was even recently repeated in an article by a leading lawyer at the Department of Justice, wondering how the Court of Justice could ever consider the amount of data problematic when the police had no direct access.[57]

The emphatically stated goal of the Danish government in revising the Retention Order in 2021–2022, was to retain as much data as possible while still complying with the 'insane' and 'deluded' *La Quadrature du Net 'I'* judgment.[58] Concerns about violations of privacy were countered with anecdotes of imaginary crimes potentially remaining unsolved, and no other possible methods of aiding the police in their work seem to have been considered.[59] Strikingly, despite multiple claims of the invaluable usefulness of the retained data, no statistics were provided, as they were apparently unavailable.[60] Meanwhile, a re-examination of more than 5,000 judgments following the reveal of faulty telephony data found no cases where the retained data had been presented as decisive proof.[61] Additionally, for a short period of time in 2022 after *Garda Síochána*, the police could not access retained data for solving serious crimes. If the data is such a pivotal tool, it is worth noting that the lack of access seemingly did not result in fewer solved cases, at least none that were brought to the attention of the public.

Looking further into the lack of statistics it becomes clear that the IT systems of the Danish Police apparently do not support the creation of such. The systems are old, developed as case-working systems aimed at helping the police, without a tagging or classification system from which statistical information could be drawn.[62] Therefore, the only statistics available are the numbers forwarded to the EU on successful requests for access to the retained data.[63] There are no statistics on the number of unsuccessful requests, though they could have served as proof that the court warrant is an effective guarantee against misuse, and not just a rubber stamp. There is also no knowledge of how many cases the data helped solve, though it has apparently never been used as decisive or solitary proof of guilt. Also unknown is how much of the requested data concerned recent events and therefore would have been available anyway without the retention order, as the companies typically use and thus retain most of the information for their bookkeeping and to correct errors, for a period of two weeks. In short, all that has been presented to the public and the parliament is anecdotal evidence and vague statements of usefulness, peppered with tales of imagined crimes which the data could potentially help solve. Bearing in mind that, since *Digital Rights Ireland*, the Court of Justice has been very clear on the amount

---

[57] Holst-Christensen (n 46), p. 96.
[58] *Folketingstidende 2021-22*, tillæg F, møde 21, pp 21–34 at 15:59
[59] ibid, at 15:41.
[60] Rigspolitiet (National Police), 'L 93 - 2021-22 - Bilag 25' (Appendix 25) (11 January 2022) <https://www.ft.dk/samling/20211/lovforslag/L93/bilag/25/2525702/index.htm> accessed 12 May 2023; Minister of Justice, 'L 93 - 2021-22 - Endeligt Svar På Spørgsmål 21' (Final Answer to Question 12) (12 January 2022) <https://www.ft.dk/samling/20211/lovforslag/L93/spm/21/svar/1845626/2512032/index.htm> accessed 12 May 2023.
[61] Ritzau, 'Fejl i teledata fører ikke til genoptagelse af sager' (Mistakes in teledata do not lead to reopening of cases) (*Politiken*, 3 February 2021) <https://politiken.dk/indland/art8088477/Fejl-i-teledata-f%C3%B8rer-ikke-til-genoptagelse-af-sager> accessed 12 May 2023.
[62] Retsudvalget (Legal Affairs Committee), 'Bilag 608 Statistik vedrørende logningsbekendtgørelsens anvendelse udarbejdet til brug for afrapportering af EU-Kommissionen' (Appendix 608 Statistics regarding use of the Retention Order created for reporting to the EU Commission) (*Folketinget*, 19 June 2009) <https://www.ft.dk/samling/20081/almdel/REU/bilag/608/index.htm> accessed 21 June 2023.
[63] See 'Statistik over Indgreb i Meddelelseshemmeligheden' (Statistics on Interferences of the Right to private communication) <https://www.ft.dk/samling/20051/lovforslag/L217/bilag/26/274306.pdf> accessed 21 June 2023 for an example.

of data, in and by itself, being a problem, the lack of evidence is startling, especially when coupled with the legally mandated revisions continuously being postponed due to, inter alia, lack of evidence on which to base a revision, a problem no one seems to have attempted to resolve.

The lack of publicly available evidence is also visible in the decision of whether to order general, undifferentiated retention, based on threat assessments carried out by various official units who typically make an annual report to this purpose, with the content often classified as confidential, and only summaries available to the public. The reports are also not available in full detail to any court who might be tasked with trying the proportionality of the general retention. Notably, the official assessment of the level of threats against the State of Denmark has been continuously 'severe' since 2014, calling into question whether the situation is indeed an exception.[64]

3.3 What is not in the rules?

As important as examining the contents of the regulation is, what is not regulated is equally interesting. The rules hold no mention of any form of supervision or oversight from an independent agency, nor of individual access to effective remedies.[65] Citizens may potentially take their cases to court, but this is both costly and slow, and the Danish courts are traditionally hesitant to examine legislation which does not noticeably or specifically effect the plaintiff, calling into question the effectiveness of such a remedy.[66] This is even more noticeable in light of both the Court of Justice and the European Court of Human Rights (ECtHR) emphasising the importance of such measures when implementing large-scale retention of data.[67]

4. Conclusion

Although now revised to purportedly be in concordance with the fundamental rights of the Charter, the Danish retention legislation is still grounded in a desire to retain as much data as possible, exemplified by the so-called targeted retention covering upwards of 67% of the population, and leaving serious doubts as to the respect for fundamental rights. Whether the retention itself, particularly the extent hereof, is a violation of privacy for the many persons whose data is retained has never been seriously questioned, let alone debated, as the various governments in charge have been completely unwilling to even consider the question. This lack of debate is, in and of itself, problematic. The impression left by actions such as the repeated postponement of legally mandated revisions, lacklustre reactions to pivotal judgments from the Court of Justice, apparent invisibility of relevant case-law from

---

[64] Christensen and Lentz (n 57).
[65] These would have counted as additional procedural safeguards, according to established EctHR case law, holding that the more intrusive an interference, the stronger procedural safeguards are needed. See e.g. ECtHR, Szabó and Vissy v. Hungary, no. 37138/14, 12 January 2016.
[66] Christensen and Lentz (n 57); See also *Foreningen imod Ulovlig Logning mod Justitsministeriet* (The Association against Illegal Retention v the Ministry of Justice) [2022] Danish Supreme Court BS-26847/2021-HJR.
[67] Christensen (n 48), pp 149–57, 210–11.

the ECtHR, and the proposal of legislation carrying a 'significant litigation risk', to mention but a few, is one of a state so intent on preventing terrorism, and crime in general, it willingly runs the risk of violating both EU law, and the European Convention on Human Rights. Something is, indeed, if not completely rotten, then definitely wrong, in the State of Denmark.

16
Belgium's New Data Retention Legislation
Third Time Lucky, or Three Strikes and You're Out?

Vanessa Franssen and Catherine Van de Heyning

1. Introduction

In Belgian law, the retention of communications data goes back to an Act of 13 June 2005 on electronic communications (ECA).[1] This Act provided for an obligation to retain both identification (or subscriber) data and traffic and location data, as rendered possible by Article 15 of the ePrivacy Directive of 2002.[2] The latter, which still is in the process of being reformed,[3] constitutes a key piece of European legislation in the field of data protection. As a *lex specialis* to the 1995 Data Protection Directive[4] (meanwhile replaced by the General Data Protection Regulation (GDPR)),[5] it guarantees the confidentiality of electronic communications.[6] As a result, it is prohibited to intercept, store or surveil the content of such communications, as well as the related traffic data. Certain exceptions are however possible, such as to prevent, investigate, detect, and prosecute criminal offences, provided that they are necessary, appropriate, and proportionate (Article 15(1) ePrivacy Directive). While the latter exception formed the basis of the first data retention regime in Belgium, data retention remained theoretical because the Royal Decree determining the conditions of application was never adopted.[7]

The real start of data retention under Belgian law was marked by the adoption of the Act of 30 July 2013,[8] which transposed—with some delay—the 2006 Data Retention

---

[1] *Moniteur belge* (ie the Belgian Official Journal), 20 June 2005.
[2] Directive 2002/58/EC of the European Parliament and of the Council of 12 July 2002 concerning the processing of personal data and the protection of privacy in the electronic communications sector (Directive on privacy and electronic communications) [2002] OJ L 201/37.
[3] European Commission, Proposal for a Regulation of the European Parliament and of the Council concerning the respect for private life and the protection of personal data in electronic communications and repealing Directive 2002/58/EC (Regulation on Privacy and Electronic Communications) [2017] COM/2017/010 final - 2017/03 (COD), 10 January 2017 ('ePrivacy Proposal').
[4] Directive 95/46/CE of the European Parliament and of the Council of 24 October 1995 on the protection of individuals with regard to the processing of personal data and on the free movement of such data [1995] OJ L 281/31.
[5] Regulation 2016/679 of the European Parliament and of the Council of 27 April 2016 on the protection of natural persons with regard to the processing of personal data and on the free movement of such data, and repealing Directive 95/46/EC (General Data Protection Regulation) [2016] OJ L 119/1.
[6] ePrivacy Directive, Art 5(1).
[7] F Coudert and F Verbruggen, 'Conservation des données de communications électroniques en Belgique : un juste équilibre ?', in V Franssen and D Flore (eds), *Société numérique et droit pénal. Belgique, France, Europe* (Brussels, Larcier/Bruylant 2019) 246.
[8] Act of 30 July 2013 amending Articles 2, 126, and 145 of the Act of 13 June 2005 on electronic communications and Article 90*decies* of the Code of Criminal Procedure, *Moniteur belge*, 23 August 2013.

Directive,[9] adopted in the wake of the terrorist attacks in Madrid and London. The 2013 Act amended the ECA and the Code of Criminal Procedure (CCP), thereby creating an actual legal obligation to retain identification and traffic data and regulating the access of judicial authorities to such data. Nevertheless, its success did not last for very long: two years later, in 2015, the Constitutional Court annulled the 2013 Act.[10] In its judgment, the Constitutional Court faithfully followed the reasoning of the Court of Justice of the European Union (CJEU) in *Digital Rights Ireland*,[11] whereby the latter Court had invalidated the Data Retention Directive.

Ever since, the Belgian legislator (like the European)[12] has been searching to strike the right (ie CJEU-proof) balance between the right to respect for private life and the right to data protection (enshrined in Articles 7 and 8 of the Charter of Fundamental Rights of the EU (Charter), on the one hand, and the effectiveness of criminal investigations (and ultimately the protection of other fundamental rights, such as the right to life),[13] on the other.[14]

The provisional[15] last step in this search for an equilibrium is the adoption of the Act of 20 July 2022 (2022 Data Retention Act or 2022 Act)[16] after the annulment in April 2021 by the Constitutional Court[17] of the successor of the aforementioned 2013 Act, that is, the Act of 29 May 2016 (2016 Data Retention Act or 2016 Act).[18] This annulment was the direct impact of the CJEU's Grand Chamber ruling in *La Quadrature du Net 'I'*,[19] which critically

---

[9] Directive 2006/24/EC of the European Parliament and of the Council of 15 March 2006 on the retention of data generated or processed in connection with the provision of publicly available electronic communications services or of public communications networks and amending Directive 2002/58/EC [2006] OJ L 105/54.

[10] Constitutional Court, Case 84/2015, 11 June 2015. For further analysis, see C Conings and F Verbruggen, 'Grondwettelijk Hof plaatst reparateurs dataretentiewet voor moeilijke opdracht', *Juristenkrant*, 24 June 2015, No 312, 1, 3; C Forget, 'L'obligation de conservation des "métadonnées": la fin d'une longue saga juridique ?' (2017) *Journal des Tribunaux* 237; C Van de Heyning, 'Data Retention in Belgium' in M Zubik, J Podkowik, and R Rybski (eds), *European Constitutional Courts towards Data Retention Laws* (Springer 2021) 53–74.

[11] CJEU, Judgment of 8 April 2014, *Digital Rights Ireland and Seitlinger and others* (C-293/12 and C-594/12) ECLI:EU:C:2014:238.

[12] At EU level, the European Commission and the Member States have tried to find a common ground for new EU-wide data retention legislation, but these attempts have not yet resulted in a legislative proposal. See eg European Commission, *Non-paper on the way forward on data retention* [2021] WK 7294/2021 INIT, 10 June 2021. See also A Juszczak and E Sason, 'Recalibrating Data Retention in the EU. The Jurisprudence of the Court of Justice of the EU on Data Retention – Is this the End or is this the Beginning?' (2021) *Eucrim*, section IV.4, available at <https://doi.org/10.30709/eucrim-2021-020> accessed 15 July 2024. In Spring 2023 a 'High-Level Expert Group on access to data for effective law enforcement' was created, chaired by the European Commission and the Member State holding the presidency of the Council of the EU. The High-Level Expert Group is expected to propose, by mid-2024, 'recommendations for the further development of Union policies and legislation to enhance and improve access to data for the purpose of effective law enforcement'. It identified data retention, along with encryption and anonymisation, as the most pressing issues to address. High-Level Expert Group on access to data for effective law enforcement, *Scoping paper*, annex to Presidency of the Council of the EU, [2023] ST-8281-2023-INIT, 13 April 2023, 3 and 5, available at <https://data.consilium.europa.eu/doc/document/ST-8281-2023-INIT/en/pdf> accessed 15 July 2024.

[13] See eg F Verbruggen, . Royer, and H Severijns, 'Reconsidering the Blanket-data-retention-taboo, for Human Rights' Sake ? (1 October 2018) European Law Blog <https://europeanlawblog.eu/2018/10/01/reconsidering-the-blanket-data-retention-taboo-for-human-rights-sake/> accessed 15 July 2024.

[14] For more details on the legal framework between 2013 and 2019, see F Coudert and F Verbruggen, 'Conservation des données de communications électroniques en Belgique' (n 7) 245–66.

[15] As we explain in section 4, it is unlikely that the 2022 Act is the last step in this process.

[16] Act of 20 July 2022 on the gathering and retention of identification data and metadata in the sector of electronic communications and on the production of that data to the authorities, *Moniteur belge*, 8 August 2022.

[17] Constitutional Court, Case No 57/2021, 22 April 2021.

[18] Act of 29 May 2016 on the gathering and retention of data in the sector of electronic communications, *Moniteur belge*, 18 July 2016.

[19] CJEU, Judgment of 6 October 2020, *La Quadrature du Net and others* (C-511/18, C-512/18 and C-520/18) ECLI:EU:C:2020:791 ('*La Quadrature du Net 'I'*').

accessed the Belgian (and the French) data retention regime and caused a profound crisis among national judicial authorities. The latter feared that the CJEU case law would undermine a large number of criminal investigations in which retained communications data had been used.[20] Even if the most extreme and immediate effects of this annulment could be avoided thanks to the application of the rules on admissibility of illegally obtained evidence, the need for a new legal framework remained high.

In this chapter, we will first sketch the 2016 data retention regime which was found incompatible with EU law in *La Quadrature du Net 'I'* and summarise the CJEU's main points of criticism as well as its requirements for future data retention, including those put forward in more recent judgments (section 2). Subsequently, we will briefly present the impact of the CJEU's case law at national level (section 3), before introducing the new legal framework that was adopted in the Summer of 2022 (section 4). Whereas, at first sight, the 2022 Data Retention Act seems to comply with the CJEU's prohibition on general and indiscriminate data retention, a closer analysis will reveal that several features of the new legal regime might still raise questions. For instance, while the regime is targeted in name, the criteria chosen by the Belgian legislator de facto result in data retention covering (almost) the entire territory (and thus all citizens). Moreover, in terms of access to retained data, the new legal regime continues to present certain problems. Therefore, this chapter will critically assess the new legislation in light of the CJEU's case law and reflect on the future destiny of Belgium's data retention regime.[21]

2. The Belgian Legislator in Search of EU-Proof Data Retention Legislation

2.1 Main features of the old data retention regime

As indicated, after the 2013 Act was found incompatible with EU law and annulled by the Constitutional Court, the Belgian legislator tried to address the concerns of the CJEU with the adoption of the 2016 Data Retention Act. At the time, the CJEU's case law was limited to the *Digital Rights Ireland* case; its outright condemnation of national laws providing for general and indiscriminate data retention in *Tele2 Sverige*[22] had yet to come.

Under the 2016 Act, Article 126 ECA imposed upon operators of electronic communications established in Belgium a *general obligation to retain* identification data, on the one hand, and traffic and location data, on the other. The obligation was general and indiscriminate as it encompassed the data of all users of electronic communications services in Belgium, without requiring the existence of a suspicion of a criminal offence against the persons concerned. The data retention period was set at 12 months, for identification data starting from the date at which communication was last possible

---

[20] See eg P Heymans and D Hiroux, 'Grondwettelijk Hof vernietigt wet op bijhouden van telefoondata: wat betekent dat voor jou? En voor politie en parket?', Interview with P Van Linthout, investigating judge, *VRT nws*, 22 April 2021, available at <https://www.vrt.be/vrtnws/nl/2021/04/07/dataretentie/> accessed 15 July 2024. This concern is shared by law enforcement authorities across the EU: SIRIUS EU Digital Evidence Situation Report (2022) 6, 10, 44–47, and 54.
[21] This chapter was finalised in June 2024, based upon the state of law as of 30 April 2024.
[22] CJEU, Judgment of 21 December 2016, *Tele2 Sverige* (C-203/15 and C-698/15) ECLI:EU:C:2016:970.

using the service at hand and, for traffic and location data, starting from the date of the communication.

As regards *access* to retained data, the Belgian legislator had chosen to take a gradual approach in function of the gravity of the offence under investigation, thereby hoping to meet the requirements of proportionality and necessity. The procedural conditions of access were (and still are) defined by the CCP, in particular Articles 46*bis* CCP (identification data) and 88*bis* CCP (traffic and location data).[23]

According to Article 46*bis*, § 1, last paragraph CCP, the district public prosecutor was entitled to order the *production of identification data* for a period of six months preceding the order if the offence was not likely to result in a prison sentence of one year or more. For more serious offences, access was possible during 12 months. The term 'identification data'[24] comprised, for instance, the telephone number, the International Mobile Equipment Identity (IMEI) number of a cell phone, the name and surname of the user of the service, and his/her (postal or email) address. Moreover, in practice, the date of the creation of an email account and the IP address used at that moment were also considered identification data,[25] even if such data would rather be labelled traffic data under EU law.

The *production of traffic and location data* required, according to Article 88*bis* CCP, in principle the authorisation of an investigating judge, leading the criminal investigation (ie in the context of a judicial inquiry) or intervening only punctually during the public prosecutor's investigation (ie by a so-called mini judicial inquiry (*mini-instruction*)).[26] In some cases, however, the district public prosecutor also had the power to require the production of such data. Regarding the period of access, Article 88*bis*, § 2 CCP made a three-fold distinction in function of the severity of the offence: (1) in case of a terrorist offence, the investigating judge could require the data during 12 months preceding his/her decision; (2) for the offences listed in Article 90*ter*, §§ 2 and 4 CCP (ie offences for which the investigating judge may order a covert interception, search or recording of non-publicly accessible communications or data from an IT system, in short: the 'wiretap' offences), offences committed in the context of a criminal organisation or offences which can result in a prison sentence of five years or more, the period of access was limited to nine months; and (3) for all other less serious offences but nonetheless punishable with imprisonment of one year or more, the access was only possible during six months.

This combination of a general data retention obligation with a gradual approach at the level of access to retained data was the Belgium's attempt to meet the requirements of the CJEU set forth in *Digital Rights Ireland*, while at the same time protecting the 'goldmine'[27]

---

[23] It should be pointed out that these legal provisions also apply to the production of future data and data in the possession of service providers that are not covered by the general data retention obligation of Article 126 ECA, such as OTT service providers, as long as they offer, in a targeted manner, services in Belgium. For further analysis, see B Flumian and V Franssen, 'Le nouveau cadre légal en matière de conservation des données électroniques: "Old wine in new bottles" pour les autorités judiciaires ?' in V Franssen and A Masset (eds), *Le droit pénal et la procédure pénale en constante évolution* (Anthemis 2022) 320–21 and the references mentioned therein.

[24] CCP, Art 46*bis*, § 1, para 1.

[25] This is illustrated by the Belgian *Yahoo!* case. See V Franssen and O Leroux, 'Les mesures d'enquête concernant l'internet: une évaluation critique de la nouvelle législation belge' in V Franssen and D Flore (eds), *Société numérique et droit pénal. Belgique, France, Europe* (Larcier/Bruylant 2019) 197 para 71.

[26] For a presentation of the Belgian criminal investigation and the role of the investigating judge, see AL Claes, A Werding, and V Franssen, 'The Belgian Juge d'Instruction and the EPPO Regulation: (Ir)reconcilable?' (2021) 6 European Papers 357, 363–66.

[27] F Verbruggen, L Collage, and J Huysmans, 'België ziet Europese sterren: enkele aandachtspunten voor de strafrechtspraktijk' in *Straf- en strafprocesrecht*, Themis, vol 122 (Intersentia 2022) 184ff.

that communications data constitutes for criminal investigations in the digital era. Nevertheless, many scholars were quite critical of the 2016 Data Retention Act,[28] and the CJEU proved them right.

2.2 The Belgian legislator sent back to square one by the CJEU

2.2.1 Introduction

The 2016 Data Retention Act was indeed soon after its adoption attacked before the Constitutional Court, which decided to pass the 'hot potato' onto the CJEU. In its reference for a preliminary ruling the Constitutional Court[29] raised several questions, which were joined with a related set of questions posed by the French *Conseil d'État*[30] in the *La Quadrature du Net 'I'* case. The CJEU judgment of 6 October 2020 was nothing less than an earthquake to national judicial authorities, even if the Court mainly confirmed what it had already decided in *Tele2 Sverige*. At the same time, the CJEU also created a few 'openings' which were meant to meet some concerns of law enforcement.

In what follows, we will give an overview of the Court's case law, focusing on the most questionable features of the 2016 Data Retention Act,[31] and its requirements for future EU-proof data retention. In doing so, we will also give an account of the CJEU's more recent case law, in which it further clarified certain issues.

2.2.2 New red card for general and indiscriminate retention of traffic and location data

Ever since *Digital Rights Ireland*, the CJEU has reiterated that traffic and location data is 'not less sensitive ... than the actual content of communications' as that data 'may allow' to draw 'very precise conclusions' on the private life of the persons concerned.[32] The *general and indiscriminate retention* of such data without informing these persons 'is likely to cause' the feeling 'that their private lives are the subject of constant surveillance'[33] and thus constitutes a 'particularly serious' interference in the rights enshrined in Articles 7 and 8 of the Charter.[34] In other words, such data retention is in violation of EU law. Considering the 2016 Act obliged operators of electronic communications services to retain traffic and location data in a general and indiscriminate way, it was thus contrary to EU law.

---

[28] See eg Coudert and Verbruggen, 'Conservation des données de communications électroniques en Belgique' (n 7) 265-65. Elsewhere, the efforts of the Belgian legislator in the 2016 Act to make the data retention regime more proportionate by restricting and differentiating the conditions of access to the retained data based on the gravity of the offences have been welcomed. Verbruggen, Royer, and Severijns, 'Reconsidering the blanket-data-retention-taboo' (n 13) para 7.
[29] Constitutional Court, Case No 96/2018, 19 July 2018.
[30] Contrary to the questions of the Belgian Constitutional Court, those of the French *Conseil d'État* centred essentially in the retention of data to safeguard national security.
[31] For a more extensive analysis, see Flumian and Franssen, 'Le nouveau cadre légal en matière de conservation des données électroniques' (n 23) 321-329; C. Van de Heyning, 'Het moeilijke evenwicht tussen privacy & veiligheid: de impact van het debat over het bewaren van communicatiegegevens' (2022) 2 *Radices* 132, 132-48.
[32] See eg *Digital Rights Ireland* (n 11) para 27; *Tele2 Sverige* (n 22) para 99; *La Quadrature du Net 'I'* (n 19) para 117.
[33] *Digital Rights Ireland* (n 11) para 37; *Tele2 Sverige* (n 22) para 100.
[34] *Tele2 Sverige* (n 22) para 100; *La Quadrature du Net 'I'* (n 19) para 177.

Despite this obvious violation, the Belgian Constitutional Court tried to test the CJEU's position by stressing that the general obligation laid down in the 2016 Act was necessary to meet the positive obligations that follow from Articles 3 and 8 of the European Convention on Human Rights (ECHR) and the corresponding provisions of the Charter, as the latter require a legal framework that allows effective criminal investigations and effective punishment of, for instance, sexual abuse of minors.[35] Even if this argument goes to the core of the concerns of law enforcement, the CJEU did not buy into it:

> Even the positive obligations of the Member States which may arise, depending on the circumstances, from Articles 3, 4 and 7 of the Charter and relating ... to the establishment of rules to facilitate effective action to combat criminal offences cannot have the effect of justifying interference that is as serious as that entailed by legislation providing for the retention of traffic and location data with the fundamental rights, enshrined in Articles 7 and 8 of the Charter, of practically the entire population, *without there being a link, at least an indirect one, between the data of the persons concerned and the objective pursued*.[36]

2.2.3 Targeted retention of traffic and location data for the purposes of fighting serious crime: A difficult 'tactic' to implement

Targeted retention thus seems the only option for traffic and location data. Indeed, in order to comply with the principle of proportionality, the CJEU repeated in *La Quadrature du Net 'I'* that retention of traffic and location data is only possible for the purpose of combating serious crime,[37] must be targeted, namely based on objective and non-discriminatory criteria 'that establish a connection between the data to be retained and the objective pursued',[38] and limited in time to what is 'strictly necessary', as required by Article 15(1) of the ePrivacy Directive.[39] The CJEU gave some indications as to what constitute objective and non-discriminatory criteria that could justify targeted data retention, namely (i) a 'geographical area and/or a group of persons likely to be involved, in one way or another, in a serious crime, or (ii) persons who could, for other reasons, contribute, through their data being retained, to combating serious crime'.[40] In case of a geographical criterion, the Court suggested that 'the competent national authorities [could] consider, on the basis of objective and non-discriminatory factors, that there exists, in one or more geographical areas, a situation characterised by a high risk of preparation or commission of serious criminal offences'.[41]

These indications, which echoed the ones given in *Tele2 Sverige*,[42] had however been received quite critically by law enforcement authorities: in their view, targeted retention was at odds with the basic logic of data retention[43] which, unlike an investigative measure,

---

[35] *La Quadrature du Net 'I'* (n 19) para 78. On the importance of this argument, see also Verbruggen, Royer, and Severijns, 'Reconsidering the blanket-data-retention-taboo' (n 13) para 5.
[36] ibid para 145 (emphasis added).
[37] ibid paras 140–151. Cf *Tele2 Sverige* (n 22) paras 109–111.
[38] *Tele2 Sverige* (n 22) para 110; ibid para 133.
[39] ibid para 164. Cf *Tele2 Sverige* (n 22) para 108.
[40] ibid para 144.
[41] ibid para 150.
[42] *Tele2 Sverige* (n 22) para 111.
[43] This point of view was echoed in the submissions of the Belgian government in the annulment proceedings concerning the 2016 Data Retention Act. Constitutional Court, Case 96/2018, 19 July 2018, paras A.5.12, A.8.3, and A.13.3. See Verbruggen, Royer, and Severijns, 'Reconsidering the blanket-data-retention-taboo' (n 13) para 4.

constitutes a precautionary measure, preceding the detection of an offence, the opening of a criminal investigation and the identification of a suspect,[44] and thus it is impossible to target certain geographical areas or (groups of) persons beforehand. As this scepticism was reiterated in the Constitutional Court's reference for a preliminary ruling,[45] the CJEU clarified in *La Quadrature du Net 'I'*: '[t]hose areas may include places with a high incidence of serious crime, places that are particularly vulnerable to the commission of serious criminal offences, such as places or infrastructure which regularly receive a very high volume of visitors, or strategic locations, such as airports, stations or tollbooth areas'.[46] As explained in section 4.1, the Belgian legislator took this guidance at heart in the 2022 Data Retention Act.

In more recent judgments, the CJEU has continued to provide some additional elements of clarification, as the concept of targeted data retention clearly puzzles many national legislators and authorities. In the Irish *Garda Síochána* case, the Court explained with respect to the average crime rate when used as a geographical criterion that it is not necessary for the authorities to have 'specific indications as to the preparation or commission, in the areas concerned, of acts of serious crime'.[47] Moreover, to reassure Member States, the Court emphasised that 'the criterion drawn from the average rate of serious crime is entirely unconnected with any potentially discriminatory factors'.[48] That said, the Court also highlighted that it is important to update the selected geographical zones 'in accordance with changes in the circumstances that justified their selection, thus making it possible to react to developments in the fight against serious crime'.[49]

As regards personal criteria for targeted data retention, the CJEU has in the meantime made further suggestions too. Member States could, for instance, target 'persons who, on the basis of an identification, are the subject of an investigation or other measures of current surveillance or of a reference in the national criminal record relating to an earlier conviction for serious crimes with a high risk of reoffending'.[50] This would not be discriminatory in the Court's view. One may, however, wonder whether this approach is not stigmatising.

Finally, the Court opened the door to other potential objective and non-discriminatory criteria,[51] thus inviting national legislators to reflect for themselves.

Another related question concerns what is to be understood as *serious crime* and at which level—the Member States or the EU—that notion is to be defined. Until the CJEU's recent ruling in *Bolzano*,[52] there could be two possible readings of the CJEU's case law.

On the one hand, it could be argued that the CJEU reserved a wide margin for Member States to define this notion. When the Member States adopted the Data Retention Directive in 2006, they explicitly agreed that this notion is to be 'defined by each Member State in its national law' in order to preserve national diversity.[53] In *Ministerio Fiscal*, for instance, the Court did not indicate what constitutes a 'serious' crime, as this might vary from one

---

[44] SIRIUS EU Digital Evidence Situation Report (2022) 53–54.
[45] *La Quadrature du Net 'I'* (n 19) para 76.
[46] ibid para 150.
[47] CJEU, Judgment of 5 April 2022, *Commissioner of An Garda Síochána* (C-140/20) ECLI:EU:C:2022:258 para 80.
[48] ibid para 80.
[49] ibid para 82.
[50] ibid para 78.
[51] ibid para 83.
[52] CJEU, Judgment of 30 April 2024, *Procura della Repubblica presso il Tribunale di Bolzano* (C-178/22), ECLI:EU:C:2024:371 ('*Bolzano*').
[53] Data Retention Directive, Art 1(1).

country to another and it would go beyond the competence of the EU to establish a categorisation of crimes based on their severity. Rather, it limited itself to stating that, in the light of the principle of proportionality, a serious interference with Articles 7 and 8 of the Charter can only be justified by the objective of fighting 'serious' crime.[54]

Yet, on the other hand, one could argue that there were some indications that the concept of serious crime was evolving—slowly—into an EU one.[55] In its judgments, the CJEU repeatedly mentioned organised crime and terrorism as examples of serious offences,[56] examples that were also mentioned in Recital 9 of the Data Retention Directive. Pushed by the national authorities involved, the Court indicated in *La Quadrature du Net 'I'* that serious crime also includes 'particularly serious child pornography offences, such as the acquisition, dissemination, transmission or making available online of child pornography',[57] which are offences for which the EU legislator has adopted minimum rules. This reference to so-called 'Eurocrimes'—which have increased substantially since 2006 and particularly since the entry into force of the Lisbon Treaty—could suggest a pathway for a future EU definition of serious crime.[58]

In *Bolzano*, a case relating to access to retained traffic and location data in the context of a criminal investigation by the Italian Public Prosecutor's Office on aggravated theft, the CJEU provided most *welcome clarification*, taking a quite nuanced two-step approach. On the one hand, the Court explicitly ruled that it is for the Member States to define the notion of 'serious crime' considering the EU has not (yet!) legislated in this regard.[59] It also stressed that 'the definition of criminal offences ... reflects both social realities and legal traditions, which vary not only between the Member States but also over time'.[60] On the other hand, the CJEU emphasised that the Member States must exercise their competence 'in line with EU law', in particular the requirements set out by Article 15(1) of the ePrivacy Directive, in light of the Charter and the general principles of EU law, especially the principle of proportionality.[61] In the case at hand, national law defined serious crime 'by reference to a maximum term of imprisonment of at least three years'.[62] This threshold is an objective criterion[63] which, in the CJEU's view, does not seem 'excessively low' and is not 'necessarily

---

[54] CJEU, Judgment of 2 October 2018, *Ministerio Fiscal* (C-207/16) ECLI:EU:C:2018:788 para 56. Interestingly, the Court used quotation marks when referring to the notion of 'serious' crime.

[55] The need for an autonomous EU definition of 'serious crime' has also been advocated by Advocate-General Szpunar. CJEU, First Opinion of AG Szpunar of 27 October 2022, Case C-470/21, *La Quadrature du Net and Fédération des fournisseurs d'accès à Internet associatifs and Franciliens.net and French Data Network*, para 74.

[56] *Digital Rights Ireland* (n 11) para 51; *Tele2 Sverige* (n 22) para 103.

[57] *La Quadrature du Net 'I'* (n 19) para 154.

[58] For one, Article 83(1) TFEU defines the EU's legislative competence with respect to 'areas of particularly serious crime with a cross-border dimension'; for another, in sector-specific EU legislation too one may find indications of 'harmonised' offences that are regarded as serious offences. For instance, Directive (EU) 2018/1673 of the European Parliament and of the Council of 23 October 2018 on combating money laundering by criminal law ([2018] OJ L 284/22) makes a subtle distinction between serious and less serious offences, despite the existence of EU minimum rules. See V Franssen, AL Claes, and D Flore, 'La lutte contre le blanchiment par le biais du droit pénal: la compétence et le rôle de l'Union européenne' in M Marty and F Kirmann (eds), *Le droit criminel à l'épreuve de l'infraction de blanchiment. Regards croisés luxembourgeois, français et belge* (Larcier 2023) 32–33. For another attempt to distil an EU concept of serious crime from the existing EU legislation and case law, see L Van Roy and S Royer, 'De nieuwe dataretentiewetgeving: over oude ketels en nieuwe soep' (2023) Nullum Crimen 1, 8–11.

[59] *Bolzano* (n 52) paras 44 and 46.

[60] ibid para 45.

[61] ibid paras 44, 47, and 48.

[62] ibid para 52.

[63] ibid para 54.

contrary to the principle of proportionality'.[64] In principle, such threshold is thus acceptable. However, at the same time, the CJEU insisted that the court or independent administrative body which is asked to authorise access to the retained data should assess, as part of its proportionality examination balancing the needs of the investigation and the rights of privacy and data protection of the person concerned, whether the facts in the case at hand indeed constitute serious crime.[65] The court or independent administrative authority must indeed 'be entitled to refuse or restrict' the access to the data if the offence in point 'is *manifestly* not a serious offence'.[66] Put differently, it is not because the offence as such (aggravated theft in the case at hand) meets the objective legal threshold for serious crime, that the concrete case is actually serious crime (for instance, the theft of a object of minor value such as a loaf of bread or, as in the case at hand,[67] a mobile phone).

The CJEU thus imposes an important obligation *both* on the legislator and on the authorising court or independent administrative authority. The former needs to define serious crime in an objective and restricted[68] manner. The latter must assess in every single case whether the facts are really serious, justifying a serious interference with Articles 7 and 8, as well as 11 (freedom of expression) of the Charter. In doing so, the Court—rightfully—tries to evacuate the risk that prosecuting authorities would incorrectly label a case as a serious offence to meet the legal threshold in order to get access to the retained data (see also section 4.2). It explicitly gives the court or body authorising the access to the data the power to look beyond the label and, possibly, even question the legislator's threshold for serious crime.

2.2.4 Green card for general and indiscriminate retention of identification data

Whereas general and indiscriminate retention is unacceptable for traffic and location data, the CJEU spelt out in *La Quadrature du Net 'I'* that 'data relating to the civil identity of persons who have used [the electronic communications] services'—a term it also used in *Ministerio Fiscal* and which seems to correspond (more or less) to the identification data defined previously in the Data Retention Directive—is considered much less sensitive as they do not allow to draw precise conclusions on a person's private life.[69] Consequently, the retention of such data (and their subsequent access)[70] cannot be classified as a serious interference with the Charter rights.[71] Therefore, the Court considers national law may require that such data is retained in a general way, affecting all users of electronic communications services.[72] Such data retention does not have to be limited in time and may serve the fight against crime in general, even if not serious, or the safeguarding of public security.[73]

---

[64] ibid paras 56 and 58.
[65] ibid para 60.
[66] ibid paras 60 and 62 (emphasis added).
[67] In particular, the Italian referring court questioned whether offences 'which cause only a limited social disturbance and which are punishable only on foot of a complaint by a private party, in particular low-value thefts such as mobile phone or bicycle theft' can be considered serious crime. *Bolzano*, ibid para 21.
[68] The CJEU indeed stressed that the definition given by national law 'must not be so broad that access becomes the rule rather than the exception'; it 'cannot cover the vast majority of criminal offences'. *Bolzano*, ibid para 55.
[69] *Ministerio Fiscal* (n 54) para 60. More recently confirmed in CJEU, Judgment of 30 April 2024, *La Quadrature du Net and Fédération des fournisseurs d'accès à Internet associatifs and Franciliens.net and French Data Network* (C-470/21) ECLI:EU:C:2024:37 ('*La Quadrature du Net 'II'*') para 96.
[70] ibid para 61.
[71] *La Quadrature du Net 'I'* (n 19) para 157.
[72] ibid para 159.
[73] ibid para. 159 ('without imposing a specific time limit'). Cf *La Quadrature du Net 'II'* (n 69) para 96.

To conclude, with respect to identification data, the 2016 Data Retention Act was in conformity with EU law; in fact, it even provided for more guarantees than required by the CJEU (eg data retention limited to 12 months).

2.2.5 Conditions for access to retained data: Indispensable but not enough

As explained (in section 2.1), the Belgian legislator had placed his bet in 2016 on offering more guarantees and a gradual approach at the level of access to retained data, considering that one of the problems in the Data Retention Directive pointed out by the CJEU was the lack of material and procedural conditions to limit the access to and subsequent use of the retained data by competent authorities to what is strictly necessary.[74] In particular, the Court had indicated that the access should be limited to fighting serious offences,[75] but that this requirement alone was not enough.[76] Other material and procedural conditions, such as a prior review carried out by a court or by an independent administrative body,[77] 'except in cases of validly established urgency',[78] were indispensable too. The persons to whose data access has been granted should be informed of this by the authority in point 'as soon as that notification is no longer liable to jeopardise the investigations being undertaken by those authorities'.[79]

In contrast, 'data relating to the civil identity' of the users of electronic communications services can be retained to fight crime in general. Therefore, access to such data may be granted for the purpose of any offence, provided that the possibility of access is limited in time.[80] In this respect, the 2016 Act definitely met the requirements of EU law.

In *La Quadrature du Net 'I'*, the Court however brought an *important clarification*,[81] insisting on the fact that the objective pursued by the access to the data should be identical to the one for which the data was retained, unless the objective justifying retention is ranked lower in the Court's hierarchy of objectives.[82] By no means, data retained for the purpose of combating serious crime (or to safeguard national security) could be used to investigate and prosecute 'an ordinary criminal offence'.[83] By contrast, 'in accordance with the principle of proportionality', if the data has been retained for the purpose of fighting serious crime, access to the data 'may . . . be justified by the objective of safeguarding national security'[84]—or put differently, *qui peut le plus, peut le moins*.[85] In recent case law, the Court has continued to further clarify this point.[86]

---

[74] *Digital Rights Ireland* (n 11) para 61. Cf *Tele2 Sverige* (n 22) para 118.
[75] ibid para 61.
[76] *Tele2 Sverige* (n 22) para 119.
[77] *Digital Rights Ireland* (n 11) para 62.
[78] *Tele2 Sverige* (n 22) para 120.
[79] ibid para 121 Cf *La Quadrature du Net 'I'* (n 19) para 190.
[80] *Ministerio Fiscal* (n 54) para 62.
[81] Cf *Tele2 Sverige* (n 22) para 119, where the Court was still somewhat less explicit.
[82] The Court clearly considers national security more important that the fight against serious crime, just like the latter is more important than the fight against crime in general, even if this distinction has been contested by both privacy experts and national governments. For further analysis, see Van de Heyning, 'Het moeilijke evenwicht tussen privacy & veiligheid' (n 31) 144–45. See also G Robinson, 'Targeted Retention of Communications Metadata: Future-proofing The Fight Against Serious Crime in Europe?' (2023) 8 European Papers 713, 722.
[83] *La Quadrature du Net 'I'* (n 19) para 166.
[84] ibid para 166.
[85] French expression for 'who can do more, can do less'.
[86] *Garda Síochána* (n 47) paras 96–100.

As the Belgian legislation provided for general and indiscriminate data retention, for both identification data and traffic and location data, its approach was flawed from the very start, a flaw that could not be corrected by imposing stricter conditions for the access to the data, despite the arguments put forward by the Belgian government.[87] In more recent case law, the CJEU has explicitly confirmed this.[88]

Meanwhile, the procedural requirement of a *prior review by a court or an independent administrative body* has also been further elaborated on by the CJEU. In *Prokuratuur*, the Court specified that to qualify as an independent administrative body, 'that authority must be a third party in relation to the authority which requests access to the data, in order that the former is able to carry out the review objectively and impartially and free from any external influence'.[89] More in particular, that authority 'must not be involved in the conduct of the criminal investigation in question' and have 'a neutral stance vis-à-vis the parties to the criminal proceedings'.[90] This is not the case for 'a public prosecutor's office which directs the investigation procedure and, where appropriate, brings the public prosecution'.[91] Even if the public prosecutor has the duty to verify both incriminating and exculpatory evidence and to guarantee the lawfulness of the pre-trial procedure, he/she cannot be regarded as a third party to the proceedings.[92] *A fortiori*, as the Court ruled in *Garda Síochána*, a police officer does not meet this requirement of independence and impartiality.[93]

In Belgian law, this requirement in principle does not appear problematic as the public prosecutor can only access identification data on the basis of Article 46*bis* CCP. Solely an investigating judge can order access to location and traffic data. There are, however, some exceptions. For instance, in cases of emergency or *flagrant délit* (ie when the author of certain serious offences is caught in the act), the public prosecutor can access location and traffic data. For certain offences, the investigating judge is to sanction this decision within 24 hours after the order by the public prosecutor; for others, this confirmation is not required.[94] One may question whether these exceptional powers for the public prosecutor are in line with the CJEU's case law.[95] In this respect, it is worth pointing out that the CJEU has recently confirmed that 'it is essential that the access ... to the retained data be subject, *except in cases of duly justified urgency*, to a prior review'.[96] In other words, in case of urgency, such review can be omitted. Elsewhere, the Court ruled that the review by a court or an independent administrative authority 'must take place within a short time' in 'cases of duly justified urgency'.[97] One may thus conclude that these exceptional powers, which continue to exist in the 2022 Act, are in conformity with the requirements of the CJEU.

---

[87] Constitutional Court, Case No 96/2018, 19 July 2018, paras A.10.5 and A.15. See Verbruggen, Royer, and Severijns, 'Reconsidering the blanket-data-retention-taboo' (n 13) para 3.

[88] CJEU, Judgment of 2 March 2021, *Prokuratuur* (C-746/18) ECLI:EU:C:2021:152 para 35; *Bolzano* (n 52) para 36 ('other factors relating to the proportionality of a request for access, such as the length of the period in respect of which access to such data is sought, cannot have the effect that the objective of preventing, investigating, detecting and prosecuting criminal offences in general is capable of justifying such access').

[89] *Prokuratuur*, ibid para 54.

[90] ibid para 54.

[91] ibid para 55.

[92] ibid para 56.

[93] *Garda Síochána* (n 47) paras 111–114.

[94] CCP, Art 88*bis*, §1, paras 6–8.

[95] For further analysis, see Flumian and Franssen, 'Le nouveau cadre légal en matière de conservation des données électroniques' (n 23) 346–47, 352.

[96] *Bolzano* (n 52) para 43 (emphasis added).

[97] *Prokuratuur* (n 88) para 51.

Finally, as indicated (section 2.2.3), the CJEU also emphasised in *Bolzano* that the requirement of the seriousness of the offence must be tested *in concreto*,[98] making the role of the court or independent administrative body ever more important. Indeed, the latter must be entitled to exclude access to traffic and location data if the offence in the case at hand does 'manifestly' not constitute serious crime.[99]

2.2.6 New 'game' opportunities created by the CJEU: National security and IP addresses of the source of the connection

So far, the impression may be the CJEU mainly confirmed its earlier case law in *La Quadrature du Net 'I'*. It did however more than that.

One novelty in the ruling is that the CJEU decided to accept general and indiscriminate retention of traffic and location data for the purpose of safeguarding *national security*, provided that strict procedural conditions are met.[100] A more detailed analysis of these criteria is however beyond the scope of this chapter, which focuses on data retention for the purpose of fighting crime.

Another novelty introduced by *La Quadrature du Net 'I'*, which is more important for this contribution, is the exception created for (certain) *IP addresses*, notwithstanding they are regarded as traffic data under EU law. The CJEU indeed considers that Article 15(1) of the ePrivacy Directive, read in the light of the Charter, 'does not preclude legislative measures that ... provide, for the purposes of safeguarding national security, combating serious crime and preventing serious threats to public security, for the general and indiscriminate retention of *IP addresses assigned to the source of an Internet connection* for a period that is limited in time to what is strictly necessary'.[101] Even if those addresses are traffic data, they are 'less sensitive than other traffic data' because 'they are *generated independently of any particular communication and mainly serve to identify*, through providers of electronic communications services, the natural person who owns the terminal equipment from which an Internet communication is made'.[102] The Court also considered that, 'where an offence is committed online, the IP address might be the only means of investigation enabling the person to whom that address was assigned at the time of the commission of the offence to be identified'.[103] Therefore, the CJEU concluded that the general and indiscriminate retention of this type of IP address can be justified in light of the proportionality principle to fight serious crime, provided that they are used neither to track a user's online activity nor to produce a detailed profile of that person.[104]

Despite this new possibility, the 2016 Data Retention Act remained problematic because IP addresses needed for the purpose of identification were treated as identification data, which service providers were obliged to retain regardless of the seriousness of the offence.

Mostly recently, in *La Quadrature du Net 'II'*, the CJEU however seems to have taken a *significant step back* on the requirements regarding the retention of IP addresses put

---

[98] *Bolzano* (n 52) para 60.
[99] *Bolzano*, ibid para 62.
[100] For further analysis, see eg Flumian and Franssen, 'Le nouveau cadre légal en matière de conservation des données électroniques' (n 23) 324–25 and 328; Van de Heyning, 'Het moeilijke evenwicht tussen privacy & veiligheid' (n 31) 141–42.
[101] *La Quadrature du Net 'I'* (n 19) para 168, emphasis added.
[102] ibid para 152, emphasis added.
[103] ibid para 154. See also para 152.
[104] ibid paras 153 and 156.

forward in *La Quadrature du Net 'I'*. The potential impact of this new case law on Belgian law will be analysed in more detail when evaluating the 2022 Data Retention Act (see section 4.2).

3. The National Impact of *La Quadrature du Net 'I'*: A Hard Ball to Catch

3.1 The inevitable strike home of the Constitutional Court

With its ruling in *La Quadrature du Net 'I'*, the CJEU did not offer much leeway to the Belgian Constitutional Court, all the more since the former also replied negatively to the latter's last prejudicial question concerning the possibility to 'maintain on a temporary basis the effects of [the 2016 Data Retention Act] in order to avoid legal uncertainty and to enable the data previously collected and retained to continue to be used for the objectives pursued by the law'.[105] Unlike the French *Conseil d'État*,[106] the Belgian Constitutional Court had already shown in the past that it faithfully follows the case law of the CJEU (see section 1).

Consequently, the inevitable happened: the 2016 Data Retention Act was annulled in April 2021,[107] creating considerable uncertainty as to whether the retained data that had already been collected by law enforcement authorities in ongoing criminal investigations could still be used as evidence in court. The Constitutional Court however opened a backdoor by reminding trial courts that they retain the power to rule on the admissibility of the evidence collected under the annulled Act.[108] In Belgian law, the rules on admissibility of illegally obtained evidence are laid down in Article 32 of the Preliminary Title to the CCP. The question is whether these rules meet the requirements set out by the CJEU at the end of the *La Quadrature du Net 'I'* judgment. In the absence of EU legislation on the admissibility of evidence,[109] the CJEU indeed put forward several requirements, drawn from earlier case law (though unrelated to the criminal law field).[110] Briefly summarised, national courts are to exclude the retained data obtained contrary to EU law in criminal proceedings where

---

[105] ibid paras 79 and 213–220.
[106] French Conseil d'État, Case 393099, 21 April 2021, available at <https://www.legifrance.gouv.fr/ceta/id/CETATEXT000043411127> accessed 15 July 2024. For a critical analysis, see T Christakis, 'French Council of State Discovers the "Philosopher's Stone" of Data Retention', *about:intel*, 23 April 2021, available at <https://aboutintel.eu/france-council-of-state-ruling/> accessed 15 July 2024. For a more in-depth analysis, see the Chapter 11 by M Lassalle in this volume.
[107] Constitutional Court, Case No 57/2021, 22 April 2021. For an analysis of this judgment, see M Giacometti and A Rizzo, 'La Cour constitutionnelle a-t-elle sonné le glas de la conservation des données de communications en vue de leur utilisation dans le cadre des procédures pénales ?' (2021) 9–10 *Revue de droit pénal et de criminologie* 934.
[108] Constitutional Court, Case No 57/2021, 22 April 2021, para B.24.3.
[109] Many academics have already emphasised the need to adopt EU rules on the admissibility of evidence, which is possible on the basis of Article 82(2), para 2, a) TFEU. See eg E Sellier and A Weyembergh, *Criminal Procedural Laws Across the European Union—A Comparative Analysis of Selected Main Differences and the Impact They Have Over the Development of EU Legislation*, Study commissioned by the LIBE Committee of the European Parliament (2018) 63–55 available at < https://www.europarl.europa.eu/meetdocs/2014_2019/plmrep/COMMITTEES/LIBE/DV/2018/10-10/IPOL_STU2018604977_EN.pdf> accessed 15 July 2024; K Ligeti, B Garamvölgyi, A Ondrejová, and M von Galen, 'Admissibility of Evidence in Criminal Proceedings in the EU' (2020) 3 *Eucrim* 201; European Law Institute (ELI), Proposal for a Directive of the European Parliament and the Council on Mutual Admissibility of Evidence and Electronic Evidence in Criminal Proceedings (Vienna, ELI, 2023).
[110] *La Quadrature du Net 'I'* (n 19) paras 221–228.

(1) the suspects are 'not in a position to comment effectively on [that] evidence', (2) the evidence pertains 'to a field of which the judges have no knowledge', and (3) it is 'likely to have a preponderant influence on the findings of fact'.[111] Yet, the precise extent of these requirements (eg which fields judges have no knowledge of?) still requires further clarification.[112]

3.2 Belgian authorities playing extra time?

After the annulment of the 2016 Data Retention Act, Belgian judicial authorities faced two major problems. First, what to do with data that is retained in violation of EU law and has already been used in ongoing criminal cases? Second, is it still possible to require the production of traffic and location data based on the legal provisions in the CCP?

As suggested by the Constitutional Court, the first question could be tackled with the rules on admissibility of evidence, which in essence lead to nullity only in three scenarios: (1) when the evidence has been collected in violation of a formal legal requirement whose non-respect is sanctioned with nullity; (2) when the illegality undermines the reliability of the evidence; or (3) when the use of the illegal evidence is contrary to the right to a fair trial. The first scenario is rather exceptional as few national requirements are sanctioned this way today and no EU rule is. The other two hypotheses of nullity are not applied frequently either due to a restrictive interpretation by the Belgian *Cour de cassation* (Supreme Court).[113] Consequently, it is unlikely that retained data to which access has been granted before the annulment of the 2016 Act (or even before the publication of the Constitutional Court's judgment in the Official Journal) will be excluded by the courts. So far, the Supreme Court has ruled on this issue in four cases, and each time concluded that the evidence is admissible.[114] This way, Belgian judicial authorities were able to save ongoing investigations.

The second question, regarding future data collection, was more challenging. While the problems for identification data under the 2016 Act were confined to IP addresses as they were all treated alike, without distinguishing the less sensitive ones from the more sensitive ones, and without limiting their retention to the fight against serious crime,[115] the problems for traffic and location data were sizeable. Indeed, after the annulment, judicial authorities could only require the production of (past) traffic and location data to the extent that the

---

[111] *Prokuratuur* (n 88) para 44.

[112] A more in-depth analysis of these requirements would call for a separate contribution. See S Careel and F Verbruggen, 'Digital Evidence in Criminal Matters: Belgian Pride and Prejudice' in V Franssen and S Tosza (eds), *The Cambridge Handbook of Digital Evidence in Criminal Investigations* (CUP 2025) 224-6; Verbruggen, Collage, and Huysmans (n 27), 'België ziet Europese sterren' 192–93, para 62; C Van de Heyning, 'Het gebruik van communicatiegegevens bewaard op basis van de vernietigde dataretentiewet: Cassatie schijnt zijn licht', case comment under Cass. 25 January 2022 (2022) *Tijdschrift voor Strafrecht* 162; F Dumortier and C Forget, 'La fin de l'obligation de conservation systématique et indifférenciée des "métadonnées" contrecarrée par des exceptions de principe', case comment under CJEU 6 October 2020 (2021) *Journal des Tribunaux* 867–68, E Maes and M Panzavolta, 'Op zoek naar normatief principe voor uitsluiting van onrechtmatig bewijs in tijdperk van 'mass data gathering'', *Juristenkrant*, 24 February 2021, No 424, 16 ; E Maes and S Careel, 'Toegang tot bewaarde telecomdata en het gebruik ervan in strafzaken : sust Antigoon de gemoederen ?', *Juristenkrant*, 7 April 2021, No 427, 6 ; P Tersago, 'Dataretentiewet opnieuw vernietigd. Wat zijn de gevolgen voor het bewijs in strafzaken ?', case comment under Constitutional Court 22 April 2021 (2021) *Revue de droit judiciaire et de la preuve/Tijdschrift voor Procesrecht en Bewijsrecht* 171–74.

[113] For a succinct analysis, see eg Tersago, 'Dataretentiewet opnieuw vernietigd' (n 112) 169–71.

[114] Cass., 11 January 2022, No. P.21.1245.N; Cass., 25 January 2022, No. P.21.1353.N, *T. Strafr.*, 2022, No. 3, p. 160, case comment C Van de Heyning; Cass., 29 March 2022, No. P.21.1422.N; Cass., 29 March 2022, No. P.22.0078.N.

[115] Constitutional Court, Case No. 57/2021, 22 April 2021, paras B.17–B.18.

data is kept by service providers for commercial or technical reasons, as they are allowed to do by Article 5(2) of the ePrivacy Directive, and only with prior authorisation of a judge, excluding the powers given to the public prosecutor's office in certain cases. This explains why the adoption of new data retention legislation was urgently needed.

4. Third Attempt: Playing Ball in the CJEU's Courtyard

4.1 Main features of Belgium's new data retention regime

The Belgian Minister of Justice started preparing a new legal framework for data retention shortly after the annulment of the 2016 Data Retention Act.[116] A thoroughly prepared[117] bill was introduced in Parliament on 17 March 2022.[118] It proposed to amend the ECA creating a new data retention regime with diversification based on the nature of the data, the purpose and the duration of retention. Notwithstanding critique from privacy experts[119] and the Belgian Data Protection Authority[120] (for more details, see section 4.2), the 2022 Data Retention Act was adopted and published in the Official Journal in August 2022.

In the first place, the new law reaffirms the general retention of *identification data* for the purpose of fighting crime and protecting the public order and national security as both the CJEU and the Constitutional Court had approved such data retention regime. Contrary to the old law, the types of identification data are now listed in the law itself[121] and the previous list was extended to seventeen categories of data, which comprise the personal data of the user such as name, address, telephone number, and email address, as well as information on the subscription and activation of the service, and data regarding the means and reference of payment.[122] Like under the 2016 Act, those data must be retained for a period of 12 months after the end of the use of the service provided.[123]

New is that the *IP address of the origin of the communication* is also expressly considered identification data and thus retained on a general basis to fight (any) crime. That entails the

---

[116] This contribution only focuses on the rules in the new Belgian legislation applicable to the retention of identification and communication data for the fight against crime, protection of public order and national security. In addition, the legislation also provides for a framework of retention for emergency services, to ensure security and functioning of electronic communications services and to avoid and tackle abuse of those services.

[117] For more details on the preparation of this bill and the various actors consulted, see Flumian and Franssen, 'Le nouveau cadre légal en matière de conservation des données électroniques' (n 23) 332–33.

[118] Bill on the collection and retention of identification data and metadata in the electronic communications sector and their provision to authorities, *Doc. parl.*, Ch. représ., sess. 2021-2022, No. 55-2572/001.

[119] C Berthélémy, 'New Belgian data retention law: a European blueprint?', *EDRi*, 17 November 2021, available at <https://edri.org/our-work/new-belgian-data-retention-law-a-european-blueprint/> accessed 15 July 2024; L Klingert, 'Moving Towards Mass Surveillance? Belgian Parliament Approves Data Retention Law' *The Brussels Times*, 8 July 2022, available at <https://www.brusselstimes.com/251735/moving-towards-mass-surveillance-belgian-approves-data-retention-law> accessed 15 July 2024.

[120] Data protection authority, Opinion No 108/2021 of 28 June 2021 on a preliminary draft law on the collection and retention of identification, traffic, and location data in the electronic communications sector and access to them by the authorities and on a draft royal decree amending the Royal Decree of 19 September 2013 implementing Article 126 of the Act of 13 June 2005 on electronic communications (CO-A-2021-099), *Doc. parl.*, Ch. représ., sess. 2021-2022, No. 55-2572/001, 720 and 777.

[121] Under the old regime, the types of data were listed in a Royal Decree, which was considered problematic by the Constitutional Court in another judgment on the requirement to identify the users of prepaid cellphone cards. Constitutional Court, Case No. 158/2021, 18 November 2021. See Flumian and Franssen, 'Le nouveau cadre légal en matière de conservation des données électroniques' (n 23) 334.

[122] ECA, Art 126, § 1, 1°–17°.

[123] ibid § 2, para 1.

IP address that served for subscription or activation of the service and the source port of the connection and the timestamp,[124] as well as the IP address at the source of the connection, the timestamp of assignment, and, in the case of shared use of an IP address of the end user, the ports assigned to the latter.[125] Those IP addresses may be kept for a period of 12 months after the end of the session.[126]

In the second place, the 2022 Act introduces a new complex regime of data retention regarding *traffic and location data*, now referred to as 'metadata' in the ECA.[127] Article 126/2, § 1 ECA defines 'communication' as 'information exchanged or transmitted between a finite number of parties by means of a publicly available electronic communications service'. According to Article 126/2, § 2 ECA, ten types of metadata should be retained, which largely correspond to the traffic and location data that had to be retained under the 2016 Act.[128] That list of data includes:

- the description and technical characteristics of the electronic communications service that was used during the communication, including all numbers to which the call is routed in case of call forwarding or call transfer;
- the IP address of the addressee and the timestamp of assignment;
- the date and exact time of the start and end of the session of the service in question;
- the date and exact time of the start and end of the call the data allowing the identification and localisation of the cells or other network connection points of the mobile network, which were used for the communication, from the start to the end of the communication;
- the exact dates and times of these different locations, the volume of data uploaded and downloaded during the duration of the session;
- as far as mobile electronic communications services are concerned, the date and time of connection and end thereof between the device and the network, as well as the location of the terminal equipment and the date and time of this location whenever the operator wants to know which terminal equipment is connected to its network;
- and, interestingly, any other data regarding the addressee of the communication that would be available in the future thanks to technological developments.[129]

New is that the retention of metadata is no longer a general obligation applicable to all users of electronic communications on the entire Belgian territory, but based on a set of *geographical criteria*, as suggested by the CJEU. First, metadata must be retained when generated in a high-crime zone, namely judicial districts or police zones where per 1,000 inhabitants at least three serious offences have occurred per year in the last three years.[130] An offence is considered serious if listed in Article 90*ter*, §§ 2 and 4 of the CCP (ie the 'wiretap'

---

[124] ibid § 1, 4°.
[125] ibid § 1, 15°.
[126] ibid § 2, para 2.
[127] ECA, Art 2, 93°. This terminological change was made to anticipate the adoption of the ePrivacy Regulation; the Belgian definition is even a literal translation of Article 4(2), (c) of the Commission's Proposal for a Regulation. Unfortunately, this change was not made in the CCP. See Flumian and Franssen, 'Le nouveau cadre légal en matière de conservation des données électroniques' (n 23) 333–34 and 346.
[128] Like identification data, metadata are now listed in the Act itself.
[129] For more details on this last open-defined type of data and the applicable procedure, see Flumian and Franssen, 'Le nouveau cadre légal en matière de conservation des données électroniques' (n 23) 336.
[130] ECA, Art 126/3 § 1.

provision; see section 2.1). In the aforementioned zones the compulsory period of retention varies depending on the prevalence rate of serious crime. It is six months in case of three to four serious crimes per 1,000 inhabitants per year, nine months in case of five or six serious crimes per 1,000 inhabitants, and 12 months in case of seven or more serious crimes per 1,000 inhabitants per year. Second, metadata must also be retained in a list of 13 areas that are particularly exposed to threats against national security or the commission of serious crime (eg harbours and airports),[131] eight zones where there is a potential serious threat to the vital interests of the country or the essential needs of the population (eg parliament),[132] and six zones where there is a potentially serious threat to the interests of international institutions established in the national territory (eg NATO premises).[133] Meanwhile, the Executive has further determined the perimeter of these zones of retention.[134]

Furthermore, it is important to point out that the *personal scope of application* of the data retention regime has also changed due to another Act, namely the Act of 21 December 2021 implementing the European Electronic Communications Code.[135] That Act redefined the term 'operator'. As a result, whereas before, the data retention obligation was essentially limited to operators of networks established in Belgium, today all operators of electronic communications services are under an obligation to retain identification data and metadata, including so-called 'Over-The-Top' providers.[136] To counterbalance this extension, Article 126/1, § 1, para 2 ECA as amended by the 2022 Data Retention Act states that only data 'generated or processed' by the service provider in the course of the service should be retained. Thus, the 2022 Act does not impose on service providers to retain data they would normally not require from their users or process.[137] This limitation is important in light of the principle of data minimisation.[138]

In addition to rules regarding the retention of these data, the CCP settles which authority can *access* the retained data on which conditions and the period of access. Interestingly, the conditions on access for judicial authorities have not substantially changed[139] compared to the 2016 Data Retention Act, which was already based on a gradual (ie proportionate) approach depending on the seriousness of the offence under investigation (see section 2.1). While those rules were not scrutinised by the CJEU in *La Quadrature du Net 'I'*,[140] at least one aspect of those rules seems problematic in light of the subsequent case law of the Court: the power of the public prosecutor to require the production of metadata in case of harassment by means of an electronic communications service.[141] As the CJEU ruled in *Prokuratuur*, a public prosecutor is not sufficiently independent and impartial to

---

[131] ibid § 3.
[132] ibid § 4.
[133] ibid § 5.
[134] Ministerial Decree of 30 March 2023 implementing Article 126/3, § 1, of the Act of 13 June 2005 on electronic communications with a view to establishing the list of judicial districts and police zones subject to the data retention obligation, together with the retention period, *Moniteur belge*, 4 April 2023 (Ministerial Decree of 30 March 2023).
[135] Act of 21 December 2021 implementing the European Electronic Communications Code and amending various legal provisions relating to electronic communications, *Moniteur belge*, 31 December 2021.
[136] Careel and Verbruggen, 'Digital Evidence in Criminal Matters: Belgian Pride and Prejudice' (n 112) 224.
[137] For further details, see Flumian and Franssen, 'Le nouveau cadre légal en matière de conservation des données électroniques' (n 23) 337–38.
[138] GDPR, Art. 5(1)(c).
[139] For an analysis of some punctual changes, see Flumian and Franssen, 'Le nouveau cadre légal en matière de conservation des données électroniques' (n 23) 344–47.
[140] Indeed, none of the three questions of the Constitutional Court concerned the rules on *access* to retained data.
[141] CCP, Art 88*bis*, § 1, para 9.

authorise such access (see section 2.2.5). Unfortunately, that power of the public prosecutor remains intact under the 2022 Act and might cause problems in the future.[142] In contrast, as explained (section 2.2.5), the power of the public prosecutor to require the production of metadata in case of emergency[143] seems to meet the CJEU's requirements.

The new law also intends to provide more *transparency* on the *use* of these retained data. Therefore, the Belgian Institute for Postal Services and Telecommunications shall send annual statistics to the Minister of Justice on the production of retained data to the judicial authorities and the intelligence services.[144] These statistics are also transmitted to parliament so that it can monitor the application of data retention legislation. Such statistics shall include: (1) the cases in which retained data has been produced to the competent authorities, (2) the time elapsed between the date on which the data is retained and the date on which the competent authorities requested its production, and (3) the cases in which requests for retained data could not be granted.

Finally, it is worthwhile to mention that the 2022 Act provides that the use of *encryption* by an operator should not prevent the execution of a targeted request by a competent authority for the purpose of end-user identification, detection, and localisation of the communication.[145] Whereas the Act reaffirms that the use of encryption is free, it nevertheless requires operators to design the applied encryption in such a manner that they would still be capable of complying with production orders for subscriber and traffic data issued by judicial authorities.[146]

4.2 A new pitch to the Constitutional Court and the CJEU: Meatball or curveball?

With the 2022 Act the Belgian legislator once again hoped to walk the tightrope between the protection of personal data and privacy on the one hand, and data retention for protecting national security and fighting crime on the other. But did he succeed in striking the right balance? This question will soon have to be answered by the Constitutional Court, where no less than five requests for annulment are currently pending[147]—unless the Court would prefer to call upon the CJEU's help (again). In this section, we will make a first attempt to assess the 2022 Data Retention Act in light of the CJEU's case law.

The following Table 16.1 summarises how the requirements of the CJEU presented in section 2.2. have been translated into Belgian law.

---

[142] See also F Dumortier and C Forget, 'La loi du 20 juillet 2022 ou l'art de dissimuler l'obligation de conservation systématique et indifférenciée des métadonnées', *Journal des Tribunaux*, 2023, p 421, paras 36–37.
[143] CCP, Art 88*bis*, § 1, paras 6–8.
[144] ECA, Art 127/1, § 7.
[145] ECA, Art 107, § 3.
[146] B Flumian and V Franssen, 'Le nouveau cadre légal en matière de conservation des données électroniques' (n 23) 348–49.
[147] Constitutional Court, Cases No 7907, 7929, 7930, 7931 and 7932, available at <https://www.const-court.be/fr/judgments/pending-cases>. The Court ruled on these cases in September 2024, after the drafting of this chapter was concluded. In its nearly 200-page judgment, the Court basically approved the Belgian law, including on certain points where, in our view, further clarification by the CJEU would have been desirable. At the same time, the Court also referred a few preliminary questions to the CJEU, though only concerning the data retention rules for operators to prevent fraud and malicious use on their networks as well as harassment of end users. Constitutional Court, Case No. 97/2024, 26 September 2024.

Table 16.1 Comparison CJEU case with the 2022 Act

Data category	CJEU case law	Belgian law
Identification data	General retention for fighting crime in general, even without a specific time limit	General retention of identification data for fighting crime in general, for 12 months, exceptionally 6 months (Art 126, § 2 ECA)
	Access limited in time, for the purpose of fighting crime in general	Access limited to 6 or 12 months, depending on the seriousness of the offence (Art 127/1, § 3, para. 2 ECA and Art 46*bis*, § 1, last para. CCP)
IP addresses of source of the connection	General retention for fighting serious crime or safeguarding national security	General retention of IP addresses of the source of the connection for 12 months for fighting crime in general (Art 126, § 1, 15° and 127/1, § 2, 6° and 8° ECA)
	Access limited in time and only for the purpose for which the data is retained	Access limited to 6 or 12 months, depending on the seriousness of the offence, including crime that is not serious (Art 127/1, § 3, para. 2 ECA and Art 46*bis*, § 1 CCP)
		But if the IP addresses would allow to track the internet user's clickstream access limited to fighting serious crime or safeguarding national security (Art 127/1, § 3, para. 4 ECA)
Traffic and location data	General retention only in case of serious and imminent threat to national security	General retention of metadata only if the Coordination Organ identifies a serious threat to the entire territory of Belgium (Art 126/3, § 3 ECA)
	Targeted retention only for fighting serious crime, limited in time, based on objective and non-discriminatory criteria	Retention of metadata only for fighting serious crime listed in Article 90*ter*, §§ 2 and 4 CCP, for 6, 9 or 12 months, based on geographical criteria (Art. 126/3 ECA): - high-crime zones - zones particularly exposed to threats against national security or for the commission of serious crime - zones of vital interest to the country - zones of interest to international institutions established in the territory
	Access limited in time and only for the purpose for which the data is retained, and, except for urgency, with prior authorisation of a court or an independent administrative authority	Access differentiated in time (6–9–12 months) depending on the seriousness of the offence (Art 88*bis*, § 2 CCP, defining serious crime as offences punishable with at least one year of imprisonment), ordered by the investigating judge, but exceptions for the public prosecutor (Art. 88*bis*, § 1, paras 6–9 CCP)

Globally speaking, Belgian legislation now appears to be in line with the case law of the CJEU. Yet, upon a closer look, several problems come to the fore.

First of all, one could question whether the new legislation corresponds to the underlying *ratio* of the CJEU's case law, that is, limiting the protection of personal data and privacy to fight crime and protect the national security only in as far as necessary. As stressed by the CJEU (and the Constitutional Court) on several occasions, data retention should be the exception, not the rule.[148] But is this really true under the 2022 Act?

Second, it can be questioned whether the retention of IP addresses of the source of the connection goes beyond the limitations imposed by the CJEU, as they are retained for any type of crime (not just serious crime) and their regime applies to related traffic data (such as the timestamp of assignment). The case law of the CJEU is, however, not coherent in this regard and therefore makes it hard to assess how the Court would rule on the Belgian framework.

The Belgian legislator relied on *La Quadrature du Net 'I'* to impose a general retention of IP addresses of the origin of the communication for a period of 12 months with a diversified period of access by law enforcement to identification data, namely access for six months prior to the warrant for fighting crimes punishable with a prison sentence below one year[149] and protecting the public order, and access of 12 months prior to the warrant for fighting more serious offences punishable with a prison sentence of one year or more, addressing serious threats to the public order and protecting national security[150]. However, in *La Quadrature du Net 'I'* and *SpaceNet*,[151] the CJEU restricted the retention of such data to fighting serious crime, protecting national security and the public order against serious threats. This appeared at odds with the 2022 Act because the latter allows for the retention of IP addresses for all offences. The new Act only makes a distinction based on the seriousness of the offence at the level of the access to the retained data (six versus 12 months, depending on whether the term of imprisonment is below one year or not). In addition, to meet the critical comments of the legislative branch of the Belgian *Conseil d'État*[152] and the Belgian Data Protection Authority, the legislator added that such IP addresses cannot be accessed by judicial authorities if they would allow to track a person's online activities, unless such access would be requested for the purposes of safeguarding national security, fighting serious crime, preventing serious threats to public security, or protecting the vital interests of a person.[153] Nevertheless, this limitation of access appeared insufficient to pass the CJEU's test given the objective of retention (ie fighting crime in general).

Yet, in the more recent case *La Quadrature du Net 'II'*, the CJEU has mitigated its former requirements in a notable way. In this case, the Court indeed argued that 'the general and indiscriminate retention of a set – *even a vast set* – *of static and dynamic IP addresses* used by a person in a given period *does not necessarily constitute, in every case, a serious interference* with the fundamental rights guaranteed by Articles 7, 8 and 11 of the Charter'.[154] Therefore, 'the general and indiscriminate retention of IP addresses may, as the case may

---

[148] *La Quadrature du Net 'I'* (n 19) para 111; *La Quadrature du Net 'II'* (n 69) para 66.
[149] To be more precise, reference is made to the concrete prison sentence that the offence would warrant ('*Pour des infractions qui ne sont pas de nature à entraîner un emprisonnement correctionnel principal d'un an ou une peine plus lourde*'), not to the legal minimum or maximum term of the imprisonment.
[150] CCP, Art 46*bis*.
[151] CJEU, Judgment of 27 October 2022, *SpaceNet* (C-793/19 and C-794/19) ECLI:EU:C:2022:702 paras 97–101.
[152] The legislative branch of the Belgian *Conseil d'État* (Council of State) reviews draft bills on their legality and quality. Its opinions are non-binding but highly authoritative. The competences of the *Conseil d'État* are regulated in the Acts on the Council of State of 12 January 1973, *Moniteur belge*, 21 March 1973.
[153] ECA, Art 127/1, § 3, para 4. Flumian and Franssen, 'Le nouveau cadre légal en matière de conservation des données électroniques' (n 23) 335.
[154] *La Quadrature du Net 'II'* (n 69) para 79 (emphasis added).

be, be justified by the objective of *combating criminal offences in general* where it is genuinely ruled out that that retention could give rise to serious interferences with the private life of the person concerned due to the possibility of drawing precise conclusions about that person by, inter alia, linking those IP addresses with a set of traffic or location data which have also been retained by those providers'.[155] As a consequence, if national law imposes a system of retention that guarantees a 'watertight separation' of the different categories of data retained,[156] in particular separating IP addresses (and data relating to civil identity) from other traffic and location data, such retention would be acceptable in a general and indiscriminate manner even for offences that are not serious[157] (in the case at hand, the data was retained for identifying offenders of copyright infringements). One could argue that the CJEU further fine-tuned its previous case law by providing an exemption to its previous principle that IP addresses may be retained for fighting serious crime only, namely in so far as there is a strict separation between the categories of retained data.[158] However, given the decisive wording of the Court in the previous case law on the appreciation of the retention of IP addresses as a serious interference with private life, it appears that the CJEU is simply taking a step back[159] enabling undifferentiated retention of (all) IP addresses (not just those of the source of the connection) for fighting crime.[160]

In view of this more recent case law, the 2022 Act generally appears in line with the CJEU's requirements. Still, Belgian law would have to be complemented with a requirement of a watertight separation of IP addresses from other data and it should provide for 'regular review by a public authority other than that which seeks to obtain access to the personal data retained by the providers of electronic communications services'.[161]

Third, with respect to traffic and location data, the 2022 Act raises several questions, in particular the geographical criteria used to target the retention of data and the definition of serious crime.

The latter is indeed defined in different ways. At the level of retention, the notion of serious crime corresponds to the 'wiretap list' of offences.[162] This long list of offences is not based on an express term of imprisonment (or another objective criterion) and has been extended on several occasions, whenever the legislator deemed so necessary.[163] At the level of access, the law puts forward two different (but largely overlapping) definitions of serious crime, an explicit one[164] and an implicit one,[165] which are broader than the definition

---

[155] ibid para 82 (emphasis added).
[156] ibid para 84.
[157] ibid para 85.
[158] This could be deduced from the CJEU's wording, namely that the retention of IP addresses 'not necessarily constitute' a serious infringement of private life, suggesting that in principle it does.
[159] See in particular *La Quadrature du Net 'II'* (n 69) para 77.
[160] It is worth noting that the CJEU went beyond what Advocate-General Szpunar had proposed. The latter's proposal consisted in widening the retention of IP addresses of the source of the connection to all 'online criminal offences' for which the IP address is 'the *only means* of investigation' to identify the offender—a proposal that raised new questions, especially in terms of delineating such online offences. CJEU, First Opinion of AG Szpunar of 27 October 2022, Case C-470/21, *La Quadrature du Net 'II'* (n 69) para 83 (original emphasis). See Robinson, 'Targeted Retention of Communications Metadata' (n 82) 732.
[161] *La Quadrature du Net 'II'* (n 69) para 89.
[162] ECA, Art 126/3, § 1.
[163] For a critical analysis, see Flumian and Franssen, 'Le nouveau cadre légal en matière de conservation des données électroniques' (n 23) 351–52. Cf Van Roy and Royer, 'De nieuwe dataretentiewetgeving: over oude ketels en nieuwe soep' (n 58) p 14, para 44.
[164] ECA, Art 127/1, § 1.
[165] CCP, Art 88*bis*, § 2.

of serious crime on which the retention is based. Indeed, access to retained traffic and location data is essentially[166] possible for offences punishable with at least one year of imprisonment.[167]

The existence of distinct definition of serious crime for the purposes of retention and access is not coherent. It will be for the CJEU to assess whether a threshold of one year of imprisonment, which refers to the concrete prison sentence that can be imposed[168] and thus enables access to retained metadata for the large majority of offences under Belgian law, is in conformity with its requirements as set out in *Bolzano* (see section 2.2.3.).

Next, we will focus on the criteria chosen by the Belgian legislator to target the retention of metadata as they are the most contentious aspect in the new data retention regime.

From the outset, the Belgian Data Protection Authority voiced a number of concerns in this respect. Indeed, in its opinion on a preliminary version of the bill, the Data Protection Authority questioned the lack of transparency on the practical impact of the newly proposed data retention rules.[169] There was no impact analysis of these rules, nor were any concrete numbers provided during the parliamentary process. Moreover, the Data Protection Authority took aim at the manner of calculating the ratio of three serious crimes per 1,000 citizens in a particular judicial district or police zone. The ratio would be based on the National General Database (NGD).[170] This database holds all the data of ongoing and past criminal complaints and records. It is searchable on police zone as well as on incrimination assigned to the case. As such, it is an easy tool to determine the ratio per police zone. Nevertheless, it can be argued that the NGD is not a self-evident objective standard for assessing the geographical crime risk.[171] First, police zones may apply differential standards when registering offences in this database, which may result in a different outcome as to risk assessment. For instance, in case of a group of persons involved in drug trafficking, one police zone may opt for the incrimination of drug dealing in an organisation, whereas another zone may prefer to register this criminal activity as two separate offences, namely drug dealing and membership of a criminal organisation. In the first scenario the criminal activity would result in just one registration in the NGD, whereas in the second this would lead to two registrations. In consequence, the manner of registration would have an impact on reaching the three to 1,000 threshold and, therefore, in turn on the retention of location and traffic data in a particular area. Moreover, the numbers in the NGD only indicate how many cases the police recorded, but not whether an actual crime occurred. For example, in case of a suspicious death, the police might register the case as manslaughter. The investigation could later show that, in fact, it was an accidental death. Finally, the Data Protection Authority warned that police officers may be inclined to initially qualify criminal facts as a serious offence, even though a judge may later on requalify (or 'relabel') the facts and opt for another incrimination that does not constitute serious

---

[166] In addition, Article 127/1, § 1 ECA includes certain economic offences (eg in the area of market abuse) which are punished with (high) criminal fines.
[167] CCP, Art 88*bis*, § 2.
[168] See n 149.
[169] Belgian Data Protection Authority, Opinion No. 108/2021, *Doc. parl.*, Ch. représ., sess. 2021-2022, No. 55-2572/001, 720 and 777.
[170] In French: *Banque de données Nationale Générale*.
[171] The Control Organ for Police Information stated that information in the NGD cannot be labelled *ab initio* as objective. Control Organ for Police Information, Opinion COC-DPA-A No. 007/2018, 23 October 2018, DA180007, available at <http://www.controleorgaan.be/files/DA180007-FR.pdf> accessed 15 July 2024.

crime, given that the three to 1,000 ratio is based on the initial legal qualification chosen by the police.[172] Therefore, the Data Protection Authority proposed to make the assessment on a database whose statistical data is based on qualitative principles defined by law. Moreover, it argued that the assessment should take into account the actual convictions by courts.[173]

In reaction to these concerns, the government implicitly conceded that the NGD might not be fully accurate, highlighting that it does not entail all criminal activities but only those that have come to the police's attention. Yet alternatively, if the calculus would be founded on the number of convictions, the analysis of occurrence of serious crime and, thus, data retention would be based on a situation in the past as it might take years before a case is tried definitively by a court.[174] Therefore, the NGD is currently the only objective tool available to Belgian authorities for such risk-based assessment of crime. Improving the quality of the data registered in the NGD and enhancing standardisation of police practices as to the choice of offence to label a criminal event should, however, be a priority.

Finally, the 2022 Act could be criticised for trying to maintain, in practice, general retention of location and traffic data for the purpose of fighting serious crime as it uses such lenient criteria for delineating geographical zones that the retention obligation in fact spans almost the entirety of Belgium.[175] Article 1 of the Ministerial Decree of 30 March 2023 provides that location and traffic data would still be retained in all judicial arrondissements of Belgium for 12 months, that is, the maximum period of retention, as was the case in the previously annulled legislation, except for the less populated regions of Eupen and Arlon. Yet even in these areas the data could still be retained for a period of nine months.[176] This outcome follows from the fact that the legislation uses a low minimum threshold for designating an area as a high-risk area (ie three (complaints of) serious offences per 1,000 citizens in that area), the lack of harmonised rules on how to qualify such offences in the NGD, as explained above, and the extended list of locations and facilities included in the law to justify retention of location and traffic data. The counterargument for this finding is that Belgium is a densely built and populated country in consequence of which most people live in the vicinity of one of the designated places for retention or in a high-crime area. It will be interesting to see how the CJEU will deal with these arguments and develop further guidance on the interpretation of 'targeted retention'.

5. Conclusion

After two earlier attempts struck down by the Courts, it is to be seen whether the Belgium's third attempt will result to be another failure.

---

[172] Belgian Data Protection Authority, Opinion No. 108/2021, para 123.
[173] ibid para 124.
[174] Bill on the collection and retention of identification data and metadata in the electronic communications sector and their provision to authorities, 68.
[175] See Robinson, 'Targeted Retention of Communications Metadata' (n 82) 735; Dumortier and Forget, 'La loi du 20 juillet 2022 ou l'art de dissimuler' (n 142) 410, paras 26 and 413, para 41.
[176] Ministerial Decree of 30 March 2023, Art 2. This outcome was already predicted by P Breyer, '"Targeted" Data Retention: Online map shows what the Belgian government wants to hide' (7 June 2022) available at <http://www.patrick-breyer.de/en/targeted-data-retention-online-map-shows-what-the-belgian-government-wants-to-hide/> accessed 15 July 2024.

First, under the 2022 Act, the retention of IP addresses of the source of the connection is required for all offences, without limitation to serious crime as the CJEU prescribed. Only the access conditions are related to the seriousness of the offence. Nevertheless, in light of the most recent case law of the CJEU, the 2022 Act will most likely pass this test as the Court no longer restricts retention of IP addresses to serious offences.

Second, the definition of serious crime raises several questions, even after the CJEU's clarifications in *Bolzano*. For one, the notion is defined in a different manner for retention and access purposes. For another, it spans a large number of offences, especially in the way it is determined at the level of access to retained data.

Third, the new regime of targeted retention of traffic and location data in practice covers (almost) the entire Belgian territory due to the chosen crime risk ratio. Moreover, the way in which the crime risk assessment is made raises concerns because the statistics of the NGD are based on how offences are registered by the police at the beginning of a case, and for instance not on how those offences are eventually labelled by a court if the case results in a conviction.

If the CJEU would be called to evaluate, once again, the Belgian data retention legislation,[177] the Belgian government will have to convince the CJEU that its approach complies with the proportionality principle. For sure, the Belgian legislator has made substantial efforts to take the CJEU's guidance at heart[178] by elaborating a very detailed legal framework based on geographical criteria[179] and differentiated access conditions, while keeping in mind the needs of law enforcement. In our view, if Belgium wants to have a chance at convincing the CJEU that such balance can be struck, the government will have to invest in building more accurate crime statistics and in enhancing transparency regarding the real impact of the data retention framework and the measures to limit the retention of metadata to what is strictly necessary.

The future will tell if the Belgian legislator has succeeded in marrying the CJEU's requirements with the needs of law enforcement. In the affirmative, the Belgian legal framework might very well become an example for other Member States that seek to design a meaningful targeted data retention regime.

---

[177] As indicated above (n 147), the Constitutional Court has referred new preliminary questions to the CJEU after this chapter was finalised, but it is unlikely these questions will be the end of the story.

[178] The new Belgian legislation is, for instance, much more limited in scope and more proportionate than the Russian law that recently resulted in a flagrant violation of Article 8 ECHR: *Podchasov v Russia* (App No 33696/19) 13 February 2024. For a first analysis, see S Royer, 'Europees Mensenrechtenhof principieel voor encryptie van communicatie', *Juristenkrant*, 6 March 2024, No 485, 1–2.

[179] According to some authors, the CJEU has opened the door to 'quasi' general data retention when it included strategic locations in its suggestions for targeted retention based on geographical criteria. See Van Roy and Royer, 'De nieuwe dataretentiewetgeving: over oude ketels en nieuwe soep' (n 58) p 15, para 48.

17
The Swedish Data Retention Saga
From EU Initiator to Penalty Payments, Reviewed and Revised National Rules

Maria Bergström

1. Introduction

In the words of the Swedish Government Official Report 2023:22 on data retention and access to electronic information, data retention is 'an obligation for providers of electronic communications networks and services, such as mobile operators, to retain electronic communications data'.[1] Data retention includes data about the communication but not the content itself. Data on communication includes who communicated with whom, when, and where they were when the communication took place. In Sweden, data retention for law enforcement purposes has existed since the 1990s, but today EU law plays a major role in legislation on data retention for law enforcement purposes.[2] In this context, it should be mentioned that this Government Official Report, like other forms of Swedish preparatory works, are central in the Swedish lawmaking process, and also have a strong position as sources of law in Sweden.[3]

After this brief introduction, the chapter provides a contextual and historical, but also dual European and national, analysis of the Swedish data retention saga evolving around a number of legal paradoxes. First, the Swedish support for data retention legislation on the EU level, and the extended Swedish implementation process (section 2); second, the penalty payments for non-implementation, and the adoption of Swedish implementing legislation (section 3); third, the annulment of the 2006 Data Retention Directive, and reviewed national legislation (section 4); fourth; the request for a preliminary ruling from the Stockholm Administrative Court of Appeal and the following continuous clarification by the Court of Justice of the European Union (CJEU) of the required safeguards for data retention to be lawful, and revised national legislation in the absence of a general EU legislative framework (section 5). The Swedish data retention saga provides a rich example of the interrelation between national and European law and the legal processes that led to legal changes both on national and European levels, including an analysis of data retention, but with focus more on lawmaking and judicial processes rather than data retention as such

---

[1] Swedish Government Official Reports, SOU 2023:22 *Datalagring och åtkomst till elektronisk information*, at p 31.
[2] SOU 2023:22, at p 32.
[3] See eg P H Lindblom, '1. Inledning: Rätt och rättstillämpning', in Claes Sandgren. *Norstedts juridiska handbok* (17th edn, Norstedts Juridik AB, 2001).

and in detail: in other words, multilevel governance, judicial dialogue, and dynamic EU lawmaking.[4]

In modern lawmaking, there are a number of different and often contrasting interests at stake, and the final legislative act needs to carefully balance these interests. For example, as has been mentioned concerning the drafting of the e-evidence legislative package, that legislative process included an extensive stakeholder and expert consultation process. The proposals by the Commission thereby tried to strike an 'extremely delicate balance between effective and efficient criminal investigations (for police and judicial authorities), legal certainty (for technology companies) and fundamental rights protection (of suspects and other users).'[5] The interests at stake in this example closely resemble the interests at stake when regulating data retention, where it can be assumed that high-quality legislation carefully balances effective and efficient criminal investigations, legal certainty, and fundamental rights protection. With the help of these interests at stake as a starting point, this chapter thereby aims to answer the research question: did the various political and legal avenues in EU lawmaking help develop legally acceptable requirements for data retention in the European Union? In order to do so, the following derived questions aims to be answered in the individual sections: did the: (1) extended implementation process; (2) penalty payments; (3) annulment of the Data Retention Directive; and (4) preliminary references improve the quality of the data retention legislation in the Union and in Sweden, in respect of effective and efficient criminal investigations, legal certainty, and fundamental rights protection?

In answering these questions, and contributing to this volume's second part on adaptations of policy and amendments to legislation in Sweden, this chapter is providing some insights into the traditions of the Swedish legal system in general, and the quality of data retention regulation in particular.

2. The Swedish Support for EU Data Retention Rules, Swedish Parliamentary Control, and the Extended Implementation Process

The adoption of the 2006 Data Retention Directive[6] must be seen in the context of the EU's fight against organized crime and terrorism following the terrorist attacks in Madrid 11 March 2004[7] and London on 7 July 2005.[8] On 28 April 2004, France, Ireland, Sweden,

---

[4] On judicial dialogue, see eg F Casarosa and M Moraru (eds), *The Practice of Judicial Interaction in the Field of Fundamental Rights: The Added Value of the Charter of Fundamental Rights of the EU* (Edward Elgar 2022).

[5] V Franssen, 'The European Commission's E-evidence Proposal: Toward an EU-wide Obligation for Service Providers to Cooperate with Law Enforcement?' European Law Blog, 12 October 2018, available at <https://europeanlawblog.eu/2018/10/12/the-european-commissions-e-evidence-proposal-toward-an-eu-wide-obligation-for-service-providers-to-cooperate-with-law-enforcement/> accessed 15 July 2024.

[6] Directive 2006/24/EC of the European Parliament and of the Council of 15 March 2006 on the retention of data generated or processed in connection with the provision of publicly available electronic communications services or of public communications networks and amending Directive 2002/58/EC, OJ 2006, L 105/54 ('Data Retention Directive').

[7] 2004 Madrid train bombings—Wikipedia, at <https://en.wikipedia.org/wiki/2004_Madrid_train_bombings> accessed 25 September 2024.

[8] 2005 London bombings—Wikipedia, at <https://en.wikipedia.org/wiki/7_July_2005_London_bombings> accessed 25 September 2024.

and the UK submitted a proposal to the Council for a framework decision[9] on data retention for the purposes of the prevention, investigation, detection, and prosecution of criminal offences, including terrorism.[10] Although agreeing that the proposed legal basis under the so-called third pillar would be correct in some respects, the proposal would affect existing directives including the ePrivacy Directive.[11] Therefore the Commission was of the opinion that the determination of the categories of data to be retained and of the relevant retention period fell within the competence of the Community legislature, and the Commission reserved the right to submit a proposal for a Directive under the first pillar.[12]

After the extraordinary Justice and Home Affairs Council on 13 July 2005, a plenary session on retention of communications data was held by the UK Presidency of the EU at the informal Justice and Home Affairs Meeting in Newcastle on 8 September 2005.[13] At this plenary session chaired by the UK Home Secretary, presentations were herd from policy and industry representatives including the National Crime Squad, the European Internet Services Providers Association, and the European Telecommunications Network Operators' Association, which provides good examples of some of the stakeholders in this field. At this stage in time, with full focus on combating organized crime and terrorism, no digital rights groups working for civil liberties were invited to give presentations.

At the following meeting on 1 and 2 December 2005,[14] an agreement was reached by the Council.[15] In this meeting, the Council decided to seek the adoption of a Directive based on the EC Treaty and the first pillar rather than pursuing the adoption of a framework decision under the third pillar.[16] This meant that the Member States had no veto, and the Council adopted the Data Retention Directive by qualified majority at the Justice and Home Affairs meeting on 21 February 2006 in Brussels under the Austrian presidency. Only the Irish and Slovak delegations voted against the proposal,[17] whereas Sweden that was represented by Minister of Justice Mr Thomas Bodström (Social Democratic Party, S) and Minister for Migration and Asylum Policy, Ms Barbro Holmberg (Social Democratic Party, S) voted for. According to various Swedish Newspapers and News Reports still available today, and

---

[9] The use of framework decisions for the adoption of legislative acts in police and judicial cooperation in criminal justice matters within the so-called third pillar, were abandoned after the coming into force of the Lisbon Treaty, after which the pillar structure was abandoned and such measures can be adopted by directives.

[10] Council Document 8958/04.

[11] Directive 2002/58/EC of the European Parliament and of the Council of 12 July 2002 concerning the processing of personal data and the protection of privacy in the electronic communications sector (Directive on privacy and electronic communications) [2002] OJ L 201/37 ('ePrivacy Directive').

[12] CJEU, Judgment of 10 February 2009, *Ireland/Parliament and Council* (C-301/06, ECR 2009 p I-593) ECLI:EU:C:2009:68 ('*Ireland v Parliament and Council*'), paras 18–21.

[13] Justice and Homa Affairs Informal, < https://web.archive.org/web/20130424070331/http://www.eu2006.at/en/News/Council_Conclusions/JAISch lussfolgerungen.pdf> (9 September 2005) accessed 4 January 2025. Archived from the original on 27 October 2008, link at <https://en.wikipedia.org/wiki/Data_Retention_Directive> accessed 25 September 2024.

[14] Press Release, Justice and Home Affairs, Brussels, 21 February 2006, provisional version, available at < https://web.archive.org/web/20130424070331/http://www.eu2006.at/en/News/Council_Conclusions/JAISch lussfolgerungen.pdf > at p 2, accessed 1 November 2024.

[15] See also Data Retention Directive—Wikipedia (n 13).

[16] *Ireland v Parliament and Council* (n 12) para 21.

[17] Press Release, Justice and Home Affairs, Brussels, 21 February 2006, provisional version, at <https://web. archive.org/web/20130424070331/http://www.eu2006.at/en/News/Council_Conclusions/JAISchlussfolgerun gen.pdf> p 8, accessed 4 January 2025.

the Swedish version of Wikipedia, former Swedish Minister of Justice Thomas Bodström initiated the Data Retention Directive.[18] According to the English version of Wikipedia, Bodström was heavily criticized by advocates of privacy and liberal think tanks, 'as he is said to have worked towards giving the police the possibility of monitoring people who might be involved in minor crimes, as well as other things that could be seen as intrusive to privacy'.[19] This may be somewhat surprising given his other professions. Perhaps less so given his former profession as professional footballer during his law studies, but more so as practising defence lawyer. Yet, many of the proposals he was criticized for, have more recently been introduced, in particular by the current Minister of Justice Mr Gunnar Strömmer (Moderate Party, M), who is also a lawyer by profession, and previously manager of the non-profit *Centrum för Rättvisa*,[20] cl<aiming to be Sweden's first public interest law firm with the mission to protect individual fundamental rights and freedoms.[21] As a consequence of the change of government from a Social Democratic government under Prime Minister Göran Persson, to a coalition government under Prime Minister Fredrik Reinfeldt (M) including also the Liberal Party (*Folkpartiet, FP*), the Centre Party (*Centerpartiet, C*), and the Christian Democrats (*Kristdemokraterna, KD*) following the 2006 government election,[22] Ms Beatrice Ask (M) became Minister of Justice.

The Data Retention Directive placed an obligation on providers of publicly available electronic communications services and of public communications networks to retain certain communications data for law enforcement purposed. The Directive regulated the retention of traffic and location data, and data necessary to identify the subscriber or registered user by the aforementioned providers, while making it clear that no content data should be retained under its provisions. Although the retention of specific categories of data were to be provided only to the competent national authorities for a time period between 6 and 24 months, this entailed major consequences for telecommunications operators, Internet Service Providers (ISPs), and citizens.

Even before the adoption of the Data Retention Directive, Article 15(1) of the ePrivacy Directive allowed EU Member States to adopt legislative measures for the retention of traffic and location data when such measures constitute:

> a necessary, appropriate and proportionate measure within a democratic society to safeguard national security (i.e. State security), defence, public security, and the prevention, investigation, detection and prosecution of criminal offences or of unauthorised use of the electronic communication system ... To this end, Member States may, inter alia, adopt legislative measures providing for the retention of data for a limited period justified on the grounds laid down in this paragraph. All the measures referred to in this paragraph shall be

---

[18] See eg *Kritiserad datalag kan snart bli verklighet*, SVT Nyheter, at <|https://www.svt.se/nyheter/inrikes/kritiserad-datalag-blir-snart-verklighet> accessed 15 July 2024) and Thomas Bodström—Wikipedia, at <https://sv.wikipedia.org/wiki/Thomas_Bodstr%C3%B6m> accessed 15 July 2024.

[19] ibid, with further references.

[20] Gunnar Strömmer—Wikipedia, at <https://en.wikipedia.org/wiki/Gunnar_Str%C3%B6mmer> accessed 15 July 2024.

[21] *Centrum för rättvisa, Om oss*, at <https://centrumforrattvisa.se/om-oss/> accessed 15 July 2024), only available in Swedish.

[22] *Tidigare regeringsbildningar och statsminister, Sveriges riksdag*, at <https://www.riksdagen.se/sv/sa-fungerar-riksdagen/demokrati/sa-bildas-regeringen/tidigare-regeringsbildningar-och-statsministrar/s> accessed 4 January 2025, only available in Swedish.

in accordance with the general principles of Community law, including those referred to in Article 6(1) and (2) of the Treaty on European Union.[23]

These conditions under which data retention measures may be adopted significantly resemble the exceptions to the right to privacy laid out in Article 8(2) of the European Convention on Human Rights (ECHR):[24]

Article 8: '1. Everyone has the right to respect for his private and family life, his home and his correspondence. 2. There shall be no interference by a public authority with the exercise of this right except such as is in accordance with the law and is necessary in a democratic society in the interests of national security, public safety or the economic well-being of the country, for the prevention of disorder or crime, for the protection of health or morals, or for the protection of the rights and freedoms of others.'

Yet, the Data Retention Directive amending the ePrivacy Directive was formally adopted on 15 March 2006.[25] It covered fixed and mobile telephony, and internet access, email and telephony, and had to be implemented by 15 September 2007.[26] According to Article 15(3) of the Directive, each Member State may postpone application of the Directive to the retention of communications data relating to internet data, upon notification of the Council and the Commission by way of a declaration. Sweden submitted such a declaration and had until 15 March 2009 to implement the Directive in this latter respect. Thereby, the stipulated implementation time was between 18 to 36 months. The Member States had to take necessary measures to ensure that any intentional access to, or transfer of, data retained was punishable by penalties, including administrative or criminal penalties, that are effective, proportionate, and dissuasive. Each Member State had further to designate a public authority to be responsible for monitoring the application within its territory of the provisions adopted regarding the security of stored data.

Since only the Irish and Slovak delegations had voted against the Data Retention Directive,[27] it was of little surprise that it was Ireland that on 6 July 2006 brought the first, direct action, to annul the Data Retention Directive under Article 263 TFEU, with the support of the Slovak Republic. Ireland claimed that the court should annul the Data Retention Directive on the ground that it could not be based on the internal market legal basis since its 'centre of gravity' does not concern the functioning of the internal market, and that the sole or at least its principal objective, was the investigation, detection, and prosecution of crime.[28] On 10 February 2009, the Grand Chamber of the CJEU however dismissed that

---

[23] Article 15(1) ePrivacy Directive.
[24] Convention for the Protection of Human Rights and Fundamental Freedoms (European Convention on Human Rights, as amended).
[25] For more details about the EU lawmaking process leading up to the adoption of the Data Retention Directive, see besides EUR-Lex, at <https://eur-lex.europa.eu/legal-content/EN/HIS/?uri=celex:32006L0024> accessed 15 July 2024, see also eg EU Monitor, at <https://www.eumonitor.eu/9353000/1/j9vvik7m1c3gyxp/vi8rm2zhtnw1> accessed 15 July 2024 with links to the explanatory memorandum, considerations, and legal provisions.
[26] Article 15 Data Retention Directive.
[27] Press Release, Justice and Home Affairs, Brussels, 21 February 2006, provisional version, at <https://web.archive.org/web/20130424070331/http://www.eu2006.at/en/News/Council_Conclusions/JAISchlussfolgerungen.pdf> 8, accessed 4 January 2025.
[28] *Ireland/Parliament and Council* (n 12) para 58.

action underlining the fact that the internal market legal basis could be used in particular where disparities exist between national rules having a direct effect on the functioning of the internal market, and that there were legislative and technical disparities between the national provisions governing the retention of data by service providers.[29] Here it should perhaps be noted that the EU Charter only became legally binding only later that year, on 1 December 2009, when the Lisbon Treaty entered into force.

Although Sweden had previously been in favour of the Data Retention Directive, the implementation was substantially delayed due to fundamental rights concerns after the change of government in 2006, which resulted in minimum implementation of the Directive.[30] According to the new government's opinion, the fundamental purpose of the Data Retention Directive—to ensure that data is available for the purposes of investigation, disclosure, and prosecution of serious crimes—was already achieved in Sweden to a large extent with the support of current rules.[31] Although the implementation deadline for the Directive in its entirety was 15 March 2009, on 23 October 2009, former Minister of Justice, now Member of the *Riksdag*, Swedish Parliament (MP), Mr Thomas Bodström (S) directed an 'interpellation' in the *Riksdag*, that is, a constitutional question, to his successor, Minister of Justice Ms Beatrice Ask (M): "Does the Minister of Justice intend to come back with a proposal to legislate on the obligation to save traffic data, and if so, when will such a proposal be made?"[32] According to the Swedish Constitution, all members of the *Riksdag* have the right to address questions to the government as part of parliamentary control, which is a fundamental precondition for a democratic system of parliamentary government. According to the *Riksdag's* homepage in English, Parliamentary control 'is designed to help the government and public agencies to work in an efficient manner, in conformity with the rule of law, and to help citizens feel that they can trust the way in which the public agencies exercise their powers.'[33]

Well aware of the risk of penalty payments under Article 260 TFEU of at least 30 million EUR after the CJEU on 4 February 2010 ruled against Sweden for non-implementation and failure to fulfil obligations under Article 258 TFEU,[34] yet another government election, in 2010, probably came in the way. The official reason was however slightly different: 'We think that the EU's decision should be followed. But in this case, we have considered that it is actually more important to ensure that the reasons for privacy are carefully weighed against the reasons for law enforcement', said Beatrice Ask, Minister of Justice (M).[35] Politically, there had been divided opinions about how long the traffic data should be saved, who should pay for the storage, the state or the suppliers, and finally in October 2009, Beatrice Ask had

---

[29] ibid paras 63 and 66.
[30] T Konstadinides, 'Mass Surveillance and Data Protection in EU Law—The Data Retention Directive Saga' in M Bergström and A Jonsson Cornell, *European Police and Criminal Law Co-operation* (Hart Publishing 2014) 69–84, at 80.
[31] *Sverige: Datalagringsdirektivet är onödigt*, Europaportalen, at <https://www.europaportalen.se/2011/09/sverige-datalagringsdirektivet-ar-onodigt> (1 September 2011) accessed 15 July 2024, in which the answer to the Commission was cited.
[32] *Interpellation 2009/10:46 av Boström, Thomas (s)*, Sveriges Riksdag, at <https://www.riksdagen.se/sv/dokument-och-lagar/dokument/interpellation/trafikdata_gx1046/> accessed 4 January 2025, only available in Swedish.
[33] *Sveriges riksdag*, at <https://www.riksdagen.se/en/how-the-riksdag-works/what-does-the-riksdag-do/examines-the-work-of-the-government/> accessed 15 July 2024.
[34] CJEU, Judgment of 4 February 2010, *European Commission v Kingdom of Sweden* (C185/09) ECLI:EU:C:2010:59, available only in Swedish.
[35] Translated from a newspaper article: *Miljonsmäll för EU trots*, Aftonbladet, at: <https://www.aftonbladet.se/nyheter/a/8w5mVr/miljonsmall--for-eu-trots> (11 February 2010) accessed 15 July 2024, only available in Swedish.

announced that nothing will be decided before the election since the government wanted to wait for the outcome of a Government Official Report 'on police methods',[36] which partly concerned the same issues.[37]

On 12 March 2010, a little more than a month after the judgment of the CJEU against Sweden for non-implementation of the Data Retention Directive and one year after the final implementation deadline, MP Thomas Bodström (S) filed an official complaint with the Committee on the Constitution (*Konstitutionsutskottet, KU*). The various instruments of parliamentary control are set out in Sweden's Constitution, and according to Chapter 13 of the Instrument of Government, the Committee of the Constitution has a special task to ensure that the government observes existing regulation.[38] In this respect, MP Bodström wanted the Committee on the Constitution to examine the reasons for the government's and the Minister of Justice's negligence with regard to the introduction of the Data Retention Directive. Besides the right to address questions to the government, all members of the *Riksdag* have the right to report government ministers to the Committee on the Constitution. If the *Riksdag* no longer has confidence in a minister or in the Prime Minister, it can decide to make a declaration of no confidence.

In its almost 300-page report for 2010/11, the Committee of the Constitution examined the implementation of the Data Retention Directive in detail, on 15 pages,[39] and after carefully constructing a timeline and examining documents by the Ministry of Justice and Ministry of Foreign Affairs. The Committee noted that the implementation of the Directive would have been legally possible without coordination with the question of how the regulatory framework for the law enforcement authorities' access to the stored data should be designed, but that the government assessed that the implementation of the Directive in Swedish law should nevertheless be considered in a broader context.[40]

The Committee further underlined the importance of the government demanding longer implementation times in particular when negotiating directives in which issues of privacy are concerned. The Committee's review showed that the preparation of the proposal for the implementation of the Directive had entailed difficult trade-offs, not least with regard to the protection of privacy of individuals. Hereby the Committee of the Constitution underlined two important needs for Sweden. Firstly, to enable a full-fledged preparation of implementing provisions, including time to take a position on the difficult trade-offs that such directives often entail. Secondly, to ensure that the *Riksdag*, in cases where implementation requires a decision on new laws or legislative amendments, has sufficient time to make its decision in accordance with the provisions of the Instrument of Government on the decision-making procedure for restricting the rights and freedoms of individuals.[41]

The Committee's evaluation ended on 3 December 2010 when the Government Bill 2010/11 proposing amendments to the Code of Judicial Procedure and the Electronic

---

[36] Swedish Government Official Reports: SOU 2009:1 *En mer rättssäker inhämtning av elektronisk kommunikation i brottsbekämpningen*.
[37] *Miljonsmäll för EU trots*, Aftonbladet, at <https://www.aftonbladet.se/nyheter/a/8w5mVr/miljonsmall--for-eu-trots> (11 February 2010) accessed 15 July 2024, newspaper article only available in Swedish.
[38] Information available on the homepage of the Swedish Parliament: <https://www.riksdagen.se/en/how-the-riksdag-works/what-does-the-riksdag-do/examines-the-work-of-the-government/> accessed 15 July 2024.
[39] KU 2010/11:KU20, Section 2.1 '*Hanteringen av datalagringsdirektivets genomförande*' 65–79, available in Swedish at <https://data.riksdagen.se/fil/3249EF38-C06C-46FE-BE2C-4EB746120B00> accessed 15 July 2024.
[40] ibid.
[41] ibid.

Communications Act[42] in order to implement the Data Retention Directive, was presented.[43] The amendments were proposed to enter into force on 1 July 2011.

Notable is that the statement of opinion by the Council of Legislation (*Lagrådet*), consisting of one former Supreme Court Judge, one Supreme Administrative Court Judge, and one Supreme Court Judge, did not include any criticism of the proposals in the Government Bill. Instead their view was that the proposal in all essential respects complied with what was prescribed in the Data Retention Directive and might, in corresponding parts, be considered to constitute a justifiable interference with personal integrity in order to bring about the necessary law enforcement measures. On two points, *Lagrådet* ascertained that the government went further than what the Data Retention Directive prescribed. Firstly, it was proposed that information about failed calls should be stored, and secondly information about the location where a communication ends when using mobile communication equipment should be stored. *Lagrådet* concluded that, in context, this additional information may be considered marginal intrusions into personal privacy, well justified by their importance in revealing, investigating, and prosecuting crimes.[44] On its homepage, the following can be read about *Lagrådet* that is somewhat comparable with constitutional courts in other countries, although their scrutiny only concern proposed legislation, and they can only issue advisory opinions:[45]

> The Council on Legislation (Swedish: Lagrådet) scrutinizes draft bills which the Government intends to submit to Parliament. A parliamentary standing committee can also request a statement of opinion in a legislative matter.
>
> The Council on Legislation consists of one or more divisions—with a maximum of five. Each division has three members, of whom at least one must be a justice of the Supreme Court and at least one a justice of the Supreme Administrative Court.
>
> Draft bills are presented to the Council by civil servants or parliamentary officials who have been involved in the preparation process. One important feature of the Council's work is to consider whether the draft bill is compatible with the constitution and general legal principles.
>
> The Council on Legislation's views are of an advisory nature, and are not binding on the Government or Parliament. The Council's statement of opinion is a public document which is included in the Government bill or standing committee statement, together with the draft text.

3. A Swedish Commissioner, Penalty Payments for Non-implementation, and the Adoption of Swedish Implementing Legislation

According to Chapter 2 of the Instrument of Government, there are a number of constitutional conditions for restricting rights and freedoms.[46] Besides requirements such as

---

[42] Electronic Communications Act (2003:389).
[43] Government Bill (*prop*) 2010/11:46, only available in Swedish.
[44] *Lagrådets yttrande, utdrag ur protokoll vid sammanträde* 2010-11-17, attachment to Government Bill (*prop*) 2010/11:46, at p 126, only available in Swedish.
[45] *Lagrådet*, at <https://www.lagradet.se/in-english/> accessed 15 July 2024.
[46] Instrument of Government in English translation can be found at <https://www.riksdagen.se/globalassets/05.-sa-fungerar-riksdagen/demokrati/the-instrument-of-government-2023-eng.pdf> accessed 15 July 2024.

restrictions need to be included in legislative acts, these include a minority protection rule under section 22 to hold certain draft government bills in abeyance for a minimum of 12 months if supported by at least ten members of the *Riksdag*. This kind of minority protection can be used concerning government bills that interfere with civil liberties, and the Committee of the Constitution had already stated that the current proposal was of this kind.[47] A proposal can still be adopted if supported by at least five-sixths of those voting in the *Riksdag*.[48]

If the *Riksdag* had not decided to hold the provisions of the government bill in abeyance, the government bill submitted to it, which would have partially implemented the Directive, would have entered into force on 1 July 2011.[49] Beatrice Ask (M) on 14 December 2010 sounded relatively positive about the implementation of the Data Retention Directive, arguing that this kind of data is already collected and stored today, and that the Directive is rather about what to oblige operators to save and on what terms it is saved. She further argued that in this way, there will be more order, as there will be rules for who can extract data, in what context and how quickly the operators must delete stored data.[50]

Nevertheless, the Left Party (*Vänsterpartiet*, V), wanted to use the Constitution's minority protection rule to delay the Data Retention Directive for a year,[51] in the same way as happened with another controversial law infringing privacy rights.[52] The Green Party were also critical and wanted the government to take the initiative to renegotiate it claiming it is a gross violation of privacy.[53] In connection with the *Riksdag's* consideration of the Justice Committee's report,[54] in which the government's bill on the implementation of the Data Retention Directive is discussed,[55] it was requested, among other things, that the proposal for an Act amending the Electronic Communications Act[56] included in the bill should be held in abeyance for at least 12 months due to the fact that the bill entailed such restriction of freedoms and rights.[57]

Accordingly, with the support of Members of the *Riksdag* spanning from the Left Party (*Vänsterpartiet*, V), and the Green Party (*Miljöpartiet*, MP) to the Sweden Democrats (*Sverigedemokraterna*, SD),[58] on 16 March 2011, the *Riksdag* decided to refer the proposal to the Committee on Justice for a period of at least 12 months.[59] In accordance with the provisions in Chapter 2, section 22, first paragraph, of the Instrument of Government, 281

---

[47] KU 2010/11:KU20 (n 39, with further reference to yttr. 2010/11:KU3y p 20).
[48] Chapter 2, Section 22, first paragraph, of the Instrument of Government.
[49] KU 2010/11:KU20 (n 39) 79.
[50] *Swedish Television News* at < https://www.svt.se/nyheter/inrikes/kritiserad-datalag-blir-snart-verklighet> accessed 1 November 2024, only available in Swedish.
[51] *Swedish Television News* at <https://www.svt.se/kultur/datalagringen-kan-fastna-i-riksdagen> (16 December 2010) accessed 15 July 2024, only available in Swedish.
[52] The so-called FRA law, see eg <https://en.wikipedia.org/wiki/National_Defence_Radio_Establishment#Legal_framework> accessed 15 July 2024.
[53] *Swedish Television News* at <https://www.svt.se/kultur/datalagringen-kan-fastna-i-riksdagen> 16 December 2010) accessed 15 July 2024, only available in Swedish.
[54] Report by the Justice Committee, bet. 2010/11:JuU14.
[55] Bill 2010/11:46.
[56] Electronic Communications Act (2003:389).
[57] In accordance with Chapter 2, Section 22, first paragraph, of the Instrument of Government.
[58] Section 11 of the *Riksdag's* minutes 2010/11:73, only available in Swedish at <https://data.riksdagen.se/fil/967EA19D-62BA-4FDF-A756-B9753B81D3DF> accessed 15 July 2024.
[59] See section 7 (debate) and 11 (decision) of the *Riksdag's* minutes 2010/11:73, only available in Swedish at <https://data.riksdagen.se/fil/967EA19D-62BA-4FDF-A756-B9753B81D3DF> accessed 15 July 2024.

and less than five-sixths of those voting in the *Riksdag* had voted for the proposal to be adopted, whereas 62 had voted for abeyance. The votes were spread amongst the parties in government (M, FP, C, and KD) and in opposition,[60] with those voting for the proposal included: 109 S, 107 M, 24 FP, 23 C, 18 KD, and those for abeyance: 25 MP, 18 SD, 19 V. Six members of parliament were absent: 3 S, 2 SD, 1 KD.[61]

Following the decision by the *Riksdag* to postpone adoption of transposing legislation for 12 months,[62] on 6 April 2011, the Commission decided to refer a case to the CJEU under Article 260 TFEU seeking the imposition of a financial penalty on Sweden.[63] According to the newssite *Europaportalen*, it was the former Swedish EU minister and at the time EU Commissioner Cecilia Malmström (former Liberals (*Liberalerna, L*)) who was responsible for the decision by the Commission.[64] If the CJEU were to rule against Sweden, Sweden would have to pay approximately SEK 85,000 per day since the previous ruling on 4 February 2010, at the time amounting to almost SEK 37 million, and will continue to grow until Sweden implements the Directive.[65] If the CJEU ruled against Sweden a second time, Malmström proposed that the fine will increase to SEK 370,000 per day until the Directive is implemented. According to Cecilia Malmström's press secretary, the amount of the fine is based on several different criteria, 'including how serious the offense is judged to be, how much time has passed since the country should have introduced the Directive and the size of the country'.[66]

On 18 April 2011, Sweden's EU Commissioner, Ms Cecilia Malmström presented a long-awaited evaluation that should have been published already in September 2010, of how the Data Retention Directive works in the EU Member States.[67] According to the evaluation, the Data Retention Directive has been implemented in many different ways, and Malmström said that the Commission aimed at presenting amendments to the Directive towards the end of 2011.[68] According to *Europaportalen*, opponents wanted it abolished altogether and the Brussels-based organization, European Digital Rights wrote in a shadow

---

[60] Tidigare regeringsbildningar och statsministrar, Sverige Riksdag, at <https://www.riksdagen.se/sv/sa-fungerar-riksdagen/demokrati/sa-bildas-regeringen/tidigare-regeringsbildningar-och-statsministrar/> accessed 15 July 2024, only available in Swedish.

[61] Section 11 of the *Riksdag's* minutes 2010/11:73, only available in Swedish at <https://data.riksdagen.se/fil/967EA19D-62BA-4FDF-A756-B9753B81D3DF> accessed 15 July 2024.

[62] European Commission, Report from the Commission to the Council and the European Parliament— Evaluation report on the Data Retention Directive (Directive 2006/24/EC), COM(2011)225 final, at <https://eur-lex.europa.eu/legal-content/EN/TXT/PDF/?uri=CELEX:52011DC0225> accessed 15 July 2024 at p 21.

[63] KU 2010/11:KU20, p 78. Available in Swedish at <https://data.riksdagen.se/fil/3249EF38-C06C-46FE-BE2C-4EB746120B00>, referring to Commission Press Release (IP/11/409).

[64] The EU Commission proposes million fines for Sweden at <https://www-europaportalen-se.translate.goog/2011/04/kommissionen-foreslar-miljonboter-for-sverige?_x_tr_sch=http&_x_tr_sl=sv&_x_tr_tl=en&_x_tr_hl=sv&_x_tr_pto=wapp> (6 April 2011) accessed 15 July 2024.

[65] *EU-kommissionen föreslår miljonböter för Sverige, Europaportalen*, at https://www.europaportalen.se/2011/04/kommissionen-foreslar-miljonboter-for-sverige (6 April 2011) accessed 15 July 2024.

[66] *EU-kommissionen föreslår miljonböter för Sverige, Europaportalen*, at <https://www.europaportalen.se/2011/04/kommissionen-foreslar-miljonboter-for-sverige> (6 April 2011) accessed 15 July 2024. See also CJEU, Judgment of 30 May 2013, *European Commission v Kingdom of Sweden* (C-270/11) ECLI:EU:C:2013:339 ('*European Commission v Kingdom of Sweden II*').

[67] European Commission, Report from the Commission to the Council and the European Parliament— Evaluation report on the Data Retention Directive (Directive 2006/24/EC), COM(2011)225 final, at <https://eur-lex.europa.eu/legal-content/EN/TXT/PDF/?uri=CELEX:52011DC0225> accessed 15 July 2024.

[68] *Spretig datalagring ska styras upp, Europaportalen* at <https://www-europaportalen-se.translate.goog/2011/04/spretig-datalagring-ska-styras-upp?_x_tr_sl=sv&_x_tr_tl=en&_x_tr_hl=sv&_x_tr_pto=wapp> (18 April 2011) accessed 15 July 2024.

report that the Commission's evaluation shows that the Directive 'has failed to respect the fundamental rights of Europe's citizens, it has failed to harmonize the European single market and it has failed as a necessary instrument to fight crime'.[69] At the time, only Sweden and Austria had still not implemented the Directive at all,[70] 'due to doubts as to its compliance with fundamental rights',[71] but in Germany for example, the implementing legislation had already been annulled by the Federal Constitutional Court in 2010.[72] Besides this case, the Bulgarian Supreme Administrative Court (2008), the Romanian Constitutional Court (2009), the Cypriot Supreme Court (2011), and the Czech Constitutional Court (2011) had ruled that national data retention laws were incompatible with national constitutions or, in some cases, also with the European Convention on Human Rights, ECHR.[73] In parallel to these cases, complaints challenging both national implementing provisions and the Data Retention Directive were brought before national constitutional and supreme courts in Ireland, Austria, Poland, Slovenia, Slovakia, and Romania.[74] As is well known, the cases before the Irish and the Austrian courts came before the CJEU as requests for preliminary rulings and were later joined.[75]

Still, in a second judgment of 30 May 2013,[76] the CJEU declared that Sweden had failed to comply with the previous case brought against Sweden,[77] and ordered a lumpsum payment. The justifications put forward by Sweden, that the delay in complying with the previous judgment was attributed to 'extraordinary internal difficulties connected with specific aspects of the legislative procedure, to the extensive political debate on the transposition of the Data Retention Directive, and to the issues raised in terms of difficult choices involving weighing the protection of privacy against the need to combat crime effectively',[78] could not be upheld by the court. These indirect attempts to challenge the Directive were unsuccessful, but as has been argued, the CJEU could not assess the validity of the Data Retention Directive 'in light of the allegations that the Directive had led to disproportionate interference with fundamental rights'.[79] Rather, is has been suggested that these Member States should have challenged the Directive on the grounds that it lacked proportionality referring to the CJEU's jurisprudence on general principles,[80] that is, despite the EU Charter of Fundamental Rights not being legally binding at the time.

---

[69] ibid.
[70] European Commission, Report from the Commission to the Council and the European Parliament—Evaluation report on the Data Retention Directive (Directive 2006/24/EC), COM(2011)225 final, at p 21.
[71] J Podkowik, R Rybski, and M. Zubik, 'Judicial Dialogue on Data Retention Laws: A Breakthrough for European Constitutional Courts?' (2021) 19(5) International Journal of Constitutional Law 1597–1631 at 1602.
[72] Judgment of the Federal Constitutional Court of 2 March 2010, 1 BvR 256/08, 263/08, and 586/08= BVerfGE 125, 260 (with dissenting opinions of two judges). See eg M Albers, 'Data Retention in Germany' in M Zubik, J Podkowik, and R Rybski (eds), *European Constitutional Courts towards Data Retention Laws: Law, Governance and Technology Series* (vol 45, Springer 2021) 117–36.
[73] Podkowik, Rybski, and Zubik, 'Judicial Dialogue on Data Retention Laws' (n 71) 1603ff. See also T Konstadinides, 'Destroying Democracy on the Ground of Defending it? The Data Retention Directive, the Surveillance State and Our Constitutional Ecosystem' (2011) 36(5) European Law Review 722–36.
[74] Podkowik, Rybski, and Zubik, ibid 1603ff.
[75] CJEU, Judgment of 8 April 2014, *Digital Rights Ireland and Seitlinger and others* (C-293/12 and C-594/12) ECLI:EU:C:2014:238.
[76] *European Commission v Kingdom of Sweden II* (n 66).
[77] ibid. Cf CJEU, Judgment of 29 July 2010, *European Commission v Republic of Austria* (C-189/09) ECLI:EU:C:2010:455.
[78] *European Commission v Kingdom of Sweden II*, ibid, para 54.
[79] Podkowik, Rybski, and Zubik, 'Judicial Dialogue on Data Retention Laws' (n 71) at 1603.
[80] ibid at 1603.

In a way, the Data Retention Directive could possibly have been indirectly challenged, in a preliminary reference case from the Supreme Court in Sweden. On 19 April 2012, the CJEU gave its ruling in the *Bonnier Audio* case,[81] that concerned copyright infringements of an exclusive right for audiobooks available via internet. Due to unclear wording of the Data Retention Directive and lack of limitation by the CJEU of the use of the Data Retention Directive for 'any offence committed using telecom networks, including copyright infringements',[82] Member States were not excluded from using the Data Retention Directive to enforce intellectual property rights. The court concluded that the Data Retention Directive must be interpreted as not precluding the application of national legislation that permits an internet service provider in civil proceedings to be ordered to give a copyright holder information on the subscriber to whom the internet service provider provided an IP address, which was allegedly used in an infringement, although that legislation does not fall within the material scope of the Data Retention Directive. This meant that Member States were allowed to widen the scope of the Directive beyond law enforcement authorities to natural and legal persons, as in this case despite the fact that Sweden had not yet implemented the Data Retention Directive. Still, future private party requests to access personal data need to be authorized by a national judge, taking the principle of proportionality into account, balancing Article 7 and respect for private and family life with Article 17 and right to (intellectual) property of the EU Charter.[83]

It was not until 1 May 2012 that Sweden had formally implemented the Data Retention Directive when the legislative amendments adopted by the Swedish *Riksdag* on 21 March 2012 came into force.[84] The Member States had been given the choice for the service providers to retain data between 6 and 24 months, and the Swedish *Riksdag* had opted for 6 months, although the Swedish Government Official Report had suggested one year.[85] About a year later, on 30 May 2013 Sweden was fined 3 million EUR for its belated implementation.[86] In light of Sweden's full implementation, the Commission had however made a partial withdrawal of the case.[87] The Commission stated that 'in accordance with its practice in cases where a Member State transposes a Directive at a moment in time where the infringement has already reached the stage of a second referral to the Court, the Commission decided to withdraw the request for a penalty payment while maintaining the request to condemn Sweden to pay a lump sum'.[88] Still, this was the first time Sweden was fined in an

---

[81] CJEU, Judgment of 19 April 2012, *Bonnier Audio AB and others v Perfect Communication Sweden AB* (C-461/10) ECLI:EU:C:2012:219.
[82] Konstadinides, 'Mass Surveillance and Data Protection in EU Law' (n 30) at 80.
[83] ibid at 81.
[84] The Data Retention Directive was mainly implemented by changes to the now repealed Electronic Communications Act (2003:389) (*Lagen (2003:389) om elektronisk kommunikation (LEK)*), that has now been replaced by the new Electronic Communications Act (2022:482), one of 41 posts that also implemented Directive (EU) 2018/1972 of the European Parliament and of the Council of 11 December 2018 establishing the European Electronic Communications Code (Recast) OJ 2018, L 321/36. See further <https://eur-lex.europa.eu/legal-content/EN/NIM/?uri=uriserv:OJ.L_.2018.321.01.0036.01.ENG> accessed 15 July 2024.
[85] SOU 2007:76, p 24 and 173 ff.
[86] *European Commission v Kingdom of Sweden II* (n 66).
[87] Konstadinides, 'Mass Surveillance and Data Protection in EU Law' (n 30) at 80, with reference to European Commission Press Release, 'Data Retention: Commission takes Germany to Court Requesting that Fines be Imposed' IP/12/530, 31 May 2012, available at <https://ec.europa.eu/commission/presscorner/api/files/document/print/en/ip_12_530/IP_12_530_EN.pdf> accessed 25 September 2024.
[88] European Commission Press Release, 'Data Retention: Commission takes Germany to Court Requesting that Fines be Imposed' IP/12/530, 31 May 2012, <https://ec.europa.eu/commission/presscorner/api/files/document/print/en/ip_12_530/IP_12_530_EN.pdf> accessed 1 November 2024.

Article 260(2) TFEU proceeding.[89] It can be noted that the Data Retention Directive was not examined against the EU Charter in this case.

About a year later, on 8 April 2014, the data retention saga took an entirely different turn, when the CJEU in the indirect challenges in the two requests for preliminary references brought before it from Ireland and Austria in joined cases C-293/12 and 594/12, in short most often referred to as *Digital Rights Ireland*, annulled the Data Retention Directive in a Grand Chamber ruling.[90] Thereby the CJEU ruled that the Data Retention Directive entailed a serious interference with the fundamental rights to privacy and data protection as protected in the EU Charter, and that the EU legislature, exceeded 'the limits imposed by compliance with the principle of proportionality in the light of Articles 7, 8 and 52(1) of the Charter'.[91] Against the background of the numerous contributions in this volume analysing this case in depth,[92] in brief, the Data Retention Directive was annulled with reference to an elaborate application of the proportionality principle and Articles 7, 8, and 52(1) of the EU Charter, whereas mandatory safeguards were enumerated to protect privacy in any future EU legislation on data retention.[93]

Following the CJEU:s ruling in *Digital Rights Ireland* on 8 April 2014, the fine of 3 million EUR imposed for non-implementation on 30 May 2013, was paid back after the Commission's lawyers had been looking into the issue.[94] This might have ended the Swedish data retention saga, but despite the Commission's previous allegation that Sweden requested too few preliminary references in its action against Sweden in 2004,[95] this has clearly changed over time.[96]

4. Invalidation of National Legislation after the Annulment of the 2006 EU Data Retention Directive?

Following the judgment in *Digital Rights Ireland* on 8 April 2014, Swedish internet service provider (ISP) Bahnhof deleted all retained records and stopped collecting customer information, and called on other providers to do the same.[97] According to ZDNet, the rest of the industry followed, including the largest telco Telia, and Tele2, Three, and ComHem.[98]

---

[89] EU-domstolen dömer Sverige till miljonböter (europaportalen.se), at <https://www.europaportalen.se/2013/05/eu-domstolen-domer-sverige-till-miljonboter> (31 May 2012) accessed 15 July 2024.
[90] *Digital Rights Ireland* (n 75).
[91] ibid para 69.
[92] Being one of the most analysed CJEU cases, a vast amount of further references can be found in the other chapters of this volume. For some examples of reactions to the ruling, see eg 'EU Court slams Data Retention Directive', EurActiv, 9 April 2014, available at <https://www.euractiv.com/section/justice-home-affairs/news/eu-court-slams-data-retention-directive/https://www.euractiv.com/section/justice-home-affairs/news/eu-court-slams-data-retention-directive/> accessed 15 July 2024.
[93] *Digital Rights Ireland* (n 75) paras 56ff.
[94] Sverige får tillbaka böter för datalagring—DN.se, at <https://www.dn.se/ekonomi/sverige-far-tillbaka-boter-for-datalagring/> (11 April 2014) accessed 15 July 2024.
[95] The infringement procedure against Sweden, 2003/2161, C (2004) 3899, and before that the formal notice by the Commission dated 1 April 2004 (SG (2004) D/201417). No further steps were taken after an amendment of the Swedish laws.
[96] See the insightful report by U Bernitz, 'Förhandsavgöranden av EU-domstolen 1995-2020: Genomslag och betydelse i Sverige', Sieps 2021:2.
[97] Data retention—Wikipedia (n 13), with reference to <https://www.pcworld.com/article/444812/swedish-isp-deletes-all-retained-customer-data-in-wake-of-eu-court-ruling.html> (10 April 2014) accessed 15 July 2024.
[98] Swedish data retention back in full swing minus one ISP | ZDNET, at <https://www.zdnet.com/article/swedish-data-retention-back-in-full-swing-minus-one-isp/> (29 October 2014) accessed 15 July 2024.

Although the CJEU had ruled that the Data Retention Directive seriously interfered with fundamental privacy rights, the Swedish implementation law was still in place. Yet, upon this statement, the Swedish Post and Telecom Authority (*Post- och telestyrelsen, PTS*) that monitors the electronic communications and postal sectors in Sweden,[99] first said that they will no longer take action against an internet service provider that erased all retained communications metadata, 'even though there is still a law in place compelling providers to retain such data'.[100] This clearly created a legally uncertain situation that was also criticized by the Swedish Police. As a temporary solution the Police were now aiming to request information about customers and traffic that the operators save for their own needs, without the data retention rules requiring it. This may fill some of the vacuum that had arisen after the judgment and PTS's position.[101] While data retention is an important tool for law enforcement authorities, ISPs need legal certainty on how to act including whether to retain any data and if so what kind of data, as well as whether to make costly investments to this end.

To come to terms with this situation, a one man investigation initiated by Justice Minister Beatrice Ask (M) and led by the former chairman of the Supreme Administrative Court, Sten Heckscher, with Professor in Public International Law, Iain Cameron as expert, concluded that Sweden could continue to retain data since the Swedish provisions neither contravened EU law nor the ECHR.[102] According to the investigation,[103] the overall assessment was that the Swedish regulatory framework on the storage and disclosure of data fell within the framework set by the general principles of EU and European law and the requirement of respect for fundamental rights. In view of the fact that EU and European law only sets out certain minimum requirements for the protection of privacy that must be met in national law, the investigation nevertheless considered that there was reason to reflect on some regulatory changes in order to further strengthen the protection of personal privacy. Following this outcome, and an administrative court decision,[104] the PTS reversed its course.[105]

As a result, Bahnhof faced a SEK 5 million fine with a deadline of 24 November 2014 unless it resumed storing data.[106] Bahnhof then filed a complaint with the European Commission, arguing that Sweden did not follow the judgment of the CJEU and the EU Charter.[107] In June 2014, PTS ordered Tele2 to resume data retention. Tele2 complied with

---

[99] The homepage of PTS available also in English at <https://www.pts.se/en/about-pts/> accessed 25 September 2024.
[100] Data retention—Wikipedia (n 13), with reference to <https://www.pcworld.com/article/444845/sweden-wont-enforce-data-retention-law-against-isp-that-deleted-metadata.html> (11 April 2014) accessed 15 July 2024.
[101] Polisen ser väg runt datalagringsdom, SVT Nyheter, at <https://www.svt.se/nyheter/inrikes/polisen-ser-vag-runt-datalagringsdom> 8 May 2014.
[102] Ministry Publications Series: Ds 2014:23 *Datalagring, EU-rätten och svensk rätt*, published 13 June 2014 <https://www.zdnet.com/article/swedish-data-retention-back-in-full-swing-minus-one-isp/> (29 October 2014) accessed 15 July 2024.
[103] See also O Lynskey, 'Tele2 Sverige AB and Watson et al: Continuity and Radical Change', European Law Blog, 12 January 2017 at <https://www.europeanlawblog.eu/pub/tele2-sverige-ab-and-watson-et-al-continuity-and-radical-change/release/1> accessed 4 January 2025.
[104] Swedish data retention back in full swing minus one ISP | ZDNET, at <https://www.zdnet.com/article/swedish-data-retention-back-in-full-swing-minus-one-isp/> accessed 15 July 2024, 29 October 2014.
[105] Data retention—Wikipedia (n 13).
[106] ibid, with reference to <https://web.archive.org/web/20170807070723/https://gigaom.com/2014/10/29/swedish-isp-bahnhof-threatened-with-fine-for-not-storing-customer-data-for-law-enforcement/> (29 October 2014) accessed 4 January 2025; and < https://web.archive.org/web/20170807070723/https://gigaom.com/2014/10/29/swedish-isp-bahnhof-threatened-with-fine-for-not-storing-customer-data-for-law-enforcement/> (29 October 2014) accessed 1 November 2024.
[107] ibid, with reference to H Alexandersson, 'The Swedish Data Retention Drama' (27 October 2014) available at <https://hax.5july.org/2014/10/27/the-swedish-data-retention-drama/> accessed 27 September 2024.

the order but appealed the decision to the Administrative Court of Stockholm (*Förvaltningsrätten*).[108] Before the Administrative Court of Stockholm, Tele2 argued that the Swedish implementation should be reversed following the Directive being declared invalid, including the fact that the Swedish implementation went further than the Directive, including registration of failed telephone calls and the geographic endpoint of a mobile communications. The appeal was rejected in October 2014,[109] but was appealed to the Administrative Court of Appeal (*Kammarrätten*) that sent a request for a preliminary ruling to the CJEU. As with the Data Retention Directive, the CJEU held that blanket data retention of all communications of all citizens' communications to combat crime contravened EU Law.[110]

5. The Request for a Preliminary Ruling from the Stockholm Administrative Court of Appeal and the Continuous Clarification by the CJEU of the Required Safeguards for Data Retention to be Lawful, and Revised National Legislation in the Absence of a General EU Legislative Framework

As seen in the previous section, the judgment of the CJEU in *Digital Rights Ireland* did not automatically result in the invalidation of national implementation legislation of the now annulled Data Retention Directive. Yet, it served as the basis for a number of national procedures that challenged the loss of the empowering authority of the Data Retention Directive. This led to a number of national and CJEU judgments, including the Grand Chamber ruling of 21 December 2016 in joined cases C-203/15 and C-698/15 *Tele2 Sverige AB and Watson et al* respectively.[111] The CJEU had been asked by a Swedish and British court respectively to consider the scope and effect of its judgment in *Digital Rights Ireland*. Case C-203/15 originated from the Stockholm Administrative Court of Appeal and the challenge of the PTS decision by Tele2. Despite being set in the context of the ePrivacy Directive, this was one of the first cases in which the CJEU made clarifications of the required safeguards for data retention to be lawful in the absence of an EU legal framework. This case, like the *Digital Rights Ireland* case, has been extensively analysed by legal scholars. To provide but one example, Professor Iain Cameron, who took part in the first one-man investigation as expert,[112] concluded that it would have been better if the Court would have followed the Advocate General's proposal,[113] to make the Member States justify their systems of retention and access before national supreme or constitutional courts.[114]

---

[108] ibid, with reference to <https://www.zdnet.com/article/swedish-data-retention-back-in-full-swing-minus-one-isp/> accessed 27 September 2024.
[109] Swedish data retention back in full swing minus one ISP | ZDNET, at <https://www.zdnet.com/article/swedish-data-retention-back-in-full-swing-minus-one-isp> (29 October 2014) accessed 15 July 2024.
[110] *Poliser ser väg runt datalagringsdom*, SVT Nyheter, at <https://www.svt.se/nyheter/inrikes/polisen-ser-vag-runt-datalagringsdom> (8 May 2014) accessed 25 September 2024.
[111] CJEU, Judgment of 21 December 2016, *Tele2 Sverige* (C-203/15 and C-698/15) ECLI:EU:C:2016:970.
[112] Ministry Publications Series: Ds 2014:23 *Datalagring, EU-rätten och svensk rätt*, published 13 June 2014.
[113] *Opinion of Advocate General Saugmansgaard Øe of 19 July 2016 in Tele2 Sverige* (C-203/15 and C-698/15), ECLI:EU:C:2016:572 ('*AG Opinion Tele2 Sverige*'). See also V Franssen, 'The Future of National Data Retention Obligations—How to Apply Digital Rights Ireland at National Level?' European Law Blog (25 July 2016) at <https://europeanlawblog.eu/2016/07/25/the-future-of-national-data-retention-obligations-how-to-apply-digital-rights-ireland-at-national-level/> accessed 15 July 2024.
[114] I Cameron, 'Balancing Data Protection and Law Enforcement Needs: Tele2 Sverige and Watson' (2017) 54 Common Market Law Review 1467–1496.

In this case, the CJEU had the opportunity to 'specify the interpretation to be given in a national context to the judgment in Digital Rights Ireland'.[115] As a result, the CJEU prioritized the protection of privacy in a way that put pressure for new Swedish legislation with a somewhat narrower scope.[116] In contrast to the annulment of national data retention laws in Bulgaria, Czech Republic, Cyprus, Germany, and Romania, based on an assessment of the proportionality of the relevant measures, the *Tele2 Sverige* judgment involved the finding that blanket retention was unlawful per se.[117]

The Administrative Court of Appeal in its subsequent judgment declared the Swedish law incompatible with EU law and annulled the decision by the PTS.[118] According to Chapter 15 section 1 of the new Electronic Communications Act,[119] the judgment of the Administrative Court of Appeal may not be appealed. As a result, the service providers could no longer be required to retain data for law enforcement purposes[120] The result was unsatisfactory, not least from the Police Authority's point of view. Soon, revised and more limited national legislation was introduced that came into force on 1 October 2019.[121] It has been noted that the Swedish constitution or any other Swedish law lack clear equivalent to the general provisions on the protection of personal integrity that are part of the EU Charter. The basic legal starting point regarding privacy protection can therefore be said to differ between Union and Swedish law.[122] In a subsequent case of 2 March 2021, the CJEU clarified that access, for the purposes in the criminal field, to a set of traffic or location data in respect of electronic communications, allowing precise conclusions to be drawn concerning a person's private life, is permitted only in order to combat serious crime or prevent serious threats to public security.[123] In this respect, the influence of the EU Charter provisions cannot be understated.[124]

In Sweden, the ePrivacy Directive has been implemented mainly through the new Electronic Communications Act.[125] At the time of the *Tele2 Sverige* judgment, the retention

---

[115] Eclan, 'Tele2 Sverige AB v Post- och telestyrelsen and Secretary of State for the Home Department v Tom Watson, Peter Brice, Geoffrey Lewis', at <https://eclan.eu/en/eu-case-law/tele2-sverige-ab-v-post-och-telestyrelsen-and-secretary-of-state-for-the-home-department-v-tom-watson-peter-brice-geoffrey-lewis> accessed 15 July 2024.

[116] See also Bernitz (n 96) 44.

[117] Lynskey (n 103); 'Case C-203/15, Tele2 Sverige—Swedish data retention despite Digital Rights Ireland', EU Law Radar, <https://eulawradar.com/case-c-20315-tele2-sverige-swedish-data-retention-despite-digital-rights-ireland/> (17 June 2015) accessed 15 July 2024; see also Podkowik, Rybski, and Zubik, 'Judicial Dialogue on Data Retention Laws' (n 71) 1597–1631.

[118] Judgment by the Administrative Court of Appeal of 7 Mars 2017 in case nr 7380-14, referred to as RK 2017:1.

[119] Electronic Communications Act (2022:482).

[120] Bernitz (n 96).

[121] See further Government Bill (*Prop.*) 2018/19:86, *Datalagring vid brottsbekämpning—anpassningar till EU-rätten*.

[122] Bernitz (n 96) 46, referring to the Grand Chamber CJEU, Judgment of 2 March 2021, *Prokuratuur* (C-746/18) ECLI:EU:C:2021:152. See also Data retention across the EU | European Union Agency for Fundamental Rights (europa.eu), at <https://fra.europa.eu/en/publication/2017/data-retention-across-eu> accessed 15 July 2024, that looks at amendments to national retention laws in 2016, after the *Digital Rights Ireland* judgment.

[123] *Prokuratuur* (n 122) at 60. For subsequent EU and national cases, see A Juszczak and E Sason, 'Recalibrating Data Retention in the EU' (2021) 4 eucrim, at <https://eucrim.eu/articles/recalibrating-data-retention-in-the-eu/> accessed 15 July 2024. See also the Full Court CJEU, Judgment of 30 April 2024, *La Quadrature du Net a.o. c. Premier Ministre and Ministre de la Culture* (C-470/21) ECLI:EU:C:2024:370 ('*La Quadrature du Net 'II'*'), commented by X Groussot and A Engel, Op-Ed: 'The Devil is in the (Procedural) Details—the Court's Judgment in La Quadrature du Net' (13 May 2024), EU Law Live at <https://eulawlive.com/op-ed-the-devil-is-in-the-procedural-details-the-courts-judgment-in-la-quadrature-du-net-by-xavier-groussot-and-annegret-engel/> accessed 15 July 2024.

[124] See also Bernitz (n 96) at 46, referring *Prokuratuur* (n 122) at 60.

[125] Electronic Communications Act (2022:482).

obligation was general and unlimited 'in the sense that it covered all telephony, messaging and broadband services provided by the traditional telecoms operators'.[126] This meant that after *Tele2 Sverige*, such general and unlimited retention obligations exceeded what was strictly necessary and could not in accordance with the ePrivacy Directive be considered justified in a democratic society. As a result, new rules on data retention entered into force on 1 October 2019 that limited the retention obligations and differentiated between the retention periods.[127] According to *Tele2 Sverige*, EU law does not prevent a Member State from adopting legislation permitting, as a preventive measure, the targeted retention of traffic and location data, for the purpose of fighting serious crime, provided that 'the retention of data is limited, with respect to the categories of data to be retained, the means of communication affected, the persons concerned and the retention period adopted, to what is strictly necessary'.[128]

After *Tele2 Sverige*, many subsequent CJEU cases have followed, making it necessary to yet again amend the Swedish rules. The Swedish Government Official Report SOU 2023:22 lists and analyses six Grand Chamber Cases all related to targeted retention to combat crime: *Ministerio Fiscal*,[129] *La Quadrature du Net 'I'*,[130] *Privacy International*,[131] *Prokuratuur*,[132] *Garda Síochána*,[133] and *Space Net*.[134] Since then, a number of other cases have been delivered of which only the Full Court ruling in *La Quadrature du Net 'II'* that concerned the protection of copyright and limits to access data retained, will be mentioned.

As a result of the CJEU judgments, other Member States including Germany, France, Belgium, and Denmark have adapted their data retention rules to EU law, and the Government Report drew the conclusions that there may be reason to amend also Swedish legislation. According to SOU 2023:22, proposals on data retention to protect national security, and targeted retention to combat serious crime should be submitted. In this respect, targeted refers to retention of data that is limited to a specific geographical area, to a specific group of people or to some other distinguishing criterion, such as technical criteria.[135]

Concerning national security retention, the report proposes that a new specialist decision-making body be the supervisory body since a decision on national security detention by the Swedish Security Service must be subject to effective supervision.[136] In addition, there will be special rules for retention to combat serious crimes that do not constitute a threat to national security. Thereby, the report proposes two forms of targeted retention to combat serious crime, that is, geographically targeted retention, and extended targeted retention. Geographically targeted retention must only take place in areas 'in which objective criteria indicate that there is a comparatively higher probability of serious crime than in

---

[126] SOU 2023:22, at 32.
[127] SOU 2023:22, at 32, and Government Bill 2018/19:86.
[128] *Tele2 Sverige* (n 111) para 108, where the requirements were more closely developed in the subsequent paragraphs (109–112).
[129] CJEU, Judgment of 2 October 2018, *Ministerio Fiscal* (C-207/16) ECLI:EU:C:2018:788.
[130] CJEU, Judgment of 6 October 2020, *La Quadrature du Net and others* (C-511/18, C-512/18 and C-520/18) ECLI:EU:C:2020:791 ('*La Quadrature du Net 'I'*').
[131] CJEU, Judgment of 6 October 2020, *Privacy International* (C-623/17) ECLI:EU:C:2020:790.
[132] *Prokuratuur* (n 122).
[133] CJEU, Judgment of 5 April 2022, *Commissioner of An Garda Síochána* (C-140/20) ECLI:EU:C:2022:258.
[134] CJEU, Judgment of 27 October 2022, *SpaceNet* (C-793/19 and C-794/19) ECLI:EU:C:2022:702.
[135] SOU 2023:22 at p 33.
[136] ibid at 33–34 and 181–247.

other areas'.[137] In this respect, the report argues that geographically targeted retention must be based on the official statistics on reported crimes presented by the Swedish National Council for Crime Prevention (*Brottsförebyggande rådet, Brå*) and with the municipalities as geographical units. The PTS must annually prescribe the municipalities that are to be subject to geographically targeted retention.[138] Accordingly, *Brå* has been given this task,[139] and produces documentation with statistics of reported offences, which can form the basis for considerations of the introduction of geographically targeted retention of electronic communications data.[140]

Geographically targeted retention is meant to be complemented by so-called extended targeted retention, that may concern: '1. a limited geographical area in which serious crime has occurred or in which it is probable that serious crime will occur, 2. a site worthy of protection, 3. a person convicted of serious offences, 4. a person that has been subject to secret coercive measures, or 5. an equipment or subscription identity that has been used in a serious crime or serious criminal activity or that it may reasonably be assumed may be used in a serious crime or serious criminal activity'.[141] The Swedish Police authority, the Swedish Security Service, and Swedish Customs are suggested to be able to decide on extended targeted retention.[142]

The retention period both for geographically targeted retention and extended targeted retention is proposed to be one year. These proposed rules were proposed to enter into force between 1 July 2024 and 1 July 2025, but are still within the Swedish lawmaking process.[143] As is customary, the government forwards the finished report to relevant public agencies, organizations, and municipalities in order to hear their opinions on the proposals. This is known as referral of a report for consideration. Amongst the long list of more than 50 invited actors to provide opinions on the proposals in SOU 2023:22 before 1 November 2023, some familiar actors can be found such as, Bahnhof AB, the Administrative Court of Stockholm, the Administrative Court of Appeals of Stockholm, PTS, Tele2 Sverige AB, and the Law Faculty at the University of Uppsala, just to mention a few.[144] Anyone, including private individuals, is entitled to obtain a copy of the report and to submit comments. The next step of the legislative process, is that the Council on Legislation (*Lagrådet*) will examine the proposal.[145] No doubt, this time, this report will be much more interesting to read.

When it comes to geographically targeted retention and the proposed model to ascertain in which areas this should be possible, much can be said against the proposed model although it would probably meet the requirements of law enforcement and effective and efficient criminal investigations. However, the simple fact put forward by Gustaf Almkvist in his opinion for the Law Faculty at the University of Uppsala, that the result of the suggested model would be that about 70% of Sweden's population would be covered by the

---

[137] ibid at p 34 and 249–324.
[138] ibid at p 34.
[139] *Regeringsbeslut* Ju2023/1666, 6 July 2023.
[140] *Brottsförebyggande rådet—Årsredovisning* 2023, p 15.
[141] SOU 2023:22 at 34–35.
[142] ibid 35.
[143] This paragraph largely builds on SOU 2023:22, ibid, at 31ff.
[144] Remiss av SOU 2023:22 Datalagring och åtkomst till elektronisk information—Regeringen.se <https://www.regeringen.se/remisser/2023/07/remiss-av-sou-202322-datalagring-och-atkomst-till-elektronisk-information/> accessed 15 July 2024.
[145] The Homepage of the Riksdag: Makes laws, Sveriges riksdag (riksdagen.se), at <https://www.riksdagen.se/en/how-the-riksdag-works/what-does-the-riksdag-do/makes-laws/> accessed 15 July 2024.

geographically targeted retention, gives serious doubts about the model. The reason for the high percentage is that most of Sweden's most populous municipalities are included in the 132 municipalities that would be subject to the retention obligations.[146] Although these calculations differ from the calculations in the report itself including the attached expert opinion, the previous rejection by the CJEU of broad, general retention, entails there would be little difference between such a scheme and the now proposed. Hardly a model that would be compatible with EU Law as developed in the case law of the CJEU for example in *SpaceNet*.[147]

6. Conclusions—Trial and Error or Business as Usual? Multilevel Governance, Judicial Dialogue, and Dynamic EU Lawmaking towards Legally Acceptable Requirements for Data Retention?

The Swedish Data Retention Saga has provided a rich example of the interrelation between national and European law and the legal processes that led to legal changes both on national and European level, including an analysis of data retention, but with focus more on lawmaking and judicial processes rather than data retention as such and in detail.

Initially in this chapter, we assumed that high-quality legislation carefully balances effective and efficient criminal investigations, legal certainty, and fundamental rights protection. With the help of these interests at stake as a starting point, this chapter had in aim to answer the research question: did the various political and legal avenues in EU lawmaking help develop legally acceptable requirements for data retention in the European Union? In order to do so, the following derived questions were aimed to be answered in the individual sections: did the: (1) extended implementation process; (2) penalty payments; (3) annulment of the Data Retention Directive; and (4) preliminary references, improve the quality of the data retention legislation in the Union and in Sweden, in respect of effective and efficient criminal investigations, legal certainty, and fundamental rights protection?

As a result, those derived questions have been answered in the individual sections. Firstly, in section 2 in which the Swedish support for EU data retention rules, and the extended implementation process were presented and analysed, the underlying question was: did the extended implementation process improve the quality of the data retention legislation in the Union and in Sweden, in respect of effective and efficient criminal investigations, legal certainty, and fundamental rights protection? Since the main concern in the national implementation process was fundamental rights oriented, and the report of the Committee of the Constitution emphasized the importance of longer implementation times, in particular concerning directives in which issues of privacy are concerned, these processes at least put fundamental rights protection in focus as well as the importance of multifaceted lawmaking processes.

Secondly, in section 3 in which the penalty payments for non-implementation, and the adoption of Swedish implementing legislation were presented and analysed, the underlying

---

[146] Uppsala universitet (juridiska fakulteten) (regeringen.se), at <https://www.regeringen.se/contentassets/99890fe966574c16b0e30600c543893e/uppsala-universitet-juridiska-fakulteten.pdf> accessed 15 July 2024.
[147] *SpaceNet* (n 133).

question was: did the penalty payments improve the quality of the data retention legislation in the Union and in Sweden, in respect of effective and efficient criminal investigations, legal certainty, and fundamental rights protection? The answer to this question mainly concerns efficiency and effectiveness of EU law and the application of the loyalty principle, and less so data retention as such. Still, it may have a bearing also on fundamental rights protection and legal certainty.

Thirdly, in section 4 in which the annulment of the Data Retention Directive and reviewed national legislation were presented and analysed, the underlying question was: did the annulment of the Data Retention Directive improve the quality of the data retention legislation in the Union and in Sweden, in respect of effective and efficient criminal investigations, legal certainty, and fundamental rights protection? Perhaps not directly, and this is also really an issue about legal certainty, but in the long run the annulment of the Data Retention Directive most probably led to improved fundamental rights protection in particular given the enhanced role of the EU Charter provisions.

Fourthly, in section 5 in which the request for a preliminary ruling from the Stockholm Administrative Court of Appeal and the following continuous clarification by the CJEU of the required safeguards for data retention to be lawful, and revised national legislation in the absence of a general EU legislative framework, were presented and analysed, the underlying question was: did the preliminary references, improve the quality of the data retention legislation in the Union and in Sweden, in respect of effective and efficient criminal investigations, legal certainty, and fundamental rights protection? The answer to this final question is that the balancing of the underlying interests has been corrected towards more focus on fundamental rights protection although the main challenge most probably is legal uncertainty due to the case-by-case rulemaking by the CJEU. The increasing number of (Grand Chamber) cases is however developing the field in the absence of a more general EU legislative framework. In this respect it is not possible to underestimate the importance of legal certainty and lawmaking by individual cases certainly has its challenges. The direct challenges brought before the CJEU is also an illustration of the importance of preparing the cases well. Would it have been possible to argue the fundamental rights concerns already earlier before the EU Charter became binding with the Lisbon Treaty coming into effect?

In answering these questions, and contributing to this volume's second section on adaptations of policy and amendments to legislation in Sweden, this chapter has hopefully provided some insights into the traditions of the Swedish legal system in general, and the quality of data retention regulation in particular.

18
Data Retention and Law Enforcement Access to Personal Data in India

Shweta Reddy Degalahal

1. Introduction

India has had a tenuous relationship[1] with safeguarding the privacy rights of its citizens. For the longest time, the existence of the right to privacy has been questioned by the courts and the Union Government.[2] This changed in 2017, when the right to privacy was given the status of a constitutional right and not just a statutory right by the Supreme Court's interpretation of the larger right to life under article 21 of the Constitution in the now widely referred to as the *Puttaswamy* judgment.[3] The litigation in 2017 was born out of a legal challenge to the Aadhaar project, which is a unique identity project that provides the residents of India with a unique identity number after they submit their biometric information. The project was challenged on the grounds of infringing the right to privacy and concerns around State applies to State agencies in addition to the private sector.

During the course of the hearing of the *Puttaswamy* case, the Union Government constituted a committee chaired by a former judge of the Supreme Court, which was tasked with reviewing the data protection issues in the country and draft their version of the data protection bill.[4] The report provided an extensive analysis of the state of data protection in the country including the potential harms to individuals due to the absence of legislation that takes into account the development of the digital economy of the country.[5] The Committee drafted the first version of the data protection legislation[6] in 2018 after the affirmation of the constitutional right to privacy and it was modelled heavily on Europe's General Data Protection Regulation. The draft Bill was introduced in the Parliament in 2019 and then sent to a Joint Parliamentary Committee for further reviews and suggestions.[7] The report of the Joint Parliamentary Committee was released to the general public along with another

---

[1] Planning Commission, Government of India, *Report of the Group of Experts on Privacy* (2012); Ministry of Personnel, Public Grievances & Pensions, *Right to Privacy Bill, 2011* (Press Information Bureau 2011).
[2] *MP Sharma & Ors v Satish Chandra and Ors* (1954) 1 SCR 1077; *Kharak Singh v State of Uttar Pradesh* [1964] 1 SCR 332.
[3] *Justice KS Puttaswamy and Anr v Union of India and Others* (2017) 10 SCC 1.
[4] ibid 26C.
[5] Committee of Experts under the Chairmanship of Justice B N Srikrishna, 'A Free and Fair Digital Economy; Protecting Privacy, Empowering Indians' (2018) <https://www.meity.gov.in/writereaddata/files/Data_Protection_Committee_Report.pdf> accessed 11 July 2024.
[6] Draft Personal Data Protection Bill 2018.
[7] Lok Sabha, 'Bill for reference to Joint Committee' (Lok Sabha, 11 December 2019) <https://loksabhadocs.nic.in/lobmk/17/Second/SLOB11.12.2019_.pdf?ref=static.internetfreedom.in> accessed 11 July 2024.

version of the draft Bill in 2021.[8] The second version of the draft was once again withdrawn in August 2022.

At the end of 2022, the Ministry of Electronics and Information Technology released the third version of the draft bill titled Digital Personal Data Protection Bill 2022.[9] This version has been heavily criticized[10] for the dilution of the notice provisions,[11] wide exemptions provided to the government agencies, and its failure to address the questions of surveillance reform, especially after the Pegasus scandal in the country. In 2023, the Digital Personal Data Protection Act (the Act)[12] passed in both houses of the Parliament and received the Presidential assent. Pursuant to its publication in the Official Gazette, the Act is now considered to be enacted in India. However, the law is still not in effect: the Union Government has to provide notice of the date from which the law will be in effect. Additionally, there will be a phased roll-out of the law with different provisions being enacted on different dates.[13]

Currently, almost all legal provisions related to regulating technology, including obligations of intermediaries towards individuals and towards law enforcement agencies, originate from only one legislation: the Information Technology Act 2000. Introduced 23 years ago, the legislation has gone through periodic amendments to address the changes in the technological environment of the country. However, news reports suggest that this legislation is going to be overhauled in its entirety and was expected to be replaced with the Digital India Act in 2023.[14]

The objective of this chapter is to provide an overview of the privacy and data protection landscape in the country and examine its interaction with the requirements on data retention and law enforcement's powers to access personal data, specifically with respect to the telecommunications and electronic communications data. Firstly, the right to privacy as interpreted in the *Puttaswamy* judgment will be explained. As part of the judgment, the

---

[8] Indranth Gupta and Paarth Naithani, 'An Assessment of the JPC Report on PDP Bill, 2019'(Economic and Political Weekly, 30 July 2022) <https://www.epw.in/engage/article/assessment-jpc-report-pdp-bill-2019> accessed 11 July 2024.
Rakesh Mohan Chaturvedi, 'Data Protection Bill: Parliamentary Panel Adopts Draft Report', *The Economic Times* (23 November 2021) <https://economictimes.indiatimes.com/news/india/parliamentary-panel-adopts-draft-report-on-data-protection-bill/articleshow/87858918.cms> accessed 11 July 2024.
[9] Digital Personal Data Protection Bill 2022.
[10] 'IFF's First Read of the Draft Digital Personal Data Protection Bill, 2022' (*Internet Freedom Foundation*, 18 November 2022) <https://internetfreedom.in/iffs-first-read-of-the-draft-digital-personal-data-protection-bill-2022/> accessed 11 July 2024; 'The Centre for Internet and Society's Comments and Recommendations to the: The Digital Data Protection Bill 2022 — The Centre for Internet and Society' <https://cis-india.org/internet-governance/blog/cis-comments-recommendations-to-digital-data-protection-bill> accessed 11 July 2024; 'Apar Gupta Writes: Digital Data Protection Bill Uses Brevity and Vagueness to Empower Government, Undermine Privacy' (*The Indian Express*, 20 November 2022) <https://indianexpress.com/article/opinion/columns/apar-gupta-writes-digital-data-protection-bill-brevity-vagueness-empower-government-undermine-privacy-8279134/> accessed 11 July 2024; Sukanya Shantha, '"Vague Wording, Unguided Powers": Experts on New Draft Digital Data Protection Bill' *The Wire* <https://thewire.in/tech/experts-comment-on-new-data-protection-bill> accessed 11 July 2024.
[11] Section 6 of the Bill required the notice to consist of the description of personal data categories that were to be collected and the purpose of processing such data. However, this has been slightly improved in the Act (section 5) which additionally requires information related to the manner in which a data principal can exercise her rights as well as the procedure to complain to the data protection board.
[12] The Digital Personal Data Protection Act 2023 <https://www.meity.gov.in/writereaddata/files/Digital%20Personal%20Data%20Protection%20Act%202023.pdf>.
[13] The Digital Personal Data Protection Act 2023, section 1(2).
[14] Aashish Aryan, 'Digital India Bill Draft Bill Likely to Open for Public Consultation within 15 Days' *The Economic Times* (27 June 2023) <https://economictimes.indiatimes.com/tech/technology/digital-india-bill-draft-likely-within-15-days/articleshow/101287865.cms?from=mdr> accessed 11 July 2024. At the time of writing the chapter, the legislation has not been released to the general public.

Supreme Court obligated the Union Government to operationalize the right to informational privacy by introducing a data protection legislation for the citizens of the country. The general obligations and the exemptions to these obligations under the notified data protection legislation will be provided. Subsequently, the fragmented nature of the data retention requirements that are currently in force will be provided. Additionally, the legal provisions related to the law enforcement access to data will also be provided. Despite not falling under the scope of data retention, it is the author's opinion that the fragmented nature of drafting of the data retention requirements coupled with legally questionable powers of the law enforcement to access data, it is possible that entities might be required to retain data that are not directly provided for under the retention requirements but are provided for under the law enforcement access to data. Hence, legal provisions that allow law enforcement to request or summon access to data will also be examined before the conclusion of the chapter.

2. Right to Privacy in India

The Indian Constitution doesn't have an explicit reference to the right to privacy. Any implicit interpretation of the existence of the constitutional right was quashed by the Supreme Court in *M P Sharma v Satish Chandra*[15] and *Kharak Sign v State of Uttar Pradesh*.[16] The former case was decided by an eight-judge bench while the latter was decided by a six-judge bench and both the denied the existence of a right to privacy. So for the interpretation of the existence of a constitutional right to privacy to be legally valid, a bench with more than eight judges was necessary.

A fresh round of petitions requiring such an interpretation began in 2012 with a petition[17] before the Supreme Court that questioned the legal validity of the Aadhaar project due to its implications on the fundamental rights of the citizens. The project involved assigning a twelve-digit unique identity number to all the Indian residents after collecting their biometric information, primary objective of which was to enhance the efficiency of welfare delivery schemes in the country. The constitutional validity of the project was challenged based on multiple reasons, among which was an argument of infringement of privacy as a result of the compilation of the demographic biometric data. Multiple petitions[18] challenging other aspects of the Aadhaar project were also filed in the high courts of different states in the country which were subsequently clubbed with the 2012 petition before the Supreme Court which has been referred to as the *Puttaswamy* judgment.

On the 24 August 2017, a nine-judge bench of the Supreme Court of India in Justice *K S Puttaswamy and Anr v Union of India & others*[19] (*Puttaswamy*) pronounced that the constitutional right of privacy was integral to Part III of the Indian Constitution along with the other fundamental rights and freedoms. The judgment lay to bed inconsistencies over the

---

[15] (1954) 1 SCR 1077.
[16] (1964) 1 SCR 332.
[17] *Puttaswamy* (n 3).
[18] *S Raju v Govt of India and Others*, WP(C) No. 439 of 2012; *Aruna Roy & Anr v Union of India & Ors*, WP No 833 of 2013; *S G Vombatkere & Anr v Union of India & Ors* WP No 829 of 2013; *Unique Identification Authority of India & another v Central Bureau of Investigation* (Crl) No(s) 2524/2014.
[19] *Puttaswamy* (n 3).

explicit existence of the right to privacy over jurisprudence spanning multiple decades. The judgment had a total of six opinions: the plurality opinion was signed by four judges and the other five judges drafted individual concurring opinions.

The operative part of the judgment that was signed by all the nine judges and hence is binding on all future cases holds[20] that the right to privacy is an intrinsic part of the right to life and liberty under article 21 of the Constitution and the previous cases of *M P Sharma*[21] and *Kharak Singh*[22] that hold that privacy is not protected under the Constitution are overruled to that extent. It recognizes that privacy rights of the individual can be reasonably restricted and are not absolute in nature. They also recognize the effect of State's interference in the fulfilment of the privacy rights and present a three-pronged approach to restrict privacy. The three-pronged approach requires an act that has a potential to infringe on the privacy of the individuals to be (a) based in the law, (b) address a legitimate state aim, and (c) be proportional to the objective that is sought to be achieved. These three analytical steps to determine the legal validity of the restriction originate from the procedural and content-based safeguards as part of a restriction on article 21 of the Constitution[23] (protection of life and personal liberty).

The majority opinion and the concurring opinions take into consideration international jurisprudence on privacy and data protection. One of the main contentions of the government was that privacy deserved statutory protection and did not rise up to the standards of a constitutional right. The Court had to examine if the existence of statutory protection did not warrant privacy the status of a constitutional right. In doing so, the Court argued that recognizing the constitutional element of a right made it immune from the proclivities of the legislative majorities which cannot be said for statutory rights.[24] Privacy of an individual was considered to be a core part of their personal liberty and hence warranted the status of a constitutional right.[25] Despite being signed by only four of the judges, the plurality opinion authored by Justice D Y Chandrachud has been highly regarded for its views. Neither of the opinions explicitly discuss the right to data protection, however the plurality opinion discusses the importance of informational privacy in the context of the technological developments. The plurality opinion also refers to the key cases from Europe on data retention of electronic communications[26] without any specific additional guidance on its relevance or as lessons for the Indian context.

In addition to affirm the existence of a constitutional right to privacy, the Court acknowledged[27] the need for a data protection legislation to safeguard the rights of the citizens of the country. After this acknowledgement, there began multiple iterations of drafts which were either withdrawn or sent to parliamentary standing committee for further deliberations. Finally, in 2022 the most recent draft of the Digital Personal Data Protection Bill was released for public consultations.

---

[20] ibid 544.
[21] (1954) 1 SCR 1077.
[22] (1964) 1 SCR 332.
[23] *Puttaswamy* (n 3) 254
[24] ibid 214.
[25] ibid 221.
[26] ibid 188, 190.
[27] ibid 253, 532.

3. Data Protection Legislation in India

As stated earlier, India enacted recently a cross-sectoral data protection legislation, the Digital Personal Data Protection Act 2023. This version of legislation has undergone multiple revisions since 2018. This section will lay down the legal provisions relating to the general obligations of data fiduciaries and the exemptions to complying with such obligations under the Digital Personal Data Protection Act 2023.

3.1 General obligations

This and the previous iterations of the draft data protection legislation have used the term 'data fiduciary' for the entity that determines the means and purposes of processing personal data,[28] where the influence from the definition of 'controller' in the European General Data Protection Regulation (GDPR)[29] is obvious. Despite the use of this term, there does not seem to be any inclusion of specific obligations related to the general notions of fiduciary responsibilities. The Act does not differentiate between personal data and sensitive personal data. The 2018 and 2019 versions of the draft legislation had specific definition of sensitive personal data (along the lines of the GDPR) and related grounds for processing such data.[30] The rationale for omitting the definition or any other higher compliance requirements for personal data of a sensitive nature has not been provided by the drafters of the Act.

The details that need to be provided by the data fiduciaries to the data principal (the natural person to whom the personal data relates to)[31] at the time of data collection have been diluted relative to the previous versions, that is, under the proposed requirements, data fiduciaries need to provide details related to the nature of data collection, the purpose of data collection, the manner in which to exercise data principal rights under the Act, as well as the procedure to approach the Data Protection Board in the event of any complaints.[32] The retention provision requires data fiduciaries to either cease retaining the personal data or erase personal data upon request of the data principal and completion of the purpose of collection of data unless retention is necessary for compliance with any applicable law.[33] Despite the usage of the term retention by the drafters, the obligation does not explicitly lay down additional *ex ante* safeguards or balancing tests that need to be conducted prior to retaining personal data in accordance with applicable law. This means that the existence of any such safeguards or tests need to be looked for in the legislations that have explicit data retention requirements.

---

[28] Section 2(i) Digital Personal Data Protection Act 2023.
[29] GDPR, Art 4(7): Regulation (EU) 2016/679 on the protection of natural persons with regard to the processing of personal data and on the free movement of such data, and repealing Directive 95/46/EC (General Data Protection Regulation) [04.05.2016] OJ L119/1.
[30] R Mihir, 'Digital Personal Data Protection Act, 2023: A Missed Opportunity for Horizontal Equality' (*Supreme Court Observer*, 23 August 2023) <https://www.scobserver.in/journal/digital-personal-data-protection-act-2023-a-missed-opportunity-for-horizontal-equality/>.
[31] Section 2(j) Digital Personal Data Protection Act 2023 (similar to the definition of data subject under the General Data Protection Regulation).
[32] Section 5 ibid.
[33] Section 8(7) ibid.

3.2 Exemptions under the Act

The most pressing concern in relation to law enforcement access to personal data of individuals and mandatory data retention procedures is the provision on exemptions[34] from the application of the law. Personal data that is processed in the interest of prevention, detection, investigation, or prosecution of any offence or contravention of any law is exempt from the application of the provisions of the Act apart from the requirements around cross-border data transfer.[35] Additionally, the Central Government has the power to exempt any agency of the State from the application of the bill in the interest of security, sovereignty, and integrity of the country, friendly relations with foreign states, maintenance of public order, or preventing incitement of any related cognizable offence.[36] The personal data that is provided to the Central Government by these exempted agencies is also exempted from the application of the Act.[37]

The Central Government has the power to exempt[38] data fiduciaries from the obligations relating to providing a privacy notice in different languages,[39] the erasure of personal data upon request by the data principal,[40] and the data principals' right to seek information regarding their personal data that is being processed. The exemption has to be granted based on the volume and nature of the personal data processed, however no other additional guidelines on this analysis has been provided as of now.

As it can be observed, the provisions that grant the powers to the Central Government to grant exemptions to other data fiduciaries or permit significantly lax data protection measures in cases where personal data processing is for security and public order measures are not narrowly worded. The independence of the data protection board that is expected to be constituted under the Act has been questioned consistently.[41] Even though the composition of the data protection board including the process of selection, terms and conditions of the appointment of the members, the removal of the chairperson or the other members has been mentioned in the Act, the final call on the appointment is still solely determined by the Central Government.[42] The lack of independence of the data protection board means that there may not be oversight over the actions of the Central Government.

4. Data Retention in India

The data retention requirements that are applicable to service providers, intermediaries, and other entities are not stated in one national legislation. These requirements are located in the primary legislation of Information Technology Act 2000 and subordinate rules that derive its legitimacy from the primary legislation.

---

[34] Section 17 ibid.
[35] Section 17(1)(c) ibid.
[36] Section 17(2)(a) ibid.
[37] Section 17(2)(a) ibid.
[38] Section 17(3) ibid.
[39] Section 5(2) ibid.
[40] Section 8(7) ibid.
[41] Anuskha Jain and Prateek Waghre, 'IFF's First Read of the Draft Digital Personal Data Protection Bill, 2023' (*Internet Freedom Foundation*, 3 August 2023) <https://internetfreedom.in/iffs-first-read-of-the-draft-digital-personal-data-protection-bill-2023/> accessed 11 July 2024.
[42] Chapters 5 and 6 Digital Personal Data Protection Act 2023.

4.1 Information Technology Act 2000

The primary provision for data retention/preservation is found in the Information Technology Act 2000. An amendment to the Information Technology Act 2000 was introduced in the Lok Sabha[43] in 2006 and was stalled for a couple of years. However, the Information Technology (Amendment) Act 2008 was passed towards the end of the 2008, a month after one of the most devastating terrorist attacks in the country. This amendment introduced the requirement of preservation and retention of information by intermediaries.[44] Whether this was directly in response to national security concerns can only be speculated, as no such announcement was made through the official channels and the amendment was passed in the Lok Sabha without any discussion. According to section 67C of the Information Technology (Amendment) Act 2008, intermediaries had to preserve and retain information that is specified by the Union Government. The form and duration of the retained information is also determined by the Central Government. In case of the intermediaries intentionally or knowingly did not comply with the retention requirements, they could be subjected to imprisonment for up to three years and a fine. The specific rules regarding retention and security of information by intermediaries providing digital locker facilities[45] has been explicitly drafted.[46] The rules regarding intermediaries that do not provide such facilities has not been notified, despite news reports indicating the start of the process of drafting such rules.[47]

In order to enhance cybersecurity and prevent the spread or intrusion of computer contaminant in the country, the Central Government has the power to authorize any agency of the government to monitor and collect the traffic data that is generated.[48] The provision does not explicitly equate enhancing cybersecurity of the country to national security. However, lack of specificity in terms of cybersecurity of which infrastructures of the country can result in a potentially wide scope. This is concerning also due to the definition of traffic data for the purposes of the provision which includes data that is identifying or can identify an individual, location, origin, destination of the communication, and any related information.[49] The procedural framework for the issuance of directions relating to traffic data is provided under the Information Technology (Procedure and Safeguards for Monitoring and Collecting Traffic Data or Information) Rules 2009.[50] According to the procedural framework, purposes of monitoring can include 'identifying or tracking of any person who

---

[43] The Lower house of the Indian Parliament, literally meaning the house of the people. Legislative proposals need to be passed in the Lower house and the Upper house of the Parliament and then assented by the President to be an enacted legislation.

[44] Section 2(1)(w) Information Technology Act 2000.

[45] A scheme that provides for a secure personal electronic space for storing documents by the user of the facilities. Ministry of Electronics and Information Technology 'Digital Locker' <https://www.meity.gov.in/digital-locker> accessed 25 September 2024.

[46] Information Technology (Preservation and Retention of Information by Intermediaries Providing Digital Locker Facilities) Rules 2016.

[47] Surabhi Agarwal, 'Tech Companies like Gmail, WhatsApp May Be Asked to Store User Information' *The Economic Times* (14 October 2016) <https://economictimes.indiatimes.com/tech/ites/tech-companies-like-gmail-whatsapp-may-be-asked-to-store-user-information/articleshow/54839888.cms?utm_source=contentofinterest&utm_medium=text&utm_campaign=cppst> accessed 11 July 2024.

[48] Section 69B Information Technology Act 2000.

[49] Section 69B(4)(ii) ibid.

[50] Information Technology (Procedure and Safeguards for Monitoring and Collecting Traffic Data or Information) Rules 2009 <https://upload.indiacode.nic.in/showfile?actid=AC_CEN_45_76_00001_200021_1517807324077&type=rule&filename=ru_cen_45_0_00028_1519711141735.pdf> accessed 25 September 2024.

has breached, or is suspected of having breached or being likely to breach cybersecurity', 'forecasting of imminent cyber incidents', or 'any other matter relating to cybersecurity' among other purposes. The framework does not necessarily narrow down the scope of the retention and monitoring requirement from the primary legislation with use of phrases like 'being likely to breach cybersecurity'. The procedural framework specifies the period of retention as nine months from the receipt of direction or creation of record—for the records that concern the directions for monitoring or collecting the traffic data[51]—and not specifically for the data that has been collected or monitored. The framework does prohibit the authorized agency to further disclose the data that has been collected for purposes other than that of enhancing cybersecurity.[52]

4.2 The Indian Computer Emergency Response Team (Cert-In) Rules

The Indian Computer Emergency Response Team (Cert-In) issued new directions under section 70B of the Information Technology Act 2000 in relation to information security practices, procedure, prevention, response, and reporting of cyber incidents.[53] These directions were issued without public consultations and is especially troubling due to ambiguity around the key terms such as service providers, intermediaries, and body corporates as the scope of application of the directions depends on the definitions of these terms. The rules require service providers that fall within the scope to 'mandatorily enable logs of all ICT systems'[54] the details of which are expected to be stored for a period of 180 days. The rules require one copy of this data to be stored within the Indian jurisdiction (soft data localization measures). This is tricky in case of VPN service providers and even messaging platforms such as Signal[55] and Proton[56] as they claim that they do not retain any logs by design as a privacy preserving measure. Additionally, in case of any cancellation or withdrawal of registration of their services by the users, the service providers are expected to retain the data that has been used for registration with data centers, virtual private server providers, VPN service providers and cloud service providers for a period of five years or more as mandated by the law.[57] This data includes user information such as names, email addresses, contact information, and IP addresses.

---

[51] Section 8(1) Information Technology (Procedure and Safeguards for monitoring and collecting traffic data or information) Rules 2009.

[52] Section 10, Information Technology (Procedure and Safeguards for monitoring and collecting traffic data or information) Rules 2009.

[53] Indian Computer Emergency Response Team, 'Directions under sub-section (6) of section 70B of the Information Technology Act, 2000 relating to information security practices, procedure, prevention, response and reporting of cyber incidents for Safe & Trusted Internet' (*Ministry of Electronics and Information Technology*, 28 April 2022) <https://www.cert-in.org.in/PDF/CERT-In_Directions_70B_28.04.2022.pdf> accessed 9 July 2023.

[54] Indian Computer Emergency Response Team, 'Directions under sub-section (6) of section 70B of the Information Technology Act, 2000 relating to information security practices, procedure, prevention, response and reporting of cyber incidents for Safe & Trusted Internet' 2022, Direction 4.

[55] David Delima, 'Recent Subpoena Response Reveals Exactly How Much Data Signal Collects about You' (*HT Tech*, 28 April 2021) <https://tech.hindustantimes.com/mobile/news/recent-court-filing-reveals-exactly-how-much-data-signal-collects-about-you-71619595504148.html> accessed 11 July 2024.

[56] Proton Team, 'Indian Government Can Spy on Indian Internet Users in Real Time' (*Proton VPN Blog*, 11 November 2022) <https://protonvpn.com/blog/indian-real-time-surveillance/> accessed 11 July 2024.

[57] Indian Computer Emergency Response Team, 'Directions under sub-section (6) of section 70B of the Information Technology Act, 2000 relating to information security practices, procedure, prevention, response and reporting of cyber incidents for Safe & Trusted Internet', Direction 5.

5. Law Enforcement Access to Retained Personal Data

Apart from the explicit provisions on retaining certain categories of data, certain legal obligations either require real time access to some information or require service providers to cooperate with law enforcement as and when required and provide them with the required information. Though there is no explicit legal obligation regarding retaining data categories that law enforcement can seek access to, the ability of law enforcement to request or even summon such data means that service providers may need to retain such data in the first instance. Hence, the following sections will lay down relevant legal provisions of the legislations that provide legitimacy to the access requests by the law enforcement.

5.1 Criminal Procedure Code 1973

The provisions under Criminal Procedure Code 1973 (CrPC) are do not mandate the service providers to retain specific categories of data. However, the code sets out requirements for law enforcement access to data that is already in the possession of the relevant service providers. Section 91 of the CrPC allows a court or a police officer to issue either a summons or a written order requiring submission of 'any document or other thing' that is 'necessary or desirable' for the purposes of an investigation. A document or a thing for the purposes of this section is extremely wide and only letters, postcards, telegrams, and things which are in the custody of the postal or a telegraph authority are explicitly excluded from the scope of this provision.[58] The broad authority provided under section 91 CrPC is preferred by law enforcement authorities to request access to data despite the existence of more specific provisions under the Information Technology Act 2000 and its corresponding rules and procedures.[59]

On the other hand, section 92 of the CrPC lays down the procedure to request access to letters and telegrams and other things that are under the custody of the postal or telegraph authority. The summons under this section cannot be issued by a competent police officer but must be issued post approval from the competent judicial authority. The scope of the provision is narrower than the previous one limiting itself to only those documents or things that are under the custody of the postal or the telegraph authority. Ironically, what this means is a judicial approval is needed to request production of documents related to telegraphs but a police officer can seek user data from Facebook without any judicial safeguards under section 91 of the CrPC. Based on the transparency report that was submitted for the period of July to December 2022, 63,852 requests for user data were received from the state agencies in the country, of which 68.26% were provided with some of the data that has been produced by the user. For the same time period, 8,170 of preservation requests were submitted which require Facebook to preserve the relevant account information temporarily till the legal process that needs to be conducted to access the data is completed.[60]

---

[58] Criminal Procedure Code 1973, section 91(3).
[59] Justin Hemmings, Sreenidhi Srinivasan and Peter Swire, 'How Stricter Procedures in Existing Law May Provide a Useful Path for Cloud Act Executive Agreements' (*Cross-Border Data Forum*, 16 November 2018) <https://www.crossborderdataforum.org/how-stricter-procedures-in-existing-law-may-provide-a-useful-path-for-cloud-act-executive-agreements/> accessed 11 July 2024.
[60] Meta, 'Government Requests for User Data | Transparency Center' <https://transparency.fb.com/data/government-data-requests/country/in/> accessed 11 July 2024.

Facebook has just been used as an example in this instance. Similar summoning powers can be exercised against any of the service providers operating in the country.

The criminal codes of the country underwent a major overhaul at the end of 2023. The criminal codes consist of the Indian Penal Code 1860, Code of Criminal Procedure 1898, and the Indian Evidence Act 1872. All three codes pre-dated the independence of the country and were drafted by the colonial powers with very different objectives. Hence, the overhaul of the codes was an approach towards 'decolonizing' the law. This chapter will not delve further into the meaning of decolonization or whether the newly introduced legislations actually achieved the said objective. Instead, the following section will merely focus on the legal provisions relevant to data retention and law enforcement access to personal data.

The Bharatiya Nyaya Sanhita (BNS),[61] Bharatiya Nagrik Suraksha Sanhita (BNSS),[62] and the Bharatiya Sakshya Adhiniyam (BSA)[63] replaced the earlier mentioned legislations respectively and received the assent from the President in December 2023 and are set to come into force in July 2024 as per the notification[64] issued by the Ministry of Home Affairs. Like its predecessor, the BNSS also permits the court to summon any document or material that is necessary for an investigation.[65] However, unlike its predecessor there is an explicit mention of 'communication devices that contain digital evidence' in the relevant provision. Even though the earlier provision under the now soon to be irrelevant CrPC permitted similar summons, the explicit mention of communication devices can have severe consequences. Summoning an entire communication device instead of specific information from the communication device can provide the courts and law enforcement potential access to lots of information that might not be necessary for the proceedings in question. The nature in which such issues will be handled will probably have to be determined by additional guidelines from the court in a way that the Digital Personal Data Protection Act 2023 is not violated and neither is the right to privacy of the individual under article 21 of the Constitution.

5.2 Indian Telegraph Act 1885

The Unified Access Services License (UASL) agreements[66] bind the licensee, that is, the telecommunications provider, and the licensor, that is, the Department of Telecommunication, to specific terms that permit the licensee to provide wireless or wireline services in a

---

[61] The Bharatiya Nyaya Sanhita 2023 (English Translation: The Indian Penal Code).
[62] The Bharatiya Nagrik Surakhsa Sanhita 2023 (English Translation: The Indian Citizen Protection Code).
[63] The Bharatiya Sakshya Adhiniyam 2023 (English Translation: The Indian Evidence Act).
[64] Ministry of Home Affairs, Notification CG-DL-E-24022024-252353 <https://www.mha.gov.in/sites/default/files/BhartiyaNyayaSanhita_24022024.pdf>; Ministry of Home Affairs, Notification CG-DL-E-24022024-252354 <https://www.mha.gov.in/sites/default/files/BharatiyaNagarikSurakshaSanhita_24022024.pdf>; Ministry of Home Affairs, Notification CG-DL-E-24022024-252352 <https://www.mha.gov.in/sites/default/files/BharatiyaSakshyaAdhiniyam_24022024.pdf> all accessed 2 September 2024.
[65] The Bharatiya Nagrik Surakhsa Sanhita 2023, section 94(1).
[66] Department of Telecommunications, 'Introduction to Erstwhile Unified Access Services/Cellular Mobile Services' <https://dot.gov.in/access-services/introduction-unified-access-servicescellular-mobile-services> accessed 11 July 2024.

particular service area.[67] These agreements are drafted under are drafted under the authority provided by the Indian Telegraph Act 1885. According to the terms of the agreement,[68] the licensee is expected to provide access to its subscriber database to the licensor and is also tasked with maintaining an updated list of the subscribers. The licensee is also required to maintain call detail records, exchange details records, IP detail records. These records should be archived for a minimum period of two years and with an option to extend the retention available to the licensor.[69] The retention period was increased to two years from one year via an amendment on 21 December 2021[70] without public consultation or affected stakeholders' consultation. The circular does not provide for additional information on the necessity of the increase in retention period of the call data records which makes the assessment of the existence of legitimate aim difficult. The licensee is also required to provide the licensor or an agency authorized by the licensor the geographical location of the subscriber upon request.[71]

5.3 Centralized Monitoring Systems

It has been speculated that the Centralized Monitoring System, essentially a surveillance system, was initiated as a response to the tragic terrorist attack that took place in Mumbai on 26 November 2008. To strengthen national security structure of the country, this system was conceived in 2009 to create a centralized system to monitor telecommunications and internet traffic in the country.[72] This includes monitoring of the text messages, social media, and telecommunications data including landlines and mobile phones.[73] The infrastructure was being developed in a way that direct monitoring and interception could be undertaken without any manual intervention from the telecom service providers.[74] Now, law enforcement authorities need not request the telecom service providers to monitor and provide access to the required user information. Instead they can simply monitor or access such information through the centralized system.

Prior to the introduction of the system, telecom service providers installed lawful interception systems that allowed them to conducted targeted surveillance of citizens based on

---

[67] Government of India, Ministry of Communications Department of Telecommunications, 'License agreement for Unified License' (Department of Telecommunications) <https://dot.gov.in/sites/default/files/Upda ted%20UL-AGREEMENT%20up%20to%2031%20Mar%2023.pdf?download=1> accessed 11 July 2024.
[68] ibid clause 39.19.
[69] ibid clause 39.20.
[70] Ministry of Communications, Department of Telecommunications, 'No 20-271/2010 AS-I (Vol.-III)' (Department of Telecommunications, 21 December 2021) <https://dot.gov.in/sites/default/files/21122021%20 UL%20CDR%20two%20years.pdf> accessed 11 July 2024.
[71] Government of India, Ministry of Communications Department of Telecommunications, "License agreement for Unified License", clause 39.23(x).
[72] Press Information Bureau 'Centralised System to Monitor Communications' (Press Information Bureau, 26 November 2009) <https://pib.gov.in/newsite/PrintRelease.aspx?relid=54679> accessed 11 July 2024.
[73] Anjani Trivedi, 'In India, Prism-like Surveillance Slips Under the Radar' [2013] *Time* <https://world.time. com/2013/06/30/in-india-prism-like-surveillance-slips-under-the-radar/?ref=static.internetfreedom.in#ixzz2Y pWhRsrB> accessed 11 July 2024.
[74] 'Watch the Watchmen Series Part 2: The Centralised Monitoring System' (*Internet Freedom Foundation*, 14 September 2020) <https://internetfreedom.in/watch-the-watchmen-series-part-2-the-centralised-monitor ing-system/> accessed 11 July 2024; Addison Litton, 'The State of Surveillance in India: The Central Monitoring System's Chilling Effect on Self-Expression' 14 Washington University Global Studies Law Review 799.

requests by the law enforcement. Amendments were made to the UASL licences in 2013[75] that facilitated this by requiring the service providers to provide dark optic fibre connectivity to the nearest point of presence of the Centralized Monitoring Systems network. Due to an obligation on the telecom service providers to integrate interception store and forward servicers with the lawful interception systems, all data that is intercepted by the telecom service providers is automatically transmitted to the regional monitoring centres which is connected to the Centralized Monitoring System.[76]

This system was introduced in the country when there was neither an explicit right to privacy nor was there even a draft of the data protection legislation. In the absence of any extensive data protection or privacy safeguards, oversight over the functioning of the system and the collection and interception of data was important. In 2013, in response to a question on the oversight mechanism and procedural safeguards that the Centralized Monitoring System is subjected to, the Minister of State in the Ministry of Communications and Information Technology stated that the oversight mechanism was dictated by section 5(2) of the Indian Telegraph Act 1885 read with rule 419A of the Indian Telegraph (Amendment) Rules 2007.[77] The system, (along with two others, NETRA[78] and NATGRID[79]) has been challenged in the Delhi High Court in 2020,[80] on grounds that the direct and easy access to intercept, monitor, store, and analyse the telecommunication and internet communications in bulk is an infringement of the fundamental right to privacy of the individuals under article 21 of the Indian Constitution. The legal proceedings are still ongoing and could be one of the most important case related to surveillance in the country after the confirmation of the explicit constitutional right to privacy.

5.4 Information Technology (Reasonable Security Practices and Procedures and Sensitive Personal Data or Information) Rules 2011

The Information Technology (Reasonable Security Practices and Procedures and Sensitive Personal Data or Information) (SPDI) Rules were drafted under section 43A of the Information Technology Act 2000. Despite the bare minimum requirements, these rules

---

[75] Department of Telecommunications, 'Amendment 2 of 2013, Amendment to the Unified Access Services (UAS) Licence agreement' (Department of Telecommunication, June 2013) <https://dms.dot.gov.in/access-services/amendments-access-service-licences?order=field_access_services_date&sort=asc&page=4> accessed 25 September 2024.

[76] Maria Xynou, 'India's Central Monitoring System (CMS): Something to Worry About? — The Centre for Internet and Society' (Centre for Internet and Society, 30 January 2014) <https://cis-india.org/internet-governance/blog/india-central-monitoring-system-something-to-worry-about?ref=static.internetfreedom.in> accessed 11 July 2024.

[77] *Centre for public interest litigation & Another v Union of India & Others* Writ Petition (Civil) No. 8998 of 2020.

[78] Network Traffic Analysis, developed by the Centre for Artificial Intelligence—a laboratory under the Defence Research and Development organization. It monitors internet traffic for the use of specific keywords. Writ Petition (Civil) No. 8998 of 2020.

[79] National Intelligence Grid is attached to the Office of the Ministry of Home Affairs. It's a framework that is expected to gather information to enhance the counter terrorism capability of the country by connecting the approved security/law enforcement agencies to designated data providers; Anushka Jain, 'Watch the Watchmen Series Part 1 : The National Intelligence Grid' (2 September 2020) <https://internetfreedom.in/watch-the-watchmen-part-1-the-national-intelligence-grid/> accessed 11 July 2024.

[80] *Centre for public interest litigation & Another v Union of India & Others* Writ Petition (Civil) No. 8998 of 2020; Matter is subjudice. More details can be found at: Software Freedom Law Center, 'Legal Challenge by CPIL and SFLC.IN to Surveillance Projects CMS, NATGRID and NETRA' (24 March 2022) <https://sflc.in/legal-challenge-cpil-and-sflcin-surveillance-projects-cms-natgrid-and-netra/> accessed 11 July 2024.

are the primary data protection framework of the country. The scope of application of these rules extends only to body corporates, that is, a company or association of individuals that is engaged in commercial or professional activities.[81] Government agencies are exempt from the application of the rules. These rules do not contain explicit data retention requirements. However, they do contain rather broad obligation on the body corporates to disclose information when required.

Body corporates are required to disclose sensitive personal data to government agencies without seeking consent from the provider of information on receiving a request from the government agency seeking the information along with its purpose.[82] Government agencies under these rules are authorized to seek disclosure of such information form the purpose of either verifying the identity of the provider of information or for preventing, detecting, investigating, and punishing offences.[83] The nature of offences has not been mentioned which means information can be sought for anything without any specific threshold. As the rules do not contain specific information regarding the types of sensitive personal data that can be requested from the body corporates, it may be concluded that these rules do not create additional data retention obligations. These rules will be officially repealed when the Digital Personal Data Protection Act 2023 is enacted.

5.5 Information Technology (Intermediary Guidelines and Digital Media Ethics Code) Rules 2021

The idea to break end to end encryption of messaging services began in relation to an unusual case in India. It involved a petition[84] in the Madras High Court by an individual aggrieved over defamatory attacks and verbal abuse over his involvement with committee against animal abuse. Their main prayer for relief was to link the user's social media accounts with their Aadhaar numbers to ensure swift justice to victims of cybercrime, that is, social media platforms will have to be obliged to disclose user information linked to alleged perpetrator accounts. The case quickly devolved into a discussion over the level of information the social media platforms have to share with law enforcement agencies. The case took an unexpected turn when the Madras High Court dropped the original prayer regarding Aadhaar linkage and focused on the feasibility of identifying the originator on information on end-to-end messaging services. This case is still pending, however rules mandating certain class of social media services to break encryption and provide details regarding the originator of communications while not disclosing the communication content has made data retention requirements murky once again.

The Information Technology (Intermediary Guidelines and Digital Media Ethics Code) Rules 2021 were drafted by the Union Government in exercise of their powers under section 87 if the Information Technology Act 2000 and have repealed the 2011 version of the

---

[81] Information Technology Act, 2000, section 43A Explanation (1).
[82] Information Technology (Reasonable Security Practices and Procedures and Sensitive Personal Data or Information) Rules 2011, section 6.
[83] ibid.
[84] *Antony Clement Rubin vs Union of India*, WP No. 20774 of 2018.
'SC Allows Facebook's Transfer Petition in Antony Clement Rubin v. UoI' (*Internet Freedom Foundation*, 22 October 2019) <https://internetfreedom.in/facebooks-transfer-petition-in-madras-hc-case-involving-encryption-and-traceability-allowed-after-tamil-nadu-government-withdraws-objections/> accessed 11 July 2024.

rules. These rules flow from the safe harbour provisions granted to intermediaries under section 79 of the Information Technology Act 2000. The rules increase the due diligence requirements the intermediaries need to fulfil in order to avoid liability for the content posted by their users. The Rules differentiate between social media intermediaries and significant social media intermediaries with the latter meaning intermediaries with more than 5 million registered users.[85]

Significant social media intermediary providing messaging services are required to enable the identification of the first originator of the information.[86] Such tracing must be undertaken by the significant social media intermediary if it is required by a court of relevant jurisdiction or a competent authority under section 69 of the Information Technology Act 2000 as per the Information Technology (Procedure and Safeguards for interception, monitoring and decryption of information) Rules 2009.[87] Conditions under which the traceability order can be passed include for offences related to the sovereignty and integrity of India, security of the state, friendly relations with foreign states, or public order, or in relation to rape, sexually explicit material, or child sexual abuse material, or for an offence that is punishable with imprisonment for a minimum term of five years.

Most messaging services have argued that they retain minimal user data to enable the exchange of electronic information and the protocol of end-to-end encryption is necessary to ensure privacy of the users and the security of the services provided.[88] The messaging services have argued that the first originator of the information can be identified only if they access the content of the messages resulting in breaking the protocol of end-to-end encryption.[89] With respect to communication content, the rules state that the significant social media intermediary will not be required to disclose the contents of the messages[90] and that significant social media intermediaries should be approached to identify the first originator of the message only if other less intrusive measures to identify the first originator are not available.[91] However, with respect to the prohibition of display of content, it has been argued[92] that the Information Technology Decryption[93] rules do contain powers that can provide statutory backing to demands of content of the messages. So, even if Information Technology Rules 2021 do not mandate disclosure of communication content, due to technical reasons associated with breaking end-to-end encryption, the significant social media intermediaries might have to retain communication data. Any access to such communication data though prohibited under one set of rules might have the

---

[85] Information Technology(Intermediary Guidelines and Digital Media Ethics Code) Rules, 2021 section 2(v).
[86] ibid section 5(2).
[87] Information Technology (Procedure and Safeguards for interception, monitoring and decryption of information) Rules 2009, Rule 4(2).
[88] Anushka Jain et al, 'Latest Draft Intermediary Rules: Fixing Big Tech, by Breaking Our Digital Rights?' (25 February 2021) <https://internetfreedom.in/latest-draft-intermediary-rules-fixing-big-tech-by-breaking-our-digital-rights/> accessed 11 July 2024.
[89] Meri Baghdasaryan, 'EFF and Partners Urge the Indian Government to Keep End-to-End Encryption Alive' (*Electronic Frontier Foundation*, 18 July 2022) <https://www.eff.org/deeplinks/2022/07/eff-and-partners-urge-indian-government-keep-end-end-encryption-alive> accessed 11 July 2024.
[90] Information Technology (Intermediary Guidelines and Digital Media Ethics Code) Rules 2021, section 4(2).
[91] ibid.
[92] Krishnesh Bapat and others, 'How the Intermediaries Rules Are Anti-Democratic and Unconstitutional' (*Internet Freedom Foundation*, 27 February 2021) <https://internetfreedom.in/intermediaries-rules-2021/> accessed 11 July 2024.
[93] Information Technology (Procedure and Safeguards for interception, monitoring and decryption of information) Rules 2009, Rule 4(2).

necessary statutory backing under the Information Technology Decryption rules making it rather concerning.

However, the practical implications[94] of these provisions are not yet known and are subject to challenge in the courts on grounds of infringement of privacy. It has also been argued that enabling traceability and breaking end-to-end encryption doesn't fall within the mandate provided under section 79 of the IT Act, which is the primary provision that enables safe harbour for intermediaries in India and hence is ultra vires of the legislation.[95] Facebook and WhatsApp Inc have challenged the traceability provisions in the Delhi High Court and have called the requirement unconstitutional and infringing the privacy of their users while creating an atmosphere of mass surveillance.[96]

6. Analysis with the *Puttaswamy* Test

As provided in earlier sections, the *Puttaswamy* judgment recognized the constitutional right to privacy to be a part of Article 21 of the Constitution. This judgment extensively researches international approaches to privacy and data protection and recognizes broad types of privacy interests[97] such as bodily privacy, spatial privacy, communicational privacy, and others. For the purposes of this chapter, observations regarding informational privacy provided in the plurality opinion[98] drafted by Justice Chandrachud and the concurring opinion of Justice Nariman[99] are relevant. They argue that informational privacy is a key facet of the right to privacy in accordance with the Constitution. They also contend that an individual's control over the dissemination of their information is an important aspect of safeguarding their informational privacy. The importance of control over disclosure of personal information was affirmed even in the concurring opinion of Justice Kaul.[100] Mandatory data retention and subsequent access to retained data to law enforcement is a clear infringement of informational privacy as individuals do not necessarily have control over further disclosure of their data.

The majority opinion in *Puttaswamy* acknowledges that the right to privacy of the individual is not absolute in nature. It can be restricted provided that such a restriction is (a) based in the law, (b) advances a legitimate state aim, and (c) is a proportional response to the objectives being sought. The first element of the test is self-explanatory, that is, the restriction must have a grounding in the law that is in force at the time the restriction was introduced. An analysis of the legitimate state aim is conducted to ensure that the nature and content of the law does not amount to arbitrary state action, that is, the aim should not

---

[94] Internet Society, 'Traceability and Cybersecurity' (*Internet Society*, 27 November 2020) <https://www.internetsociety.org/resources/doc/2020/traceability-and-cybersecurity-experts-workshop-series-on-encryption-in-india/> accessed 11 July 2024.

[95] Bapat and others, 'How the Intermediaries Rules Are Anti-Democratic and Unconstitutional' (n 92).

[96] Aditi Agrawal, 'Facebook, WhatsApp Sue Indian Government Over Traceability Requirement' *Forbes India* (26 May 2021) <https://www.forbesindia.com/article/take-one-big-story-of-the-day/facebook-whatsapp-sue-indian-government-over-traceability-requirement/68175/1> accessed 11 July 2024.

[97] *Puttaswamy* (n 3) p 202 referred to Bert-Jaap Koops et al, 'A Typology of Privacy' (2017) 38(2) University of Pennsylvania Journal of International Law, 566

[98] ibid 246.

[99] ibid 449.

[100] ibid 523.

suffer from arbitrariness of the State.[101] Prevention and investigation of crime[102] and for the purposes of national security[103] have been given as examples in the judgment. Justice Kaul in his concurring opinion elaborated on the test of legitimate aim by adding that such an aim must be construed narrowly to prevent arbitrariness.[104] The test of proportionality requires a determination of an existence of a rational nexus between the objects and means adopted to achieve them, that is. between the legitimate state aim and the measure adopted to achieve such an aim. Rational nexus and proportionality do not mean the same nor does analysis of a nexus lead to an answer on the proportionality of the measure. Examining rational nexus would merely lead to an analysis of whether the measure achieves the stated objective,[105] not whether it was disproportionate in achieving such a measure. While the *Puttaswamy* judgment was hailed as being one of the cornerstones of Indian constitutional cases, its lack of extensive analysis of the doctrine of proportionality was a disappointment.

This situation was partly corrected in another seminal case two years later, in a judgment widely referred to as *Puttaswamy II*,[106] which ruled on the constitutionality of the various parts of the Aadhaar (Targeted Delivery of Financial and Other Subsidies, Benefits and Services) Act 2016, a legislation that gives legal backing to the Aadhaar project mentioned in earlier sections. The majority opinion in the case refined the proportionality test that was set *Puttaswamy* to further include an analysis of (i) legitimate aim, (ii) necessity of means, (iii) a less restrictive but equally effective alternative, (iv) measure must not have a disproportionate impact on the rights holders.[107] This is a much more substantial analysis. Despite reference to the EU charter[108] and the General Data Protection Regulation[109] in the *Puttaswamy* judgment, the proportionality test as it stands currently falls short of the standard set by the EU. However, it is possible that this doctrine gets expanded on by the Courts in the many pending cases before it dealing with privacy and data protection. For the purposes of this chapter, the doctrine of proportionality as stated in *Puttaswamy II* will be referred to despite having a smaller judges bench than the *Puttaswamy* judgment to highlight the inadequacies of the current data retention and law enforcement access to personal data legal provisions.

Section 67C of the Information Technology Act 2000[110] does not specifically state the legitimate aim that is intended to be achieved as a result of the retention and preservation requirements. Section 69B of the same Act[111] on the other hand, does state the

---

[101] ibid 254.
[102] ibid 256.
[103] ibid 265.
[104] ibid 534.
[105] Aparna Chandra, 'Proportionality in India: A Bridge to Nowhere?' (2020) 3 University of Oxford Human Rights Hub Journal.
[106] *Puttaswamy* (n 3).
[107] ibid 320.
[108] ibid 180.
[109] ibid 534.
[110] '67C. Preservation and retention of information by intermediaries.
 –(1) Intermediary shall preserve and retain such information as may be specified for such duration and in such manner and format as the Central Government may prescribe.
 (2) any intermediary who intentionally or knowingly contravenes the provisions of sub-section (1) shall be punished with an imprisonment for a term which may extend to three years and also be liable to fine.]'
[111] '69B. Power to authorise to monitor and collect traffic data or information through any computer resource for cyber security.–(1) The Central Government may, to enhance cyber security and for identification, analysis and prevention of intrusion or spread of computer contaminant in the country, by notification in the Official Gazette, authorise any agency of the Government to monitor and collect traffic data or information generated, transmitted, received or stored in any computer resource.

legitimate aim as enhancing cybersecurity which has a very wide scope. However, the associated procedural framework that governs the collection and monitoring of traffic data does not narrow down this State aim due to inclusion of phrases such as 'being likely to breach cybersecurity' among others. With regards to the Cert-In rules, the data retention periods, the requirement for service providers to maintain a copy of all logs of their ICT systems in India and the requirement for VPN service providers to collect and store customer data categories cannot be considered to be proportional to the State aim of enhancing cybersecurity as there are no indications of examination of any least restrictive measures or even cursory consideration of the disproportionate impact on the rights of citizens.

The Criminal Procedure Code (and its succeeding legislation) provision that enables access of 'any document' that is 'necessary or desirable' for the purpose of investigation of any offence does amount to a legitimate State aim. However, inclusion of the phrase desirable and lack of non-executive oversight over the procedure to requisition personal information does bring into question if the provision has been sufficiently narrowly tailored. The traceability requirement under the Information Technology (Intermediary Guidelines and Digital Media Ethics Code) Rules 2021 that requires significant social media intermediaries that provide messaging services to identify the first origination of specific content does have a legitimate State aim, that is, prevention, detection investigation of offences that is related to sovereignty, integrity, or security of the country, friendly relations with foreign states, and public order, among others. However, this requirement may not pass the proportionality test as it is difficult to understand how identifying the first originator of an information is aiding the State in achieving its aim. Apart from questioning the technical feasibility of identifying the first originator,[112] the first originator of the message does not necessarily have to be the creator of the content. The disproportionate impact on the rights of the citizens is also significant.

It cannot be definitely said that the above-mentioned requirements related to data retention and law enforcement access to use of personal data pass the threefold test laid out by the *Puttaswamy* judgment. More often than not, the legitimate State aims are defined in an extremely broad manner or the measures implemented to achieve the State aims are unnecessarily intrusive.

---

(2) The intermediary or any person in-charge or the computer resource shall, when called upon by the agency which has been authorised under sub-section (1), provide technical assistance and extend all facilities to such agency to enable online access or to secure and provide online access to the computer resource generating, transmitting, receiving or storing such traffic data or information.

(3) The procedure and safeguards for monitoring and collecting traffic data or information, shall be such as may be prescribed.

(4) Any intermediary who intentionally or knowingly contravenes the provisions of sub-section (2) shall be punished with an imprisonment for a term which any extend to three years and shall also be liable to fine.

Explanation.–For the purposes of this section,–

(i) ―computer contaminant‖ shall have the meaning assigned to it in section 43;

(ii) ―traffic data‖ means any data identifying or purporting to identify any person, computer system or computer network or location to or from which the communication is or may be transmitted and includes communications origin, destination, route, time, data, size, duration or type of underlying service and any other information.]'

[112] Vasudev Devadasan, 'Intermediary Guidelines and the Digital Public Sphere: Tracing First Originators' (*Indian Constitutional Law and Philosophy*, 10 April 2021) <https://indconlawphil.wordpress.com/2021/04/10/intermediary-guidelines-and-the-digital-public-sphere-tracing-first-originators/> accessed 11 July 2024.

7. Conclusion

This chapter has essentially been an exercise in gathering information pertaining to data retention and law enforcement access to retained data by scouring thorough myriad legislations. Indian citizens have been granted the constitutional right to privacy only in 2017 after decades of judicial inconsistency. Some of the data retentional and law enforcement access to data requirements such as the ones originating from the Centralized Monitoring Systems or the Unified access services licences did come into force prior to 2017. Laxity in accounting for privacy rights could be granted at that time. However, apart from the fact that prior systems need to be changed, the more severe requirements such as the ones originating from the Information Technology Rules 2021, the renewed criminal procedure codes originated much later and should have accounted for the test set forth in the *Puttaswamy* judgment, even in the absence of a data protection legislation.

The fragmentation of the provisions related to data retention and law enforcement access to use of retained data makes it difficult to get an accurate representation of the extent of potentially unwarranted surveillance. Even in cases where there are clear legal requirements, the vague drafting of state aims, lack of clear scope of applicability of the legislation make it difficult to extensively analyse the proportionality of these requirements. Considering that litigation regarding some of the legislations mentioned in this chapter are still pending and the wide exemptions provided to government agencies under the data protection legislation, oversight over enforcement of these powers of the law enforcement is crucial.

Yet, institutional accountability and independent oversight is lacking. This is by no means a novel realization. The understanding that State institutions will be granted exemptions for certain processing of personal data is not unsurprising. However, what is surprising is the lack of sufficient parliamentary oversight or judicial approval over the process that impacts the constitutional right of the citizens. The need for such an oversight has in fact been submitting in 2018 by the Srikrishna Committee on their report on data protection in India.[113]

The primary legislations the Information Technology Act 2000 and the Digital Personal Data Protection Act 2023 provides the Union Government with wide-ranging powers to draft the specificities of the legal requirements of the provisions to future rules or subordinate legislations. These powers are granted without much legislative guidance or meaningful safeguards that check the potential heavy handedness of the Union Government. The only safeguard left maybe that of judicial oversight *ex post facto* enforcement of the subordinate rules or legislations. Similar judicial oversight resulted in striking down specific provisions of the Aadhaar Act due to their noncompliance with the *Puttaswamy* test.[114] However, with vague assertions of protection of national security from the Executive and speculations over even the independence of the judiciary, it is uncertain if judicial oversight is a valid safeguard to protect the privacy rights of the individuals.

---

[113] Committee of Experts under the Chairmanship of Justice B.N Srikrishna, 'A Free and Fair Digital Economy; Protecting Privacy, Empowering Indians' (2018) <https://www.meity.gov.in/writereaddata/files/Data_Protection_Committee_Report.pdf> accessed 11 July 2024.

[114] 'Constitutionality of Aadhaar Act: Judgment Summary' (*Supreme Court Observer*) <https://www.scobserver.in/reports/constitutionality-of-aadhaar-justice-k-s-puttaswamy-union-of-india-judgment-in-plain-english/> accessed 11 July 2024.

India has a vibrant and active civil society. Campaigns against net neutrality,[115] in favour of privacy safeguards in the Aadhaar project,[116] and litigation against the validity of internet shutdowns[117] have all been spearheaded by various civil society organizations and advocacy groups in the country. These organizations have also been known to represent the affected individuals and communities in courts and have impressive knowledge of the effect of privacy infringing measures on the people. However, these organizations seldom have the opportunity to participate in the legislative process as the draft legislations are not always released for public consultations. Additionally, it is acknowledged that matters of national security make transparency of operations difficult. However, the legal obligations on intermediaries and service providers requires them to provide access to user data even in cases where the law enforcement is ensuring public order or is preventing or investigations any offence. Surely, the level of opacity in operations for these conditions need not be as high as that of national security.

The legislations that provide legitimacy to some of the existing surveillance measures are decades old. Just as the surveillance measures have adapted to the changes in technologies, the overarching legislations providing them legitimacy should be updated in a transparent process. The introduction and enactment of a data protection legislation that provides the individuals with adequate redressals and lays down effective accountability and oversight mechanisms over the powers of the Executive was considered to be the need of the hour. However, the enacted data protection legislation leaves the rights wanting more. But the rules to be prescribed that will make the data protection legislation in force could be a reason for hope.

---

[115] Internet Freedom Foundation, 'SaveTheInternet.In' (Internet Freedom Foundation) <https://internetfreedom.in/campaigns-savetheinternet/> accessed 11 July 2024.

[116] Anoo Bhuyan, 'Aadhaar Isn't Just About Privacy. There Are 30 Challenges the Govt Is Facing in Supreme Court' (The Wire) <https://thewire.in/government/aadhaar-privacy-government-supreme-court> accessed 11 July 2024.

[117] 'KeepItOn: Fighting Internet Shutdowns around the World' (*Access Now*) <https://www.accessnow.org/campaign/keepiton/> accessed 11 July 2024.

19
Regulating Data Retention in Japan

Xenofon V Kontargyris

1. Introduction

In Japan, the terms 'data retention' and 'records retention' are typically defined and regulated across a number of legal frameworks pertaining to various areas of human and economic activity. Before looking in detail into these rules, it is useful to put together an overview of how the two terms are commonly understood.

The concept of 'data retention' in Japan generally refers to the practice of storing and preserving electronic data or personal information collected or generated by businesses or organizations.[1] However, there is no specific legal definition of 'data retention' in Japanese legislation nor has comprehensive legislation on data retention been adopted in Japan so far.

Data retention requirements are primarily addressed in sector-specific laws and regulations with foundational concepts, such as the country's Civil or Commercial Codes. A lot of provisions related to retention found in sector-specific laws that were adopted later than the Japanese Act on the Protection of Personal Information (APPI), which is Japan's cornerstone privacy law governing the handling of personal data,[2] are heavily inspired by the APPI. These sectoral laws generally outline the obligations of data handlers regarding the collection, use, disclosure, and disposal of data and records. They often include provisions on retention periods, security measures, and conditions for the lawful storage of personal or other types of data.[3]

The specific definitions and requirements for data retention can vary depending on the sector and the nature of the data involved.[4] For instance, financial institutions, telecommunications providers, and healthcare organizations have their own specific data retention obligations outlined in sector-specific laws and regulations.[5]

'Records retention' in Japan typically refers to the preservation and maintenance of various types of records and documents, both in physical and electronic formats.[6] Records

---

[1] For detailed information on how 'data retention' is understood in Japan and other major countries around the world, refer to S Gutwirth et al, *European Data Protection: Coming of Age* (Springer 2013).

[2] Fujita, Masahito, 'Data Retention Policies and Practices in Japan' in Proceedings of the 3rd International Conference on Information Systems Security and Privacy (ICISSP 2017), 330–36. Porto, Portugal: SCITEPRESS, 2017.

[3] Graham Greenleaf, *Data Protection Law in Asia* (Edward Elgar 2014).

[4] Nakamura Hisao, 'The Evolution of Data Protection Laws in Japan: The Struggle between Individual Rights and Public Interests' International Data Privacy Law 2, no. 3 (2012): 145–51.

[5] Satake Masako, 'Data Retention Policies in Japan' in Proceedings of the 2014 International Conference on Information Networking (ICOIN) IEEE (2014) 526–31.

[6] <https://www.archives.go.jp/english/news/pdf/121130_01_01.pdf> accessed 17 December 2023; Fukuzawa Noboru, 'Development of Records and Archives Administration in Japan' The American Archivist 45, no. 4 (1982): 346–53; Greenleaf, *Data Protection Law in Asia* (n 3); Kawabe Hiroko and Mitsuhiro Maeda, 'Records Management and Archives Administration in Japan: Current State and Issues' Records Management Journal

retention is essential for legal, regulatory, and operational purposes, ensuring that relevant documents are retained for specific periods of time as required by law or industry-specific guidelines.

The concrete definition and requirements for records retention can vary across different sectors as well as among different types of documents. For example, accounting records, corporate minutes, contracts, tax-related documents, and employee records may have distinct retention periods and regulations set forth in sector-specific laws, such as the Regulations on Corporate Accounting of Japan's Ministry of Justice, tax laws, labour laws, or specific regulations applicable to particular industries.

It is important to keep in mind that while 'data retention' in Japan primarily focuses on electronic data and personal information, 'records retention' is a broader term encompassing various types of documents that may be required to be retained for legal, regulatory, or operational purposes.[7] After presenting basic information on both concepts the rest of this chapter will solely focus on data retention and the way it is regulated in Japan.

2. The Meiji Restoration and Origins of the Right to Privacy in Japan's Constitution

In many aspects of its social, political, and economic life, Japan experienced a profound transformation in the period between 1868 to 1912, the so-called Meiji Era from the name of the reigning 122nd Emperor on the Chrysanthemums Throne at the time.[8] This is also true as far as the legislative landscape in the country is concerned: during the Meiji period and following the reorganization and centralization of Japan's government and public administration around the Emperor, most basic laws underwent an extensive overhaul[9] which was characterized by a tendency to import into Japan notions and interpretations of legal norms from Western jurisdictions, most notably from the USA.[10] In this context, the Meiji Era is the period when the concepts of 'data retention' and 'records retention' can be

---

28, no. 2 (2018): 198–210; Shimomura Hidehiko, 'The Japanese Archival System: A Comparative View', The American Archivist 39, no. 2 (1976): 151–61.

[7] For additional information about the difference between 'data retention' and 'records retention' and the way the two concepts are understood in Japan, refer to: K O'Neal, 'What's the Difference Between Information Management and Data Management?' available at <https://www.firstsanfranciscopartners.com/blog/difference-between-information-management-data-management/> accessed 17 December 2023; M Kolodziej, 'Records Management vs Information Management: Is There a Difference?' available at <https://www.accesscorp.com/blog/records-management-vs-information-management/> accessed 17 December 2023; A Cunningham, 'Data Retention vs. Records Management: What's the Difference?' (2014) Information Management Journal 48, no. 1: 30–34; R Touray, 'A Review of Records Management in Organisations' (2021) 8 Open Access Library Journal 1–23, available at <https://www.scirp.org/journal/paperinformation.aspx?paperid=113666> accessed 17 December 2023; K Dan, S Blackburne, B Reed et al, 'Reviews' (1997) 25(2) Archives & Manuscripts 346–422, available at <https://publications.archivists.org.au/index.php/asa/article/view/8663> accessed 17 December 2023.

[8] For a comprehensive summary about the Meiji Restoration refer to <https://www.britannica.com/event/Meiji-Restoration> accessed 17 December 2023.

[9] <http://afe.easia.columbia.edu/special/japan_1750_meiji.htm> accessed 17 December 2023; M Izuru, 'Modernization of Japan's Administrative System, Japanese Modernization Lecture Series, Japan International Cooperation Agency (JICA)' available at <https://www.jica.go.jp/dsp-chair/english/chair/modernization/index.html> accessed 17 December 2023; C Cooper, *The Meiji Restoration: Japan as a Global Nation*, Robert Hellyer and Harald Fuess (eds) (CUP 2020).

[10] Cooper, ibid.

traced for the first time in Japanese legislation. The first significant law in this regard was the Public Archives Act of 1909.[11] This act aimed to preserve government documents of historical value. It established the National Archives of Japan and specified rules for document preservation and access.

After the Second World War, Japan experienced significant changes in its legal framework. In 1947, the post-war Japanese Constitution was adopted, which guaranteed the right to privacy.[12] Concretely, Article 13 in Chapter III 'Rights and Duties of the People' of the Japanese Constitution reads: 'All of the people shall be respected as individuals. Their right to life, liberty, and the pursuit of happiness shall, to the extent that it does not interfere with the public welfare, be the supreme consideration in legislation and in other governmental affairs'.[13] The constitution of Japan technically applies only to the relationship between the state and the individual.[14] However, courts in the country have consistently referred to the

---

[11] Ogawa Chiyoko (1991) 'Archives in Japan: The State of the Art' 54(4) The American Archivist 546–54; Koga Takashi (2007) 'Overview of Archives and Archival Issues in Japan' available at <https://repository.kulib.kyoto-u.ac.jp/dspace/handle/2433/72837> accessed 17 December 2023.

[12] The one from 1947 was not Japan's first Constitution. In brief Japan's constitutional history can be summarized as follows:

Meiji Constitution (1889): This was Japan's first modern constitution, established during the Meiji era. It established a constitutional monarchy with a parliamentary government. However, power remained primarily in the hands of the Emperor and his advisors, limiting democratic representation.

Post-World War II Constitution (1947): Following Japan's defeat in World War II, the country underwent a major constitutional overhaul under the Allied occupation led by General Douglas MacArthur. The new constitution, often referred to as the 'Peace Constitution' or the 'MacArthur Constitution', was promulgated on November 3, 1946. It established a parliamentary democracy, guaranteeing fundamental human rights, pacifism, and the renunciation of war as a sovereign right.

The Heisei Era Revisions: While the core principles of the post-war constitution remained intact, there were debates and discussions about amending certain articles, particularly Article 9, which renounces war and prohibits maintaining military forces. During the Heisei era (1989–2019), there were talks about reinterpretations rather than amendments to maintain Japan's Self-Defense Forces.

Current discussions and developments: in recent years, discussions around constitutional revisions have continued, focusing on aspects like clarifying the status of the Self-Defense Forces, revising emergency powers, and adjusting the balance between individual rights and public interests. However, amending the constitution requires a two-thirds majority in both houses of the National Diet (Japan's parliament) and majority support in a national referendum, making significant revisions challenging.

[13] <https://japan.kantei.go.jp/constitution_and_government_of_japan/constitution_e.html> accessed 17 December 2023.

[14] While analysis of the way Japan's Constitution has been interpreted by courts when regulating the affairs between Japanese state and private citizens is beyond the scope of this chapter, in brief, Japanese courts interpret the Constitution of Japan as a fundamental framework that guides the relationship between the state and private individuals. Several key principles and articles within the Constitution inform this relationship:

Protection of Rights: The Constitution guarantees various rights to individuals, including freedom of speech, assembly, religion, and equality under the law. Courts play a crucial role in upholding these rights, ensuring that laws and government actions do not infringe upon them.

Limiting State Power: The Constitution includes checks and balances on the powers of the government and public authorities. Courts interpret and enforce these limitations, ensuring that government actions are within the bounds of constitutional authority. For instance, Article 13 guarantees the right to be free from searches and seizures without probable cause, as part of the wider right of liberty in private life.

Judicial Review: The Japanese judiciary practices judicial review, which allows courts to assess the constitutionality of laws and government actions. If a law or action is deemed unconstitutional, courts can declare it invalid or order corrective measures.

State Responsibility: The Constitution imposes responsibilities on the state to protect the welfare and rights of its citizens. Courts can hold the government accountable for failing to fulfil these obligations.

Interpreting Article 9: Article 9, renouncing war and prohibiting the maintenance of military forces, has been subject to interpretation by the courts. While Japan maintains the Self-Defense Forces, the courts have addressed cases related to the constitutional boundaries of self-defence and collective security.

For further details see Handbook on the Research Report on the Constitution of Japan, Research Commission on the Constitution, House of Councilors, Japan, 2005, available at <https://www.sangiin.go.jp/eng/report/ehb/ehb.pdf> accessed 17 December 2023.

standards of the constitutional right to privacy when applying the Civil Code in disputes between private individuals.[15] As a result, the 'right to privacy' for individuals is derived from a general right to the 'pursuit of happiness', a right which is generally undermined by invasions of privacy.[16] The country's Supreme Court generally defines 'the right to privacy' as one which prohibits reckless or otherwise arbitrary disclosure of information about an individual's private life.[17] Article 13 of the Constitution provides that citizens' liberty in private life shall be protected against the exercise of public authority.[18] Consequently, it can be construed that, as one of individuals' liberties in private life, every person has the liberty of protecting their own personal information from being disclosed to a third party or made public without valid reason.[19]

This constitutional provision laid the foundation for later legislation related to data and records retention in Japan in the way these notions are commonly understood in modern laws and jurisprudence. In this chapter, an analysis is attempted on the most important of these laws. While Japanese data protection and privacy laws have been at the core of rules regarding these two notions, there are several other overarching or sector-specific legal frameworks which aim to regulate the notions of data and records retention in the country.

3. The Civil Code of Japan

Before focusing on laws containing manifest provisions on data and records retention, it is worth explaining how the two notions and, more precisely, the requirements essentially stemming from the need to retain data and records are systematized in Japan's Civil Code.[20]

The Japanese Civil Code primarily focuses on civil rights, obligations, and contracts. While it does not specifically address data and records retention, certain provisions and concepts enshrined within it can be relevant in the context of data and records management.[21] The most relevant of these concepts are the following:[22]

---

[15] Y Orito and M Kiyoshi, 'Privacy Protection in Japan: Cultural Influence on the Universal Value' (2005) available at <https://www.semanticscholar.org/paper/Privacy-Protection-in-Japan%3A-Cultural-Influence-on-Orito-Murata/b11ecaf37c4c73134d66e69afe33d3e97ce506f417> accessed 17 December 2023.
[16] Megan Richardson, *The Right to Privacy: Origins and Influence of a Nineteenth-Century Idea* (CUP 2017).
[17] Miyashita Hiroshi, 'The Evolving Concept of Data Privacy in Japanese Law' (2011) 1(4) International Data Privacy Law 229–38.
[18] Emma A Imparato, 'The Right to Privacy in East Asian Constitutionalism in Comparative Perspective: The Case of China and Japan' (2023) DPCE Online, [S.l.], v. 55, n. 4 available at <https://www.dpceonline.it/index.php/dpceonline/article/view/1732> accessed 17 December 2023.
[19] See also 1965 (A) No. 1187, judgment of the Grand Bench of the Supreme Court of December 24, 1969, Keishu Vol. 23, No. 12, at 1625.
[20] An English translation of the Japanese Civil Code can be found on <https://www.japaneselawtranslation.go.jp/en/laws/view/3494/en> accessed 17 December 2023.
[21] Kaori Ishii, 'Advancements in the Personal Information Protection System in Japan' (2020) 1(3) Global Privacy Law Review 164–72.
[22] Shusei Ono, 'Comparative Law and the Civil Code of Japan' (1996) 24(02) Hitotsubashi Journal of Law and Politics 27–45.

3.1 Obligation to keep records

In various provisions of the Civil Code, it is foreseen that individuals and entities have an obligation to keep records.[23] While these provisions do not explicitly refer to data or electronic records, they establish a general principle that parties may have a duty to maintain accurate and reliable records to support their legal rights and obligations.

3.2 Legal personality of entities

Chapter 3 of the Civil Code stipulates rules relating to legal personality for entities such as corporations, associations, and organizations. These provisions acknowledge that entities have rights and obligations similar to individuals. Consequently, entities are expected to maintain records and data necessary for fulfilling their legal obligations, such as accounting records, corporate minutes, and transactional documents.

3.3 Preservation of evidence

Another concept the Japanese Civil Code addresses is the preservation of evidence. It establishes a duty for individuals and entities to preserve evidence relevant to legal disputes. This can be interpreted broadly to include the retention of data, documents, and records that may serve as evidence in civil proceedings.

3.4 Limitation period

The Civil Code also sets forth conditions around limitation period for bringing a legal claim. In this context, there are specifications around the time limit within which a claim must be initiated. In the context of data and records retention, relevant provisions indirectly suggest that relevant records should be retained for a duration that exceeds the limitation period to ensure the availability of evidence, if required.

---

[23] In Japan, the requirements to keep records related to civil matters are outlined in the Civil Code. While the Civil Code addresses various aspects of civil law, it does not specifically provide an exhaustive list of record-keeping requirements. However, it establishes general principles regarding records and documentation in civil matters. The following are some of the most prominent record-keeping requirements found in the Japanese Civil Code:
   Documentary Evidence: The Civil Code emphasizes the importance of documentary evidence in civil transactions. It states that written documents often serve as proof of agreements, transactions, and legal relationships between parties.
   Contractual Records: Parties involved in civil transactions, agreements, and contracts are encouraged to maintain written records or documents that outline the terms, conditions, and details of the agreements. These records serve as evidence in case of disputes.
   Evidence in Disputes: In case of litigation or disputes, parties can present documentary evidence, including written records, contracts, correspondence, and other documents, to support their claims or defences.

4. The Japanese Act on Protection of Personal Information and its Cornerstone Role for Regulating Retention in Japan

4.1 A summary of the evolution of the Japanese law on data privacy

The APPI was enacted in 1988 as the first comprehensive law in Japan to address the protection of personal information. While it did not explicitly regulate data retention periods, it established basic principles for the handling of personal data, including the need for consent, purpose specification, and security measures.[24]

In 2003, the APPI was amended to strengthen privacy protections. These amendments included provisions related to the appropriate collection, use, and disclosure of personal information. While the amendments did not introduce specific data retention requirements, they emphasized the importance of implementing appropriate security measures and establishing internal rules for data management.[25]

In 2005, the Japanese government issued, for the first time, guidelines to assist businesses and organizations in complying with the APPI.[26] These guidelines covered various aspects of personal data protection, including data retention. They recommended that organizations establish internal rules for data retention and disposal, considering the purposes of data usage and legal requirements.[27]

In 2015, significant amendments to the APPI were passed to strengthen data protection regulations. The amended law introduced stricter requirements for obtaining consent, expanded the definition of personal information, and enhanced individual rights regarding data access and correction. While it did not introduce specific data retention periods, it emphasized the importance of establishing retention rules based on the purposes of data usage.

The amended APPI came into full effect in 2017. It established the Personal Information Protection Commission (PPC) as an independent administrative authority responsible for overseeing and enforcing data protection regulations. The PPC provides guidelines and recommendations on various aspects of data protection, including data retention and disposal.

The APPI was then amended in 2020, with amended provisions fully entering into effect on 1 April 2022, further enhancing Japan's data privacy regime and making it even more compatible with GDPR standards, following the EU Commission granting Japan an adequacy decision for its privacy framework in 2019.

The latest amendment of the Act took place in 2021 and brought the public sector rules for data protection in Japan within the realm of the APPI.

For a more detailed overview of Japan's Civil Code refer to Ono Shusei, 'Comparative Law and the Civil Code of Japan (I)' (1996) 24 Hitotsubashi Journal of Law and Politics 27-4; and Ono Shusei, 'Comparative Law and the Civil Code of Japan (II)' (1997) 25 Hitotsubashi Journal of Law and Politics 29-5.

[24] Greenleaf, *Data Protection Law in Asia* (n 3).
[25] ibid.
[26] Cabinet Office Guidelines on Personal Information Protection. For a summary of these Guidelines and how they have developed over the years refer to: <https://www.aplawjapan.com/archives/pdf/data-protection-202009.pdf> accessed 17 December 2023.
[27] Greenleaf, *Data Protection Law in Asia* (n 3).

4.2 How has APPI shaped thinking and regulatory treatment of data and records retention in Japan?

Before focusing on how APPI is shaping the issue of data retention in Japan, it is important to elaborate on how the terms 'personal information' and 'personal data' as well as a number of other similar terms are defined in the Japanese privacy law. In particular, APPI differentiates between various types of data:

1. Personal information (個人情報) in the APPI means 'information about a living individual which can identify the specific individual by name, date of birth or other description contained in such information including such information as will allow easy reference to other data and will thereby enable the identification of the specific individual'.[28]
2. Sensitive personal information (要配慮個人情報) means 'personal information as to an identifiable person's race, creed, social status, medical history, criminal record, the fact of having suffered damage by a crime, or other identifiers or their equivalent prescribed by Cabinet Order as those of requiring special care so as not to cause unjust discrimination, prejudice or other disadvantages to that person'.[29]
3. Personal data (個人データ) means 'personal information compiled in a personal information database or the equivalent'.[30]
4. Pseudonymized personal information (仮名加工情報) means 'information relating to an individual that can be prepared in a way that makes it not possible to identify a specific individual unless collated with other information'.[31]
5. Anonymized personal information (匿名加工情報) means 'information relating to an individual that can be prepared in a way that makes it not possible to identify a specific individual by taking any of the measures prescribed ... and also make it not possible to restore that personal information'.[32]
6. Information related to personal information (個人関連情報) means 'information relating to a living individual which does not fall under personal information, pseudonymized personal information and anonymized personal information'.[33]
7. Personal data the business holds (保有個人データ) means 'personal data which a business handling personal information has the authority to disclose; to correct, add or delete content from; to cease to use; to erase; or to cease to provide to a third party, other than what Cabinet Order provides for as data which is likely to harm the public interest or other interests if its existence or non-existence is made clear'.[34]

---

[28] See Art 2 APPI. An official bilingual version of the law is available here: <https://www.japaneselawtranslation.go.jp/en/laws/view/4241> accessed 17 December 2023.
[29] ibid.
[30] ibid.
[31] ibid.
[32] ibid.
[33] ibid.
[34] ibid.

Generally speaking, 'personal information' is understood in the context of the APPI as one single set of personal information, while 'personal data' as a rule indicates collective sets of personal information that are stored in a systematic and/or searchable manner. This distinction is important because certain requirements of the APPI, including the requirement for deletion once the purpose for which personal data is maintained ceases to exist, only apply to personal data, that is, systematically organized and searchable collections of personal information, and not to personal information as single sets of data related to a living person. Nevertheless, it should be noted that an increasing number of businesses in the country tend to adjust their data management programs and treat personal information as personal data, regardless of whether it is maintained in organized data collections or on a standalone basis, bringing the reality of data handling in the country closer to EU standards, assumingly as a result of the growing recognition of EU's GDPR in Japan, following the adequacy decision the country has received from the EU regarding privacy compliance.[35] Lastly, it is interesting to note that, although no specific additional compliance requirements are called out in the APPI as far as sensitive personal data is concerned, organizations handling such data are required to maintain stricter compliance standards and put elevated security measures in place to adequately safeguard such information. This requirement essentially results in more prominent attention and intensified efforts to demonstrate compliance with the APPI by organizations typically processing such sensitive information, for example, medical device manufacturers and healthcare service providers.

The APPI represents nowadays the most important piece of legislation around data retention in Japan. To a great extent, sectoral laws that will be analyzed in the rest of this Chapter essentially transpose APPI's spirit in different types of activities and market sectors. The requirements stipulated in the APPI which, directly or indirectly, influence thinking around data retention in Japan are as follows:[36]

a. Purpose Limitation: APPI requires organizations to clearly define the purpose for which personal information is collected and to retain the information only for as long as necessary to achieve that purpose.
b. Lawful Cause for Retention: Personal information should be retained based on a lawful cause. APPI specifies several lawful causes, including compliance with a legal obligation, protection of vital interests, performance of a contract, or legitimate interests pursued by the organization or a third party.
c. Period of Retention: APPI does not explicitly specify the period for data retention, but it requires organizations to establish internal rules for retention periods based on the purpose of use and other relevant factors. The retention periods should be clearly communicated to the individuals whose data is being collected.
d. Notification of Retention: When collecting personal information, organizations must notify the individuals of the purpose of use and the period of retention, unless such

---

[35] Commission Implementing Decision (EU) 2019/419 of 23 January 2019 pursuant to Regulation (EU) 2016/679 of the European Parliament and of the Council on the adequate protection of personal data by Japan under the Act on the Protection of Personal Information 2019 C/2019/304 OJ L 76/1–58.
[36] K Ueno, 'Data Privacy in Japan: A Comprehensive Analysis of the Act on the Protection of Personal Information (APPI)' (Springer 2018); K Nakamura, 'Japan: The Amended Act on the Protection of Personal Information' (2017) 7(2) International Data Privacy Law 163–74; K Nishimura, 'The Amended Act on the Protection of Personal Information in Japan: The New Regulation Trend in Japan and Asia-Pacific' (2017) Data Privacy in the Asia-Pacific 79–100.

information is already publicly available or if it would involve a disproportionate effort to provide the notification.
e. Secure Storage: Organizations are required to implement appropriate security measures to protect personal information from unauthorized access, loss, destruction, alteration, or leakage during storage and retention. The security measures should be regularly reviewed and updated as necessary.
f. Data Subject Rights: APPI grants individuals certain rights regarding their personal information, including the right to request access, correction, suspension of use, erasure, and cessation of third-party provision. Organizations must establish procedures to handle these requests within a reasonable timeframe.
g. Third-Party Provision: Personal information should not be provided to third parties without the consent of the individual, except in specific cases permitted by APPI. When providing personal information to third parties, organizations must exercise appropriate supervision over the recipient to ensure the security of the information.
h. Recordkeeping: APPI requires organizations to keep records of the handling of personal information, including the purpose of use, details of third-party provision, and period of retention. These records should be retained for at least two years and should be made available to data subjects upon request.
i. Data Disposal: When personal information is no longer necessary for the purpose of use or the retention period has expired, organizations must dispose of the information in a manner that prevents unauthorized access or restoration.

4.3 The Commission on Protection of Personal Information and its role in enforcement of privacy legislation, including obligations relevant to data retention

The Commission on Protection of Personal Information (PPC) is Japan's independent administrative agency responsible for protecting personal information and enforcing the APPI.

While the APPI does not provide specific retention periods for different types of data, it requires organizations to clearly define the purpose of data retention and to dispose of personal information in a timely manner once it is no longer necessary to retain it, as detailed above.[37]

The PPC plays a key role in enforcing data retention obligations under the APPI. It conducts various activities to ensure compliance and protect individuals' personal information. These activities can include:[38]

---

[37] Ministry of Internal Affairs and Communications, 'Overview of the Act on the Protection of Personal Information' (2015) Tokyo: Ministry of Internal Affairs and Communications, available here: <https://www.soumu.go.jp/english/soumu/index.html> accessed 17 December 2023.

[38] T Ito, 'The Amended Act on the Protection of Personal Information: A Step Forward for Japan' (2016) Data Protection Laws of the World 79–89; K Ishikawa, 'The Role and Activities of the Personal Information Protection Commission of Japan' (2014) 128 Privacy Laws & Business International Report 23–25; Y Oshima and M Sakai, 'The Enforcement of Personal Data Protection Law in Japan' (2020) 1(3) Global Privacy Law Review 173–79, available at <https://kluwerlawonline.com/journalarticle/Global+Privacy+Law+Review/1.3/GPLR2020094> accessed 17 December 2023.

a. Guidance and Recommendations: The PPC provides guidance and recommendations to businesses and organizations on how to comply with the APPI's requirements. This includes providing advice on establishing appropriate data retention policies and procedures.
b. Inspections and Audits: The PPC has the authority to conduct inspections and audits of organizations to assess their compliance with the APPI. During these inspections, the PPC can review data retention practices to ensure they are in line with the law.
c. Complaint Handling: The PPC accepts and investigates complaints related to violations of personal information protection. If a complaint involves data retention obligations, the PPC may investigate the organization's practices and take appropriate action.
d. Administrative Actions: If the PPC determines that an organization has violated the APPI, it has the power to take administrative actions against them. These actions may include issuing warnings, ordering corrective measures, or imposing administrative fines.

5. Japan's Commercial Code and its Provisions Related to Data Retention

The Commercial Code[39] in Japan contains provisions related to data retention obligations for companies. The most important elements of these provisions are:[40]

a. Business Correspondence: The Commercial Code requires companies to retain business correspondence. Business correspondence refers to letters, telegrams, electronic communications, and other written or electronic communications exchanged in the course of business. This includes correspondence with customers, suppliers, business partners, and other relevant parties.
The Commercial Code does not specify a concrete retention period for business correspondence. However, it is generally advisable to retain business correspondence for a reasonable period to preserve historical documentation and facilitate the resolution of any disputes that may arise.
b. Commercial Books and Documents: The Commercial Code also mandates the retention of various commercial books and documents. These include:

---

[39] A translation of the Japanese Commercial Code in English is available here: <https://www.japaneselawtranslation.go.jp/en/laws/view/4293> accessed 17 December 2023.

[40] T Fujita, '"De-codification" of the Commercial Code in Japan' <https://www.gcoe.j.u-tokyo.ac.jp/pdf/GCOESOFTLAW-2012-5.pdf> (2013) accessed 4 January 2025; John Owen Haley, 'The Spirit of Japanese Law' (University of Georgia Press 2006); Like R Nottage, 'The Development of Comparative Law in Japan' in Mathias Reimann and Reinhard Zimmermann (eds), *The Oxford Handbook of Comparative Law* (2nd edn, OUP 2019) 201–27; E Jenks, 'The Japanese Commercial Code' (1932) 14(1) Journal of Comparative Legislation and International Law 62–65 available at <http://www.jstor.org/stable/753729> accessed 30 September 2024; Shuya Hayashi. 'Business Law in Japan, Cases and Comments: Intellectual Property, Civil, Commercial and International Private Law: Writings in Honor of Harold Baum' (2015) 18(1) Social Science Japan Journal 127–29.

- General Ledger: The general ledger contains a record of all transactions and financial information of the company. It must be retained for a reasonable period to support financial reporting and provide an audit trail of the company's financial activities.
- Subsidiary Ledgers: Subsidiary ledgers are subsidiary records that provide more detailed information on specific accounts or transactions. These may include accounts payable and accounts receivable ledgers, inventory records, and other subsidiary records relevant to the company's operations. The retention period for subsidiary ledgers should be determined based on the company's internal policies and legal requirements.
- Invoices and Receipts: The Commercial Code requires companies to retain invoices and receipts issued or received in the course of business. These documents support the recognition of revenue, expenses, and tax-related matters.
- Contracts and Agreements: Companies should retain copies of contracts and agreements entered into in the course of business. These documents serve as evidence of the rights, obligations, and terms agreed upon by the parties involved.
- Minutes of General Meetings of Shareholders and Board of Directors: The Commercial Code mandates the retention of minutes of general meetings of shareholders and board of directors' meetings. These minutes record the decisions made, discussions held, and voting results during these meetings.

The Commercial Code does not provide specific retention periods for commercial books and documents. The retention periods should be determined based on legal requirements, accounting standards, industry practices, and the company's internal policies. It is generally advisable to retain commercial books and documents for a reasonable period to ensure compliance with potential legal, regulatory, and audit requirements. However, this has admittedly led to Japanese companies predominantly adopting rather conservative approaches towards data and documents retention, a tendency which poses increasing challenges in terms of data storage resources, in parallel to maintenance of physical company records for continuously prolonged periods of time.

Inspection and Access: The Commercial Code provides shareholders and other relevant parties with the right to inspect certain commercial books and documents of the company. Shareholders have the right to request access to the shareholders' register and minutes of general meetings of shareholders. Other commercial books and documents may be subject to inspection by authorized individuals or entities as provided by law or in accordance with the company's internal rules.

6. Rules with Relevance to Data Retention in Japan's Medical Practitioners Act

The Medical Practitioners Act[41] in Japan focuses on regulations pertaining to medical practitioners and the practice of medicine. While the act does not explicitly address data and document retention rules, there are general obligations and considerations related to data

---

[41] A translation of Japan's Medical Practitioners Act in English can be found here: <https://www.japaneselawtranslation.go.jp/en/laws/view/3992/en> accessed 17 December 2023.

protection and record-keeping that medical practitioners in Japan should be aware of. Here are some key points to consider:

1. Medical Records: Medical practitioners in Japan are obligated to maintain accurate and complete medical records for their patients. These records include information about patient diagnoses, treatment plans, medications, test results, and other relevant medical information.
   - Retention Period: While the Medical Practitioners Act does not specify a specific retention period for medical records, medical practitioners are generally advised to retain these records for a reasonable period. The retention period may vary depending on factors such as the type of medical condition, the age of the patient, and other legal or professional considerations.
   - Confidentiality: Medical practitioners have a duty to protect the confidentiality and privacy of patient information. They must ensure that medical records are stored securely and accessible only to authorized personnel.
2. Act on the Protection of Personal Information: If medical practitioners handle personal information, such as patient data or employee records, they must comply with the APPI. This law sets out requirements for the collection, use, and retention of personal information, including the obligation to retain personal data only for the necessary period and within the scope of the intended purpose.
   - Consent: Medical practitioners should obtain the informed consent of patients before collecting, using, or disclosing their personal information, except in cases permitted by law.
   - Security Measures: The APPI also requires medical practitioners to implement appropriate security measures to protect personal information from unauthorized access, loss, or leakage.
3. Guidelines and Professional Standards: In addition to legal obligations, medical practitioners in Japan should also follow guidelines and professional standards set by medical associations and organizations. These guidelines may provide recommendations on data and document retention practices, ensuring the accuracy of medical records, and safeguarding patient information.

7. Data Retention Requirements Applicable for Telecommunications Service Providers in Japan

Telecommunications service providers in Japan must observe a series of obligations regarding data retention. The main of these requirements include:[42]

---

[42] Thomas J Shaw, 'Information Security and Privacy: A Practical Guide for Global Executives, Lawyers, and Technologists' (American Bar Association 2012)'; Ian Walden, *Telecommunications Law and Regulation* (5th edn, OUP 2018); Noriya Ishikawa and Akiko Takiguchi, 'Amended Telecommunications Business Act' available at <https://www.nishimura.com/sites/default/files/newsletters/file/data_protection_230512_en.pdf> accessed on 17 December 2023; Roya Akhavan-Majid, 'Telecommunications Policymaking in Japan: The 1980s and beyond' (1990) 14(2) Telecommunications Policy 159–68 (1990); S Beraha, H Kobayashi, C B Han et al, 'The Technology, Media and Telecommunications Review: Japan' available at <https://thelawreviews.co.uk/title/the-technology-media-and-telecommunications-review/japan> accessed 17 December 2023; Richard Coopey, *Information Technology Policy: An International History* (1st edn, OUP 2004); John Ure (ed), *Telecommunications Development in Asia* (Hong Kong University Press 2008).

Call Data Records (CDR) Retention: Telecommunications service providers are required to retain certain CDRs for a specified period. This includes information such as the calling and called party's telephone numbers, the date and time of the call, and the duration of the call. The specific retention period is determined by the Ministry of Internal Affairs and Communications (MIC) and may vary based on the type of telecommunications service provided.

Subscriber Information Retention: Telecommunications service providers must retain subscriber information for a certain period as prescribed by the MIC. Subscriber information typically includes details such as the customer's name, address, telephone number, and any other information collected during the registration or provision of telecommunications services.

Lawful Intercept Data Retention: Telecommunications service providers are required to retain certain data related to lawful intercept activities. Law enforcement agencies may request the interception of telecommunications under certain circumstances,[43] and providers are obligated to retain the intercepted data as specified by the relevant laws and regulations.

Records of Service Provision: Telecommunications service providers must maintain records related to their service provision. These records may include details of contracts or agreements with customers, records of billing and payment transactions, customer complaints, and any other relevant information related to the provision of telecommunications services.

Data Security and Confidentiality: Telecommunications service providers are required to implement appropriate measures to protect the retained data from unauthorized access, loss, or disclosure. They must establish safeguards to ensure the security and confidentiality of the data they retain.

Retention Period: The specific data retention periods are typically determined by the MIC through ministerial ordinances. These retention periods may vary depending on the type of data involved and the nature of the telecommunications services provided.

---

[43] Japan's regulations regarding the interception of communications by enforcement agencies are primarily found in the Act on Wiretapping for Criminal Investigation. Here are some key aspects:

Legal Oversight: Interception is regulated by strict legal procedures. Law enforcement agencies must obtain a court-issued warrant before conducting any interception activities.

Criminal Investigation Requirement: Interception is typically allowed only in cases involving serious crimes, such as organized crime, terrorism, drug trafficking, and other significant offences. It is not used for minor infractions.

Court Authorization: Law enforcement agencies must present compelling evidence to a judge or a panel of judges to justify the need for interception. The court evaluates the necessity and proportionality of the interception request before granting a warrant.

Duration and Scope: Warrants specify the duration and scope of the interception. They are not open-ended and must be specific about the communication channels, individuals involved, and the time frame for which interception is permitted.

Confidentiality and Privacy Protection: There are strict protocols in place to protect the privacy of individuals not involved in criminal activities. Monitoring activities are to be limited to the specified targets mentioned in the warrant.

Oversight and Accountability: There are provisions for oversight to ensure that interception activities comply with legal requirements. Oversight committees or authorities monitor the use of interception powers to prevent misuse or abuse.

Penalties for Abuse: Misuse of interception powers or conducting unauthorized surveillance can result in severe penalties for law enforcement officials involved.

For more details see <https://www.waseda.jp/folaw/icl/assets/uploads/2014/05/A02859211-00-000190056.pdf> accessed 17 December 2023.

Data Sharing and Disclosure: Telecommunications service providers should comply with the applicable laws and regulations regarding the sharing and disclosure of customer data. They must respect customer privacy and obtain appropriate consent or follow lawful procedures when sharing or disclosing customer data to third parties.

8. Data Retention Obligations in Japan's Healthcare Industry—Rules for Medical Device Manufacturers and Healthcare Providers

A traditionally important market sector in Japan is healthcare.[44] Japanese medical device manufacturers enjoy a worldwide reputation[45] for the level of precision and the focus on minimal invasiveness of their products. At the same time, the country's ageing population[46] has been a somewhat unconventional factor for the generally advanced level of healthcare services in the country. Given this prominence for Japanese economy and importance for the country's social cohesion, both sectors are highly regulated in Japan. In fact, the country's quality standards for manufacturing of medical devices are generally regarded of equal rigour at those required by US' Federal Drugs Administration (FDA). Among others, the rules in force for medical device manufacturers and healthcare providers contain obligations regarding data retention. Below is an overview of these obligations that apply to Japan's manufacturers of healthcare products and health practitioners:

8.1 Medical Device Manufacturers

a. Quality Management System: Medical device manufacturers are typically required to establish and maintain a quality management system (QMS) in accordance with the Pharmaceutical Affairs Law (PAL) and related regulations. This includes requirements for data retention.[47]
b. Device Master Records: Manufacturers are obligated to maintain Device Master Records (DMRs) containing comprehensive information about the design,

---

[44] For a concise yet illustrative analysis of how healthcare has historically evolved in Japan refer to 'The Transition and Characteristics of Japan's Healthcare System', JICA-IUJ Case material series Tokyo, available at <https://www.jica.go.jp/Resource/jica-ri/research/jica-dsp/l75nbg000019c4qr-att/case_iuj_04.pdf> accessed 17 December 2023.

[45] T Sugahara, 'Challenges and Prospects in the Medical Device Industry: Heading toward a Leading Japanese Industry' (2023) 37 Journal of International Economic Studies 55–67.

[46] For latest data and statistics around Japan's ageing population issue refer to <https://www.mitsui.com/mgssi/en/report/detail/__icsFiles/afieldfile/2023/08/30/2307k_suzuki_e_2.pdf> accessed 17 December 2023.

[47] Japan Pharmaceutical Manufacturers Association, Pharmaceutical Administration and Regulations in Japan (2020), available at <https://www.jpma.or.jp/english/about/parj/eki4g600000078c0-att/2020.pdf> accessed 17 December 2023; S Nagasaka, B Lang, M Shintani, and S Ueno, 'An Overview of Pharmaceutical and Medical Device Regulation in Japan', Morgan Lewis-TMI, available at <https://www.morganlewis.com/-/media/files/publication/outside-publication/article/overview_pharma_device_reg.ashx> accessed 17 December 2023; S Nozawa, 'Evolution of Japanese Regulatory System and Agencies' (2022) 2(2) RF Quarterly 4–16, published online 27 June 2022 at <https://bit.ly/3nlcwet> accessed 17 December 2023; Y Nippousha, 'Supplement II to Japanese Pharmaceutical Excipients' (Yakuji Nippo 2018); M Hideki, 'Medical Affairs in Pharmaceutical Companies and Related Pharmaceutical Regulations in Japan' (2021) 8 Frontiers in Medicine.

development, manufacturing, and quality control of their medical devices. These records should be retained for a specified period, which may vary depending on the type of device and its classification.

c. Complaint Handling Records: Manufacturers must retain records of complaints received about their medical devices, including investigation details, corrective actions taken, and outcomes. These records are important for monitoring device performance and addressing safety concerns.

d. Adverse Event Reporting: Manufacturers are required to keep records of any adverse events associated with their medical devices and report them to the relevant authorities. Retention periods for these records may be defined by applicable regulations.

e. Labelling and Instructions: Manufacturers should retain records of device labelling, instructions for use, and any updates or changes made to these documents.

8.2 Healthcare providers

a. Medical Records: Healthcare providers have a duty to maintain medical records for their patients in accordance with the APPI and related regulations. These records should include patient information, medical history, diagnoses, treatments, medications, and other relevant data.[48]

b. Retention Period: The retention period for medical records can vary depending on the type of healthcare provider and the applicable regulations. Generally, medical records should be retained for a certain number of years from the last treatment or discharge of the patient.

c. Privacy and Data Protection: Healthcare providers must ensure the security and confidentiality of patient data, including appropriate measures to protect against unauthorized access, loss, or disclosure.

d. Consent and Authorization: Providers should retain records of patient consent and authorization for the collection, use, and disclosure of their personal and medical information.

---

[48] Katsunori Kai, Zuichiro Sato, and Zuko Nagamizu, 'Medical Law in Japan' (3rd edn, Kluwer Law Intl 2020); S Matsuda, 'Health Policy in Japan—Current Situation and Future Challenges' (2019) 2(1) JMA Journal 1–10; M Mimura, H Abe, and T Yamamoto, *The Pharma Legal Handbook: Japan*, Nishimura & Asahi, available at <https://www.nishimura.com/en/knowledge/publications/20220801-89201> accessed 17 December 2023; Patient Disclosure Rights in Japan's Healthcare System (1998), available at <https://www.pacificbridgemedical.com/publication/patient-disclosure-rights-in-japan-s-healthcare-system/> accessed 17 December 2023; R Leflar, 'Informed Consent and Patient's Rights in Japan' (1996) 33 Houston Law Review; R Leftar, 'The Law of Medical Misadventure in Japan' (2012) 87(1) Symposium on Medical Malpractice and Compensation in Global Perspective: Part II; A Hagihara, M Nishi, and K Nobutomo, 'Standard of Care and Liability in Medical Malpractice Litigation in Japan' (2003) 65(2) Health Policy 119–27; Y Tejima, 'Tort and Compensation in Japan: Medical Malpractice and Adverse Effects from Pharmaceuticals' (1993) 15 University of Harvard Law Review 728; K Nakajima, C Keyes, T Kuroyanagi, and K Tatara, 'Medical Malpractice and Legal Resolution Systems in Japan' (2001) 285 JAMA: The Journal of the American Medical Association 1632–40; D G Pozgar, *Legal Aspects of Health Care Administration* (13th edn, Jones and Bartlett 2019); J Eba and K Nakamura, 'Overview of the Ethical Guidelines for Medical and Biological Research Involving Human Subjects in Japan' 52(6) (2002) Japanese Journal of Clinical Oncology 539–44; E Feldman, 'Medical Ethics the Japanese Way' (1985) 15(5) The Hastings Center Report 21–24; R Ishiwata and A Sakai, 'The Physician–Patient Relationship and Medical Ethics in Japan' (1994) 3(1) Cambridge Quarterly of Healthcare Ethics 60–66; T Yuichiro, 'Medical Privacy Issues in Ageing Japan' (2017) 18(1) Australian Journal of Asian Law, Article 6: 77–94.

e. Incident and Accident Reports: Healthcare providers may be required to retain incident and accident reports, including any investigations and actions taken to address patient safety incidents or adverse events.

8.3 A deep-dive into obligations related to data retention in Good Manufacturing Practice Guidelines in Japan—an attempt to safeguard quality and ensure accountability in the provision of healthcare

In Japan, Good Manufacturing Practice (GMP) guidelines are established to ensure the quality, safety, and efficacy of pharmaceuticals, including medical devices. While GMP guidelines primarily focus on manufacturing processes and quality control, they do address certain obligations regarding data retention. Here is an overview of the key obligations around retention found in the GMP guidelines in Japan:[49]

a. Document Control: GMP guidelines emphasize the importance of maintaining controlled documents, including records, throughout the manufacturing process. This includes procedures, specifications, protocols, batch records, and other relevant documents.
b. Batch Records: GMP guidelines require the creation and retention of batch records for each batch or lot of pharmaceutical products. These records should contain information about the manufacturing process, including raw material identification, equipment used, processing parameters, sampling and testing results, packaging details, and any deviations or changes made during production.
c. Quality Control Records: GMP guidelines mandate the retention of quality control records, including test results, analytical data, stability studies, and any other quality control-related information. These records help ensure the quality and compliance of pharmaceutical products.
d. Equipment Calibration and Maintenance Records: Manufacturers are required to maintain records related to the calibration and maintenance of equipment used in the manufacturing process. These records should include details of calibration procedures, dates of calibration, results, and any corrective actions taken.
e. Deviation and Change Control Records: GMP guidelines require the retention of records related to deviations from established procedures or changes made to the manufacturing process. These records should document the nature of the deviation or change, investigations conducted, risk assessments, corrective actions, and any impact on product quality.

---

[49] Shayne C Gad, *Pharmaceutical Manufacturing Handbook: Regulations and Quality* (Wiley 2008); T Kudo, 'GMP System of Japan, 1st India-Japan Medical Products Regulation Symposium' 18–19 May 2016, available at <https://www.mhlw.go.jp/file/04-Houdouhappyou-11123000-Iyakushokuhinkyoku-Shinsakanrika/gmp.pdf> accessed 17 December 2023; S H Willig and R J Stoker, *Good Manufacturing Practices for Pharmaceuticals: A Plan for Total Quality Control* (4th edn, Basil New York 1997); Carmen Medina, *Compliance Handbook for Pharmaceuticals, Medical Devices, and Biologics* (1st edn, CRC Press 2004); K S Niazi, *Handbook of Pharmaceutical Manufacturing Formulations: Semisolid Products* (2nd edn, CRC Press 2009); M K Müller et al, 'Quality Assurance for Biopharmaceuticals: An Overview of Regulations, Methods and Problems', (1996) 71(6) Pharmaceutica Acta Helvetiae 421–38; O Doblhoff-Dier and R Bliem, 'Quality Control and Assurance from the Development to the Production of Biopharmaceuticals' (1999) 17 Trends in Biotechnology 266–70.

f. Training Records: GMP guidelines highlight the importance of training employees involved in manufacturing processes. Manufacturers should maintain records of employee training, including training programs, topics covered, dates, and employee signatures or acknowledgments.

g. Data Retention Period: While the GMP guidelines do not specify a uniform retention period for all types of data, manufacturers are generally expected to retain it for a period defined by applicable laws, regulations, and company policies. The retention periods may vary depending on the specific types of data, product type, and regulatory requirements.

9. Conclusion

To sum it up, data retention regulations for telecommunication and healthcare service providers and manufacturers in Japan are shaped by a framework that prioritizes the protection of sensitive information while ensuring compliance. The country's legal landscape imposes obligations on businesses to retain specific data for designated periods which vary based on the nature of the information and the purpose for which it is collected.

It could be argued that Japan's regulatory environment attempts to strike a balance between fostering innovation and safeguarding retained data and records as well as the rights associated to them, such as privacy. However, recent regulatory developments, including the amendment to the APPI in 2022, have heightened focus on stricter data protection measures and increased penalties for non-compliance, underlining the evolving nature of data retention requirements. Slowly but gradually, Japan seems to follow more European patterns and go further than soft compliance and, thus, enforcement of applicable rules on a range of topics around data and the wider digital economy, including data retention. Rules are becoming more challenging to comply with, auditing efforts on behalf of authorities intensify and, in case of violations, 'publicly name and shame' is not enough anymore, with concrete penalties, financial, administrative, or even penal ones, being handed down. This is a trend clearly visible in the two market sectors examined more closely in this chapter.

Telecommunications and healthcare providers alike operating in Japan must stay vigilant, ensuring adherence to these evolving regulations, implementing robust data management practices, and regularly reviewing and updating their retention policies to align with the dynamic regulatory landscape. Ultimately, regulators and enforcement authorities wish to reaffirm that compliance with data retention regulations expected from Japanese telecommunications and healthcare organizations not only fosters trust among consumers and stakeholders but also reinforces Japan's commitment to upholding data privacy and security standards in the digital age.

20
Regulating Access

A Brief Overview of US Regulations on Access to Communications Data

Bryce Clayton Newell

1. Introduction

European data retention law has had a tumultuous existence over the past two decades. Whether lawmakers can require communications service providers to retain subscriber and communications-related data, or when and to what extent they can do so under blanket or more targeted data retention rules, has become a complicated question under the evolving jurisprudence of the Court of Justice of the European Union ('CJEU'). Across the Atlantic, related legislation in the United States has also evolved, but the questions have been different. Rather than seeking to mandate data retention, US legislation has focused on regulating access (by law enforcement and others) to communications data held by private companies under whatever data retention policy each company chooses to institute. More recent amendments have, for example, addressed whether the government can compel service providers to turn over data held outside the physical boundaries of the United States.[1] In this chapter, I provide an overview of the US legislation, primarily provisions of the Stored Communications Act ('SCA'). The chapter is framed for European scholars and professionals, who may find the US approach interesting or useful when considering the options available to European legislators as the data retention debate continues in Europe.

2. Regulating Access to Communications Data in US Law

In contrast to the EU's Data Retention Directive and the CJEU case law that has evolved over the past couple of decades, the United States has not promulgated a general data retention law. Rather, US law regulates law enforcement access to data in some contexts and provides mechanisms whereby law enforcement agencies can access privately held data or demand that private companies preserve data in their systems prior to formally requesting access. As Reidenberg noted very clearly, 'United States law is essentially silent on data retention but regulates access to data held in the private sector by public authorities'.[2] A narrow example

---

[1] See 18 U.S.C. § 2713.
[2] Joel R Reidenberg, *The Data Surveillance State in Europe and the United States*, 49 Wake Forest L Rev 583, 585 (2014) (citing Joel R Reidenberg, *Resolving Conflicting International Data Privacy Rules in Cyberspace*, 52 Stan L Rev 1315, 1345 (2000)).

of federal law that does address mandatory data retention is the Bank Secrecy Act of 1970,[3] which requires banks to retain certain customer banking records and to create 'reports that would be useful in criminal, tax, or regulatory investigations or proceedings'.[4] Some state laws limit data retention in some contexts or require data retention and destruction policies.[5] But most of these laws do not directly target communications-related data.

Legal provisions that regulate law enforcement access to data frequently create tension with privacy interests. As the Supreme Court of the United States stated in its 1977 decision, *Whalen v Roe*, 'the enforcement of the criminal laws all require the orderly preservation of great quantities of information, much of which is personal in character and potentially embarrassing or harmful if disclosed'.[6] Generally, under US law, law enforcement access to information held by private communications companies requires a judicial warrant under the Fourth Amendment to the US Constitution and/or various forms of court order or subpoena as outlined in federal laws such as the SCA (for communications data held in electronic storage)[7] and related laws governing communications interception[8] and the use of pen registers and trap-and-trace devices to capture dialling and other traffic data.[9] When comparing US law to the issues covered by the Data Retention Directive and the CJEU's subsequent case law, the most relevant federal law is the SCA. As such, my focus in the following paragraphs is providing a succinct overview of the SCA.

2.1 The Stored Communications Act

The Stored Communications Act was adopted by Congress in 1986 as part of the Electronic Communications Privacy Act ('ECPA'). The law regulates access to communications data held in 'electronic storage' or by a 'remote computing service'.[10] The law differentiates between the 'contents' of communication and 'non-content' data related to the communication (such as traffic data, addressing information, and IP addresses). The SCA does not mandate data retention, except for a requirement to preserve records upon request by law enforcement for a (renewable) 90-day period during which law enforcement must seek a warrant or court order to gain access to the preserved data.[11] Since 2018, these preservation orders cover all communications data held by the service provider, regardless of whether the data is stored within the US or internationally.[12] The SCA primarily prohibits unauthorized access to communications data held in such storage and outlines when and how law enforcement may compel access to such data and when service providers may voluntarily grant access without incurring legal liability. Under the SCA, 'electronic storage' refers to:

---

[3] Bank Secrecy Act of 1970, 31 USC § 5311 et seq.
[4] Daniel Solove and Paul Schwartz, *Information Privacy Law* (7th edn, Wolters Kluwer 2021) 304.
[5] See eg New Jersey Genetic Privacy Act, N.J.S.A. §§ 10:5–43 et seq; Illinois Biometric Information Privacy Act, 740 ILCS 14/10 (2008).
[6] *Whalen v Roe*, 429 U.S. 589, 605 (1977).
[7] 18 U.S.C. §§ 2701–11.
[8] ibid §§ 2510–23.
[9] ibid §§ 3121–27.
[10] ibid § 2703(a)–(b).
[11] ibid § 2703(f); see also § 2704.
[12] ibid § 2713.

(A) any temporary, intermediate storage of a wire or electronic communication incidental to the electronic transmission thereof; and
(B) any storage of such communication by an electronic communications service for purposes of backup protection of such communication.[13]

Importantly, when considering whether the disclosure of data is required, voluntary, or prohibited, the SCA distinguishes between the 'contents' of a communication and the 'non-content' information related to such communications (eg metadata). Although the European debate on data retention relates to the retention of traffic and location data, leaving content data out of scope of any European regulation on data retention, I present the US rules on both content and non-content data for reasons of completeness.

2.2 Content data

With some exceptions, the SCA limits communications service providers from disclosing or sharing the contents of a subscriber's communications with other parties, including law enforcement.[14] The law also differentiates between content data held in storage for 180 days or less (heightened protection) and content data which has been in storage for more than 180 days (lesser protection). Under section 2703(a), if communications data has been held in electronic storage for 'one hundred and eighty days or less', communications service providers are required to disclose the contents of a communication to law enforcement or other government agencies upon issuance of a warrant. If the data has been in storage for *more* than 180 days, the government can compel disclosure by issuing a warrant[15] or by issuing an administrative subpoena or obtaining a court order (which may require issuing prior notice to the subscriber in some cases).[16] The warrant and court order provisions effectively preserve prior judicial review of requests for access to data. The allowance for an administrative subpoena bypasses prior judicial review but does require prior notice to the subscriber unless the government provides a written certification that prior notice would result in certain adverse results (in such cases, notification may be delayed for up to 90 days).[17]

Exceptions to the general prohibition on disclosure applies to a service provider divulging subscriber communications data to a law enforcement agency under certain circumstances. For example, the SCA also allows communications service providers to *voluntarily* disclose the contents of a subscriber's communications to law enforcement 'if the provider, in good faith, believes that an emergency involving danger of death or serious physical injury to any person requires disclosure without delay of communications relating to the emergency'[18] or when the 'the contents ... were inadvertently obtained by the service provider [and] appear to pertain to the commission of a crime'.[19] Additionally, US law

---

[13] ibid § 2510(17).
[14] ibid § 2702(a).
[15] ibid § 2703(b).
[16] ibid §§ 2703(b)(1)(B), 2703(d).
[17] ibid § 2705(a)(B).
[18] ibid § 2702(b)(8).
[19] ibid § 2702(b)(7).

allows broad access to electronic communications data (in storage or through interception) when the communications are 'readily accessible to the general public',[20] a catch-all provision that immunizes law enforcement and others from accessing publicly accessible communications data such as those on some social media platforms.

2.3 Non-content data

Under section 2703(c), law enforcement can compel a service provider to provide access to certain non-content data related to a subscriber's communications by obtaining an administrative subpoena, a court order under section 2703(d), or a traditional warrant. Such data includes a subscriber's:

> name; address; local and long distance telephone connection records, or records of session times and durations; length of service (including start date) and types of service utilized; telephone or instrument number or other subscriber number or identity, including any temporarily assigned network address; and means and source of payment for such service (including any credit card or bank account number).[21]

There is no distinction based on the number of days the records have been in electronic storage. Interestingly, the law also provides certain protections for subscriber information held by 'video tape service providers' (including streaming media content providers) including rental or viewing histories related to 'audio visual materials'.[22] Relatedly, whenever a 'cable operator' (ISP) receives a court order for subscriber information, a separate federal law requires the cable operator to notify the subscriber and provide the subscriber with 'the opportunity to prohibit or limit such disclosure' before the ISP can disclose the identity of its subscriber to a third party.[23]

The SCA allows communications service providers to *voluntarily* disclose non-content information about a subscriber or their communications to law enforcement 'if the provider, in good faith, believes that an emergency involving danger of death or serious physical injury to any person requires disclosure without delay of information relating to the emergency'.[24] ISPs are not compelled to reveal IP addresses or other types of user-identifying information (communications metadata) to non-governmental entities. Such disclosure is allowed on a voluntary basis, as the law states that service providers 'may disclose a record or other information pertaining to a subscriber . . . to any person other than a governmental entity'.[25] Importantly, for comparative purposes, this allowance for voluntary disclosure does not require prior judicial review and, as such, would run afoul of the prior review requirements laid out in decisions of the CJEU.

---

[20] ibid § 2511(2)(g)(i).
[21] ibid § 2703(c)(2).
[22] ibid § 2710. This provision was added by the Video Privacy Protection Act of 1988 (commonly referred to as the 'VPPA').
[23] 47 U.S.C. 551(c)(2)(C)(i).
[24] 18 U.S.C. § 2702(c)(4).
[25] ibid § 2703(c)(1)(A).

2.4 The Fourth Amendment and non-content data

Because the SCA provides broad access to non-content data (communications metadata), federal courts have also addressed how and to what extent the Fourth Amendment regulates such access to data. As a general constitutional provision related to search and seizure, the Fourth Amendment regulates investigative efforts by government agents, including those who seek to access or acquire user, subscriber, or customer data. Whenever government action constitutes an unreasonable search or seizure (that is, when the action would violate a person's reasonable expectations of privacy or interfere impermissibly with private property interests), the Fourth Amendment requires the government to secure a judicial warrant prior to conducting a search or committing a seizure.

However, federal courts have held that law enforcement can compel service providers to provide access to subscriber or user IP address information through court orders under § 2703(d) under a less stringent standard than the probable cause standard required for a warrant.[26] This is because federal and state courts have generally held that IP addresses and other 'non-content' subscriber information do not attract Fourth Amendment protection; that is, they do not implicate any reasonable expectation of privacy.[27] For example, the First Circuit has found that 'individuals do not have a legitimate expectation of privacy in subscriber information, such as email and IP addresses, that individuals disclose during the ordinary use of the internet'.[28] As such, ISPs can be compelled to disclose IP address information linked to a particular user to the government without a warrant, since the Fourth Amendment's protections do not apply.

These decisions have been based on the so-called 'third party doctrine' announced in cases like *Smith v Maryland*,[29] which held that '[A] person has no legitimate expectation of privacy in information he voluntarily turns over to third parties.' For example, in *United States v Forrester*,[30] the Ninth Circuit examined surveillance techniques that uncovered, among other things, IP addresses of users, and found that:

> e-mail and Internet users have no expectation of privacy in the to/from addresses of their messages or the IP addresses of the websites they visit because they should know that this information is provided to and used by Internet service providers for the specific purpose of directing the routing of information. Like telephone numbers, which provide instructions to the 'switching equipment that processed those numbers,' e-mail to/from addresses and IP addresses are not merely passively conveyed through third party equipment, but rather are voluntarily turned over in order to direct the third party's servers.[31]

---

[26] See *United States v Hood*, 920 F.3d 87, 92 (1st Cir. 2019); *United States v Morel*, 922 F.3d 1, 9 (1st Cir. 2019); *United States v Monroe*, unpublished opinion, 2021 WL 8567708 (1st Cir. 2021).
[27] See eg *United States v Kennedy*, 81 F. Supp. 2d 1103, 1110 (D. Kan. 2000); *State v Evers*, 175 N.J. 355, 372 (2003); *Guest v Leis*, 255 F.3d 325, 335 (6th Cir. 2001); *United States v Perrine*, 518 F.3d 1196, 1204 (10th Cir. 2008) ('Every federal court to address this issue has held that subscriber information provided to an internet provider is not protected by the Fourth Amendment's privacy expectation').
[28] *Brantley v Florida Attorney General*, 2021 WL 3077017 (11th Cir. 2020) (unpublished), citing *United States v Trader*, 981 F.3d 961 (11th Cir. 2020).
[29] *Smith v Maryland*, 442 U.S. 735, 743–44 (1979).
[30] *United States v Forrester*, 512 F.3d 500 (2008).
[31] *United States v Forrester*, 512 F.3d 503 (2008), citing *Smith v Maryland*, 442 U.S. 735 (1979).

However, the Supreme Court of the United States has held that only a judicially granted warrant is sufficient to acquire even non-content communications data when there is a particularly acute and 'legitimate privacy interest in records held by a third party'.[32] In *Carpenter v United States*, the Court held that this interest existed in relation to historical cell-site location information stored by a wireless service provider, finding that 'an order issued under § 2703(d) is not a permissible mechanism for accessing historical cell-site records'[33] due to how invasive the disclosure of historical geolocation information can be to individual privacy interests. As such, heightened protection for non-content subscriber information and associated records only acquires Fourth Amendment protections when they meet this higher standard, and it is unclear how far this reasoning will affect records besides geolocational data.

2.5 Beyond the SCA

Moving beyond the SCA, and federal law all together, it is worth noting that US states have been adopting a growing patchwork of consumer data privacy laws that have borrowed ideas from data protection law and made some state-level US data privacy law look a bit more like data protection law. As of 3 July 2024, at least nineteen states have enacted broad consumer data privacy laws that effect the topography of data privacy, data retention, and law-enforcement-access-to-data regulations in the US. These laws incorporate data minimization and purpose specification obligations on data collection and data retention practices, but they generally clear covered businesses from explicit data retention obligations or liability for cooperating with law enforcement agencies after receiving data access requests. Some state-level data privacy laws define IP addresses as a type of 'personal information' or 'personal data'. For example, the California Consumer Privacy Act (CCPA) includes 'Internet Protocol address' as an example of information that constitutes 'personal information' under the statute.[34] IP addresses are subject to the same broad data minimization and purpose limitation principles as other forms of personal information under the CCPA.[35] However, the CCPA, like other state privacy laws, does not require retention of data that would otherwise be purged or deleted 'in the ordinary course of business'.[36]

3. Connections and Conclusions

As noted above, the US does not have broadly applicable rules on data retention, except in a few very narrow circumstances that generally fall outside the context of communications and communication-related data (eg banking-related data held by financial institutions). Rather, US law relies on rules related to accessing communications-related data that are already in the hands of providers (presumably collected for commercial purposes, which

---

[32] *Carpenter v United States*, 585 U.S. 296, 319 (2018).
[33] ibid 585 U.S. 296, 317 (2018).
[34] Cal. Civ. Code § 1798.140(v)(1)(A). The CCPA also defines IP addresses as a form of 'Unique identifier' and 'unique personal identifier'. Cal. Civ. Code § 1798.140(aj).
[35] ibid § 1798.100(c).
[36] ibid § 1798.145(j)(2).

is generally only constrained by state-level consumer data privacy laws such as the CCPA). This is likely due, at least in part, to the fact that the US has also never had a comprehensive data privacy or data protection law.

The SCA, insofar as it requires law enforcement authorities to first obtain a warrant or court order prior to compelling a service provider to provide access to non-content data in the hands of the providers remains relatively consistent with the CJEU's requirement of prior review. However, provisions in the SCA which allow access to such data under an administrative subpoena or by other means, for example, may not. The SCA's provisions on notice to subscribers are also more limited than the CJEU's case law would require, as access to non-content data is generally not subject to any notice requirements. As a consequence, US law offers some good ideas for regulating access to communications metadata that fall in line with the CJEU's evolving requirements and enumerated safeguards, but it also falls short in several ways (eg the absence of a notification requirement, opportunities for voluntary disclosure to non-governmental entities, and exceptions to the requirements for prior judicial review of access requests through a warrant or court order in some contexts).

In cases involving data retention issues, the CJEU's evolving case law has demonstrated a gradual shift towards a focus on developing rules and outlining key safeguards that relate to access to retained data by competent authorities, rather than simply just on data retention rules themselves. In this light, can looking to other jurisdictions, like the US, which do not have broadly applicable data retention rules but instead focus on regulating law enforcement access to data, provide insights that may be useful for reimagining European data retention debates moving forward? Certainly, US law is far from perfect and does not hold all the answers. However, shifting focus from data retention to access to data could provide one way to think beyond the decades-old debates about data retention obligations in Europe, and the US case at least shows one example of an access-focused system of rules.

PART III
PUBLIC POLICY, TECHNOLOGY, AND SOCIETAL IMPACT

21
The Judicialization of EU Data Retention Law
Epistemic Injustice and the Construction of an Unequal Surveillance Regime

Maria Tzanou

1. Introduction

Data retention—the subject matter of this edited collection—refers to a long line of legislative, policy, and mainly judicial developments at both the European Union (EU) and the Member States' level, concerning the retention of traffic[1] and location[2] telecommunications data by electronic communications service providers (hereinafter 'ECSPs'), in order to make them available for law enforcement and national security purposes. The so-called 'data retention saga'[3] commenced in 2006 with the adoption of the Data Retention Directive,[4] following the terrorist attacks in Madrid (2004) and London (2005). The Directive aimed to harmonize rules on the retention of communications metadata by ECSPs in order to ensure that these were available to law enforcement authorities. The Data Retention Directive was invalidated by the Court of Justice of the EU (CJEU),[5] who has shaped thereafter in a series of rulings the ongoing development of the data retention framework across the EU Member States and has established a set of red lines and rules regarding 'prohibited' and 'permissible' data retention in the areas of law enforcement and national security. Indeed, the Court—judicialization—has been at the steering wheel of both the EU and Member States' data retention frameworks.

This chapter employs the theory of judicialization of EU law to critically examine data retention. Judicialization is broadly understood as the 'reliance on courts and judicial means for addressing public policy questions, and political controversies'.[6] Judicialization focuses

---

[1] Traffic data refers to 'any data processed for the purpose of the conveyance of a communication on an electronic communications network or for the billing thereof'. See Art 2(b) of Directive 2002/58/EC of the European Parliament and of the Council of 12 July 2002 concerning the processing of personal data and the protection of privacy in the electronic communications sector [2002] OJ L 201/37 (ePrivacy Directive).

[2] Location data refers to 'any data processed in an electronic communications network, indicating the geographic position of the terminal equipment of a user of a publicly available electronic communications service'. See Art 2(c) of ePrivacy Directive.

[3] Maria Tzanou and Spyridoula Karyda, 'Privacy International and Quadrature Du Net: One Step Forward Two Steps Back in the Data Retention Saga?' (2022) European Public Law 123; Mark Cole and Franziska Boehm, 'EU Data Retention – Finally Abolished? Eight Years in Light of Article 8' (2014) Critical Q Legis & L 58, 78; Edoardo Celeste, 'The Court of Justice and the Ban on Bulk Data Retention: Expansive Potential and Future Scenarios', (2019) 15 Eur Const L Rev 134, 135.

[4] Directive 2006/24/EC of the European Parliament and of the Council of 15 March 2006 on the retention of data generated or processed in connection with the provision of publicly available electronic communications services or of public communications networks and amending Directive 2002/58/EC [2006] OJ L 105/54.

[5] CJEU, Judgment of 8 April 2014, *Digital Rights Ireland and Seitlinger and others* (C-293/12 and C-594/12) ECLI:EU:C:2014:238).

[6] Ran Hirschl, 'The Judicialization of Politics' in Robert Goodin (ed) *The Oxford Handbook of Political Science* (OUP 2011) 253.

on the significant role that the CJEU has played in shaping the European Union's ever increasing integration[7] and is, therefore, considered a theoretical framework at the heart of the EU legal order.[8] Data retention constitutes an important case study of judicialization because while it does not have as its focus internal market integration under which the main theories of the judicialization of Europe were developed, it nevertheless matches well to general theories of judicialization. Indeed, as the discussion will show, data retention presents several key aspects identified in judicialization frameworks of the EU in general, such as *constitutionalization*,[9] *principal agent theory*,[10] *positive* and *negative* judicialization,[11] *judicial activism*[12] and the construction of new realities or regimes, playing out as '*direct design*' by the CJEU rather than mere codification or modification.[13] This is a significant finding as data retention focuses on matters particularly sensitive to Member States such as surveillance for law enforcement and—even—national security purposes.

However, and more importantly, the present analysis aims to combine debates on data retention and judicialization and move them both forward by asking an until now neglected question: judicialization *for whom*? Who are the main beneficiaries of the judicialization of data retention? Are data privacy law outcomes equally distributed in the context of data retention surveillance? What are the epistemic implications of the construction of targeted surveillance as by default permissible?

The above questions matter for both data retention and judicialization theories. While the CJEU's case law on data retention (often referred to as the 'data retention saga')[14] has attracted a significant amount of scholarship[15] (including the present book) and public policy debates, little attention has been paid to the distribution of its societal consequences[16] and to its epistemic implications. These are crucial because they concern the outcomes and the collective ramifications of the construction by the CJEU of what constitutes—lawful—state surveillance across all EU countries.

On the other hand, while judicialization of the EU theories started developing more than 40 years ago since the early 1980s and the Court's alleged 'activism' has been challenged for decades by politicians, media, and academics,[17] such discussions have mostly missed out

---

[7] Elaine Fahey and Fabien Terpan, 'Torn between Institutionalisation & Judicialisation: The Demise of the EU-US Privacy Shield' (2021) 28 Ind J Global Legal Stud 205, 207.

[8] ibid.

[9] Eric Stein, 'Lawyers, Judges, and the Making of a Transnational Constitution' (1981) American Journal of International Law 1.

[10] Gareth Davies, 'The European Union Legislature as an Agent of the European Court of Justice' (2016) JCMS 846.

[11] Fahey and Terpan (n 7).

[12] Mark Dawson, 'The Political Face of Judicial Activism: Europe's Law-Politics Imbalance' in M Dawson, B De Witte, and E Muir (eds) *Judicial Activism at the European Court of Justice* (Edward Elgar 2013) 11.

[13] Ninke Mussche and Dries Lens, 'The ECJ's Construction of an EU Mobility Regime- Judicialization and the Posting of Third-country Nationals' (2019) 57 JCMS 1247, 1252.

[14] See above.

[15] See inter alia Maria Tzanou, *The Fundamental Right to Data Protection: Normative Value in the Context of Counter-Terrorism Surveillance* (Hart Publishing 2017); Valsamis Mitsilegas et al, 'Data Retention and the Future of Large-Scale Surveillance: The Evolution and Contestation of Judicial Benchmarks' (2022) ELJ 1; Ian Cameron, 'Metadata Retention and National Security: Privacy International and La Quadrature Du Net' (2021) CML Rev 1422.

[16] For instance, Tzanou and Karyda discuss this in one paragraph in a journal article spanning over 40 pages. See Tzanou and Karyda (n 3) 139.

[17] Daniel Kelemen, 'Judicialization, Democracy and European Integration' (2013) Representations 295.

broader problems regarding the Court's construction and framing of concepts that might lead to deficits of *substantive justice*.[18] Indeed, questions on what role EU law in general, and EU data protection law in particular, can play in eliminating privilege, or class, race, and sex inequalities—albeit crucial—are rarely (if ever) considered by the CJEU and the extensive literature surrounding its judgments.[19] This absence is all the more noteworthy given that the Court has developed an impressive case-law on fundamental rights and more specifically data retention, which has distinguished it even from human rights specialized courts such as the European Court of Human Rights (ECtHR), generating observations, such as from a current ECtHR judge that 'the Strasbourg Court lags behind the Luxembourg Court, which remains the lighthouse for privacy rights in Europe'.[20]

In this regard, the main contribution of this study is to broaden our imagination about the ways of moving the judicialization of data retention forward so that it can advance substantive justice. It argues that judicialization even when widely considered as a victory for fundamental rights—as in the case of data retention—it might overlook substantive justice concerns. The chapter demonstrates this by providing evidence on how 'targeted surveillance' has been treated by the CJEU as opposed to 'mass surveillance' and what distributional and epistemic injustice consequences this approach has produced. The chapter is, therefore, likely to influence academic debates in the area by bringing at the fore an until now underexplored perspective in data retention; the ultimate hope is that it can prompt the Court to rethink its case law.

The chapter proceeds as follows: section 2.1 provides an overview of the main features of the judicialization of the EU general theoretical frameworks. Section 2.2 applies these to the judicialization of data retention to identify its key aspects and trends. Section 3 investigates the targeted data retention problem by exploring its underlying assumptions (3.1) as well as its distributive (3.2) and epistemic injustice implications (3.3). Section 4 re-imagines data retention and puts forward two normative propositions regarding the role the CJEU can play in addressing structural inequalities. Section 5 provides conclusions.

2. The Judicialization of Data Retention

2.1 The judicialization of the EU: theories, impact, and resistance

Judicialization is broadly defined by political scientists as the 'reliance on courts and judicial means for addressing core moral predicaments, public policy questions, and political controversies'.[21] As a concept, it is often seen as describing an evolution rather than a static situation that comprises both an increasing reliance on courts in a given political system as well as a growing tendency of these courts to actively exercise their power of judicial

---

[18] Maria Tzanou, 'The Future of EU Data Privacy Law: Towards a More Egalitarian Data Privacy' (2020) Journal of International and Comparative Law 449, 454.
[19] Daniela Caruso and Fernanda Nicola, 'Legal Scholarship and External Critique in EU Law' in Tamara Perišin and Siniša Rodin (eds), *The Transformation or Reconstitution of Europe: The Critical Legal Studies Perspective on the Role of the Courts in the European Union* (Hart Publishing 2018) 221, 230; Tzanou, ibid.
[20] Opinion of Judge Pinto De Albuquerque in ECtHR (Grand Chamber), *Big Brother Watch and others v UK*, Applications nos. 58170/13, 62322/14 and 24960/15, 25 May 2021, para 59.
[21] Hirschl, 'The Judicialization of Politics' (n 6) 253.

review.[22] Judicialization has generated a broad scholarship at the national,[23] regional,[24] and international levels,[25] with scholars describing this trend as 'governing with judges'[26] or 'juristocracy';[27] viewing judges as 'legislators in robes',[28] and suggesting that we are living in a 'judicial era'.[29] Indeed, the last few decades have seen a 'dramatic increase' in the number and types of national and transnational courts and tribunals;[30] an 'ever-growing significance of courts and judges in determining political and policy-making outcomes worldwide';[31] and 'criticism of, resistance to, and occasional backlash against expanded judicial power'.[32]

In the EU, a rich scholarship has developed over the past decades analysing the considerable role, the CJEU (previously the European Court of Justice (ECJ)) has played in shaping the EU's ever deeper 'integration through law'[33] or 'judicial integration'.[34] Indeed, the CJEU has been characterized as one of 'the most influential supranational courts' serving as the apex judicial body of the European Union, a 450 million-person association.[35]

A closer look at the different trends identified in the CJEU's judicialization of European integration is useful for the present analysis. Early literature saw the influence of the CJEU on the Community's market integration as the *constitutionalization* of the Community legal order.[36] By establishing the principles of direct effect[37] and primacy of EU law over national law,[38] the Court interpreted the European Community Treaties and legislation in a 'constitutional mode',[39] ascribing to them effects typical of constitutional law, while at the same time systematically advancing the legal interpretation and institutional evolution of the Community—EU—[40] in a way that was 'more or less detached from the will of Member

---

[22] Fahey and Terpan (n 7), 211; Doreen Lustig and Joseph Weiler, 'Judicial Review in the Contemporary World— Retrospective and Prospective' (2018) I•CON 315.

[23] See inter alia Christine Landfried, 'The Judicialization of Politics in Germany' (1994) Int'l Pol Sci Rev 113; Tokujin Matsudaira, 'Judicialization of Politics and the Japanese Supreme Court' (2010) Washington University Law Review 1559, 1559.

[24] See inter alia Rachel Sieder et al (eds), *The Judicialization of Politics in Latin America* (Springer 2005); Björn Dressel (ed), *The Judicialization of Politics in Asia* (Routledge 2012).

[25] See Anne-Marie Slaughter, 'Judicial Globalization' (2000) Virginia Journal of International Law 1103.

[26] Alec Stone Sweet, 'Judicialization and the Construction of Governance' (1999) Comparative Political Studies 147.

[27] Ran Hirschl, *Towards Juristocracy: The Origins and Consequences of the New Constitutionalism* (Harvard University Press 2004); Ran Hirschl, '"Juristocracy" – Political, not Juridical' (The Good Society, Penn State University Press 2004).

[28] Kenneth Shepsle, 'Old Questions and New Answers About Institutions: The Riker Objection Revisited' in Barry Weingast and Donald Wittman (eds), *The Oxford Handbook of Political Economy* (OUP 2006) 1031.

[29] Erin Delaney and Rosalind Dixon (eds) *Comparative Judicial Review* (Edward Elgar 2018).

[30] Ran Hirschl, 'The Global Expansion of Judicial Power' in Lee Epstein et al (eds) *Oxford Handbook of Comparative Judicial Behaviour* (OUP 2023) <https://papers.ssrn.com/sol3/papers.cfm?abstract_id=4373693> accessed 15 July 2024.

[31] ibid.

[32] ibid.

[33] Stein (n 9). See also Sabine Saurugger and Fabien Terpan, *The Court of Justice of the European Union and the Politics of Law* (Bloomsbury Publishing 2017).

[34] Anne-Marie Burley and Walter Mattli, 'Europe Before the Court: A Political Theory of Legal Integration' (1993) 47 Int'l Org 41.

[35] Hirschl, 'The Global Expansion of Judicial Power' (n 30).

[36] Stein (n 9).

[37] Case 26-62 *Van Gend en Loos*, ECLI:EU:C:1963:1.

[38] Case 6-64 *Flaminio Costa v ENEL*, ECLI:EU:C:1964:66.

[39] Stein (n 9).

[40] Karen Alter, *Establishing the Supremacy of European Law: The Making of an International Rule of Law in Europe* (OUP 2001); Dieter Grimm, 'The Democratic Costs of Constitutionalization: The European Case' (2015) European Law Journal 460; Joseph Weiler, 'The Transformation of Europe' (1991) The Yale Law Journal 2403.

States'.[41] In this way, the Court has been seen as exerting its judicial control 'to address major public policy issues and political disputes'.[42]

In this context, scholars have viewed the CJEU as a 'trustee Court' acting as a trustee of the values enshrined in the constitutive Treaties,[43] with the powers of a *super-agent* as it appears virtually impossible for Member States to reverse the Court's rulings on constitutional Treaty law.[44] The 'super-agent' theory to qualify the Court can be seen at both the vertical and the horizontal levels. At the vertical level, the Court is considered to have the power to serve the Treaties' objectives in a position of structural supremacy over the member states and dominate, therefore, the evolutionary process of the EU.[45] At the horizontal level, it has been argued that the Court as a 'super-agent' has such a substantial degree of control over the EU legislature that it can be characterized as the 'principal agent' while the other legislative bodies (the Council and the Parliament) act as 'agents' of the 'principle agent' Court.[46]

Judicialization is considered to have had a significant impact not only on the integration of the EU, but also on the—vertical—distribution of competences between the EU and its Member States. According to the 'absorption' theory, the CJEU has gradually expanded the competences of the EU[47] in a way that it allowed it to find national measures that were not part of the EU competence, to be in conflict with EU law.[48] Arguably, the main beneficiaries of the judicialization of Europe are considered to be the four fundamental freedoms (free movement of goods, persons, services, and capital),[49] which were 'transformed from objective principles for legislation into subjective rights of the market participants who could claim them against the Member States before national courts'.[50]

Judicialization has therefore had an important effect on the EU's legislation, leading to both codification and modification of the law. Indeed, it has been observed that EU internal market legal instruments (Regulations and Directives) are in fact an exercise in codifying the CJEU's case law.[51] Going even further, Mussche and Lens argued that judicialization also plays out as 'Direct Design' by the Court. According to this view, the CJEU can lead to the 'construction of entirely new legal realities or regimes' often bypassing any legislative process.[52]

Judicialization—and in particular the adjudication of important cases—may trigger resistance.[53] Resistance may come in different forms and patterns ranging from merely

---

[41] Grimm (n 40); Mussche and Lens 'The ECJ's Construction of an EU Mobility Regime- Judicialization and the Posting of Third-country Nationals' (2019); Alec Stone Sweet and Thomas Brunell, 'Trustee Courts and the Judicialization of International Regimes' (2013) Journal of Law and Courts 61.
[42] Kelemen (n 17) 259.
[43] Stone Sweet and Brunell (n 41).
[44] ibid.
[45] ibid; Mussche and Lens (n 41) 1249.
[46] Davies (n 10).
[47] Weiler, 'The Transformation of Europe' (n 40); Mussche and Lens (n 41) 1252.
[48] Mussche and Lens (n 41) 1252.
[49] Weiler, 'The Transformation of Europe' (n 40); Mussche and Lens (n 41) 1252.
[50] Grimm (n 40) 467.
[51] Davies (n 10); Susanne Schmidt, *European Court of Justice and the Policy Process: The Shadow of Case Law* (OUP 2018)
[52] Mussche and Lens (n 41) 1259.
[53] See inter alia Mikael Rask Madsen, 'Resistance to the European Court of Human Rights: The Institutional and Sociological Consequences of Principled Resistance' in Marten Breuer (ed.) *Principled Resistance to ECtHR Judgments—A New Paradigm?* (Springer Verlag 2019) <https://papers.ssrn.com/sol3/papers.cfm?abstract_id=3387347> accessed 15 July 2024; Mikael Rask Madsen, Pola Cebulak, and Micha Wiebusch, 'Backlash against International Courts: Explaining the Forms and Patterns of Resistance to International Courts' (2018) Int'l

seeking to change or reverse the direction of the law (often referred to as pushback) to challenging or overturning the authority of the Court (often referred to as backlash). The CJEU's rulings over the years have been the subject of critique by a variety of actors ranging from national courts (including Constitutional and Supreme courts) to governments, politicians, academics, and the media.[54] Indeed, the CJEU has been accused numerous times of producing a 'far-reaching case-law' that amounts to 'judicial activism'.[55] However, while resistance may have as its aim the delegitimization of the Court, it is not always detrimental.[56] In fact, and crucial to the present discussion, resistance or critique to the CJEU might in the long term change the direction of the case-law to allow it to take into account more neglected epistemological perspectives,[57] thus, consolidating its institutional role.

2.2 The judicialization of data retention: from *constitutionalization* to *resistance*

It is a truism to state that the EU data retention regime[58] has been shaped by the CJEU. In fact, the main characteristic of the so-called data retention saga is its high degree of judicialization, which placed the Court at the steering wheel of both the EU and Member States' retention frameworks. This has manifested both as negative and positive judicialization which form a useful analytical distinction[59] to study data retention. Negative judicialization has the potential to challenge a legal regime, while positive judicialization would instead enhance it by guaranteeing its proper functioning.[60]

As seen above, in the aftermath of the terrorist attacks in Madrid (2004) and London (2005), the EU adopted the so-called Data Retention Directive, which aimed to harmonize rules on the retention of communications metadata by ECSPs in order to ensure that these were available to law enforcement authorities.[61] The first instance of judicialization

---

J L Context; Karen J Alter and Mikael Rask Madsen, 'Beyond Backlash: The Consequences of Adjudicating Mega-Politics' (2021) 84 Law & Contemp Probs; Karen J Alter, 'The European Legal System and Domestic Policy: Spillover or Backlash' (2000) *Int'l Org* 489; Karen Alter, James Gathii, and Laurence Helfer, 'Backlash Against International Courts in West, East and Southern Africa: Causes and Consequences' (2016) Eur J Int'l Law 293; Erik Voeten, 'Populism and Backlashes Against International Courts' (2020) *Persp On Pol* 407; Wayne Sandholtz, Yining Bei, and Kayla Caldwell, 'Backlash and International Human Rights Courts' in Alison Brysk and Michael Stohl (eds) *Contracting Human Rights* (Edward Elgar 2018).

[54] Kelemen (n 17).
[55] See inter alia Alter *Establishing the Supremacy of European Law* (n 40); Bill Davies, *Resisting the European Court of Justice: West Germany's Confrontation with European Law, 1949-1979* (CUP 2012); Arthur Dyevre, 'Domestic Judicial Defiance in the European Union: A Systemic Threat to the Authority of EU Law?' (2016) 35 Yearbook of European Law 106; Harm Schepel, 'Reconstructing Constitutionalization: Law and Politics in the European Court of Justice' (2000) Oxford Journal of Legal Studies 457; Grimm (n 40); Richard Bellamy, 'The Democratic Constitution: Why Europeans Should Avoid American Style Constitutional Judicial Review' (2008) European Political Science 9; Andreas Follesdal and Simon Hix, 'Why There is a Democratic Deficit in the EU: A Response to Majone and Moravcsik' (2006) JCMS 533; Fritz Scharpf, 'Legitimacy in the Multilevel European Polity' (2009) European Political Science Review 173.
[56] Madsen, 'Resistance to the European Court of Human Rights' (n 53).
[57] ibid. For an elaboration in this argument, see below.
[58] Data retention refers to the obligation of Electronic Communications' Service Providers (ECSPs) to retain traffic and location data (metadata) so that they can be accessed by relevant national authorities for law enforcement and national security purposes. See Tzanou, *The Fundamental Right to Data Protection* (n 15) 72.
[59] Fahey and Terpan (n 7) 213.
[60] ibid.
[61] Art 1(1) Data Retention Directive.

commenced in 2009 in *Ireland v Parliament and Council*, which focused on a procedural, rather than a substantive, challenge of the Data Retention Directive concerning its legal basis.[62] The Court confirmed that the appropriate legal basis for the adoption of the Directive was the (then) first rather than the third pillar, but left—the elephant in the room—the question about the fundamental rights implications of the Data Retention Directive untouched.[63]

A landmark momentum of *negative judicialization* followed some years later, in 2014, with *Digital Rights Ireland*,[64] where the CJEU invalidated the Data Retention Directive ruling that indiscriminate bulk metadata retention was incompatible with EU fundamental rights.[65] This decision marked the beginning of the *constitutionalization* of data retention.[66] As in the context of the general judicialization theory of the EU discussed above, the constitutionalization of data retention commenced with the interpretation of an instrument of EU secondary law (here, the Data Retention Directive) in a 'constitutional mode' through the application of the EU Charter of fundamental rights.

After *Digital Rights Ireland*, the path has been one of *positive judicialization*.[67] As this ruling created a lack of an established data retention regime at the EU level, a further question arose about the applicability of EU fundamental rights this time on Member States' data retention laws. In 2017, in *Tele2 Sverige*,[68] the CJEU held that national data retention frameworks fell within the scope of EU law,[69] and EU fundamental rights and the *Digital Rights Ireland* principles applied to national laws implementing the invalidated Data Retention Directive.[70] In 2018, in *Ministerio Fiscal*[71] the Court confirmed again that EU law applies to national data retention frameworks and clarified that only serious interferences with the rights to personal and family life (Article 7 Charter) and with the protection of personal data (Article 8 Charter) are required to satisfy the criterion of the seriousness of the crime at issue.[72]

This expansive judicialization continued in 2020 in *Privacy International*.[73] The issue this time concerned the applicability of EU law to domestic data retention legislation adopted to safeguard national security.[74] It should be recalled that pursuant to Article 4(2) of the Treaty on European Union (TEU), 'national security remains the *sole responsibility* of each Member State';[75] nevertheless, the CJEU clarified in *Privacy International* that

---

[62] CJEU, Case C-301/06 *Ireland v Parliament and Council*, ECLI:EU:C:2009:68. See Ester Herlin-Karnell, 'Case C-301/06, Ireland v. Parliament and Council, Judgment of the Court (Grand Chamber) of 10 February 2009', (2009) CMLR 1667; TJ McIntyre, 'Data Retention in Ireland: Privacy, Policy and Proportionality' (2008) CLSR 326.

[63] Tzanou, *The Fundamental Right to Data Protection* (n 15) 73.

[64] CJEU, Judgment of 8 April 2014, *Digital Rights Ireland and Seitlinger and others* (C-293/12 and C-594/12) ECLI:EU:C:2014:238.

[65] ibid para 57.

[66] See also Maria Tzanou and Plixavra Vogiatzoglou, 'National Security and New Forms of Surveillance: From the Data Retention Saga to a Data Subject Centred Approach' (2024) *European Papers* (forthcoming).

[67] *Digital Rights Ireland* (n 64) paras 60–68. For a detailed discussion of the case, see inter alia, Tzanou, *The Fundamental Right to Data Protection* (n 15) 81–88.

[68] CJEU, Judgment of 21 December 2016, *Tele2 Sverige* (C-203/15 and C-698/15) ECLI:EU:C:2016:970.

[69] ibid paras 64–81.

[70] ibid paras 103 and 108.

[71] CJEU, Judgment of 2 October 2018, *Ministerio Fiscal* (C-207/16) ECLI:EU:C:2018:788.

[72] ibid paras 55–56.

[73] CJEU, Judgment of 6 October 2020, *Privacy International* (C-623/17) ECLI:EU:C:2020:790.

[74] For a detailed analysis, see Tzanou and Karyda (n 3); Mitsilegas et al (n 15).

[75] Emphasis added.

national laws that require ECSPs to retain metadata or grant access to this to national authorities for the purpose of national security fall within the scope of EU law; while, national laws that do not impose any obligations on ECSPs, but directly implement national security measures fall outside its scope.[76]

It can, thus, be observed that judicialization saw the Court advancing legal interpretation and constitutional evolution of rules regarding communications surveillance in a way that was detached from the will of member states. Indeed, the Court exerted its judicial control to address a major public issue, namely data retention in the context of law enforcement and national surveillance by encroaching on Member States' competences. A degree of *absorption* can, therefore, be observed in the context of the judicialization of data retention, with the CJEU gradually expanding the competences of the EU in a way that it allowed it to find national retention measures in the field of national security, which has traditionally been outside the scope of the European integration, to be in conflict with EU law. The Court thus established itself as a *trustee* of the Charter and EU fundamental rights and as 'an important actor in the national security landscape'[77] with the powers of a *super-agent* in the context of data retention.

However, regardless of the normative implications of the expansive judicialization of the scope of EU law in national data retention matters, the Court has been sensitive to the threat of 'non-compliance' by Member States. *La Quadrature Du Net 'I'*,[78] which was delivered on the same day as *Privacy International*, marked an important shift from the CJEU's prohibitive approach to bulk data retention as established in *Digital Rights Ireland* to a more nuanced one that opened the door for bulk data retention measures when required for counterterrorism purposes.[79] As I have argued elsewhere, this re-evaluation of data retention models which occurred within the judicialization process can be seen as a 'proceduralisation of surveillance', under which instead of prohibitive rules, data retention measures could be gradually permitted on the basis of a set of procedures, criteria, and safeguards under which they should operate.[80] This approach is in accordance with the general judicialization scholarship, which has refuted the idea that the CJEU works entirely autonomously in furthering European integration,[81] arguing that the Court is open to adjust its rulings to perceived risk of legislative override, taking into account Member States' resistance.[82]

The most significant contribution of *La Quadrature du Net 'I'* is that it developed a typology of permissible national data retention laws by providing comprehensive guidance on how national surveillance measures can be constructed to comply with EU fundamental rights.[83] Pursuant to the CJEU's taxonomy, the compatibility of different data retention

---

[76] *Privacy International* (n 73) para 103. Tzanou and Karyda (n 3) 127.

[77] Monika Zalnieriute, 'A Struggle for Competence: National Security, Surveillance and the Scope of EU Law at Court of Justice of European Union' (2022) 85(1) MLR 198, 199.

[78] CJEU, Judgment of 6 October 2020, *La Quadrature du Net and others* (C-511/18, C-512/18 and C-520/18) ECLI:EU:C:2020:791 ('*La Quadrature du Net 'I'*').

[79] Tzanou and Karyda (n 3) 154.

[80] ibid.

[81] Clifford Carrubba et al., 'Judicial Behaviour under Political Constraints: Evidence From The European Court Of Justice' (2008) American Political Science Review 435; Olof Larsson and Daniel Naurin, 'Judicial Independence and Political Uncertainty: How the Risk of Override Impacts on the Court of Justice of the EU' (2016) International Organization 377.

[82] Mussche and Lens (n 41); Michael Blauberger and Susanne Schmidt, 'The European Court of Justice and its Political Impact' (2017) West European Politics 907.

[83] For a detailed taxonomy based on the CJEU's guidance, see Tzanou and Karyda (n 3) 132–36.

regimes with EU fundamental rights depends on several different factors, including (1) the purposes for which surveillance can be undertaken; (2) the conditions under which data retention is allowed; (3) the applicable safeguards; and (4) the possibility of extending the retention laws beyond a certain amount of time.[84] This list is 'so prescriptive that at times the Court seems to be assuming a *quasi-legislative* role'.[85] The judicialization, therefore, that occurred in *La Quadrature du Net 'I'* goes beyond mere codification; it entails *direct design* by the Court and the construction of permissible data retention legal regimes at the national, rather than the EU, level.

Finally, the most recent wave of judicialization has seen further challenges against national retention laws brought by individuals (*Prokuratuur*[86] delivered in 2021 and *Garda Síochána*[87] delivered in 2022) and ECSPs (*SpaceNet*[88] delivered in 2022). In these cases, the Court reiterated the application of EU fundamental rights to national retention measures, while confirming the more nuanced, proceduralized approach to data retention established in *La Quadrature Du Net 'I'*.[89]

Overall, judicialization is an important theoretical framework to study data retention. It evidences an evolutionary process with the Court at its heart, characterized by a significant numerical increase of data retention cases and by a substantive *constitutionalization* of the area, with the CJEU acting as a *super-agent* and *directly designing* new legal regimes at the national level, including in a field where Member States enjoy exclusive competence, such as national security.

This *judicial activism* has unavoidably triggered *resistance* by Member States.[90] For instance, government voices in France argued that the CJEU's interpretation would undermine security services, in particular when dealing with terrorist threats.[91] In fact, the CJEU was accused of misinterpreting the scope of the national security clause and acting outside its competences (*ultra vires*).[92] The Conseil d'État in its judgment did not pursue the *ultra vires* path, but nevertheless deviated significantly from the pronouncements of the CJEU by essentially allowing 'a permanent' national data retention regime[93] on the basis that the terrorist threat in France is ongoing and other less intrusive measures proposed by the Court, such as targeted retention did not allow the identification of unknown terrorist threats.[94] The judicialization of data protection has, therefore, produced significant pushback and even backlash to the extent that national authorities raised *ultra vires* concerns. This resistance focuses on two main themes: first, the challenges faced by national authorities to

---

[84] ibid, 132.
[85] ibid.
[86] CJEU, Judgment of 2 March 2021, *Prokuratuur* (C-746/18) ECLI:EU:C:2021:152.
[87] CJEU, Judgment of 5 April 2022, *Commissioner of An Garda Síochána* (C-140/20) ECLI:EU:C:2022:258).
[88] CJEU, Judgment of 27 October 2022, *SpaceNet* (C-793/19 and C-794/19) ECLI:EU:C:2022:702.
[89] See also more recent cases: CJEU, Judgment of 30 April 2024, *La Quadrature du Net a.o. c. Premier Ministre and Ministre de la Culture* (C-470/21) ECLI:EU:C:2024:370 ('*La Quadrature du Net 'II'*) and CJEU, Judgment of 30 April 2024, *Procura della Repubblica presso il Tribunale di Bolzano* (C-178/22) ECLI:EU:C:2024:371.
[90] Marcin Rojszczak, 'The Uncertain Future of Data Retention Laws in the EU: Is a Legislative Reset Possible?' (2021) Computer Law & Security Review 105572; Marcin Rojszczak, 'National Security and Retention of Telecommunications Data in Light of Recent Case Law of the European Courts' (2021) European Constitutional Law Review 607, 625.
[91] Laura Kayali, 'France seeks to bypass EU top court on data retention' (3.03.2021) *Politico* <https://cli.re/RwEqKe> accessed 15 July 2024.
[92] Mathieu Pollet, 'Données de connexion: le Conseil d'État va devoir choisir entre froisser le Gouvernement ou les institutions européennes' (16.04.2021) Euractiv France <https://cli.re/jYrVp1> accessed 15 July 2024.
[93] Rojszczak, 'National Security and Retention of Telecommunications Data' (n 90) 628.
[94] Conseil d'État, Case 393099, 21 April 2021, ECLI:FR:CEASS:2021:393099.20210421.

implement the Court's data retention jurisprudence (mainly raised by national governments and courts), and second, criticisms of the Court's legal reasoning and interpretative results (mainly raised by legal scholars).

Yet, as will be argued in the remainder of this chapter, little attention has been paid to the distributional outcomes and the epistemic justice consequences of this judicialization in terms of substantive justice. The crucial questions regarding who the main beneficiaries of the judicialization of data retention are, and whether data privacy law outcomes are equally distributed in the context of electronic communications' surveillance have been overlooked by both the Court and its critics. The chapter turns its attention to these by focusing on the targeted surveillance problem.

3. A Hierarchy of Surveillance: The 'Targeted Retention' Problem and its Consequences

3.1 Mass versus targeted surveillance and the underlying assumptions

A fundamental issue that the data retention scholarship has so far overlooked is the way in which data retention is framed and addressed by the CJEU. Since the initial constitutionalization cases, the Court has constructed a key distinction between bulk data retention of metadata which is prohibited and targeted data retention which is permitted. More specifically, the CJEU has held that the 'general and indiscriminate retention of all traffic and location data',[95] covering 'in a *generalised manner*, all persons and all means of electronic communication as well as all traffic data without any differentiation, limitation or exception'[96] is prohibited as it presents a disproportionate interference with the fundamental rights to privacy (Article 7 Charter), data protection (Article 8 Charter), and, since *Tele2 Sverige*, freedom of expression (Article 11 Charter).[97] By contrast, the 'targeted retention' of metadata, is permitted as 'a preventive measure'[98] for the purpose of fighting serious crime and safeguarding national security, provided that it is compliant with certain conditions.[99]

This legal distinction between mass and targeted data retention and the concomitant conceptualization of mass retention as *impermissible* is based on the widely shared perception that mass surveillance affects 'everyone' as it sweeps up communications data of the entire population, including those of 'innocent people'.[100] In the words of the Court, the problem with mass data retention is that it is 'comprehensive in that it affects *all persons* using electronic communication services, even though those persons are not, even indirectly, in a situation that is liable to give rise to criminal proceedings. It therefore applies even

---

[95] *Tele2 Sverige* (n 68) para 97.
[96] *Digital Rights Ireland* (n 64) para 57. Emphasis added.
[97] *Tele2 Sverige* (n 68) para 107.
[98] ibid para 108.
[99] The retention of data is limited with respect to the categories of data to be retained, the means of communication affected, the persons concerned and the retention period adopted. See ibid para 108.
[100] Seda Gürses et al, 'Crypto and Empire: The Contradictions of Counter-surveillance Advocacy' (2016) *Media, Culture & Society* 576.

to persons for whom there is no evidence capable of suggesting that their conduct might have a *link*, even an indirect or remote one, with serious criminal offences'.[101]

By contrast, targeted retention is framed as *permissible* because it is 'portrayed as the collection of the data and communications of those who are considered to be the *legitimate targets* of government investigation and repression'.[102] As the Court has explained, targeted retention is allowed because it is based on a *relationship* between the data which must be retained and a threat to public security.[103] This *link* or *relationship* may be established on the basis of '(i) data pertaining to a *particular time* period and/or *geographical area* and/or a *group of persons* likely to be involved, in one way or another, in a serious crime, or (ii) persons who could, for other reasons, contribute, through their data being retained, to fighting crime'.[104] Indeed, these persons are constructed as the legitimate targets of 'targeted' data retention even if their potential link to serious crime is not a personal one, but temporal or geographical.

This chapter contends that this construction by the CJEU of a legal distinction between *impermissible* surveillance (mass retention) versus *permissible* surveillance (targeted retention) is problematic and has serious epistemic implications. It is problematic because it involves assumptions about whose experiences of data retention 'are to be addressed and whose ignored' and, thus, suffers from cognitive flaws. More crucially, it may lead to epistemic injustice because it implies a judicially constructed hierarchy of EU data protection problems: those that concern the experiences of the majority are deemed more important than those of minoritized data subjects. The next section discusses these issues by focusing on retention targeting geographical areas of interest.

3.2 The problem with the targeted surveillance of geographical spaces

Pursuant to the Court, a geographical criterion may be used for the permitted targeted data retention. This would target communications in 'one or more geographical areas' based on 'objective and non-discriminatory factors', demonstrating the existence of 'a situation characterised by a high risk of preparation for or commission of serious criminal offences'.[105]

The geographic criterion may appear neutral at first instance, but its symbolic and normative implications cannot be ignored. As critical scholars have demonstrated, spaces are socially constructed and matter in terms of distribution of resources, benefits and collective or societal problems.[106] As an American scholar observed, 'resources and benefits (e.g., higher property values, well-funded schools, newer amenities) concentrate in "White spaces," and collective or societal problems (e.g., poverty, over-policing, underfunded schools) accumulate in non-White spaces'.[107] In the United States, 'segregation' understood

---

[101] *Tele2 Sverige* (n 68) para 105. Emphasis added.
[102] Gürses et al (n 100).
[103] See *Tele2 Sverige* (n 68) para 106.
[104] ibid para 106. Emphasis added.
[105] *La Quadrature du Net 'I'* (n 78) para 150.
[106] Rashida Richardson, 'Racial Segregation and the Data-Driven Society: How Our Failure to Reckon with Root Causes Perpetuates Separate and Unequal Realities' (2021) Berkeley Technology Law Journal 1051; Mary Anne Franks, 'Democratic Surveillance' (2017) 30 Harvard Journal of Law and Technology 425; Michele Gilman and Rebecca Green, 'The Surveillance Gap: The Harms of Extreme Privacy and Data Marginalization' (2018) 42 New York University Review of Law & Social Change 253.
[107] Richardson, ibid 1067. See also Martha Minow, *Making All the Difference: Inclusion, Exclusion, and American Law* (Cornell University Press 1990) 21; Elijah Anderson, 'The White Space' (2015) *Socio. Race &*

as 'a systematic spatial separation and social exclusion of groups' has occurred over the years on the basis of race and ethnicity (often referred to as 'racial segregation').

Spatial concentrations of privilege (or disadvantage) are evident in the European societies as well. Indeed, the more affluent neighbourhoods are viewed as 'safer', whereas sites of concentrated disadvantages and societal problems are often considered spaces of higher risk of disorder or 'crime hot spots', where a greater degree of law enforcement presence, targeting, and surveillance practices are expected.[108] Hotspot policing not only concentrates criminal justice arrests and incarcerations in more disadvantaged neighbourhoods, it also produces skewed feedback-loop effects of crime data that justify further police presence in the same disadvantaged neighbourhoods.[109] Thus, 'crime hotspots' render disadvantaged spaces more visible to state surveillance.

This problem goes beyond physical spaces and affects personal data that constitute the focus of the present analysis. In fact, predictive policing uses so-called crime-focused geographic information systems and technology tools—in other words targeted data retention—to capture, store, combine and analyse data relevant to specific geographic areas in order to draw up predictive crime maps.[110] However, as critical geographic information science scholars note, these approaches and technologies may 'offer distorted representations of social reality ... [because] data production can only yield a small selection from the sum total of all possible data available [and] as such, data are inherently partial [and] selective'.[111] What is more, these crime data are then commonly used as training data for data-driven predictive policing technologies, feeding the established inequalities in society into the algorithms.[112] In addition to the problematic reliability of such data analysis tools, data retention targeting geographical spaces focuses mainly on specific 'street crimes' (eg burglary) which demonstrate an element of physicality and have a more obvious connection to geographic spaces, ignoring other potential—digital—offences which lack geographic boundaries but present potential higher societal costs, such as blue collar crimes (corporate crimes, fraud, etc).[113] This selective focus on a specific subset of crimes and locations 'serves to mask or legitimize disproportionate and often discriminatory policing of certain areas or communities'.[114]

At a symbolic level, the judicial construction of targeted geographical retention as hierarchically less invasive compared to mass surveillance—and hence permissible—demonstrates cognitive ignorance of spatial concentrations of privilege and disadvantage, of their consequences and of how these interlink with systemic social ills such as poverty,

---

Ethnicity 10; Sheryll Cashin, 'Drifting Apart: How Wealth and Race Segregation Are Reshaping the American Dream' Georgetown Law Faculty Publications and Other Works 1698; Clarissa Rile Hayward, *Urban Space and American Political Development: Identity, Interest, Action* (Routledge 2009).

[108] Richardson ibid. See also Orla Lynskey, 'Criminal Justice Profiling and EU Data Protection Law: Precarious Protection from Predictive Policing' (2019) Int'l J L Context 162; Andrew Selbst, 'Disparate Impact in Big Data Policing' (2017) Georgia Law Review 109.
[109] Richardson ibid.
[110] See also the German Federal Constitutional which has declared the use of the Palantir software by police in Hesse and Hamburg unconstitutional. 1 BvR 1547/19 and 1 BvR 2634/20, judgment of 16 February 2023.
[111] Brian Jordan Jefferson, 'Policing, Data, and Power-geometry: Intersections of Crime Analytics and Race During Urban Restructuring' (2018) Urban Geography 1247, 1249. See also Rob Kitchin, *The Data Revolution: Big Data, Open Data, Data Infrastructures and their Consequences* (Sage 2014).
[112] Richardson (n 106).
[113] ibid.
[114] ibid 1080.

discrimination, gendered, racial, and socioeconomic subordination. This judicial distinction might lead to differentiation (and breed further indifference) between the majority (all of us/'innocent'/affected by surveillance) and the 'others' (identified as legitimate targets of surveillance due to the geographic area they reside).

In this form of approved by the CJEU 'targeted governance',[115] the logics of information, surveillance, and prediction are carried out through data-driven assessment of systemic threats based on geographical conceptualizations of risk. The data retention judicialization singles out those outside the norm (the ones residing in alleged 'crime hot spots' and disadvantaged areas) for disproportionate harm.[116] In fact, the distinction between permitted 'targeted surveillance' of spaces and prohibited 'mass surveillance' is structurally *subordinating*. It disproportionality targets certain racial and religious minorities for surveillance 'deterring them from entering society on their own terms and, in effect, erasing aspects of their identities from society'[117] due to their links to specific geographical spaces. It appears, thus, that the judicialization of data retention has given its blessing to the 'surveillance violence'[118] of affected communities—privacy violations that often lead inexorably to material and psychological harm[119] both at the individual and the societal level.

The legal distinction between targeted and mass retention also has significant cognitive implications because it constructs the legal boundaries of what is considered permissible and what impermissible surveillance on the basis of normative assumptions of 'social space (and its denizens), disorder, and crime, as well as . . . political priorities'.[120] This conclusion reinforces the notion, mainly discussed in the law and political economy literature,[121] that 'economic and distributional systems are creatures of law'[122]—in the present case of judicialization.

To sum up, the judicialization of data retention, therefore, seems to have produced a normative hierarchy of beneficiaries as well: the data protection of the majority matters more than the data protection rights of the less advantaged who have the misfortune to reside in higher risk areas (historically subject to increased surveillance).[123] This entails the inherent assumption that diminished levels of data protection are acceptable for data pertaining to individuals living in certain geographical areas on the grounds that these might be legitimate targets of surveillance or 'suspects by default' and, therefore, in this case crime fighting and national security objectives take priority over their fundamental rights. Data protection law outcomes, therefore, are not equally distributed in the context of electronic communications' surveillance; certain individuals and targeted groups linked to specific geographical spaces are subject to 'greater suspicion, differential treatment, and more punitive and exclusionary outcomes'.[124]

---

[115] Ari Ezra Waldman, 'Gender Data in the Automated Administrative State' (2023) Columbia Law Review <https://papers.ssrn.com/sol3/papers.cfm?abstract_id=4358437> accessed 15 July 2024.
[116] ibid.
[117] Scott Skinner-Thompson, *Privacy at the Margins* (CUP 2020) 2.
[118] ibid 3.
[119] ibid.
[120] Richardson (n 106).
[121] See eg Jedediah Britton-Purdy, David Grewal, Amy Kapczynski, and K Sabeel Rahman, 'Building a Law-and-Political Economy Framework: Beyond the Twentieth-Century Synthesis' (2020) 129 Yale Law Journal 1784.
[122] Waldman (n 115).
[123] Franks (n 106); Tzanou, 'The Future of EU Data Privacy Law' (n 18).
[124] Rashida Richardson and Amba Kak, 'Suspect Development Systems: Databasing Marginality and Enforcing Discipline' (2022) U Mich J L Reform 813.

Admittedly, the Court has laid down several substantive and procedural conditions and safeguards against the risks of abuse, applicable to targeted surveillance that must be carried out 'on the basis of objective and non-discriminatory factors'.[125] Yet, the unequal distribution of data retention cannot simply be fixed by proceduralized conditions and safeguards while mass surveillance (affecting the majority) remains prohibited. To put it differently, I argue that targeted surveillance cannot be framed as less problematic and thus, legally and socially acceptable because it is constrained by conditions and safeguards.

3.3 The judicialization of data retention and epistemic injustice

Beyond the distributive normative implications of the judicialization of data retention, this chapter contends that the judicial construction of prohibitive mass surveillance and permitted targeted surveillance has created a further problem of *epistemic injustice*.

In her groundbreaking work, Miranda Fricker theorizes the intersection of social epistemology with theories of justice. Fricker identifies two distinctively epistemic forms of injustice: *testimonial injustice*, that 'occurs when prejudice causes a hearer to give a deflated level of credibility to a speaker's word' and *hermeneutical injustice* that 'occurs when a gap in collective interpretive resources puts someone at an unfair disadvantage when it comes to making sense of their social experiences'.[126] I focus here on the second form of epistemic injustice, hermeneutical injustice, which is relevant to the present analysis. Hermeneutical injustice is always structural because it arises when a society lacks the interpretive resources to make sense of a speaker's experience, because they or members of their social group have been 'prejudicially marginalized in meaning-making activities'.[127] The example used by Fricker to explain hermeneutical injustice is illuminating. As Fricker explains, prior to the introduction of the concept of sexual harassment into public and institutional discourse, people tended to interpret women's experiences and trauma at unwanted sexual advances as 'hysterical reactions to innocent flirtation'.[128] Sexually harassed women suffered hermeneutical injustice because they lacked the interpretive resources to make sense of the injustice they were suffering, due to their prejudicial epistemic marginalization: women were expected to put up with what was considered 'normal' male behaviour.[129]

While Fricker's hermeneutical injustice theory focuses primarily on the individual level and proposes epistemic virtue as a solution,[130] it is an important analytical framework through which the problem of targeted data retention could be examined. Unlike Fricker, however, who focuses on the speaker's experiences (for example, the ones of the harassed women), I look at hermeneutical injustice at the *institutional* (here the *judicial*) level; and in particular, *how* epistemic injustice may be constructed through judicialization. Feminist

---

[125] *La Quadrature du Net 'I'* (n 78) para 150.
[126] Miranda Fricker, *Epistemic Injustice: Power and the Ethics of Knowing* (OUP 2007) 1.
[127] ibid 158–59; Elizabeth Anderson, 'Epistemic Justice as a Virtue of Social Institutions' (2012) Social Epistemoly 163, 166.
[128] Fricker (n 126) 158–59; Anderson, ibid 166.
[129] Fricker, ibid.
[130] ibid.

theory has long discussed 'the way in which relations of power can constrain women's ability to understand their own experiences'.[131] As Nancy Hartsock noted, 'the dominated live in a world structured by others for their purposes—purposes that at the very least are not our own and that are in various degrees inimical to our development and even existence'.[132] Social institutions and practices are structured 'to favour the powerful' and, from an epistemological point of view, 'the powerful have an unfair advantage in structuring collective social understandings'.[133] This entails that 'in the hermeneutical context of social understanding . . . if understandings are structured a certain way, then so are the social facts'.[134]

Let us now consider the problem of the judicial construction of permissible targeted retention through the above lenses. When the Court framed data retention targeting specific geographical sites as by default acceptable and, therefore, allowed it, it constructed a hermeneutical social understanding of surveillance that favours the more powerful (the majority who is considered as 'innocent') as opposed to the powerless (who are considered 'suspects by default' and therefore legitimate targets of surveillance). What is crucial and cannot go unnoticed here is that this social understanding, that replicates widely shared views in politics and academia, is cemented by the apex judicial institution in the EU legal order, the Court of Justice of the EU. This hermeneutical injustice may lead to epistemic harms. The powerless subjected to increased (permissible, targeted) data retention may find their social experience of surveillance as obscured from collective understanding due to this institutional hermeneutical marginalization. This has been described as 'epistemic domination', where the majority holds unwarranted epistemic power in shaping collective understandings and social standards.[135]

To sum up, it is crucial to consider the institutional hermeneutical injustice implications of judicialization which go beyond its normative and distributive consequences. This is because the epistemic injustice harms are not merely theoretical; they can construct and cement long-lasting reality bias[136] and social understandings about the experiences of the less powerful (and of the more advantaged) and might affect the trust of the less privileged in the judiciary and public institutions more generally.[137] Combatting epistemic injustice, thus, becomes urgent for 'the functioning of democracy, since privacy is a core value inherent to a liberal democratic and pluralist society'.[138] As I argue in the next section, judicialization—the CJEU—still has an important role to play into this rethinking of data retention.

---

[131] ibid 148.
[132] Nancy Hartsock, *The Feminist Standpoint Revisited and Other Essays* (Westview Press 1998) 241.
[133] Fricker (n 126) 148.
[134] ibid.
[135] Amandine Catala, 'Democracy, Trust, and Epistemic Justice' (2015) Monist 424. See also Federica Liveriero, 'Epistemic Injustice in the Political Domain: Powerless Citizens and Institutional Reform' (2020) Ethical Theory and Moral Practice 797; Jose Medina, *The Epistemology of Resistance: Gender and Racial Oppression, Epistemic Injustice and Resistant Imaginations* (OUP 2013).
[136] Anderson (n 127) 169.
[137] Tzanou, 'The Future of EU Data Privacy Law' (n 18) 465.
[138] European Union Agency for Fundamental Rights (FRA), 'Facial Recognition Technology: Fundamental Rights Considerations in the Context of Law Enforcement' (2019) 20 <https://fra.europa.eu/en/publication/2019/facial-recognition-technology-fundamental-rights-considerations-context-law> 28, accessed 27 September 2024.

4. Re-imagining Data Retention

The reflection on the normative and epistemic implications of the judicialization of data retention does not have as its aim to add yet another academic critique of the Court's case law. It rather intends to broaden our imagination about moving judicialization forward in a way that contributes to substantive justice. The question, thus becomes: can judicialization deal with distributional and epistemic injustices? What role can the CJEU play in this regard?

Perhaps to the reader's surprise, I argue that judicialization is important and the CJEU can play a significant role in addressing structural issues. How can the data retention judicialization be reimagined so that it accounts for the experiences of both advantaged and less powerful groups? I make two *normative* propositions in this respect.

The first requires that EU data protection law *should* be *egalitarian*: it should be equally distributed to and equally enjoyed by all persons.[139] This means that data retention outcomes *should* be equally distributed to the majority and the less advantaged. It cannot, therefore, be accepted that the starting point of assessment of targeted geographical surveillance is different from mass surveillance. Either both are prohibited under fundamental rights or both are deemed permissible on the basis of similar safeguards.

Second, judicialization as a dynamic, rather than a static, process *should* pay due attention to questions of epistemic injustice. Indeed, creating the conditions for epistemic justice should be a primary goal of judicialization. This means that the Court needs to concern itself with questions on what role its case law can play in eliminating privilege, class, race, and gender inequalities.[140] It could do so by broadening its methodological perspectives by engaging with the analytical, conceptual, and empirical toolkits of research agendas and methods such as the 'law and society' movement (LSM), critical legal studies, critical race theory, feminist epistemology, and post-colonial legal studies.[141] It is crucial to interrogate EU data retention (and protection) case law through different lenses to 'critically revisit ... epistemologies which underlie the conceptual frameworks now in circulation'.[142] The employment of these methods can reveal 'blind spots' in data retention law that 'fail to account for the inherent power asymmetries and structural disempowerment' of disadvantaged groups.[143] Methods and analytical frameworks matter not only to identify the problematic distributive consequences of the EU data protection judicialization, but also to provide a more explicit recognition of the—often neglected—interests at stake when adjudicating relevant cases.[144] In other words, using such frameworks to interrogate current power structures can help to address questions of epistemic injustice. Finally, these conceptual frameworks can guide the construction of new realities and regimes,[145] which as seen above have arisen both through the judicialization of data retention and of EU law in general.

---

[139] Tzanou, 'The Future of EU Data Privacy Law' (n 18).
[140] ibid.
[141] See Peer Zumbansen, 'Transnational Law as Socio-Legal Theory and Critique: Prospects for Law and Society in a Divided World' (2019) Buffalo Law Review 909, 912; Thérèse Murphy, 'Human Rights in Technological Times' in Roger Brownsword, Eloise Scotford, and Karen Yeung (eds), *The Oxford Handbook of Law, Regulation and Technology* (OUP 2017) 953.
[142] Zumbansen, ibid 916.
[143] ibid 920.
[144] Tzanou, 'The Future of EU Data Privacy Law' (n 18) 468.
[145] Katharine Bartlett, 'Feminist Legal Methods' (1990) 103 Harvard Law Review 829, 830.

Admittedly, the above normative proposals are not easy to achieve. Going back to the judicialization discussion, resistance has been a powerful response to and constraint of judicialization. Yet, the general judicialization of the EU legal order theories have shown that the Court can be both restrained but also pushed towards new directions through resistance. This, however, requires a shift of focus, from Member States' pushback to the constitutionalization of surveillance, to deeper neglected epistemic justice questions that concern the distributive outcomes of the Court's case law.

5. Conclusion

The study of the judicialization of EU data retention has revealed a dynamic process of substantive *constitutionalization* of surveillance, characterized by elements of *judicial activism*, with the CJEU acting as a *super-agent* and directly *designing* new legal regimes at the national level, including in a field where Member States enjoy exclusive competence, such as national security.

Despite the resistance that this judicialization has produced, scarce attention has been paid to the *distributional outcomes* and *epistemic consequences* of the judicialization of data retention. The crucial questions regarding who are the main beneficiaries of the judicialization of data retention and whether data privacy law outcomes are equally distributed in the context of electronic communications' surveillance have been overlooked by both the Court and its critics.

This chapter employed the case study of targeted surveillance of geographical spaces to demonstrate this problem. Since the initial judicialization of data retention cases, the Court has constructed a key distinction between bulk data retention of metadata which is prohibited and targeted data retention which is permitted. The permissibility of targeted retention focusing on geographical spaces is a valuable case study in the neglected risks posed by judicialization: how it allocates fundamental rights' protection, how it forces legibility, and how it excludes; all these elements demonstrate the significant institutional role that the Court plays in this area.

The case study of targeted data retention showed that data privacy law outcomes (and the legal boundaries between prohibited and permissive data retention) *are not equally distributed* in the context of electronic communications' surveillance; certain individuals and targeted groups linked to specific geographical spaces are subject to greater suspicion and more exclusionary, differential treatment. This distinction involves assumptions about whose experiences of data retention 'are to be addressed and whose ignored' and implies a judicially constructed hierarchy of EU data protection problems: those that concern the experiences of the majority are deemed more important than those of minoritized data subjects.

Further to the problematic distributive consequences that this construction by the CJEU of a legal distinction between *impermissible* surveillance (mass retention) versus *permissible* surveillance (targeted retention) has produced, the chapter argued that the judicialization of data retention raises issues of *institutional epistemic injustice*. This is because it constructs an hermeneutical social understanding of permitted surveillance that favours the more powerful to the detriment of the less privileged. Therefore, while the judicialization of data retention establishes several procedural conditions and safeguards, it fails to scrutinize the role of policies, practices, and ultimately the role of the Court itself in engendering the problems it sought to mitigate.[146]

Nevertheless, this chapter submitted that the study of the neglected aspects of the judicialization of data retention is significant in broadening our imagination about the ways of moving judicialization forward. It, thus, embarked in reimagining judicialization so that it can advance substantive justice. It argued that judicialization is important and matters to the less privileged and the CJEU can play a significant role in addressing structural issues. This requires a focus on *egalitarian* and *epistemic justice* objectives and could be achieved by challenging institutional and social assumptions that create unequal structural surveillance regimes and realities and contribute to the differential treatment of individuals and groups. It requires that EU data retention (and indeed data protection) law *should* be *egalitarian*: data retention outcomes should be equally distributed to all persons. It, therefore, rejects interpretations that adopt a different starting point for the judicial assessment of targeted geographical surveillance compared to the one used for mass surveillance. In this regard, the chapter argued that two paths are available: either both mass and targeted surveillance are prohibited under fundamental rights or both are deemed permissible on the basis of similar safeguards. Finally, judicialization *should* pay due attention to questions of epistemic injustice. Indeed, creating the conditions for epistemic justice should be one of the main aims of judicialization if this purports to serve, rather than undermine, substantive justice objectives.

---

[146] Richardson (n 106).

22
Data Retention as a Matter of Constitutional Law

Marco Bassini

1. Introduction

The 'data retention saga' is a term often used to describe the unprecedented wave of judgments from the Court of Justice of the European Union (CJEU) in the past decade that has contributed to the shaping of the applicable legal regime in the European Union. However, the constitutional courts of various Member States played an equally important role in orchestrating the interaction[1] between the respective legal systems. Constitutional courts not only played a part in reacting to the most resounding and well-known CJEU case—*Digital Rights Ireland*[2]—which was without any doubt *the* leading case; they had already paved the way for a vibrant interaction on this matter. Such a deep involvement of the constitutional courts reflects the huge impact of data retention on fundamental rights; however, it also signifies the difficulty of striking a balance between the interests at stake in a matter that features important political considerations. Sometimes, constitutional courts were called to action with a view to safeguarding and preserving the choices made by domestic lawmakers vis-à-vis an allegedly trenchant approach of the CJEU. This is not to claim that constitutional courts took a political role, disobeying their genuine legal mandate; nevertheless, this observation reflects the actual dynamics going on between European and domestic courts (including ordinary courts), with constitutional adjudication playing a role in 'testing the waters' and interacting with the CJEU, particularly as a 'filtering mechanism', that is, by trying to obtain feedback from Luxembourg on the efforts made by national lawmakers. The fact that so many constitutional courts took the floor in this domain[3] proves that, despite the guidance offered by the CJEU in *Digital Rights Ireland*, there was inherent bewilderment among lawmakers on the proper framing of a new legal regime that could prove consistent with the CJEU ruling(s). At the same time, the entrance on the scene of constitutional courts in this phase reflected the disputed status of this subject matter and the tricky intersection among various societal interests and policies, not always under the clear umbrella of the EU sphere of competences. Despite the

---

[1] Ludovica Benedizione and Eleonora Paris, 'Preliminary Reference and Dialogue Between Courts as Tool for Reflection on the EU System of Multilevel Protection of Rights: The Case of the *Data Retention Directive*' (2015) 16(6) German Law Journal 1727.

[2] CJEU, Judgment of 8 April 2014, *Digital Rights Ireland and Seitlinger and others* (C-293/12 and C-594/12) ECLI:EU:C:2014:238.

[3] For an overview of the constitutional courts' stances when faced with *Digital Rights Ireland*, see Eleni Kosta, 'The Way to Luxembourg: National Court Decisions on the Compatibility of the Data Retention Directive with the Rights to Privacy and Data Protection' (2013) 10(3) SCRIPTed 339.

CJEU holding in *Ireland v Parliament*[4] that the Data Retention Directive[5] fell within the competence of the EU as it merely regulated the obligations of service providers to retain data (and not the access of public authorities to such data), the stance of the EU, and of the CJEU in particular, did in fact have a huge impact on the Member States' room for manoeuvre in the prevention, identification, and prosecution of crimes.[6] So, if it cannot be disputed that the legal regimes in force in a plurality of Member States had to be aligned with the guidelines issued by the CJEU, it is also true that predicting the success of lawmaking efforts was anything but an easy job. This was all the more true in the light of the reluctance of the EU (or, perhaps, of Member States) to replace the Data Retention Directive once it had been invalidated, most probably because of the foreseeable problems in finding consensus on a future regulation on this subject. This reluctance reveals a certain degree of hypocrisy among the EU institutions: while the CJEU was firmly using its scrutiny in a reactive mode on the compatibility between privacy rights and various pieces of national legislation implemented in the vacuum generated by the invalidation of the Data Retention Directive, the EU lawmakers failed to preventively offer any remedy in terms of legislative initiatives.[7]

It is, likewise, remarkable that the judgments released by the CJEU after *Digital Rights Ireland* had to review the compatibility of Member States law with Article 15 of the ePrivacy Directive,[8] which at present is the only legal ground in the EU legal system that legitimizes the adoption of data retention obligations. This sounds even more paradoxical if one thinks that, in 2006, with the adoption of the Data Retention Directive, the EU created a specific framework with a view to harmonizing Member States' legal systems. As result of the invalidation of the Data Retention Directive, EU law only indirectly regulates data retention obligations through a provision that reproduces the exemptions and restrictions on a range of rights and obligations provided by Article 13 of the (now repealed) Directive 95/46/EC. This is a visible failure to regulate this subject matter, reflecting the silent self-restraint of EU institutions. However, the fact that the EU did not establish a detailed and comprehensive framework after the 2014 *Digital Rights Ireland* decision led to the factual empowerment of the CJEU, which is the only institutional actor that could not help but model, albeit indirectly, a legal regime for data retention compatible with the fundamental rights protected by the Charter.[9]

So, given the legislative inertia of the EU, it was up to the CJEU to propose some pillars for this subject matter: this is nothing new in the recent case law on privacy and data

---

[4] CJEU, Judgment of 10 February 2009, *Ireland/Parliament and Council* (C-301/06, ECR 2009 p. I-593) ECLI:EU:C:2009:68 ('*Ireland v Parliament*').

[5] Directive 2006/24/EC of the European Parliament and of the Council of 15 March 2006 on the retention of data generated or processed in connection with the provision of publicly available electronic communications services or of public communications networks and amending Directive 2002/58/EC, [2006] OJ L 105/54.

[6] For some remarks on the far-reaching impact of the data retention saga, see Monika Zalnieriute, 'A Struggle for Competence: National Security, Surveillance and the Scope of EU Law at the Court of Justice of European Union' (2022) 85(1) MLR 198.

[7] Giulia Formici and Edoardo Celeste, 'Constitutionalizing Mass Surveillance in the EU: Civil Society Demands, Judicial Activism and Legislative Inertia' (2024) German Law Journal, First View.

[8] Directive 2002/58/EC of the European Parliament and of the Council of 12 July 2002 concerning the processing of personal data and the protection of privacy in the electronic communications sector (Directive on privacy and electronic communications) [2002] OJ L 201/37.

[9] Maja Brkan, 'The Court of Justice of the EU, Privacy and Data Protection: Judge-made Law as a Leitmotif in Fundamental Rights Protection' in Maja Brkan and Evangelia Psychogiopoulou (eds), *Courts, Privacy and Data Protection in the Digital Environment* (Edward Elgar 2017).

protection in Europe. Commentators have highlighted judicial activism as one of the driving forces that has marked the shifting paradigm of data protection and other fundamental rights in the digital age.[10] However, the fact that the definition of legal boundaries is left to the CJEU with such broad latitude may trigger concerns, from a constitutional perspective, concerning the principle of the separation of powers. This is not to criticize the role that the CJEU has played in this respect, as its clear objective has been to safeguard fundamental rights; rather, the extent to which the CJEU had to solve the legislative vacuum by resorting to the umbrella of Article 15 of the ePrivacy Directive is remarkable.

Against this background, the role of constitutional courts can be observed in at least three phases: when paving the way for the CJEU to invalidate the Data Retention Directive (whether directly, by referring preliminary questions, or indirectly, by avoiding this option); when acting as the intermediary between national legal systems and CJEU scrutiny on the content of the relevant provisions; and when reviewing the appropriateness of the domestic provisions adopted in the aftermath of the CJEU decisions. Wishing to capture the contribution of constitutional courts to the framing of data retention as a matter of constitutional law as well, this chapter will delve into some particular judgments, without any expectation of carrying out an exhaustive overview. It will first look at the German and Romanian constitutional courts' judgments in the pre-*Digital Rights Ireland* era to highlight the tension between the EU legal order and the national legal orders (section 2). The chapter will then analyse the attitude of the Belgian Constitutional Court, to emphasize its ability to have a say in the search for a compromise (section 3). Finally, it will illustrate how, in the approach of the Portuguese Constitutional Court, the data retention saga played a role as a driver for a change in attitude vis-à-vis EU law.

Accordingly, this chapter will frame data retention as a constitutional law problem, with a view to exploring the interaction in this field between the CJEU (and thus the EU legal system) and constitutional courts (and their respective legal orders).[11] As scholars have commented widely on the Irish High Court's and the Austrian Constitutional Court's references to the CJEU[12] that paved the way for the *Digital Rights Ireland* judgment, this chapter—without neglecting the key role of those rulings—will focus on courts offering interesting insights into the relationship with EU law. This piece will also emphasize how constitutional courts played a different role and how this influenced their approach towards data retention measures.[13]

---

[10] Oreste Pollicino, *Judicial Protection of Fundamental Rights on the Internet: A Road Towards Digital Constitutionalism?* (Hart Publishing 2021).

[11] Marek Zubik, Jan Podkowik, and Robert Rybski, 'Judicial Dialogue on Data Retention Laws in Europe in the Digital Age: Concluding Remarks' in Marek Zubik, Jan Podkowik, and Robert Rybski (eds), *European Constitutional Courts towards Data Retention* (Springer 2021).

[12] Among others, see Axel Anderl and Alona Klammer, 'Data Retention in Austria' in Zubik, Podkowik, and Rybski, ibid; David Fennelly, 'Data Retention in Ireland', in Zubik, Podkowik, and Rybski, ibid. Also see Barbara Grabowska-Moroz, 'Data Retention in the European Union', in Zubik, Podkowik, and Rybski, ibid; and Arianna Vedaschi and Valerio Lubello, 'Data Retention and its Implications for the Fundamental Right to Privacy' (2015) 20 Tilburg Law Review 14. For a deeper overview on the data retention saga from a constitutional law perspective, see Giulia Formici, *La disciplina della data retention tra esigenza securitarie e tutela dei diritti fondamentali. Un'analisi comparata* (Giappichelli 2021).

[13] On the role of constitutionalism see Darinka Piqani, 'Arguments for a Holistic Approach in European Constitutionalism: What Role for National Institutions in Avoiding Constitutional Conflicts between National Constitutions and EU Law' (2012) 8 ECLR 493, 509.

2. Constitutional Pride

The German and Romanian constitutional courts are among those[14] that had the chance to review the compatibility of the national rules implementing the Data Retention Directive with the respective constitutional provisions on the right to private life (including confidentiality of communications) before the *Digital Rights Ireland* case.

It is widely accepted among constitutional law scholars that the German Federal Constitutional Court (*Bundesverfassungsgericht* (BVerfG)) ranks among the most authoritative such court in Europe.[15] Special regard is therefore given to its jurisprudence, most notably on the most politically sensitive matters such as the relationship with the EU legal system.[16] In this respect, and particularly on the relationship with the EU catalogue of fundamental rights, the BVerfG also proved to adhere to quite a conservative and 'suspicious' approach, which reflected the well-known *Solange* doctrine.[17] According to this doctrine, the BVerfG would refrain from reviewing the compatibility of mandatory EU law provisions, on the assumption that, in the EU legal order, fundamental rights enjoy a level of protection equal to the protection provided by the Basic Law. Within this framing of the relationship with EU law, the notion of constitutional identity plays a key role,[18] as it draws a line between the undisputed supremacy of EU law and the preservation of the fundamental rights protected by the Basic Law (*Grundgesetz*).[19] It is also worth recalling that, through the domestic case law, data protection gained a solid status as a fundamental right in Germany well before the relevant EU primary and secondary law provisions came into force.

This being the relevant context, the approach of the BVerfG to the case of data retention tells us a great deal about its attitude to the EU legal order, especially when the latter challenges the system of protection of fundamental rights established by the Basic Law.

It is no coincidence, perhaps, that the BVerfG was among the first constitutional adjudicators to rule on data retention, and that it did so well before the *Digital Rights Ireland* case. In 2010,[20] requested to review the constitutionality of the provisions of the Telecommunications Act that had implemented the Data Retention Directive in 2007, the

---

[14] The supreme and constitutional courts in other jurisdictions also reviewed the compatibility of the respective data retention laws with the national legal system before the *Digital Rights Ireland* case: Supreme Administrative Court of Bulgaria, 25 October 2008, no 13627/2008; Supreme Court of Cyprus, 1 February 2011, app nos 65/2009, 78/2009, 82/2009, and 15/2010-22/2010; and Czech Constitutional Court, 22 March 2011, no 23/2011. For an overview of these judgments, which will not be directly analysed in this contribution, see Cristiana Markou, 'The Cyprus and other EU Court Rulings on Data Retention: The Directive as a Privacy Bomb' (2012) 28 Computer Law & Security Review 468; Cristiana Markou, 'Data Retention in Cyprus in the Light of EU Data Retention Law' in Zubik, Podkowik, and Rybski (n 11); Radim Polčák, 'Data Retention in the Czech Republic' in Zubik, Podkowik, and Rybski (n 11); Alexander Kashumov, 'Data Retention in Bulgaria' in Zubik, Podkowik, and Rybski (n 11); Pavel Molek, 'Unconstitutionality of the Czech Implementation of the Data Retention Directive; Decision of 22 March 2021, Pl. ÚS 24/10' (2012) 8 ECLR 338.

[15] For an interesting overview of the rise and evolution of the BVerfG, see Michela Hailbronner, 'Rethinking the Rise of the German Constitutional Court: From Anti-Nazism to Value Formalism' (2014) 12(3) IJCL 626.

[16] Oreste Pollicino, 'The European "Market" for Constitutional Ideas. Abuse of a Judicial Dominant Position?' (2020) <https://verfassungsblog.de/the-european-market-for-constitutional-ideas> accessed 20 July 2023.

[17] This doctrine is rooted, in particular, in the judgments BVerfG, 29 May 1974, BvR 37, 271, 2 BvL 52/71 (*Solange I*) and BVerfG, 22 October 1986, BvR 73, 339, 2 BvR 197/83 (*Solange II*).

[18] In the case at issue, see Dietrich Westphal, 'German Federal Constitutional Court delivers Roadmap for National Data Retention Laws – Without Transferral to CJEU' (2011) 5 Vienna J on Int'l Const L 222, 229.

[19] On the approach until 2015 of the BVerfG vis-à-vis preliminary references to the CJEU, see Eva Julia Lohse, 'The German Constitutional Court and Preliminary References – Still a Match not Made in Heaven?' (2015) 16(6) German Law Journal 1491.

[20] BVerfG, 2 March 2010, 1 BvR 256/08, 1 BvR 586/08, 1 BvR 263/08.

BVerfG found a brilliant way to escape from the 'perils' of a possible preliminary reference to the CJEU. Instead of focusing on the problem of determining who held the lawmaking competence, and thus going beyond the first problem addressed by the CJEU in its case law, the BVerfG reasoned that, while the provisions establishing obligations on providers in respect of the retention of data fell within the scope of the EU's lawmaking powers (having been harmonized through the Data Retention Directive), those governing the use of and access to data that were subject to retention obligations had not been subject to harmonization. This line of reasoning was consistent with the 2009 judgment of the CJEU in Case C-301/06, in which it found the Data Retention Directive to be properly grounded on the harmonization of the internal market pillar. The distinction drawn between the rules on retention and the rules on the use of and access to personal data made it possible for the BVerfG to autonomously review the compatibility of the domestic provisions with the fundamental rights yardsticks enshrined in the Basic Law without any need to refer a preliminary question to the CJEU.[21] By this move,[22] a reference to the CJEU was deemed unnecessary and the BVerfG could enforce the Basic Law provisions protecting fundamental rights. One might think that the BVerfG could simply have found that a reference to the CJEU was not required in order to review the conflict between the relevant provisions (not taking into consideration the implementation of the Data Retention Directive) and fundamental rights. However, those who are familiar with the attitude of the German court vis-à-vis EU law will quickly note that this move was a perfectly consistent *escamotage* to avoid giving the floor to the CJEU[23] on a matter with sensitive effects on data protection, a fundamental right deeply rooted in the German constitutional tradition.[24]

Being among the first courts to adjudicate on this matter, the BVerfG aimed to deliver an influential precedent that was likely to have a huge impact on other courts in the EU. One could nonetheless wonder whether the *distinguo* at the heart of the 2010 BVerfG decision played any role in the reasoning and interpretative strategies of the constitutional and ordinary courts, in the aftermath of the *Digital Rights Ireland* case, to justify a margin for manoeuvre for the Member States despite the invalidation of the Data Retention Directive.

Setting this question aside, it is worth noting that, in its 2010 judgment, the BVerfG did in fact go beyond its 'self-restraint'. As noted by Albers,[25] it also reviewed the domestic legislation implementing the mandatory provisions of the Data Retention Directive (and not just the legislation transposing the non-mandatory provisions), revisiting the traditional

---

[21] It is worth noting that the BVerfG itself made its first request for a preliminary ruling to the CJEU (Case C-62/14) only in 2014 in the well-known *Gauweiler* case (BVerfG, 21 June 2016, 2 BvR 2728/13, 2 BvE 13/13, 2 BvR 2731/13, 2 BvR 2730/13, 2 BvR 2729/13).

[22] Katja de Vries, Rocco Bellanova, Paul de Hert, and Serge Gutwirth, 'The German Constitutional Court Judgment on Data Retention: Proportionality Overrides Unlimited Surveillance (Doesn't It?)', in Serge Gutwirth, Yves Poullet, Paul de Hert, and Ronald Leenes (eds), *Computers, Privacy and Data Protection: An Element of Choice* (Springer 2011) 12.

[23] This line of reasoning made it possible for the German Constitutional Court to deliver its judgment without disregarding the essence of the *Solange* doctrine, under which it was committed to refrain from exercising its jurisdiction to review the compatibility of domestic provisions implementing EU mandatory norms with the Basic Law. This self-restraint from the German Constitutional Court applies to the extent that the fundamental rights established by the Basic Law enjoy equivalent protection in the legal system of the European Union. See *Solange I*, *Solange II* (n 17).

[24] Christian DeSimone, 'Pitting Karlsruhe Against Luxembourg? German Data Protection and the Contested Implementation of the EU Data Retention Directive' (2010) 11(3) German Law Journal 29; Anna-Bettina Kaiser, 'German Data Retention Provisions Unconstitutional In Their Present Form; Decision of 2 March 2010, *NJW* 2010, p. 833' (2010) 6 ECLR 503, 504–05.

[25] Marion Albers, 'Data Retention in Germany' in Zubik, Podkowik, and Rybski (n 11) 122.

Solange approach as a consequence of what scholars defined as 'functional delimitation construction'.[26] In a nutshell, this extension of the reach of the constitutional scrutiny was not seen as impermissible, as long as its goal was to confirm the constitutionality of provisions implementing EU law. It must be recalled that, at the time, the CJEU had not yet been requested to review the compatibility of the Data Retention Directive with fundamental rights. This control by the CJEU was purely hypothetical and a mere possibility at the time: there was no certainty that the CJEU would have taken the floor on this profile, and this paved the way for the actual extension of the inherently limited review that the BVerfG could practically exercise.[27] The authoritative guidance of the BVerfG thus definitely, albeit indirectly, had an impact in Europe at a time when national courts were struggling with the national transpositions of the Data Retention Directive. In a way, the CJEU could also have been indirectly influenced by such a significant precedent in the *Digital Rights Ireland* case. In coherence with the German legal tradition, this ruling—which held Articles 113a and 113b of the *Telekommunikastionsgesetz* (TKG) and Article 100g, para 1, no 1 of the Criminal Procedure Code for breach of Article 10, para 1, of the Basic Law to be unconstitutional—developed a set of requirements based on the respective constitutional framework, with a view to assessing the compatibility of the interferences posed by the contested provisions with the privacy (ie freedom and confidentiality) of individual correspondence and telecommunications. The provisions were found to lack proportionality, despite meeting the requirement of legality and serving a legitimate interest.[28]

By contrast, the BVerfG did not take a position on the vexed question that years later would capture both national courts' and the CJEU's interest, that is, whether untargeted retention could amount to a form of impermissible mass surveillance contrary to the fundamental rights protected by constitutions and human rights covenants. Nonetheless, it is quite interesting that when the BVerfG focused on its proportionality-driven perspective it made a significant point by affirming that data retention 'without cause' is not per se prohibited, even if such an interference must meet the proportionality test.[29] On this specific point, however, the BVerfG recently released a new judgment in which it could not avoid revisiting its view on data retention without cause, as result of the CJEU's stance in *SpaceNet*.[30] As the CJEU found the obligation of telecommunications service providers

---

[26] ibid.
[27] ibid, where the author emphasizes that this 'new approach' is grounded on two reasons: the political pressure for a quick decision (resulting from the huge number of complaints and the vocal protests ongoing at the time in Germany), and the desire of the BVerfG to be at the forefront of the European judicial debate with a judgment that could be a source of inspiration and guidance for others.
[28] As noted by de Vries et al (n 22) 6–7, the BVerfG applied a 'privacy test' consistent with the three-prong scrutiny enshrined in Article 8, para 2, ECHR. However, in the ECtHR scheme, proportionality is assessed in the context of the 'necessary in a democratic society' criterion, whereas in the reasoning of the BVerfG it is autonomously considered as the third step of the test. Furthermore, the authors point out another remarkable difference that explains the relevance of the proportionality requirement in the case at issue. While the ECtHR considers the adoption of appropriate safeguards to mitigate the impact of interference with the fundamental right to private and family life to be a component of the legality requirement, the BVerfG sees the adoption of these safeguards as part of the assessment of the proportionality of an interference.
[29] Albers (n 25) 125 notes that a key role in the line of reasoning of the BVerfG in this respect was played by the difference between retention of data and access to data. Retrieval of data is, in fact, seen as taking place 'in a second step . . . and carried out on a case-by-case basis following legally defined criteria', ibid 126. Moreover, in the retention phase the distributed nature of storage is considered by the Constitutional Court to be of help in mitigating the impact on fundamental rights, as it means that data are not available on a general basis to public authorities as a whole, but are retained by the respective service providers.
[30] CJEU, Judgment of 27 October 2022, *SpaceNet* (C-793/19 and C-794/19) ECLI:EU:C:2022:702.

to store data without cause (which was reintroduced by the German Parliament in 2015 in the 'second data retention' regime[31]) to be incompatible with EU law, the BVerfG was eventually able to rule the national provisions inapplicable in August 2023.[32] As a result, despite the important guidance offered in its 2010 ruling, there has been no 'happy ending' for the paternalistic attitude of the BVerfG in the field of data retention. In fact, the Federal Administrative Tribunal before which the data retention obligations had been challenged[33] ultimately deemed it necessary to request the CJEU to rule on the compatibility of the national provisions with EU law, without any apparent opportunity for constitutional scrutiny.[34]

The *SpaceNet* judgment indirectly had a '*cul-de-sac* effect' on the BVerfG. Despite its ability to follow an autonomous line of reasoning,[35] and its room to build on certain *distinguo*, the BVerfG could not but acknowledge that the national provisions failed 'to address the principles of specificity and clarity emphasized by the CJEU in order to even consider the possibility of data retention regimes and therefore may not be applied to the primacy of EU law'.[36]

Another remarkable aspect lies in the ability of the BVerfG to enforce Article 10 of the Basic Law despite its old-fashioned[37] wording. In the same way as for the CJEU case law, whereas technology developments played a role in shaping new threats and challenges to fundamental rights, it cannot be disputed that the provisions protecting the fundamental rights at stake, no matter whether or not they captured a given state of art, turned out to be effective safeguards. There was therefore no need to revisit traditional rights that already had robust constitutional entrenchment, especially in Germany; instead, the focus of the BVerfG's reasoning is on enforcement, that is, on the ability to make the provisions protecting the right to privacy 'living safeguards' even vis-à-vis the threats of the digital society.

Keeping the focus on the case law that preceded the landmark *Digital Rights Ireland* judgment, it is worth noting that the BVerfG was not the only court to rule on this matter at that early stage of the data retention saga. Among others, the Romanian Constitutional Court (RCC) was the first constitutional tribunal to engage (whether directly or indirectly) with the CJEU and the EU legal system on data retention.[38] The RCC issued two judgments, one in 2009[39] and the other in 2014,[40] and these, respectively, found to be unconstitutional the national law transposing the Data Retention Directive and a national law passed in the

---

[31] See in particular Chapter 7 by Matthias Bäcker, 'Data Retention in Germany—Not a Never-ending Story After All?' in this volume.
[32] BVerfG, 14 August 2023, 6 C 6.22 and 6 C 7.22.
[33] For a detailed description of the background to this case, see Sven Braun, 'German Data Retention Law Nullified, Again' (2023) 3 EDPL 353. See also Bäcker (n 31).
[34] It is quite telling that, even prior to the adoption of a specific constitutional judgment on the compatibility of the second data retention regime, the *SpaceNet* CJEU case was found to mark a point of no return for the applicability of the German law provisions. See, for instance, BVerfG, 14–15 February 2023, 1 BvR 141/15, 1 BvR 2683/16, 1 BvR 2845/16, in which a BVerfG chamber dismissed some constitutional complaints concerning the disputed provisions of the German Telecommunications Act on being satisfied that the CJEU had already found them incompatible with EU law.
[35] See Braun (n 33) 354.
[36] ibid 355.
[37] de Vries et al (n 22) 5.
[38] Simona Șandru, 'Data Retention in Romania' in Zubik, Podkowik, and Rybski (n 11).
[39] RCC, 8 October 2009, no 1258. See Adrian Bannon, 'Romania Retrenches on Data Retention' (2010) 24(2) International Review of Law, Computer & Technology 145; Cian C. Murphy, 'Romanian Constitutional Court, Decision No. 1258 of 8 October 2009' (2010) 47(3) CMLR 933.
[40] RCC, 8 July 2013, no 440.

aftermath of the first ruling. The Romanian cases also show the ability of the RCC to 'fine-tune' the approach of the lawmakers to data retention, which is something similar to what the CJEU has done over the last decade in modelling the compliance of Member States' legislation with Article 15 of the ePrivacy Directive.

Interestingly enough, in its first judgment the RCC took a different approach to that taken in the 2010 German case just a few months later. Although the RCC took into account the inherent distinction between retention and retrieval of data, it came to a partly different conclusion. In the view of the RCC, the main critical aspect of a data retention scheme lies in the first stage, that is, in the storage of data. While retaining data can meet the proportionality requirement, the bulk retention of data cannot: it is disproportionate by nature.[41] According to the Romanian judges, the core of the threat to fundamental rights is thus derived from the blanket retention[42] of data, which is likely to overturn not only the presumption of innocence for individuals but also, ultimately, the relationship between the protection of the right to privacy as a rule and the interference with this right as an exception to the rule.

Also in this respect the purely legal line of reasoning cannot be disentangled from its political significance and the underlying doctrines applicable to the relationship with the EU legal system. As pointed out in the legal literature,[43] by focusing on the 'retention phase' the RCC was implicitly positioning itself as a critic of the Data Retention Directive, even though its review concerned the domestic implementing provisions. In this context, the RCC did not hesitate to directly scrutinize the norms enshrined in Romanian Law no 298/2008 and declare this law to be unconstitutional because of the violation of Article 53 of the Constitution. The lack of a worked-through and solid constitutional doctrine on the relationship with EU law, which was also the result of the relatively 'young' status of Romania as a Member State of the EU, may have influenced the approach of the Court.[44] In the end, the RCC also relied, in its reasoning, on the proportionality requirement, but found it relevant to the retention obligations rather than to the provisions on the use of and access to data. In this way, a first clue into what the CJEU case law would have addressed at a later stage, after the invalidation of the Data Retention Directive, became visible.

Paradoxically, the second judgment rendered by the RCC soon after the *Digital Rights Ireland* case in 2014 invalidated the law that had been passed in 2012 to avoid the risk of an infringement procedure by the EU Commission after the 2009 judgment.

3. Lack of Constitutional Pride?

The Belgian Constitutional Court (BCC), commonly regarded as sympathetic to the European integration process[45] and to the EU legal system, had no hesitation in 2015 in

---

[41] de Vries et al (n 22) 14.
[42] ibid 14.
[43] ibid 15: according to the authors, the Court performed 'a frontal attack on national law 298/2008, but also on the Directive itself'.
[44] It is no coincidence that the reasoning of the Romanian Constitutional Court was inspired more by the case law of the ECtHR than the CJEU jurisprudence. In any case, for a deeper analysis of the reasoning of the RCC in this respect see Viorica Viță, 'The Romanian Constitutional Court and the Principle of Primacy: To Refer or Not to Refer?' (2015) 16 German Law Journal 1623, 1648–61.
[45] For a broader perspective, see Patricia Popelier and Catherine Van de Heyning, 'The Belgian Constitution: The Efficacy Approach to European and Global Governance' in Anneli Albi and Samo Bardutzky

declaring to be unconstitutional the national law transposing the Data Retention Directive, soon after its invalidation by the CJEU.[46] The judgment by which the Belgian judges 'drew the consequences' from the CJEU landmark decision did not, however, escape criticism for its plain adherence to the CJEU ruling.

Of course, it was not difficult for the national judges to take a position on the constitutionality of the provisions transposing the Data Retention Directive, after the latter had been invalidated. The CJEU provided valuable guidelines on the flaws in the Data Retention Directive, and these were likely to affect the national transposing provisions. However, it could not be taken for granted that the outcome of the rulings would have been the same, especially considering the common practice of national courts to elaborate on distinguishing arguments.

In the 2015 ruling,[47] the BCC found that the Belgian Act on Electronic Communication violated the constitutional principles of equality and non-discrimination (Articles 10 and 11), which are to be read in conjunction with the rights enshrined in Articles 7 and 8 of the Charter and also with Article 52 of the Constitution.[48] Thus, the BCC invalidated these provisions, despite the attempts made by the Belgian government to claim that certain norms were autonomous from the Data Retention Directive and could then possibly 'survive' as an expression of the Member State's discretion in regulating the retention of personal data. Curiously, the BCC first mentioned the relevant Charter provisions and then found the legislation under scrutiny to contradict the Constitution 'read in conjunction' with the former. Scholars have pointed to the 'lack of constitutional pride'[49] emerging in this statement, which mirrors the 'fascination for "higher" norms' and is consistent with the 'cosmopolitan' attitude of the BCC.[50]

In the view of the BCC, there were no substantial differences between the Data Retention Directive and the Belgian legislation transposing it. For this reason, the BCC could easily reproduce the same reasoning as the CJEU with regard to the aspects of the Data Retention Directive implemented by the national legislation that were found to be incompatible with the provisions of the Charter.

Later on, however, the Belgian legislator, under pressure from the law enforcement authorities, took to the floor once again and modified the existing provisions to strike a compromise between the 'lessons' given by the CJEU and the BCC and the need to safeguard the effectiveness of investigative powers. It was pointed out that the BCC, knowing in advance about this foreseeable discontent, could have used the occasion to go beyond the CJEU's reasoning and further explain its focus on national law. The BCC's stance sounded like a simple 'confirmation' of the CJEU judgment, and this did not contribute towards an

---

(eds), *National Constitutions in European and Global Governance: Democracy, Rights, the Rule of Law* (Asser Press 2019).

[46] BCC, 11 June 2015, no 84/2015.
[47] Laurens Naudts, 'Belgian Constitutional Court Nullifies Belgian Data Retention Law' (2015) 3 EDPL 208, 209–10.
[48] ibid 210, where the author highlights that the Belgian court failed to properly articulate the connection between the constitutional provisions and the provisions of the Charter protecting the right to privacy and data protection.
[49] Paul de Hert, 'Courts, Privacy and Data Protection in Belgium: Fundamental Rights that Might As Well be Struck from the Constitution', in Maja Brkan and Evangelia Psychogiopoulou (eds), *Courts, Privacy and Data Protection in the Digital Environment* (Edward Elgar 2017) 75.
[50] ibid 78.

easing of the tension with the law enforcement authorities raised by the invalidation of the relevant provisions; the enforcement authorities felt deprived of valuable tools for the accomplishment of their institutional tasks.[51]

The new provisions introduced to 'fill the gap' maintained the position as regards the bulk retention of data, but accompanied this with additional safeguards, in the hope of fulfilling the requirements set forth by the CJEU, albeit theoretically, in its 2014 ruling.[52] The Belgian Parliament passed the new law on the assumption—made explicit in the preparatory works—that the requirements laid down by the CJEU in the *Digital Rights Ireland* case were understood as alternative rather than cumulative conditions.[53] According to this view, the more severe interference with the right to privacy and data protection in the retention phase could be counterbalanced by the adoption of safeguards applicable to the subsequent access and use phase.[54] However, in 2016 another remarkable judgment came into play: the *Tele2 Sverige* case.[55] In this judgment, the CJEU not only laid down another legal ground for reviewing the compatibility of data retention provisions but also started to model a 'statute' of data retention with a particular focus on the need to prevent mass surveillance. This was an unfortunate coincidence for the Belgian lawmaker, which had just reacted to the negative impact of *Digital Rights Ireland* and the subsequent BCC ruling on the domestic legal system.

Against this background, the BCC had a new chance to rule on data retention, which on this occasion was turned into a request for a preliminary ruling referred to the CJEU that resulted in the *La Quadrature du Net 'I'* ruling.[56] This case demonstrates the contribution that constitutional courts can offer in the interaction between legal systems on a disputed matter like data retention that presents a challenging connection to the competences reserved to Member States or for which the Member States in any case retain a higher discretion.

The reference to the CJEU made by the BCC was perhaps surprising but is most likely justified by the desire to give the CJEU the say on the fine-tuning of the data retention regime as outlined in the previous cases, especially in the light of the pressure from the national authorities. One might suppose that the BCC did not want to take responsibility for a new stance that could have a significant impact on the status quo. Regardless of the political background, the choice to refer the preliminary question resulted in a partial reshaping of the guidelines provided by the CJEU in the *Tele2 Sverige* case, leading to a new compromise between the competing interests at stake. As is known, the CJEU had clarified that the bulk (ie untargeted) retention of data for the purpose of countering crime could be justified with respect to subscriber data but was not permissible if applied to traffic and location data. As result, Member States could only establish targeted retention obligations

---

[51] Naudts (n 47) 210. As the author notes, the Belgian court did not deem it necessary to consider other aspects deserving clarification on which the plaintiffs had raised specific claims, such as the impact on other fundamental rights (ie freedom of expression, fair trial). For this reason, the judgment failed to provide effective guidance for the Belgian lawmaker that could be beneficial for the drafting of new provisions on this matter. Another disputed aspect, namely whether evidence obtained on the basis of the now-invalidated rules had to be considered illegal, was not clarified.

[52] Catherine Van de Heyning, 'Data Retention in Belgium', in Zubik, Podkowik, and Rybski (n 11) 55.

[53] Formici, *La disciplina della data retention* (n 12) 300.

[54] ibid.

[55] CJEU, Judgment of 21 December 2016, *Tele2 Sverige and Watson* (C-203/15 and C-698/15) ECLI:EU:C:2016:970 ('*Tele2 Sverige*').

[56] CJEU, Judgment of 6 October 2020, *La Quadrature du Net and others* (C-511/18, C-512/18 and C-520/18) ECLI:EU:C:2020:791 ('*La Quadrature du Net 'I'*').

applicable to these data for the purpose of fighting crime. However, the Belgian law passed in the aftermath of the *Digital Rights Ireland* case required the general retention of these categories of data, but just established more severe safeguards with respect to their use. The *La Quadrature du Net 'I'* case led the CJEU to revisit its previous approach and find a more balanced compromise between the protection of privacy and personal data and the fight against serious crime.

It is worth noting, at the outset, that the CJEU rejected a very important claim that there existed positive obligations, inherently based on Articles 4 and 6 of the Charter, that bound the Member States to prevent or punish certain crimes. In the absence of a collective right to security,[57] the CJEU escaped from the need to strike a new balance between the rights and interests at stake.

However, in a part of the judgment that an author has ranked among the 'wins' for the law enforcement community,[58] the CJEU revisited its previous case law with specific respect to traffic and location data. On the one hand, the CJEU had found the indiscriminate retention of these data to be compatible with fundamental rights when it comes to serious threats to national security. As noted by scholars,[59] in these circumstances the CJEU's departure from its precedents should not in any way prejudice the applicability of the more severe restrictions on access to data set out in the *Tele2 Sverige* judgment. On the other hand, the CJEU paved the way for the general retention of IP addresses in order both to fight serious crime and to combat threats to national security, qualifying the same as subscribers' data.

These conclusions constituted a significant concession[60] to law enforcement authorities, whose pressure was, in a way, voiced by the BCC. The reasoning of the CJEU was supported by the need to assist the national authorities with preventing or combating crimes such as online child abuse, for which the use of IP addresses constitutes an essential (and indispensable) way to identify perpetrators. The distinction between the conditions under which bulk data retention is permissible (combating a threat to national security) and those under which it is not (fighting serious crime) symbolizes a significant evolution in the CJEU case law. After the CJEU judgment, the BCC court had an easy route to take the floor again and declare to be unconstitutional some provisions of the 2016 law on data retention, applying de facto the conclusions reached by the CJEU.[61]

Despite the apparently 'negative' outcome of the decision, the interaction between the Belgian legal system (by virtue of the role of the BCC) and the CJEU resulted in a reward that was much more important reward than it first appeared to be. As a consequence of the annulment of these provisions, in July 2022 Belgium adopted a new piece of legislation on data retention, in an attempt to align the national law with the guidelines of the CJEU case law and (it was hoped) mark a point of no return in the difficult search for a compromise.[62]

---

[57] Juraj Sajfer, 'Bulk Data Interception/Retention Judgments of the CJEU – A Victory and a Defeat for Privacy' (2020) European Law Blog <https://europeanlawblog.eu/2020/10/26/bulk-data-interception-retention-judgments-of-the-cjeu-a-victory-and-a-defeat-for-privacy> accessed 20 July 2023.
[58] ibid.
[59] ibid.
[60] See Catherine Van de Heyning, 'The Belgian Constitutional Court's Data Retention Judgment: A Revolution that Wasn't' (2022) Diritti Comparati <https://www.diritticomparati.it/the-belgian-constitutional-courts-data-retention-judgment-a-revolution-that-wasnt> accessed 20 July 2023.
[61] BCC, 22 April 2021, no 57.
[62] On the differences with the French Council of State approach, see Formici and Celeste (n 7).

4. From Constitutional Indifference to Constitutional Obedience

The Portuguese 'national drama' is perhaps one of the most interesting examples of the frustration experienced by national governments because of the allegedly one-sided and 'blind' approach of the CJEU in the data retention saga. While in Belgium the BCC indirectly voiced the national authorities' discontent with the outcome of *Digital Rights Ireland*, in Portugal an intense debate took place, culminating in a proposal (eventually dismissed) to amend the Constitution in order to empower the competent authorities to access metadata, in contrast to the trend emerging in the CJEU case law.[63]

The recent turmoil, however, which was labelled as 'a national constitutional crisis'[64] came as the result of a surprisingly late move by the Portuguese Constitutional Court (PCC), which only in its judgment of 19 April 2022[65]—and after a previous decision in which it refused to refer a preliminary question to the CJEU[66]—declared the national provisions requiring the indiscriminate retention of traffic and location data for one year to be unconstitutional. However, ultimately aligning the national law with the standard set by the CJEU required the PCC to revisit its traditional understanding of the relationship between EU law and national constitutional law. This point of no return was marked in 2020 by the PCC in what scholars have named its '*Solange* moment'.[67] In judgment no 422/2020 the PCC developed in-depth reasoning on its competence to review the compatibility of EU law with national constitutional provisions. In this way, the PCC made explicit 'the constitutional mandate of friendliness towards EU integration'[68] and could in more detail elaborate on the primacy clause enshrined in Article 8(4) of the Constitution to determine the limits to the enforcement of EU law vis-à-vis the national constitutional order. The fact that the moment when such a groundbreaking change came into play fell between the two judgments of the PCC concerning the validity of national legislation on data retention explains both the difference of approach of the PCC in the two stances and the deep political background to the data retention saga, an aspect that the case law of the constitutional courts perhaps highlights better than the CJEU's case law. Curiously enough, the approach vis-à-vis EU law played a leading role in the shift from a position that was in blatant contrast with the CJEU case law to a position of plain alignment with the latter through the invalidation of the relevant national provisions.

Once again, the 'original sin' lies in the absence of crystal-clear consequences of the invalidation of EU law acts such as directives. As is well known, the deadlock revolves around

---

[63] Also worth mentioning is the petition filed by the Attorney-General for the invalidation of the ruling under which the Constitutional Court eventually declared unconstitutional the domestic norms on data retention, which was rejected in case no 382/2002.

[64] Teresa Violante, 'How the Data Retention Legislation Led to a National Constitutional Crisis in Portugal' (2022) *Verfassungsblog* <https://verfassungsblog.de/how-the-data-retention-legislation-led-to-a-national-constitutional-crisis-in-portugal/#:~:text=09%20Juni%202022-,How%20the%20Data%20Retention%20Legislation%20Led%20to%20a%20National%20Constitutional,to%20metadata%20on%20personal%20communications> accessed 20 July 2023.

[65] PCC, 13 July 2017, no 420/2017.

[66] PCC Court, 19 April 2022, no 268/2022.

[67] Rui Tavares Lanceiro, 'The Portuguese Constitutional Court Judgment 422/2020 – A 'Solange' Moment?' (2020) EULawLive <https://eulawlive.com/op-ed-the-portuguese-constitutional-court-judgment-422-2020-a-solange-moment-by-rui-tavares-lanceiro> accessed 20 July 2023.

[68] See also Violante, 'How the Data Retention Legislation Led to a National Constitutional Crisis in Portugal' (n 64).

the implications of the invalidation of EU law acts that Member States have transposed into their respective legal systems. The legal literature and EU Treaties stick to the principle that it is up to national courts to invalidate Member State law, whereas the competence of the CJEU is limited to EU law. Accordingly, no automatic consequence can be derived for Member States from the invalidation of an act of EU law. Although many constitutional (or supreme) courts, sooner or later, drew the necessary consequences from the *Digital Rights Ireland* ruling, by revoking or invalidating the domestic provisions implementing the Data Retention Directive, this was not the case in Portugal, at least until the PCC could reframe the relationship between constitutional law and EU law with a far-reaching judgment. Faced with the CJEU case law that followed the *Digital Rights Ireland* case to further circumscribe the scope of permissible data retention measures based on Article 15 of the ePrivacy Directive, the Portuguese authorities failed to address the problem. As scholars have remarked, this failure was the combined effect of 'a delusional legislator, an absent data protection supervisor, and an erratic Constitutional Court'.[69]

Focusing on the PCC,[70] it is worth comparing the two steps that mark the shifting approach of the constitutional judges on the basis of different framings of the relationship with EU law.

The PCC first had the chance to rule on the national data retention law in 2017, when it was requested to deliver a concrete review on appeal from a lower court. The point at issue concerned the compatibility with the Constitution—namely with Articles 18 and 34—of provisions allowing public prosecutors to access basic data subject to untargeted retention. It is worth recalling that the legal status of key sets of information such as IP addresses would only be clarified by the CJEU in its judgment in *La Quadrature du Net 'I'* in 2020. At the time of the PCC ruling, there was no certainty about the status of subscribers', or basic, data. Instead of seeking interpretative aid from the CJEU through a request for a preliminary ruling, the PCC seized the opportunity to set out its line of reasoning and thus avoid any interaction with Luxembourg: the PCC, passively adhering to the guidelines released by the Public Prosecutor Cybercrime Office in 2015, on the one hand made it clear that the invalidation of the Data Retention Directive did not have any automatic consequence for the transposing provisions in the national legislation and, on the other hand, specified that the CJEU case law only concerned the untargeted retention of traffic data and location data, without affecting the status of basic data.[71] In reaching its first conclusion, the PCC emphasized that implementing provisions rely on an autonomous source of validity and legitimacy; in this way, the PCC could develop its reasoned opinion in reliance only on the constitutional provisions, without any need to address (via a preliminary question) the compatibility of the contested norms with EU law and the Charter. In the end, the PCC

---

[69] Francisco Pereira Coutinho, 'Data Retention in Portugal: Big Brother is (No Longer) Watching' (2022) ssrn.com, forthcoming in Inês Quadros and Miguel Gorjão-Henriques, *APDE*, 2022, 22 <https://papers.ssrn.com/sol3/papers.cfm?abstract_id=4216870> accessed 20 July 2023.

[70] On which, in Francisco Pereira Coutinho's words, '[I]ronically, much of the blame for the delay rests'; see Francisco Pereira Coutinho, 'Better Late Than Never: Blanket Data Retention Struck Down at Last by the Portuguese Constitutional Court' (2022) Diritti Comparati <https://www.diritticomparati.it/better-late-than-never-blanket-data-retention-struck-down-at-last-by-the-portuguese-constitutional-court/#:~:text=In%20C ase%20268%2F2022%2C%20several,constitutional%20rights%20to%20privacy%2C%20data> accessed 20 July 2023.

[71] See Teresa Violante, 'Data Retention in Portugal', in Zubik, Podkowik, and Rybski (n 11) 183.

disregarded the *Simmenthal*[72] mandate[73] and upheld the constitutionality of the national legislation. As scholars have observed,[74] the PCC did not even notice that any provision requiring the retention of data, despite the invalidation of the Data Retention Directive, would fall within the scope of Article 15 of the ePrivacy Directive and must therefore conform to the provisions of the Charter.

Only a few years later the PCC had a second chance, in the context of an abstract constitutional review, to adjudicate on the national legislation on data retention. 'Wearing the lenses' of a reshaped relationship with EU law, the PCC could eventually invalidate the relevant provisions of Portuguese law establishing traffic and location data retention obligations. The PCC reasoned that these provisions 'organically stemmed from a national source of law whose formal validity could never be affected by a ruling of the Court of Justice'.[75] Relying on a well-known quotation from the Spanish Constitutional Tribunal,[76] it stated that EU law retains 'primacy' but not 'supremacy' over national law, in order to signify that EU law can never repeal national provisions, the latter being a prerogative of the parliament (as lawmaker) or the PCC (when exercising its abstract review). Therefore, the PCC found it necessary to obey the duty of sincere cooperation (Article 4(3) TEU) in order to interpret the constitutional provisions on fundamental rights in accordance with the Charter and the case law of the CJEU. The adhesion to the principle of consistent interpretation allowed the PCC to draw the necessary consequences from its review, at the same time abiding by EU law and the Treaties and complying with the clause enshrined in Article 8(4) of the Constitution.[77] The PCC could, in other words, 'filter' the findings of the abundant CJEU case law through its constitutional fundamental rights-based review of the national law.

The PCC ruling of 2022 marked the end of the 'hypocrisy' of the Portuguese authorities vis-à-vis data retention. The so-called 'erratic' PCC could set aside its original approach and inaugurate a new constitutional awareness of the implications of data retention for fundamental rights: it is no coincidence that the PCC rejected the attempt made by the General Public Prosecutor to restrict the effects of the judgment. Most notably, however, the contribution of the PCC can be seen in its relationship with other authorities that were likewise responsible (perhaps more than the PCC) for the delay in addressing the flaws in the data retention legislation: in the aftermath of the 2022 judgment, the attempt to introduce a constitutional revision to overcome the PCC ruling was ruled out of the political agenda, and the dismissal of the bill was accompanied by the acknowledgment that this subject matter

---

[72] 'A national court which is called upon, within the limits of its jurisdiction, to apply provisions of Community law is under a duty to give full effect to those provisions, if necessary refusing of its own motion to apply any conflicting provision of national legislation, even if adopted subsequently, and it is not necessary for the court to request or await the prior setting aside of such provisions by legislative or other constitutional means'. See Case 106/67 *Simmenthal* (1978) ECLI:EU:C:1978:49.
[73] See Coutinho, 'Data Retention in Portugal' (n 69) 30–31.
[74] ibid 31.
[75] ibid.
[76] See Spanish Constitutional Tribunal, 13 December 2004, Declaration no 1/2004 on the Treaty establishing a Constitution for Europe.
[77] As noted by Coutinho in 'Data Retention in Portugal' (n 69) 32, this approach 'is perfectly aligned with the obligation to apply EU law provisions in the *conditions prescribed* by EU law (Article 8(4) of the Portuguese Constitution), which is based on the pluralistic constitutional assumption of the existence of a systematic compatibility regarding the protection of fundamental rights between the Portuguese and European constitutional orders'. On this aspect, see also Violante, 'How the Data Retention Legislation Led to a National Constitutional Crisis in Portugal' (n 64).

must be debated at EU level.[78] It is a late, yet favourable, move forward: but will the EU take this step?

5. Concluding Remarks

This chapter aimed to capture the significant role played by constitutional courts in the difficult interaction between national legal orders and the EU legal order with respect to the specific domain of data retention. It is generally accepted that Member States have shown a degree of reluctance towards the findings of the CJEU in its case law, and still today are far from a full alignment with the data retention regime as modelled by the CJEU. It is likewise common knowledge that Member States had to face a quite unprecedented chain of legal evolutions, such as the invalidation of a directive already subject to transposition and the absence of automatic legal effects in national legal systems, combined with the relevance of a more limited yet valid legal ground for retention measures such as Article 15 of the ePrivacy Directive, which in turn triggered a new wave of judicial activism by the CJEU. The goal of this chapter was to go beyond these common observations to highlight the various ways in which constitutional courts could interpret their role as the 'junction point' between the supranational and the national legal orders.

Bearing this goal in mind, the chapter has stressed that it was not the subject matter of data retention per se that determined the 'gap' between the legal orders, but rather the degree of 'friendliness' with EU law and of engagement with the CJEU. The chapter selected some specific cases and tried to capture the overall impact on the approach adopted by Member States vis-à-vis the data retention saga of the doctrines on the relationship with EU law and its system of protection of fundamental rights. In doing so, the chapter shed some light on the potential of constitutional provisions protecting privacy, secrecy of communications, and comparable interests (sometimes also freedom of expression), where these exist, to censor national legislation disproportionately interfering with fundamental rights. This does not mean denying the role of the Charter and its applicability on a matter that definitely falls within the scope of competence of EU law. On the contrary, this remark should highlight the consistency among the different layers in the multilevel protection of fundamental rights, and the need for 'mutual enrichment' between the understandings of fundamental rights in the national legal orders and in the EU legal order. At the same time, this should suggest that EU institutions (and especially the CJEU) should use 'caution' in the light of the risks of conflict that may arise in connection with too broad a framing of the right to privacy, which commentators have also pointed out with respect to other domains[79] in the context of the digital age. Additionally, the potential offered by national constitutions to work not *against* but *together with* the Charter (and the ECHR, of course) should bring to an end the debate on the need to frame ad hoc provisions protecting fundamental rights in the digital age, which is at the heart of the expansionistic rhetoric of digital constitutionalism.

---

[78] See again Violante, 'How the Data Retention Legislation Led to a National Constitutional Crisis in Portugal' ibid.
[79] Pollicino, *Judicial Protection of Fundamental Rights on the Internet* (n 10).

Finally, after directing most of the criticism towards Member States, one question is still waiting for a response: could the EU have done something to avoid almost a decade of CJEU judicial activism triggered by the inconsistent implementation by Member States of provisions that are now grounded on Article 15 of the ePrivacy Directive but in the end, whether directly or indirectly, are the ultimate result of the 'securitarian season' of the EU dating back to 2006?[80] By posing this question, I do not intend to exonerate Member States from their responsibilities for too often being 'deaf' to the CJEU warnings, but rather to suggest an answer that other authors have adopted when commenting on constitutional courts' delayed stances and to apply it to a possible legislative solution: better late than never.

---

[80] For a balance on the alleged failure of harmonization in the field of data retention before the *Digital Rights Ireland* case, see Theodore Konstadinides, 'Destroying Democracy On the Ground of Defending It? The Data Retention Directive, The Surveillance State and Our Constitutional Ecosystem' (2012) 1(xi) European Current Law.

23

Passenger Name Records

Necessary Data Retention to Fight Crime and Terrorism, or Threatening Privacy and Data Protection?

Lucas M Haitsma, Oskar J Gstrein, and Heinrich Winter

1. Introduction and Methodology

Human dignity prevails in societies where people are both secure *and* free. While state-of-the-art technology might make a considerable contribution to protecting security, its use should not come at the cost of sacrificing fundamental rights and freedoms.[1] Nevertheless, law enforcement agencies (LEAs) are increasingly relying on data and data-driven techniques to increase their capacity for information processing, as well as the efficiency and effectiveness in detecting and preventing crime.[2] To preserve the rights to privacy and data protection, institutions such as courts, human rights bodies and academics advocate for comprehensive regulation of the use of innovative data-driven technology in the sector.[3]

The growing desire to 'datafy' security on the one hand, and the need to protect the fundamental rights to privacy and data protection on the other hand, also becomes visible in the context of the PNR Directive.[4] This Directive allows for collecting, processing, and retaining data relating to passengers using air transport within, as well as to and from Europe.[5] LEAs of EU Member States have been keen to demonstrate that there is a necessity for PNR data. In their view, it is an effective means to combat crime, which makes the collection, processing, and retention of such data both necessary and proportionate to address the aim of protecting national security.[6] However, the effects and results of the

---

[1] Commissioner for Human Rights, 'Human Rights in Europe Should Not Buckle Under Mass Surveillance' (12 February 2016), available at <https://www.coe.int/en/web/commissioner/-/human-rights-in-europe-should-not-buckle-under-mass-surveillance> (all websites accessed 22 November 2023).

[2] Diana Dimitrova, 'Surveillance at the Borders: Travellers and their Data Protection Rights' in Gloria González, Rosamunde van Brakel, and Paul de Hert (eds), *Research Handbook on Privacy and Data Protection Law Values, Norms and Global Politics* (Edward Elgar 2022) 304.

[3] ibid 303–34; Sara Roda, 'Shortcomings of the Passenger Name Record Directive in Light of Opinion 1/15 of the Court of Justice of the European Union' (2020) 6(1) EDPL Rev, 66–83; Susanna Villani, 'Some Further Reflections on the Directive (EU) 2016/68 on PNR Data in the Light of the CJEU Opinion 1/15 of 26 July 2017' (2018) 101 *Revista de Derecho Politico* 900–28; Christian Thönnes, 'A Cautious Green Light for Technology-driven Mass Surveillance: The Advocate General's Opinion on the PNR Directive', *VerfBlog* (28 January 2022) <doi:10.17176/20220128-180359-0>, available at <https://verfassungsblog.de/green-light/>.

[4] Directive (EU) 2016/681 of 27 April 2016 on the use of passenger name record (PNR) data for the prevention, detection, investigation and prosecution of terrorist offences and serious crime. OJ 2016, L 119/132.

[5] Lena Ulbricht, 'When Big Data Meet Securitization. Algorithmic Regulation with Passenger Name Records' (2018) 3 European Journal for Security Research 141.

[6] European Commission, COM(2020) 305 final, 'Report From the Commission to the European Parliament and The Council On the review of Directive 2016/681 on the use of passenger name record (PNR) data for the prevention, detection, investigation and prosecution of terrorist offences and serious crime' 6–7.

collection, processing, and retention of PNR data remain largely unclear. This raises questions about the effectiveness of the PNR regime, especially when it comes to necessity and proportionality with regard to the rights to privacy and data protection as enshrined in Articles 7 and 8 of the Charter of Fundamental Rights ('Charter').[7] Even stronger, some legal scholars and human rights bodies argued that the PNR Directive does not seem to be compliant with this legal framework, and the use and retention of data stemming from the PNR regime should be—at least—subject to more stringent safeguards.[8] To address such concerns, the Court of Justice of the European Union (CJEU) delivered a landmark judgment in the *Ligue des droits humains* case on 21 June 2022, responding to a preliminary reference from Belgium.[9]

This chapter considers if the PNR Directive, following the findings of the CJEU in *Ligue des droits humains*, is compatible with the rights to privacy and data protection. To this extent, the retention of passenger data provided by air carriers based on the PNR Directive is examined in light of established data retention jurisprudence regulating the retention of PNR data as well as electronic communications data. Furthermore, this chapter also considers whether the Directive is fit for its purpose of combating serious crime and terrorism. To answer this question, we make use of relevant literature, legislative frameworks and organizational documents, case law, preliminary references by national courts to the CJEU, Opinions of Advocate-Generals (AGs), as well as review reports by civil society organizations, researchers, and others. These sources are used to explore the context, current state of affairs, and analyse the compatibility of the PNR Directive with the right to privacy and data protection.

In section 2, the historical context and contents of the PNR Directive are presented. Furthermore, the rights to privacy and data protection will be delineated. In section 3, the *Ligue des droits humains* judgment and the safeguards on the PNR Directive introduced by the CJEU will be summarized. In section 4, the central question whether the PNR Directive is compatible with the fundamental rights to privacy and data protection will be discussed. In particular, *Ligue des droits humains* will be considered in light of applicable data retention case law including *PNR Canada*,[10] as well as case law from the more publicly discussed electronic communication sector. In addition, it will be considered if the PNR is fit for the purpose of combating serious crime and terrorism. In conclusion, we submit that while the CJEU in *Ligue des droits humains* introduces several commendable measures for safeguarding the right to privacy and data protection, the judges avoid the question whether the PNR Directive is fundamentally necessary for combating serious crimes and terrorism.

---

[7] European Commission, COM(2020) 305 final, 1–12.; Kristina Irion and Romy van Es, 'PNR Act Review September 2021' (2021) University of Amsterdam 9; Caterina Rodelli, 'Analysis: Will the PNR Directive entrench automated suspicion?', *accessnow* (17 February 2022), available at <https://www.accessnow.org/pnr-directive-eu-security-privacy-risks/>.

[8] Sara Roda, 'Shortcomings of the Passenger Name Record Directive in Light of Opinion 1/15 of the Court of Justice of the European Union' 2020; Susanna Villani, 'Some Further Reflections on the Directive (EU) 2016/68 on PNR Data in the Light of the CJEU Opinion 1/15 of 26 July 2017' 2018; Thönnes, 'A Cautious Green Light' (n 3).

[9] CJEU, Judgment of 21 June 2022, *Ligue des droits humains ASBL v Conseil des ministers* (C-817/19), ECLI:EU:C:2022:491.

[10] CJEU, Opinion 1/15 (*EU–Canada PNR Agreement*), of 26 July 2017 (Digital Reports) ECLI:EU:C:2017:592 ('*PNR Canada*').

2. The Regulation of PNR Data

2.1 Historical context

PNR data can be understood as information provided by passengers to air carriers. The data contains travel dates, travel itinerary, ticket information, contact details including addresses and phone numbers, travel agents, payment information, seat number, and baggage information.[11] PNR data differs from Advanced Passenger Information (API) data, which refers to the electronically readable part of a passport and includes passenger names, dates of birth, nationality, and passport number.

On an international level, countries such as the United States and Canada in the early 2000s argued that terrorist attacks—or the seemingly persistent threat thereof—required the adoption of legal frameworks and policies to enable the use of API and PNR data to combat serious crime and terrorism.[12] European airlines flying to and from these third countries were thus obligated to supply PNR data for automated processing.[13] This raised doubts about the compatibility of foreign PNR laws with the stringent data protection and privacy legislation in the EU, which requires an 'adequate level of protection' to be ensured by third countries.[14] As a result, the EU, with varying success attempted to negotiate and conclude agreements with the United States and Canada regarding the transfer and use of PNR data.[15] After several attempts, an agreement was concluded with the United States, while such an agreement with Canada was ultimately factually prevented through the CJEU judgment on *PNR Canada*.[16]

Within the European Union, attempts to regulate PNR data were also made via legislative proposals in 2007 and 2011.[17] In both instances, the proposals were rejected due to conflicts with the right to privacy and concerns of mass surveillance.[18] These rejections made

---

[11] Directive (EU) 2016/681 of 27 April 2016 on the use of passenger name record (PNR) data for the prevention, detection, investigation and prosecution of terrorist offences and serious crime [2016] OJ L 119/132 (PNR Directive), Annex I.

[12] David Lowe, 'The European Union's Passenger Name Record Data Directive 2016/681: Is It Fit For Purpose?' (2016) 16(5) International Criminal Law Review 859; Christian Kaunert, Sarah Léonard, and Alex MacKenzie, 'The Social Construction of an EU Interest In Counter-Terrorism: US Influence and Internal Struggles in the Cases of PNR and SWIFT' (2012) 21 European Security 483–90.

[13] Julia Wojnowska-Radzińska, 'Pre-emptive Data Surveillance and Challenges for Fundamental Rights' in Julia Wojnowska-Radzińska, *Implications of Pre-emptive Data Surveillance for Fundamental Rights in the European Union* (Brill Nijhoff 2023) 66–87.

[14] ibid 66–67; Lowe (n 12) 860.

[15] ibid 66–87; Elif Mendos Kuşkonmaz, 'Birth of PNR Data and the EU–US PNR Agreement' in Elif Mendos Kuşkonmaz, *Privacy and Border Controls in the Fight against Terrorism* (Brill Nijhoff 2021) 120–26.

[16] ibid 66–87; Mendos Kuşkonmaz, ibid 127–44; Agreement between the United States of America and the European Union on the use and transfer of passenger name records to the United States Department of Homeland Security [2012] OJ L 119/132.

[17] European Commission, 'Proposal for a Council framework decision on the use of Passenger Name Record (PNR) for law enforcement purposes', COM(2007) 654 final; European Commission, 'Proposal for a Directive of the Council and the European Parliament on the use of Passenger Name Record data for the prevention, detection, investigation and prosecution of terrorist offences and serious crime, 2011/0023(COD).

[18] European Data Protection Supervisor, 'Opinion 110/1: Opinion of the European Data Protection Supervisor on the draft Proposal for a Council Framework Decision on the use of Passenger Name Record (PNR) data for law enforcement purposes' (1 May 2008), OJ C 110/1, paras 23–32, 100; European Parliament, 'What Happened in Parliament on EU PNR from 2011 to Early 2015?' (2016) available at <https://www.europarl.europa.eu/news/en/press-room/20150123BKG12902/eu-passenger-name-record-pnr-directive-an-overview/3/what-happened-in-parliament-on-eu-pnr-from-2011-to-early-2015> accessed 26 September 2024.

it unlikely that the use of PNR data would be regulated on EU level, until a number of high-profile terrorist attacks took place in some EU Member States, thus reviving calls for the adoption of a PNR framework.[19] In addition to these attacks, there were concerns relating to returning radicalized foreign fighters with EU citizenship, who had gone to support organizations such as the Islamic State.[20] Hence, discussions on the 2011 proposal were revived and while once again met with scepticism regarding its necessity and proportionality, as well as renewed concerns about mass surveillance, it was ultimately amended and swiftly adopted.[21] Relative to the previous proposals, this one included more safeguards to comply with fundamental rights—particularly with regard to the right to data protection and privacy.[22] In conclusion, on 27 April 2016, the EU adopted a PNR Directive with an implementation deadline for the Member States of May 2018.[23]

2.2 The PNR Directive

The PNR Directive provides a legal basis for the collection, retention, processing, and use of passenger name records data for combating serious crime and terrorism.[24] The Directive calls upon Member States to oblige air carriers to collect and transfer PNR data relating to extra-EU flights, and possibly intra-EU flights, to a single designated Passenger Information Unit (PIU) established in each Member State.[25] PIUs are police or intelligence units established under the PNR directive within each Member State.[26] These units employ personnel specialized in data analytics and information sharing for counterterrorism and crime prevention purposes.[27] PNR data must be delivered by the airline 24–48 hours before flight departure and immediately after the closure of the flight.[28] The role of PIUs is then to assess, process, and analyse this data by automated means against relevant databases and risk criteria to identify threats of serious crimes and terrorism.[29]

---

[19] European Parliament, 'Legislative Train Schedule: EU passenger name record' (2022), available at <https://www.europarl.europa.eu/legislative-train/theme-area-of-justice-and-fundamental-rights/file-eu-passenger-name-record-(european-pnr)> accessed 26 September 2024; Lowe (n 12) 883.

[20] Edwin Bakker, Christophe Paulussen, and Eva Entenmann, 'Returning Jihadist Foreign Fighters' (2014) 25 Security and Human Rights 15–16; European Parliament, ibid.

[21] European Commission, 'Proposal for a Directive of the Council and the European Parliament on the use of Passenger Name Record data for the prevention, detection, investigation and prosecution of terrorist offences and serious crime' 2007; Resolution (EU) 2015/2063 of 25 November 2015 on the prevention of radicalisation and recruitment of European citizens by terrorist organizations [2017] OJ C 366/101; European Data Protection Supervisor, 'Opinion 5/2015: Second Opinion on the Proposal for a Directive of the European Parliament and of the Council on the Use of Passenger Name Record Data for the Prevention, Detection, Investigation and Prosecution of Terrorist Offences and Serious Crime' (24 September 2015) paras 12–31, 62–66.

[22] Susanna Villani, 'Some Further Reflections on the Directive (EU) 2016/68 on PNR Data in the Light of the CJEU Opinion 1/15 of 26 July 2017' (2018) 913–15.

[23] PNR Directive (n 11).

[24] Migration and Home Affairs, 'Passenger Name Record (PNR)' (2022), available at <https://home-affairs.ec.europa.eu/policies/law-enforcement-cooperation/passenger-data_en>; PNR Directive, preamble para 12, Annex II; Directive 2017/541 (2017). Directive (EU) 2017/541 of the European Parliament and of the Council of 15 March 2017 on Combating Terrorism and Replacing Council Framework Decision 2002/475/JHA and Amending Council Decision 2005/671/JHA (OJ 2017, L 88), Art 3.

[25] PNR Directive (n 11) Art 4, preamble, para 10.

[26] PNR Directive (n 11) Art 4; Georgios Glouftsios and Matthias Leese, 'Epistemic Fusion: Passenger Information Units and the Making of International Security' (2022) 49(1) Review of International Studies 126.

[27] ibid.

[28] PNR Directive (n 11) Art 8(3).

[29] ibid Art 4; SWD(2020) 128 final, 'Commission staff working document accompanying the document: Report From the Commission to the European Parliament and the Council on the review of Directive 2016/681 on the

When processing PNR data against relevant databases, national, European, and international databases are used.[30] On the national level, one can think of law enforcement databases or watchlists containing information on suspected or known criminals.[31] On the European level, the Schengen Information System is a database that enables border authorities to exchange information, and consult alerts relating to missing persons or potentially stolen objects and documents.[32] International databases—such as those of Interpol—provide up-to-date information on crimes and criminals, and stolen travel documents.[33]

In addition to processing PNR data against relevant databases, this data is also processed against risk criteria indicating a heightened risk of a threat. Such criteria includes bookings stemming from agencies known to be used by traffickers, inconvenient and overly expensive travel routes, or luggage that does not correlate to the duration of travel.[34] Any threats of serious crimes or terrorism flagged via automated analysis are manually reviewed by the PIU to determine if action needs to be taken by law enforcement.[35]

Where relevant to combating serious crime and terrorism, PNR data and the results of its processing is exchanged with, or can be requested by, PIUs in other Member States.[36] Additionally, PNR data and the results of its analysis can be shared, requested, and further processed by a list of competent authorities adopted by a Member State in order to further combat serious crime and terrorism.[37] The PNR Directive allows for the data collected by the PIUs and subsequent results of its processing to be shared with and requested by Europol.[38]

When it comes to safeguards concerning the guaranteeing of fundamental rights, the PNR Directive firstly requires that collected PNR data cannot be retained for more than five years.[39] Furthermore, it must be 'depersonalised' after six months by removing any data elements that could be used to identify passengers including elements such as names, addresses, contact information, and all forms of payment information.[40] The collection and subsequent processing of sensitive data is also prohibited.[41] The five-year retention period is deemed necessary for the identification of criminal associations and behavioural patterns, and given the lengthy nature of serious crime and terrorism investigations.[42] In addition, all PNR data must be collected via the 'push-method'; air carriers transfer the requested data, as opposed to public authorities having direct access.[43]

---

use of passenger name record (PNR) data for the prevention, detection, investigation and prosecution of terrorist offences and serious crime' 24; United Nations, 'Gotravel Technical Introduction' (2021) available at <https://www.un.org/cttravel/ru/goTravel> accessed 26 September 2024.

[30] Dimitrova (n 2) 310.
[31] Douwe Korff, 'Opinion on the broader and core issues arising in the PNR Case currently before the CJEU (Case C-817/19)' (2021) 58, 66 available at <https://papers.ssrn.com/sol3/papers.cfm?abstract_id=4436951> accessed 26 September 2024.
[32] ibid; European Commission, 'SIS II - Second generation Schengen Information System (2022) available at <https://knowledge4policy.ec.europa.eu/dataset/ds00009_en>.
[33] Dimitrova (n 2); Korff (n 31) 65.
[34] SWD(2020) 128 final (n 29) 24.
[35] PNR Directive (n 11) Art 6(6–7).
[36] ibid Art 9.
[37] ibid Art 7.
[38] ibid, preamble para 23, Art 10.
[39] ibid, preamble para 25, 37, Art 12(1).
[40] ibid, Art 12(2).
[41] ibid, preamble para 37.
[42] European Commission, COM(2020) 305 final, 8.
[43] PNR Directive (n 11), preamble para 16, Art 8(2).

Secondly, regarding the processing and analysis of PNR data, the Directive stipulates that this must be done in a non-discriminatory manner, according to criteria that are predetermined, targeted, proportionate, and specific.[44] The criteria used must be set and regularly reviewed by the PIU, the respective data protection officer, and the designated competent authorities.[45] Any decisions taken based on the assessment cannot be taken solely on the basis of automated processing.[46] Finally, Member States must establish or assign a national supervisory authority to observe the legality of the processing of PNR data, address investigative complaints, and safeguard the rights of citizens.[47]

2.3 The right to privacy and data protection

Article 7 of the Charter pertains to the right to respect for private and family life, home, and communications.[48] Article 8 of the Charter pertains specifically to personal data protection and stipulates that such data must be processed fairly, for specific purposes and on the basis of individual consent, or another legitimate aim as specifically prescribed by law.[49] According to Article 52(1) of the Charter, any limitation placed on these rights must be provided for by law. Furthermore, such limitations must be necessary in light of a specific legitimate aim that meets the objectives and interests of the EU (eg protection of national security, detection of crime), using the least intrusive means able to reach the aim, and not disproportionately affect ('sacrifice') other rights.[50] Still, while proportionality is essential in scrutinizing any surveillance measure, there is a lack of a uniform approach to assessing proportionality across Member States. Articles 7 and 8 of the Charter correspond to Article 8 ECHR, which encompasses both rights and stipulates that any interference must be necessary about interests such as national security, public safety, the prevention of disorder or crime, and the protection of the rights and freedoms of others.[51]

3. *Ligue des droits humains*

On 21 June 2022, the CJEU issued its judgment in *Ligue des droits humains* in response to the preliminary reference submitted by Belgium.[52] The case was the result of an action

---

[44] ibid Art 6(4).
[45] ibid Art 6(4).; Lowe (n 12) 875; SWD(2020) 128 final (n 29), 16.
[46] ibid preamble para 20, Art 6(4)(5), Art 7(6).
[47] ibid, Art 15.
[48] Charter of Fundamental Rights of the European Union [2012] OJ C 326/391, Art 7.
[49] ibid Art 8.
[50] ibid Art 52(1); Lorenzo Dalla Corte, 'A Right to a Rule: On the Substance and Essence of the Fundamental Right to Personal Data Protection' in Dara Hallinan, Ronald Leenes, Serge Gutwirth, and Paul de Hert (eds), *Data Protection and Privacy: Data Protection and Democracy* (Hart Publishing 2020) 42–53.
[51] ibid Art 52; European Convention for the Protection of Human Rights and Fundamental Freedoms, as amended by Protocols Nos. 11 and 14, ETS 5, 4 November 1950, Art 8; Amnon Lehavi, Pierre Larouche, Matej Accetto, Nadezhda Purtova, and Lior Zemer, 'The Human Right to Privacy and Personal Data Protection: Local-to-Global Governance in the Digital Era' (2016) 1 Law Schools Global League 12–13.
[52] Court of Justice of the European Union, 'Summary of the request for a preliminary ruling from Belgium *in case C-817/19 Ligue des droits humains*' (31 October 2019), available at <https://curia.europa.eu/juris/showPdf.jsf?text=&docid=225831&pageIndex=0&doclang=en&mode=req&dir=&occ=first&part=1&cid=5910456> 40–42 accessed 27 September 2024.

of annulment of the PNR Directive and its transposition into Belgian law stipulating that it infringed on Articles 7, 8, and 52(1) of the Charter.[53] The CJEU in its judgment interpreted the PNR Directive in light of Articles 7, 8, and 52(1) of the Charter and considered the validity of the Directive.[54] The CJEU held that the PNR Directive pursues an objective interest, is appropriate for meeting that interest, and is limited to what is proportional and strictly necessary.[55] The CJEU thus found nothing capable of jeopardizing the validity of the PNR Directive.[56] The following subsections highlight the most relevant aspects of the *Ligue des droits humains* judgment, clarifying the interpretation of the PNR Directive by the judges in Luxembourg.

3.1 Interference with the right to private life and data protection

In considering whether the PNR Directive entailed an interference with the right to Articles 7 and 8 of the Charter, the CJEU found that there was undeniably a serious interference with the rights guaranteed by these Articles.[57] Firstly, it was found that the PNR data collected and processed on the basis of the PNR Directive included data capable of identifying precise information about air passengers.[58] Hence, it affected and was subject to the requirements laid down in Articles 7 and 8 of the Charter.[59] It was acknowledged that inferences could be made about travel itinerary and habits, relationships between people, financial situations of passengers, their diet and health, as well as further sensitive information on the basis of data obtained from other 'relevant databases'.[60] Secondly, the CJEU stated that communicating personal data to third parties, as well as allowing for its retention and use by third parties, constitutes an interference with Article 7 and 8 of the Charter.[61] With PNR data this is the case when airlines submit the data to PIUs, as well as when this data is subsequently shared with, retained, or used by other PIUs, competent authorities, or Europol.[62] Thirdly, the scope of the PNR Directive as it pertains to extra-EU flights, and its possible application to intra-EU flights, was found to increase the seriousness of the interference.[63] Fourthly, the judges found that the seriousness of the interference was further demonstrated by the fact that the PNR data of a large population of the EU can be retained and accessed, automatically processed, and repersonalized for a particularly long period of time.[64] Therefore, the CJEU concluded that the PNR Directive created a surveillance regime that

---

[53] ibid.
[54] Court of Justice of the European Union, 'Press Release No 105/22 on *Case C-817/19 Ligue des droits humains*' (21 June 2022), available at <https://curia.europa.eu/jcms/upload/docs/application/pdf/2022-06/cp220105en.pdf> 1, accessed 27 September 2024.
[55] ibid.
[56] ibid; EDRI, 'Mass surveillance of external travellers may go on, says EU's highest court' (6 July 2022) available at <https://edri.org/our-work/mass-surveillance-of-external-travellers-may-go-on-says-eus-highest-court/>; Christian Thönnes, 'A Directive Altered Beyond Recognition on the Court of Justice of the European Union's PNR decision (C-817/19)' *VerfBlog* (23 June 2022) <doi: 10.17176/20220623-153431-0> available at <https://verfassungsblog.de/pnr-recognition/> accessed 27 September 2024.
[57] *Ligue des droits humains* (n 9) para 111.
[58] ibid paras 100, 104.
[59] ibid paras 93–95.
[60] ibid para 100, 104.
[61] ibid para 96.
[62] ibid paras 96–97.
[63] ibid paras 98–99.
[64] ibid paras 106–110.

was 'continuous, untargeted, and systematic', and enabled the automated processing and assessing of potentially every individual that made use of air transportation services within the EU.[65]

3.2 The pursuit of an objective interest

As Articles 7 and 8 of the Charter are not absolute rights, interference with these rights must, in accordance with Article 52(1) CFEU, be both necessary and proportional. In this sense, interferences that limit these rights must be done in the pursuit of an objective of interest of the EU, or the need to protect the rights and freedoms of others, and must not go beyond what is strictly necessary.[66] With regards to the objective interest, the CJEU stated that the objective of the PNR Directive is to ensure the internal security of the EU and those within it, while protecting the fundamental rights to privacy and data protection of passengers.[67]

3.3 Appropriateness of the processing of PNR data for meeting the objective interest

The CJEU then went on to consider the appropriateness of the automated processing of PNR data in light of the interest pursued. Here, the CJEU noted that the number of false positives generated by automated processing was substantial, as five out of six individuals between 2018 and 2019 were incorrectly flagged by way of automated processing as posing a threat, upon non-automated review (human review).[68] The CJEU stated that this was capable of limiting the appropriateness of the PNR system, but—maybe surprisingly—did not find that the PNR system as such is entirely inappropriate.[69] The CJEU stated that the appropriateness of the PNR Directive 'essentially depends' on the proper verification of automated results by non-automated means in order to safeguard against false positives.[70] The CJEU went on to argue, based on the review of the PNR Directive by the European Commission, that the automated processing of PNR data had contributed to the identification of passengers that posed a risk of terrorism or serious offences, thereby indicating that the objectives of the Directives are met.[71]

3.4 Sufficiently clear and precise terminology

In *Ligue des droits humains* the CJEU introduced several more restrictive interpretations surrounding the terminology of the PNR Directive.[72] Firstly, the CJEU found that a number of terms such as 'general remarks', 'contact information', 'payment and billing information',

---

[65] ibid para 111.
[66] ibid para 112–18; Art 7, Art 8, Charter (n 48) Arts 7, 8, and 52(1).
[67] *Ligue des droits humains* (n 9) para 121.
[68] ibid para 106, 123.
[69] ibid para 123.
[70] ibid para 124.
[71] ibid paras 123–124.
[72] Christian Thönnes, 'A Directive Altered Beyond Recognition' (n 56).

any and all 'advanced passenger information', were not sufficiently clear and precise, and thus in some instances went beyond what was strictly necessary.[73] Here the CJEU stated that the same terms were previously deemed to be insufficiently clear and precise in *PNR Canada*.[74] As such the CJEU interpreted these definitions in the context of the PNR Directive, in order to limit their scope and bring them in line with Articles 7, 8, and 52(1) of the Charter.[75]

In particular, it was noted here that the PNR data collected had to pertain to a specific person and flight and be limited to what was necessary to prevent, detect, investigate, and prosecute terrorist offences and serious crime.[76] The CJEU thus found that the phrase 'address and contact information (telephone number and email address)' should be interpreted as pertaining only to the information of the passenger on whose behalf the flight reservation was made.[77] 'All forms of payment information, including billing address' was stated to refer exclusively to payment methods and billing of the air ticket and not to other information unrelated to the flight.[78] With regard to the category 'general remarks' under heading 12 of Annex I of the PNR Directive, the CJEU decided that in order to comply with Articles 7, 8, and 52(1) of the Charter, and limit the ability to include further sensitive data, only the information expressly listed under that heading could be collected.[79] Finally, the category allowing for the collection of 'any advanced passenger information' should be interpreted as referring to only those data mentioned under heading 18 of that Annex.[80]

3.5 The scope of application of the PNR Directive

With regards to the collection and processing of PNR data on extra-EU flights, the CJEU argued that collecting and processing data of all *extra-EU* passengers did not go beyond what was necessary to combat terrorism, as limiting this scope would defeat the purpose of the Directive.[81] In contrast, the court found that the indiscriminate collection and processing on *intra-EU* flights went beyond what was necessary and thus disproportionate.[82] The CJEU then stipulated that in the event of a genuine and present, or foreseeable *terrorist* threat, the PNR system can be applied to all *intra-EU* flights for a limited period of time and subject to the review of a court or independent body.[83] However, in the context of *serious crime*, the PNR system can only be applied to specific travel routes, travel patterns, or airports selected by Member States in which there are indications capable of justifying the necessity, proportionality, and effectiveness of that application.[84]

---

[73] *Ligue des droits humains* (n 9) paras 125, 126, 128, 130–140.
[74] *PNR Canada* (n 10) paras 157–161.
[75] *Ligue des droits humains* (n 9) paras 125, 126, 128, 130–140.
[76] ibid para 128.
[77] ibid para 131.
[78] ibid para 132.
[79] ibid paras 128, 136; PNR Directive (n 11), Annex I.
[80] ibid paras 137–140.
[81] ibid paras 161–162.
[82] ibid paras 173.
[83] ibid paras 171–172.
[84] ibid paras 170–174.

3.6 The retention period of PNR data

Regarding the retention of PNR data for the purposes of subsequent assessment and disclosure, the CJEU distinguished between the initial retention period of six months and the subsequent retention period of five years.[85] It found that the initial retention period of six months, regardless of a link to involvement of a data subject in terrorism or serious crime, does not go beyond what is strictly necessary, as this enables the identification of passengers not previously suspected of such acts.[86] However, the CJEU decided that the indiscriminate retention of data for a period exceeding six months and up to five years without any link, even an indirect one, between the retention and the objectives pursued by the PNR Directive went beyond what was necessary.[87] Before linking this interpretation by the CJEU to the overarching theme of data retention in section 4.A.b, we continue by summarizing the key findings of the judgment below.

3.7 Processing PNR data with algorithmic systems and artificial intelligence

To ensure further compliance with Articles 7, 8, and 52(1) of the Charter, the CJEU introduced several safeguards pertaining to the algorithmic systems used for processing PNR data and generating the assessment criteria. Firstly, the CJEU introduced safeguards to limit the possibility of mining and analysing 'relevant databases' together with PNR to generate further inferences and specific profiles.[88] The court clarified that 'relevant databases' refers only to those regarding persons or objects actively sought or under alert, and the databases relied on must be reviewed by the PIU as being relevant for the fight against terrorism and serious crime.[89]

Secondly, the CJEU drew on the Opinion of Advocate-General Pitruzzella,[90] in stating that processing PNR data against criteria that were 'pre-determined' precluded the use of self-learning artificial intelligence technologies to modify the assessment process, the assessment criteria, and their weighting.[91] The CJEU stated that using artificial intelligence systems for these purposes was only permissible provided there was a human intervention or review.[92]

Thirdly, the CJEU emphasized that PIUs must review all positive matches stemming from the automated processing of PNR data. This review must be done via non-automated means to identify false positives and exclude discriminatory results.[93] The review must be governed by clear and precise rules that ensure that positive matches are analysed and verified in a uniform manner.[94]

---

[85] ibid para 252.
[86] ibid para 255.
[87] ibid 256–259.
[88] ibid paras 183–184.
[89] ibid paras 187–191.
[90] Opinion of Advocate General Pitruzzella of 27 January 2022, *Ligue des droits humains* (C-817/19) ECLI:EU:C:2022:65 ('*AG Opinion Ligue des droits humains*').
[91] *Ligue des droits humains* (n 9) para 194.
[92] ibid para 195.
[93] ibid paras 179, 203.
[94] ibid paras 205–206.

Finally, the CJEU introduced a form of a notification obligation. Namely, passengers must be able to understand the pre-determined criteria, non-automated review process, and the workings of the automated systems used to exercise their judicial remedies.[95] The judges further prescribed that the automated processing activities must be able to be reviewed by the data protection officer of the PIU, the national supervisory authority, and national courts.[96]

4. Discussion: Is the PNR System Compatible with European Data Retention Case Law?

This section examines the extent to which the PNR Directive, as interpreted by the CJEU in *Ligue des droits humains*, is compatible with the right to privacy and data protection. To this extent, section 4.1 examines the CJEU's alignment of the Directive with pre-existing data retention case law regulating the retention of PNR data and electronic communications data. This includes *PNR Canada* and CJEU data retention jurisprudence from the electronic communications sector. Furthermore, section 4.2 analyses whether the PNR system in its current form contributes to, and is thus necessary for, combating serious crime and terrorism.

4.1 Aligning the PNR Directive with European data retention case law

In its preliminary reference to the CJEU, the Belgian court explicitly asked whether the CJEU data retention case law, including *PNR Canada* and jurisprudence from the electronic communications sector, are transposable and applicable to the PNR Directive.[97] The question of transposability is of importance, as it clarifies whether the standards safeguarding the rights to privacy and data protection established in those cases are applicable and compatible with the PNR Directive, in light of the CJEU findings in *Ligue des droits humains*. *PNR Canada* is of relevance as this is the only instance where the CJEU explicitly addresses the issue of automated processing of PNR data and compatibility with the right to privacy and data protection. Through *PNR Canada*, the CJEU prevented the conclusion of a PNR agreement between the EU and Canada by identifying several weaknesses in the draft agreement relating to Articles 7 and 8 of the Charter, thus arguing that the agreement was incompatible with those provisions.[98]

Furthermore, while this chapter focuses on PNR data, this field of data retention can be compared with the much more prominent and publicly discussed collection, retention, and analysis of data from the electronic communications sector, central to this present volume. This is also appealing since more detailed and comprehensive case law is available for the latter. Both case law from the CJEU, as well as the European Court of Human

---

[95] ibid para 210.
[96] ibid paras 211–212.
[97] Court of Justice of the European Union, 'Summary of the request for a preliminary ruling from Belgium in case C-817/19', paras 60–64, 91.
[98] E Carpanelli and N Lazzerini, 'PNR: Passenger Name Record, Problems Not Resolved? The EU PNR Conundrum After Opinion 1/15 CJEU' (2017) 42 Air & Space Law 380.

Rights (ECtHR) can be considered to draw analogies. On the Luxembourg side this includes cases such as *Digital Rights Ireland*,[99] *Tele2 Sverige*,[100] *Privacy International*,[101] *La Quadrature du Net 'I'*,[102] *SpaceNet*,[103] *Garda Síochána*,[104] *La Quadrature du Net 'II'*,[105] as well as *Bolzano*.[106] On the Strasbourg side of the ECtHR one could consider *Big Brother Watch and others*.[107]

4.1.1 PNR Canada

Starting with *PNR Canada*, the Belgian court noted the difference in scope between the PNR Directive and PNR system described in *PNR Canada*. Specifically, the Directive enables a more generalized and indiscriminate form of collection, transfer, and processing than *PNR Canada*, which was limited to air travel between Canada and the EU.[108] Firstly, the CJEU stated that the PNR system constituted an interference similar in nature to that discussed in *PNR Canada*, yet went further due to its scope of application to extra-EU flights, and possible application to intra-EU flights.[109] Secondly, the CJEU limited the scope of insufficiently clear and precise terminology from the PNR Directive stating that many of the same terms were deemed insufficiently clear and precise in *PNR Canada*.[110] Thirdly, in finding that limiting the collection and processing of PNR data of all *extra-EU* passengers would defeat the purpose of the PNR Directive, the CJEU referred to the same argument put forth by the CJEU in *PNR Canada*.[111] Fourthly, citing the same measure prescribed in *PNR Canada*, the Court required that a link to involvement in serious crime and terrorism be established in order to justify the prolonged retention of PNR data.[112] Lastly, the CJEU in *Ligue des droits humains* introduced a notification obligation similar to that in *PNR Canada*, and similarly emphasized the importance of non-automated reviews.[113] Hence, in summary the transposability of these prominent features of *PNR Canada* to the PNR framework seems evident.

4.1.2 Analogies to data retention case law from the electronic communications sector

In its preliminary reference, Belgium questioned whether the case law regulating the indiscriminate retention of electronic communications data could be transposed to

---

[99] CJEU, Judgment of 8 April 2014, *Digital Rights Ireland and Seitlinger and others* (C-293/12 and C-594/12) ECLI:EU:C:2014:238.
[100] CJEU, Judgment of 21 December 2016, *Tele2 Sverige* (C-203/15 and C-698/15) ECLI:EU:C:2016:970.
[101] CJEU, Judgment of 6 October 2020, *Privacy International* (C-623/17) ECLI:EU:C:2020:790.
[102] CJEU, Judgment of 6 October 2020, *La Quadrature du Net and others* (C-511/18, C-512/18 and C-520/18) ECLI:EU:C:2020:791 ('*La Quadrature du Net 'I'*').
[103] CJEU, Judgment of 27 October 2022, *SpaceNet* (C-793/19 and C-794/19) ECLI:EU:C:2022:702.
[104] CJEU, Judgment of 5 April 2022, *Commissioner of An Garda Síochána* (C-140/20) ECLI:EU:C:2022:258.
[105] CJEU, Judgment of 30 April 2024, *La Quadrature du Net a.o. c. Premier Ministre and Ministre de la Culture* (C-470/21) ECLI:EU:C:2024:370 ('*La Quadrature du Net 'II'*').
[106] CJEU, Judgment of 30 April 2024, *Procura della Repubblica presso il Tribunale di Bolzano* (C-178/22) ECLI:EU:C:2024:37.
[107] ECtHR, *Big Brother Watch and others v the United Kingdom* [GC], nos. 58170/13 and 2 others, 25 May 2021.
[108] Court of Justice of the European Union, 'Summary of the request for a preliminary ruling from Belgium in case C-817/19' paras 63–64; *PNR Canada* (n 10) para 150.
[109] *Ligue des droits humains* (n 9) paras 109–110; *PNR Canada* ibid para 150.
[110] *Ligue des droits humains* ibid paras 125–140; *PNR Canada* ibid paras 154, 157–165.
[111] *Ligue des droits humains* ibid para 161; *PNR Canada* ibid para 187
[112] *Ligue des droits humains* ibid paras 256–259; *PNR Canada* paras 204–206.
[113] *Ligue des droits humains* ibid para 210; *PNR Canada* ibid paras 220, 223.

indiscriminate collection, transfer, and processing of PNR data.[114] In response to this question, Advocate-General Pitruzella clearly stated in their opinion regarding *Ligue des droits humains* that this body of case law could not be equally applied to PNR Data.[115] Firstly, the AG argued that in *PNR Canada* no parallels were drawn between PNR data and electronic communications data.[116] Secondly, the AG argued that while specific private and professional information could be inferred from PNR data, this information only pertained to a specific context of life, namely air travel. As such, the AG argued that this is less intrusive than access to the content, traffic, and location data from electronic communications. The AG argued that PNR data is sufficiently limited to an exhaustive list, less sensitive, and applies to a smaller population.[117]

In *Ligue des droits humains,* the CJEU does not explicitly answer the question posed by Belgium about the transposability of its data retention jurisprudence to the PNR context. Nevertheless, in contrast to the AG opinion, the CJEU prescribes measures effectively aligning the PNR Directive with the data retention case law and makes references to several relevant cases. In relation to making a distinction between threats of terrorism and serious crime, similar distinctions can be found in *Digital Rights Ireland, Tele2 Sverige, Privacy International, La Quadrature du Net 'I'*, and *Garda Síochána*, with explicit reference being made by the Luxembourg judges to the last two.[118] In the context of needing to establish a link between the retention of data and the objectives pursued by the PNR Directive, this approach is also established in *Digital Rights Ireland* and *Tele2 Sverige*.[119] On this point, the CJEU also argued in *Digital Rights Ireland, Tele2 Sverige, Privacy International, La Quadrature du Net 'I'*, as well as more recently in *La Quadrature du Net 'II'* and *Bolzano*, that indiscriminate retention of data for prolonged periods of time goes beyond what is strictly necessary.[120] Finally, safeguards have been introduced to various phases of the assessment process in the context of the PNR Directive, which resemble the end-to-end safeguard requirement established in *Big Brother Watch and others.*

Therefore, while the AG in their opinion argues for a clear distinction from the PNR framework and the electronic communications framework regulating data retention, the CJEU seems to head in a direction of converging on some principles as specifically outlined above. This suggests that the case law relating to electronic communications is not only transposable to the context of the PNR Directive, but that the CJEU has also interpreted the PNR Directive to ensure compatibility with the safeguards for the right to privacy and data protection.

---

[114] Court of Justice of the European Union, 'Summary of the request for a preliminary ruling from Belgium in case C-817/19' paras 60–62.
[115] AG Opinion *Ligue des droits humains* (n 90) para 199.
[116] ibid para 190.
[117] ibid paras 192–199.
[118] ibid paras 172–174; CJEU, *Privacy International* (n 101) paras 74–75; *La Quadrature du Net 'I'* (n 102) para 168; *Garda Síochána* (n 104) paras 58–59, 62; *Tele2 Sverige* (n 100) para 119.
[119] *Ligue des droits humains* (n 9) paras 256–259; *Digital Rights Ireland* (n 99) paras 63–66; *Tele2 Sverige* (n 100) paras 110–111; *La Quadrature du Net 'I'* (n 102) paras 140–151.
[120] *Digital Rights Ireland* (n 99) paras 56–58, 63–65, 69; *Tele2 Sverige* (n 100) paras 110–111; *Privacy International* (n 101) para 82; Case C-511/18, *La Quadrature du Net 'I'* (n 102) para 168; *La Quadrature du Net 'II'* (n 105) para 93, 164–165; *Bolzano* (n 106) para 35.

4.2 Does the PNR Directive contribute to the fight against serious crime and terrorism?

The CJEU introduces several measures to align the PNR directive with existing case law safeguarding the right to privacy and data protection. However, it refrains from assessing the effectiveness of the directive. The issue of effectiveness is of relevance to determining if the infringement on the fundamental rights of passengers stemming from the collection and processing of PNR data is necessary for reaching the objectives of the PNR Directive. This issue is addressed in the following paragraphs.

4.2.1 Obstacles to the PNR Directive's effectiveness

When evaluating the PNR Directive, two issues in particular seem to impede its effectiveness. These are false positives stemming from the automated processing of PNR data, and the poor quality of PNR data itself. Firstly, the automated processing operations of PNR data leads to a substantial rate of false positives, as was observed in the European Commissions' review of the PNR Directive and acknowledged in *Ligue des droits humains*.[121] Such a substantial rate of false positives, despite undoubtedly having a negative impact on the suitability of the PNR system in meeting its objectives, has been seemingly laid aside by the CJEU.[122] The judges stipulate that the appropriateness of the PNR system, in light of these false positives, is essentially dependent on the successful non-automated review of the results of processing.[123] Interestingly, the court states that the PIU itself is the one tasked with laying down clear and precise rules governing such a review, and must document such reviews for the purpose of verifying its lawfulness and for self-monitoring.[124]

However, whether such safeguards are adequate for ensuring a high level of protection of the rights to privacy and data protection can be called into question upon closer scrutiny. Firstly, each PIU in each Member State is able to create their own, and potentially substantially different, rules that guide the review process.[125] The CJEU provided no further guidance or parameters regarding this non-automated review process, other than that these criteria should enable agents to verify if a match concerns effectively an individual who might be involved in terrorism or serious crime.[126] This lack of guidance places a considerable amount of discretion and trust in Member States to develop and implement appropriate rules and criteria. It seems unlikely that such standards will be adequately equivalent throughout the EU, which enables varying levels of effectiveness in terms of reducing the number of false positives. Therefore, the level of protection of Articles 7 and 8 of the Charter might suffer.[127]

Secondly, it can be questioned if it is realistic to expect that PIUs are able to effectively review all potential false positives, as in the PNR review by the European Commission it was stated that these manual reviews can 'significantly increase' the workload of the PIUs.[128] Finally, competent authorities, where they rely on the results of the processing of PNR data,

---

[121] *Ligue des droits humains* (n 9) paras 123–124; SWD(2020) 128 final (n 29) 28, 30.
[122] EDRI (n 56); Thönnes, 'A Directive Altered Beyond Recognition' (n 56).
[123] *Ligue des droits humains* (n 9) para 124.
[124] ibid paras 203–207.
[125] ibid paras 203–207.
[126] ibid para 206; EDRI (n 56).
[127] EDRI, ibid.
[128] SWD(2020) 128 final (n 29) 46.

are instructed to also ensure the lawfulness of the individual review.[129] However, the lawfulness of the individual review is dictated by the PIUs ability to follow its own self-written criteria. Hence, the check is only useful in ensuring that the PIU follows its own rules, but not in checking the quality and effectiveness of the rules with regards to reducing false positives as such.

In addition to the problems relating to the review of the considerable numbers of false positives, the effectiveness and appropriateness of the PNR system is challenged by the arguably poor quality of PNR data. The CJEU, in *Ligue des droits humains*, acknowledges the issue of false positives as hindering the appropriateness of the PNR system, yet seems to overlook the issue of data quality.[130] PNR data is declaratory in nature as it is provided by passengers to air carriers who subsequently submit the data to PIUs for automated processing.[131] Given that air carriers and passengers' primary focus is on efficient travel instead of ensuring the quality of PNR data sets, the data submitted to PIUs frequently suffers from inaccuracies.[132] In particular, the data submitted contains spelling errors, omitted or misplaced variables, or fictious information filled in due to last-minute flight changes.[133] Furthermore, when PNR data and the results of its processing are shared with other PIUs, this often occurs unsystematically and in a piecemeal way.[134] The issue of data quality is particularly problematic as it undermines the ability for PIUs to accurately and effectively analyse the submitted data and yield meaningful results for combating serious crime and terrorism.[135] The poor quality of PNR data also impedes the ability to rely on the data and results of its processing to inform new targeting rules.[136]

4.2.2 Demonstrating the effectiveness of the PNR Directive

Despite the issues of false positives and data quality, in *Ligue des droits humains* the CJEU found that the PNR Directive was appropriate for achieving the objective of combating serious crimes and terrorism. The CJEU stated that the appropriateness of the system could be demonstrated based on evidence in the European Commission's review of the PNR Directive.[137] According to the European Commission, case studies and interviews showed that the collection, processing, and analysis of PNR data has proven instrumental to the identification of potential terrorists or persons involved in serious crimes, the arrest of persons previously unknown to law enforcement, and the prevention of serious crimes.[138] Data retained after the arrival of passengers was said to also be effectively used to investigate, prosecute, and unravel criminal networks subsequent to crimes being committed.[139] Furthermore, PNR data is also used proactively to examine and identify the travel

---

[129] *Ligue des droits humains* (n 9) paras 208–209.
[130] ibid para 106.
[131] SWD(2020) 128 final (n 29) 41–42; Glouftsios and Leese (n 26) 134.
[132] SWD(2020) ibid; Glouftsios and Leese ibid 134.
[133] SWD(2020) ibid 41–42.
[134] Glouftsios and Leese (n 26) 134.
[135] SWD(2020) 128 final (n 29) 41–42.
[136] Glouftsios and Leese (n 26) 136–38; Council of the European Union, 'Final Report Future Group on Travel Intelligence and Border Management' (2022) 57, available at <https://www.statewatch.org/media/3307/eu-council-europol-frontex-travel-intelligence-future-group-6767-22.pdf> accessed 27 September 2024.
[137] *Ligue des droits humains* (n 9) paras 123–124; European Commission, COM(2020) 305 final, 6–11.
[138] European Commission, COM(2020) 305 final, 6–7; European Commission, COM(2020) 605 final, 'Communication from the Commission on the EU Security Union Strategy' 22.
[139] SWD(2020) 128 final (n 29) 25.

behaviours of terrorists and those committing serious crime in order to formulate risk profiles for carrying out risk assessments.[140] The Commission stressed that these results could only have been achieved by way of using PNR data.[141]

To investigate the European Commission's claims, the evidence available in the Member State reports must be considered. For instance, a thorough review from the Netherlands finds that information regarding the input data is known, namely the collection and processing of the data relating to 61,431,852 passengers between 2019 and 2021. However, the output information in terms of achieved results stemming from this collection and processing is unknown.[142] Such lack of information is a result of the use of the PNR data not being documented in any record-keeping systems, which, as stated in the report, makes it 'hardly possible' to determine what role PNR data play in criminal investigations.[143] The report does state that there is a high demand for the data which may indicate its usefulness—or at least attractiveness. However, to date there are no known criminal case decisions where PNR data was used as evidence. Furthermore, the report states that no conclusions can be drawn about the effectiveness of the use of PNR data, and particularly the extent to which the same results could be achieved without the PNR Directive.[144]

Unlike the Netherlands, reports from Germany and France argue that clear conclusions can be drawn regarding the effectiveness of the use of PNR data. German institutions argue this effectiveness can be observed in the statistics of 2020, as PNR data enabled the execution of 813 arrest warrants, the processing of 547 'hits' pertaining to politically motivated crime, and the prevention of unauthorized entry in 249 instances.[145] Furthermore, Germany cited an example in which the federal police, on the basis of an evaluation of PNR data, arrested a US citizen transiting in Frankfurt for war crimes committed in former Yugoslavia.[146] French institutions have argued that the use of PNR data has enabled customs to illuminate illicit financial practices. This resulted in a number of tobacco seizures.[147] French police also stated that hits within the PNR system have led to cases being transferred to the prosecution authorities, as well as a number of flagged individuals being detained.[148] Finally, France stated that the use of PNR data has been useful in detecting and investigating signals of terrorism.[149]

Different Member States, the European Commission, and the CJEU appear to use varying means to evaluate and draw conclusions about the effectiveness of the PNR data in combating serious crime and terrorism. Germany and the Netherlands both use statistics to illustrate the effectiveness of the PNR Directive, yet reach differing conclusions as to the effectiveness of the PNR data. France argues for the necessity of PNR data yet

---

[140] ibid.
[141] European Commission, COM(2020) 305 final, 6–8.
[142] Irion and van Es (n 7) 4.
[143] ibid 4–5.
[144] ibid 4–5.
[145] Bundespolizei, 'Jahresbericht 2020' (2020), available at <https://www.bundespolizei.de/Web/DE/Service/Mediathek/Jahresberichte/jahresbericht_2020_file.pdf?__blob=publicationFile&v=5> accessed 27 September 2024, 37.
[146] ibid 70.
[147] Christophe Hypolite, 'API-PNR: an overview of the French system and the challenges faced', WCO News (2018), available at <https://mag.wcoomd.org/magazine/wco-news-82/api-pnr-an-overview-of-the-french-system-and-the-challenges-faced/> accessed 27 September 2024.
[148] ibid.
[149] ibid.

does not substantiate this further with any statistical data. The European Commission, and subsequently the CJEU in *Ligue des droits humains*, argue for the effectiveness of the PNR Directive, yet demonstrate this using qualitative case studies and interviews.[150] Conversely, in *PNR Canada*, the CJEU relied on concrete statistics to demonstrate the effectiveness and appropriateness of PNR data.[151] Thus, the role of PNR data in supporting criminal investigations within the EU does not appear equally consistent, measured, substantiated, and demonstrable.[152]

While law enforcement agencies and intelligence services either have a high demand for this data, or believe that it is an appropriate and effective means for combatting terrorism and serious crime, there is arguably a lack of EU wide statistical evidence or solid qualitative reporting to substantiate such claims.[153] If fully harmonized reporting seems too far-fetched in terms of competences for European institutions, one might at least consider the adoption of consistent standards across Member States. It remains unclear if this lack of comparable data stems from a lack of results and insights within the Member States themselves, or if the current situation results from a lack of standardized collection of statistics and recording practices.[154] Regardless of the reason for a lack of statistics and the lack of data to support the claims, the result is that the appropriateness of the collection and processing of PNR data in the form of a concrete contribution to the fight against serious crime and terrorism throughout the EU can currently not be clearly demonstrated.

4.2.3 Is the PNR Directive necessary?

In summary, the PNR system as established by the PNR Directive suffers from a high rate of false positives and issues stemming from poor data quality. Both undermine the effectiveness of the system and its appropriateness for achieving the objectives of the directive. These issues are either overlooked or seem insufficiently addressed by the CJEU. In particular, it remains unclear how the prescribed safeguards, such as that of the non-automated review, can be operationalized in a uniform and effective manner across member states and how the issue of data quality can be resolved. It additionally cannot be clearly demonstrated at the EU level to which extent the PNR system contributes to the fight against serious crime and terrorism. This raises the question as to the necessity of the PNR Directive as a tool for combating serious crime and terrorism.

As discussed in the literature, the EU already has a plethora of systems for the purpose of analysing passenger data and tracking their movements, sometimes giving rise to the label of 'Fortress Europe', or 'Panopticon Europe'.[155] This includes increasingly interoperable and searchable supranational databases, which can be used for the identification of

---

[150] *Ligue des droits humains* (n 9) para 123.
[151] *PNR Canada* (n 10) paras 56, 152–53.
[152] Korff (n 31) 115–19.
[153] ibid.
[154] SWD(2020) 128 final (n 29) 36–37.
[155] This includes the currently used Schengen Information System (SIS II), Visa Information System (VIS), The European Asylum Dactyloscopy Database (Eurodac) databases. See Dimitrova (n 2) 306; Rocco Bellanova & Georgios Glouftsios, 'Formatting European Security Integration through Database Interoperability' (2022) 31(3) European Security; Douwe Korff, 'Opinion on the Broader and Core Issues Arising in the PNR Case Currently before the CJEU (Case C-817/19)' (2021) 127–28; Christian Thönnes, Stefan Salomon, Elspeth Guild, and Evelien Brouwer, 'The Future of the European Security Architecture: A Debate Series', *VerfBlog* (8 May 2023) <doi: 10.17176/20230508-204615-0> available at <https://verfassungsblog.de/pnr-debate/> accessed 27 September 2024.

national security threats.[156] The CJEU also recently reaffirmed in *La Quadrature du Net 'II'* and *Bolzano* the possibility of storing telephone records and IP addresses, and clarified the applicable conditions.[157] Additionally, automated predictive threat detection instruments like the European Travel Information and Authorisation System are under development, and there are possibilities for profiling based on the proposed regulation to prevent and combat child sexual abuse.[158] In light of this emerging digital security infrastructure in the European Union and the lack of evidence clearly demonstrating the effectiveness of the PNR Directive, it becomes questionable what the added value of the PNR regime is.[159] Despite these points of concern, there is interest in even expanding the PNR system to other forms of transportation,[160] and the EU has proposed new legal bases for the use of PNR data and its combination with other data sources.[161] Furthermore, Member States have actively been seeking out how to circumvent the safeguards laid down in the PNR judgment.[162] These developments suggest that the EU and its member states remain keen to continue to collect, process, and use PNR data despite the discussed shortcomings.

5. Conclusion

In *Ligue des droits humains*, the CJEU introduces several measures that seek to align the PNR Directive with existing data retention case law relevant to Articles 7, 8, and 52(1) of the Charter. This includes sharpened definitions of various provisions, reducing the scope of the PNR Directive and the length of retention, as well as imposing several data protection safeguards pertaining to the review of collection, processing and retention activities, notification of passengers, automated processing, and the non-automated review of positive matches. The newly introduced measures suggest an interpretation of the PNR Directive that aims to bring the Directive in line with pre-existing data retention case law from the electronic communications sector and *PNR Canada*.

This chapter further considers whether the PNR system is fit for the purpose of combating serious crime and terrorism. In *Ligue des droits humains* the CJEU seems to set this issue aside, despite striking the core of the legal framework. The purpose of the PNR

---

[156] Bellanova and Glouftsios, ibid; Thönnes et al, ibid; Christian Thönnes and Niovi Vavoula, 'Automated Predictive Threat Detection after Ligue des Droits Humains', *VerfBlog* (8 May 2023) <doi: 10.17176/20230508-204551-0> accessed 27 September 2024; Council of the European Union, 'Final Report Future Group on Travel Intelligence and Border Management' (2022); European Parliamentary Research Service, 'Artificial intelligence at EU borders: Overview of applications and key issues' (2021), available at <https://www.europarl.europa.eu/RegData/etudes/IDAN/2021/690706/EPRS_IDA(2021)690706_EN.pdf> accessed 27 September 2024; Migration and Home Affairs, 'Entry/Exit System' (2023), available at <https://home-affairs.ec.europa.eu/policies/schengen-borders-and-visa/smart-borders/entry-exit-system_en>.
[157] *La Quadrature du Net 'II'* (n 105); *Bolzano* (n 106).
[158] Thönnes and Vavoula (n 156).
[159] Thönnes et al, 'The Future of the European Security Architecture' (n 155).
[160] SWD(2020) 128 final (n 29) 39–40.
[161] Council of the European Union, 'Air travel data: Council adopts position on EU laws about data collection and processing' (2023), available at <https://www.consilium.europa.eu/en/press/press-releases/2023/06/21/air-travel-data-council-adopts-position-on-eu-laws-about-data-collection-and-processing/> accessed 27 September 2024.
[162] Statewatch, 'EU: Travel surveillance: member states seek to circumvent court judgment on PNR' (2022), available at <https://www.statewatch.org/news/2022/september/eu-travel-surveillance-member-states-seek-to-circumvent-court-judgment-on-pnr/> accessed 27 September 2024.

Directive is to enable effective advanced assessments of passengers for the purpose of detecting, preventing, investigating, and prosecuting terrorism and serious crime. The PNR system, even with a broad and indiscriminate scope, has to date not consistently produced demonstrable and convincing results across the EU. Furthermore, the issues of a substantial margin of false positives and poor data quality contribute to the inaccuracy and arguably inappropriateness of the PNR system in achieving its purpose. The judgment in *Ligue des droits humains* drastically reduces this scope which, while being a positive development in relation to Articles 7 and 8 of the Charter, raises the question of what this will mean for the already few demonstrable results of this system.

Thus, while the CJEU in *Ligue des droits humains* introduces several important measures for safeguarding the right to privacy and data protection, it avoids the question whether the PNR Directive is fundamentally necessary for combating serious crimes and terrorism. Certainly, one might question whether this is for a court to decide. However, in *Ligue des droits humains*, the CJEU interprets the law in a way that leads to the adoption of 'window dressing' safeguards. This allows it to bring the Directive in line with existing case law on data retention, thereby providing a route to compliance with Articles 7, 8, and 52(1) of the Charter. Nevertheless, one might argue that the result is to breathe life into a Directive that so far appears ill-suited to achieve the objectives for which it was designed.

24
Data Retention and Automated Processing of Personal Data

Unpacking the CJEU's Approach

Niovi Vavoula

1. Introduction

As the volumes of metadata have grown exponentially, security and intelligence services have resorted to sophisticated tools of automated processing, including automated analysis, which have been developed thanks to increasing computational powers to enhance their abilities to process data. In the abundant amount of case law concerning the processing of metadata for law enforcement purposes, the Court of Justice of the European Union (CJEU) considered in *La Quadrature du Net 'I'*[1] one form of such automated analysis in connection with the processing of traffic and locations data in pursuing national security interests. The Court delivered its findings on the type of automated analysis that was challenged in *La Quadrature du Net 'I'* largely based on its earlier observations in *PNR Canada* on the use of automated processing in the context of Passenger Information Record (PNR) data analysed for law enforcement purposes in border controls.[2] The findings of the CJEU were further elaborated in *Ligue des droits humains*, which also concerned the processing of PNR data,[3] this time in light of the PNR Directive.[4] The latest contribution to the emerging checklist comes from the judgment in *La Quadrature du Net 'II'*, also on retention of telecommunications metadata.[5]

This chapter aims to analyse the state of play of the CJEU case law on automated processing following the judgments in *PNR Canada*, *La Quadrature du Net 'I'*, and *Ligue des droits humains*, to establish the criteria and conditions under which automated processing is permissible as a law enforcement tool and compatible with the right to respect for private life,[6] the right to protection of personal data,[7] the right to non-discrimination,[8] and

---

[1] CJEU, Judgment of 6 October 2020, *La Quadrature du Net and others* (C-511/18, C-512/18 and C-520/18) ECLI:EU:C:2020:791 ('*La Quadrature du Net 'I'*').
[2] CJEU, Opinion 1/15 (*EU–Canada PNR Agreement*), of 26 July 2017 (Digital Reports) ECLI:EU:C:2017:592 ('*PNR Canada*').
[3] CJEU, Judgment of 21 June 2022, *Ligue des droits humains ASBL v Conseil des ministres* (C-817/19), ECLI:EU:C:2022:491 ('*Ligue des droits humains*').
[4] Directive 2016/681 of 27 April 2016 on the use of passenger name record (PNR) data for the prevention, detection, investigation and prosecution of terrorist offences and serious crime [2016]OJ L 119/32.
[5] CJEU, Judgment of 30 April 2024, *La Quadrature du Net a.o. c. Premier Ministre and Ministre de la Culture* (C-470/21) ECLI:EU:C:2024:370 ('*La Quadrature du Net 'II'*').
[6] EU Charter of Fundamental Rights ('Charter') Article 7.
[7] ibid Article 8.
[8] ibid Article 21.

the right to an effective remedy.[9] Having provided a concise examination of the CJEU case law, section 3 provides an appraisal of selected issues emanating from the case law, namely the transplantation of the CJEU's standards to other contexts of automated processing, outstanding matters for further elaboration in subsequent cases, the relationship with the right not to be subjected to automated decision-making under Article 11 of the Law Enforcement Directive (LED),[10] and the relationship with the AI Act.[11]

2. Automated Analysis: The Evolution of the CJEU Case Law

2.1 The first steps: *PNR Canada*

The European Courts have been confronted with questions regarding the compatibility of automated processing of personal data primarily with the rights to respect for private life (and protection of personal data). As early as in 2008, in *S and Marper v the United Kingdom*, the European Court of Human Rights (ECtHR) formalised the principle according to which in relation to automated processing of personal data the need for additional safeguards is 'all the greater ... not least when such data are used for police purposes'.[12] Since then, both Courts have reiterated this principle on various occasions with the CJEU linking the existence of safeguards with the requirement of ensuring proportionate legislation and effective protection from the risk of abuse.[13] This judicial dialogue between the Court has solidified a broad consensus that automated processing in its different forms and irrespective of the specific context within which it takes place requires concrete rules and standards to effectively protect the rights of individuals. This is all the more the case in the law enforcement domain, whereby some degree of secrecy is necessary so as not to jeopardise criminal investigations.

---

[9] ibid Article 47.
[10] Directive 2016/680 of 27 April 2016 on the protection of natural persons with regard to the processing of personal data by competent authorities for the purposes of the prevention, investigation, detection, or prosecution of criminal offences or the execution of criminal penalties, and on the free movement of such data, and repealing Council Framework Decision 2008/977/JHA [2016] OJ L 119/89 ('LED').
[11] Regulation 2024/1689 of the European Parliament and of the Council of 13 June 2024 laying down harmonised rules on artificial intelligence and amending Regulations (EC) No 300/2008, (EU) No 167/2013, (EU) No 168/2013, (EU) 2018/858, (EU) 2018/1139, and (EU) 2019/2144 and Directives 2014/90/EU, (EU) 2016/797 and (EU) 2020/1828 (Artificial Intelligence Act) [2024] OJ L 2024/1689 ('AI Act').
[12] ECtHR, *S and Marper v the United Kingdom*, nos. 30562/04 and 30566/04 4 December 2008, para 103.
[13] Including the judgments that are discussed in this chapter. See CJEU, Judgment of 8 April 2014, *Digital Rights Ireland and Seitlinger and others* (C-293/12 and C-594/12) ECLI:EU:C:2014:238 para 55; CJEU, Judgment of 6 October 2015, *Maximillian Schrems v Data Protection Commissioner* (C-362/14) ECLI:EU:C:2015:650 ('*Schrems I*'), para 91; *PNR Canada* (n 2) paras 140–141; CJEU, Judgment of 16 July 2020, . (C-311/18) ECLI:EU:C:2020:559 ('*Schrems II*'), para 176; CJEU, Judgment of 6 October 2020, *Privacy International* (C-623/17) ECLI:EU:C:2020:790, para 68; *La Quadrature du Net 'I'* (n 1) para 132; CJEU, Judgment of 5 April 2022, *Commissioner of An Garda Síochána* (C-140/20) ECLI:EU:C:2022:258 para 54; *Ligue des droits humains* (n 3) para 117; CJEU, Judgment of 22 November 2022, *WM and Sovim SA v Luxembourg Business Registers* (C-37/20 and C-601/20) ECLI:EU:C:2022:912 ('*WM and Sovim*'), para 65; *La Quadrature du Net 'II'* (n 5) para 153. For the ECtHR, see ECtHR, *MK v France*, no. 19522/09, 18 April 2013, para 35; ECtHR, *Breyer v Germany*, no. 50001/12, 30 January 2020, para 78; ECtHR, *Big Brother Watch and others v the United Kingdom* [GC], nos. 58170/13 and 2 others, 25 May 2021, para 330; ECtHR, *Centrum för rättvisa v Sweden* [GC], no. 35252/08, 25 May 2021, para 244; ECtHR, *Glukhin v Russia*, no. 11519/20, 4 July 2023, para 52; *ex ante* and *ex post* ECtHR, *Podchasov v Russia*, no. 33696/19, 13 February 2024, para 62; ECtHR, *Škoberne v Slovenia*, no. 19920/20, 13 February 2024, para 55.

The crystallisation of the increased safeguards in the CJEU case law started materialising much later with the first decisive step taken by the Court in the context of the processing of PNR data for law enforcement purposes. The processing of PNR data has been the subject of CJEU litigation on three occasions, with the first case—*Parliament v Council*—concerning the transfer of PNR data to the United States Bureau of Customs and Border Protection pursuant to an international agreement on PNR records. The European Parliament challenged the legal basis of the agreement, with the Court opining that the processing concerned public security and the activities of the state in relation to criminal law and the fight against terrorism.[14] Thus, the Court did not deal with the compatibility of the processing of PNR data with fundamental rights, let alone the extent to which they are subject automated analysis by the US authorities. The second time was the charm. In *PNR Canada*, the Court had the opportunity to engage with such questions when asked to assess the compatibility with the EU Charter of Fundamental Rights ('Charter') of the draft EU–Canada Passenger Name Record (PNR) Agreement that was then being negotiated, concluding that it could not be concluded in its original form. The agreement followed the expiration of a previous one from 2005.[15] Among the particularities of the processing of PNR data under the draft Agreement is that Canada's border pre-screening programme entails automated cross-checking and analysis of information concerning individuals buying an air ticket to Canada with a view to identifying supposedly high-risk travellers, who would then be subjected to secondary screening to be admitted to the country.[16] As part of this operation, airline companies, regardless of where they are based, are obliged by law to share passenger information with the Canadian border control authority.

With regard to automated processing of PNR data as part of Canada's border control pre-screening operation, the CJEU made various observations,[17] which provided the basis for the Court's subsequent analysis in the other judgments examined in this chapter. In particular, as the Agreement was deemed to essentially be 'an intelligence tool',[18] the Court acknowledged some margin of error, which appears to be significant, as the analyses are carried out on the basis of unverified personal data and pre-established models and criteria.[19] It also linked the extent of the interference with the pre-established models and criteria and the databases that type of data processing is based on.[20] First, according to the

---

[14] CJEU, Judgment of 30 May 2006, *Parliament v Council and Commission* (C-317/04 and C-318/04) ECLI:EU:C:2006:346 ('*Parliament v Council*'). For an analysis see Valsamis Mitsilegas, *EU Criminal Law* (2nd edn, Hart 2022). Also see Elif Mendos Kuskonmaz, *Privacy and Border Controls in the Fight against Terrorism: A Fundamental Rights Analysis of Passenger Data Sharing* (Brill Nijhoff 2021).

[15] Council Decision 2006/230/EC of 18 July 2005 on the conclusion of an Agreement between the European Community and the Government of Canada on the processing of API/PNR data [2006] OJ L82/14; Agreement between the European Community and the Government of Canada on the processing of Advance Passenger Information and Passenger Name Record data [2006] OJ L 82/15.

[16] For information on Canada's passenger pre-screening see David Lyon, 'Airport Screening, Surveillance, and Social Sorting: Canadian Responses to 9/11 in Context' (2006) 48(3) Canadian Journal of Criminology and Criminal Justice 397; Peter Hobbing, 'Tracing Terrorists: The EU-Canada Agreement in PNR Matters' (CEPS Special Report, September 2008).

[17] *PNR Canada* (n 2) paras 190–211. For commentary see Christopher Docksey, 'Opinion 1/15: Privacy and Security, Finding the Balance' (2017) 24(6) Maastricht Journal of European and Comparative Law 768; Arianna Vedaschi, 'The European Court of Justice on the EU-Canada Passenger Name Record Agreement' (2018) 14 European Constitutional Law Review 410; Edoardo Celeste, 'The Court of Justice and the Ban on Bulk Data Retention: Expansive Potential and Future Scenarios' (2019) 15(1) European Constitutional Law Review 134.

[18] *PNR Canada*, ibid para 130.

[19] ibid paras 169–170.

[20] ibid para 172.

Court, 'the pre-established models and criteria should be specific and reliable, making it possible ... to arrive at results targeting individuals who might be under a "reasonable suspicion" of participation in terrorist offences or serious transnational crime and should be non-discriminatory'.[21] Second, if the automated analysis involves cross-checking of other databases, these 'must be reliable, up to date and limited to those used by Canada in relation to the fight against terrorism and serious transnational crime'.[22] Third, any positive result obtained following the automated processing of that data must be subject to an individual, non-automated re-examination before an individual measure adversely affecting the air passengers concerned is adopted.[23] Finally, the reliability and topicality of the databases, models, and criteria should, taking account of statistical data and the results of international research, be covered by the joint review of the implementation of the Agreement.[24]

2.2 The second step: *La Quadrature du Net 'I'*

In *La Quadrature du Net 'I'*, the CJEU reiterated the requirements laid down in *PNR Canada* and added some important clarifications, even though the context in which the autonomous analysis took place as well as the data against which that analysis was carried out was different.[25] In particular, one of the questions dealt with in *La Quadrature du Net 'I'* concerned French law, namely Article L. 851-3 of the Internal Security Code (Code de la sécurité intérieure (CSI)), according to which providers of electronic communications services are required to install automated data processing techniques on their networks to detect links that might constitute a terrorist threat.[26] These techniques entail the use of algorithms that analyse traffic and location data to detect suspicious patterns of behaviour of persons using telephony and internet services with a view to safeguarding national security.[27] Such automated processing does not allow the identification of the persons to whom the information or documents relate. According to Maxwell, due to the opacity of the techniques involved, the legal provision has been called 'the black box provision'.[28]

To assess the legality of automated analysis of traffic and location data, the CJEU first addressed whether that practice triggered the protection of fundamental rights under the Charter, namely Article 7 on the right to privacy and Article 8 on the right to protection of personal data. As a preliminary point, the Court clarified that though automated analysis does not, as such, allow the identification of users whose data is being analysed, this does not prevent such data from being classified as 'personal data'. Since the procedure allows the

---

[21] ibid para 172.
[22] ibid para 172.
[23] ibid para 173. On this point, the CJEU recognised that the draft Agreement itself contained a provision prohibiting the sole automated decision-making, and interestingly, it did not list it among the requirements mentioned in its *ratio decidendi*.
[24] ibid para 174. Similar to the CJEU's finding on the prohibition on the sole automated decision, this requirement was not later mentioned in its *ratio decidendi*.
[25] In *Privacy International* (n 13), which was delivered on the same date as *La Quadrature du Net 'I'*, the UK surveillance regime that was subject of the preliminary ruling set out a 'selective' operation' to filter through the retained data, but the legality of that operation in and by itself was not disputed.
[26] For a thorough analysis of the relevant French law in *La Quadrature du Net 'I'* and the judgment itself, please Chapter 11 by Maxime Lassalle in this volume.
[27] Winston J Maxwell, 'Systematic Government Access to Private Sector Data in France' in Fred H Cate and James X Dempsey (eds), *Bulk Collection* (OUP 2017) 55-56.
[28] ibid.

individual(s) concerned by the data, the automated analysis of which has shown that there may be a terrorist threat, to be identified at a later stage through authorisation by the Prime Minister, all persons whose data has been the subject of automated analysis can potentially be identified from that data. In other words, this technique provided the possibility of de-anonymising the traffic and location data, which could allow the individual concerned to be indirectly identified. As such, the provision concerns the processing of information relating, to an identifiable person, which according to the definition of personal data, suffices for data to be considered as personal.[29] The Court framed automated analysis of traffic and location data as 'general and indiscriminate processing' of data since the analysis involves screening all traffic and location data of all users of electronic communications services.[30] That processing is independent of the subsequent collection of data relating to the persons identified following that automated analysis.

In light of the above, in addition to possible compatibility issues with the rights of privacy and personal data protection, the Court found that that personal data processing also triggered a question pertaining to the confidentiality of communications, in relation to the right to privacy, which encompasses the right to respect communications.[31] It may also have a deterrent effect on the exercise of freedom of expression, which is enshrined in Article 11 of the Charter.[32] The right to an effective remedy under Article 47 of the Charter was referenced too, but in relation to the requirement for notifying individuals whose traffic and location data are automatically analysed. There, the Court opined that:

> [T]he competent national authority is obliged to publish information of a general nature relating to that analysis without having to notify the persons concerned individually. However, if the data matches the parameters specified in the measure authorising automated analysis and that authority identifies the person concerned in order to analyse in greater depth the data concerning him or her, it is necessary to notify that person individually. That notification must, however, occur only to the extent that and as soon as it is no longer liable to jeopardise the tasks for which those authorities are responsible.[33]

The Court further highlighted that this type of personal data processing amounted to a *serious* interference with the aforementioned rights taking into account two factors. First, it involved the monitoring of the metadata 'generally and indiscriminately' of all persons using electronic communication systems, including persons with respect to whom there is no evidence capable of suggesting that their conduct might have a link, even an indirect or remote one, with terrorist activities.[34] Second, the processing may reveal the nature of the information consulted online.[35] These factors though do not outright exclude the use of automated analysis as a technique, they nonetheless impact the outcome of the proportionality test. The CJEU recalled its findings in the earlier paragraphs of the judgment on the strict necessity test for generalised and indiscriminate *collection* of traffic and location

---

[29] *La Quadrature du Net 'I'* (n 1) para 171.
[30] ibid para 172.
[31] ibid para 173.
[32] ibid.
[33] ibid para 191.
[34] ibid para 174.
[35] ibid.

data for national security purposes. In this respect, the Court concluded that the objective of national security justifies such collection.[36] National security has been understood as:

> the primary interest in protecting the essential functions of the State and the fundamental interests of society and encompasses the prevention and punishment of activities capable of seriously destabilising the fundamental constitutional, political, economic or social structures of a country and, in particular, of directly threatening society, the population or the State itself, such as terrorist activities.[37]

The Court reiterated that automated analysis is not completely ruled out due to its general and indiscriminate nature. It can be justified where conducted to safeguard against serious national security threats, including terrorism.[38] In other words, the gravity of 'serious' national security threats including, but not exhausted to, terrorism, could serve as a legitimate aim to justify the serious infringement. In line with its findings on mass data retention regimes for national security purposes earlier in the judgment, the CJEU also noted that a national security threat must be 'genuine and present or foreseeable'[39] and the interference must be for a strictly limited period.[40] Furthermore, the decision of the body authorising the automated analysis must be subject to an effective review by a body whose decision is binding.[41] The review must verify that a serious threat to national security exists and 'the conditions and safeguards' that must be laid down are observed.[42]

Importantly, the CJEU added certain requirements specifically for automated analysis. Building on the requirements mentioned in *PNR Canada*, the Court opined that the 'pre-established models and criteria' (algorithms) should not only be specific and reliable but also non-discriminatory.[43] In this regard, the CJEU stressed the discriminatory effect of pre-established models and criteria that are designed on the premise that individuals' protected characteristics may be relevant for the prevention of terrorism.[44] Therefore, the Court found that the models or criteria for conducting an automated analysis cannot be based on sensitive data *in isolation*.[45] It also acknowledged the need to regularly re-examine the algorithms and databases to ensure they remain reliable, up to date and non-discriminatory, and limited to what is strictly necessary to achieve the intended purposes.[46]

Finally, concerning individual and public oversight, the competent national authority should publish information of a general nature about the automated analysis taking place without having to notify the persons concerned individually. However, if the data matches

---

[36] ibid para 175.
[37] ibid para 135.
[38] ibid para 177.
[39] ibid.
[40] ibid para 178.
[41] ibid para 179.
[42] ibid. The meaning of the 'conditions and safeguards' mentioned in the relevant paragraph are not detailed by the Court so far as the Charter right infringement by automated analysis is concerned. It is unclear whether the Court refers to the requirements it considers later in terms of those requirements that need to be observed to enable that pre-established models and criteria are non-discriminatory, accurate and up to date, because observing those requirements seems to be tied into regular assessment of the systems as opposed to reviewing the authorisation of the system per se.
[43] ibid para 180.
[44] ibid.
[45] ibid para 181. Emphasis added.
[46] ibid para 182.

the parameters specified in the measure authorising automated analysis and that authority identifies the person concerned in order to analyse in greater depth the data concerning him or her, it is necessary to notify that person individually. That notification must, however, occur only to the extent that and as soon as it is no longer liable to jeopardise the tasks for which those authorities are responsible.[47]

2.3 The third step: *Ligue des droits humains*

The third step in this jurisprudential chain is the judgment of 21 June 2022 on the interpretation of the PNR Directive. The case was initiated by Ligue des droits humains, a non-governmental organisation, seeking annulment of the Belgian law implementing the PNR Directive.[48] This resulted in a decision by the Belgian Constitutional Court (Grondwettelijk Hof) to submit no less than ten preliminary questions to the CJEU. These questions related to a series of aspects concerning the processing of passengers' personal data, including the use of data for law enforcement and security purposes, the applicability of the regime to intra-EU flights, the retention of PNR data and automated decision-making. The CJEU stressed various flawed and unclear provisions of the PNR Directive, but chose not to invalidate it, approach that one could probably have expected in light of the approach taken in *Digital Rights Ireland*.[49] As mentioned by Brouwer, this approach may be seen as reflecting the dilemma of the judges 'between the aim of preserving national sovereignty within the field of national security on the one hand, and the necessity to have transparent and harmonised rules to protect the fundamental rights of passengers on the other'.[50] Another factor that may explain why the PNR Directive was not invalidated may have to do with the legal vacuum that was created post-*Digital Rights Ireland*, which provided a contextual disincentive for creating a similar regulatory gap in the PNR arena.

Among the various aspects discussed in the judgment, the Court analysed the use of passenger data for automated risk assessments. According to the PNR Directive, air carriers must transfer the PNR data of all their passengers, which are collected by them during booking a flight, between 24 and 48 hours prior to the scheduled flight departure to the Passenger Information Units (PIUs). The latter are the national police units of the Member State of destination, in charge of receiving, processing, and sharing PNR data with the competent national authorities, Europol, and third countries. According to Article 6 of the PNR Directive, the PIUs, among others, are entrusted with the task of conducting 'an assessment of passengers prior to their scheduled arrival in or departure from the Member State to identify persons who require further examination by the competent authorities' and,

---

[47] ibid para 191.
[48] Loi du 25 décembre 2016 relative au traitement des données des passagers, Official publication: Moniteur Belge; Publication date: 25/01/2017; Page number: 12905-12918.
[49] For a critique see Evelien Brouwer, 'Ligue des droits humains and the Validity of the PNR Directive: Balancing Individual Rights and State Powers in Times of New Technologies' (2023) 60(3) Common Market Law Review 839; Christian Thönnes, 'A Directive Altered beyond Recognition: On the Court of Justice of the European Union's PNR decision (C-817/19)' (*Verfassungsblog*, 23 June 2022) <https://verfassungsblog.de/pnr-recognition/> accessed 10 July 2024; Kristina Irion, 'Repairing the EU Passenger Name Record Directive: The ECJ's judgment in Ligue des droits humains (Case C-817/19)' (European Law Blog, 11 October 2022) <https://europeanlawblog.eu/2022/10/11/repairing-the-eu-passenger-name-record-directive-the-ecjs-judgment-in-ligue-des-droits-humains-case-c-817-19/> accessed 10 July 2024.
[50] Brouwer, ibid 840.

'where relevant, by Europol' in view of the fact that such persons may be involved in a terrorist offence or serious crime. Such advance assessment comprises of two elements: a comparison of PNR data against databases relevant for the purposes of preventing, detecting, investigating, and prosecuting terrorist offences and serious crime, and processing of PNR data against pre-determined criteria.[51]

Building on its findings in *PNR Canada* and *La Quadrature du Net 'I'*, the CJEU developed even more elaborate safeguards on automated processing of PNR data to conduct advance assessments of air travellers. In a nutshell, echoing *PNR Canada*, the Court acknowledged that automated processing 'necessarily presents a fairly substantial margin of error, since it is carried out on the basis of unverified personal data and is based on pre-determined criteria'.[52] Then, the Court opined that it must be ensured that no decision that produces an adverse legal effect on a person or significantly affects a person may be taken by the competent authorities only by reason of the automated processing of the PNR data.[53] Therefore, the PIUs may only transfer PNR data to national authorities after individual review by non-automated means, and national supervisory authorities, data protection officers and the PIUs must be provided with 'the material and human resources necessary to carry out their review under the PNR Directive'.[54] Furthermore, the national law transposing the Directive must lay down clear and precise rules for the determination of the databases and criteria to be used without relying on other methods not referred in the Directive.[55]

Unpacking each of these elements, the Court examined the databases against which the PNR data can be compared. Article 6(3)(a) of the PNR Directive provides that the data may be compared against 'databases relevant for the purposes of preventing, detecting, investigating and prosecuting terrorist offences and serious crime, including databases on persons or objects sought or under alert, in accordance with Union, international and national rules applicable to such databases'. Applying a strict necessity test, the Court found that the term 'relevant' does not describe in a sufficiently clear and precise manner the databases against which the PNR data can be compared.[56] Thus, the Court essentially rewrote the provision as meaning that the *only* databases that can be compared are those on persons or objects sought or under alert, in accordance with Union, international and national rules applicable to such databases.[57] Given that the assessment must take place in a non-discriminatory manner, the criteria for the databases must be targeted, proportionate, and specific, and must be set and regularly reviewed by the PIUs in cooperation with the competent authorities.[58] Entry into the databases on persons sought or under alert must be based on objective and non-discriminatory factors, defined in EU, international, and national rules applicable to such databases.[59] In addition, the databases against which the PNR data may be compared 'must be used in relation to the fight against terrorist offences and serious crime having an objective link even if only an indirect one with the carriage

[51] PNR Directive, Art 6(3).
[52] *Ligue des droits humains* (n 3) para 178.
[53] ibid paras 179–180.
[54] ibid para 180.
[55] ibid.
[56] ibid para 187.
[57] ibid para 188.
[58] ibid para 189.
[59] ibid para 190. See by analogy, *Garda Síochána* (n 13) para 78.

of passengers by air'.[60] Moreover, the databases used must be managed by the competent authorities with regard to EU databases as well as international databases, be exploited by those authorities in the context of their mission to combat terrorist offences and serious crime.[61]

The next step for the CJEU was to examine the risks of algorithm-based decision-making and identify limitations to the development and use of automated risk assessments. Indeed, according to Article 6(3)(b) of the PNR Directive the PIU of a Member State may process PNR data against pre-determined criteria to identify persons who may be involved in a terrorist offence or serious crime. Furthermore, Article 6(4) states that this assessment must be carried out in a non-discriminatory way and that the pre-determined criteria must be 'targeted, proportionate and specific'. In his Opinion, Advocate-General Pitruzzella held that the definition of 'pre-determined' criteria precludes the use of artificial intelligence in self-learning systems, which 'whilst it may be more precise, is difficult to interpret, even for the operators carrying out the automated processing'.[62] The Court followed the Advocate-General's approach concluding that the PNR Directive precludes the use of AI 'in self-learning systems ("machine learning"), capable of modifying without human intervention or review the assessment process and, in particular, the assessment criteria on which the result of the application of that process is based as well as the weighting of those criteria'.[63] It was acknowledged that the use of such technology would be liable to make the individual review of positive matches and monitoring of lawfulness impossible.[64] It might also be impossible to understand the reason why a given program arrived at a positive match and to challenge the non-discriminatory nature of the results, given the 'opacity which characterises the way in which artificial intelligence works', depriving data subjects of their right to effective judicial protection as protected in Article 47 of the Charter.[65]

In other words, the Court banned the use of self-learning AI systems, as long as such use is capable of modifying without human intervention or review the assessment process, the assessment criteria, and the weighing of those criteria. This does not mean that the Court supported an outright prohibition on the use of all self-learning algorithms; however as Thönnes has highlighted,[66] this may cover most of today's available AI technologies. That said, it is possible that AI could, in the future, incorporate methods of supervised and reinforced learning where autonomous learning is intertwined with human interventions.[67] Therefore, the prohibition on self-learning algorithms is a positive step forward— but without further legal elaboration security agencies could circumvent this prohibition if they just use the right AI systems. At the same time, I am not sure the Court meant to prohibit self-learning systems which '(1) are capable of modifying their assessment criteria without any human intervention of review (this notably open logical distinction does not matter much at the moment), and/or (2) are too opaque to allow for effective judicial

---

[60] ibid para 191.
[61] ibid para 192.
[62] Janneke Gerards and Raphaële Xenidis, 'Algorithmic Discrimination in Europe: Challenges and opportunities for gender equality and non-discrimination law' (Publications Office of the EU 2021) 33.
[63] *Ligue des droits humains* (n 3) para 194.
[64] ibid para 195.
[65] ibid.
[66] Thönnes (n 49).
[67] Reuben Binns and Michael Veale, 'Is that your Final Decision? Multi-stage Profiling, Selective Effects, and Article 22 of the GDPR' (2021) 11(4) International Data Privacy Law 319.

remedy against their recommendations'.[68] In para 194 of *Ligue des droits humains* the CJEU is clear that the AI systems that are prohibited are those that have the characteristic under (1) and that their opacity under (2) is the reason for such prohibition.

Then, the CJEU defined four standards for the use of pre-determined criteria that must be fulfilled to ensure their non-discriminatory and proportionate use. First, to avoid discrimination, which involves both direct and indirect discrimination,[69] the criteria must be defined in such a way that 'while worded in a neutral fashion, their application does not place persons having the protected characteristics at a particular disadvantage'.[70] Second, the CJEU elaborated on what 'targeted, proportionate and specific' pre-determined criteria mean. Individuals who must be targeted are those 'who might be reasonably suspected of involvement in terrorist offences or serious crime'.[71] Third, to bolster the reliability and proportionality of (the use of) those criteria, they must take consideration specific features in the factual conduct of persons when preparing and engaging in air travel which, following the findings of and experience acquired by the competent authorities, might suggest that the persons acting in that way may be involved in terrorist offences or serious crime.[72] Therefore, 'incriminating' as well as 'exonerating' circumstances, must be taken into account.[73] Finally, the CJEU recalled the need for regular review of the pre-determined criteria, so that the criteria are updated in accordance with the circumstances justifying their being taken into consideration, but also taking into account acquired experience to reduce as much as possible the number of false positives.[74]

In addition, the Court underlined the need for compliance with the aforementioned safeguards throughout the process of processing the data.[75] Beyond devising pre-determined criteria and the determination of the database against which processing must take place, the individual review of any positive match by non-automated means must be ensured to identify, 'as much as possible', any 'false positives' (also to exclude any discriminatory results).[76] This review obligation concerns matched against both databases and pre-determined criteria.[77] The results of the automated processing operations must not transfer the results of those automated processing operations to the competent authorities if, following that review, there is nothing capable of giving rise, to the requisite legal standard, to a reasonable suspicion of involvement in terrorist offences or serious crime in respect of the persons identified by means of those automated processing operations or when they have reason to believe that those processing operations lead to discriminatory results.[78] The verification of a match must take place based on 'clear and precise rules capable of providing guidance and support for the analysis carried out by the agents in charge of the individual review', laid down by the Member States to 'guarantee a uniform administrative practice within the PIU that observes the principle of non-discrimination'.[79] At the same time, there is an obligation

---

[68] Thönnes (n 49).
[69] *Ligue des droits humains* (n 3) para 197.
[70] ibid.
[71] ibid para 198.
[72] ibid para 199.
[73] ibid para 200.
[74] ibid para 201.
[75] ibid para 202.
[76] ibid para 203.
[77] ibid.
[78] ibid para 205.
[79] ibid.

for PIUs to also establish a clear and precise manner, objective review criteria.[80] On the one hand, such criteria will enable the authorities to verify whether and to what extent a positive match effectively concerns an individual who may be involved in terrorist offences or serious crime. On the other hand, these criteria must ensure the 'non-discriminatory nature of automated processing operations, and especially the pre-determined criteria and databases used'.[81] At the same time, Member States and their national PIUs are offered a wide discretionary power to decide on what they consider as 'clear and precise and objective review criteria'.[82] Finally, on all the processing operations PIUs must maintain relevant documentation, including in the context of the individual review by non-automated means, for the purpose of verifying its lawfulness and for the purpose of self-monitoring.[83]

In any case, the competent authorities receiving the results from the PIUs must not take any decision that produces an adverse legal effect on a person or significantly affects a person only by reason of the automated processing of PNR data, which means, in connection with the advance assessment, that they must take into consideration and, where applicable, give preference to the result of the individual review conducted by non-automated means by the PIU over that obtained by automated processing.[84]

The last part of the Court's assessment on these aspects concerns the obligations for Member States to protect the right to effective legal protection and to ensure effective oversight mechanisms.[85] These are particularly significant considering that the PNR operations take place in border decisions, based on automated processing of personal data or risk assessment, whereby individuals may have limited access to lawyers and possibility to understand the language and the legal system of an EU Member State. To safeguard individuals' right to judicial redress, as laid down in Article 13(1) of the PNR Directive, the competent authorities must ensure that the person concerned is able to understand how those criteria and those programs work, to decide 'with full knowledge of the relevant facts' whether or not to exercise their right to the judicial redress and challenge the unlawful and discriminatory nature of the pre-determined criteria.[86] The Court was mindful to add that this does not mean that that person, during the administrative procedure, must become aware of the pre-determined assessment criteria and programs applying those criteria.[87] This raises questions as to whether there exists a right to meaningful information. How can a person who is not allowed to embark on a flight or to enter the territory of a Member State, on the basis of a prior PNR assessment, address the possibly discriminatory nature of such assessment or calculate his or her chances for a successful judicial review? Furthermore, the court responsible for reviewing the legality of the decision adopted by the competent authorities as well as, except in the case of threats to State security, the persons concerned themselves

---

[80] ibid para 206.
[81] ibid.
[82] ibid.
[83] ibid para 207.
[84] ibid para 208.
[85] ibid para 209.
[86] ibid para 210.
[87] ibid. Drawing from CJEU, Judgment of 24 November 2020, *RNNS v Minister van Buitenlandse Zaken* (C-225/19 and C-226/19) ECLI:EU:C:2020:951 and CJEU, Judgment 4 June 2023, *ZZ* (C-300/11) ECLI:EU:C:2013:363 ('ZZ'). These judgments both concern immigration law First, the ECJ obliges Member States to ensure that individuals have access to national courts which are empowered to review the legality of the use of pre-determined criteria and the programs applying those criteria. Second, Member States must also guarantee access to courts which are able to examine all the grounds and evidence on the basis of which PNR decisions were taken.

must have had an opportunity to examine 'both all the grounds and the evidence on the basis of which the decision was taken'.[88]

Finally, the Court referred to the necessary role of data protection officers and national supervisory authorities 'to ensure the monitoring of the lawfulness of the automated processing carried out by the PIU'.[89] The Court clarified that the monitoring covers among others whether those operations are not discriminatory. This is an important pronouncement because it denotes the value of data protection law as safeguarding other fundamental rights, including non-discrimination and the need for data protection authorities to have a broader overview of the fundamental rights implications beyond the strict contours of data protection. For this purpose, the data protection officer must have access to all data processed by the PIU, that access must necessarily cover the pre-determined criteria and databases used by that unit in order to guarantee effectiveness and a high level of data protection that that officer must ensure.[90] Similarly, the investigations, inspections, and audits to be carried out by national supervisory authorities may also concern those pre-determined criteria and databases.

2.4 The fourth step: *La Quadrature du Net 'II'*

The latest addition in the CJEU case law detailing the safeguards for automated processing of personal data to be compatible with fundamental rights is the *La Quadrature du Net 'II'* judgment of 30 April 2024. The applicants in the main proceedings brought action before the French Council of State to seek the annulment of the decision of the Prime Minister to reject their request to repeal Decree No 2010-236, which regulated the powers of Hadopi, the authority assigned to protect works covered by copyright or related rights against infringements of those rights committed on electronic communications networks used for the provision of online public communication services with respect to the prosecution of copyright infringement on the internet.[91] In particular, French law provides for a specific graduated response mechanism, operated by Hadopi's Commission for the protection of rights. According to this mechanism, sworn officials, approved by the Minister of Culture and operating within rightholder organisations, are given the power to collect from peer-to-peer networks the IP addresses of users making available content infringing copyright. Those IP addresses, the processing of which is authorised directly by the French National Commission for Information Technology and Civil Liberties (CNIL), are reported to Hadopi, which may thus obtain from providers of electronic communications services the corresponding data concerning the civic identity of those users (the subscriber's surname and first names, postal address and email addresses, telephone number, and the address of the subscriber's telephone installation) and send a first recommendation to the alleged infringer. In case of persistent copyright violations, a second recommendation may be provided to the person identified through the IP address, before referring the matter, at the 'third strike', to the public prosecutor's service.

---

[88] *Ligue des droits humains* (n 3) para 211.
[89] ibid para 212.
[90] ibid.
[91] In this sense, it is classified as a public authority within the meaning of Article 3 of the LED.

The CJEU was confronted with questions regarding the requirement for prior review by a court or an independent administrative body before a public authority accesses data relating to the civil identity associated with an IP address of users to fight less serious crimes, namely those related to the protection of copyright and related rights. Compared to the previous case law which had a continuity and one judgment built on the findings of the other, this case is different in that it concerns the manner of that review and particularly whether it could be entirely automated in view of its massive scale. The French Government submitted in that regard that such a review, which is of a purely objective nature, is intended essentially to verify that the report referred to Hadopi contains all the required information and data, without Hadopi being required to carry out any assessment of that information or data.[92] The Court disagreed opining that a prior review may in no case be entirely automated, since:

> in the case of a criminal investigation, it is a requirement of such a review, in any event, that the court or independent administrative body concerned must be able to strike a fair balance between, on the one hand, the legitimate interests relating to the needs of the investigation in the context of combating crime and, on the other hand, the fundamental rights to respect for private life and protection of personal data of the persons whose data are concerned by the access.[93]

This balancing requires intervention of a natural person, all the more so where the automatic nature and large scale of the data processing (due to the number of instances of counterfeiting detected) in question poses privacy risks.[94] The Court found that an entirely automated review is not, as a rule, capable of ensuring that the access does not go beyond the limits of what is strictly necessary and that the persons whose personal data are concerned have effective safeguards against the risks of abuse and against any unlawful access to or use of those data.[95] That said, verification of some of the information contained in the rightholder organisations' reports can be automated.[96]

Furthermore, the Court confirmed that processing of personal data 'must go hand in hand with reviews by natural persons' and that checks in essentially automated manner is not sufficient.[97] Furthermore, automated processing is likely to involve a certain number of false positives and importantly there is a risk of potentially very significant amount of personal data be misused by third parties for unlawful or abusive purposes. Therefore, the data processing system used by a public authority must the subject, at regular intervals, of a review by an independent body acting as a third party in relation to that authority, intended to verify the integrity of the system, including the effective safeguards against the risks of abuse and against any unlawful access to or use of those data which that system must ensure as well as the effectiveness and reliability of that system in detecting offending conduct liable to be classified, if repeated, as gross negligence or counterfeiting.[98] The Court stressed

---

[92] *La Quadrature du Net 'II'* (n 5) para 147.
[93] ibid para 148.
[94] ibid para 149.
[95] ibid para 150.
[96] ibid para 151.
[97] ibid para 155.
[98] ibid para 156.

the applicability of the LED in this case[99] and the applicability of its substantive and procedural safeguards.[100]

3. The Potential and Limitations of the CJEU's Approach

The Court's findings provide food for thought in many respects; through their incremental creation, various issues have progressively been addressed, whereas a series of questions and protection gaps remain. This section will unpack certain key aspects arising from the emerging jurisprudence and relate to the transplantation of the CJEU's standards to other contexts of automated processing (section 3.1), outstanding issues for further elaboration in subsequent cases (section 3.2), the relationship with the right not to be subjected to automated decision-making under Article 11 of the LED (section 3.3) and the relationship with the AI Act (section 3.4).

3.1 The transplantation of the CJEU's standards to multiple contexts

A key question arising from the jurisprudence of the CJEU is the applicability of the Court's standards to a multiplicity of contexts. An answer in favour of the transplantability of the CJEU's safeguards would be grounded on the fact that there is clear continuity in the existing case law, which concerns two types of cases; *PNR Canada* and *Ligue des droits humains* scrutinise the automated processing of PNR data, whereas *La Quadrature du Net 'I'* involves the automated analysis of telecommunication metadata. In the latter case it is clear that the CJEU picked up and further developed the safeguards from *PNR Canada*, which were afterwards fledged in an even fuller manner in *Ligue des droits humains*. On first sight, one might be tempted to consider the two contexts as somewhat unrelated due to the different logic behind the automated tools involved; after all an algorithm analysing telecommunication metadata does not operate in a manner similar to algorithmic profiling of passengers. Furthermore, automated analysis in the context of telecommunications metadata is permissible to safeguard national security, in recognition of the seriousness of the interference with the rights to privacy and personal data protection. In turn, automated processing of PNR data concerns fighting terrorism and serious crimes, thus to safeguard public security purposes and does not concern *prima facie* national security, although terrorism can be considered as a matter of national security as well.[101] This means that there is a slight difference in the scope, whereby automated analysis of telecommunication metadata is permissible for national security purposes, but such analysis is permissible for broader purposes when it involves PNR data.

Notwithstanding this convolution, the Court's flexible approach allows for imagining the applicability of its standards—perhaps with some modifications and adaptations—in the other contexts as well. For example, the standards could apply in the context of money

---

[99] ibid para 157.
[100] ibid paras 161–163.
[101] *La Quadrature du Net 'I'* (n 1) para 135.

laundering obligations to obliged entities[102] in accordance with the 6th Anti-Money Laundering Directive.[103] Another example is the case of two EU large-scale IT systems for third-country nationals, the European Travel Information and Authorisation System (ETIAS) and the Visa Information System (VIS). Automated processing is embedded in the operationalisation of the forthcoming ETIAS to enable assessing the applications for travel authorisations by visa free applicants[104] and the revised VIS for the assessment of applications for short-stay (Schengen) visas.[105]

In particular, the ETIAS Regulation requires visa free travellers to apply online for travel authorisation prior to travelling to the Schengen area and disclosing a series of personal data including biographical data, travel arrangements, home and email address, phone number, level of education, and current occupation. Based on that information, ETIAS will operate as a pre-emptive control mechanism: the data provided will be subject to automated checks against: (a) the other IT systems, Europol data and the Interpol databases Stolen and Lost Travel Document database (SLTD) and the Interpol Documents Associated with Notices databases (TDAWN); (b) screening rules, enabling profiling on the basis of risk indicators, developed by the ETIAS Central Unit, within the European Border and Coast Guard Agency; and (c) a dedicated watchlist of persons suspected of terrorist or serious crime. The aim of the automated processing is to determine whether the presence of the ETIAS applicant in the territory of the Member States would pose a security, irregular migration or high epidemic risk. If automated processing reveals a verified hit, then the application will be processed manually (human in the loop) by the responsible ETIAS National Unit. Similarly (subject to minor differences), in the case of VIS, Schengen visa applicants' data will be subject to automated processing to assist visa authorities in the examination of applications by flagging potential risky travellers. Flagging an applicant as potentially risk will take place not because of any specific actions they have engaged in but because they display particular category traits in a probabilistic logic devoid of concrete evidence.

As argued elsewhere, the standards of the CJEU should be applied *mutandis mutandis* for various reasons; first, automated processing is explicitly mandated by EU law, whereas in both cases of data retention and PNR processing this is a choice of the public authorities involved to implement EU policies; second, the by default discriminatory nature of immigration law, which creates a divide between the citizen and the foreigner, thus necessitating all the more taking into account the potential biases in the design and implementation of automated processing schemes; and third, PNR data and data stored in IT systems have an inherent kinship as they involve travellers' data in the broader sense. Finally, the ETIAS

---

[102] Zhiyuan Chen and others, 'Machine Learning Techniques for Anti-money Laundering (AML) Solutions in Suspicious Transaction Detection: A Review' (2018) 57 Knowledge and Information Systems 245–85.
[103] Directive 2024/1640 of the European Parliament and of the Council of 31 May 2024 on the mechanisms to be put in place by Member States for the prevention of the use of the financial system for the purposes of money laundering or terrorist financing, amending Directive (EU) 2019/1937, and amending and repealing Directive (EU) 2015/849 [2024] OJ L 2024/1640 ('6th Anti-Money Laundering Directive').
[104] Regulation 2018/1240 of the European Parliament and of the Council of 12 September 2018 establishing a European Travel Information and Authorisation System (ETIAS) and amending Regulations (EU) No 1077/2011, (EU) No 515/2014, (EU) 2016/399, (EU) 2016/1624 and (EU) 2017/2226 [2018] OJ L 236/1 ('ETIAS Regulation').
[105] Regulation 2021/1134 of the European Parliament and of the Council of 7 July 2021 amending Regulations (EC) No 767/2008, (EC) No 810/2009, (EU) 2016/399, (EU) 2017/2226, (EU) 2018/1240, (EU) 2018/1860, (EU) 2018/1861, (EU) 2019/817 and (EU) 2019/1896 of the European Parliament and of the Council and repealing Council Decisions 2004/512/EC and 2008/633/JHA, for the purpose of reforming the Visa Information System [2021] OJ L 248/11 ('revised VIS Regulation').

and VIS rules themselves refer to the need for the algorithms to be targeted and proportionate, and add the need to safeguard the principle of non-discrimination, thus pointing to the direction that the CJEU's apply. Their application here allows to conclude about the lack of proportionality of the underlying rules not least due to the lack of reliability of the databases and information that will create statistical data based on which the risk profiles will be generated, thus affecting the reliability of the pre-established models and criteria.[106]

Whereas ETIAS and VIS may be seen as having a distinct status, there are other schemes that undertake to automatically identify previously unknown material or persons in large data pools in order to protect public security where the CJEU's standards should apply. The Court's findings may be relevant in the case of online content moderation for counter-terrorism purposes, in line with the TERREG Regulation,[107] and to detect child sexual abuse material (CSAM) online, pursuant to a 2022 Commission proposal on this matter.[108] Particularly the latter is important because the proposed Regulation, among other things, authorises competent national courts or independent administrative authorities, upon request by designated national 'Coordinating Authorities', to issue detection orders,[109] which allow providers of hosting services, such as Facebook or YouTube, or interpersonal communication services, such as WhatsApp, to use automated systems to detect and report not only known, but also new child sexual abuse material and grooming. While known CSAM can be recognised through an image's digital quasi-fingerprint (so-called hashes), this is not possible for unknown CSAM, which is only possible by training self-learning algorithms based on pattern recognition in previously classified CSAM material and then unleashing them on all users of the service in question.[110]

As stressed elsewhere,[111] the CJEU's safeguards are not respected in multiple respects. First, the transparency and legal contestability are doubtful. The proposed Regulation allows—but does not require private providers—to use the screening software developed by the EU Centre on Child Sexual Abuse software (an agency specifically created for the Regulation's implementation),[112] thus opening the door for non-transparent, commercial software. It is not clear how supervisory authorities can guarantee that the software in use is compliant with non-discrimination. In the name of security, the CSAM proposal deliberately curtails access to databases of indicators and source codes for supervisory authorities or affected persons.[113] Furthermore, automated processing in the context of CSAM will rely on technological tools that are not considered fully reliable and may result in high false

---

[106] For additional analysis see Niovi Vavoula, 'Tr-AI-nsforming Migration, Asylum and Border Management in the EU: The Roles of the AI Act, Interoperable Large-scale IT Systems and EU Migration Agencies' (forthcoming Computer Law & Security Review).

[107] Regulation 2021/784 of the European Parliament and of the Council of 29 April 2021 on addressing the dissemination of terrorist content online [2021] OJ L 172/79 ('TERREG Regulation').

[108] European Commission, 'Proposal for a Regulation of the European Parliament and of the Council laying down rules to prevent and combat child sexual abuse' (COM)2022 209 final ('CSAM Proposal').

[109] ibid Art 7(1).

[110] For criticism see Linette de Swart and others, 'Complementary Impact Assessment of the proposal for a regulation laying down the rules to prevent and combat child sexual abuse' (commissioned by the European Parliament Research Service, 2023).

[111] Christian Thönnes and Niovi Vavoula, 'Automated Predictive Threat Detection after Ligue des Droits Humains—Implications for ETIAS and CSAM (Part II)' (*Verfassungsblog*, 12 May 2023) <https://verfassungsblog.de/pnr-threat-detection-ii/> accessed 10 July 2024.

[112] CSAM Proposal (n 108) Art 10(2).

[113] ibid Art 46.

positive rates.[114] The Court links the severity of interferences with fundamental rights to the reliability of the technology used—the higher a system's false positive rate, the higher its interference with fundamental rights. According to *Ligue des droits humains*, systems with a 'fairly substantial number of false positives', 'depend on the proper functioning of the subsequent verification of the results ... by non-automated means'[115] to guarantee their proportionality, guided by clear and precise rules. The proposed Regulation contains no precise rules for that purpose, only stipulating that the EU Centre on Child Sexual Abuse should throw out manifestly unfounded reports,[116] and stating that the training data must be chosen in a diligent assessment.[117]

3.2 Room for further elaboration

Whereas the four judgments, particularly *Ligue des droits humains*, provide comprehensive standards for conducting proportionate automated analysis, upon closer inspection there is still room for further elaboration. This sub-section will consider the possibility of developing more elaborate standards for auditing the algorithmic models, measuring the reliability of databases, addressing intersectional discrimination and conducting supervision to monitor the lawfulness of automated processing.

3.2.1 Auditing algorithms

First, whereas in all three judgments, the Court insists on ongoing review of algorithmic models that may resonate with the lively debate on algorithmic transparency and unboxing the proverbial 'Black Box' by auditing algorithms.[118] There is however not a single line of authority on the best practices of algorithmic auditing.[119] As far as EU data protection law is concerned, discussions unfolded as to the extent to which the relevant national law may comprise aspects of algorithmic analysis, despite not explicitly requiring it.[120] Some mechanisms, which have sprung from the privacy impact assessment policies and practices,[121] such as a Data Protection Impact Assessment, do however involve algorithmic auditing but only before commissioning the algorithmic systems.[122] They may potentially be useful but

---

[114] Linette de Swart and others, 'Complementary Impact Assessment of the proposal for a regulation laying down the rules to prevent and combat child sexual abuse' (commissioned by the European Parliament Research Service, 2023).

[115] *Ligue des droits humains* (n 3) para 124.

[116] CSAM Proposal (n 108) Art 48(2).

[117] ibid Art 36(1).

[118] Tal Zarsky, 'The Trouble with Algorithmic Decisions: An Analytic Road Map to Examine Efficiency and Fairness in Automated and Opaque Decision Making' (2016) 41(1) Science, Technology, & Human Values 118; Jennifer Cobbe and Jatinder Singh, 'Reviewable Automated Decision Making' (2020) 39 Computer Law & Security Review 1. Algorithmic transparency is considered as a requirement of 'trustworthy' AI in ethics guidelines, soft-law instruments and (draft) legislation. See High-Level Expert Group on Artificial Intelligence, 'Ethics Guidelines for Trustworthy AI (April 2019); Council of Europe, Declaration by the Committee of Ministers on the manipulative capabilities of algorithmic processes, Decl(13/02/2019) 1.

[119] 'Examining the Black-Box: Tools for Assessing Algorithmic Systems' (*Ada Lovelace Institute*, 29 April 2020). <https://www.adalovelaceinstitute.org/report/examining-the-black-box-tools-for-assessing-algorithmic-systems/> accessed 10 July 2024.

[120] Bryce Goodman, 'Discrimination, Data Sanitisation and Auditing in the European Union's General Data Protection Regulation' (2016) 2(4) European Data Protection Law Review 493.

[121] See eg Paul de Hert, 'A Human Rights Perspective on Privacy and Data Protection Impact Assessments' in David Wright and Paul de Hert, *Privacy Impact Assessment* (Springer 2021).

[122] Regulation 2016/679 of the European Parliament and of the Council of 27 April 2016 on the protection of natural persons with regard to the processing of personal data and on the free movement of such data, and

may not require an ongoing assessment once the system is commissioned. In endorsing the ongoing revision of algorithmic systems based on a number of factors, the CJEU seems to be hinting towards the addressing what internal audits of surveillance regimes that are based on algorithmic models may comprise.[123]

3.2.2 Assessing the reliability of databases

Another issue that must be elaborated is how to assess and measure the reliability and up-to-date character of a database against automated processing takes place. In general, the larger the database, storing millions of datasets and accessed by multiple end-users and for different purposes, the more likely it is that the database may be unreliable by storing unlawfully collected data, or data that are not up-to-date or incorrect. For example, it cannot be ruled out that certain databases that on paper may seem to be reliable, in practice they are not. The CJEU does not make a distinction between EU and international databases and does not provide any indication as to what are the standards for a database to cease being considered as reliable. Examples of incorrect, incomplete, or unlawfully stored data in both international and EU databases are multiple: at international level, with regard to the Interpol databases, especially TDAWN, recent reports have unearthed the abuse of the notices by certain countries in the pursuit of political objectives, repressing freedom of expression or persecuting members of the political opposition beyond their borders.[124] EU databases have also attracted criticism for storing millions of unlawful or incorrect records.[125] As for Europol data, their reliability cannot be determined and scarce information exists in that regard. What is publicly known is that in drawing up the Serious Organised Crime Threat Assessment (SOCTA) report in 2013, the agency was willing to make use of data that, judged by its own assessment methods, was considered 'not confirmed'.[126] In that regard, it has been reported that Europol may consider certain partners as trustworthy and thus not conduct a close examination of the reliability of the data received.[127]

3.2.3 Intersectional discrimination

The Court has made significant efforts to address the discriminatory effects of automated processing.[128] Whereas in *PNR Canada* the Court did not consider the principle

repealing Directive 95/46/EC (General Data Protection Regulation) [2016] OJ L 119/1 ('GDPR'), Art 35. Also see LED, Art 27. On the application of a data protection impact assessment to algorithmic accountability and transparency see Margot E Kaminski and Gianclaudio Malgieri, 'Algorithmic impact assessments under the GDPR: producing multi-layered explanations' (2021) 11(2) International Data Privacy Law 125.

[123] For an example of good practices regarding safeguards against the automated decision making to meet the GDPR requirements see Article 29 Data Protection Working Party, 'Guidelines on Automated individual decision-making and profiling for the purposes of Regulation 2016/679' (3 October 2017).
[124] Rasmus Wandall and others, 'Misuse of Interpol's Red Notices and impact on human rights—recent developments' (Study for the Subcommittee on Human Rights (DROI) of the European Parliament, P 603.472, January 2019).
[125] Niovi Vavoula, *Immigration and Privacy in the Law of the EU* (Brill Nijhoff 2022) 184–86, 278–79, 281–82, 357–60. See EU Fundamental Rights Agency (FRA), 'Under Watchful Eyes: Biometrics, EU IT-systems and Fundamental Rights' (2018) 81–98; European Court of Auditors, 'EU Information Systems Supporting Border Control - A Strong Tool, but More Focus Needed on Timely and Complete Data' (2019).
[126] 'Europol: "4x4" intelligence handling codes includes "dodgy data"' (*Statewatch*, 7 January 2013) <https://www.statewatch.org/news/2013/january/europol-4x4-intelligence-handling-codes-includes-dodgy-data/> accessed 10 July 2024.
[127] ibid.
[128] Andrea Romei and Salvatore Ruggieri, 'Discrimination Data Analysis: A Multi-disciplinary Bibliography' in B Custers and others (eds), *Discrimination and Privacy in the Information Society—Data Mining and Profiling*

of non-discrimination at all, in *La Quadrature du Net 'I'* the Court explicitly precluded the use of sensitive data from the pre-established models and criteria, when these are used *in isolation*.[129] Such sensitive data are meant those that can reveal a person's colour, race, ethnic or social origin, genetic features, language, political or any other opinion, religion, or philosophical belief, trade union membership, membership of a national minority, property, birth, disability, or sexual orientation. As acknowledged (later) in *Ligue des droits humains*, algorithmic analysis may lead to indirect discrimination, whereby the processing is not conducted by reference to a protected characteristic, such as those mentioned earlier, but by using proxies to protected characteristics. For example, using a person's address or occupation group may reveal their ethnic origin, a person's geolocation may also reveal colour, race, ethnic or social origin (for instance, in case someone's residence is located in a neighbourhood which is primarily populated by individuals originating from a specific country). Whereas recognising the impact of automated processing on non-discrimination, including indirect discrimination, is important, the pronouncement in *La Quadrature du Net 'I'* leaves open questions. A potential interpretation of this finding might be that sensitive data could be included in the dataset as long as it is introduced with non-sensitive data. The Court's numerous references to the principle of non-discrimination indicates that this kind of limited reading might not have been its intention, not least because to argue otherwise would still raise problems in relation to potentially 'indirect' differential treatment.[130] It, however, leaves the door open for permissible risk factors being based on a combination of sensitive data, such as gender and age (eg 'women below the age of x'). This is a rather low standard that allows for algorithms that would be particularly wide, resulting in a large number of erroneous matches, namely false positives that must then be weaved by the human in the loop.

Importantly, it does not take into account the potential of intersectional discrimination, understood as a form of discrimination occurring when a person is treated less favourably due to different protected grounds that, inseparably and simultaneously, operate and interact with one another. Indeed, automated systems may appear fair with respect to sensitive attributes considered separately, but be unfair with respect to intersectional subgroups.[131] It is true that intersectionality or intersectional discrimination has been partially and incrementally accepted by the CJEU. For example, in *Parris*, concerning the right of a same-sex partner to be entitled to a survivor's pension, the CJEU found that 'there is . . . no new category of discrimination resulting from the combination of more than one of those grounds' . . . that may be found to exist where discrimination based on those grounds

---

in Large Databases (Springer 2013) 109; EU Agency for Fundamental Rights (FRA), 'Big Data: Discrimination in Data-Supported Decision Making' (2018); Frederik Zuiderveen Borgesius, 'Discrimination, Artificial Intelligence, and Algorithmic Decision-Making' (Council of Europe, Directorate General of Democracy, 2018).

[129] *La Quadrature du Net 'I'* (n 3) para 181. Emphasis added.
[130] See Valsamis Mitsilegas and others, 'Data Retention and the Future of Large-Scale Surveillance: The Evolution and Contestation of Judicial Benchmarks' (2022) European Law Journal 176, 191.
[131] Alessandra Calvi, 'Exploring the Synergies between Non-Discrimination and Data Protection: What Role for EU Data Protection Law to Address Intersectional Discrimination?' (2023) 14(2) European Journal of Law & Technology; Abolfazl Asudeh and others, 'Designing Fair Ranking Schemes'(2019) Proceedings of the ACM SIGMOD International Conference on Management of Data 1259; Ke Yang, Joshua R Loftus, and Julia Stoyanovich, 'Causal Intersectionality and Fair Ranking'(2021) 192 Leibniz International Proceedings in Informatics, LIPIcs.

taken in isolation has not been established'.[132] This gap must be resolved to allow for the justiciability of intersectional discrimination claims and the protection of individuals, particularly the most vulnerable and marginalised ones. This is all the more necessary in cases of facial recognition technology; the algorithms embedded in facial recognition systems produce higher false positive matches in cases of black people and women, particularly of black women.[133] There is therefore scope for the CJEU to re-evaluate and reformulate its interpretation of discriminatory effect of automated processing when the occasion arises.

3.2.4 The 'human in the loop'

The CJEU judgments are adamant on the role of individual non-automated re-examination of a positive result before adopting a measure that may have adverse effect on the person concerned—the so-called human in the loop— because of the margin of error that may result from the automated processing. Similarly, in *La Quadrature du Net 'II'*, the Court stressed the need that prior review of conditions of access to data cannot take place in a manner entirely automated, but human intervention is necessary, The Court's standards need to be informed by significant literature on the different types of biases that may impact on the judgment of the human in the loop, influenced by what have been termed as automation bias, selective adherence bias or anchoring bias.[134] The former concept refers to situations where there is propensity to favour suggestions from automated decision-making tools. Rather pessimistically, Leese notes that 'the human reviewers lose true agency, as they can only enact what algorithmic categorizations indicate'.[135] Selective adherence or confirmation bias refers to situations where the human in the loop may have their own, culturally and historically grown biases against certain groups of individuals and therefore they may have more or less incentive to manually examine an application if the algorithmic result confirms or is at odds with their own prejudices and biases. This creates an additional layer of potential indirect or intersectional discrimination, which may be particularly difficult to detect due to the inherent opacity in decision-making. Anchoring bias refers to situations whereby the human decision-maker takes into account the first piece of evidence that is available to them, which tends to be the output of the automated processing. The standards elaborated in *Ligue des droits humains* about the need to (a) lay down clear and precise rules capable of providing guidance for the review, and aimed at (b) reliable documentation and self-monitoring, as well as (c) guaranteeing uniform administrative practices, whereby (d) the results of individual human reviews must take preference over those of automated processing are particularly important to uncover the extent to which there exist different types of biases. It is important that public or private decision-makers develop elaboration of practical handbooks with good or bad practices, cooperate within their respective fields with other bodies engaged with automated processing, organise dedicated trainings to raise

---

[132] CJEU, judgment of 24 November 2016 (C-443/15) *Parris v Trinity College and others* ECLI:EU:C:2016:897 para 80.

[133] National Institute for Standards and Technology (NIST), 'Face Recognition Vendor Test (FRVT) Part 3: Demographic Effects' (2019). See Pawel Drozdowski and others, 'Demographic Bias in Biometrics: A Survey on an Emerging Challenge' (2020) 1(2) IEEE Transactions on Technology and Society 89, 98.

[134] Saar Alon-Barkat and Madalina Busuioc, 'Human-AI Interactions in Public Sector Decision-Making: "Automation Bias" and "Selective Adherence" to Algorithmic Advice' (2023) 33(1) Journal of Public Administration Research and Theory 153.

[135] Matthias Leese, 'The New Profiling: Algorithms, Black Boxes, and the Failure of Anti-discriminatory Safeguards in the European Union' (2014) 45(5) Security Dialogue 494.

awareness about the existence of biases, which will assist in their mitigation and ultimately safeguarding the right to non-discrimination.

3.2.5 The 'human over the loop'

A final issue that requires further elaboration and potentially re-conceptualisation concerns the conduct of supervision by the national supervisory authority, typically data protection authorities, to ensure the monitoring of the lawfulness of the automated processing. According to the CJEU, this monitoring covers issues of non-discrimination. This brings to the fore two issues: first, it denotes the value of the right to personal data protection as a right that can safeguard other fundamental rights, such as the right to non-discrimination.[136] This approach was signalled already in *Huber* concerning an Austrian living in Germany who complained about his inclusion in a German database for foreigners that was much more comprehensive that any database on German nationals. In his complaint, he claimed that he had been discriminated against on the basis of nationality. The CJEU analysed the facts through the data protection lens and considered discrimination within the data protection analysis when examining the necessity of the processing, which was 'interpreted in the light of the prohibition on any discrimination on grounds of nationality'.[137] The case could be seen as signalling the instrumental nature of data protection (and privacy), which would safeguard the different rights at stake by internalising them within its internal balancing/proportionality exercise.[138] Second, it elevates national supervisory authorities as guardians of non-discrimination through data protection law by opining that their investigations, inspections, and audits may also concern those pre-determined criteria and those databases.

Data protection authorities constitute independent public authorities that supervise, through investigative and corrective powers, the application of the data protection law. They provide expert advice on data protection-related issues and handle complaints lodged against violations of EU data protection law and relevant national laws. The supervision conducted concerns all different forms of processing of personal data, including automated processing. At the same time, supervision of processing against algorithms (pre-determined models and criteria) is a particularly challenging task because the processing entails broader fundamental rights challenges that go beyond the protection of personal data, particularly in relation to the principle of non-discrimination. As a result, one might wonder whether data protection authorities have too big shoes to fill in the era of algorithms (and potentially AI). Second, the Court did not mandate how supervisory authorities should conduct their tasks, but rather allowed them to 'get their hands dirty' by investigating, inspecting or auditing the relevant pre-established criteria and databases. Advocate-General Mengozzi provided some additional insights into how supervision ought to take place noting that supervision must be 'able to cover all aspects inherent in the automated processing', 'including identifying the databases used to compare data ... and to draw

---

[136] Paul de Hert and Serge Gutwirth, 'Data Protection in the Case Law of Strasbourg and Luxembourg' in Serge Gutwirth and others (eds), *Reinventing Data Protection?* (Springer 2009); Maria Tzanou, *The Fundamental Right to Data Protection: Normative Value in the Context of Counter-Terrorism Surveillance* (Hart 2017) 24–31.

[137] CJEU, Judgment of 16 December 2008 (C-524/06) *Heinz Huber v Bundesrepublik Deutschland* EU:C:2008:724 ('*Huber*') para 66.

[138] Raphael Gellert and Serge Gutwirth, 'The Legal Construction of Privacy and Data Protection' (2013) 29 Computer Law & Security Review 530.

up the pre-determined criteria used for the analysis' and must take place both *ex ante* and *ex post*. The temporal issue raised by the Advocate-General is crucial; indeed, supervision must be on the ground and an ongoing, continuous process in order to track the data flows and how these have affected and shaped the final decision-making. Focusing solely on the human in the loop is one thing, but the pivotal role of the 'human over the loop' must also be highlighted and strengthened. For this, it is imperative that appropriate resources are allocated so that supervisory authorities have the capacity to exercise such intricate tasks.

3.3 The relationship with the right not to be subject to automated decision-making

Prohibition of *solely* automated decision-making have always found a place in EU data protection law[139] and more recently have received utmost attention as the field of artificial intelligence and machine learning has advanced.[140] Two main legal sources that impose prohibitions on solely automated decision making are Article 22 of the GDPR and Article 11 of the LED. A similar prohibition can also be found in the other EU legislation, such as Article 7(6) of the EU PNR Directive. Without intending to go into their scope or effectiveness of these provisions,[141] this chapter aims to highlight the pronouncements of the CJEU regarding the right not to be subject to automated decision-making, given that the Court seem to endorse a prohibition of automated decision-making at least in cases involving serious crime. Even in *La Quadrature du Net 'II'*, the Court was mindful to stress that an essentially automated review before access to the data by the Hadopi was not sufficient to prevent false positives and the risk of misuse of the data by third parties, but only required a periodical review of the integrity of the system by an independent body, without preventing a fully automated system as long as the substantial and procedural guarantees of the LED, as implemented by national law, existed and were applicable. Except the PNR Directive, the GDPR and the LED provide a *qualified* prohibition against fully automated decision-making and exceptionally allow solely automated decision-making in their respective contexts if certain conditions are fulfilled.[142] The Court's insistence on 'non-automatic

---

[139] Lee A Bygrave, 'Article 22 - Automated Individual Decision Making including Profiling' in Christopher Kuner, Lee A Bygrave, and Christopher Docksey (eds), *The EU General Data Protection Regulation (GDPR): A Commentary* (OUP 2020) 522.

[140] Isak Mendoza and Lee A Bygrave, 'The Right Not to Be Subject to Automated Decisions Based on Profiling' (University of Oslo Faculty of Law Research Paper No. 2017-20, 8 May 2017); Orla Lynskey, 'Criminal Justice Profiling and EU Data Protection Law: Precarious Protection from Predictive Policing' (2019) 15 International Journal of Law in Context 162.

[141] See Isak Mendoza and Lee A Bygrave, 'The Right Not to Be Subject to Automated Decisions Based on Profiling' (2017); Sandra Wachter, Brent Mittelstadt and Luciano Floridi, 'Why a Right to Explanation of Automated Decision-Making Does not Exist in the General Data Protection Regulation' (2017) 7(2) International Data Privacy Law 91; Maja Brkan 'Do Algorithms Rule the World? Algorithmic Decision-Making and Data Protection in the Framework of the GDPR and beyond' (2019) 27 International Journal of Law and Information Technology 91.

[142] Article 22(2) of the GDPR reads: '[p]aragraph 1 shall not apply if the decision: (a) is necessary for entering into, or performance of, a contract between the data subject and a data controller; (b) is authorised by Union or Member State law to which the controller is subject and which also lays down suitable measures to safeguard the data subject's rights and freedoms and legitimate interests; or (c) is based on the data subject's explicit consent'. Article 13 of the LED reads as '[m]ember States shall provide for a decision based solely on automated processing, including profiling, which produces an adverse legal effect concerning the data subject or significantly affects him or her, to be prohibited *unless* authorised by Union or Member State law to which the controller is subject and

intervention', as highlighted in *La Quadrature du Net 'I'*, seems to be absolute.[143] In its findings on non-automatic intervention, the CJEU endorses its dicta in *PNR Canada*, where the draft EU–Canada PNR Agreement in fact contained an absolute prohibition on automated decision-making.[144] There is thus room for clarification as to the basis on which such absolute prohibition (by requiring 'non-human intervention') is endorsed by the CJEU, considering that not all fully automated decisions would directly be incompatible with the Charter, since the GDPR and the LED allow exceptions to the prohibition. As highlighted elsewhere,[145] one way of viewing this could be to limit the Court's findings to the facts of the case. The automated analysis in question amounted to a derogation from the principle of confidentiality of communications for national security purposes, as set out in Article 15 of the ePrivacy Directive[146] because of the obligations imposed upon electronic communications service providers (*lex specialis*) and by extension the Charter applied. This interpretation, however, may raise an issue as to the relationship between *lex specialis* and *lex generalis* data protection law to the extent that the respective derogations constitute personal data processing.[147] In fact, the Court recognised in *La Quadrature du Net 'I'* the relationship between the ePrivacy Directive and the GDPR when it considered the legality of the retention of subscriber information.[148] In particular, it referred to Article 23 of the GDPR, which allows Member States to restrict the application of obligations and individual rights based on a number of grounds, one of which is to safeguard national security, defence, and public security.[149] Considering that the right not to be subjected to solely automated decision-making is one such right, fully automated decisions are, in theory and as a matter of exception, allowed by virtue of Article 23 of the GDPR, subject to the qualifications set out in that Article. Member States are limited as to the extent to which they may resort to the exceptions under Article 23, as they may only be exercised for a purpose specified in the Article, without interfering with the essence of fundamental rights and in accordance with the requirements of necessity and proportionality. In a way, the prohibition against solely automated decision-making under secondary legislation is still not an absolute prohibition as the Court portrayed it in its analysis on automated analysis of personal data in *La Quadrature du Net 'I'*. Clarity in terms of the reasoning of the Court in upholding a prohibition as such is necessary to understand the implications of the ruling in automated decision systems beyond this case, as—at least in theory—the secondary legislation allows for a derogation from the prohibition, albeit it must be scrutinised in light of fundamental rights protection.

---

which provides appropriate safeguards for the rights and freedoms of the data subject, at least the right to obtain human intervention on the part of the controller.' Emphasis added.

[143] *La Quadrature du Net 'I'* (n 1) para 182.
[144] *PNR Canada* (n 2) para 173.
[145] Mitsilegas and others, 'Data Retention and the Future of Large-Scale Surveillance: The Evolution and Contestation of Judicial Benchmarks' (2022).
[146] Directive 2002/58/EC of the European Parliament and of the Council of 12 July 2002 concerning the processing of personal data and the protection of privacy in the electronic communications sector (Directive on privacy and electronic communications) [2002] OJ L 201/37 ('ePrivacy Directive').
[147] On the relationship between the ePrivacy Directive and the GDPR see European Data Protection Board (EDPB), 'Opinion 5/2019 on the interplay between the ePrivacy Directive and the GDPR, in particular regarding the competence, tasks and powers of data protection authorities' (12 March 2019).
[148] *La Quadrature du Net 'I'* (n 1) para 202.
[149] ibid para 209.

3.4 The relationship with the AI Act

The final issue that this chapter aims to examine is the future of automated processing in light of the adoption of the AI Act, the text of which was agreed on. It is true that not all automated processing involves the use of AI; automated processing may operate based on rules-based systems that rely on knowledge elicited from experts and use predefined rules to make decisions, drawing upon practical experience and domain-specific knowledge. Machine learning systems infer procedures from examples and perform logical analysis. Machine learning systems are a sub-set of AI, as defined in the AI Act,[150] thus activating its safeguards. The AI Act adopts a risk-based approach, whereby different levels of risk (unacceptable, high, limited, and minimal) corresponding to certain AI systems and leading to regulation of varying levels of density.[151] The AI Act may compound the existing patchwork of EU data processing related instruments. For example, the exclusion of national security systems from the scope of the AI Act under Article 4 has significant implication for data retention schemes, whereby in accordance with *La Quadrature du Net 'I'*, automated analysis of traffic and location data is permissible to safeguard national security. As a result, in such cases, the safeguards of the AI Act will not apply, but the standards of the CJEU will. This is not the same as regards automated processing to conduct risk assessments of individuals, which according to Annex III of the AI Act, AI systems assessing the risk of a natural person offending or re-offending *not* solely on the basis of the profiling of natural persons, as referred to in Article 3(4) of LED, or to assess personality traits and characteristics or past criminal behaviour of natural persons or groups are classified as high risk. This leads to a series of legal obligations imposed on their providers, users, and third parties laid down in Articles 8–51 of the AI Act. In turn, according to Article 5(1)(d) of the AI Act, the use of an AI system for making risk assessments of natural persons in order to assess or predict the risk of a natural person committing a criminal offence, based solely on the profiling of a natural person or on assessing their personality traits and characteristics are prohibited. As a result, the AI Act adds another layer of standards and safeguards which must be applied in conjunction with the CJEU's standards.

4. Conclusion

This chapter aimed to provide a concise synthesis of the CJEU approach to automated processing of personal data and analyse its benefits and flaws to inform future jurisprudential development. As evidenced by the progressive elaboration of a rather comprehensive set of standards and safeguards—in line with the long-standing dicta that automated processing requires greater safeguards—judges have risen to the occasion by demonstrating a growing understanding of the underlying issues of automated processing, be it AI-powered or not. These safeguards have been pronounced in cases concerning two separate contexts;

---

[150] Article 3(1) defines AI as 'a machine-based system designed to operate with varying levels of autonomy and may exhibit adaptiveness after deployment and that, for a given set of explicit or implicit objectives, infers, from the input it receives, how to generate outputs such as predictions, content, recommendations, or decisions that can influence real or virtual environments'.
[151] See Athina Sachoulidou and Niovi Vavoula, 'Artificial Intelligence and Surveillance' in James Sperling and Sonia Lucarelli (eds), *Handbook on Governance and the EU* (Edward Elgar, forthcoming 2024).

automated analysis of telecommunications metadata on the one hand, and automated processing of PNR data. Yet, so far the case law appears internally consistent growing the appetite for their potential application in other domains where automated processing is foreseen or permitted under EU law. At the same time, the case law appears to be somewhat disconnected from EU data protection law, specifically the qualified prohibition of automated decision-making raising an eyebrow as to whether the respective articles in the GDPR and the LED should be reformed. In any case, the existing pronouncements leave much to be desired from the CJEU when faced with similar questions in future cases; the technical nature of automated processing and the significant risks for the right to non-discrimination create the need for more in depth safeguards on numerous fronts and potential reconceptualisation of the law on non-discrimination due to its inherent limited approach of the CJEU in 'traditional', non-technology related cases. In an era of AI and omnipresence of personal data processing, it remains to be see how the CJEU will further develop its case law and how the ECtHR will continue their constrictive dialogue.

25
Automated Analysis in the AFSJ and Digital Single Market Monitoring
An Effaced Nexus

Maria Grazia Porcedda

1. Introduction

Judgments issued by the Court of Justice of the European Union (CJEU) and the European Court of Human Rights (ECtHR) have progressively defined the contours of permissible practices of data processing for evidentiary purposes. In the data retention saga, the CJEU has considered the seriousness of the interference of evidentiary measures in light of the objectives that may justify such interferences, painting a matrix of permissible measures for the collection of e-evidence. In *La Quadrature du Net 'I'*, the automated analysis of metadata is understood as the 'screening of all metadata retained by providers'.[1] For the Court, it constitutes a particularly serious interference justified to counter a serious threat to national security that is shown to be genuine and present or foreseeable. In its case law on bulk data collection, the ECtHR breaks a system of intelligence gathering into four stages deemed to be progressively more intrusive into the right to privacy, where the automated application of explicit selectors (stage two) is not considered as serious an interference as the retention of data such as in the guise of an intelligence report (stage four).

Both Courts, irrespective of their different remits and the context of the cases they adjudicated on, thus authorize the use of automated analysis of data. In so doing, they implicitly endorse the gatekeeping role of private sector entities in charge of such data under the increasingly interchangeable hat of 'electronic communication services' and 'information society services'. The two Courts also sanction a practice that developed and arguably thrived in the margins of the law.

In this chapter I examine CJEU and ECtHR mass surveillance case law on automated analysis to bring to the fore the effaced role of monitoring by 'electronic communication services' and 'information society services' (section 2). Building on scholarship on the fragmentary EU rules on monitoring[2] and the gatekeeping role of the private

---

[1] CJEU, Judgment of 6 October 2020, *La Quadrature du Net and others* (C-511/18, C-512/18 and C-520/18) ECLI:EU:C:2020:791 ('*La Quadrature du Net 'I'*) para 172.

[2] Sophie Stalla-Bourdillon, 'Online Monitoring, Filtering, Blocking... What is the Difference? Where to Draw the Line?' (2013) 29 Computer Law & Security Review, 702–12; Rojszczak, 'Online Content Filtering in EU Law – A Coherent Framework or Jigsaw Puzzle?' (2022) 47 Computer Law & Security Review; Maria Grazia Porcedda, *Cybersecurity, Privacy and Data Protection in EU Law: A Law, Policy and Technology Analysis* (Hart Publishing 2023) chs 6 and 7.

sector,[3] I produce original research on the diachronic evolution of rules on 'electronic communication services' and 'information society services', which were once distinct entities but have become increasingly interchangeable (section 3) to the effect that protections against monitoring have been seriously diluted. I then review the implications of the nexus between automated analysis and monitoring as against the broader architecture of EU information technology law (section 4).[4] I will show how the role of intermediaries in automated analysis relates to the nexus between legislation in the Digital Single Market (DSM) and Area of Freedom, Security and Justice (AFSJ), and is difficult to address in light of the 'effacement of information technology from the law' and the 'indeterminacy loop' that characterize EU DSM law. Unpacking these dynamics is crucial for the development of meaningful recommendations.

The 'effacement of information technology from the law' and 'indeterminacy loop'[5] explain dynamics of de-politicization of technology in the 1980s that were instrumental to the creation of the Common Market and the adoption of future-proof regulation supportive of innovation. The effacement of technology results in an indeterminacy loop, whereby lawmakers and courts rarely, if ever, engage with actual technologies to determine if they meet or undermine legislative goals. There are thus no mechanisms to foster or ban actual technologies, since the responsibility for doing so has shifted from legal processes to the market.

Private sector entities gather, analyse, and retain data under multiple frameworks that classify them differently (electronic communication or information society services) depending on the nature of the activities they conduct. These frameworks are premised on the effacement of information technology from the law, which leads to overlook the tools that implement such provisions and how such tools often egregiously undermine the fundamental right objectives underpinning such legislation. As a result of such an effacement, monitoring provisions ignore and arguably aggravate the content/metadata divide, with serious implications for the protection of the essence of the right to private life. Since technology is effaced from the law, the Courts' assessment is tech-agnostic, so that judgments amplify the effacement of information technology from the law and thus foster high levels of indeterminacy.

I conclude the chapter with a recommendation to assess the permissibility of automated analysis in light of provisions on monitoring and the uncertain divide on content and metadata, pending significant legislative developments, to question the need for siloed legislation and to actively engage with the technological state of the art to attempt to steer it.

---

[3] Among many: Uta Kohl, 'The Rise and Rise of Online Intermediaries in the Governance of the Internet and Beyond – Connectivity Intermediaries' (Part 1) (2012) 26 International Review of Law, Computers and Technology (2–3); Lilian Edwards, 'With Great Power Comes Great Responsibility' in Lilian Edwards (ed) *Information Technology Law* (Hart Publishing 2019); Giancarlo Frosio and Sunimal Mendis, 'Monitoring and Filtering: European Reform or Global Trend?' in Giancarlo Frosio (ed), *Oxford Handbook of Online Intermediary Liability* (OUP 2020); Valsamis Mitsilegas, Elspeth Guild, Elif Kuskonmaz, and Niovi Vavoula 'Data Retention and the Future of Large-scale Surveillance: The Evolution and Contestation of Judicial Benchmarks' (2022) 29(1–2) European Law Journal 14; Grazia Porcedda, *Cybersecurity*, ibid. See also debates under 'digital constitutionalism', 'private regulation', and 'private ordering'.

[4] Grazia Porcedda, *Cybersecurity*, ibid; Maria Grazia Porcedda, 'The Effacement of Information Technology from EU Law: The Need for Collaborative Approaches to Redesign the EU's Regulatory Architecture', in F Bieker, S De Conca, I Schiering, N Gruschka, and M Jensen, *Proceedings of the 18th IFIP Summer School 2023: Advances in Information and Communication Technology* (Springer, forthcoming).

[5] Grazia Porcedda, *Cybersecurity*, ibid 141–56.

2. Automated Analysis in CJEU Data Retention and ECtHR Mass Surveillance Case Law

This section examines automated analysis in recent landmark mass surveillance cases of the CJEU and ECtHR. I first examine the approach of the CJEU in *La Quadrature du Net 'I'* and, to a lesser extent, *Privacy International*[6] and *La Quadrature du Net 'II'*,[7] where automated analysis features obliquely. I then analyse the approach of the Grand Chamber of the ECtHR in *Centrum för Rättvisa v Sweden*[8] and *Big Brother Awards v UK*,[9] which act as the minimum standard of protection of the right to private life, especially when EU law does not apply. I finally place automated analysis in the context of electronic communication and intermediation services, thus building a bridge with section three.

2.1 Automated analysis in the CJEU data retention saga after *La Quadrature du Net 'I'*

Automated analysis is one of several measures authorised by national data retention law concerning the retention and access of traffic, location, and related data that have come under scrutiny of the CJEU since *Privacy International* and *La Quadrature du Net 'I'*.[10]

Table 25.1 shows permissible measures, the interference they cause to the rights to private life and data protection, the objectives of general interest that justify such interferences[11] and the safeguards that must be put in place to make such interferences proportionate. Automated analysis is second from the top, among the measures deemed to cause a particularly serious interference in *La Quadrature du Net 'I'*.

Missing from Table 25.1 are measures prohibited by the Court, which include the preventative general and indiscriminate retention of traffic and location data[12] for any offences and to combat market abuse offences including insider dealing.[13] The Court also found the general and indiscriminate retention of personal data relating to access to online public communication services and hosting service providers impermissible.[14] Another unlawful measure is the centralized processing of requests for access to data issued by the police in the context of the investigation or prosecution of serious criminal offences by a police officer.[15] For the Court, the degree of interference of a measure is the same for retention and for access, although legislation governing access to retained data 'cannot be limited to requiring that the authorities' access to such data should correspond to the objective pursued

---

[6] CJEU, Judgment of 6 October 2020, *Privacy International* (C-623/17) ECLI:EU:C:2020:790.
[7] CJEU, Judgment of 30 April 2024, *La Quadrature du Net a.o. c. Premier Ministre and Ministre de la Culture* (C-470/21) ECLI:EU:C:2024:370 ('*La Quadrature du Net 'II'*').
[8] ECtHR, *Centrum för Rättvisa v Sweden* [GC], no. 35252/08, 25 May 2021.
[9] ECtHR, *Big Brother Watch and others v the United Kingdom* [GC], nos. 58170/13 and 2 others, 25 May 2021.
[10] CJEU, Judgment of 2 March 2021, *Prokuratuur* (C-746/18) ECLI:EU:C:2021:152; CJEU, Judgment of 5 April 2022, *Commissioner of An Garda Síochána* (C-140/20) ECLI:EU:C:2022:258; CJEU, Judgment of 20 September 2022, *VD and SR* (C-339/20 and C-397/20) ECLI:EU:C:2022:703 ('*VD and SR*'); CJEU, Judgment of 27 October 2022, *SpaceNet* (C-793/19 and C-794/19) ECLI:EU:C:2022:702.
[11] Provided there is a connection between such objectives and the data being processed.
[12] *La Quadrature du Net 'I'* (n 1) para 229 (1).
[13] *VD and SR* (n 10) para 108 (1).
[14] *La Quadrature du Net 'I'* (n 1) para 229 (3).
[15] *Garda Síochána* (n 10) para 129 (2).

Table 25.1 Matrix of interference and permissibility of measures in *La Quadrature du Net 'I'* (LQdN I) and *'II'* (LQdN II)

	Measure	Obj. of general interest	Binding decision	Verify objective of general interest	Verify observance of safeguards	Verify prior necessity	Effectiveness
Particularly serious interference	recourse to an instruction requiring providers of electronic communication services to retain, generally and indiscriminately, traffic and location data (§ 229 LQdN I)	serious threat to national security that is shown to be genuine and present or foreseeable	X	X	X		X
	automated analysis *inter alia* of <u>traffic and location data</u> (§ 229 LQdN I)		X	X	X		X
	real-time collection *inter alia* of <u>traffic and location data</u> <u>(can be expedited)</u> (§ 229 LQdN I)		X			X	X
	• Including real-time collection of technical data concerning the <u>location</u> of the terminal equipment used		X			X	X
Serious interference	targeted retention of traffic and location data limited according to the categories of persons concerned or using a geographical criterion (§ 229 LQdN I)	safeguarding national security, combating serious crime and preventing serious threats to public security					
	general and indiscriminate retention of IP addresses assigned to the source of an Internet connection (§ 229 LQdN I)						
	general and indiscriminate retention of IP addresses drawing precise conclusions about [a] person (§82 LQdN II)	combating serious crime			X		
	Electronic communication services to undertake the expedited retention of traffic and location data in their possession (§ 229 LQdN I)	combating serious crime and, a fortiori, safeguarding national security					X
	general and indiscriminate retention of data relating to the civil identity of users (§ 229 LQdN I)	safeguarding national security, combating serious crime and preventing serious threats to public security					
Interference not serious in principle	general and indiscriminate retention of a set of static and dynamic IP addresses used by a person in a given period (§ 79, 82 LQdN II)	Combating serious crime, criminal offences in general					
	retention and access to traffic and location data as authorized by Art 6 ePrivacy Directive (§98 LQdN II)	combating criminal offences in general					X

Limits to measure			Other safeguards			
Time (extendable)	Time	Factors: objective, non-discriminatory	Compliance with substantive/ procedural conditions	Effective against risks of abuse	Valid terrorist suspicion	Watertight separation
X			X			
					X	
					X	
X		X	X			
	X		X			
						X
		X				
			X			
						X
				X		X

by that legislation, but must also lay down the substantive and procedural conditions governing that use'.[16]

Automated analysis came to the fore in *La Quadrature du Net 'I'*, where the French *Conseil d'État* asked the CJEU to assess the compatibility of L-851.3 of the *Code de la sécurité intérieure* (CSI) with Article 15(1) ePrivacy Directive,[17] read in the light of Articles 7, 8, 11, and 52(1) Charter of Fundamental Rights of the EU (Charter).[18] For the referring court, L-851.3 'requires providers of electronic communications services to implement, on their networks, measures allowing ... the automated analysis and real-time collection of traffic and location data'[19] without directly identifying data subjects, to detect links 'that might constitute a terrorist threat'.[20]

The CJEU preliminarily notes that automated analysis pursuant to Article L. 851-3 is performed on data that cannot be considered to be anonymous, because such data concern persons that can be identified.[21] As a result, automated analysis falls within the scope of data protection law.[22] Following the Court, that automated analysis:

> corresponds, in essence, to a *screening* of all the traffic and location data retained by providers of electronic communications services, which is **carried out by those providers at the request of the competent national authorities applying the parameters set by the latter**. It follows that all data of users of electronic communications systems is *verified if it corresponds to those parameters*. Therefore, such automated analysis must be considered as involving, for the providers of electronic communications services concerned, the undertaking on behalf of the competent authority of *general and indiscriminate processing*, in the form of the use of that data *with the assistance of an automated operation*, within the meaning of Article 4(2) of Regulation 2016/679, *covering all traffic and location data of all users* of electronic communications systems. That processing is independent of the subsequent collection of data relating to the persons identified following that automated analysis.[23]

The CJEU finds the interference caused by such a measure with rights enshrined in the Charter to be particularly serious due to its breadth, depth, and wholesale nature. The measure covers, 'generally and indiscriminately, the data of persons using electronic communication systems', 'is likely to reveal the nature of the information consulted online' and 'is applied generally to all persons',[24] including people that do not have links with terrorist activities. As with time-limited general and indiscriminate retention, such a serious interference can 'meet the requirement of proportionality only in situations in which a Member State is facing a serious threat to national security which is shown to be genuine and present

---

[16] *La Quadrature du Net 'I'* (n 1) para 177.
[17] Directive 2002/58/EC of the European Parliament and of the Council of 12 July 2002 concerning the processing of personal data and the protection of privacy in the electronic communications sector (Directive on privacy and electronic communications) [2002] OJ L 201/37.
[18] Charter of Fundamental Rights of the European Union [2012] OJ C326/391 (Charter). See further on this issue Maxime Lassalle, Chapter 11 of this volume.
[19] *La Quadrature du Net 'I'* (n 1) para 169.
[20] ibid para 170. The measure is described at para 43.
[21] ibid para 171.
[22] ibid para 172.
[23] ibid para 172. L-851.3 is described at paras 43 and 41.
[24] ibid para 174.

or foreseeable, and provided that the duration of that retention is limited to what is strictly necessary'.[25]

The safeguards placed on the performance of automated analysis are also similar to those required for time-limited general and indiscriminate retention measures. Legislation authorizing automated analysis 'must lay down the substantive and procedural conditions governing'[26] access to such data by authorities and 'be subject to effective review, either by a court or by an independent administrative body whose decision is binding, the aim of that review being to verify that a situation justifying that measure exists and that the conditions and safeguards that must be laid down are observed'.[27]

The Court identifies parameters akin to caveats of efficacy for the 'pre-established models and criteria', that is, the algorithms and selectors for automated analysis. First, the models and criteria should be reliable, that is they should enable to identify individuals that raise a reasonable suspicion of involvement in terrorist offences. Secondly, the models and criteria should be non-discriminatory. Thus, algorithms and selectors for automated analysis cannot draw on sensitive data[28] in isolation. Finally, in light of the potential for false positives inherent in the use of automated analysis, 'any positive result obtained following automated processing must be subject to an individual re-examination by non-automated means before an individual measure adversely affecting the persons concerned is adopted'.[29] The algorithms, selectors and databases used for automated analysis should also be subject to 'regular re-examination'.[30] The CJEU reiterates that the processing of content data by Electronic Communication Services (hereafter ECSs) is prohibited.[31]

Mitsilegas, Guild, Kuskonmaz, and Vavoula note these criteria are adapted from the Court's discussion of automated analysis in *PNR Canada*.[32] It is important to note that the constraints and safeguards placed on the use of automated analysis apply solely to ECSs in the context of data protection law (section 2.3).

Automated analysis also appears in *La Quadrature du Net 'II'*, which stems from a dispute concerning the French decree 'System for the management of measures for the protection of works on the Internet' pursuant to Article 331-21 of the Intellectual Property Code (IPC).[33] The decree authorizes the French public authority Hadopi 'to establish a system for the automated processing of personal data'[34] of individuals suspected of infringing the IPC, which the Court divides into 'upstream' and 'downstream'[35] data processing measures. At face value, 'upstream' processing appears to relate to the mass filtering of IP addresses to detect intellectual property infringements, while 'downstream' processing seems to concern the matching of IP addresses with the civil identity of the holders of those IP addresses.

The Court focuses on 'downstream processing' as a derogation from Articles 5 and 15 ePrivacy Directive and an interference with Charter rights. A serious interference with Article 7 only arises if downstream measures allow to draw precise conclusions about

---

[25] ibid para 177.
[26] ibid para 176.
[27] ibid para 179.
[28] ibid para 181.
[29] ibid para 182.
[30] ibid para 182.
[31] ibid.
[32] Mitsilegas et al (n 3).
[33] *La Quadrature du Net 'II'* (n 7) para 2.
[34] ibid para 26.
[35] ibid paras 54–55.

individuals concerned, which can be avoided by enforcing 'watertight separation between the categories of data retained' following a number of criteria.[36] When measures would allow to track the clickstream of individuals concerned, they must be accompanied by prior review, which cannot be fully automated.[37] Thus, the Court refers to 'automated analysis' only obliquely, as a necessity 'explained by the massive number of instances of counterfeiting detected'[38] which 'carry a real risk of systemic impunity'.[39] However, on account of its liability to detect false positives or to be misused, the Court finds that automated analysis must be subject to periodic independent review to ensure its integrity and effectiveness.[40]

2.2 Automated analysis in the ECtHR judgments of *Big Brother Watch* and *Centrum för Rättvisa*

In its case law, the ECtHR defers to the CJEU for the assessment of data retention regimes of ECHR Contracting States that are also EU Member States.[41] For what concerns intelligence gathering other than that based on data retention legislation, the ECtHR reviews the permissibility of processing not only 'metadata' but also content data, and draws a distinction between the levels of intrusiveness of data gathering and of access to data already gathered.

In *Centrum för Rättvisa* and *Big Brother Watch*, the ECtHR Grand Chamber examines the compatibility of bulk interception of cross-border communications by intelligence services in Sweden and the United Kingdom respectively with Article 8 ECHR. It does so in light of 'end-to-end safeguards' to interception, meaning that the assessment of necessity and proportionality is to be carried out at all stages of the process. Indeed, the ECtHR subdivides the bulk interception of (cross-border) communications into four ideal stages, as the court takes them to be[42] in light of 'limited information about the manner in which those regimes operate'.[43] The stages, shown in Table 25.2, are identically described in both judgments.[44]

Following the Venice Commission's finding that the 'the main interference with privacy occur[s] when stored personal data [are] processed and/or accessed by the agencies',[45] the ECtHR treats 'bulk interception as a gradual process in which the degree of interference with individuals' Article 8 rights increases as the process progresses'.[46] This approach is shown in Figure 25.1. In its analysis of the permissibility of the intrusion with privacy rights, the Court carries out a joint assessment of the four stages' accordance with the law and their necessity in a democratic society.[47]

At the heart of the pragmatic approach taken by the Court lie concerns around the harmful implications of technological development for the security of Contracting States

---

[36] ibid paras 82 and 84–89.
[37] ibid para 151.
[38] ibid para 154.
[39] ibid para 119.
[40] ibid para 156.
[41] eg *Big Brother Watch* (n 9) para 467.
[42] ibid para 325.
[43] ibid para 323.
[44] *Centrum för Rättvisa* (n 8) paras 239–45; *Big Brother Watch* (n 9) paras 325–30.
[45] *Centrum för Rättvisa*, ibid para 244; *Big Brother Watch*, ibid para 30.
[46] *Centrum för Rättvisa*, ibid para 239; *Big Brother Watch*, ibid para 325.
[47] eg *Big Brother Watch*, ibid para 334.

Table 25.2 Stages of a system of bulk intelligence gathering

	Stages	Description	Interference
I	'(a) the interception and initial retention of communications and related communications data (that is, the traffic data belonging to the intercepted communications), "(or "packets" of electronic communications)'	'electronic communications (or "packets" of electronic communications) will belong to a large number of individuals, many of whom will be of no interest whatsoever to the intelligence services. Some communications of a type unlikely to be of intelligence interest may be filtered out at this stage.'	'not...aparticularly significant Interference'
II	'(b) the application of specific selectors to the retained communications/related communications data';	'The initial searching, which is mostly automated... when different types of selectors, including "strong selectors" (such as an email address) and/or complex queries are applied to the retained packets of communications and related communications data. This may be the stage where the process begins to target individuals through the use of strong selectors.'	
III	'(c) the examination of selected communications/related communications data by analysts';	'intercept material is examined for the first time by an analyst.'	
IV	'(d) the subsequent retention of data and use of the "final product", including the sharing of data with third parties'.	'when the intercept material is actually used by the intelligence services. This may involve the creation of an intelligence report, the disseminating of the material to other intelligence services within the intercepting State, or even the transmission of material to foreign intelligence services.'	'the need for safeguards will be at its highest'

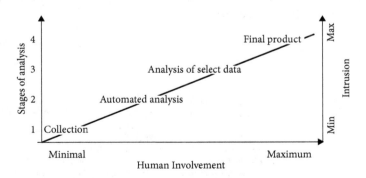

Figure 25.1 Diagram of intrusiveness of data collection according to human involvement.

and their citizens. The ECtHR grants a wide margin of appreciation to ECHR Contracting States[48]—arguably ampler than the CJEU to EU Member States—in light of the complexity of new threats, which include global terrorism, cyber-attacks and the sexual exploitation of children.

The Court acknowledges that bulk interception is a 'valuable technological capacity to identify new threats in the digital domain',[49] which differs from targeted data collection in light of its international focus, foreign intelligence and counter-espionage objective and application.[50] In particular, bulk interception is applied to data flows through 'packets', instead of devices. On this basis, the ECtHR defines a regime of end-to-end safeguards based on continuous supervision and assessment: bulk gathering must first be independently authorized, it must be supervised throughout and it finally must be subject to *ex post facto* review.[51] The Court draws two lists of safeguards to reduce the State's margin of appreciation, one for targeted interceptions, the other for bulk interception.[52] Thus, the ECtHR identifies minimum requirements that apply to the regime of bulk intelligence-gathering as a whole, rather than its single components.

As noted, the automated nature of the processing is among the reasons why bulk retention differs from targeted retention:

> While bulk interception is not necessarily used to target specified individuals, it evidently can be—and is—used for this purpose. However, when this is the case, the targeted individuals' devices are not monitored. Rather, individuals are 'targeted' by the application of strong selectors (such as their email addresses) to the communications intercepted in bulk by the intelligence services. Only those 'packets' of the targeted individuals' communications which were travelling across the bearers selected by the intelligence services will have been intercepted in this way, and only those intercepted communications which matched either a strong selector or complex query could be examined by an analyst.[53]

Thus, the interference caused by automated processing with privacy rights may be significant, but not the most serious because individuals are targeted through the use of strong selectors rather than through their devices. Although the Court draws from *S and Marper v UK* to justify the need for safeguards at this stage,[54] automated analysis is not deemed to be as intrusive as other stages shown in Table 25.2 and Figure 25.1, due to the limited human involvement in the intelligence-gathering process.

---

[48] *Big Brother Watch*, ibid paras 38–39, subject to safeguards.
[49] *Centrum för Rättvisa* (n 8) para 237; *Big Brother Watch*, ibid para 323.
[50] *Centrum för Rättvisa*, ibid paras 254–61; *Big Brother Watch*, ibid paras 341, 344–46.
[51] *Centrum för Rättvisa*, ibid para 264; *Big Brother Watch*, ibid para 350.
[52] *Centrum för Rättvisa*, ibid para 275; *Big Brother Watch*, ibid paras 335, 361.
[53] *Centrum för Rättvisa*, ibid para 260; *Big Brother Watch*, ibid para 346. See para 417 and also para 96 on RIPA.
[54] *S and Marper v the United Kingdom*, nos. 30562/04 and 30566/04 4 December 2008. In *Centrum för Rättvisa* (n 8) para 244; *Big Brother Watch* (n 9) para 326.

2.3 Automated analysis, electronic communication and intermediation services

The two Courts engage with automated 'analysis' or processing under different circumstances. The CJEU engages with it as one of the discrete national measures in the context of references for preliminary ruling, while the ECtHR considers automated processing as a component of a hypothetical regime of bulk intelligence-gathering. In general, the two courts take different views as to the intrusiveness of automated analysis into rights, and the ECtHR seems to treat automated analysis more favourably than the CJEU, although with signs of cross-fertilization.

For the ECtHR, automated analysis is not particularly intrusive because of the limited human involvement it entails. Judge Pinto de Albuquerque finds the distinction between types of interception to be the weakest argument of *Big Brother Watch*, insofar as it gives 'the impression that bulk interception based on strong selectors is less intrusive than the old-fashioned monitoring of an individual's devices'.[55] He finds the former to be 'a potentially much more intrusive form of interference with Article 8 rights than the mere monitoring of' devices, citing to this effect *Digital Rights Ireland*.[56] On this point, 'General Michael Hayden, former director of both the NSA and the CIA' has been reported to say '"We kill people based on metadata"'.[57]

The CJEU has deemed automated analysis a very serious interference, permissible only to respond to a genuine, and at least foreseeable, serious threat to national security. This approach was met favourably by Rojszczak, who suggests that automated analysis (algorithmic retention) with the safeguards identified by the CJEU and the ECtHR could represent a reasonable compromise for data collection between sweeping preventative retention and ineffective targeted retention.[58] Mitsilegas and colleagues consider it to be a step in the right direction but note the absence of accepted methods for algorithmic auditing and that the safeguards identified by the Court may be insufficient to protect against the risks of indirect algorithmic bias.[59] Furthermore, they note the decision questions the interplay between automated analysis and automated decision-making enshrined in Articles 22 and 23 GDPR, a pressing matter due the development of artificial intelligence automated decision-making tools.[60] On point, *La Quadrature du Net 'II'* discounts the full automation of prior review in the context of intellectual property infringement proceedings.[61]

---

[55] Partly Concurring and Partly Dissenting Opinion of by Judge Pinto de Albuquerque in *Big Brother Watch*, ibid para 12.
[56] Partly Concurring and Partly Dissenting Opinion of by Judge Pinto de Albuquerque in *Big Brother Watch*, ibid, referring to para 346 of the judgment.
[57] Stephen Farrell, Farzaneh Badiei, Bruce Schenier, and Steven M Bellovin, 'Reflections on Ten Years Past the Snowden Revelations', *Request For Comments 9446* (Internet Engineering Task Force 2023) <https://datatracker.ietf.org/doc/rfc9446/> accessed 15 July 2024, citing L Ferran, 'Ex-NSA Chief: "We Kill People Based on Metadata"', ABC News, May 2014, <https://abcnews.go.com/blogs/headlines/2014/05/ex-nsa-chief-we-kill-people-based-on-metadata> accessed 27 September 2024.
[58] Marcin Rojszczak, 'National Security and Retention of Telecommunications Data in Light of Recent Case Law of the European Courts' (2021) 17 European Constitutional Law Review, 608, 630, and 634.
[59] Mitsilegas et al 16.
[60] ibid 16–17 and 31.
[61] *La Quadrature du Net 'II'* (n 7) paras 148–51.

However, in keeping with Murphy's observation of cross-fertilization between the CJEU and ECtHR in mass surveillance cases,[62] there are signs of convergence. In *La Quadrature du Net 'II'* concerning measures that are 'the result of essentially automated data processing',[63] the CJEU finds that 'the intensity of the infringement of the right [to privacy] is likely to increase as the graduated response procedure ... progresses through its various stages'.[64] Those stages entail the progressive acquisition of information on individuals concerned, making the Court's reasoning evocative of *Big Brother Watch* (see Figure 25.1). More importantly, both courts authorize the use of automated data analysis, subject to different safeguards in their judgments (compare Tables 25.1 and 25.3). The contemporary ecosystem of online communication and intermediation services within which automated analysis is used does not form part of the courts' reasoning, except for a consideration of whether the analysis is performed by the service provider or by the public authorities themselves. The ECtHR rightly notes little knowledge is available about the practical operations of regimes of bulk data gathering, which limits the analysis to the hypothetical system as the Court takes it to be. As for the CJEU, such an ecosystem is implicit in the discussion of data retention measures and instrumental in determining the applicability of EU law. The public-private partnership that is data retention has not escaped commentators.

Rojszczak recalls how the introduction of the Data Retention Directive[65] caused a dispute among Member States as to whether a security measure 'constitutes an element of harmonization of internal market rules'.[66] He adds that, in the data retention saga, the CJEU has had to interpret 'Article 4(2) of the TEU' so as to respect the national identity of states, without hindering 'the standardisation of telecommunication rules applied within the internal market'.[67] Mistilegas and colleagues note that by emphasizing the statutory role of the private sector in retaining data and preventing public authorities from directly accessing retained data 'the Court recognised the privatisation of surveillance as a key factor to ensure the applicability of EU law'.[68]

One fundamental observation is that the ecosystem of private-public data retention measures is much more complex in 2024 than it was in 2006. *La Quadrature du Net 'I'* and *'II'* offer a glimpse into such a complexity within the remit of the questions posed to the CJEU.

The referring Court in the joined case of *Ordre des Barreaux* (C-512/18) asked the CJEU whether the provisions of the eCommerce Directive,[69] read in the light the Charter, preclude 'national legislation which requires providers of access to online public communication services and hosting service providers to retain, generally and indiscriminately, inter

---

[62] Maria Helen Murphy, 'Algorithmic Surveillance: The Collection Conundrum' (2017) 31 International Review of Law, Computers & Technology 12, 226. There, she urges to question whether the strengthening of safeguards can meet the challenges of mass collection and algorithmic processing (235).
[63] *La Quadrature du Net 'II'* (n 7) para 154.
[64] ibid para 140.
[65] Directive 2006/24/EC of the European Parliament and of the Council of 15 March 2006 on the retention of data generated or processed in connection with the provision of publicly available electronic communications services or of public communications networks and amending Directive 2002/58/EC [2006] OJ L 105/54.
[66] Rojszczak, 'National Security' (n 58) 608.
[67] ibid 616.
[68] Mistilegas, Guild, Kuskonmaz, and Vavoula (n 3) 6.
[69] Directive 2000/31/EC on certain legal aspects of information society services, in particular electronic commerce, in the internal market (Directive on Electronic Commerce) [2002] OJ L178/1.

alia, personal data relating to those services'. These are Information Society Services (ISSs), which, following the *Skype Communications* (and *Google*) cases, are classed as ECSs to the extent that they consist wholly or mainly in the conveyance of signals on electronic communications networks,[70] and thus come under the remit of the ePrivacy Directive.[71] The Court suggests that the referring court may find that some of the service providers are ECSs.[72]

Thus, the conditions disciplining automated analysis by ISSs are not discussed by the Court. The CJEU draws from Recitals 14 and 15 eCommerce Directive to clarify that obligations, derogations, and limitations relating to the protection of personal data and the confidentiality of communications are disciplined by data protection and e-privacy legislation, rather than the eCommerce Directive framework[73] disciplining hosting and transmission intermediaries. The meaningfulness of such a distinction must be discussed in light of today's e-communication and intermediation ecosystem.

Before I do so, it is important to note that the measures at stake in *La Quadrature du Net 'II'* apply both to ECS and ISSs.[74] The wording of the judgment suggests that ISSs are mainly involved in data processing 'upstream', while ECSs are mainly involved in data processing 'downstream', but this matter is for further research. The referring court did not raise questions around monitoring under eCommerce legislation and, on its part, the CJEU does not bring up the eCommerce Directive nor its case law on monitoring for intellectual property infringement (see sections 3.2 and 3.3). By limiting the analysis to 'downstream' data processing, the judgment eschews the complexities of the e-communication and intermediation ecosystem, to which I turn now.

3. Automated Analysis in the Digital Single Market: E-communication, Online Intermediation Services, and Monitoring

The importance of discussing what falls within the scope of an ECS becomes clear in light of the invalidated Data Retention Directive and the ePrivacy Directive, which apply to publicly available ECSs in public electronic communications networks. The ecosystem of e-communication and online intermediation services, within which automated analysis can be used, has developed over three decades that bore witness to the liberalization of Telcos and commercialization of the internet. Here I analyse such an evolution along two lines: silos and monitoring.

First, e-communication and intermediation services have traditionally been regulated in silos. This remains the case even though the lines between silos have deteriorated due to

---

[70] Case C-142/18, *Skype Communications*, EU:C:2019:460 ; Case C-193/18, *Google*, EU:C:2019:498. Cited in LQdN, C-511/18, paras 204–205.
[71] Directive 2002/58/EC of the European Parliament and of the Council of 12 July 2002 concerning the processing of personal data and the protection of privacy in the electronic communications sector (Directive on privacy and electronic communications) [2002] OJ L 201/37, as amended by Directive 2009/136/EC of 25 November 2009.
[72] *La Quadrature du Net 'I'* (n 1) para 203.
[73] ibid para 199.
[74] *La Quadrature du Net 'II'* (n 7) para 23, citing the French transposition of the European Electronic Communications Code and the E-commerce Directive.

'convergence'.[75] Silos are however kept in place by non-prejudice clauses found within the respective frameworks.

Secondly, rules for innovative online services after the liberalization of telcos created new powers for private and public actors that necessitated the creation of safeguards against the risk of dragnet surveillance. This, however, is not to say that monitoring was altogether banned. In fact, the wide margins of uncertainty generated by the effacement of technology from the law (section four) created room for harnessing monitoring, such as automated analysis, to support a variety of interests.

In the following, I split the analysis between three periods: 1998–2007, 2008–2017, and 2017–present. The period between 1998 and 2007 saw the development of a framework for telecommunications and online intermediation services which erected the barriers between e-communication services and information society services, to allow the latter to thrive. The unease of the divide started to show between 2008 and 2017. The last period saw a major overhaul of the regulation of data protection, e-communication and intermediation services in which the divide is left unaddressed through non-prejudice clauses, as against the overlap of the services over which such regulation is enforced. I conclude the analysis with an overview of the confusing and fragmented rules on monitoring that enable the use of automated analysis.

3.1 The evolution of rules on digital service provision and monitoring: from neat distinction to blurred lines between ECSs, ISSs and monitoring clauses

The Data Retention Directive was an exception to the ePrivacy Directive, in turn the *lex specialis* of the Data Protection Directive. The ePrivacy Directive repealed the 1997 Directive on the processing of personal data and privacy in telecommunications, obsoleted by the uptake of mobile telephony, internet connectivity, and the demise of state communication monopolies at the turn of the millennium as part of the e-communications reform known as 'Telecoms Package'. The Framework Directive[76] advocated a single regulatory framework for all transmission networks and services in light of '[t]he convergence of the telecommunications, media and information technology sectors', but separated 'the regulation of transmission from the regulation of content'.[77]

This made sense in light of the limited functional equivalence between telcos, broadcasting/media, and internet service providers: traditional telephony functions, media fruition and web hosting were all clearly distinguishable. The exercise of editorial control, the carriage or storage of content, interoperability, and interconnectivity were consequently regulated in silos, often involving a complex structure of non-communicating national regulatory (supervisory) authorities.

---

[75] Whereby 'electronic technology is bringing all modes of communication into one grand system', Ithiel De Sola Pool, *The Technologies of Freedom* (Harvard University Press 1983), cited in Andrew Murray, *Information Technology Law. The Law and Society* (3rd edn, OUP 2019) 50.

[76] Directive 2002/21/EC on a common regulatory framework for electronic communications networks and services (Framework Directive), OJ L108 [2009] OJ L 337, as amended by Directive 2009/140/EC of 25 November 2009.

[77] ibid, Rec 5.

The 'Telecoms Package' was limited to the grid, shown at the bottom of Figure 25.2, which is inspired by Benkler's institutional ecology of information production.[78] Benkler's ecology is made of physical, logical, and content layers that represent 'the basic functions involved in mediated human communication'.[79] Figure 25.2 illustrates the categories of services corresponding to each layer, their function, the corresponding area of (EU) regulation, and concerns growing around these services. Without the aim of being exhaustive, entities include networking services providing connectivity, organizations dedicated to interoperability through protocols and software producers, as well as content hosts and providers.

Thus, entities providing the network and access to telecommunications to the public, known as ECSs, were governed by e-communication and e-privacy frameworks; component and device providers were covered by new Approach Frameworks, which are however beyond this discussion.[80] Entities enabling interoperability, such as public international organizations (the International Telecommunications Union) and private international organizations (eg International Organization for Standardization) or even private organizations (eg the ICANN), known as standards-developing organizations and standards-setting organizations, were governed by global administrative,[81] public and private international law; software developers were under limited constraints beyond intellectual property, and e-commerce frameworks. Entities performing editorial control were governed by media and privacy frameworks. Finally, entities hosting content but not exercising editorial control, known as intermediaries or ISSs, were governed by e-commerce frameworks (defined in, but independent of, new Approach Frameworks).

The focus here is on ECSs and ISSs, whose core definitions have not changed since they were first introduced. Directive 98/48/EC defined Information Society Services as 'any service normally provided for remuneration, at a distance, by electronic means and at the individual request of a recipient of services'.[82] The Commission endeavoured to observe developments in ISSs, 'in light of the convergence between telecommunications, information technology and media, and adopt rules as may be required'.[83]

This was done in 2000 with the eCommerce Directive, which laid down rules for mere conduit (common carriers), caching and hosting services[84] to support innovation in a way that was also expedient to the discharge of duties by Member States. The regime established limitation of liability for the content transmitted, cached, or hosted by intermediaries, provided they abstained from certain behaviours and fully cooperate with authorities when required to do so. To enjoy immunity from liability under the eCommerce Directive, conduit

---

[78] Yochai Benkler, *The Wealth of Networks: How Social Production Transforms Markets and Freedoms* (Yale University Press 2006) 392.
[79] ibid. Note that what is borrowed from Benkler is the ecology and not the ethos of 'regulatory abstinence' he argues for at 393 to aid the growth of information technology systems.
[80] eg Directive 98/34/EC laying down a procedure for the provision of information in the field of technical standards and regulations [1998] OJ L 204/37. For a discussion of the problematic influence of the New Legislative Approach, see Grazia Porcedda, *Cybersecurity* (n 2) 148–54, 180.
[81] Benedict Kingsbury, Nico Krisch, and Richard B. Stewart, 'The Emergence of Global Administrative Law' (2005) 68 Law and Contemporary Problems 68, 15–61.
[82] Art 1(2) of the now repealed Directive 98/48/EC of the European Parliament and of the Council of 20 July 1998 amending Directive 98/34/EC laying down a procedure for the provision of information in the field of technical standards and regulations [1998] OJ L 217/18.
[83] Dir 98/48/EC, Rec 27.
[84] eCommerce Directive, Arts 12–14.

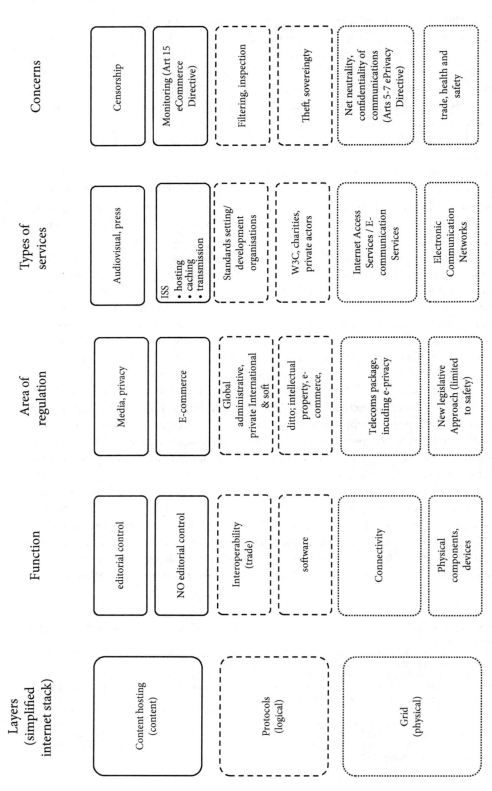

Figure 25.2 Simplified internet stack and early regulatory setup of digital service providers: distinction between ECSs, ISSs, and related concerns.

services were, among other prohibitions, not to initiate the transmission of information,[85] caching services were not to modify the information cached, and hosting services were not to have *actual knowledge* of illegal activity or information and, as regards claims for damages, be aware of facts or circumstances from which the illegal activity or information is apparent. Kohl notes that the rewards of immunity are counterbalanced by the regulatory pressures imposed especially on common carriers, which were turned into gatekeepers because the 'ripple effect of regulation via intermediaries is much greater than would be achievable by any direct action against primary wrongdoers'.[86]

Indeed, communication services were subject to retention regimes via the Data Retention and ePrivacy Directives. Together with electronic communications networks (ECNs[87]), 'electronic communications services' were defined in the Framework Directive as:

> a service normally provided <u>for remuneration</u> which consists <u>wholly or mainly in the conveyance of signals</u> <u>on electronic communications networks</u>, . . . ; it <u>does not include information society services</u>, as defined in Article 1 of Directive 98/34/EC, **which do not consist wholly or mainly in the conveyance of signals on electronic communications networks.**[88]

Thus, the Framework Directive addressed the conveyance of signals while the eCommerce Directive limited liability for the content transmitted through signals. The potential for overlap between ECSs and ISSs was acknowledged at recital level by both the eCommerce Directive and the Framework Directive. ISSs 'include services consisting of the transmission of information via a communication network, in providing access to a communication network or in hosting information provided by a recipient of the service',[89] which covers Internet Access Providers. Both instruments meant to cover traditional electronic email, but the eCommerce Directive only for trade, business or professional purposes;[90] electronic mail used by natural persons for other purposes, including their use for the conclusion of contracts between such persons, was only classed as an ECS. Voice telephony was an ECS.[91] The Framework Directive further acknowledged that 'the same undertaking, for example an Internet service provider, can offer both an electronic communications service, such as access to the Internet, and services not covered under this Directive, such as the provision of web-based content'.[92] The risk of regulatory redundance and conflict was discounted since most ISSs 'do not consist wholly or mainly in the conveyance of signals on electronic communications networks'.[93]

---

[85] For a critique of the passive nature of mere conduit, see Sophie Stalla-Bourdillon, Evangelia Papadaki, and Tim Chown, 'From Porn to Cybersecurity Passing by Copyright: How Mass Surveillance technologies are Gaining Legitimacy . . . The Case of Deep Packet Inspection Technologies' (2014) 30 Computer Law & Security Review 6, 671.
[86] Kohl, 'The Rise and Rise of Online Intermediaries' (n 3) 191.
[87] Framework Dir (n 76), Arts 2(a) and 2(d).
[88] ibid Art 2(c).
[89] eCommerce Directive, Rec 18.
[90] ibid.
[91] Framework Dir (n 76), Rec 10.
[92] ibid.
[93] ibid.

In terms of monitoring that involves the processing of personal data, ISSs that were also ECSs had to comply with the rules on confidentiality contained in Article 5 and, to a lesser extent, Articles 6 and 9 of the ePrivacy Directive and related data retention obligations. As for ISS that were not ECSs, Article 15 eCommerce Directive prohibited Member Stats from imposing 'a general obligation on providers [when providing mere conduit, caching and hosting services] to monitor the information which they transmit or store, nor a general obligation actively to seek facts or circumstances indicating illegal activity'. However, that provision does not prohibit service providers from monitoring *tout court*. Indeed, the eCommerce Directive did not 'preclude the development and effective operation ... of technical systems of protection and identification and of technical surveillance instruments made possible by digital technology within the limits'[94] of data protection legislation, which took precedence over the eCommerce Directive.[95] The only other safeguard against dragnet surveillance was the risk of losing immunity from liability after acquiring *actual knowledge* of illegal activity. Note, however, that the divide between content and metadata only applied for ECSs and that the protection afforded by data protection law before the adoption of the Lisbon Treaty was circumscribed.

Against this background, there was ample room for the development of private and public surveillance, including automated analysis, which has been amply documented by the media, privacy, internet, and telecommunications literature under labels such as censorship, violations of confidentiality, filtering, inspection, net neutrality, and exceptional access.[96] This will be discussed again in section 4.

3.2 2008–2017: The uneasy divide between ECSs and ISSs begins to show

Changes occurring between 2008 and 2017 took place against the entry into force of the Lisbon Treaty, with its revamped national security clause,[97] expanded competences in the Area of Freedom, Security and Justice (AFSJ) and new legal bases for data protection.[98] The Charter acquired the status of primary law and with it the rights to private life and personal data protection, as well as the stringent obligation for measures to respect the essence of fundamental rights.[99] This period saw a partial overhaul of the legislative framework, the introduction of new instruments and the adoption of landmark judgments for e-communications and intermediation services.

---

[94] eCommerce Directive, Rec 40.
[95] ibid Art 1(5)(b).
[96] Among many, see Stalla-Bourdillon, 'Online Monitoring, Filtering, Blocking' (n 2) 702–12; Chris Marsden, *Network Neutrality: From Policy to Law to Regulation* (Manchester University Press 2017); Bert-Jaap Koops and Eleni Kosta, 'Looking for Some Light Through the Lens of "Cryptowar" History: Policy Options for Law Enforcement Authorities against "Going Dark"' (2018) 34 Computer Law & Security Review 890–900; TJ McIntyre, 'Internet Censorship in the United Kingdom: National Schemes and European Norms' in Lilian Edwards (ed), *Law, Policy and the Internet* (Hart Publishing 2019); Grazia Porcedda, *Cybersecurity* (n 2) ch 6.
[97] Rojszczak, 'National Security' (n 58) 612.
[98] Consolidated versions of the Treaty on European Union (TEU) and the Treaty on the Functioning of the European Union (TFEU) [2016] OJ C202/1 (Lisbon Treaty), Arts 39 TEU and 16 TFEU.
[99] Charter (n 18) Arts 7, 8, and 52.

On the legislative front, Article 5(3) ePrivacy Directive was amended in 2009 to require consent to the placing of trackers on users' devices. This provision applies both to ECSs and ISSs, thus addressing the legal grey area pertaining to ISSs that were not ECSs and therefore escaped rules on the confidentiality of communications. Kosta notes that, by broadening the scope of Article 5(3) in such a manner, 'the European legislator overreaches the scope of the ePrivacy Directive, as specified in Article 3'.[100] As a result of these changes, more, yet unspecified, ISSs were brought under the umbrella of ECSs.

A second legislative novelty was the invalidation of the Data Retention Directive as a result of *Digital Rights Ireland*.[101] Citing Brown, Kohl notes the Data Retention Directive was anyway quickly obsoleted by the rapid development of ISSs that worked as substitutes for traditional means of telecommunications, such as 'blogs, social networking sites, video platforms, instant messaging, Usenet or peer-to-peer services and web-based [cloud-based, ndr] email ... or Internet telephony'.[102] The evolving technological landscape also forced the overhaul of the data protection framework and the adoption, among others, of the GDPR,[103] which came to fruition in 2018 (section 3.3).

The final legislative novelty was the introduction of the Open Internet Regulation (OIR),[104] which supplies a European response to the complex issue of 'net neutrality', for which I defer to Marsden.[105] The OIR lays down rules to safeguard equal and non-discriminatory treatment of traffic in the provision of internet access services and related end-users' rights[106] addressing providers of electronic communications to the public (ECSs and partly ISSs), Internet Access Services (ECS and potentially ISSs) and regulated intra-EU communications.[107] Open internet access rights are without prejudice to law related to the lawfulness of the content, applications or services.[108]

At Article 3(3) the OIR lays down rules on permissible monitoring for providers of Internet Access Services (IASs). The principle is that IASs 'shall treat all traffic equally, when providing internet access services, without discrimination, restriction or interference'. This does not preclude traffic management measures that are reasonable insofar as they are based on 'objectively different technical quality of service requirements of specific categories of traffic' and do 'not *monitor the specific content*'.[109] However, IASs can 'block,

---

[100] Eleni Kosta, 'Peeking into the Cookie Jar: The European Approach Towards the Regulation of Cookies' (2013) 21(4) International Journal of Law and Information Technology 384.

[101] CJEU, Judgment of 8 April 2014, *Digital Rights Ireland and Seitlinger and others* (C-293/12 and C-594/12) ECLI:EU:C:2014:238.

[102] Kohl (2011), 202 citing Ian Brown, 'Communications Data Retention in an Evolving Internet' (2011) 19 International Journal of Law and Information Technology 2, 95, 97ff.

[103] Regulation (EU) 2016/679 on the protection of natural persons with regard to the processing of personal data and on the free movement of such data, and repealing Directive 95/46/EC (General Data Protection Regulation) [2016] OJ L119/1 (GDPR).

[104] Regulation (EU) 2015/2120 laying down measures concerning open internet access and amending Directive 2002/22/EC on universal service and users' rights relating to electronic communications networks and services and Regulation (EU) 531/2012 on roaming on public mobile communications networks within the Union [2015] OJ L310/1.

[105] Marsden, *Network Neutrality* (n 96), especially ch 4.

[106] OIR, Art 1(1).

[107] ibid Art 2(1) to (3).

[108] ibid Art 3(1).

[109] Other requirements are transparency, proportionality, non-discrimination, time-limitedness based on necessity, and OIR, ibid Art 3(3).

slow down, alter, restrict, interfere with, degrade or *discriminate between specific content, applications or services, or specific categories thereof*'[110] on a short-time basis on grounds of necessity to comply with Union legislative acts, or national legislation that complies with Union law, preserve the integrity and security of the network, of services provided via that network, and of the terminal equipment of end-users and prevent impending network congestion. As such, the OIR provides a legal basis for automated data analysis for IASs.

The processing of personal data for traffic management purposes is allowed only if necessary and proportionate, and in compliance with data protection law, including the ePrivacy Directive. Accordingly, monitoring based on 'traffic data, ie information contained in the IP packet header and in some -unspecified- case transport layer (eg TCP) header, are allowed'.[111] The emphasis on specific content is intentional and will be discussed later.

On the judicial front, the CJEU made three crucial pronouncements that affected the interpretation of confidentiality and monitoring for ECSs and ISSs: the aforementioned *Digital Rights Ireland, Scarlet Extended* and *SABAM*.[112] Stalla-Bourdillon et al rightly say these judgments should be read together.[113]

With *Digital Rights Ireland*, the Court not only invalidated the Data Retention Directive, but also expressed *a contrario* that an encroachment into the content of communications was liable to violate the essence of fundamental rights.[114] A few years earlier, the Court had examined the compatibility of an injunction sought by copyright management firm SABAM requiring two intermediaries to instal a filtering system to monitor all data relating to their customers in order to prevent any future infringement of intellectual property rights. The ISSs were Scarlet Extended SA, a Belgian Internet Access Provider, and Netlog NV, a social networking platform, respectively involved in the *Scarlet Extended* and *SABAM* cases. To identify the movement of electronic files containing musical, cinematographic, or audio-visual work, such a preventative system was to filter all electronic communications passing via the ISSs' services, applying indiscriminately to all customers for an unlimited period of time. At the heart of the judgments was a form of automated analysis measure: a deep-packet inspection system marketed by the company Audible Magic.

The Court found in *Scarlet Extended* that to oblige an ISS to implement such a filter by means of an injunction would amount to actively carry out general monitoring, which violates Article 15 eCommerce Directive.[115] The Court did not, however, find the measure to be incompatible with EU law solely based on the infringement of the monitoring clause in the eCommerce Directive. Since at stake was the availability of effective remedies for the aggrieved intellectual property right holder, the Court justified its decision by reading the eCommerce Directive, copyright legislation and data protection law in light of fundamental rights, namely the freedom to conduct a business, the protection of personal data and freedom of information.[116]

---

[110] ibid Art 3(3)(a)–(c).
[111] Grazia Porcedda, *Cybersecurity* (n 2) 187. See also Body of European Regulators for Electronic Communications (BEREC), BEREC Guidelines 'Guidelines on the Implementation of the Open Internet Regulation, BoR (20) 112'.
[112] CJEU, Judgment of 24 November 2011, *Scarlet Extended* (C-70/10, ECR 2011 p. I-11959) ECLI:EU:C:2011:771; CJEU, Judgment of 16 February 2012, *SABAM* (C-360/10) ECLI:EU:C:2012:85.
[113] Stalla-Bourdillon, Papadaki, and Chown (n 85) 686.
[114] *Digital Rights Ireland*, para 39.
[115] *Scarlet Extended* (n 112) para 40.
[116] ibid para 54.

The *SABAM* judgment followed similar argumentative lines. The contested filtering system processes personal data because it involves 'the identification, systematic analysis and processing of information connected with the profiles created on the social network by its users',[117] a reasoning visible also in *La Quadrature du Net 'I'* and *'II'* (section 2.1). Stalla-Bourdillon, Papadaki, and Chown point out that the Court does not 'say expressly that the DPI practice at stake violates the principle of confidentiality of communications and does not mention Article 15 of the data protection Directive which could seem relevant in such a scenario'.[118] Drawing from the analysis of additional CJEU and UK cases, Stalla-Bourdillon observes that preventative mass surveillance is 'admitted without much difficulty'.[119]

Remarkably, an earlier adoption of the OIR could have led to a different result in the case of *Scarlet Extended SA*. Furthermore, the pronouncements just discussed rule out dragnet surveillance, but not surveillance as such, including automated analysis; Edwards notes how subsequent case law drew indeed the contours of permissible *ex ante* filtering,[120] and thus monitoring and surveillance. Such permissibility is only implied in *La Quadrature due Net 'II'*, as 'upstream' processing did not form part of the reference for preliminary ruling.

To appreciate the magnitude of the potential for public and private surveillance, we must read judgments on data retention and filtering together and in light of recent legislative changes, which are discussed next.

3.3 After 2018: ECSs and ISSs overlapping *de facto*, but not *de iure*

The greater convergence created by the latest technological developments has spurred legislative changes in data protection, e-communication, and intermediation that affect the relationship between ECSs and ISSs, relationship further refined by case law. Notwithstanding changes in these and germane fields, such as copyright, media, and AI, the siloed regulatory setup of the early 2000 is still in place.

The year 2018 saw the entry into force of the GDPR and the recast of the 'Telecoms Package' as the European Electronic Communications Code (EECC).[121] The GDPR engenders a horizontal data protection framework that implements the fundamental right to the protection of personal data; a Regulation overhauling the ePrivacy Directive has been stalled for years,[122] pending which a *lex specialis* was adopted in 2021.[123]

The GDPR strengthens the accountability system on which the applicable data protection law pivots, and introduces new safeguards around profiling, the processing of special

---

[117] *SABAM* (n 112) para 49.
[118] Stalla-Bourdillon, Papadaki, and Chown (n 85) 677.
[119] Stalla-Bourdillon, 'Online Monitoring, Filtering, Blocking' (n 2) 709.
[120] Discussing *Telekabel UPC*, C-314/12: Edwards, 'With Great Power Comes Great Responsibility' (n 3) 280.
[121] Directive (EU) 2018/1972 of 11 December 2018 establishing the European Electronic Communications Code [2018] OJ L321/36 (EECC).
[122] European Commission, Proposal for a Regulation of the European Parliament and of the Council concerning the respect for private life and the protection of personal data in electronic communications and repealing Directive 2002/58/EC (Regulation on Privacy and Electronic Communications)' COM (2017) 10 final.
[123] Regulation (EU) 2021/1232 on a temporary derogation from certain provisions of Directive 2002/58/EC as regards the use of technologies by providers of number-independent interpersonal communications services for the processing of personal and other data for the purpose of combating online child sexual abuse [2021] OJ L274/41.

categories of personal data, and automated individual decisions. These point to the permissibility of automated analysis under specific conditions, as discussed by Mitsilegas et al.[124] Recital 21 clarifies the GDPR is not prejudicial to the eCommerce Directive and the latter's liability rules of mere conduit, caching, and hosting ISSs.[125]

The EECC is a complex Directive that lays down a harmonized framework for the regulation of electronic communications networks, electronic communications services, associated facilities and associated services, and certain aspects of terminal equipment.[126] The EECC contains many important provisions, such as the establishment of affordable universal service, which are however outside the scope of this research.[127] For this discussion, the biggest change contained in the EECC is the inclusion of additional ISSs under the scope of the 'Telecom' framework, namely interpersonal communication, 'over-the-top' (OTT) services. These services have the same functionality of telephony and text messaging but are offered '"over the top" of the network[,] without the direct involvement of a network operator or Internet Service Provider. Examples... include Skype (voice and video calling), WhatsApp (messaging), Google (search), Spotify (music) and Netflix (video content)'.[128] This is because of the functional equivalence between ECSs and ISSs, whereby 'from the point of view of the consumer, some ECS and ISS may be very similar or indeed may substitute for one another',[129] which the previous regulatory framework did not account for.[130]

ECSs include IASs as defined in the OIR, services consisting wholly or mainly in the conveyance of signals[131] and 'interpersonal communications service'. These enable non-ancillary 'direct interpersonal and interactive exchange of information via electronic communications networks between a finite number of persons', and can be number-based or number-independent.[132]

The EECC is not to prejudice, among others, the protection of personal data and privacy, content regulation, and audiovisual policy and the OIR.[133] Annex 1 provides for the maximum list of conditions which may be attached to general authorizations for ECSs and networks, including interactions with the ePrivacy Directive concerning personal data, privacy, legal interception, and security of public networks against unauthorized access. The EECC also addresses the cross-over with the eCommerce Directive:

> In the absence of relevant rules of Union law, content, applications and services are considered to be lawful or harmful in accordance with national ... law. It is a task for the Member States, not for providers of electronic communications networks or services, to decide, in accordance with due process, whether content, applications or services are

---

[124] See Mitsilegas et al (n 3).
[125] For an alternative discussion, see Giovanni Sartor, 'Liabilities of Internet users and providers' in M Cremona (ed), *New Technologies and EU Law* (OUP 2017) 179–84.
[126] EECC, Art 1.
[127] EECC, Part III, Title I, and Annex V.
[128] European Parliament, *Regulating Electronic Communications. A Level Playing Field for Telecoms and OTTs?* Briefing, September 2016, 1.
[129] ibid 5.
[130] The European Parliament notes that national regulatory authorities, for instance in Spain and France, consider OTTs that offer voice telephony to be ECSs but struggled to impose telecom legislation onto OTT providers: European Parliament, ibid.
[131] eg transmission services used for the provision of machine-to-machine services and for broadcasting, EECC Art 2(4)(c).
[132] ibid Arts 2(5)–(7).
[133] ibid Arts 1(3)(b)–(d).

lawful or harmful. This Directive and Directive 2002/58/EC are without prejudice to Directive 2000/31/EC, which, inter alia, contains a 'mere conduit' rule for intermediary service providers, as defined therein.[134]

In between the adoption of the EECC and the deadline for its transposition at national level, the CJEU held in *Skype* that the 'fact that the VoIP service provided by SkypeOut is also covered by the definition of "information society service"... in no way implies that it cannot be classified as an' ECS.[135] 'Only information society services... that do not consist wholly or mainly in the conveyance of signals on electronic communications networks are excluded from the definition of' ECSs. Thus, an ISS comes within the scope of application of e-communications legislation 'provided that it consists wholly or mainly in the conveyance of signals on electronic communications networks'.[136] In its judgment, the Court clarifies the conditions under which intermediaries can be brought under the scope of the definition of ECSs, which applies to SkypeOut.

Conversely, 'a web-based email service which does not itself provide internet access, such as the Gmail service provided by Google LLC' is not an ECS under the Framework Directive 'because it does not consist wholly or mainly in the conveyance of signals on electronic communications networks'.[137] However, all email services are now captured by the EECC notion of interpersonal communications service.[138] The EECC constitutes the most significant shift in the categorization of online services since the introduction of the early framework and arguably demonstrates the broadening of monitoring enabled by the eCommerce Directive, alongside data retention and open internet frameworks. Indeed, following the EECC and the stalling of the ePrivacy Regulation, the EU legislator adopted Regulation (EU) 2021/1232.[139]

Regulation 2021/1232 legitimizes measures used by number independent interpersonal communication services within the meaning of the EECC in derogation from Articles 5(1) and 6(1) ePrivacy Directive, to combat online child sexual abuse, until August 2024.

Following Recital 8, the interference with the 'confidentiality of communications, cannot be justified merely on the grounds that providers were using certain technologies at a time when number-independent interpersonal communications services did not fall within the definition of "electronic communications services"'. After recalling Article 52 Charter, however, Recital 8 simply states, 'Where such limitations permanently involve a general and indiscriminate monitoring and analysis of the communications of all users, they interfere with the right to confidentiality of communications'. This is remarkable, insofar as such an interference has been found to be impermissible by the Court under data retention case law, but also suggestive of the type of measures that ISS had been adopting under the GDPR.[140]

---

[134] ibid, Rec 270. There are also provisions about Radio Local Area Networks and Art 12 eCommerce Directive on mere conduit and restrictions at Annex 1(c)(4).

[135] *Skype Communications*, Case C-142/18, para 46. For a commentary, see Marcin Rojszczak, 'OTT Regulation Framework in the Context of CJEU Skype case and European Electronic Communications Code' (2020) 38 Computer Law and Security Review 38, 1–14, <https://doi.org/10.1016/j.clsr.2020.105439> accessed 27 September 2024.

[136] CJEU, Judgment of 5 June 2019, *Skype Communications* (C-142/18) ECLI:EU:C:2019:460, para 48.

[137] CJEU, Judgment of 13 June 2019, *Google* (C-193/18) ECLI:EU:C:2019:498.

[138] EECC, Rec 17.

[139] Regulation (EU) 2021/1232.

[140] ibid Rec 9.

Measures are 'specific technologies for the processing of personal and other data to the extent strictly necessary to detect online child sexual abuse on their services and report it and to remove online child sexual abuse material from their services', with the 'exclusion of "the scanning of audio communications"'.[141]

Such measures must respect the 'state of the art in the industry' and be 'the least privacy-intrusive' and 'to the extent that they are used to *scan text* in communications, they are not able to *deduce the substance of the content* of the communications but are solely able to *detect patterns* which point to possible online child sexual abuse' (see further section 4).

On the eCommerce Directive side, the cases of *Glawischnig-Piesczek*[142] and, jointly, *YouTube and Cyando*[143] shed light on the interpretation of Article 15 eCommerce Directive on the prohibition of general monitoring. The first case concerns court proceedings for defamation brought by Austrian politician Glawischnig-Piesczek against Facebook. The CJEU finds Article 15(1) eCommerce Directive not to preclude the imposition of monitoring obligations 'in a specific case'.[144] An injunction requiring a 'host provider to block access to the information stored, the content of which is identical to the content previously declared to be illegal, or to remove that information, irrespective of who requested the storage of that information' does not amount to 'an obligation to monitor generally the information which it stores, or a general obligation actively to seek facts or circumstances indicating illegal activity'.[145] Still, the injunction '*may* not be pursued by imposing an excessive obligation on the host provider'.[146] The obligation in *Glawischnig-Piesczek* was not excessive because it was 'limited to information containing the elements specified in the injunction' and did not require 'the host provider to carry out an independent assessment, since the latter has recourse to *automated search tools and technologies*'.[147]

The second set of cases pertains to the infringement of the intellectual property rights held by Mr Peterson and Elsevier perpetrated by users of the hosting platforms *YouTube and Cyando*. The Grand Chamber found that the activity of the operators in the main proceedings falls within scope of Article 14 (1) eCommerce Directive, if the operator does not play an active role of such a kind as to give it knowledge of or control over content uploaded to the platform. Active role means not to create, select, view, or monitor content uploaded to the platform. Use of 'technological measures aimed at detecting, among the videos communicated to the public via its platform, content which may infringe copyright', does not mean 'that operator plays an active role giving it knowledge of and control over the content of those videos'.[148]

The exemption from liability applies if the host has knowledge of or awareness of specific illegal acts committed by its users relating to protected content that was uploaded to its platform, which excludes awareness in a general sense. A systemic analysis of the wording, objective, scheme, and context of the eCommerce Directive leads the Court to refer to specific illegal information and activities committed by the users of the hosting services.[149]

---

[141] ibid Art 1.
[142] CJEU, Judgment of 3 October 2019, *Glawischnig-Piesczek* (C-18/18) ECLI:EU:C:2019:821.
[143] CJEU, Judgment of 22 June 2021, *YouTube & Cyando* (C-682/18 and C-683/18) ECLI:EU:C:2021:503.
[144] *Glawischnig-Piesczek* (n 141) para 34.
[145] ibid para 37.
[146] ibid para 44.
[147] ibid para 46.
[148] *YouTube & Cyando* (n 142) para 109.
[149] ibid para 112.

The Court remarks whether 'information society service providers who adopt measures which seek specifically to combat [copyright] infringements are to be excluded from the rules on exemption from liability'.[150] This hints to a policy matter that was subsequently addressed by the Digital Services Act (DSA)[151] amending the eCommerce Directive.

The DSA updates the eCommerce Directive in light of the significant evolution of intermediaries 'by setting out harmonized rules for a safe, predictable and trusted online environment that facilitates innovation and in which fundamental rights enshrined in the Charter ... are effectively protected'.[152] The 101-page, 93-article long Regulation updates the liability framework for providers of intermediary services and lays down due diligence obligations, implementation, and enforcement rules. The categories benefitting from 'conditional exemption' from liability remain the same—mere conduit, caching, and hosting.[153]

The DSA still contains a provision prohibiting general monitoring or to seek active fact-finding. Thus, 'no general obligation to monitor the information which providers of intermediary services transmit or store, nor actively to seek facts or circumstances indicating illegal activity shall be imposed on those providers'.[154] However, following Article 7 on 'Voluntary own-initiative investigations and legal compliance', intermediaries 'shall not lose their exemptions from liability 'solely because they, in good faith and in a diligent manner, carry out voluntary own-initiative investigations into, or take other measures aimed at detecting, identifying and removing, or disabling access to, illegal content, or take the necessary measures to comply with' legal requirements. Where automated tools are used to conduct such activities, the intermediaries must take reasonable measures to ensure that relevant technology is sufficiently reliable to limit to the maximum extent possible the rate of errors.[155]

The DSA contemplates the use of partly or fully automated 'activities' in the context of recommender systems and content moderation[156] but excludes their sole use for the sake of setting up points of contact.[157] All intermediaries are expected to disclose the use of automated means as part of their transparency reporting obligations.[158]

The DSA acknowledges the EECC insofar as it excludes from its scope interpersonal communication services, such as emails or private messaging services. Where such services allow the making available of information to a potentially unlimited number of recipients, not determined by the sender of the communication, such as through public groups or open channels, the DSA still applies.[159] The DSA is without prejudice, among others, to Regulations 2021/784 addressing the dissemination of terrorist content online, Regulation 2021/1232(11) on temporary derogation from certain provisions of the ePrivacy Directive, and the ePrivacy Directive itself.[160]

---

[150] ibid para 109.
[151] Regulation (EU) 2022/2065 on a Single Market For Digital Services and amending Directive 2000/31/EC (Digital Services Act), OJ L277/1 (DSA).
[152] ibid Art 1(1).
[153] ibid Arts 4–6 contain small but significant edits to the definitions of mere conduit, caching, and hosting, which are however beyond the scope of this work and are therefore not discussed here.
[154] ibid Art 8.
[155] ibid Recital 26; see also Rec 54.
[156] ibid Art 3(s) and (t).
[157] ibid Art 12.
[158] ibid Art 15.
[159] ibid Rec 14.
[160] ibid Rec 10.

3.4 Summary of the regulatory overlap of telecommunication and intermediation services

In sum, over time the scope of ECSs has broadened to include an increasing number of ISSs. Stalla-Bourdillon's impression in 2013 of a legislative and judicial trend 'towards the enlargement of the category of providers of publicly available electronic communications'[161] has turned out to be correct and lasting.

ISSs have thus become subject to the principle of confidentiality of content data enshrined in Article 5 of the ePrivacy Directive and the exceptions enabled by data retention legislation. Entities that are both ECSs and ISSs must also observe the provisions of the ePrivacy Directive, when processing traffic and location data for their own business purposes and for compliance with requests by Member States under national data retention law. Although metadata are afforded less protection than content data, which forms part of the essence of the right to private life, there is awareness that the processing of metadata can be as intrusive as content data.[162] The admissibility of automated analysis for national security purposes and economic offences has been confirmed by case law. However, questions remain around the reconciliation between the strict use of automated analysis in the context of state security and relaxed use of automated analysis in the context of economic crime or misconduct, which are left unanswered by *La Quadrature du Net II*.

Furthermore, Internet Access Services must not monitor specific content. BEREC has clarified that traffic data does not amount to specific content. Upon request by BEREC, the European Data Protection Board (EDPB) clarified that domain names, unique resource identifiers (URLs), and Transport Layer payload must be considered as content data.[163] This finding has not, to the best of my knowledge, been confirmed in case law on the OIR or data retention measures.

ISSs that are not ECSs cannot be required to engage in (GDPR-compliant?) general monitoring on behalf of Member States, but can monitor in 'specific cases' or in a way that strategically stays below the threshold of the acquisition of 'specific knowledge'. The hurried adoption of Regulation 2021/1232 after the entry into force of the EECC may suggest that ISSs applied automated analysis to all data, irrespective of the metadata/content divide effected by the ePrivacy Directive. Processing of this kind has been found by the CJEU to be seriously intrusive and confined to use for the sake of combatting serious and present threats to national security. Regulation 2021/1232 derogates from the ePrivacy Directive to enable the scanning of text, but in a way that does not allow to deduce the substance of the content. The Regulation does not explain what elements of a packet can be examined, which begs the questions of how the measure can respect the content/metadata divide.

For what concerns liability, the DSA has heeded the comments of the Court in *YouTube and Cyando* to clarify that voluntary own-motion analyses do not result in the acquisition of specific knowledge and does therefore not deprive ISSs of the exemptions they enjoy. If Article 15 of the eCommerce Directive already seemed 'an empty shell' to Stalla-Bourdillon in 2013,[164] the DSA has given the fatal blow, signalling the shift from negligence-based

---

[161] Stalla-Bourdillon, 'Online Monitoring, Filtering, Blocking' (n 2) 708.
[162] See section 2 above.
[163] European Data Protection Board, Letter to BEREC. Data protection issues in the context of Regulation (EU) 2015/2120, OUT2019-0055, 3 December 2019.
[164] Stalla-Bourdillon, 'Online Monitoring, Filtering, Blocking (n 2) 712.

liability to proactive private ordering responsibility, anticipated by Frosio, Mendis, and Kuczerawy.[165]

These misaligned rules are part of the complex and fragmentary framework of monitoring provisions across the Digital Single Market.[166] These rules are the result of the siloed approach to the regulation of online services and the arbitrary regulatory fault lines stand to benefit different players. Arguably the ECS and ePrivacy Directive are beneficial to Member States' public authorities, while ISSs rules benefit the private sector. What is in the collectivity's best interest remains to be determined and is partly discussed in the following section.

4. Automated analysis, the Single market-AFSJ nexus, and the effacement of technology from EU law: ways forward

In section 2 I synthesized the CJEU and ECtHR approach to automated analysis in landmark mass surveillance cases. In section 3 I explained how the regulatory ecosystem of e-communication and intermediation services in which automated analysis takes place has evolved over time and how such an ecosystem operates at present. In particular, conceptual categories originating from regulatory siloes are still in place but have become blurred, watering down to the point of no use the few protections against private surveillance embedded in single instruments. In this section I connect those conversations in light of two mechanisms I conceptualized in previous work, the procedural interconnection between the DSM and the AFSJ, and the effacement of technology from EU law.[167]

The different approach of the CJEU vis-à-vis the compatibility with EU law of the UK RIPA in *Privacy International* and Article L. 851-3 of the French CSI in *La Quadrature du Net 'I'* offers a good starting point to reflect on the DSM–AFSJ nexus. Rojszczak notes that, in *Privacy International*, requiring ECSs to forward retained data to national competent authorities for the latter to perform automated analysis was deemed incompatible with EU law, as opposed to asking ECSs to perform automated analysis via parameters set by national authorities, which was deemed compatible in *La Quadrature du Net 'I'*.[168] Unless the Court considered it permissible for national competent authorities to perform automated analysis on traffic data without asking the ECSs to forward retained data,[169] the approach in *La Quadrature du Net 'I'* is the only viable approach compatible with EU law.

In this way, the EU court implicitly acknowledges the gatekeeping role of the private sector. This is unsurprising in light of the procedural interconnection between the DSM and the AFSJ: since the liberalization of Telecommunications, EU law has implicitly allowed national public authorities to co-opt private sector entities to access communications

---

[165] Giancarlo Frosio, 'The Death of "No Monitoring Obligations": A Story of Untameable Monsters' (2017) 8 Journal of Intellectual Property, Information Technology and E-Commerce Law 3; Aleksandra Kuczerawy, 'General Monitoring Obligations: a New Cornerstone of Internet Regulation in the EU?' in CiTiP (ed), *Rethinking IT and IP Law—Celebrating 30 Years CiTiP* (Intersentia 2019); Frosio and Mendis, 'Monitoring and Filtering' (n 3).
[166] Stalla-Bourdillon, 'Online Monitoring, Filtering, Blocking' (n 2); Frosio, 'The Death of "No Monitoring Obligations"' (n 164); Rojszczak, 'Online Content Filtering in EU Law' (n 2); Grazia Porcedda, *Cybersecurity* (n 2), chs 5 and 6. With respect to copyright, Frosio and Mendis, 'Monitoring and Filtering' (n 3).
[167] Grazia Porcedda, *Cybersecurity* (n 2) ch 5, 141–156; also chs 6 and 7.
[168] Rojszczak, 'National Security' (n 58) 621–25.
[169] eg by splitting the cables or otherwise intercept data from core communication systems.

data needed for law enforcement and intelligence purposes. The ePrivacy Directive and the invalidated Data Retention Directive are two among many legislative examples of this implicit nexus.[170]

In recognizing the gatekeeping role of ECSs, the Court uses the private sector (as well as the national judiciary) as a counterbalance against the executive power of Member States. While such an approach may be understandable from a historical perspective, what is striking is that it overlooks the extremely intrusive automated analysis that private entities perform for their own purposes. ISSs and ECSs have done so for years taking advantage of the nooks and crannies afforded by information technology law, exemplified by the blunt and fragmentary confidentiality and no-monitoring provisions contained in the e-communication, intermediation, privacy, and data protection frameworks analysed earlier.

Up until this point, the technology of automated analysis has been left out of this discussion. This was not an oversight, but an intentional omission. In its case law, European Courts—the CJEU more so than the ECtHR—engage only in passing with the functioning of automated analysis. As discussed above, in *La Quadrature du Net 'I'* the Court speaks of the 'screening of all the traffic and location data' and 'data of users of ECSs is verified if it corresponds to those parameters'.[171] In *SABAM*, the Court discusses a filtering system involving 'the identification, systematic analysis and processing of information connected with the profiles created on the social network by its users'.[172] In *YouTube*,[173] the Court finds that implementing technological 'measures aimed at detecting ... content which may infringe copyright' does not amount to viewing or monitoring or otherwise playing an active role. In *Big Brother Watch* and *Centrum för Rättvisa*, the ECtHR traces a difference between the monitoring of packets and individuals' devices. There is no or little discussion of the meaning of 'detecting', 'identification', 'monitoring', 'packets', 'profiles', 'systematic', 'screening', 'viewing' etc. Similarly, there is no discussion of what parts of a packet correspond to traffic and location data, as against the view taken by the EDPB in its response to BEREC (section 3).

Legislation is no different. Taking Regulation 2021/1232 as an example, terms such as 'systematically filter' and 'scan text', 'detect patterns' 'deduce the substance' are not defined. At Recital 7,

> webmail and messaging services ... use specific technologies ... to detect online child sexual abuse on their services and report it to law enforcement authorities ... by scanning either the *content*, such as images and text, or the traffic data of communications using, in some instances, historical data. The technology used for those activities could be hashing technology for images and videos and classifiers and artificial intelligence for analysing text or traffic data.

The legislation does not engage in a discussion of where to draw the line between content and metadata, which is inherently ambiguous as each layer of a packet has its own payload

---

[170] For instance, see the Directive (EU) 2017/541 on combating terrorism and replacing Council Framework Decision 2002/475/JHA and amending Council Decision 2005/671/JHA [2017] OJ L88/6.
[171] *La Quadrature du Net 'I'* (n 1) para 172.
[172] *SABAM* (n 112) para 49.
[173] *YouTube & Cyando,* para 109.

or content,[174] but which is crucial to decide whether the essence of the right to private life is breached beyond repair.

The reluctance to identify technology is in keeping with the historically determined approach to law-making in technology law, aimed at spurring digital innovation. In such an approach, the law deals with technological 'functions', such as 'detecting', 'filtering', 'monitoring', and 'screening', rather than specific instances of technology. The law does not provide for mechanisms to identify the 'state of the art' nor concrete examples of tools, techniques, and technologies. Technology itself is 'effaced from the law', causing a disconnect between regulation and technology development. It is thus for regulatees to identify the technical measures (alongside organizational and operational) for compliance among those made available by the market, whether or not 'appropriate' measures are actually on offer.[175]

Disputes arise years after the adoption of legislation, and often necessitate interpretive input from the CJEU or redress of last resort from the ECtHR. European higher courts are cautious not to engage in judicial activism in matters that should have best been addressed by EU and national decision-makers or national courts. So, if the applicable law does not address technology, it is unlikely higher Courts will, as exemplified by the cases discussed in these pages. Such an approach was confirmed in the *NAP* case, where the determination of the appropriateness of state of the art measures to protect against data breaches and minimize their impact was delegated to the referring court.[176] Rather, the case-by-case approach, in which a national legislative measure is assessed against EU secondary and primary law, prevents a holistic assessment of the impact of the same technological measures used across different sectors of the DSM and to fulfil the objectives of AFSJ instruments. If neither the law nor judges addresses actual technologies, we are confronted with a technology 'indeterminacy loop' in the law. What is more, technological indeterminacy makes it possible to adopt technological solutions that compress the essence without anybody taking notice.

In a previous work of mine, I demonstrate how such a high-level approach has led to the normalization of deep-packet inspection, the technology which many commentators believe to be behind Article L. 851-3 of the French CSI and which is seamlessly applied to copyright enforcement, investigations into child sexual abuse material, malware prevention and network congestion.[177] The measure exemplifies how the avoidance of an engagement with technology analysis opens up the possibility to encroach on the essence of the right to private life, in the guise of the content of communications, and personal data protection, in the guise of meaningful conditions for purpose limitation.[178] Therein, I discuss how the 'effacement of technology from the law' and 'indeterminacy loop' have made it possible for

---

[174] For a helpful visualization of packet metadata and content: Stalla-Bourdillon, Papadaki, and Chown (n 85) 672.

[175] See Grazia Porcedda, *Cybersecurity* (n 2), ch 5; Maria Grazia Porcedda, 'The GDPR as a Cyber Risk Management System: the ECJ Cautiously Tackles Data Breaches in the NAP case' (*European Law Blog* 4/2024) <https://europeanlawblog.eu/2024/01/23/the-gdpr-as-a-cyber-risk-management-system-the-ecj-cautiously-tackles-data-breaches-in-the-nap-case/> accessed 15 July 2024.

[176] CJEU, Judgment of 23 December 2023, *Natsionalna agentsia za prihodite* (C-) ECLI:EU:C:2023:986 ('*NAP*'); Maria Grazia Porcedda, 'The GDPR as a Cyber Risk Management System' (4/2024).

[177] See discussion in Grazia Porcedda, *Cybersecurity* (n 2) 233–34.

[178] CJEU, Opinion 1/15 (*EU–Canada PNR Agreement*), of 26 July 2017 (Digital Reports) ECLI:EU:C:2017:592 para 150.

the essence of data protection, in the guise of minimum measures of integrity and confidentiality, to be determined *de facto* by the market.

What, then? Stalla-Bourdillon and Rojszczak independently and a decade from each other recommend the adoption of one dedicated legal basis for filtering and monitoring.[179] Such an approach cannot meaningfully happen without engaging in a review of the technology across sectors revealing the inefficacy and detriment of the siloed regulatory approach that has survived to this day. The key concern is that, by ignoring the 'revolving door' between DSM and AFSJ measures, we may be inflicting upon ourselves the shortcomings described in the 'blind men and an elephant' parable.[180] In the tale, blind(folded) people who do not know what an elephant is experience the animal for the first time by touching it. They each touch a different part of the body and describe what they feel, which is different from what the other people can feel. The parable shows the limitations of subjective experience and, by extension for this research, the shortcomings of siloed analysis. The recommendation is, therefore, the need to extend the judicial review to the technological implementation of the law, and possibly even start from the technology, rather than the law. This recommendation is subversive insofar as it neither aligns with the architecture of EU technology law, nor with the practice of European courts, and especially the CJEU, insofar as information technology law is concerned.

Such an approach would, among other things, require scrutinizing or reverse-engineering technological solutions and keeping up-to-date lists of technology that meet the state of the art in a manner that best addresses the triplet of democracy, rule of law, and respect for human rights to which European democracies are constitutionally committed. Perhaps a specific form of automated analysis would result in the best possible reconciliation between the requirements of public authorities, individuals, and the collectivity. But until the point when the technology involved is seriously scrutinized, we are just like the blindfolded people with the elephant: in the dark.

5. Conclusion

In this chapter I have examined CJEU and ECtHR case law on automated analysis as a measure of mass surveillance to bring to the fore the effaced role of monitoring by intermediaries within the courts' jurisprudence. Building on scholarship on fragmentary EU rules on monitoring and private sector gatekeeping, I analysed the evolution of rules on 'electronic communication services' and 'information society services', which were once distinct entities but have become increasingly interchangeable to the effect that protections against surveillance are diluted. I demonstrate how monitoring/automated analysis by intermediaries is inherent in the nexus between the DSM and the AFSJ and is worrisome on account of the 'effacement of information technology from the law' and 'indeterminacy loop' dynamics that characterize EU information technology law.

---

[179] Stalla-Bourdillon, 'Online Monitoring, Filtering, Blocking' (n 2); Rojszczak, Online Content Filtering in EU Law' (n 2).
[180] The story is attributed to Buddhist, Hindu, and Jain texts, eg the Tittha Sutta, Udāna 6.4, Khuddaka Nikaya; Idries Saha, *The Elephant in The Dark* (Octagon Press 1974).

While the adoption of a clear legal basis for monitoring or filtering proposed by some would go some way to help the problem, it would not work without extending judicial review to the technological implementation of the law, to confront the technological state of the art behind 'automated analysis' and its manifold features.[181] Such an approach could help exposing the potential contradictions of case law generated by the effacement of technology from the applicable law.

The ultimate goal should be a reform of data retention law that tackles its two limitations. The first is the siloed and technology neutral approach to monitoring rules, born to favour disruptive innovators, but which is untenable in light of today's intermediation ecosystem. The second is the DSM–AFSJ nexus and the private–public partnerships it creates, where the private sector may be given the—also untenable—upper hand in the attempt to enforce Union law. To paraphrase and adapt a common ECtHR refrain, these limitations may create a system of private surveillance set up to protect the fabric of EU law that may undermine or even destroy the proper functioning of democratic processes under the cloak of defending them.

---

[181] J L Hall, MD Aaron, A Andersdotter, B Jones, N Feamster, and M Knodel, 'A Survey of Worldwide Censorship Techniques, RFC 9505' (Internet Engineering Task Force 2023) <https://datatracker.ietf.org/doc/rfc9505/> accessed 15 July 2024.

26
On Administrative and Surveillance Vulnerability and the Digital Government in the EU

Maria-Lucia Rebrean and Gianclaudio Malgieri

1. Introduction

In pursuit of efficiency, cost-effectiveness, and cost reduction, administrative bodies across the European Union (EU) are embracing digital transformation at differing paces.[1] The resulting digitalization process, though promising, brings about many perils, including for example the exacerbation of existing social divisions, inequalities,[2] vulnerability, and surveillance practices. At the heart of public service digitalization lies the integration of data-based decision-making processes, such as the use of machine learning algorithms across administrative sectors, to derive socially significant decisions.[3] This metamorphosis raises significant risks to the fulfilment of rights. The individual's position when their (fundamental) rights are at risk due to power-imbalances that result from, among other factors, digitalization processes is described under the term 'vulnerability'.[4]

The concept of 'vulnerability' is increasingly being used by the European Court of Human Rights (ECtHR),[5] but it has yet to be employed in this juridical body in relation to state digitalization processes. Departing from a description of data subject vulnerability, which focuses on the risks to rights, such as the rights to privacy[6] or the right to

---

[1] Saar Alon-Barkat and Madalina Busuioc, 'Human–AI Interactions in Public Sector Decision Making: "Automation Bias" and "Selective Adherence" to Algorithmic Advice' (2023) 33 Journal of Public Administration Research and Theory 153.

[2] JAM van Deursen and EJ Helsper, 'The Third-Level Digital Divide: Who Benefits Most from Being Online?' (2015) 10 Communication and Information Technologies Annual <https://doi.org/10.1108/S2050-20602015000 0010002> accessed 3 July 2023; European Commission, Joint Research Centre, *AI Watch: European Landscape on the Use of Artificial Intelligence by the Public Sector* (Publications Office 2022) <https://data.europa.eu/doi/10.2760/39336> accessed 10 December 2023; Sofia Ranchordas and Luisa Scarcella, 'Automated Government for Vulnerable Citizens: Intermediating Rights' [2021] SSRN Electronic Journal <https://www.ssrn.com/abstract=3938032> accessed 3 July 2023; Sofia Ranchordas, 'Empathy in the Digital Administrative State' [2021] SSRN Electronic Journal 1341.

[3] Michael Kearns and Aaron Roth, *The Ethical Algorithm: The Science of Socially Aware Algorithm Design* (OUP 2019) 6.

[4] Gianclaudio Malgieri and Jędrzej Niklas, 'Vulnerable Data Subjects' (2020) 37 Computer Law & Security Review 1.

[5] Lourdes Peroni and Alexandra Timmer, 'Vulnerable Groups: The Promise of an Emerging Concept in European Human Rights Convention Law' (2013) 11 International Journal of Constitutional Law 1056.

[6] United Nations, 'Universal Declaration of Human Rights' <https://www.un.org/en/about-us/universal-declaration-of-human-rights> accessed 10 December 2023 Art 12; Council of Europe, 'European Convention on Human Rights' Art 8; European Union, 'Charter of Fundamental Rights of the European Union. Official Journal of the European Union' [2012] Official Journal of the European Union Art 7.

data protection[7] that stem from the power-imbalanced relationship between data subjects and data controllers,[8] we describe how vulnerability can be understood in the context of the EU Member States' digitalizing public administration. The latter form of vulnerability, also referred to as 'administrative vulnerability', was recently formulated to denote the risk to rights that result from the power-imbalanced state-individual relations,[9] and that can be enhanced by administrative digitalization processes.[10]

A comprehensive understanding of administrative vulnerability is essential because, unlike commercial digitalization processes, public service digitalization often does not permit an individual to refuse, postpone, or control the sharing, processing, or retention of their data. The data subject's inability to meaningfully impact a state's data-based activities which concern them stems from the individual's dependency on the outcome of the decisions issued by public administration bodies. These outcomes are either rights enabling or restricting. Consequently, the state's data collection, retention, and processing, as well as the use of risk-inducing technologies across public service sectors, must be thoroughly and strictly regulated as to reduce the likelihood of harm materialization and normalized surveillance practices. In this chapter, we argue that the concept of human vulnerability is inherent to reflections on surveillance and data retention. Further, this chapter proposes an extension of administrative vulnerability to 'surveillance vulnerability'. The extension permits to focus not only on the interconnection between datafication, data retention and surveillance, but also to analyse it considering its possible implications for the EU's legal landscape.

While the regulation of public service digitalization processes remains primarily addressed at national level, the EU has, over the last decades, drafted, endorsed, and funded a significant number of frameworks and projects that sustain the aforementioned transition. Most prominently, these regulatory efforts range from but are not limited to the eGovernment Declaration,[11] the Interoperable Europe Act,[12] the upcoming Artificial Intelligence Act,[13] and the General Data Protection Regulation (GDPR).[14] In view of this chapter's analysis of vulnerability in digital public administration, the GDPR plays an important role as it sets out requirements for fair data processing practices, provides individuals with data subject rights, and prohibits decisions from being taken solely on the basis of automated systems. In parallel the GDPR also provides sufficient room for states to enforce their power and lead harmful data processing activities through exemptions to the aforementioned prohibition.[15]

---

[7] Charter, Art 8.
[8] Malgieri and Niklas (n 4).
[9] See eg Martha Albertson Fineman, 'The Vulnerable Subject: Anchoring Equality in the Human Condition', in Martha Albertson Fineman (ed) *Transcending the Boundaries of Law* (Routledge-Cavendish 2008).
[10] See eg Sofia Ranchordas and Malou Beck, 'Vulnerability' in M Kaufmann and H Mork Lomell (eds), *Handbook on Digital Criminology* (De Gruyter 2024, forthcoming) (9 October 2023) <https://papers.ssrn.com/abstract=4596689> accessed 10 December 2023.
[11] 'Ministerial Declaration on eGovernment - the Tallinn Declaration | Shaping Europe's Digital Future' (6 October 2017) <https://digital-strategy.ec.europa.eu/en/news/ministerial-declaration-egovernment-tallinn-declaration> accessed 10 December 2023.
[12] European Commission, 'Proposal for a Regulation of the European Parliament and of the Council Laying down Measures for a High Level of Public Sector Interoperability across the Union (Interoperable Europe Act)' 1.
[13] European Parliament, Amendments by the European Parliament to the Commission proposal—Regulation (EU) 2024/... of... laying down harmonized rules on artificial intelligence (and amending Regulations (EC) No 300/2008, (EU) No 167/2013, (EU) No 168/2013, (EU) 2018/858, (EU) 2018/1139, and (EU) 2019/2144 and Directives 2014/90/EU, (EU) 2019/797, and (EU) 2020/1828 (Artificial Intelligence Act).
[14] Regulation (EU) 2016/679 on the protection of natural persons with regard to the processing of personal data and on the free movement of such data, and repealing Directive 95/46/EC (General Data Protection Regulation) [2016] OJ L119/1 (GDPR) Art 22.
[15] GDPR (n 14), Art 22(2).

The present chapter begins by outlining the benefits and challenges of EU public service digitalization. This genealogy is followed by an explanation of vulnerability and the derived 'administrative' and 'surveillance' vulnerability. The provided explanation is pivotal to the understanding of the necessity of strong regulatory safeguards data protection and to discussing the role of (EU digital) law in mediating power imbalances that are enhanced through digitalization processes. The chapter then continues with an analysis of how administrative and surveillance vulnerability can be minimized by means of transparency, explainability, and accountability-oriented safeguards.

2. Digitalizing Public Services in the European Union

The digitalization of public services across the EU Member States is underpinned by datafication, that is, the conversion of information into data.[16] Juxtaposing technological development, the accumulation of data facilitated the adoption of automated systems, into core governmental sectors, for example law enforcement, welfare allocation, and fraud detection.[17] This digitalization process can be classified in two streams. The first is the use of technical tools to automate routine administrative tasks, while the second involves the employment of machine-learning algorithms to improve or augment decisions and decision-making processes.[18] The digitalization of routine activities birthed the so-called eGovernment, whereas the digital transformation of state processes became the digital government.[19] Digital governments develop either as an augmentation of pre-existing bureaucratic structures, for example The Netherlands,[20] or as a novel set of governmental institutions, for example Estonia,[21] with each EU Member State proposing their own digitalization agenda.[22]

eGovernment processes, such as data and entry tracking, have been observed to serve cost-reduction and increase productivity because they provide public administrators time to address more demanding tasks.[23] The employed systems support real-time, detailed data analysis, simplify governance procedures,[24] and improve human resource allocation

---

[16] See eg Ulises A Mejias and Nick Couldry, 'Datafication' (2019) 8 Internet Policy Review. <https://policyreview.info/concepts/datafication> accessed 10 December 2023; Joanna Redden, 'Democratic Governance in an Age of Datafication: Lessons from Mapping Government Discourses and Practices' (2018) 5 Big Data & Society 2053951718809145.

[17] P Yulu, 'Machine Learning in Governments: Benefits, Challenges and Future Directions' (2021) 13 eJournal of eDemocracy 203; European Commission. Joint Research Centre AI Watch: European Landscape on the Use of Artificial Intelligence by the Public Sector (2022).

[18] Michael Veale and Irina Brass, 'Administration by Algorithm? Public Management Meets Public Sector Machine Learning' (2019) <https://papers.ssrn.com/abstract=3375391> accessed 10 December 2023.

[19] Ranchordas and Scarcella (n 2) 382.

[20] Ronald E Leenes, 'Local E-Government in the Netherlands: From Ambitious Policy Goals to Harsh Reality' (2004) Austrian Academy of Sciences 1.

[21] R Kattel and I Mergel (eds), 'Estonia's Digital Transformation: Mission Mystique and the Hiding Hand', *Great Policy Successes* (1st edn, OUP 2019).

[22] A full list of national strategies for government digitalization can be found here: Joint Research Centre, AI Watch: European Landscape on the Use of Artificial Intelligence by the Public Sector (European Commission 2022) 64–67.

[23] Noella Edelmann, Karin Steiner, and Gianluca Misuraca, 'The View from the Inside: A Case Study on the Perceptions of Digital Transformation Phases in Public Administrations' (2023) 4(2) Digital Government: Research and Practice 7:1.

[24] A Chatzimallis and others, 'Deliverable 2.1 AI4Gov Holistic Regulatory Framework V1' (2023) <https://ai4gov-project.eu/wp-content/uploads/2023/07/AI4Gov_D2.1_AI4Gov-Holistic-Regulatory-Framework.pdf> accessed 27 September 2024.

for more severe cases. Digital government transformation aims to afford citizens greater access to administrative services, provide additional transparency, procedural clarity, and customer-friendly tools.[25] Anticipating these benefits, the EU launched several policy and financial initiatives that boost governmental digitalization.

Early efforts in the EU include the 2009 Malmö Declaration which also recognizes the benefit of eGovernment for the achievement of EU policy goals.[26] The subsequent 2011–2015 eGovernment Action Plan monitors and evaluates processes for technological integration in public administration,[27] whilst the 2017 eGovernment Declaration aims to ensure 'user-centric digital public services for citizens'.[28] The following 2016–2020 eGovernment Action Plan (the Plan) addresses several principles that should underpin the digitalization of public administration.[29] These principles strive to ensure that services are primarily digitally delivered (digital by default) and that individuals only provide their data once to public administration bodies, and that those bodies should be able to use it across sectors (only once principle).[30] The Plan aims to increase inclusiveness and accessibility, openness, and transparency, and supports public administrators in providing digital public services across borders (cross-border by default) while ensuring seamless operation (interoperability-by-default) and trust in digital services (trustworthiness and security).[31] These principles have been strengthened in the 2020 Berlin Declaration,[32] the Digital Decade Initiative, and, most importantly, through the proposed Interoperable Europe Act and the Artificial Intelligence Act. Despite the support demonstrated by the sheer number of initiatives, lawmakers, scholars, and civil society organizations warn about the threats raised by governmental digitalization processes.

According to Wirtz et al, challenges of the digitalization of administration touch upon the following four categories: (1) technological implementation; (2) law and regulation challenges; (3) ethical; and (4) societal.[33] Evidently, challenges regarding technology implementation encompass matters such as technical security, financial feasibility, black-boxes, system and data quality,[34] as well as low possibility of adaptability to a given political context and the reproduction of originally inscribed values throughout the technology's

---

[25] Franklin Dehousse and Karel Van Hecke, 'The European Union and eGovernment' (2006) 59 Studia Diplomatica 135, 1.
[26] 'Ministerial Declaration on eGovernment' <https://www.mt.ro/web14/documente/date-deschise/reglementari/Ministerial-declaration-on-egovernment_Malmo_2009.pdf> accessed 27 September 2024.
[27] European Commission, 'The European eGovernment Action Plan 2011-2015 Harnessing ICT to Promote Smart, Sustainable & Innovative Government' <https://eur-lex.europa.eu/LexUriServ/LexUriServ.do?uri=SEC:2010:1539:FIN:EN:PDF> accessed 27 September 2024.
[28] 'Ministerial Declaration on eGovernment - the Tallinn Declaration' (n 11).
[29] European Commission, 'Communication from the Commission to the European Parliament, the Council, the European Economic and Social Committee and the Committee of the regions EU eGovernment Action Plan 2016-2020 Accelerating the Digital Transformation of Government' 19.04.2016 <https://eur-lex.europa.eu/legal-content/EN/TXT/?uri=CELEX%3A52016DC0179> accessed 10 December 2023.
[30] ibid 1.
[31] ibid.
[32] 'Berlin Declaration on Digital Society and Value-Based Digital Government | Shaping Europe's Digital Future' (8 December 2020) <https://digital-strategy.ec.europa.eu/en/news/berlin-declaration-digital-society-and-value-based-digital-government> accessed 10 December 2023.
[33] Bernd W Wirtz, Jan C Weyerer, and Carolin Geyer, 'Artificial Intelligence and the Public Sector—Applications and Challenges' (2019) 42 International Journal of Public Administration 596; European Commission. Joint Research Centre AI Watch: European Landscape on the Use of Artificial Intelligence by the Public Sector (2022).
[34] ibid.

lifecycle.[35] Technical challenges are deeply interlinked with human history that exhibited and continues to exhibit discriminatory and oppressive patterns.[36]

Legal challenges refer to the difficulties that arise in relation to the governance of the integrated systems.[37] These challenges question how the EU's proposed frameworks fulfil their purpose. While the regulatory and financial initiatives mentioned above suggest a strong interest in adopting digital technologies in digital governments across Member States, the other three categories of challenges indicate that this is not a straightforward endeavour. The adoption and proposal of a large number of legal initiatives has raised questions about how these frameworks interact, and whether they are sufficiently complementary.[38] Though this chapter will not be discussing all initiatives, we will later consider whether the transparency and accountability measures proposed by the GDPR provide adequate safeguards in this context.

Ethical challenges raise doubts of whether the development of some technologies is ethical in the first place, and evaluate how social norms, standards, and ethics are inscribed in technology design.[39] Here, Dignum emphasizes that because systems do not possess emotions such as regret, they are simply incapable of responding to the moral dilemmas that they aim to solve.[40] Because of machine learning, systems may also deviate from the ethical principles and norms that were originally prescribed, and use the discretion that street-level bureaucrats must execute when making administrative decisions to derive morally unsuitable decisions.[41] These challenges could become more pronounced as ethical principles and norms may not even be technically translatable or transmissible to machines.[42]

Social challenges are those that range from the social acceptance or trust in technology to the effect of technology adoption on inequality,[43] the digital divide, and digital literacy. Trust, also an underpinning principle coined by the EU, can be stained by the reassignment of responsibilities from government officials to automated systems, which casts doubt on the administration's function and legitimacy.[44] Despite their hazardous nature, public

---

[35] Maranke Wieringa, 'What to Account for When Accounting for Algorithms: A Systematic Literature Review on Algorithmic Accountability', *Proceedings of the 2020 Conference on Fairness, Accountability, and Transparency* (Association for Computing Machinery 2020) 4 <https://dl.acm.org/doi/10.1145/3351095.3372833> accessed 4 July 2023.
[36] Yulu (n 17) 207–08.
[37] Wirtz, Weyerer, and Geyer (n 33).
[38] See eg A Bogucki and others, 'The AI Act and Emerging EU Digital Acquis Overlaps, Gaps and Inconsistencies.' (CEPS 2022) <https://www.sipotra.it/wp-content/uploads/2022/09/THE-AI-ACT-AND-EMERGING-EU-DIGITAL-ACQUIS-Overlaps-gaps-and-inconsistencies.pdf> accessed 27 September 2024; Matthias Artzt and Tran Viet Dung, 'Artificial Intelligence and Data Protection: How to Reconcile Both Areas from the European Law Perspective' (2022) 7 Vietnamese Journal of Legal Sciences 39; Paweł Hajduk, 'AI Act and GDPR: On the path towards overlap of the enforcement structures (*RAILS - Blog*, 1 October 2023) <https://blog.ai-laws.org/ai-act-and-gdpr-on-the-path-towards-overlap-of-the-enforcement-structures/> accessed 10 December 2023; Jenny Bergholm, 'The GDPR and the Artificial Intelligence Regulation – It Takes Two to Tango?' (*CiTiP blog*, 6 July 2021) <https://www.law.kuleuven.be/citip/blog/the-gdpr-and-the-artificial-intelligence-regulation-it-takes-two-to-tango/> accessed 10 December 2023.
[39] Wirtz, Weyerer, and Geyer (n 33) 10–11.
[40] Virginia Dignum, *Responsible Artificial Intelligence: How to Develop and Use AI in a Responsible Way* (Springer International Publishing 2019) 35–46 <http://link.springer.com/10.1007/978-3-030-30371-6> accessed 10 December 2023.
[41] Wirtz, Weyerer, and Geyer (n 33) 11.
[42] ibid.
[43] ibid.
[44] Ryan Calo and Danielle Keats Citron, 'The Automated Administrative State: A Crisis of Legitimacy' (2021) 70 Emory Law Journal 797.

service digitalization has escaped public debate,[45] being often perceived as a normal evolution. Digital governance is citizen-driven, that is, relying on citizens to identify their own needs[46] and provide adequate information in the form of data so that the state can fulfil those needs where applicable. This shift in the right-holder's position led individuals to internalize the provision of data to the state in exchange for access to the state's services, leading to a normalization of data-based surveillance activities.[47] As Goos et al argue, 'the link between surveillance and bureaucratic organizational form illustrates the universality of surveillance'.[48]

The reliance of digital governance on data-driven decision-making activities combined with the increase of diverse and normalized forms of surveillance can be described through the concept of 'dataveillance'.[49] In this context, Birrer et al explain that the state's data retention practices that also underpin surveillance are less critically perceived by individuals as consisting of a breach of privacy compared to similar commercial practices.[50] The authors explain that data retention practices construct a modern form of state surveillance, and that states often seek loopholes through which data collection and retention practices may occur in an unrestricted manner.[51] Subsequently, the technological shift widens power asymmetries, affording the government with a stronger institutional, inhumane shape that relies on surveillance and dilutes the individual's ability to hold governmental systems accountable. In the following we consider how the development of digital government, alongside its expansive surveillance contributes to what literature has coined as 'vulnerability', and the deriving 'administrative vulnerability' and 'surveillance vulnerability'.

3. From Administrative to Surveillance Vulnerability

Vulnerability is a multifaceted concept that should be applied in the context of public service activities and the effect of digitalization on administrative structures. It implies a state of imminence, meaning that if harm occurs, the person is no longer vulnerable.[52] The concept of human vulnerability can be legally defined as the higher risks of harm to one's fundamental rights and freedoms[53] with the related incapability to mitigate those risks and face the consequences of those harms. The occurrence of higher risks is strictly related to the inherent dependencies of human beings on 'others' (parents, families, social structures, the state) to

---

[45] A Rachovitsa and Niclas Johann, 'The Human Rights Implications of the Use of AI in the Digital Welfare State: Lessons Learned from the Dutch SyRi Case' (2022) 22 Human Rights Law Review 1.
[46] OECD, 'Recommendation of the Council on Digital Government Strategies' OECD/LEGAL/0406 (2014) <https://legalinstruments.oecd.org/en/instruments/OECD-LEGAL-0406#mainText> accessed 9 January 2025, 2.2.
[47] Kerstin Goos, Michael Friedewald, C William R Webster, and Charles Leleux, 'The Co-Evolution of Surveillance Technologies and Surveillance Practices', in David Wright and Reinhard Kreissi (eds) *Surveillance in Europe* (Routledge 2014) 54.
[48] ibid.
[49] Roger Clarke, 'Information Technology and Dataveillance' (1988) 31 Communications of the ACM 498; Roger Clarke, 'Dataveillance: Delivering 1984', *Framing Technology* (Routledge 1994).
[50] Alena Birrer, Danya He, and Natascha Just, 'The State Is Watching You—A Cross-National Comparison of Data Retention in Europe' (2023) 47 Telecommunications Policy 102542.
[51] ibid.
[52] Florencia Luna, 'Identifying and Evaluating Layers of Vulnerability – a Way Forward' (2019) 19 Developing World Bioethics 86, 91.
[53] Malgieri and Niklas (n 4) 11.

satisfy their fundamental needs, their capabilities, or, in other words, their fundamental rights.[54] Such an inherent dependence may produce situations of power-imbalance when the satisfaction of one or more fundamental rights strictly depends on one or few external entities. In other words, we observe a situation of vulnerability when a powerless individual depends on some exclusive or quasi-exclusive 'enablers' of their fundamental rights and freedoms, such as in the case of digitalizing public administration. The more dependent a person is on an external enabler to satisfy their fundamental rights, the more exposed to harm to their fundamental rights they are and, thus, the more vulnerable they are.

The employed definition of vulnerability is contextual and relational/interpersonal. Its *contextuality* depends on the specific fundamental rights at issue, for example, mental or bodily integrity, privacy, data protection, non-discrimination, freedom of movement.[55] Its *interpersonal* nature depends on the specific power-imbalanced relationship at issue between the vulnerable person (at higher risk of harm) and the counterpart ('enabling' the fundamental rights of the powerless person).[56] This chapter uses the concept of 'administrative vulnerability' when focusing on the power-imbalanced relationship between individuals and the state (collecting data and taking decisions). It argues that 'surveillance vulnerability' is a specification of administrative vulnerability, focusing on the situation when the state collects information about individuals, often through ubiquitous measures, in order to make decisions across administrative sectors.

Ranchordás and Scarcella propose the first contextualized understanding of administrative vulnerability, namely 'the full or partial vulnerability to exercise rights before public authorities and participate in public life on equal terms'.[57] Departing from the assumption of universal application of vulnerability, administrative vulnerability can be differently experienced by all citizens, regardless of their socioeconomic conditions and aptitudes.[58] Building upon Mackenzie et al's developed vulnerability taxonomy, we believe that administrative vulnerability can be both dispositional (ie the vulnerability potential that characterizes an act) or occurrent (ie actual vulnerability that is perpetrated through the individual's unique socio-physical characteristics).[59] Risks-to-rights may be dispositional to all individuals who are being surveyed by digital governments due to power imbalances, but they are occurrent only for those individuals whose sensitive characteristics (eg origins or sexuality) attract additional examination of their persona or case. Though digitalization is not indispensable to administrative vulnerability, power-imbalances and dependency are. Several dimensions need to be considered in relation to power imbalances.

One key aspect in analysing state-citizen power dynamics is dependency, which relates to individuals relying on the state to grant, limit, or ensure certain rights. If a state does not grant a given right, then the individual cannot be administratively vulnerable in relation to that state because, with respect to sovereign powers, the risk-to-rights does not occur. The individual in question can only be administratively vulnerable in a moral/ethical or

---

[54] Martha LA Fineman, 'Masking Dependency: The Political Role of Family Rhetoric' (1995) 81 Virginia Law Review 2181; Fineman, 'The Vulnerable Subject' (n 9).
[55] Gianclaudio Malgieri, 'Vulnerability' in Giovanni Comandé (ed), *Elgar Encyclopedia of Law and Data Science* (Edward Elgar 2022).
[56] Gianclaudio Malgieri, *Vulnerability and Data Protection Law* (OUP 2023) Chapter 3; Jonathan Herring, *Vulnerable Adults and the Law* (OUP 2016) Chapter 2.
[57] ibid.
[58] ibid.
[59] ibid 7–9.

dispositional sense. Perhaps from a similar premise, Ranchordás and Scarcella suggest that administrative vulnerability is experienced by citizens.[60] We believe, however, that the administrative vulnerability as described can also occur in state-individual relations that are characterised by the legitimacy of residence, which can grant access to (a number of) rights. For example, EU residents can also benefit from Dutch social benefits if they are legally working and living in the Netherlands.[61] In other words, individual rights are granted by public service authorities depending on the individual's recorded presence in a given country and in accordance with the country's sovereignty.

The context of digitalization signals an additional layer of administrative vulnerability, namely that which is experienced by means of the power-imbalanced relationship between data subject and data controller[62] that is branded by information-asymmetry and opacity. An individual who is administratively vulnerable in a digital state is also vulnerable because of their position as a data subject, and may experience 'data subject vulnerability'.[63] When considering a country's data retention and collection practices, which could potentially exacerbate vulnerability among data subjects, it is crucial to take into account Malgieri and Davola's definition of (market) power as the ability to 'set data collection conditions without losing revenues or customers'.[64] The same definition can be applied to digital governments, who can set data collection conditions without ever losing the citizen's apparent willingness to provide data, and so engender mass (legal, normalized, or seemingly wanted) surveillance activities.

To expand and interpret administrative vulnerability in the context of state surveillance, as a form of case study, we should identify the context, the fundamental rights and the power relationship at issue. When an individual is under state surveillance, there are at least two levels of risks to their fundamental rights that we should observe. The first and more immediate level is the higher risk to their fundamental rights to privacy and data protection. Depending on the specific characteristics of the situation, the secret nature of surveillance, the consequent difficult means for obtaining redress and/or exercising data protection rights, the psychological consequences of feeling oneself under surveillance and the potential cascade effects of surveillance (in terms of administrative sanctions or law enforcement actions) are enough to qualify a condition of surveillance vulnerability.[65] The second and more indirect level of risk may relate to the higher risk of adverse effects on the fundamental right to—inter alia—a fair trial, non-discrimination, freedom of movement, access to welfare services, property, and freedom to conduct a business. This level of risk refers to the consequences of public decision-making based on data collected through state surveillance.

---

[60] Ranchordas and Scarcella (n 2) 416.
[61] European Commission, 'Netherlands - Employment, Social Affairs & Inclusion - European Commission' (*Employment, Social Affairs and Inclusion*, 2023) <https://ec.europa.eu/social/main.jsp?catId=1122&langId=en> accessed 3 July 2023.
[62] ibid.
[63] For a detailed account of data subject vulnerability see Malgieri and Niklas (n 4).
[64] Gianclaudio Malgieri and Antonio Davola, 'Data-Powerful' (2022), SSRN: <https://ssrn.com/abstract=4027370> or <http://dx.doi.org/10.2139/ssrn.4027370> 21.
[65] Charles Raab and David Wright, 'Surveillance: Extending the Limits of Privacy Impact Assessment' in David Wright and Paul De Hert (eds), *Privacy Impact Assessment* (Springer 2012) <https://doi.org/10.1007/978-94-007-2543-0_17> accessed 13 August 2019; David Wright and Charles D Raab, 'Constructing a Surveillance Impact Assessment' (2012) 28 Computer Law & Security Review 613.

Taking into account these considerations, in the case of state surveillance, the occurrence of individual vulnerabilities is not only possible but even likely, due to the inherent power imbalance between the parties and the important risks for fundamental rights at issue.[66] The specific rules, safeguards, and guarantees of the democratic system and the rule of law have the explicit role of mitigating the adverse effects of such a power imbalance through transparency rules, clear and easy redress mechanisms and fairness rules (ex-ante checks about state surveillance and state decisions, etc). It is then necessary to analyse the legal and practical context to understand how the risks of adverse effects on the fundamental right to privacy and data protection (and the secondary risks of discrimination, unfair trials, unfair administrative decisions, etc) are mitigated in a specific legal system and how some individuals or groups of individuals are more exposed to others in certain contexts. Accordingly, the next section will analyse how existing safeguards in the GDPR (like transparency and accountability) can offer possibilities for mitigating surveillance vulnerability.

4. Transparency and Explainability as Possible Safeguards for Administrative and Surveillance Vulnerability

Transparency is a rights-enabling tool that enables accountability, rather than an end-goal.[67] Accordingly, Pasquale's 'qualified transparency' refers to the provision of targeted information, varying in scope and depth, that is directed towards different recipient groups.[68] Implementing transparency in a manner that induces an explanation-based understanding of the (digital) law is essential for rights mobilization,[69] especially where surveillance is most prominently produced by the individual's voluntary provision of data and the normalization of surveillance-inducing digitalization processes. Transparency and explainability aid the individual's understanding of state decisions in two ways. While transparency is akin to providing clear, descriptive information as described in 'qualified transparency', explainability uses transparent description to respond to a duty to motivate a decision and to assert liability.[70] Transparency and explainability are intertwined but not interchangeable terms that elicit different expectations.

There are two moments in which transparency may be relevant when addressing administrative and subsequently surveillance vulnerability. The first moment is transparency over the surveillance measures (e.g., transparency about the existence of surveillance practices, about the parameters on which digital surveillance is based, about the functioning of the algorithms of mass surveillance, etc), while the second moment is transparency about

---

[66] Raab and Wright, ibid; Wright and Raab, ibid.
[67] Paul de Hert and Dariusz Kloza, 'Internet (Access) as a New Fundamental Right: Inflating the Current Rights Framework?' (2012) 3 European Journal of Law and Technology 1.
[68] Frank Pasquale, *The Black Box Society: The Secret Algorithms That Control Money and Information* (Harvard University Press 2016) 140–42.
[69] Margot E Kaminski, 'The Right to Explanation, Explained' (2019) 34 Berkeley Technology Law Journal 189, 204; Ida Varošanec, 'On the Path to the Future: Mapping the Notion of Transparency in the EU Regulatory Framework for AI' (2022) 36 International Review of Law, Computers & Technology 95, 97–99; Hannah van Kolfschooten and Anniek de Ruijter, 'COVID-19 and Privacy in the European Union: A Legal Perspective on Contact Tracing' (2020) 41 Contemporary Security Policy 478, 486.
[70] See also Upol Ehsan and others, 'Expanding Explainability: Towards Social Transparency in AI Systems', *Proceedings of the 2021 CHI Conference on Human Factors in Computing Systems* (Association for Computing Machinery 2021) <https://dl.acm.org/doi/10.1145/3411764.3445188> accessed 4 July 2023.

the decision-making process that might follow as a consequence of surveillance (eg transparency about enforcement actions taken on the basis of the collected data; transparency about the public administration's decision in terms of welfare services allocations or tax law procedures starting as a consequence of surveillance). Both these moments are relevant to mitigate surveillance vulnerability, but the characteristics and implications of these two different moments of transparency are very different.

4.1 Transparency over surveillance measures

Transparency over the surveillance measures, or the first moment of transparency, has been an important concept in the ECtHR case law on surveillance under Article 8 ECHR.[71] The ECtHR, in the case *Adomaitis v Lithuania* upheld that when the state conducts surveillance, transparency holds crucial value. In this instance, the interception of telephone conversations of the applicant, a prison director suspected of corruption, was permissible because it aimed at preventing corrupt acts and ensuring transparency in public service. This aligns with the legitimate objectives of maintaining order, preventing crime, and safeguarding the rights and freedoms of others.[72] As van Kolfschooten and de Ruijter suggest, the ECtHR has expressed that transparency allows individuals to invoke their (data subject) rights and should only be denied where matters of national security or public interest are balanced against the individual's rights to data protection and privacy.[73]

In various cases related to personal data collected and retained by public authorities, the ECtHR found that these authorities have an obligation to provide an 'effective and accessible procedure' to individuals concerned. This procedure should grant access to all relevant and appropriate information necessary for purposes like understanding childhood and early development,[74] establishing personal identity,[75] or tracing personal history during a past totalitarian regime.[76] However, this transparency requirement may be less strict in cases involving sensitive information concerning national security.[77]

---

[71] See eg Douwe Korff and others, 'Boundaries of Law: Exploring Transparency, Accountability, and Oversight of Government Surveillance Regimes' (5 January 2017) <https://papers.ssrn.com/abstract=2894490> accessed 17 July 2023; Teresa Scassa, 'Law Enforcement in the Age of Big Data and Surveillance Intermediaries: Transparency Challenges' (2017) 14 SCRIPTed: A Journal of Law, Technology and Society 239; David Lyon, 'Surveillance, Transparency, and Trust: Critical Challenges from the COVID-19 Pandemic', *Trust and Transparency in an Age of Surveillance* (Routledge 2021).

[72] ECtHR, *Adomaitis v Lithuania* (Application no. 14833/18, Judgment of 18 April 2022) accessed 9 January 2025 (§ 84) 2022.

[73] For example, in relation to surveillance, van Kolfschooten and de Ruijter suggest that transparency (in terms of informing the concerned individual) is an essential element in surveillance acts that trespass privacy and data protection rights. Transparency would subsequently allow the individual to mobilize their data subject rights and should only be withheld in matters of national security: van Kolfschooten and de Ruijter (n 69) 486.

[74] ECtHR, *Gaskin v United Kingdom* (Application no. 10454/83, Judgment of 7 July 1989) <https://hudoc.echr.coe.int/tur#{%22itemid%22:[%22001-57491%22]}> accessed 9 January 2025 (§§ 41–49) 1989 § 49.

[75] ECtHR, *Odièvre v France* (Application no. 422326, Judgment of 13 February 2003) <https://hudoc.echr.coe.int/eng#{%22itemid%22:[%22001-60935%22]}> [GC] 2003 §§ 41–49), identifying health risks; *Roche v the United Kingdom* [GC] 2005 § 162; *Guerra and Others v Italy* 1998 § 60; *McGinley and Egan v the United Kingdom* 1998 § 101 (Application no. 10/1997/794/995-996, Judgment of 9 June 1998) <https://hudoc.echr.coe.int/eng#{%22itemid%22:[%22001-58175%22]}> accessed 9 January 2025 (§ 101).

[76] ECtHR, *Haralambie v Romania*, 2009, § 93.

[77] ECtHR, *Leander v Sweden*, 1987, § 51; *Segerstedt-Wiberg and Others v Sweden*, 2006, § 102; *Dalea v France* (dec.) 2010.

In the case *López Ribalda and Others v Spain*,[78] the ECtHR stressed the importance of employers informing employees about data collection measures, even if only in a general manner, before implementing them. This transparency is especially crucial in employment relationships, where employers wield significant power over employees, and its absence may lead to abuses of power. However, while the provision of information to the individual being monitored is essential, it is only one aspect considered when assessing the proportionality of such measures. If information is lacking, other safeguards become even more critical.[79]

4.2 Transparency over the consequences of surveillance

To mitigate administrative and surveillance vulnerability respectively, it is also important to ensure the second moment of transparency, that is, transparency over the consequences of surveillance in particular, and the use of digital technologies within public administration in general. This form of transparency is very different from the previously described one, both in terms of legal cogency and in terms of practical implications. Indeed, as we said in the previous section, transparency over surveillance measures might be limited in cases involving sensitive information and compelling public interests, for example, in the case of national security.[80] On the other hand, transparency over administrative decisions is imposed more strictly by the EU primary and secondary law. In this section, we will try to analyse how some provisions within EU law are adequate in order to impose transparency and accountability over the 'consequences' of administrative vulnerability and surveillance.

Explainability is different from transparency also because the former is addressed towards individual accountability schemes, whereas the latter can be considered as more descriptive 'meaningful' information that varies in depth and intended recipient, being derived from Articles 13 and 14 of the GDPR.[81] Further, the requirement to disclose algorithm deployment at the time of data collection through the provision of meaningful information on the outcomes and the logic involved,[82] is a transparency-oriented measure[83] aimed at raising the individual's awareness and eliciting their response. In establishing the GDPR's *transparency* requirements, Articles 13 and 14 GDPR emphasize that supplied information must be clearly presented[84] and meaningful.[85] In line with the proposed definition of qualified transparency, achieving meaningful transparency demands the contextualization of information to the recipients[86] and their power traits.

---

[78] ECtHR, *López Ribalda and Others v Spain* [GC] 2019 § 133.
[79] ibid § 131.
[80] ECtHR, *Leander v Sweden*, 1987, § 51; *Segerstedt-Wiberg and others v Sweden*, 2006, § 102; *Dalea v France (dec.)*, 2010.
[81] Kaminski (n 69); Pasquale (n 68).
[82] GDPR Art 13(2)(f).
[83] Celine Castets-Renard, 'Accountability of Algorithms in the GDPR and Beyond: A European Legal Framework on Automated Decision-Making' (2019) 30 Fordham Intellectual Property, Media & Entertainment Law Journal 91.
[84] ibid 9.
[85] Andrew Selbst and Julia Powles, '"Meaningful Information" and the Right to Explanation', *Proceedings of the 1st Conference on Fairness, Accountability and Transparency* (PMLR 2018) 234 <https://proceedings.mlr.press/v81/selbst18a.html> accessed 3 July 2023; GDPR Arts 13(2)(f), 14(2)(g), and 15(1)(h).
[86] See also Kaminski (n 69) 211.

In turn explainability can be found under Recital 71 of the GDPR which suggests that individuals have a 'right ... to obtain an explanation of the decision reached' after solely automated processing that has legal effect. Despite not being recognized in the GDPR Articles, the WP29 guidelines alongside the succeeding scholarly analysis demonstrated that, by way of the Recital[87], the *Right to Explanation* can be interpreted under the individual's rights to express their view and contest a decision.[88] Further, in specific relation to the public sector, Article 296 of the TFEU and Article 41(2)(c) of the Charter, stipulate that public administration bodies have a duty to provide reasoning for their legal actions,[89] meaning that, regardless of decision modularity, states should explain their acts. These Articles support the provision of *Right to Explanation* at all times rather than upon request,[90] particularly when governments use digital technologies to issue decisions, that inevitably have legal effect due to the aforementioned dependency and power-imbalanced citizen-state relations.

Notwithstanding their promise as measures capable of minimizing administrative and surveillance vulnerability and their presence within varying legal frameworks, the efficacy of transparency and explainability-oriented solutions is bounded by several challenges.

5. Challenges to Implementing Transparency as a Safeguard for Administrative and Surveillance Vulnerability

Transparency requirements can quickly become ineffective when facing previously explained technological implementation challenges. Surveillance mechanisms as well as data-based, machine-learning technology that is employed within public service decision-making activities are infamous for their black-box character.[91] This opacity generates vulnerability by preventing both transparency and explainability and can only be tackled through a combination between the strict regulation of design components and the implementation of value-sensitive design. Both these measures aim to instill developers with the duty to reflect on the surveillance mechanisms that they are enabling through the system's production.[92]

The accumulation of the technology implementation challenges cascade into social as well as legal challenges. On the legal side, transparency oriented regulation manifests the transparency fallacy, that is, the erroneous belief that transparency alone is a resolution to the opaque procedures that surround technological explanation.[93] On the social side,

---

[87] 'Guidelines on Automated Individual Decision-Making and Profiling for the Purposes of Regulation 2016/679'.

[88] Kaminski (n 69) 204; Gianclaudio Malgieri, 'Automated Decision-Making in the EU Member States: The Right to Explanation and Other "Suitable Safeguards" in the National Legislations' (2019) 35 Computer Law & Security Review 1; Gianclaudio Malgieri and Giovanni Comandé, 'Why a Right to Legibility of Automated Decision-Making Exists in the General Data Protection Regulation' (2017) 7 International Data Privacy Law 243.

[89] Varošanec (n 69) 95, 97–99.

[90] See also Malgieri and Comandé (n 88) 255.

[91] Pasquale (n 68); Varošanec (n 69) 100.

[92] For decentralization of government technology production see R Csernatoni, 'New States of Emergency: Normalizing Techno-Surveillance in the Time of COVID-19' (2020) 6 Global Affairs 301; Martin Ebers, 'Standardizing AI - The Case of the European Commission's Proposal for an Artificial Intelligence Act' (6 August 2021) <https://papers.ssrn.com/abstract=3900378> accessed 5 July 2023.

[93] B Berendt, 'The AI Act Proposal: Towards the next Transparency Fallacy? Why AI Regulation Should Be Based on Principles Based on How Algorithmic Discrimination Works' (Mohr Siebeck 2022) 14 <https://people.cs.kuleuven.be/~bettina.berendt/Papers/berendt_2022c_last_author_version.pdf> accessed 27 September 2024;

Edwards and Veale argue that providing non-expert individuals with numerous and varied information will not elicit rights mobilization, but rather increases the (vulnerable) person's burden.[94] Engraving the principle of transparency within the law as the ultimate module of rights activation upholds the flawed premise of individual rationality,[95] leading to information overload or fatigue.[96] The mere presentation of descriptive information may not be sufficient in producing rights mobilization, particularly because of the individual's reduced power and resources. Under the veil of information-based empowerment, transparency requires incredible skill and knowledge for it to be meaningfully translated to accountability-seeking action.[97] In the absence of such expertise, risks-to-rights, ergo administrative and surveillance vulnerability, prevail.

Because the digital environment remains branded by cleavages resulting from the digital divide, it is difficult to manage what meaningful information means, to whom, in what context, and when.[98] There is a fundamental distinction between the type, quantity, and format in which information should be provided to users as opposed to regulators.[99] This different information provision has yet to be formalized in the law and should be contextualized to the stakeholder's power and resources. From this perspective, levelling the imbalances in surveillance activities relies on the identification of vulnerabilities and power position of each of the involved players. Where individual ex-post accountability is reliant on too many unmeasurable unknowns for example digital skills, knowledge, time, and resources, institutional safeguards should be further enforced and legally demanded.

These challenges demonstrate why systems of accountability that are rooted in transparency without explainability fail from their very beginning. This chapter suggests a cumulative interpretation of these interlinked concepts. This interpretation understands transparency as the first step to explainability, and explainability as the intermediary step to achieving accountability.[100] Without transparent information, explanations cannot be provided. In turn, convoluted explanations reduce rebuttal possibilities and, consequently, accountability. To effectively engender this cumulative process, the logic needs to be reversed and regulators should consider adapting the transparency and explainability requirements to the type of accountability they seek to achieve.

6. From Transparency and Explainability to Accountability

Bovens defines accountability as 'a relationship between an actor and a forum, in which the actor has an obligation to explain and to justify his or her conduct, the forum can pose

---

Cynthia Stohl, Michael Stohl, and Paul M Leonardi, 'Digital Age | Managing Opacity: Information Visibility and the Paradox of Transparency in the Digital Age' (2016) 10 International Journal of Communication 123, 131.

[94] L Edwards L and M Veale, 'Slave to the Algorithm? Why a "Right to an Explanation" Is Probably Not the Remedy You Are Looking For' (2017) 16 Duke Law and Technology Review 18, 67.
[95] eg Mark Leiser, 'The Problem with "Dots": Questioning the Role of Rationality in the Online Environment' (2016) 30 International Review of Law, Computers & Technology 191; Ranchordas and Scarcella (n 2).
[96] Stohl, Stohl, and Leonardi (n 93) 123, 131.
[97] Edwards and Veale (n 94) 67.
[98] Varošanec (n 69).
[99] Kaminski (n 69) 211; Pasquale (n 68) 140–88.
[100] See also Kaminski (n 69) 211.

questions and pass judgement, and the actor may face consequences'.[101] Here, the actor is the digital government which produces increased surveillance through mundane or normalized technology introduction, whereby the forum is composed of the administratively vulnerable individuals. According to Bovens, different forms of accountability can emerge, namely, administrative, political, social, and legal.[102]

Administrative accountability acknowledges independent, quasi-legal institutions that supervise various activities in their professional domain,[103] for example, the Data Protection Authorities and apply institutional-based safeguards and enable (secondary) law enforcement. Bodies, such as the European Parliament, that have a delegated role in producing accountability fall under the political accountability.[104] These bodies should also inform and foster essential public debate on the integration of surveillance-promoting technologies. Although public debate on the deployment of surveillance technologies is currently limited, it is a crucial tool for evaluating the legality of such systems.[105] Legal accountability is offered through the law by responsible authorities,[106] for example, courts. Because courts can only be reactive, they cannot always prevent the deployment of algorithmic systems, nor can they govern within a convoluted and ambiguous legal ecosystem[107]—which is the case for technology. Courts are also responsible for balancing privacy and data protection rights, which are not absolute, against the safety and efficiency discourse that surrounds broad surveillance tactics. In the digital government, legal accountability forums should decide whether surveillance technologies are held accountable as systems as opposed to their case-by-case use. For instance, Bekkum and Borgesius argue that the court ruling on the Dutch SyRI (System for Risk Indication) was insufficient in providing accountability for government-employed automated decision-making systems in the Netherlands because the institution addressed the case narrowly, without accounting for broader human rights or privacy implications.[108] Given that state surveillance technology, for example Covid-19 tracking apps,[109] are contextually deployed and surrounded by discourses of emergency, security, efficiency, etc, it is difficult to imagine that a non-contextual ruling would be issued. Nevertheless, this demonstrates the need for premeditation in technology deployment by (state) institutions in light of the risks posed by the same to fundamental rights.

Lastly, social accountability is provided through the intermediary of, for example, NGOs, aiming to achieve representation and providing a complex accountability scheme that is composed of both civil society groups and authorities.[110] These fora classification demonstrates that the responsibility to ensure accountability for surveillance activities is dispersed across actors requiring sector-specific laws.[111] Depending on whether the

---

[101] Mark Bovens, 'Analysing and Assessing Accountability: A Conceptual Framework' (2007) 13 European Law Journal 447, 447.
[102] ibid.
[103] ibid.
[104] ibid, 4.
[105] Csernatoni (n 92) 303–04; Rachovitsa and Johann (n 45) 1.
[106] Bovens (n 101) 456.
[107] Wieringa, 'What to Account For' (n 35) 4.
[108] Marvin van Bekkum and Frederik Zuiderveen Borgesius, 'Digital Welfare Fraud Detection and the Dutch SyRI Judgment' (2021) 23 European Journal of Social Security 323.
[109] eg Csernatoni (n 92).
[110] Wieringa, 'What to Account For' (n 35) 4.
[111] ibid.

accountability systems are ex-ante or ex-post, each forum should have different transparency and explainability expectations.

Ex-ante accountability reduces (digital) administrative vulnerability by seeking to mitigate data-related adverse effects in the early stages of technology deployment.[112] It requires compliance with, for example, harmonized standards,[113] data processing principles,[114] and trustworthy AI principles.[115] This accountability form is served through transparently provided information on the technology's purpose, functioning, and intent.[116] Ex-ante accountability and its associated transparency requirements should address and contextualize explanations to the administrative and political fora. Ex-ante accountability engenders pre-deployment institutional compliance and post-deployment corrections.

Ex-post accountability describes auditing mechanisms that consider a decision's processes, impacts,[117] and the system's limitations, intent, and purposes described in ex-ante accountability. Ex-post approaches are predominant in citizen-driven digital governments and should address transparent descriptions of the social and legal accountability fora. Individuals can only pursue ex-post redress mechanisms to ensure correct decision-making. Ex-post accountability prompts power-balancing and rights mobilization mechanisms that are sustained through the Charter and the GDPR (data subject) rights. Digital governance evolution should occur in tandem with accountability measures.[118] Subsequently, latency between technology development and accountability instruments should be minimized before technology adoption, and technology based surveillance should be unacceptable in the absence of sufficient accountability measures.

Taking everything into account, this section underscores that the attainment of accountability within the digitalizing public sphere necessitates a multifaceted methodology. The proposed approach, therefore, asked first how an administratively vulnerable individual can achieve a certain form of accountability, and relays that to the specific and adapted transparency and explainability requirements. Implementing this strategy serves the mitigation of administrative and surveillance vulnerability respectively because it tackles the raising challenges through different mediums.

7. Conclusion

The digitalization of public services in the EU is a double-edged sword. While it promises opportunities for efficiency and service improvement, it also raises significant risks to (fundamental) rights, that is, it produces what was defined as administrative vulnerability. In this chapter, we adopted comprehensive approach to vulnerability that takes into account

---

[112] See also Varošanec (n 69) 99.
[113] Claudio Novelli, Mariarosaria Taddeo, and Luciano Floridi, 'Accountability in Artificial Intelligence: What It Is and How It Works' [2023] AI & Society 1.
[114] GDPR Art 5.
[115] eg 'Ethics Guidelines for Trustworthy AI - Publications Office of the EU' <https://op.europa.eu/en/publication-detail/-/publication/d3988569-0434-11ea-8c1f-01aa75ed71a1> accessed 10 December 2023.
[116] M Wieringa, '"Hey SyRI, Tell Me about Algorithmic Accountability": Lessons from a Landmark Case' (2023) 5 Data & Policy 1, 12.
[117] Varošanec (n 69) 99.
[118] Ada Lovelace Institute, 'Algorithmic Accountability for the Public Sector' (*Open Government Partnership*, 23 August 2021) <https://www.opengovpartnership.org/documents/algorithmic-accountability-public-sector/> accessed 5 July 2023.

context, interpersonal relationships, and different layers of impact and introduced a preliminary assessment of the elements that compose administrative vulnerability. The concept was then expanded to respond to the state's surveillance practices. Taking a broad approach to surveillance practices, the derived 'surveillance vulnerability' focuses on the risks to rights that are associated in particular with the state's data collection, data retention, and automation practices that result in surveillance.

After describing the two interrelated concepts, we consider transparency and explainability as potential safeguards for administrative and surveillance vulnerability. We suggest that while the provision of targeted information is essential for individuals to understand public service decisions and receive explanations that allow them to exercise their rights, explainability and transparency both face significant challenges in delivering accountability. Subsequently, we identify how different forms of accountability (administrative, social, political, and legal) applied in either ex-ante or ex-post manners, serve to complete the proposed risk mitigation strategy in relation to administrative and surveillance vulnerability.

In sum, effectively addressing administrative and surveillance vulnerability requires a multifaceted approach. In this approach, it is important to first understand the nature of vulnerability and correlate it to the type of accountability that would be best attuned to address it. Then, transparency and explainability are tools used to achieve the aforementioned accountability and ensure that risks to rights are minimized.

27

Data Retention and the 'Chilling Effect' in the Context of Mass Surveillance and a Tacit Sift Towards a Hobbesian state in Western Democracies

Ivan Manokha

1. Introduction

In 2005, Giorgio Agamben observed that after the terrorist attacks of 9/11 and the subsequent adoption of measures such as the US PATRIOT Act of 2001 (officially known as the Uniting and Strengthening America by Providing Appropriate Tools Required to Intercept and Obstruct Terrorism Act), the paradigm of government in Western democracies was shifting towards a 'permanent state of exception', where emergency measures and exceptional powers become normalized and entrenched in the everyday functioning of government.[1] Not much time has elapsed since the publication of Agamben's *State of Exception*, but the transformations that we have witnessed in the intervening period have been profound. The growing digitization of everyday life and vast amounts of data that now mundane individual activities—online shopping and internet browsing, social media use, looking up directions on Google maps, or using video or audio streaming services—generate, have enabled various private and public actors to collect unprecedented amounts of information on the activities and lives of individuals. For many commercial entities the digital traces that individuals leave online have become indispensable means to generate profits. Some firms use this data as the primary source of their earnings through targeted advertising, with profits reaching gigantic amounts in some cases. Facebook, for example, with close to 3 billion monthly active users[2] that on any single day share about 5 billion items and 'like' some 4.5 billion posts, generated 85.9 billion USD in revenue in 2020, with virtually all of this revenue (about 98%) coming from targeted advertising.[3] Others use personal data as an auxiliary source of income—usually for advertisement of their own products or those of third-parties (eg online stores such as Amazon), or for finding ways to increase customer engagement and satisfaction (eg streaming platforms such as Netflix or Spotify). State governments overtly or covertly get access to private data collected by commercial actors as

---

[1] Giorgio Agamben, *State of Exception* (University of Chicago Press, 2005).
[2] Statista, 'Social Media Usage Worldwide', 8 February 2022 <https://www.statista.com/topics/1164/social-networks/> accessed 27 September 2024.
[3] Statista, 'Facebook', 18 February 2022 <https://www.statista.com/statistics/268604/annual-revenue-of-facebook/> accessed 27 September 2024.

Ivan Manokha, *Data Retention and the 'Chilling Effect' in the Context of Mass Surveillance and a Tacit Sift Towards a Hobbesian state in Western Democracies* In: *Data Retention in Europe and Beyond*. Edited by: Eleni Kosta and Irene Kamara, Oxford University Press.
© Ivan Manokha 2025. DOI: 10.1093/9780191998980.003.0027

well as employ their own means to undertake mass surveillance of citizens and foreigners. Data retention policies pursued by numerous European states—despite the invalidation of the Data Retention Directive[4] in 2014 by the Court of Justice of the European Union (CJEU)—are examples of such overt measures that 'outsource' surveillance to the private sector:[5] they require private actors to indiscriminately collect and store traffic and location data of users, in order to make them available for law enforcement purposes. In short, our individual preferences, beliefs, and activities have become an object of analysis and the ability of firms and state actors to profile and track individuals—especially with the rise of artificial intelligence (AI) and machine learning—has grown to an unprecedented extent. And this, as has been widely observed, undermines a whole range of individual rights— privacy, freedom of expression, presumption of innocence, etc—that have been fundamental to democratic societies.

In this context it may be argued that the situation in Western democracies has gone far beyond Agamben's 'permanent state of exception' as a new paradigm of government as a result of a convergence of two mutually reinforcing processes: on the one hand, there is an increasing tendency to view security as the most important value which, if necessary, may trump other values, including different individuals rights. In the field of personal data, this has involved policies of mass surveillance and bulk data collection without prior suspicion, different policies undertaken to strengthen states' 'digital sovereignty', as well as the policies of data retention that constitute the focus of this chapter. As regards actions that violate other individual rights in the name of security, examples are numerous: we may mention the CIA's extraordinary rendition of terrorist suspects to third states for interrogation, indefinite detention of terror suspects without charge or trial, restrictions on legal counselling of foreign suspects, or reinforcement of border controls and discriminatory treatment of some travellers based on their origin or religion. On the other hand, citizens of Western states are becoming more and more habituated to surveillance and personal data collection, in particular by all kinds of private actors (who is today not accustomed to suggestions of the type 'because you "liked" (purchased, viewed, listened to, visited, etc) X, you may be interested in Y?'). Such commercial profiling, based on personal data, has become a routine occurrence that hardly raises any concerns or opposition. And, as we know especially since the Snowden revelations,[6] all this data easily ends up in the hands of state agencies, either obtained directly from various private firms or by other means (for example, through purchase from data brokers[7]). As will be argued below, these two processes combined may be conceptualized as a gradual shift from a 'Lockean' to a 'Hobbesian' conception of the state and a largely implicit and unarticulated reconfiguration of a social contract, in which the paramount role of the state becomes to ensure security, at the expense of other values and fundamental liberties.

---

[4] Directive 2006/24/EC of the European Parliament and of the Council of 15 March 2006 on the retention of data generated or processed in connection with the provision of publicly available electronic communications services or of public communications networks and amending Directive 2002/58/EC [2006] OJ L 105/54.

[5] TJ McIntyre, 'Data Retention in Ireland: Privacy, Policy and Proportionality', Computer Law & Security Report, 24 no. 4 (2008) 326; Paul Bernal, 'Data Gathering, Surveillance and Human Rights: Recasting the Debate' (2016) 1(2) Journal of Cyber Policy 243.

[6] Ivan Manokha, 'Surveillance, Panopticism, and Self-Discipline in the Digital Age' (2018) 16(2) Surveillance & Society 219.

[7] Anne McKenna, 'US Agencies Buy Vast Quantities of Personal Information on the Open Market – a Legal Scholar Explains Why and What It Means for Privacy in the Age of AI', The Conversation, 29 June 2023 <https://theconversation.com/us-agencies-buy-vast-quantities-of-personal-information-on-the-open-market-a-legal-scholar-explains-why-and-what-it-means-for-privacy-in-the-age-of-ai-207707> accessed 26 September 2024.

The focus of this chapter will be on data retention policies, approached as but one instance of practices of personal data collection, and in particular on the 'chilling effect' that such policies generate. Now, the 'chilling effect'—a situation in which various actors, aware of the fact that their activity may be monitored in some way, modify the manner in which they express themselves—has already been addressed in a range of academic studies.[8] The contribution of this chapter, among other things, resides in situating it in the context of a gradual shift to a 'Hobbesian' type of state and seeing it as both, a consequence and a further catalyst of this shift. That is to say, the awareness of people of mass surveillance and of various enforcement measures (especially against those who speak up, such as whistleblowers) results in changes in the way they express themselves (as has been noted in existing studies); at the same time, self-censorship and self-policing of speech—avoidance of critique and dissent—contributes to the further growth of this 'surveillance Leviathan', and its inadvertent acceptance.

The rest of the chapter is structured as follows: the first section briefly revisits the social contract theory as expounded by Hobbes and Locke, and develops further the argument that we are witnessing a movement from a 'Lockean' to a 'Hobbesian' state in the context of the rise of digital technology. The second section focuses on various manifestations of the 'chilling effect' produced by data collection and data retention policies—in particular with respect to journalism and online behaviour of individuals—and examines their implications.

2. Digital Technology and a Shift Towards a 'Hobbesian' State

Let us start with a very brief overview of the social contract theory as developed by Hobbes and Locke. In both versions of a hypothetical agreement among individuals that establishes political authority, the goal of security plays a central role. However, in Hobbes's perspective, security becomes the sole objective, leading to the surrender of all individual natural rights, while in the Lockean tradition, security is viewed as less absolute, allowing individuals to retain various freedoms, including the freedom to alter the government.

Thomas Hobbes wrote his 'Leviathan' in 1651 during a time of great political turmoil—amid the transitional phase following the English Civil War, which saw the defeat of Charles I, and ultimately leading up to the monarchy's restoration. Appalled by the consequences of the breakdown of law and order, Hobbes develops his version of the social contract theory to ultimately justify the creation of the sovereign with unlimited powers to enforce peace and security. He examines society by deconstructing it into its fundamental elements—individuals existing in a 'state of nature', a hypothetical setting marked by the absence of any form of government—and analyses the characteristics of this state, based on the innate drives and passions that shape human behaviour within it. Because of the inherent nature

---

[8] Elizabeth Stoycheff, 'Under Surveillance: Examining Facebook's Spiral of Silence Effects in the Wake of NSA Internet Monitoring' (2016) 93(2) Journalism & Mass Communication Quarterly 296; Jonathon Penney, 'Internet Surveillance, Regulation, and Chilling Effects Online: A Comparative Case Study' (2017) 6(2) Internet Policy Review 1; Jonathon Penney, 'Chilling Effects and Transatlantic Privacy (2019) 25 European Law Journal 122; Anthony Mills, 'Now You See Me – Now You Don't: Journalists' Experiences With Surveillance' (2019) 13(6) Journalism Practice 690; Moritz Büchi, Noemi Festic, and Michael Latzer 'The Chilling Effects of Digital Dataveillance: A Theoretical Model and an Empirical Research Agenda' (2022) 9(1) Big Data & Society 1.

of human needs and desires, as well as their tendency to evolve and expand, a perpetual inclination arises for these needs and desires to demand more resources for their satisfaction than what nature provides. Consequently, a scarcity of natural resources ensues, wherein the collective sum of needs and desires surpasses the available resources. Hobbes asserts that this scarcity inevitably gives rise to competition among individuals and if some of them delay their actions until others have obtained everything they desire, there will be nothing remaining for them. Therefore, in a state of nature, individuals must be prepared to assert and safeguard their own claims. 'From this equality of ability ariseth equality of hope in the attaining of our ends. And therefore, if any two men desire the same thing which nevertheless they cannot both enjoy, they become enemies'.[9] In addition, individuals are equal in physical strength and mental agility so that even 'the weakest has strength enough to kill the strongest'.[10] Given these characteristics of human beings, Hobbes argues that the state nature, in which there is no overarching authority over individuals, is a state of war of 'every man against every man'.[11] For Hobbes, the only way for rational individuals to fulfil their utmost desire of self-preservation is to abandon the state of nature and establish an effective Sovereign or the great 'Leviathan' through a 'mutual transferring of right ... which men call contract'.[12] Thus, individuals agree to abandon the rights that they possess in the state of nature—'the natural right of every man to everything'—and transfer these rights to 'the sovereign power constituted over them by their own consent', to the 'great Leviathan called a Commonwealth'.[13] Overall, Hobbes develops his theory of the social contract as an ultimate justification of absolute sovereignty for the purposes of security, which constitutes for him the most important value that ultimately trumps everything else. As he puts it, the aim is 'the procuration of the safety of the people ... to which [the Sovereign] is obliged by the Law of Nature'.[14] Without this, 'there can be no security to any man, how strong or wise soever he be'.[15] Hobbes is so preoccupied with security, and wary of the breakdown of law and order, that he refuses to allow the possibility of any renegotiation or modification of the social contract because for him such a possibility would mean that a return to the state of nature and to the war of all against all would remain potentially possible.

John Locke proposes an alternative perspective. What he aims to defend is the cause of the first Whigs during the Exclusion Crisis of 1679–81 and seeks to justify the right of resistance against the Crown within a 'mixed constitution' (ie the sharing of powers between the Crown and the Parliament), as the English Constitution was perceived at that time. Locke asserts that government is a fiduciary power, held in trust by the people under the social compact. When this trust is violated, the people's constituent power comes into play once again. To develop this thesis Locke also starts with a hypothetical state of nature in which individuals possess natural rights, and which is governed by natural law: 'The State of Nature has a Law of Nature to govern it, which obliges every one: And Reason, which is that Law, teaches all Mankind, who will but consult it, that being all equal and independent,

---

[9] Thomas Hobbes, *Leviathan or The Matter, Forme and Power of a Commonwealth Ecclesiastical and Civil* (first published 1651, Clarendon Press 1965) 95.
[10] ibid 94.
[11] ibid 96.
[12] ibid 102.
[13] ibid 113.
[14] ibid 148.
[15] ibid 100.

no one ought to harm another in his Life, Health, Liberty, or Possessions'.[16] As in the case of Hobbes, individual security is seen as an essential value: 'the Fundamental Law of Nature' is that man is 'to be preserved, as much as possible'[17] and 'the preservation of the Society, and (as far as will consist with the public good) of every person in it'.[18] However, for Locke, the state of nature is not a condition of war, but a state of peace. Nevertheless, the creation of a political authority through a social compact is necessary because some individuals may violate natural rights of others to their property or life. For him, all individuals in the state of nature possess the right to punish such transgressors ('Every man hath a right to punish the offender, and be executioner of the law of nature'[19]) as well as the right to seek reparations, because they violate the fundamental law of nature that 'no one ought to harm another in his Life, Health, Liberty, or Possessions'.[20] But, Locke argues, 'it is unreasonable for men to be judges in their own cases; self-love will make men partial to themselves and their friends: and on the other side, that ill nature, passion and revenge will carry them too far in punishing others; and hence nothing but confusion and disorder will follow'.[21] In this respect, 'civil government is the proper remedy for the inconveniencies of the state of nature … where men may be judges in their own case, since it is easy to be imagined, that he who was so unjust as to do his brother an injury, will scarce be so just as to condemn himself for it'.[22] In other words, individuals transfer their natural rights to the political authority that will assume the responsibility of maintaining order. This can only be done through consent: 'no one can be put out of this Estate, and subjected to the Political Power of another, without his own Consent. The only way whereby any one divests himself of his Natural Liberty, and puts on the bonds of Civil Society is by agreeing with other Men to join and unite into a Community for their comfortable, safe, and peaceable living one amongst another, in a secure Enjoyment of their Properties, and a greater Security against any that are not of it … When any number of men have so consented to make one Community or Government, they are thereby presently incorporated, and make one Body Politic, wherein the Majority have a Right to act and conclude the rest'.[23] Contrary to Hobbes, the society retains the right to dissolve the government if it violates its trust and fails to secure the rights of individuals to life, liberty and property: 'if they have set limits to the duration of their legislative, and made this supreme power in any person or assembly only temporary; or else when, by the miscarriages of those in authority, it is forfeited; upon the forfeiture of their rulers, or at the determination of the time set, it reverts to the society, and the people have a right to act as supreme, and continue the legislative in themselves or place it in a new form, or new hands, as they think good'.[24]

Thus, Hobbes laid the foundation for the Western theory of the state by situating the origins of political authority in civil society (as opposed to seeing it as coming from God) but

---

[16] John Locke, *Two Treatises of Government: In the Former, The False Principles, and Foundation of Sir Robert Filmer, and His Followers, Are Detected and Overthrown. The Latter Is an Essay Concerning the True Original, Extent, and End of Civil Government* (Cambridge Texts in the History of Political Thought, (first published 1689, CUP 1999)) 271.
[17] ibid 382.
[18] ibid 356.
[19] ibid 272.
[20] ibid 271.
[21] ibid 275.
[22] ibid 276.
[23] ibid 331.
[24] ibid 428.

ended up justifying absolute monarchy to guarantee peace and security of the state. Locke extended this model to view the state as the guarantor of both security and other rights of individuals, and the objective of political society as finding the right balance between the imperatives of order and individual freedoms and liberties. The ultimate judge in these dilemmas, as argued by Locke, remains the people: 'If a controversy arise betwixt a prince and some of the people in a matter where the law is silent or doubtful, and the thing be of great consequence, I should think the proper umpire in such a case should be the body of the people'.[25] As it is widely known, it is the Lockean model that became the foundation for Western democracies which have developed a whole range of different individual rights and liberties that set limits on the ability of the government to encroach upon their liberty and autonomy, including for the purposes of security and order. However, in the last couple decades, things have started to change and we are witnessing a gradual shift towards a Hobbesian conception of the state essentially preoccupied with security. This has been a result of a convergence of two phenomena with different historical velocities and trajectories that have entered into an organic and a mutually reinforcing synthesis: on the one hand, the increasing preoccupation with security as the central goal of the state constructed in terms reminiscent of Hobbes' discussion of the state of nature as a war—'war on terror', 'cyberwar', defence of state sovereignty against migration, etc), and on the other hand, the digitization of everyday life with most routine activities of individuals now performed online and leaving some form of digital traces that can be easily collected, processed, and analysed.

As regards the former process, the pivotal event was the 9/11 terrorist attacks in the United States in 2001. This event immediately led to an unprecedented increase in surveillance and security measures in the US and, especially after the terrorist attacks in London, Madrid, and Paris, to a range of similar measures in other Western states. Thus, in October 2001 the US Congress passed the PATRIOT Act, which expanded the Foreign Intelligence Surveillance Act (FISA) granting broader surveillance powers to US law enforcement and intelligence agencies, allowing for increased monitoring of communications, including phone calls, emails, and internet usage, without the need for traditional warrants. FISA amendments of 2008 and 2012 further enhanced warrantless surveillance capabilities of US intelligence agencies to include communications between US citizens in the United States and foreign targets (the provisions often referred to as Section 702, named after the relevant section in the FISA Amendment Act). Although some of these powers were curtailed in 2015 following the revelations by Edward Snowden (in particular the unprecedented extent of mass surveillance carried out by the National Security Agency (NSA) and its 'Five Eyes' alliance partners (Australia, Canada, New Zealand, and the United Kingdom)) most of them were again reauthorized in 2018. Very similar measures were adopted by other member of the Five Eyes alliance: in the UK, the Anti-Terrorism, Crime, and Security Act (2001) and the Investigatory Powers Act (2016) (known as the 'Snooper's Charter'); in Canada, the Anti-Terrorism Act (2001), the Security of Canada Information Sharing Act (2015) and the Communications Security Establishment Act (2019); in Australia, the Anti-Terrorism Act (2004), Data Retention Legislation (2015), and the National Security Legislation Amendment (Espionage and Foreign Interference) Act (2018); finally, in New Zealand, the Terrorism Suppression Act (2002), the Telecommunications (Interception Capability

---

[25] ibid 427.

and Security) Act (2013), and the Intelligence and Security Act (2017). Analogous legislation has been passed in Western democracies outside the Five Eyes alliance, for example, the 2015 Intelligence Law (*Loi Renseignement*) and the 2017 Counterterrorism Law (*Loi relative à la lutte contre le terrorisme*) in France, or the 2016 Intelligence Services Reform Act (*Gesetz zur Reform des Verfassungsschutzes*) in Germany. More recently, many Western states also started implementing policies designed to build 'digital sovereignty', that is, 'to transform globally distributed information infrastructure into bounded national territory'.[26] While such measures are presented as a necessity to protect the state from foreign cyberattacks, industrial espionage, disinformation, and propaganda campaigns and various other security threats, the notion of 'digital sovereignty' is invested with patriotic meaning and normative ideas about 'what constitutes "good" and "bad" digital citizens'.[27] Indeed, as has been noted by a number of observers,[28] such policies are also driven by other motives, such as increased accessibility of citizens' data by intelligence actors and law enforcement agencies, and the desire to generate revenue for local internet service providers'.[29]

Data retention regulations are one of such measures adopted to increase the ability of law enforcement agencies to get access to information about individual citizens. Data retention involves a mandatory and indiscriminate storing of communications metadata by providers of electronic communications services, and subsequent access to it by public authorities for national—security and criminal—justice purposes.[30] Thus, in the case of the EU, since the early 2000s, member states started to adopt legislation for the retention of communications metadata. Among the first countries to introduce it were Italy (*Legge Pisanu*, adopted in 2005), the Netherlands (*Wet bewaarplicht telecommunicatiegegevens*, adopted in 2009), and Ireland (the Communications Act, adopted in 2011). While some attempts have been invalidated by national constitutional courts (eg in Bulgaria in 2008, in Romania in 2009, in Germany in 2010, or in the Czech Republic in 2011) and the CJEU (as in the case of the Data Retention Directive), most European countries continue data retention. In a recent study by Birrer et al,[31] 25 European countries were surveyed with respect to data retention policies (all EU member states except for Croatia, Latvia, Lithuania, and Malta, and additionally Switzerland and the UK). The study concluded that as of February 2023, 18 of these countries had legislation on bulk data retention (Belgium, Bulgaria, Czech Republic, Denmark, Estonia, Finland, France, Germany, Greece, Hungary, Ireland, Italy, Luxembourg, Poland, Spain, Sweden, Switzerland, UK). While such policies usually involve the bulk collection of metadata only—that is, the information about the location of the people engaged in a communication, and various other data such as date, time, duration, and not the content of the communication—as numerous experts and researchers have shown, such information may be extremely revealing about individuals' lives and

---

[26] Norma Möllers, 'Making Digital Territory: Cybersecurity, Techno-nationalism, and the Moral Boundaries of the State' (2021) 46(1) Science, Technology, & Human Values 112, 112.
[27] ibid 113.
[28] Anupam Chander and Uyen Le, 'Data Nationalism' (2015) 64(6) Emory Law Journal 677; Jonah Hill, 'The Growth of Data Localization Post-Snowden: Analysis and Recommendations for U.S.' (2014) 2(3) Policymakers and Industry Leaders (Lawfare Research Paper Series) 1.
[29] Julia Pohle and Thorsten Thiel, 'Digital Sovereignty' (2020) 9(4) Internet Policy Review 9.
[30] Alena Birrer, Danya He, and Natascha Just, 'The State is Watching You – A Cross-National Comparison of Data Retention in Europe' (2023) 47(4) Telecommunications Policy <https://doi.org/10.1016/j.telpol.2023.102542> accessed 27 September 2024.
[31] ibid.

identities.[32] As Snowden puts it, 'metadata can tell your surveillant the address you slept at last night and what time you got up this morning. It reveals every place you visited during your day and how long you spent there. It shows who you were in touch with and who was in touch with you. . . . With the dizzying volume of digital communications in the world, there is simply no way that every phone call could be listened to or email could be read . . . metadata is [the solution] – makes this it is precisely the first line of information that the party surveilling you requires'.[33] Indeed, as Stewart Baker of the NSA put it, '[m]etadata absolutely tells you everything about somebody's life. If you have enough metadata you don't really need content'.[34] Or, to quote an even more powerful statement, made by the former head of the NSA Michael Hayden, 'we kill people based on metadata'.[35] In addition, for the purposes of the argument developed here concerning the shift towards a Hobbesian state, it is important to mention examples of other measures that have been justified in the name of security and that violate established individual rights, but are not directly related to new technology. Among the most blatant measures one might cite the practice of extraordinary rendition, which began under Bush administration and continued during the presidency of Obama and which involved abduction and transfer to US-controlled sites or third states of terrorist suspects for interrogation, often using torture. By 2007, according to a report by the European Parliament, the CIA had conducted 1,245 flights to 'black sites' in different countries where suspects could face torture. Some of these torture sites were located in Europe, in particular in Poland.[36] Or the practice of indefinite detention of terror suspects in the United States at the Guantanamo Bay detention facility in Cuba. Detainees at Guantanamo were categorized as 'enemy combatants' and held without charge or trial, sometimes for years or even decades. The justification for their detention was to prevent them from engaging in further acts of terrorism and to gather intelligence related to terrorism. According to the available information, 779 prisoners have been held by the US military at Guantánamo since the prison opened on 11 January 2002. Of those, 739 have been released or transferred, nine have died, and 30 men are still detained.[37] We may also mention restrictions on access to legal counselling of detained immigrants imposed in countries such as the US[38] or the UK[39] as well as increased surveillance of borders and

---

[32] Jonathan Mayer, Patrick Mutchler, and John Mitchell, 'Evaluating the Privacy Properties of Telephone Metadata' (2016) 113(20) Proceedings of the National Academy of Sciences 5536. Yves-Alexandre de Montjoye, César Hidalgo, Michel Verleysen, and Vincent Blondel, 'Unique in the Crowd: The Privacy Bounds of Human Mobility' (2013) 3(1) Scientific Reports 1.

[33] Edward Snowden, *Permanent Record* (Macmillan 2019) 141.

[34] Bruce Schneier, 'NSA Doesn't Need to Spy on Your Calls to Learn Your Secrets', *Wired*, 25 March 2015 <https://www.wired.com/2015/03/data-and-goliath-nsa-metadata-spying-your-secrets/> accessed 27 September 2024.

[35] ibid.

[36] Federico Fabbrini, 'The European Court of Human Rights, Extraordinary Renditions and the Right to the Truth: Ensuring Accountability for Gross Human Rights Violations Committed in the Fight Against Terrorism' (2014) 14(1) Human Rights Law Review 85.

[37] American Civil Liberties Union, '20 Years Later, Guantánamo Remains a Disgraceful Stain on Our Nation. It Needs to End', American Civil Liberties Union, 11 January 2022 <https://www.aclu.org/news/human-rights/20-years-later-guantanamo-remains-a-disgraceful-stain-on-our-nation-it-needs-to-end> accessed 27 September 2024.

[38] Ingrid Eagly and Steven Shafer, 'A National Study of Access to Counsel in Immigration Court' (2015) 164(1) University of Pennsylvania Law Review 1.

[39] Justice 'Immigration and Asylum Appeals – a Fresh Look', London, 18 July 2018 <https://files.justice.org.uk/wp-content/uploads/2018/07/06170353/Immigration-and-Asylum-press-summary-1-1.pdf> accessed 27 September 2024.

discriminatory treatment of travellers based on their risk profile, implemented today by virtually all Western democracies.[40]

As regards the second process, everything that individuals do online—and we now all perform most of our daily activities in the digital environment connected to the internet—leaves digital traces that can be gathered, processed, and cross-referenced to provide insights about our tastes, preferences, beliefs, habits, etc. The collection of this information has become central to business models of different enterprises that use it as the main means to generate revenue. This is the case of social media platforms, such as Facebook, which generates almost all of its multi-billion revenues from targeted advertising—that is, tailored commercial offers based on user profile—as mentioned in the Introduction. The same may be said of search engines such as Google, which processes close to 5.6 billion searches per day.[41] Google's revenues progressed from 37.9 billion USD in 2011 to 256.7 billion USD in 2021, with most of the earnings (around 80%) coming from advertising,[42] of which a great deal is targeted (although the exact share of targeted advertising in Google's advertising revenue is not known). We may mention the so-called 'marketing automation solution providers', which enable any firm or platform to target customers with ads sent automatically, according to requested parameters. The leading firm in this sector is Hubspot, which earned 1.3 billion USD in 2021.[43] There are also data brokers that collect the information on individuals, mainly through the internet (although not only, especially in the case of the US), and then sell it to various customers, mostly to firms for marketing purposes. One of the leading data brokers, Acxiom, in 2021 had 23,000 servers collecting and analysing data for 500 million individuals worldwide with and up to 3,000 data points per person and earned 0.44 billion USD in 2021.[44] Finally, it is worth mentioning firms that provide various data analytics for other firms, based on a specific specialization. A relevant example—and one of the important segments in this category of business—is the social media analytics (SMA) industry. The SMA companies gather data from different social media sources and then process it to draw inferences and insights about customers of their client firms—their opinions about the brand, tastes and preferences—as well as to help them identify potential new clients.[45] One of the key SMA firms, GoodData Corporation, earned 64.5 million USD in 2021.[46] In addition, many other firms use personal data as an auxiliary source of profits. For example, in online commerce, to offer customers products based on their previous purchases; in music and video streaming, to increase user engagement with targeted suggestions; or in travel industry and online food delivery services for different marketing purposes. As these examples show, for these firms personal data is vital, and they do everything

---

[40] Antje Ellermann and Agustín Goenaga, 'Citizens in the West Should Care about Discriminatory Immigration Policies', *The Conversation*, 11 February 2019, <https://theconversation.com/citizens-in-the-west-should-care-about-discriminatory-immigration-policies-110312> accessed 27 September 2024.

[41] Statista, 'Google' (9 March 2022) <https://www.statista.com/topics/1001/google/> accessed 27 September 2024.

[42] ibid.

[43] Hubspot, 'HubSpot Reports Q4 and Full Year 2021 Results', 10 February 2022, <https://ir.hubspot.com/news/hubspot-reports-q4-and-full-year-2021-results> accessed 27 September 2024.

[44] Zippia, 'Acxiom Revenue' (2022) <https://www.zippia.com/acxiom-careers-166/revenue/#> accessed 27 September 2024.

[45] Ivan Manokha, 'Social Media Analytics Companies', in Andrea Ceron (ed) *Encyclopaedia of Technology & Politics* (Edward Elgar 2022).

[46] Mordor Intelligence, 'Social Media Analytics Market – Growth, Trends, COVID-19 Impact, and Forecasts (2022 – 2027)' (2022) <https://www.mordorintelligence.com/industry-reports/global-social-media-analytics-market> accessed 27 September 2024.

possible to collect it. But in doing so, and especially in using it for marketing purposes and targeted ads, they habituate individuals to surveillance, they normalize it and make it part of our daily lives. They also habituate individuals to surrender their privacy by requiring them to sign terms of service agreements, which are non-negotiable 'all-or-nothing' contracts, that most users sign without reading[47] (as they cannot get access to services without them, and there is little incentive to consult them as they cannot be modified).

Bringing these developments together we may observe that, on the one hand, the state adopts measures and legislation that enable it to collect different kinds of information about individuals, and, on the other, in their routine activities, individuals themselves surrender their right to privacy and render their lives transparent to various private actors. As already noted, the private data that is thereby collected by commercial entities is easily accessible to different state agencies. This is what is conceptualized here as an inadvertent reconfiguration of the social contract towards a more 'Hobbesian' form of state. Let us now turn to the 'chilling effect' and its implications in this context.

3. The Chilling Effect

The term 'chilling effect' was first introduced by Paul Freund[48] in his analysis of the compatibility of prior restraint with the First Amendment. However, it was in the US Supreme Court's First Amendment jurisprudence that the concept gained prominence,[49] especially in the late 1950s and 1960s when the Court delivered a series of rulings that invalidated various overreaching anti-communist statutes enacted during the Cold War era.[50] It has since become widely used to describe how individuals alter the way they express themselves when they know that they may be under surveillance. This concept mirrors the self-discipline and 'technologies of self' in 'panoptic' settings[51]—prisons, asylums, military barracks, factories, offices, schools, hospitals, clinics, etc—in which the 'gaze' plays the central role in disciplining the 'watched'.[52]

In the current context, marked by a gradual implicit reconfiguration of the social contract along the Hobbesian lines, we have a setting in which, especially after the Snowden revelations, individuals are aware that what they say or do may be indiscriminately monitored, recorded, tracked, and analysed. They also know that attempts to expose government

---

[47] Ivan Manokha, 'GDPR as an Instance of Neoliberal Governmentality: A Critical Analysis of the Current "Gold Standard" of Data Protection' (2023) 4(2) Political Anthropological Research on International Social Sciences 1; Insider, 'You're Not Alone, No One Reads Terms of Service Agreements' (15 November 2017) <https://www.businessinsider.com/deloitte-study-91-percent-agree-terms-of-service-without-reading-2017-11?r = US&IR = T> accessed 27 September 2024; ProPrivacy, 'Privacy Complacency: The Hidden Dangers Lurking Beneath Today's Surface–Level Data Protection' (28 January 2020) <https://proprivacy.com/privacy-news/privacy-complacency-ebook> accessed 27 September 2024.
[48] Paul Freund, 'The Supreme Court and Civil Liberties' (1951) 4(3) Vanderbilt Law Review 533.
[49] Morton Hortwitz, 'In Memoriam: William J. Brennan, Jr.' (1997) 111(1) Harvard Law Review 1.
[50] Penney, 'Chilling Effects and Transatlantic Privacy' (n 8) 122; Michael Dolich, 'Alleging a First Amendment Chilling Effect to Create a Plaintiff's Standing: A Practical Approach' (1993) 43 Drake Law Review 175.
[51] Michel Foucault, *Discipline and Punish: The Birth of the Prison* (Vintage Books 1979); Michel Foucault, 'The Eye of Power', in Colin Gordon (ed) *Power/Knowledge: Selected Interviews and Other Writings (1972–1977)* (Pantheon Books 1980).
[52] Ivan Manokha, 'Foucault's Concept of Power and the Global Discourse of Human Rights' (2009) 23(4) Global Society 429; Ivan Manokha, 'Surveillance: The DNA of Platform Capital–The Case of Cambridge Analytica Put into Perspective' (2018) 21(4) Theory & Event 891; Manokha, 'Surveillance, Panopticism, and Self-Discipline' (n 6) 219.

wrongdoing, especially in matters of security, may lead to severe punitive measures, as evidenced by the consequences that were faced by the likes of Chelsea Manning, Julian Assange, and Edward Snowden. This may have very important chilling effects, particularly on journalists and their sources, as well as on individual expression. Let us now examine these effects.

The event that enabled analysts and practitioners to see the chilling effect at work—and, as we will see shortly, in some cases to quantify some of its manifestations—were the Snowden revelations. Already prior to Snowden, 'during the Bush administration, the enactment of secret, warrantless mass surveillance to thwart terrorism created the conditions for more extensive, automated monitoring of journalists' sources in national security cases. During the Obama administration, through resort to the Patriot Act and other authorities, including the antiquated Espionage Act, the Justice Department has prosecuted more journalistic sources for leaking classified information than had all previous administrations combined'.[53] This explains a lot of hesitancy on the part of the New York Times editors to publish the revelations, in itself a clear case of the chilling effect. After the Snowden files became public, however, we entered the 'After Snowden' period[54] which was characterized by significant changes in the behaviour of reporters and their sources. As noted by Glenn Greenwald, the reporter who published the Snowden files, 'When we think we're being watched, we tend to make behavioural choices that . . . are much more compliant and much more conformist and much more submissive'.[55] Indeed, as a study conducted by the Pew Research Center in 2014 demonstrated, 14% of US investigative journalists after the Snowden revelations stated that they now refrained from pursuing stories due to surveillance concerns, and 2% even contemplated leaving the profession altogether.[56] Pen America's report, 'Global Chilling: The Impact of Mass Surveillance on International Writers', found that almost as many writers living in democracies (75%) were concerned about surveillance as in non-democracies (80%) and that the degree of self-censorship by writers in democracies, as a consequence of surveillance, is approaching that in semi-democracies and authoritarian countries.[57] A 2015 Pew Research Center study of US investigative journalists found that approximately two-thirds of the investigative journalists surveyed (64%) believed that 'the U.S. government has probably collected data about their phone calls, emails or online communications',[58] and 80% felt that their work as a journalist augmented the probability that their data was being surveilled. National security, foreign affairs and federal government reporters were even more likely (71% of them) to think the government had already collected data about their electronic communications.[59]

In a more recent study, Anthony Mills[60] sought to establish to what extent surveillance of journalists generate in them a sense of fear and prevents them from performing their role

---

[53] Steve Coll, 'Source Protection in the Age of Surveillance' in Emily Bell and Taylor Owen (eds), *Journalism After Snowden: The Future of the Free Press in the Surveillance State* (Columbia University Press 2017) 86.
[54] Emily Bell, Taylor Owen, and Smitha Khorana, 'Introduction', in Bell and Owen, ibid 6.
[55] Glenn Greenwald, 'The Surveillance State' in Bell and Owen, ibid 47.
[56] Pew Research Center, 'Social Media and the "Spiral of Silence"' (26 August 2014) <http://www.pewinternet.org/files/2014/08/PI_Social-networks-and-debate_082614.pdf> accessed 27 September 2024.
[57] PEN America, 'Global Chilling: The Impact of Mass Surveillance on International Writers' (5 January 2015) <https://pen.org/research-resources/global-chilling/> accessed 27 September 2024.
[58] Pew Research Center, 'Investigative Journalists and Digital Security: Perceptions of Vulnerability and Changes in Behavior', 5 February 2015, https://www.pewresearch.org/journalism/2015/02/05/investigative-journalists-and-digital-security/accessed 27 September 2024.
[59] ibid.
[60] Mills, 'Now You See Me' (n 8) 690.

as democratic watchdogs. The interviews with leading US and European reporters revealed the presence of a shared feeling of fear and 'paranoia' as a result of their monitoring and harassment, detention at borders, and generalized electronic surveillance. To quote just a few examples from this very insightful and rich study, one of the Guardian journalists who covered the Snowden revelations described the reactions of UK authorities as 'half-Stasi', following their destruction of the hard drives of computers of the journalists with pneumatic drills and sledgehammers. Italian journalist Stefania Maurizi, who covered the Snowden affair for L'Espresso, reported being targeted with aggressive physical surveillance 'so that I could be feeling intimidated. It actually was scary for me. I panicked. Of course, it is a chilling effect'.[61] After being stopped at the border for invalid reasons on numerous occasions, Ewan MacAskill (who had interviewed Snowden) confessed that he was 'now totally paranoid'.[62] Janine Gibson, the then-US editor of The Guardian, noted that when she was writing about the NSA, someone would start remotely deleting the text. As a result, as noted by James Bamford, 'there definitely is a growing sense of fear' which has 'a real inhibiting effect on journalists',[63] the view shared by Gavin MacFadyen, who states that electronic surveillance 'makes it almost impossible for serious journalism work'.[64] Based on these findings, Mills concludes that 'these dynamics are resulting in an intensified chilling effect' as 'the space for in-depth combative investigative reporting is shrinking' as reporters 'are becoming more cautious'.[65] It is important to add that the chilling effect affects not only reporters themselves, but also their sources on which they depend, especially when it comes to covering topics related to national security. On the one hand, the sources are now much less likely to be willing to share the information, especially when it concerns issues related to national security.[66] More importantly, because of electronic surveillance and tracking, journalists can no longer guarantee confidentiality to their sources, which has always been central to investigative reporting and its function of democratic oversight. Indeed, as the American Newspaper Guild's Code of Ethics stipulated in 1934, reporter–source confidentiality is vital for journalists to function as watchdogs of democracy and thereby 'newspapermen shall refuse to reveal confidences or disclose sources of confidential information in court or before judicial or investigative bodies'.[67] As noted by the former Guardian editor Alan Rusbridger, 'confidentiality means nothing if a third party can easily work out to whom a journalist has been talking – through their phone logs, contacts lists, e-mails, texts, etc.'[68] And even if actual emails or phone conversations are not consulted by authorities, their metadata, as noted earlier, may be highly revealing and lead to the identification of the source. As Rusbridger further observes, journalists cannot take much comfort in assurances that 'the state is not listening to the "contents" of the phone calls. A police officer or spook doesn't need to access the '"content" of any communication to work out the identity of a whistleblower or source. Welcome to the world of metadata—the accompanying information, not content—often accessible with no form of warrant or judicial oversight,

---

[61] ibid 697.
[62] ibid 699.
[63] ibid 701.
[64] ibid 701.
[65] ibid 704.
[66] Paul Lashmar, 'No More Sources?' (2017) 11(6) Journalism Practice 665.
[67] Paul Marcus, 'The Reporter's Privilege: An Analysis of the Common Law, Branzburg v. Hayes, and Recent Statutory Developments' (1984) 25 Arizona Law Review 815, 815–16.
[68] Alan Rusbridger, 'Journalism after Snowden', in Bell and Owen (n 53) 22.

and which tells so much about us'.[69] Or, as Bell et al put it, by 'leaving digital traces of the times when digital communication took place and the parties involved, metadata can and has been used to convict leakers and identify sources'.[70] Indeed, one may mention here the case of James Risen, an investigative reporter of the New York Times. When he exposed a covert CIA action to recruit a Russian scientist to provide flawed nuclear weapons designs to Iran, the authorities used metadata of his calls to identify the source—Jeffrey Alexander Sterling, a former CIA operations officer. In this context, Rusbridger concludes, 'every journalist should understand that there is no such thing as confidential digital communication. None of us have confidential sources'.[71]

Now, the Snowden revelations were also crucial in demonstrating the chilling effect on individuals. Although it affects mostly online behaviour, the importance of this should not be underestimated as more and more aspects of our lives take place in the digital environment. Indeed, as Büchi et al note, 'everyday behaviors such as researching a contentious or an entirely noncontroversial topic online, sending messages on a smartphone, or liking other people's posts on social networking sites make up the fabric of social life in the digital society'.[72]

Indeed, following the publication of the Snowden files, mass surveillance became a prevalent topic in mass media, with very extensive coverage in newspapers, journals, documentaries, news bulletins, feature films, and television series (eg *The Circle* or *Black Mirror*). This widespread coverage has raised awareness among people in Western democracies about being constantly monitored by various entities.[73] The empirical studies that were conducted in the wake of the revelations all demonstrated a significant chilling effect on individual expression, particularly online. Thus, for example a study by Pew Research Center conducted in 2014 found that while 86% of US social media users were willing to discuss government surveillance in physical settings, only 42% were willing to engage in such discussions on social media platforms.[74] In other words, almost half of the surveyed users were unwilling to talk about this topic online. Jonathon Penney's more recent studies on the online behaviour of individuals confirmed the lasting impact of the Snowden disclosures. Thus, in one of his studies showed a 30% decline in US users' Wikipedia searches for security-sensitive terms after June 2013, and another survey found that 62% of US adult internet users were less likely to discuss certain topics online, while 78% expressed increased caution in their online communication.[75] Mathews and Tucker[76] conducted a study that gathered data from the United States and ten other countries, analysing search volumes for specific keywords. The findings revealed that US users significantly reduced searches for

---

[69] ibid 22–23.
[70] Emily Bell, Taylor Owen, and Smitha Khorana, 'Introduction', in Bell and Owen (n 53) 12.
[71] WAN-IFRA, 'Trends in Newsrooms: The Urgent Need to Shield Journalism in the Age of Surveillance' (24 June 2024) *World Association of News Publishers* <https://wan-ifra.org/2014/06/trends-in-newsrooms-the-urgent-need-to-shield-journalism-in-the-age-of-surveillance/> accessed 27 September 2024.
[72] Moritz Büchi, Noemi Festic, and Michael Latzer, 'The Chilling Effects of Digital Dataveillance: A Theoretical Model and an Empirical Research Agenda' (2022) 9(1) Big Data & Society 1, 6.
[73] Alex Matthews and Catherine Tucker, 'Government Surveillance and Internet Search Behavior' (29 April 2015) <https://papers.ssrn.com/sol3/papers.cfm?abstract_id = 2412564> accessed 27 September 2024. Lee Rainie and Mary Madden, 'Americans' privacy Strategies post-Snowden' (16 March 2015) Pew Research Center <https://www.pewresearch.org/internet/2015/03/16/americans-privacy-strategies-post-snowden/> accessed 27 September 2024.
[74] Pew Research Center, 'Social Media and the 'Spiral of Silence'' (n 56).
[75] Penney, 'Internet Surveillance' (n 8) 1; Penney, 'Chilling Effects and Transatlantic Privacy' (n 8) 122.
[76] Matthews and Tucker, 'Government Surveillance and Internet Search Behavior' (n 73).

terms they believed could attract the attention of the US government, and a similar drop was observed in traffic for sensitive search terms in other countries. Similar findings were obtained by the studies of the chilling effect on online behaviour by Stoycheff.[77]

Let us now examine the implications of the 'chilling effect'. The existing analyses rightly emphasize various negative consequences that it produces for the right to freedom of expression and, with this right being one of the key individual liberties for a properly functioning democracy, for democratic politics more generally. Indeed, following Habermas,[78] we may describe democracy as a political system that constantly needs a rational–critical debate among active and engaged citizens through which personal opinions evolve into public opinion. This debate takes place in what Habermas refers to as a 'public sphere', a realm of social life where people articulate autonomous views to influence political institutions of society. For Habermas, the public sphere should allow individuals to engage in a rational–critical debate and to behave as an active 'public body' which, of course, is impossible without freedom of expression: 'Citizens behave as a public body when they confer in an unrestricted fashion — that is, with the guarantee of freedom of assembly and association and the freedom to express and publish their opinions — about matters of general interest'.[79] The 'chilling effect' clearly interferes with this ability of citizens to engage in a constructive dialogue. First, as we have seen, self-censorship that results from the 'chilling effect' reduces the participation of some individuals in the discussion of different matters, especially those that concern security and law enforcement. Second, a vibrant public sphere obviously requires the ability of individual citizens to get access to information, especially concerning various political issues and government policies. To quote Habermas once more, 'only when the exercise of political control is effectively subordinated to the democratic demand that information be accessible to the public, does the political public sphere win an institutionalised influence over the government ... The public sphere ... in which the public organises itself as the bearer of public opinion, accords with the principle of the public sphere — that principle of public information which once had to be fought for against the arcane policies of monarchies and which since that time has made possible the democratic control of state activities'.[80] As we have seen, the impact of the chilling effect on journalists and their sources interferes with this dimension of the public sphere as well. In addition, the chilling effect inhibits the ability of the 'Fourth Estate' to exercise its function of a watchdog of government. Indeed, as Thomas Carlyle who coined the term 'Fourth Estate' famously put it, it is the most important of all the estates for democracy: 'Burke said there were Three Estates in Parliament; but, in the Reporters' Gallery yonder, there sat a Fourth Estate more important far than they all. ... Printing, which comes necessarily out of Writing, I say often, is equivalent to Democracy. ... Whoever can speak, speaking now to the whole nation, becomes a power, a branch of government, with inalienable weight in law-making, ... The nation is governed by all that has tongue in the nation: Democracy is virtually there'.[81] The fear of journalists and sources to address certain issues is obviously

---

[77] Stoycheff, 'Under Surveillance' (n 8).
[78] Jürgen Habermas, 'The Public Sphere: An Encyclopedia Article', trans. Sara Lennox and Frank Lennox (1974) 3 New German Critique 49.
[79] ibid.
[80] ibid.
[81] Thomas Carlyle, *On Heroes, Hero-Worship and the Heroic in History* (first published 1840, Lincoln: University of Nebraska Press 1966) 164.

problematic in this respect. All these findings on the chilling effect of various mass surveillance policies obviously apply to the specific case of data retention policies, which constitute an instance of mass surveillance.

However, what is important to add to these implications is the manner in which the 'chilling effect' also contributes to what has been described here as an implicit reconfiguration of the social contract from a Lockean to a Hobbesian type. In a way that is similar to how individual users of different online services give up their right to privacy and resign themselves to the idea that this is how things are and there is no way to change, those reporters and individual users who engage in self-censorship analogously contribute to the formation of the Hobbesian surveillance state. In other words, here the chilling effect may be seen as both, the consequence and the cause of this slow transformation of the state in Western democracies. By renouncing to express oneself on certain issues, especially on security and law enforcement, 'because you never know what the consequences might be', individuals who thereby self-censor play a role in this tacit acceptance of the shift to the Hobbesian state.

4. Conclusion

The contribution of the present chapter to this volume resides in examining primarily the structural context within which different surveillance and data collection measures, including data retention regulations, are implemented by public and private actors. This context has been conceptualized as a largely implicit and unarticulated reconfiguration of a social contract of the social contract in Western democracies away from a 'Lockean' conception to a Hobbesian view of the state, marked by the privileging of security over other social values and individual rights. The chapter has focused on the 'chilling effect' of indiscriminate and bulk collection of data, as well as of other measures adopted in the name of security, and its implications for the functioning of the 'public sphere'. In this respect, the 'chilling effect' on journalists and their sources, as well as on individual expression, particularly online, have been approached as both, an effect and a cause of the shift towards a 'Hobbesian' state in the West. Afraid to discuss certain issues, particularly related to defence and security, journalists and individuals contribute to a tacit acceptance of this state of affairs. These developments are particularly concerning in the context of a significant rise in popularity of political movements and parties espousing radical ideologies, especially in Europe.[82] The arrival of such forces to power and having the tools of mass surveillance discussed in this chapter at their disposal might lead to the further decline of various individual liberties and accelerate the movement towards a Hobbesian type of state.

At the moment, the establishment of a 'Hobbesian' state is, of course, not a foregone conclusion. There are many instances of resistance and the fact that various pieces of national and EU legislation on surveillance and data retention, such as the Data Retention Directive, have been invalidated due to the pressure from civil society and other stakeholders is a

---

[82] Helen Milner, 'Voting for Populism in Europe: Globalization, Technological Change, and the Extreme Right (2021) 54(13) Comparative Political Studies 2286; Aurelien Mondon and Aaron Winter, *Reactionary Democracy: How Racism and the Populist Far Right Became Mainstream* (Verso 2020); Cas Mudde, *The Far Right Today* (Polity Press 2019).

clear indication of this. Nevertheless, the tendency towards an establishment of a 'surveillance Leviathan' is indisputable. Most individuals are already resigned to the idea that their privacy is constantly invaded by different private and public actors that collect, process, and analyse their routine activities. The 'chilling effect' is a manifestation of a similar (although, of course, still partial) surrender of the right to freedom of expression. Viewed in this context, data retention regulations are much more concerning than they appear at first glance.

Index

For the benefit of digital users, indexed terms that span two pages (e.g., 52–53) may, on occasion, appear on only one of those pages.

5G 236

access to
  communications data 6–7, 334, 339
  data, law enforcement vi, 296–97, 303, 312, 333–34
  data, wrongful 167, 178–79
  differentiated access 130, 274
  High-Level Expert Group on Access to Data 110, 111
  metadata 32, 72, 192, 203–4, 205–6
  retained data 15–16, 22, 43, 153, 154–55, 162–63, 166, 177, 244–45, 254–55, 309, 312, 339, 425–28
  traffic data 130, 135, 140, 142, 148, 227
accountability
  Ex-ante 469
  Ex-post 468–69
administrative
  law proceedings 123–24
  vulnerability 7–8, 455–56, 461, 462, 469–70
adverse Event Reporting 329
AI Act 397–98, 420
algorithms 24–25, 354, 400, 402, 405–6, 411–12, 413–14, 429, 455, 457, 463–64
anonymized personal information 321
Artificial Intelligence 65, 386–87, 405, 418–19, 450, 458, 471–72
Austria(n) 66, 102–3, 167, 277–78, 284–85, 287, 363, 417
automated
  analysis 76–77, 381, 397, 399, 400–3, 410, 413, 418–20, 423–53
  decision-making 397–98, 403, 410, 416–17, 418–19, 433, 468
  processing of 384, 386, 387, 390, 404, 407–8, 410, 429

Belgian
  Constitutional Court 256, 263, 363, 368–69, 403
  Data Protection Authority 265, 270, 272–73
Bulgaria 96–97, 284–85, 290, 477–79
bulk Data Collection 50, 51–52, 423, 472

Carrier Grade NAT 225–26, 233, 235, 240
Certiorari 5, 151, 152, 153–55, 157, 162
chilling effect 8, 228–29, 473, 480–85
civil identity 259, 260, 270–71, 409, 429

CJEU test
  Necessity 22, 29, 53, 65–66, 69, 70–71, 72, 74–75, 401–2, 404–5
  Proportionality 47–48, 53, 56, 64, 67, 69–70, 74, 80, 90, 92–93, 310
codification 343–44, 347, 350–51
complaint handling 324, 329
confidentiality of
  communications 2, 68–69, 143–44, 205–6, 251, 364, 401, 418–19, 435, 441, 443, 448
  data 327, 329
constitutional
  identity 183, 193, 364
constitutionalization 346–47, 349, 351, 352, 359
Council of State
  French 5, 181–90, 192, 193, 194–95, 229, 408
crime
  hotspots 354
  rate 23, 257
criminal
  courts 173
  investigations 22–23, 34, 144, 147, 171, 191, 192, 231–32, 233, 234, 252–53, 254–55, 258–59, 263–64, 276, 292–94, 392–93, 409
Cyprus
  Constitution 152
  Supreme Court 157–58, 162, 163

Data
  Banking-related data 338–39
  content vs metadata 60–61, 211–12, 424, 440
  Content data 32, 278, 335–36, 448
  Fiduciary 299–300
    Power 474–75
  geolocation data 222–23, 338
  Metadata 32, 49, 60–61, 64, 66, 72, 73, 74, 75, 79, 97–98, 102–3, 107, 109, 192, 202, 203–5, 209, 266–67, 272, 336, 337, 339, 349, 401–2, 410, 424, 430, 448, 450–51, 477–79, 481–83
  Payment data 111
  Subscriber data 111, 227, 231, 233–34, 235–36
  traffic data 118–19, 121–22, 129, 130, 132, 133–34, 136, 139, 140–42, 144, 145, 184, 193, 196, 215–16, 227, 231, 262, 270, 272–73, 280, 301–2, 310–11, 352, 373–74, 442, 448, 449
Data protection
  Authorities (DPA) 102, 143, 417–18, 468
  Essence of the right to 60, 61

Data protection (*cont.*)
  Judicialization 358
  Legal bases of 440
  Officer (DPO) 382, 408
  Principles of 66–67
  Privacy and 16–17, 18, 28, 32, 51, 76, 86–87, 287, 298, 309, 370, 377–78, 387, 425
  Right to 61, 67, 91, 151, 152, 252, 287, 320, 352, 355, 378, 417, 462
  Safeguards 457
  Shifting paradigm of 362–63
Data Protection Commissioner 5
Democracy
  Constitutional 50
  Foundations of 197–98
  Functioning of 357, 484–85
  Rule of law and 452
Denmark 25, 237–50, 477–79
Dependency 456, 461, 466
designated judge 167, 175
digital
  Government 457–58, 460, 467–68
  Services Act (DSA) 446–47
  Sovereignty 472, 476–77
Discrimination 321, 354–55, 369, 441–42
  direct 406
  indirect 406, 414–15
  Intersectional 413, 416–17
  (Principle of) non– 406–7, 408, 414–15, 417–18
distributional outcomes 352, 359
duty of sincere cooperation 171, 374

EDPB (European Data Protection Board) 97, 109–10, 112–13, 448, 450
EDPS (European Data Protection Supervisor) 97, 99–100
eGovernment Action Plan 458
electronic communications
  Code 209, 267, 443
  data 17, 18–19, 31–32, 35–36, 37, 291–92, 378, 388–89
  metadata 97, 98, 101–2, 108, 109
  network 141–42, 215, 408, 439
  providers 106
  services 42, 50–51, 66, 104–5, 253–54, 259, 266, 278, 335, 428, 445
  surveillance 359
  systems 38–39, 160, 171, 428
Encryption 268
  End to end encryption 307, 308–9
Estonia 96–97, 457, 477–79
Evidence
  admissibility of 173, 213–14, 263–64
ex ante
  approval of access 173
  judicial approval 203–4
  safeguards 299
explainability 7–8, 463, 465–66, 467, 468–69
Extraordinary Rendition 472

Facebook 303–4, 309, 412, 446, 479–80
Finland 477–79
First originator 308–9, 311
Five Eyes 476–77
Fortress Europe 393–94
France 73, 111–12, 113, 184, 190–91, 291, 351–52, 392–93, 476–77
freedom of expression 32–33, 36, 70, 104–5, 130, 259, 352, 401, 484–85

Garante 130, 141–42, 143, 145, 146
GDPR
  Data minimization 338
  Data subject 68–69, 141, 143, 323, 368, 373–74, 386, 455–56, 469
  general (and indiscriminate) obligation 226–27, 253–54, 256, 266–67, 446, 447
General Ledger 325
geographical criteria 193, 240–41, 266–67, 271, 274
Germany 79, 101–2, 117–28, 284–85, 290, 291
Good Manufacturing Practice (GMP) Guidelines 330
Google 434–35, 444, 445, 479–80

Harm 92, 154, 321, 456, 460–61, 474–75
Hierarchy of norms 113
hotspot policing 354
Human
  dignity 131, 377
  review 384

India 295–313
Information Society Services 423–24, 434–35, 437, 445
Injustice
  Epistemic 345, 356–57, 358, 359–60
  institutional 359–60
Intermediaries 301, 302, 447
  Obligations of 296
  Regulation via 437–39
  Social media intermediaries 308–9, 311, 423–24, 437–39
Internet service provider 286, 287–88, 439
IP address 21, 76, 81, 83–84, 85–87, 119, 122–23, 127, 155–56, 158–60, 161, 233–35, 262, 265–66, 270–71, 286, 337, 408–9
Italy 147, 477–79

Japan 315–31
Judicial
  Activism 347–48, 351–52, 362–63, 451
  Authorization 218–19
  Review 20, 45–46, 121, 335, 407–8

Latvia 477–79
law enforcement authorities 15, 21–22, 64, 70, 73, 106, 127, 154, 227–28, 256–57, 263–64, 281, 303, 369–70, 371, 450
LIBE committee 100

Meiji (Restoration) era 316–18
Monitoring 54–55, 102, 247, 277–78, 279, 301–2, 306, 308, 401–2, 408, 417, 433, 435, 440, 441–42, 445, 446, 447, 450, 476–77

Netherlands, The 225–36, 392–93, 457, 461, 477–79
  District Court of The Hague 228–34
  Dutch Parliament 226–27, 230
  Minister of Justice and Security 232
  Summary proceedings 228, 229, 230, 234
non-discrimination 369, 406–7, 408, 412–13, 414–15, 416–18, 461, 462
NSA (National Security Agency) 433, 476–79, 481–83

Open Internet Regulation 441
oversight
  data, of 229
  democratic 481–83
  judicial 312, 481–83
  mechanism 175, 306
  public 402–3

Panopticon Europe 393–94
passenger
  Passenger Information Unit 380
  Passenger Name Records (PNR) 56, 74, 377–95, 399, 400, 402, 403, 404, 407, 410–11, 418–19
Poland 101–2, 197–212, 284–85, 477–79
Portugal 96–97, 106–9, 372–73
positive obligations 4, 38, 81, 182, 256, 371
power imbalance 463
prior review 21–23, 71, 84, 88–90, 137, 260, 261, 336, 409, 416–17, 429–30, 433
pseudonymized personal information 321

quick freeze 19, 111, 178, 184–85, 191

reasonable expectations of privacy 337
resistance 78, 197–98
  to backlash against expanded judicial power 345–46
  judicial resistance 154
  by Member States 35–39, 351–52
risk
  of abuse 36, 37, 67, 206, 210, 398
  -based approach 420
  -based assessment/ risk assessment 273, 274, 330, 403–4
  Criteria 380
  of disorder 354
  litigation risk 244–45
  of misuse of data 418–19
  perceived risk 350
  of perpetration 71
  profiles 391–92, 411–12
  of reoffending 257
  of systemic impunity 87–88
  (un)acceptable risk 79, 92

Romania 290, 368, 477–79
rule of law 134, 165–66, 198, 199, 210–12, 280, 452

security
  Distinction between national and public security 36–37
  and IP addresses 262–63
  national security 17, 19, 30–31, 35–36, 47, 51, 52, 75, 101–2, 104–5, 109–10, 155–56, 182, 184, 268, 270, 291–92, 301, 305, 349–50, 351–52, 402, 403, 420, 440, 481–83
  national security and public order 39–40, 42, 265
  public security/safety 30–31, 38, 47
  (serious) threat to/against 37, 51, 75, 124, 182–83, 184, 190–91, 371, 448, 464
serious crime 14, 23, 68, 88, 118–19, 144, 154, 228–29, 231–32, 353, 390, 405
  combating/ to combat 17, 20, 37–38, 40–41, 51, 78, 85–86, 124, 126, 155–56, 162–63, 170–71, 194–95, 229, 240–41, 256, 260, 291–92, 381
  fight against/ fighting 16–17, 28–29, 33–34, 39–40, 41, 43, 71, 72, 87, 257, 266–67, 371, 378, 379
  incidence of 256–57
  investigating/ investigation of 23, 233
  links to 29–30
  manifestly constitute 262
  notion of/concept of/definition of 16, 135, 146, 149, 258–59, 272
  prevention of/preventing 51–52, 244–45, 391–92
  threshold for 246
  victim of 233
service provider 129, 166, 207, 220–21, 234–35, 267, 286, 287–88, 334, 335–36, 338, 339, 434–35, 439, 444
Slovakia 96–97, 101–2, 112, 113, 284–85
Snowden Revelations 45, 472, 480–81
Spain
  Spanish Criminal Law 217
  Spanish Data Retention Law 214
statistics 204–5, 208, 246, 248–49, 268, 274, 291–92, 392–93
  subsidiary ledgers 325
surveillance
  of geographical spaces 359
  legitimate targets of 354–55
  permissible 353, 355, 359–60
  targeted 55, 305–6, 344, 352, 356, 359
  vulnerability 456, 457, 460, 463–64, 466–67, 469

targeted
  advertising 479–80
  surveillance 55, 305–6, 344, 352, 355, 356, 359
technical feasibility 311
technology
  effacement of 424, 436, 449
telecom package 436
telecommunication
  data 9–10, 158, 188, 198, 199–200, 202, 203–6, 208, 209

telecommunication (*cont.*)
   service providers 199–200, 202, 204–5
   Telecommunications Data Retention Act
      (TDRA) 225–27
TERREG Regulation 412
terrorist threat 190, 385, 400–1, 428
theory
   injustice 356–57
   judicialization 349
   principal agent 343–44, 347
   social contract 473–80
   super-agent 347, 350, 351
time limits 142, 213–14, 215–16, 221
traceability 308, 309, 311
transparency 8, 65–66, 204–5, 212, 231–32, 268,
      272–73, 313, 412–13, 447, 458, 463–64, 466–
      67, 469
   administrative 468

algorithmic 413–14
qualified 463, 465
report 303–4
over surveillance 464, 465

UK 15, 101–2, 277, 449
   Regulation of Investigatory Powers Act 2000
      (RIPA) 57, 449
ultra vires 184, 309, 351–52
United States
   Fourth Amendment 334, 337
   PATRIOT Act 476–77, 481
   search and seizure 337
   Stored Communications Act 6–7, 334

violence 355
VPN service providers 302, 310–11
vulnerability 7–8, 455–70